The Semi-Official Letters of British Envoy Sir Ernest Satow from Siam, Uruguay and Morocco (1884-1895)

Edited by Ian Ruxton
With a Foreword by T.G. Otte

Copyright Notice

With regard to the main text, Crown Copyright material from the papers of Sir Ernest Satow (PRO 30/33) is reproduced by permission of The National Archives (UK) on behalf of the Controller of Her Majesty's Stationery Office. The annotations are copyright of the author, Ian C. Ruxton. The introduction is copyright T.G. Otte.

This publication may not be reproduced, stored in a retrieval system, or transmitted in any form by any means, electronic, mechanical, photocopying, recording or otherwise, without the prior written permission of the author, except for brief quotations in academic works which are welcomed as long as the source is acknowledged.

Acknowledgements by the Author

I wish to thank Professor T.G. Otte again most sincerely for his foreword.

Publisher
Lulu Press Inc., 860 Aviation Parkway, Suite 300, Morrisville, North Carolina 27560, USA.

Publication Date: April 1, 2019

ISBN: 978-1-79486-445-0

Relevant Books by the Same Author

Ruxton, Ian (ed.), *The Diaries and Letters of Sir Ernest Mason Satow (1843-1929): A Scholar-Diplomat in East Asia,* Edwin Mellen Press, 1998   (A general introduction to Satow's life and letters.)

Ruxton, Ian (ed.), *The Diaries of Sir Ernest Mason Satow, 1883-1888*, Lulu.com, 2016.

Ruxton, Ian (ed.), *The Diaries of Sir Ernest Mason Satow, 1889-1895,* Lulu.com, 2018.

Ruxton, Ian (ed.), *The Semi-Official Letters of British Envoy Sir Ernest Satow from Japan and China 1895-1906*, Lulu.com, 2007. (PRO 30/33 14/8-17. This book continues from where the present volume ends.)

See http://www.lulu.com/spotlight/ianruxton

Contents

Foreword by T.G. Otte..i

Bibliography..iv

PRO 30/33 14/1   Siam..1

PRO 30/33 14/2   Siam...78

PRO 30/33 14/3   Uruguay...141

PRO 30/33 14/4   Uruguay; Morocco..220

PRO 30/33 14/5   Morocco...261

PRO 30/33 14/6   Morocco...301

PRO 30/33 14/7   Morocco...377

PRO 30/33 14/8   Morocco...453

Foreword

T.G. Otte

Sir Ernest Satow was a diplomatic historian's diplomat, an inveterate paper-saver and a meticulous keeper of records. Readers of Ian Ruxton's previous annotated volumes of Satow's private papers will be familiar with the scholar-diplomat's diaries, kept for much of his adult life from the 1860s until just before his death in 1929. But Satow not only kept a diary, he also kept copies of his semi-official or private correspondence with his political masters in London and various colleagues in the Foreign Office and the then still separate diplomatic and consular services. Satow's papers have been well thumbed by more especially historians of the international politics of East Asia, a region with which he was associated through his profession as a diplomat and through his extracurricular activities as a student of Oriental languages and culture. Indeed, there scarcely exists a volume on any aspect of nineteenth-century Asian history that does not feature Satow's name or that does not draw on his papers.

It is perhaps worth commenting on the nature of the material brought together in this volume. In Satow's day it was described as 'private'. It was private in the sense that, although addressed to officials, it was supplementary to official despatches and telegrams, the staple items of diplomatic correspondence. The latter provided – and, indeed, continues to provide even in these days of rapid communication via e-mail and, *horribile dictu*, twitter - an official record of diplomatic exchanges. It was distributed widely amongst Britain's representatives abroad through the confidential diplomatic print series. It was also circulated within Whitehall and was often placed before the public in the shape of parliamentary *Command Papers*, better known as 'blue books' on account of their traditional dark blue paper covers. The possibility of publicity, in turn, placed a premium on economy and discretion. Indeed, in his retirement *magnum opus*, the *Guide to Diplomatic Practice*, Satow counselled that the writer of 'despatches should be careful to eschew Gallicisms or idioms borrowed from the country where he is serving. [...] Never place an adjective before a noun, if it can be spared ... . Above all, do not attempt to be witty.'[1]

Such strictures did not necessarily apply to 'private' correspondence as it was not meant to become part of the formal record. Rather such letters were meant to complement official despatches and telegrams, offering further information or analysis that was deemed too sensitive to be included in official correspondence given the risk of publication. In practice, however, the occasional private letter, or an extract from it, might be copied into the official record or reproduced in the Confidential Print.

During the years covered in this volume, Satow was posted to Siam as minister-resident and consul-general, and, from 1889 until 1895, as minister first to Uruguay and then to Morocco. Readers familiar with his diaries for the period will easily recognise certain themes emerging from his 'semi-official' letters. Meetings with foreign dignitaries, briefly touched on in his journals, frequently produced letters to senior Foreign Office clerks, in which Satow dealt in more depth and with greater candour with the issues at hand.

---

[1] Sir E.M. Satow, *A Guide to Diplomatic Practice* (2 vols., London, 1917), vol. I, § 142, p. 130.

Neither Bangkok nor Montevideo nor Fez was a diplomatic posting of the first order. Indeed, Satow was always mindful of the need to 'be on ... guard against the notion that his own post [was] the centre of international politics, and against an exaggerated estimate of the part assigned to him in the general scheme.'[2] British interests in South East Asia, Latin America and North West Africa were subsidiary to larger strategic considerations, but they were not negligible either. An amalgam of commercial interests, long-established political ties and calculations of imperial strategy defined British policy in all three regions.

In Siam trading interests, though not insignificant, were a less prominent concern. London's diplomacy was conditioned by the Thai kingdom's geographical location between British India and France's possessions in Indochina. Geopolitics and imperial defence requirements meant that the Siamese buffer-state had to be preserved as much as possible against continued French encroachments. It was in this context that Anglo-French commercial rivalry and competing claims to concessions acquired a larger significance. In these matters, Satow's legal acumen stood him in good stead (- he had studied law at Marburg university and was admitted to the bar in 1887). Indeed, the Foreign Office's legal adviser noted that he 'ha[d] quite an exceptional head for law for a layman & is a *very* able man.'[3]

Such attributes were also needed following Satow's transfer to the River Plate, where Britain's interests were of an entirely economic and financial nature. Much of the commercial life of Argentina and Uruguay was dominated by British trading houses and banking concerns. The railways in both countries were mostly British-built and operated by British companies; and not infrequently they were implicated in the corrupt practices and the involved power struggles amongst the 'unscrupulous ruffians' at Montevideo and Buenos Aires.[4] The bulk of Satow's official work was therefore taken up with commercial matters, and the protracted haggling with Uruguayan ministers over vast sums of money owed by their government to the railway companies often strained relations with Britain. Yet Satow still managed to keep them on even keel. In Victorian times, and indeed later, Latin America was seen as a diplomats' graveyard. It was testament to Satow's professionalism as a diplomatist that his career did not confirm that *dictum*.

In the autumn of 1893, Satow took up his post as minister to the Sultan of Morocco. Here he encountered rather different challenges, challenges that were more closely connected with the imperial rivalries between the European Powers. The slow decline of the Moorish kingdom shifted the focus of international attention to the future of that country. With a view to the importance of the Mediterranean sea-lines of communication for Britain's maritime power, the government in London could not afford to hold aloof from Moroccan affairs. The interior of the country was of no intrinsic strategic, let alone economic, value for Britain. The same could not be said of Tangier, one of the two principal places in Morocco, and the coastline opposite Gibraltar, for it guarded the Western entrance to the Mediterranean, and therefore had to be kept out of the hands of another European Power. Unsurprisingly, much of Satow's diplomatic activities were focused on containing French ambitions in Morocco. In addition, there was always the risk of Franco-Spanish or Hispano-Italian squabbles over all or parts of the Sultan's dominions, and this, too, required patient diplomacy to calm matters. At the same time, Satow was anxious to persuade the two Sultans with whom he

---

[2] Ibid., § 166, p. 144.
[3] Min. Davidson, n.d. [c. July 1889], Sanderson MSS, The National Archives (Public Record Office), Kew, FO 800/1 (emphasis in the original).
[4] Satow to Sanderson (private), 21 Aug. 1890, Satow MSS, TNA (PRO), PRO 30/33/14/3.

had to deal during his time at Fez to embrace the need for internal reforms and modernization so as to buttress the sultanate against the covetous ambitions of France. He had only limited success with his efforts. Indeed, he felt frustrated by Moorish procrastination, and that despite the support he received from such intriguing characters as the Sultan's redoubtable military adviser, General ('Kaïd') Harry Maclean, and Walter Harris, *The Times* newspaper's somewhat colourful correspondent in Morocco. Nor was he able to make much progress in halting the ill-treatment of, and indeed atrocities against, the Jewish population in Morocco at Mogador and other places.

In June 1895, Satow left North Africa to return to East Asia, this time as minister plenipotentiary to Japan. It is tempting to view the posting to Tokyo as the fulfilment of Satow's professional destiny. Yet it was his sojourn in Siam and his missions to the River Plate and to Fez that prepared the way for his penultimate career move.

There is one final aspect of the letters collated here that is worth noting. While Satow kept up a steady flow of correspondence with the Permanent and Assistant Under-secretaries during those years, men such as Sir Philip Currie, Sir Thomas Sanderson or Sir Percy Anderson, his exchanges with the Foreign Secretary for much of that period, the somewhat Olympian Lord Salisbury, were rather more distant. The great marquis, it seems, cared little for Satow and his posts. Not so, by contrast, his two Liberal successors, Lords Rosebery and Kimberley, who took this consummate diplomat into their confidence, as this volume shows.

Bibliography

Allen, Bernard M., *The Rt. Hon. Sir Ernest Satow, GCMG: A Memoir* London: Kegan Paul, Trench and Trubner, 1933.

Brailey, Nigel, entry on Sir Ernest Satow in the *Oxford Dictionary of National Biography*, 2004.

Brailey, Nigel (ed.), *A Diplomat in Siam*, Bangkok: Orchid Press 1994, revised 2000.

Brailey, Nigel, 'Protection or Partition: Ernest Satow and the 1880s Crisis in Britain's Siam Policy' in *Journal of Southeast Asian Studies*, 29, 1 (March 1998), pp. 63-85.

Brailey, Nigel, 'Ernest Satow and the Implementation of the Revised Treaties in Japan' in Sir Hugh Cortazzi, James Hoare, Nigel Brailey and Ayako Hotta-Lister: *The Revision of Japan's Early Commercial Treaties* (LSE / STICERD International Studies Discussion Paper IS/99/377, November 1999) pp.25-38.

Brailey, Nigel, 'Sir Ernest Satow and the 1907 Second Hague Peace Conference' in *Diplomacy & Statecraft*, Vol. 13, No. 2 (June 2002) pp. 201-228 (pub. Frank Cass, London).

Brailey, Nigel, 'Sir Ernest Satow, Japan and Asia: The Trials of a Diplomat in the Age of High Imperialism' in *The Historical Journal*, 35, 1, (1992), pp. 115-150.

Brailey, Nigel (ed.), *The Satow Siam Papers: The Private Diaries and Correspondence of Ernest Satow* (Volume 1, 1884-1885), Bangkok: The Historical Society, 1997.

Channon, Lucy, 'Sir Ernest Satow: Renowned Diplomat who retired to Ottery', in *Journal of the Ottery Heritage Society*, No. 17, Summer 2004 (Part One); No. 18, Spring 2005, (Part Two).

Coates, P.D., *The China Consuls*, Oxford: Oxford University Press, 1988.

Cortazzi, Sir Hugh & Daniels, Gordon (ed.), *Britain and Japan 1859-1991: Themes and Personalities*, London: Routledge, 1991 (includes a chapter on Satow by Dr. Peter F. Kornicki).

Cortazzi, Sir Hugh, *Collected Writings of Sir Hugh Cortazzi*, London/Tokyo: Japan Library/Edition Synapse, 2000.

Cortazzi, Sir Hugh, (ed.), *Britain and Japan: Biographical Portraits*, Vol. IV, Richmond, Surrey: Japan Library, 2002 and subsequent volumes.

Cortazzi, Sir Hugh (ed.), *British Envoys in Japan, 1859-1972*, Folkestone: Global Oriental, 2004.

Daniels, Gordon, introduction to reprint of *A Diplomat in Japan*, Oxford University Press, 1968.

Daniels, Gordon, 'The British Role in the Meiji Restoration: A Re-Interpretative Note', *Modern Asian Studies*, 2 (1968), pp. 291-313.

Hagihara (in Japan: Hagiwara) Nobutoshi, *Tōi Gake: A-nesto Sato- Nikkishō* ("Distant Cliffs: Selections from Ernest Satow's diaries"), Tokyo: Asahi Shimbunsha (2001; 14 volumes covering Satow's first period in Japan, 1861-1883).

Hoare, James E., *Japan's Treaty Ports and Foreign Settlements: The Uninvited Guests 1858-1899*, Folkestone, Kent: Japan Library, 1994.

Hoare, James E. (ed.), *Britain and Japan: Biographical Portraits*, Vol. III, Richmond, Surrey: Japan Library, 1999.

Hoare, James E., *Embassies in the East: The Story of the British and their Embassies in China, Japan and Korea from 1859 to the Present*, Richmond, Surrey: Curzon Press, 1999.

Jan, Cecilia Osteen, The East Asian Diplomatic Service and Observations of Sir Ernest Mason Satow, Florida State University (unpublished doctoral thesis) 1976, available on microfilm from University Microfilms International.

Kornicki, Peter, 'Sir Ernest Mason Satow in Japan, 1873-84', in Hugh Cortazzi (ed.), *British Envoys in Japan, 1859-1972*, Japan Society, 2004, Ch. 22, pp. 222-230.

Lensen, George Alexander (ed.), *Korea and Manchuria between Russia and Japan 1895-1904: The Observations of Sir Ernest Satow*, Sophia University, Tokyo in cooperation with The Diplomatic Press, Tallahassee, Florida (1966, reprinted 1968).

Morton, Robert and Ruxton, Ian (eds.), *The Diaries of Sir Ernest Mason Satow, 1861-1869*, Kyoto: Eureka Press, 2013. (With an Introduction by Sir David Warren)

Nagaoka, Shōzō (trans. and annotated), *A-nesuto Sato- Koushi Nikki (The Diaries of Minister Ernest Satow)*, Tokyo: Shinjinbutsu Ōraisha. Vol. 1, 1989; Vol. 2 with Fukunaga Ikuo, 1991.

Nish, Ian (ed.), *Britain and Japan: Biographical Portraits*, Vol. I, Folkestone, Kent: Japan Library, an imprint of Curzon Press Ltd. 1994; Vol. II, Richmond, Surrey: Japan Library, 1997.

Nish, Ian H., *The Anglo-Japanese Alliance: The Diplomacy of Two Island Empires, 1894-1907*, London: The Athlone Press, 1966.

Otte, T.G., *The China Question: Great Power Rivalry and British Isolation, 1894-1905*, Oxford University Press, 2007.

Otte, T.G., 'Not Proficient in Table-Thumping': Sir Ernest Satow in Peking, 1900-06, in *Diplomacy & Statecraft*, Vol. 13, No. 2 (June 2002) pp.161-200 (pub. Frank Cass, London).

Otte, T.G., *The Foreign Office Mind: The Making of British Foreign Policy, 1865-1914*, Cambridge University Press, 2011.

Otte, T.G., *An Historian in Peace and War; The Diaries of Harold Temperley,* Farnham, Surrey and Burlington, Vermont: Ashgate, 2014.

Otte, T.G., 'Satow', Chapter 7 in G.R. Berridge, Maurice Keens-Soper and T.G. Otte, *Diplomatic Theory from Machiavelli to Kissinger*, Palgrave Macmillan, 2001.

Roberts, Sir Ivor (ed.), *Satow's Diplomatic Practice*, Seventh and centenary edition, Oxford University Press, 2017.

Ruxton, Ian C. (ed.), *The Diaries and Letters of Sir Ernest Mason Satow (1843-1929): A Scholar-Diplomat in East Asia*, Lewiston, New York and Lampeter, Wales: Edwin Mellen Press, 1998.

Ruxton, Ian (ed.), *The Diaries of Sir Ernest Mason Satow, 1870-1883,* Lulu.com, 2010; Kyoto: Eureka Press, 2015. (With an Introduction by Sir Hugh Cortazzi)

Ruxton, Ian (ed.), *The Diaries of Sir Ernest Mason Satow, 1883-1888*, Lulu.com, 2016. (With an Introduction by Sir David Warren)

Ruxton, Ian (ed.), *The Diaries of Sir Ernest Mason Satow, 1889-1895*, Lulu.com, 2018. (With a Foreword by T.G. Otte)

Ruxton, Ian (ed.), *The Diaries of Sir Ernest Satow, British Minister in Tokyo 1895-1900*, Tokyo: Edition Synapse, 2003. Lulu.com, 2010. (With an Introduction by Nigel Brailey)

Ruxton, Ian (ed.), *The Diaries of Sir Ernest Satow, British Envoy in Peking, 1900-1906*, Lulu.com, Volumes One and Two, 2006. Eureka Press revised edition, 2 vols., 2016. (With an Introduction by J.E. Hoare)

Ruxton, Ian (ed.), *The Diaries of Sir Ernest Mason Satow, 1906-1911*, Kyoto: Eureka Press, 2015. (With an Introduction by Ian Nish)

Ruxton, Ian (ed.), *The Diaries of Sir Ernest Satow, 1912-1920* (2 vols.), Lulu.com, 2018. (With a Foreword by T.G. Otte)

Ruxton, Ian (ed.), *The Correspondence of Sir Ernest Satow, British Minister in Japan, 1895-1900*, Lulu.com, Volume One (2005), Volume Two (2011) Volume Three, Volume Four (2014).

Ruxton, Ian (ed.), *The Semi-Official Letters of British Envoy Sir Ernest Satow from Japan and China 1895-1906*, Lulu.com, 2006. (With an Introduction by J.E. Hoare)

Ruxton, Ian (ed.), *Sir Ernest Satow's Private Letters to W.G. Aston and F.V. Dickins: The Correspondence of a Pioneer Japanologist*, Lulu.com, 2008. (With an Introduction by Peter F. Kornicki)

Ruxton, Ian (ed.), *List of Sir Ernest Satow's General Correspondence from 1906 to 1927*, Lulu.com, 2018.

Ruxton, Ian C., 'E.M. Satow's Early Publications: A Founding Father of Modern Japanology', in *Transactions of the Asiatic Society of Japan*, 4th series, Vol. 11, 1996, pp. 151-167.

Ruxton, Ian, 'Ernest Satow, British Policy and the Meiji Restoration', *Bulletin of Kyushu Institute of Technology (Humanities and Social Sciences)*, 1997, No. 45, pp. 33-41.

Ruxton, Ian, 'Sir Ernest Satow, Minister to Japan, 1895-1900', in Hugh Cortazzi (ed.), *British Envoys in Japan, 1859-1972*, Japan Society, 2004, Ch. 8, pp. 78-88.

Ruxton, Ian, 'Sir Ernest Satow in Japan, 1862-69: Comparing his diary ('journal') and his memoir titled *A Diplomat in Japan*' in the *Journal of the International Association for Japan Studies* (IAJS), 2015, Volume 1, pp. 23-32.

Ruxton, Ian, 'Sir Ernest Satow in Japan, Britain and Europe, 1870-1883, as seen through his diaries: A chance to deepen his knowledge of Japanese culture and other matters' in the *Journal of the International Association for Japan Studies* (IAJS), 2016, Volume 2, pp. 35-44.

Ruxton, Ian, 'Sir Ernest Satow in Siam, 1884-87: Focusing on his Visits to Japan from Siam in 1884 and 1886, and his Research into Japan-Siam Relations' in the *Journal of the International Association for Japan Studies* (IAJS), 2017, Volume 3, pp. 21-30.

Satow, Sir Ernest, *The Silesian Loan and Frederick the Great*, Oxford: Clarendon Press, 1915.

Satow, Sir Ernest, *A Guide to Diplomatic Practice*, London: Longmans, Green & Co., 1917.

Satow, Sir Ernest, *International Congresses*, London: H.M.S.O., 1920.

Satow, Sir Ernest, *A Diplomat in Japan: The Inner History of the Critical Years in the Evolution of Japan when the Ports were opened and the Monarchy restored* (Originally published by Seeley, Service & Co. Ltd. in London, 1921; recently in paperback, New York & Tokyo: ICG Muse, 2000. Based on Satow's personal diaries, 1861-69.)

Satow, Sir Ernest, *Collected Works of Ernest Mason Satow*, Part 2 Collected Papers (5 volumes), London: Ganesha Publishing and Tokyo: Edition Synapse, 2001. (Reproductions of Satow's papers.)

Satow, Sir Ernest, *The Family Chronicle of the English Satows,* privately printed, Oxford, 1925.

Scott, James Brown, *The Proceedings of the Hague Peace Conferences: Translation of the Official Texts*, 2 vols., New York: Oxford University Press, 1920.

Steiner, Zara, *The Foreign Office and Foreign Policy, 1898-1914*, Cambridge University Press, 1969.

Todd, Hamish A. 'The Satow Collection of Japanese Books in the British Library: Its History and Significance' in *Daiei Toshokan shozō Chōsenbon oyobi Nihon kosho no bunkengakuteki gogakuteki kenkyū,* Fujimoto Yukio and Kosukegawa Teiji (eds.). Toyama University, 2007.

Yokohama Kaikō Shiryōkan (Yokohama Archives of History), (ed.): *Zusetsu: A-nesuto*

Sato- : Bakumatsu Ishin Igirisu Gaikōkan, (The Ernest Satow Album: Portraits of a British Diplomat in Young Japan), Yokohama: Yūrindo, 2001.

PRO 30/33 14/1   Letter Book of Semi-official Letters from Siam. (March 8, 1884 – May 7, 1885)

PRO 30/33 14/1

The notebook is labelled

"<u>Private</u> Letters E.M.S. 1884. 1885. May 27".

It contains 83 separate letters, noted mostly in full though some are in outline.

1. Satow to Cockerell[1]

Bangkok. 8 March 84.

Dear Cockerell,

   At Singapore I saw Briggs, the Agency doctor, who is on his way home on sick leave in consequence of the unfortunate accident to his eyes. He is hopeful about his case, and I shall be very glad if he is able to come back to us, as he is a very nice gentlemanlike fellow. If it should eventually turn out otherwise, I hope you will send us an efficient substitute. You can do that probably without invoking the aid of the Colonial Surgeon at Singapore, who would have to procure a man from home. If [Dr. William] Willis[2] becomes a candidate for the appointment, I shall be greatly obliged to you for any advice and assistance you can give him. His long experience in Japan would be very useful in this climate.[3]

   I seem to have dropped in here for the beginning of the hot season. The thermo[mete]r. is over 80°, but the house is large and airy, so that one does not feel it very much. The men in the Agency appear to be a very nice set of fellows, and I shall be very sorry when [W.H.] Newman goes on leave. I just caught Gould[4] before he left for Chengmai. He seems a good man, and I hope he will keep matters straight there. Having arrived here only two days ago,

---

[1] Presumably William A. Cockerell (1840-1919). Senior Clerk, Consular Department, Foreign Office, 1893-1906.

[2] Dr. William Willis (1837-1894). See Hugh Cortazzi, *Dr. Willis in Japan, 1862-1877: British medical pioneer* (London: Athlone Press, 1985)

[3] On February 27, 1884 Satow wrote to his friend Willis that the appointment was not currently vacant and explaining the advantages and disadvantages of accepting it if Briggs should retire. On December 9th Satow received a letter from Willis saying he had been appointed doctor to the Bangkok Agency and Consulate-general. He arrived on January 14, 1885. (Diary, Ruxton, 2016)

[4] Edward Blencowe Gould (1847-1916). Consular official. Student interpreter and consular assistant at Bangkok, 1868-83. Consul in Siam, 1885-1891.

PRO 30/33 14/1   Letter Book of Semi-official Letters from Siam. (March 8, 1884 – May 7, 1885)

I have not yet got to business, but if I can get the few outstanding cases settled, as I hope with Newman's assistance soon to do, life bids fair to be comparatively easy.

   Yours truly

   [Ernest Satow]

2. Satow to Sir Frederick A. Weld K.C.M.G.[5]

March 19.

Dear Sir Frederick,

   Many thanks for your note of March 2 enclosing McCarthy's report.

   I have been reading the papers that I found here relating to the Perak boundary question, & regret very much the discourteous tone of the last reply from the Siamese govt. I have taken an opportunity of telling my opinion of it to the King's private secretary, altho' it is unfortunately too late now for them to withdraw it. I cannot help thinking that if they had seen Sir H. Low's[6] memo. addressed to you of wch. a copy is enclosed in your despatch to Newman of the 13th Septr. last, they might have written differently. I telegraphed to you yesterday morning asking whether I might show it to Prince Dewan, but have not yet recd. a reply, owing perhaps to the line being interrupted. Today's mail has brought me your letters of the 11th and 13th March, to which I am sending an official acknowledgement. Pray do not take my observations amiss. I am very anxious to avoid the Siamese having any excuse for thinking or saying that we wish to encroach on their rights, especially at the present time, when it is understood that the French have designs upon part of the territory on the southeast wch. acknowledges the suzerainty of Siam. Besides, it would not be at all desirable to give the French a handle for hereafter saying that they are simply following our example when they wish to rectify their frontier on the banks of the Mekong. I know from Newman that the King said at a private audience that he would be quite ready to give way to you about the Perak boundary if it were not for his fears of the French, so that if the Govt. gives its decision agst. Siam, it is likely enough that the King may quietly acquiesce, and one can only regret the dimensions that the correspondence has assumed.

---

[5] Sir Frederick Aloysius Weld (1823-91). 14th Governor of the Straits Settlements, 1880-87.
[6] Sir Hugh Low (1824-1905). Fourth British Resident of Perak, 1877-89.

PRO 30/33 14/1   Letter Book of Semi-official Letters from Siam. (March 8, 1884 – May 7, 1885)

Wishing you a pleasant voyage and an agreeable stay in England before returning to Singapore, I remain &c.

Sir F.A. Weld K.C.M.G.

3. Satow to Cecil Clementi Smith[7]

19 March 1884.

My dear Smith,

Just a line to welcome you back to your post and to express the hope that our relations official and otherwise will be of the pleasantest. You will find that a lively correspondence has been going on about the Perak boundary question, and the Siamese have written a rather impertinent letter in Jan. last wch. has given just offence to Sir F. Weld. If I had been here, I should have insisted on its modification, for I don't think it our business to be the medium of conveying offensive insinuations to the Govr. of the Straits. I am sorry also that he shld. have made an allusion to Newman in his letter to me of the 16th, for with all due deference, I think Newman did not require to be reminded of the limits of his duty. The last paragraph of the Govr's letter of the 13th seems to convey something of a menace to Siam, which I do not feel bound to transmit, unless I get orders to do so from my own chief, when I shall of course do it cheerfully. Until the F.O. directs me otherwise it is of course my duty to keep the peace, and I have thought it advisable in sending home a copy of Sir Frederick's letter just to call Ld. Granville's[8] attention to this paragraph, & say that I propose not to communicate that part of the message to the King. In order that Sir F. Weld may not think that I am doing so behind his back, I have written the same thing to him, and I give you this explanation with the object of showing that I mean no offence by it. If I have misinterpreted his meaning, I shall in due course get a wigging from Ld. G. but in the meantime I do not want the Govr. to pitch into me, or to ask me to say to the Siamese Govt. things which I do not think myself justified in saying without instructions from my own department. I quite

---

[7] Cecil Clementi Smith (1840-1916). Colonial administrator. Colonial Secretary in the Straits Settlements from 1878, based in Singapore. Acting Governor, 1884-85. He understudied Governor Sir Frederick Weld and in 1887 succeeded him.

[8] Lord Granville (1815-91) was Foreign Secretary three times: 1851-52, 1870-74 and 1880-85.

PRO 30/33 14/1   Letter Book of Semi-official Letters from Siam. (March 8, 1884 – May 7, 1885)

recognize the quasi-independent sovereignty of Singapore, but am not its foreign minister or envoy.

This is not such a horrid hole as people at Singapore tried to make me believe. So far the temperature had been cool, and the weather perfect. One has plenty of resources, boating, riding and tennis, but not much society beyond the Agency's compound walls.

With best wishes for the success of your administration,

    Believe me &c.

P.S. Please send my letter addressed to Sir Fred[eric]k [Letter No. 2 above] after him, if he shld. have already started.

4. Satow to Sir Julian Pauncefote[9]

21 March 1884

Dear Sir Julian,

When I was at Singapore the other day, one of the barristers practising there, a Mr. Donaldson,[10] complained to me of the inconvenience arising from the want of any rules of practice in the court at Bangkok, and I ascertained on arriving here that his statement was perfectly exact. Altho' Art. 26 of the Order in Council of 1856 provides that rules of practice, regulations for the payment of witnesses, the costs of criminal prosecutions & rates of fees to be taken in civil suits may be established by H.M. Consul, no such rules &c. have ever been made. [W.H.] Newman tells me that the practice has hitherto been to levy judicial fees acc. to the scale in use in the Levant, but he thinks that they are too low, and that if we were authorized to levy fees on the China and Japan scale, the revenues would greatly benefit, while vexatious proceedings would be discouraged, a result greatly to be desired.

Another practice wch. seems to me rather irregular is the application to B/S [British

---

[9] Julian Pauncefote, 1st Baron Pauncefote (1828-1902). Known as Sir Julian Pauncefote between 1874 and 1899. British barrister, judge and diplomat. Permanent Under-Secretary of State for Foreign Affairs, 1882-1889. Later Ambassador to the United States.

[10] Probably Alexander Leathes Donaldson. The law firm of Donaldson and Burkinshaw was established in Singapore in 1874, and is still in existence as a limited liability partnership since 2014. Satow called on the firm on 10 May 1887 (diary).

PRO 30/33 14/1   Letter Book of Semi-official Letters from Siam. (March 8, 1884 – May 7, 1885)

Subjects] of eastern origin of the provisions of the Indian criminal code, while B/S of European descent are tried acc. to Engl. Law. There is no doubt some convenience in this, as the Indian Codes enable us, I am told, to punish as criminal offences certain acts for which English law provides only a civil remedy. I should be grateful to you for your advice as to whether it is advisable to continue the established usage. With regard to rules of practice and fees, would it not be possible to extend the application of the China & Japan rules to this country pending the framing of a set of rules for Siam.

I am engaged in a correspondence with the Siamese Govt. concerning the attendance of witnesses at Singapore when a criminal case has to be sent there for trial, on wch. I shall report officially when it is terminated. In the case of Ai Baa, as you may recollect they declined to send witnesses, & the consequence was that he escaped a regular trial. More recently two British-Burmese who were accused of dacoity [gang robbery] and murder had to be handed over to the authorities of Moulmein, but will no doubt escape punishment for the same reason. A third case which arose last year within the limits of the viceconsular jurisdiction of Chiengmai I hope to dispose of by sending the accused B/S to Chiengmai to await the establishment of the Court provided for by the Treaty of last year, wch. I suppose will not be long delayed.

There appears to be a fair prospect of the cases of illegal seizure of spirits belonging to B/S being shortly settled, as the King's private sec'y promises that their claims shall be paid on presentation.

The Siamese officials seem to be very friendly and I hope to continue on those terms with them.

5. Satow to Philip Currie[11]

21 March 1884.

Dear Currie,

I am informed by the King's Secy. that there is no objection to giving the desired concession to the Eastern Telegraph Extension Co., as already reported by Newman in his

---

[11] Philip Currie, 1st Baron Currie (1834-1906). Assistant Permanent Under Secretary of State for Foreign Affairs, 1882-9.

PRO 30/33 14/1   Letter Book of Semi-official Letters from Siam. (March 8, 1884 – May 7, 1885)

desp. No. 80 of 15 October last, but that certain minor points as to tariff require discussion. This information was communicated to the Co's agent at Singapore at the time, but nothing further has been heard from him. I shall be very glad when the line is completed, for it will be greatly preferable for our use to the route by Saigon to Singapore.

The Bangkok-Tavoy [Dawei] line is not yet in working order.[12] At present the Fr[ench]. telegraphists have it under their charge, and Kergeradec says they are only working it under protest until a competent staff arrives fr. England, On the other hand the Siamese tell me that the Fr. are pressing for management of all the telegraphs in Siam as a <u>quid pro quo</u> for the spirit convention. At first they asked also for control of the police on Lake Talësap on the Cambodian frontier, but owing to Siamese persistence in refucing this concession they have dropped that, and the Siamese think that by holding out on the other point, they will get the convention for nothing. In the meanwhile they mean to get rid of the Fr. telegraph people as soon as their two years engagements expire. An English telegraph engineer named [James] Marrable who arrived here a month ago is to be put in charge, he tells me, of the maintenance of all the existing lines, as the Frenchmen are only operators. I am going to suggest to the Siamese to get some Eurasian operators from India for the Bangkok-Tavoy line, in order that our telegrams may not go thro' French hands. Eurasians would be much cheaper than Europeans, and could be obtained more quickly.

I have sent two desp[atches]. covering correspondence about the Perak boundary question.[13] I am rather afraid that if this claim is pressed, the French may make it a precedent for some similar demand on the E. of Siam. I hope my declining to communicate Sir F. Weld's somewhat threatening para. to the Siamese Govt. will be approved. He seems to be very angry with them for their last letter of Jan. 23. of which Newman has already sent home a copy. I confess its tone is rather impertinent, & I have hinted as much to the King's Secy. Probably Alabaster had a hand in its concoction. These people always run to their foreign advisers when they are in difficulty, and he naturally writes them what he

---

[12] See diary for March 20,1884: "Ong Noi, H.R.H. & Minr. of Posts & Telegraphs. Says their part of the Bangkok-Tavoy line is in working order, but the Burmese part is not. No use opening until they can send a message to & fro in one day." (Ruxton, 2016, p. 65)
[13] See diary entry for March 22, 1884. (Ruxton, 2016, p. 67)

PRO 30/33 14/1   Letter Book of Semi-official Letters from Siam. (March 8, 1884 – May 7, 1885)

thinks a clever draft, wch. only makes matters worse. I don't mean to quarrel with Alabaster,[14] as he may possibly be useful.

I hope Newman's suggestion that the spirit convention shld. not be brought into operation until the pending cases of illegal confiscation are settled, will be adopted. There is fair prospect however of these claims being shortly paid, & then the sooner we can get the licensing system into working order the better. Of course it is the revenue that the Siamese care about, not the morals of the people, but it seems hard that they shld. not get more than three per cent out of the liquor traffic, and the Chinamen whose battle we have been fighting here are a precious pack of rascals. The convention will do more to reestablish our influence here than anything else, as far as I can see.

I shall do my best to keep an eye on Fr[ench]. doings, & to work smoothly with the Siamese.

There are plenty of subjects I shld. like to write to you about, but this letter is already too long.

Yrs. very truly

6. Satow to H.S.C. Clarke Jervoise[15]

25 March 1884

Dear Jervoise,

By an oversight I neglected to report at the time that I had presented to the Min[ister]. for F[oreign].A[ffairs]. L[or]d. G[ranville]'s letter accrediting me to him. The fact is, the Min[ister]. is so little more than in name, & all one's real business is transacted with the King's private secretary, which is the only excuse I can offer for this irregularity. I have now taken the earliest opportunity of repairing the omission.

The London & China Express of 22 Feb[ruary]. contains a report of Ld. Ed[mond]. Fitzmaurice's[16] reply to Dr. Cameron abt. Ai Baa's case,[17] wch. I presume is correct. Of

---

[14] Henry Alabaster was the son of James Chaloner Alabaster. The former transferred from the British China consular service to Siamese government service in 1869.

[15] Sir Harry Clarke-Jervoise (1832-1911). Head of the American and Asiatic Department, Foreign Office, 1880-1894.

[16] Lord Edmond Fitzmaurice (1846-1935). British Liberal politician. Under-Secretary of

PRO 30/33 14/1   Letter Book of Semi-official Letters from Siam. (March 8, 1884 – May 7, 1885)

course you know that the proceedings sent fr. here in acc. with instructions were those of a Siamese court, and not of the Agency.

I believe that Ai Baa cld. legally speaking still be put on his trial for murder, if it were required, but the Siamese have said nothing more abt. it, & seem quite satisfied with his having been released a short time back by Newman, just before I arrived.

I hope, if Archer is to be transferred to the Levant, that it will be done as soon as possible, both in his own interest and in that of the public service. He is losing time here that might be more profitably spent in studying Turkish, while we get no benefit from his presence here beyond his work in the office, where he attends to the shipping. Owing to the constable's time being so much taken up with the frequent arrival and departure of mails, he is of little or no use to us, and the student has to do work in the office which elsewhere, as in Japan, can well be performed by the constable, the consequence being that he gets no time for studying the language. I wish you wld, when sending a new student out, give me instructions to spare him office work as much as possible, and to employ the constable instead. I could then tell the latter that if he retains the post office for the benefit of the whole foreign population of Bangkok, he must engage an Eurasian at his own expense to distribute letters. It hardly seems reasonable that H.M.G. shld. pay him $60 a month & give him quarters, unless he discharges his duties efficiently.

 Yrs. very truly

7. Satow to Prince Devawongse[18]

[31 March 1884]

State for Foreign Affairs, 1883-85.
[17] 'DR. CAMERON asked the Under Secretary of State for Foreign Affairs, "Whether his attention has been called to the Correspondence between Mr. W.G. Palgrave, Her Majesty's Political Agent and Consul-General at Bangkok, and the Siamese Foreign Office, respecting the case of Ai baa, a coloured British subject, accused of murdering a Siamese policeman"...' (Hansard, House of Commons Debate, 19 February 1884, vol. 284 cc 1332-3).
[18] Prince Devawongse Varoprakar (1858-1923), given name Devan Udayawongse. He was at this time King Chulalongkorn's principal private secretary. Later he was Foreign Minister, 12 June 1885 – 28 June 1923.

PRO 30/33 14/1   Letter Book of Semi-official Letters from Siam. (March 8, 1884 – May 7, 1885)

Dear Prince Devawongse,

I do not know whether it will be convenient to His Majesty to receive me any day this week after the general mourning for the Duke of Albany[19] is over, but in any case I shld. like beforehand to learn exactly what is the nature of the ceremony, in order that no mistake may occur. I am of course quite ignorant of the etiquette observed here, and shld. be much obliged if you could arrange for it to be explained to me beforehand, either by yourself privately or by the proper functionary of the Ministry of Foreign Affairs. I presume of course that I shall be presented by the Minister for Foreign Affairs.

31 March 1884.   Believe me &c.[20]

8. Satow to Prince Devawongse

Dear Prince Devawongse,

Many thanks for your note about the Audience tomorrow. I will send my commission to the Min. for F.A. as you desire, tho' this I may observe is the first intimation I have recd. of such a wish. In such matters as exequaturs our instructions are to conform to the practice of the country to wch. we are apptd. I am glad to learn that the Min. for F.A. will be present to introduce me to H[is]. M[ajesty]., as I perceive from this that you follow the usage observed in other countries, & this leads me to hope that I shall receive the other marks of honour to wch. I am entitled as H.M. Repres've.

Believe me,

Yours very faithfully

April 1.

9. Satow to Prince Devawongse

---

[19] Prince Leopold, Duke of Albany (1853-84). Eighth child and youngest son of Queen Victoria and Prince Albert. He died of haemophilia aged 30.

[20] "It had been arranged that I shld. have an audience of the King today, to present letter of Queen [Victoria] acknowledging Prisdang's recall, but a telegram announcing Duke of Albany's death arrived from Parkes. Sent Newman to Min. for F.A. to inform him that my audience must be put off until the general mourning is over, & wrote also to Dewan privately." (Satow's diary, 31 March 1884)

PRO 30/33 14/1   Letter Book of Semi-official Letters from Siam. (March 8, 1884 – May 7, 1885)

Dear Prince Devawongse,

I take another sheet to reply to that part of your letter wch. relates to the affair of Mong O.[21] I have not examined into the merits of this case, because I understood that you had arranged for its settlement on the terms I proposed to you through Mr. French,[22] & wch. you appeared to me to have agreed to. I consequently am not in a position to discuss whether their losses were ever proved to be their own fault or not, but if you are willing to carry out the original understanding between us, there need be no recurrence to that matter. As you know, I am desirous that the pending cases may be settled without delay, in order that we may make a fresh start, & by the exercise of mutual forbearance, avoid the occurrence of disputes, wch. only tend to injure our amicable relations. I beg you to take these observations into friendly consideration.

Believe me
Yours very faithfully

April 1, 1884   E.S.

10. Satow to Prince Devawongse

April 5, 1884

Dear Prince Devawongse,

I have had the claims of B/S. [British Subjects] for actual losses thro' the seizure of their spirits carefully examined & am now prepared to lay them before you. The principle I have adopted in arriving at the amounts is to take the value of the property at the time of each seizure, & to add to that interest at the usual rate of one tical a catty a month, court fees & boat & gharry[23] hire actually out of pocket. The total sum amounts to 25000 ticals.

---

[21] "Mong O's claim. He said that he thought the claimant might be allowed to take away the 900 logs, without paying any duties, and get a lease of 2 or 3 y[ea]rs. for the piece of forest of w[hi]ch. the ownership was undisputed. Proposed that Mong O sh[ou]ld. present a petition to the King. I said I wl[ou]d. first show him a draft petition, & if he agreed to it, Mong O sh[ou]ld. sign." (Diary, March 12, 1884)

[22] E.H. French (1850-1935). Student Interpreter and Assistant at Bangkok, 1874-85. Vice-Consul, 1885-91 (appointed acting Vice-Consul on May 3, 1884 – diary). Consul 1891-96. He left Siam in 1894 but only formally retired two years later. (Brailey, *The Satow Siam Papers* Volume I, p. 84)

PRO 30/33 14/1   Letter Book of Semi-official Letters from Siam. (March 8, 1884 – May 7, 1885)

Will you kindly let me know when it will be convenient to you to meet me in order to discuss the question of compensation, wch. I am instructed by Ld. Granville to ask for the inconvenience & prejudice to their rights wch. the claimants have suffered thro' the intervention of the spirit farmers with a legitimate trade.

Believe me &c.

11. Satow to Pauncefote

Pauncefote

8 April /84

Dear Sir Julian

I am sending by this mail a desp[atch]. with resp[ec]t. to the recent refusal of the Siamese Govt. in several cases to send witnesses to Singapore & British Burma to give evidence in those criminal cases wch. are beyond our competence. They say, & I think with some justice, that it is a great hardship for witnesses to leave their business to go so far, especially as it often happens that they have to be brought long distances to Bangkok to give evidence at the preliminary inquiry. They suggest that the Chief Justice of Singapore might come here to try such cases, wch. wld. probably not be very often. It wld. not be a greater distance than the Chief Justice of Shanghai has sometimes to travel, & wld. be a

---

[23] A gharry was a horse-drawn cab used in India, Singapore etc.

Singapore Gharry

PRO 30/33 14/1   Letter Book of Semi-official Letters from Siam. (March 8, 1884 – May 7, 1885)

pleasant change for him fr. Singapore. I believe the Chief Justice of the Straits Settlements[24] is now at home on leave. The King's private Secy. Prince Devawongse has promised me that they will send witnesses wherever required, if they are assured that the Brit. Govt. will take their suggestion into favourable cos[iderati]on. & I hope therefore that I may be instructed to give them this assurance.

Believe me &c.

12. Satow to Currie

Currie

9/April/84

Dear Currie,

Count Kergaradec the Fr[ench]. Consul goes home by this mail on leave of absence wch. he tells me he obtained just in time to prevent his being sent off again to Annam. He was to have gone there, when Harmand[25] managed to get apptd. instead, & it is not impossible, I think, that he may after all go there, as he knows the country & language well. I do not think there is any present intention of asking Siam to agree to a rectification of boundaries towards the S. & E. as he seems to be of opinion that an indefinite neutral zone is more convenient with regard to future operations. He believes that this policy will be adopted in Tonquin, & that the mountainous tract between the more inhabited parts of the country & the S.W. provinces of China will not be taken poss[essi]on. of. It was he who recommended

---

[24] Sir Thomas Sidgreaves was the Chief Justice from 1871 to 1886.
[25] Jules Harmand (1845-1921). "Harmand's diplomatic career began as he was appointed French Consul in Bangkok. He later took up the post of French civil commissioner-general for Tonkin in June 1883, which saw him involved in the Sino-French War. In 1885 he moved to Calcutta as Consul General and in 1889 visited Chile in a plenipotentiary role. In 1894 he was involved in frontier negotiations with Siam (Thailand), while his final role in foreign diplomacy was as plenipotentiary minister in Tokyo from 1894, during conflicts between that country and China and Russia. He retired with the title of ambassador in 1907 and settled in Paris, where his interest in Southeast Asian affairs continued as an active member of several committees and societies dedicated to colonial politics and science in the region." (From https://plants.jstor.org/stable/10.5555/al.ap.person.bm000151665 accessed 5 September 2018).

PRO 30/33 14/1   Letter Book of Semi-official Letters from Siam. (March 8, 1884 – May 7, 1885)

this plan to Bourée. He still tells the Siamese that he doubts the Fr[ench]. Govt. giving the Spirit convention without a <u>quid pro quo</u>, & I understand that he leaves Bangkok with no very friendly feelings towards Siam. On the other hand, Prince Devawongse tells me the Siamese Govt. is determined not to give any quid pro quo.

I agreed with him yesterday for the satisfaction of the claim of B/S [British Subjects] whose spirits were seized, & for the payment of compensation besides. The whole amount is not more than £3,300, & bears a very small proportion of the whole trade in the article. He has promised also to give instructions not to interfere with the spirit trade, as they are anxious to get the convention carried out. The U.S. Govt. has called for a report fr. its minister here, & so has that of Holland, the former upon the advisability of concluding a convention, the latter with respect to the date at wch. it shld. be allowed to come into force.

     Yrs very truly

P.S. I have written to Sir J.P. [Julian Pauncefote – see previous letter] expressing the hope that instead of our sending murder cases to Singapore to be tried, the Chief Justice of the Straits Settlements may be empowered to hold his court here for such cases. The same difficulty we have here formerly existed in Japan until the passing of the China & Japan O. in C. [Order in Council], & I do not see any other way in wch. it can be got over. With regard to cases wch. at present ought to go to British Burma, I suppose something will be provided in the order in Council that is being framed for Chiengmai.

     E.S.

13. Satow to Cecil Smith

10 April 1884

My dear Smith,

I have read Sir H. Low's report on the robbery wch. is said to have been committed on the upper waters of the Perak river in the disputed territory, & am entirely of your opinion that it wld. be inexpedient to ask the Siamese to send orders down to Petani, at present. Fr[om]. what I can learn the Siamese Govt. is not at all disposed to admit the claim of Perak, & wld. be only too delighted to obtain any kind of direct recognition of their authority in the disputed territory. The map made by McCarthy has been shown to me, & it proves to be

PRO 30/33 14/1   Letter Book of Semi-official Letters from Siam. (March 8, 1884 – May 7, 1885)

drawn in such a manner as to show a range of mountains running straight across the river & forming in appearance a perfectly natural boundary. This map is to be sent to London as part of the Siamese case, & will be lithographed there. Its weak point is the absence of names.

I return the papers, as I perceive that they are originals.

   Yrs. very truly

    E.S.

14. Satow to Philip Currie

April 16, 1884

Dear Currie,

You will see from my desp[atch]. recording the presentation of the Queen's letter acknowledging Prisdang's[26] letters of recall that the Siamese still adhere to some of their oldfashioned notions about the manner in which foreign rr. [representatives] are recd. There was absolutely no reason why they shld. have made us get out of the carriages so far from the palace, & the rest of the consuls agree with me in theory, though they do not like to insist upon an alteration. But it seems to me time that the Siamese abandoned the remains of Oriental swagger, & I have privately told the King's Secy. that I did not like the way in wch. I was recd. though I felt certain they meant to do the proper thing.

I hope something will be done about the postoffice, so that we may be able to utilize the constable's services. The present man is getting old, & wld. probably leave if the profits of the postal agency were taken fr. him. In that case it wld. be better to get a man fr. England, who above all things ought to be a decent copyist. The work in the office is very great, & the student has not sufficient time to study. It wld. be a good thing if we could now and then send one of the men up country at public expense to look after the cases that arise there, instead of having witnesses as well as the parties brought down to Bangkok, but this could hardly be done without an additional man on the staff.

I am disposed to believe that the limitation of our powers of punishing offences has a

---

[26] Prince Prisdang (1851-1935). In 1881 he established the first permanent Siamese legation in England, presenting his credentials to Queen Victoria in 1882.

PRO 30/33 14/1   Letter Book of Semi-official Letters from Siam. (March 8, 1884 – May 7, 1885)

great deal to do with the prevalence of dacoities [robberies] & other serious crimes up country, the perpetrators of wch. are mostly Burmese. Under the existing system they are certain of impunity. On the whole I am inclined to think that it wld. be best to give Gould power to try capital crimes, as the journey from Rangoon to Chiengmai takes at least three weeks, & he wld. be better able to arrive at the merits of the case than any official who might be sent over fr. Burma.

Yours v. t.

15. Satow to Prince Devawongse
17 April 1884

Dear Prince Devawongse,

I am very glad to be able to tell you that the spirit claims, with the exception of two of the smallest, have been settled today by payment of the sums agreed upon between us, and I beg to [e]xpress to Y.R.H. [Your Royal Highness] my great satisfaction with the manner in wch. you have treated the affair.

I propose going down to Chantaboon[27] on Saturday next for a week's change of air, & shall return on Sunday the 17th.[27th?] Perhaps you will have had time before Saturday to tell me what you think abt. the case of Syed Mahomet & the draft Note to the For: Min: wch. I sent to Y.R.H. a few days ago.

Believe me

P.S. I have just learnt that the officers charged c. the payments have deducted 2½% fr. each claim & fr. the 5000 ticals compensation. It appears to me that this must have been done under a misapprehension of the nature of the arrangement betw. Y.R.H. & myself, & I beg that Y.R.H. will be so good as to inquire into the matter.

16. Satow to Gould
18 April 1884

---

[27] See PRO 30/33 17/13 'Notes of Travel in Siam. Vol. I.' Diary. Siamese mission. Travel. Chantabun visit. April 19-26, 1884. See Ian Ruxton (ed.), *The Diaries of Sir Ernest Mason Satow, 1883-1888*, Lulu.com. 2016, pp. 74-81.

PRO 30/33 14/1   Letter Book of Semi-official Letters from Siam. (March 8, 1884 – May 7, 1885)

Dear Gould,

After much cogitation I came to the conclusion that the most expeditious way of settling the case of Mong Peto & the other man accused of being concerned in the murder of Mong Bandaw wld. be to send them to Chiengmai for trial. The Siamese had declined to send witnesses abroad, & ∴[therefore] it wld. have been impossible for the Singapore or Brit: Burma courts to try the case, & to get the witnesses down here merely to establish a prima facie case agst. the defts. wch. wld. have ended in nothing, seemed a mere waste of time. As the new Treaty provides for the cases being tried at Chiengmai, it seemed best to have recourse to it. The ratifi[catio]ns. will shortly be exchanged, & the Treaty will then come into effect. Sir J. Pauncefote told me he was engaged in drafting an order in Council defining y[ou]r. powers, but in face of the express stipulations of the Treaty, it seems to me unnecessary that you shld. wait for the order.

The F.O. has called for a report as to the manner in wch. you are to be supplied with funds, & I have answered that you were to arrange matters in Rangoon, and am expecting a report fr. you on the subject.

17. Satow to Prince Devawongse
18 April 1884

Dear Prince Devawongse,

Many thanks for your note assuring me that Syed Mahomet's case will soon be settled in accordance with my desire.

I am very sorry that the absence of Chun[?] Ah Soon and Toh Mun Song shld. cause any delay in the complete settlement of these claims. The former is in China, & the latter up country, nor is there any one here who will undertake to swear their claims. That of Toh Mun Song was made up from documents existing in the Agency. If you are disposed to accept these two claims as correct, & there cannot be much doubt about them, the best way perhaps wld. be to deposit the amounts with this Agency, & I will give a receipt for the money.

I have already written a note to the Krom Tah [Kromatah, Minister of Foreign Affairs].

E.S.

PRO 30/33 14/1 Letter Book of Semi-official Letters from Siam. (March 8, 1884 – May 7, 1885)

18. Satow to Prince Devawongse

Dear Prince Devawongse,

I have just recd. a Note fr. the Krom[a]tah, offering to pay the sum of $1500 <u>out of his own private funds</u> to Syed Mahomet, with a view of avoiding unpleasant feelings betw. us. This offer, wellmeant as it is, I can hardly accept, because I do not consider that H.E. [His Excellency] is in any way personally responsible. I shld. greatly prefer not having to enter into an argumentative correspondence upon the matter, & wish it may be possible for Your R.H. [Royal Highness] to induce H.E. to withdraw this letter, & substitute for it another, offering pay[men]t. on behalf of the Customs Dept. without any personal allusions to Mr. [W.H.] Newman, wch. cannot fail to produce an unpleasant effect. I beg to enclose the Kromtah's letter for Y.R.H. perusal.

April 18/84

19. Satow to Prince Devawongse

19 April 1884

Dear Pr. Dev.

A British subject named Seyd Gunny[?] has complained to me that he has been unable for 7 yrs. past to obtain justice fr. the Rajah of Quedah in respect of certain claims agst. the Rajah & a number of his subjects for goods sold & delivered. I am desirous of taking the opportunity of the Rajah's presence in Bangkok to endeavour to obtain justice for Seyd Gunny thro' the intervention of the Siamese Govt. & beg Y.R.H. to be so good as to cause the Rajah to be detained here for a few days until I shall have had an opportunity of laying the matter before the Siamese Govt. wch. I hope to do without delay on my return fr. Chantaburi on the 27th inst.

    Believe me &c.

20. Satow to J. Russell (of the Hongkong Civil Service)

29 April/84

My dear Russell,

PRO 30/33 14/1   Letter Book of Semi-official Letters from Siam. (March 8, 1884 – May 7, 1885)

It seems strange that there shld. be any difference betw. the effect of naturalization at Hongkong & the same process at Singapore. In reply to my official application they sent me fr. the latter place a copy of a circular fr. Ld. Kimberley dated 18 May 1882, informing the Govr. that the Govt. had decided that aliens naturalized in a colony, when travelling beyond the limits of the colony shld. be placed on the same footing as aliens naturalized in Great Britain under the act of 1870. I suppose that the circular must have been recd. in Hongkong, & if I were personally acquainted c. the Col[onia]l. Secy. I wld. write privately to ask for an explanation. It is hard upon Chinese naturalized B/S [British Subjects] fr. Hongkong that they shld. not have the same privileges as those fr. the Straits Settlements. If you can throw any light upon the matter, I shld. be immensely obliged to you.

Yrs. v. t.

21. Satow to Prince Devawongse
30 April.
Dear Prince D.

I regret to have to trouble you further abt. the spirit claims. Acting upon your assurance that the 2½ per cent deducted by the Treasury officials wld. be paid, I sent the claimants to receive the money both yesterday & today, but payt. was refused on the ground that it cld. create a precedent. The claimants appear further to have been informed that Your R.H. wld. pay the 2½% out of your private purse, & that the money wld. be handed to me for delivery to them.

With regard to the two smaller cases in wch. neither claimant is in Bangkok, I am willing to take charge of the money, as agreed between us the day before yesterday.

I think it will perhaps be most expeditiously arranged if Y.R.H. will give me an interview.

I am sorry also to have to inform you that another claim has been presented to me, shown by the petition of wch. I beg to enclose a copy. If Y.R.H. on examining the case finds that the petition is in accordance c. facts, I think the petitioner will be entitled to 330 ticals with interest as calculated in the other cases.

I shld. add that of course I cannot for a moment consent to receive the money fr. Y.R.H.

PRO 30/33 14/1   Letter Book of Semi-official Letters from Siam. (March 8, 1884 – May 7, 1885)

private funds, nor to become its depository in the case of those claimants who are present in Bangkok.

The name of the officer who refused to pay the 2½% is Khun Chömni Akson, deputy of Phra Sewat.

Yrs. v. t.

22. Satow to Philip Currie

1 May 1884 [faint]

Dear Currie,

Newman is leaving Bangkok tomorrow by the usual st[eame]r., & as he intends to travel by way of Gib[raltar]. will probably not reach England much before the end of next month. He has nearly completed the period which would enable him to retire on the full pension of his present rank, but I think it would be a loss to the public service if he were to go. There is no one who possesses such an intimate knowledge of the language and ideas of the Siamese, & his manly straightforward character has made him very popular with all classes of British subjects. Would it not be possible to give him an inducement to stay on, in the shape of promotion to the rank of consul, and an increase of a couple of hundreds to his salary. For my own part, I shld. be very glad to have him back again.

y.v.t.

23. Satow to Prince Devawongse

5 May 84.

Dr. P. D.

I beg to enclose a Siamese translation of the petition of Chua Lung-hi concerning the seizure of 23 jars of spirits on the evening of the 30th April. As I said to Y.R.H. yesterday, I shall be quite satisfied if the spirit is returned to him, & the person who seized it suitably reprimanded for exceeding his duty.

I believe the Indian Govt. has expressed its willingness to construct a 2nd line fr. Moulmein to join the Siamese trunk line at Raheng, & in writing to them about the Tavoy line, it would be useful if I could give them some information about the probable time of

19

PRO 30/33 14/1   Letter Book of Semi-official Letters from Siam. (March 8, 1884 – May 7, 1885)

the line being completed as far as Raheng, & thence to the Burmese frontier, if yr. Govt. shld. be disposed to make a line by that route to Moulmein.

   Believe me

P.S. If you cld. lend me the German Spirit Convention to read, I shld. be greatly obliged.

24. Satow to Currie

7 May. 84

To Currie.

   The proceedings of the Fr[ench]. priest P[ère]. Quentrie at Chantabun, reported in a desp. that goes home by this mail, are not an isolated case of interference by the missionaries. Just after I came here a row occurred at a place called Petrin[?] about 70 m[iles]. fr[om]. Bangkok, in wch. bloodshed took place, but I have been able to ascertain the exact facts. In the case I report, I was able to hear a great deal on the spot from various persons, & the acting Fr. consul afterwards confirmed the rest. P. Quentrie, whose acquaintance I made, looks just the sort of militant apostle who wld. enjoy a row. He dwelt a good deal on the fact that the province had formerly belonged to Cambodia, & this may some day be found by the Fr[ench]. a convenient pretext for annexing this piece of territory. As it is, the Fr. maps put the boundary a good bit further north than it really is. I have advised Pr. Devawongse to publish a counter-map. But I do not hear of any questions being raised at present, except that of the police on Lake Tonlesap. There is some talk of the Fr. missionaries establishing themselves at Changmai, and the Siamese are naturally not very pleased.

   I have got all the claims for confiscated spirits settled, & the additional compensation paid into the Agency chest. The delay was not all on the Siamese side & I must say the Siamese Govt. have settled these cases without any haggling, & the claimants ought to be very glad that their stuff was seized, as they have made a considerable profit out of the transaction. If the Fr[ench]. insist upon a quid pro quo for agreeing to a date for putting the spirit convention into force, wld. it not be possible to throw them over, & to go on without their adhesion. Otherwise they will get what they want, namely the control of the whole of Lake Tonlësap, & we shall only have been playing into their hands, unless the Siamese are

PRO 30/33 14/1   Letter Book of Semi-official Letters from Siam. (March 8, 1884 – May 7, 1885)

stronger than I take them to be. Besides, we shld. be giving the Siamese a very decided proof of goodwill, wch. I think they wld. appreciate. On the other hand, supposing the spirit trade did pass out of the hands of a so called B/S, I do not think bonâ fide B[ritish]. mercantile interests wld. suffer. The carrying trade betw. this [place] & Hong Kong wld. still continue to be done under the B. flag. As for the dealers in this article, there are not a few of them who merely get naturalized in HgKg & Singapore for the purpose of coming here to trade under our protection. They go to the HgKg & Singapore authorities, & declare that they have been so many yrs. resident & are desirous of being naturalized. The said authorities having no means of verifying the statements grant a certificate, & as soon as John Chinaman gets the paper, off he comes to Siam & settles here for good. They give us a great deal of trouble, & do the B. flag no particular credit.

I wrote to the Gov[erno]rs. of Singapore & HgKg. asking for the laws wch. defined the rights of Chinese naturalized in those colonies. HgKg informed me in reply that the effect of naturalization gave the Chinaman absolutely no rights beyond the limits of the the colony, while fr. Singapore I received a copy of a circular of Ld. Kimberley's dated 28/5/82 stating that the prov[isi]ons. of the natural[izatio]n. act of 1870 with regard to pers[o]ns. naturalized in Great B[ritain].[28] apply to persons naturalized in a colony. This leaves me in a curious dilemma. Bangkok wld. be a bed of roses if one had only natives of Gr. B. to look after, but there are all the Burmese, Indians, & Arabs fr. Aden, besides these somewhat doubtful Chinese persons, who swarm in this country. We have 1500 to 2000 Asiatic B/S in Bangkok alone, & the rest are scattered over the interior beyond our reach, with no one to keep them in order. At the sapphire mines 4 days' journey fr. here are 800 Burmese, & I find that Knox & Palgrave apptd. one of them to be a sort of Vice-Consul over the others, a very good arrangement as long as the man does not exceed his authority. I think of paying them a visit as soon as travelling again becomes a possibility, but at present I cannot talk Siamese, & our staff is too limited for me to take one of the men away on a long trip.

The Bangkok-Tavoy[29] line has come to grief, & is closed for the present rainy season,

---

[28] Satow's own father Hans David Christoph Satow had been naturalized British in 1846, three years after his birth. The papers are in the National Archives.
[29] Tavoy in southeast Burma/Myanmar has been called Dawei since 1989.

PRO 30/33 14/1   Letter Book of Semi-official Letters from Siam. (March 8, 1884 – May 7, 1885)

owing to difficulties on the British-Burmese side. The Siamese are very anxious to have it put in working order again as soon as possible, & I have written to the Indian Govt. abt. it.

A Frenchman named Neiss[30] passed thro' here last week fr. the N[orth]. He left Saigon abt. 10 mos. ago, travelling up the Mekong as far as Luang Phrabang, the capital of one of the chiefs dependent on Siam. I am told that [Holt Samuel] Hallett, who belongs to [Archibald Ross] Colquhoun's party, gave a memo. to the Siamese comr. At Changmai advising him to keep an eye on Neiss' proceedings, as the latter was believed to be charged with a political mission, besides his ostensible aims of collecting butterflies & beetles, in fact nothing less than the detaching of Luang Phrabang fr. its dependency on Siam. It is certain that he remained a considerable time at Luang Phrabang, but I am inclined to believe the rest of the story to be a mare's nest [illusion]. At any rate the Siamese Govt. do not feel any anxiety about the matter. They are more disquieted by a rumour that Harmand is to be reappointed here, because that will mean bullying in store for them.

y.v.t.

25. Satow to Prince Devawongse
Devan
Dr. Pr. D.
7 May

I had a conversation with the Chan[?] Fa Ong Noi yesterday afternoon abt. telegraphs to Moulmein, & arranged c. him that I shld. communicate to the Indian Telegraph Admin[istratio]n. the substance of his recent letter to the Kromatah, expressing his hope that comm.[unicatio]n. betw. Tavoy & Bangkok wld. be established c. [with] as little delay as possible. H.R.H. [His Royal Highness] also informed me that he anticipates the completion of the Raheng telegraph by the end of next dry season, & in reply to an inquiry whether the Siam. Govt. wld. then be disposed to join the Br: Burma Govt. in making a line viâ Myawadee fr. Raheng to Moulmein, informed me that they wld. do so c. pleasure, whether the Tavoy line cld. be permanently maintained in working order or not. Of course

---

[30] Paul Marie Néis (1852-1907). French naval doctor and explorer. See diary, May 4, 1884.

PRO 30/33 14/1   Letter Book of Semi-official Letters from Siam. (March 8, 1884 – May 7, 1885)

as responsible Min[iste]r. for Telegraphs, this assurance shld. be enough, but I shld. be glad if Y.R.H. [Your Royal Highness] were able to confirm it.

     y.v.t.

26. Satow to Prince Devawongse
12/5/84

Dear Prince D.

I regret very much to be obliged to tell you that Chua Lung-hi has not been able to get his 23 jars of spirits restored to him,[31] altho' by my directions he has applied 2ce [twice], the last occasion being yesterday evening. This morning I have taken an opportunity of speaking on the matter to Phya Thap, but the latter informs me that in the absence of the Kalahom he can do nothing, & that no one else can. It is surely a very strange state of things that a Minr. going away for a prolonged absence shld. leave no one with authority to act for him, & I must protest agst. a system wch. permits Br/S to be deprived of their property without redress. It appears that the Kalahom has neglected to transmit to his subordinates H.M. orders that spirits are not to be seized. I feel persuaded, however, that Y.R.H. will not fail to take the necessary measures to ensure the faithful execution of the agreement we have entered into wth regard to the spirit traffic.

There are several matters on wch. I wish to have an opportunity of conversing with you, & hope that yr. health will soon be restored so as to permit of our having an interview. If you will kindly let me know beforehand when I may expect you I will take care to be at home.

I return with many thanks the draft of the German convention, reserving my remarks until we meet.

  Believe me

     y.v.t.

27. Satow to Director-General of Telegraphs, Simla (India)

---

[31] See Satow's diary, May 4, 1884.

PRO 30/33 14/1   Letter Book of Semi-official Letters from Siam. (March 8, 1884 – May 7, 1885)

Private & Confidential
Director-Genl. of Telegraphs, Simla
12/5/84
Dear Sir:

With ref. to my desp. of the 7th inst. on the subject of the Tavoy-Bangkok telegraph line, I beg to add that I think it wld. not be advisable, if it can be avoided, to furnish the Siamese Govt. c. any excuse for boasting of their superior foresight in having urged the construction of a line viâ Raheng in preference to the existing one by the Anya[?] Pass to Tavoy. I have read all the correspondence & cannot doubt the justice of the reasons wch. impelled Mr. Palgrave to urge the Indian Govt. to concur in his views. But those are reasons wch. cld. not well be placed before the Siamese Govt., & they could hardly be expected to have sufficient candour to appreciate their value. If it be profitable ∴ [therefore], I hope that the Tavoy line may again be put in a workable cond[itio]n. & maintained so, until the line by Raheng & Myawadee has been completed & opened for some time. Then the Siamese Govt. wld. perhaps spontaneously come to propose the abandonment of the Tavoy line, wch. I suppose the Govt. of British Burma wld. readily accept. It is because the credit, & with it the influence of this Agency is involved in the question, that I shld. prefer the proposal for the abandonment of the line not to come fr. us. One of my greatest difficulties here is that the Siamese are only too ready to impugn the acts of my predecessors, & it seems desirable therefore to avoid giving them an opportunity for crowing over their own superior wisdom & foresight. I do not send a copy of the letter fr. the Min. for F.A. because it is in parts obscure, & in others displays too much of this tone. I have informed him of my intention not to forward this letter, & he has acknowledged the justice of my reasons for this course. I may add that I have recd. fr. the King's private secretary [Prince Devawongse] a confirmation of their willingness to construct the line to Myawadee.

  yrs. very faithfully

28. Satow to Currie
15th May /84
Dear Currie,

PRO 30/33 14/1   Letter Book of Semi-official Letters from Siam. (March 8, 1884 – May 7, 1885)

The King's Secy. has given me a copy of the spirit convention concluded with Germany, & I am sending it home in a desp. of today's date. The Siamese make 2 objections to it, one of wch. is serious, the other, in my opinion, frivolous.

By our convention, & those of all the other powers but Germ. it is left to the Siamese to fix the scale of duties upon spirits, beer & wines, & all they have to do is to communicate it to the consuls. This seems a much simpler & more convenient arrangement than that insisted upon by Germany, namely that the rates shall, <u>as far as the levying of import duties</u> is concerned, be agreed upon betw. the 2 Govts. The practical effect of this stipulation is, however, to make the scale of <u>excise</u> duties a matter of negotiation betw. the 2 Govts. as the two must be identical, unless the Siamese are content to see their own spirits entirely driven out of the market. I suppose H.M.G. & all the other powers will insist upon the scale of duties being submitted to them also, as otherwise the Germans will gain the right of interfering in the Siamese excise for themselves alone, wch. is very likely their object. The result will be that the determination of the scale & the alteration of it at any subsequent time will be extremely cumbrous, & we shall not get this troublesome question off our hands for a long time to come. Surely our agreement was the most convenient to all parties, & it is difficult to see how it cld. prejudice the interests of any one, particularly the Germans, who have no spirit trade to protect, & whose beer & wines are perfectly safe. At present no similar articles are produced in Siam, nor are likely ever to be produced. If the rates of duty were left to the consuls to settle with the Siamese Govt. only those whose people trade in spirits would practically have to be consulted, but by the German arrangement every Treaty Power must give its consent, wch. I venture to think will take much longer. The Siamese objection therefore seems to me serious. Devawongse says they will ask Germany to revert to our draft. I have not offered any opinion, contenting myself simply with the observation that Germany has gone out of her way in consenting to make a convention abt. a matter in wch. she has little interest, & perh[aps]. may not like to be requested to alter it. But at the same time I am entirely of the opinion that it will be a good thing if the Siamese do get her to be satisfied with our arrangements.

The other thing the Siamese object to is the definition of the word "Germans", & their reason for wishing to get it modified appears to me to be almost childish. It only shows

PRO 30/33 14/1   Letter Book of Semi-official Letters from Siam. (March 8, 1884 – May 7, 1885)

what terror they are in of French aggression.

A good point in the German convention seems to be their care to have the word "retail" defined. B/S [British Subjects] go about the city of Bangkok & up country selling spirits for cash in quantities of a few jars at a time, a mode of distribution wch. might by some persons be regarded as retail trade. I wld. suggest that "retail" be taken to mean in quantities of less than one jar, whether to be consumed on the premises or not. Our people do not, I believe, keep liquor shops to any great extent.

I find that there are a considerable number of civil cases in wch. B/S of Asiatic origin are pltfs. [plaintiffs] agst. Siamese, that having been going on in the native court for two yrs. or more, without any result. Instead of writing letters to stir up the authorities, I have adopted the plan of sending Cording, who speaks Siamese very well, up to the courts to fight the case for our people, and it seems to promise good results.

A Mr. E.C. Davidson, who is in Siamese service will prob. call on you, to offer some information about an alternative route for a maritime canal across the Malay peninsula, wch. he examined abt. 2 mos. ago in company with an emissary of Lesseps[32] named Deloncle.[33] You may safely trust what he says about the matter. He does not appear to regard this new line of country as more practicable than that across the Isthmus of Kraw.[34]

      y.v.t.

29. Satow to Bergne[35]

17 May /84

Dear Mr. Bergne,

---

[32] Ferdinand, Vicomte de Lesseps (1805-1894). French diplomat who developed the Suez canal, opened in 1869.
[33] François Deloncle (1856-1922). French consul at Hué, Vietnam, 1883-88.
[34] The Isthmus of Kra is the narrowest part of the Malay peninsula, in southern Siam/Thailand and Burma/Myanmar. In 1897 Siam and Britain agreed that a canal would not be built so that the regional importance of Singapore would be maintained. In February 2018 the Thai Prime Minister declared it was not a priority (*The Straits Times*, February 13, 2018).
[35] Sir John Henry Gibbs Bergne (1842-1908). Superintendent of the treaty department at the Foreign Office, 1881-94.

PRO 30/33 14/1   Letter Book of Semi-official Letters from Siam. (March 8, 1884 – May 7, 1885)

I am sorry to have to tell you that the seal attached to the Queen's ratification of the Chiengmai Treaty reached us in fragments, tho' the silver case in wch. it was contained was intact. This is owing no doubt to its having been banged about in the mailbags, & if it cld. be managed on a future occasion to send such bulky things in a small case instead of in the bag, the seal wld. probably not suffer fr. the journey.

Can you tell me whether it is intended that the Siamese may at once impose duties on beer & wines in excess of three per cent, or must they wait until they begin to manufacture such articles themselves? In the absence of instructions, I think I shld. maintain that as long as Siamese beer & wines do not exist, the import duty will remain as it is.

The Siamese F.O. insisted upon my asking for an exequatur,[36] & at first made it out as for Agent & Consul General. I pointed out that my nomination having been submitted to the King & accepted by him in the usual way, there was certainly no need for his giving me an exequatur as Agent, & I doubted very much whether it was necessary for me to have one as Consul-Genl. Where it is provided by Treaty that the Queen may app[oin]t. consuls, the exercise of their functions can hardly, I shld. think, be dependent upon their having an exequatur. The Japse. however have in recent years given such docu[men]ts.

y.v.t.

30. Satow to Prince Devawongse

11 June 1884

Dear Prince D.

I agree with you that it is unfortunate that the property of Chin Siang Ho has been subjected to such cross-purposes, but before consenting to have the spirits sent down here, I think we had better consult together. As the farmer of the place where the seizure took place is, I am informed, a holder of his farm from the Royal Financial Dept., it will not be difficult I imagine, for you to deal effectually with the case. There are two things that I am entitled to ask, firstly that the farmer shld. be made to feel that he cannot with impunity violate the orders not to seize spirit wch. Y.R.H. has assured me have been given, & 2ndly

---

[36] exequatur: a written recognition of a consul by the government of the state in which he or she is stationed giving authorization to exercise appropriate powers.

PRO 30/33 14/1   Letter Book of Semi-official Letters from Siam. (March 8, 1884 – May 7, 1885)

that Siang Ho should be placed pecuniarily in the same position as if the spirits had not been seized. This is the 4th if not the 5th seizure that has taken place since the assurance given to me that such acts shld. not be repeated, & I think you will agree with me that it is time to put a stop to such proceedings.

    y.v.t.

31. Satow to Currie
13 June /84
Dear Currie,

    It is a long time since anything was written from here about the Rajah of Perak's claim to have restored to him certain territory in the occupation of Siamese Malays, & I have taken an opportunity of representing my view of the question in a desp. by this mail. The Straits people are all for annexation, and look forward to the time when the whole of the peninsula will be theirs. On the other side the French are anxious to set up similar claims on behalf of Cambodia. As I understand that H.M.G. would prefer to see Siam remain independent, it seems to me that there is nothing to be gained by supporting the Rajah of Perak, the admission of whose claim will be a signal to the French to begin nibbling in Battambong & Siemreap. Of course it is no secret among foreigners here that the Straits Govt. have demanded the territory for Perak. It is rather amusing that the Surveyor McCarthy, whom Sir F. Weld thinks such a nice fellow, on his return here from surveying the boundary, openly stated it as his opinion that Perak's claim was preposterous. This is the man that the Govr. is so anxious to take into the Singapore service.

    A draft of the answer of Siam to the Chinese claim for tribute was given to me last night, but I have had no time to enclose it in my desp. on the subject. The original letters from China I could gather the sense of, and have sent them to Hongkong to get an accurate translation made. I am going to send a copy of my desp. to Sir Harry Parkes [Minister in China, Satow's former boss in Japan] for his information. Would it not be well to give the Chinese Govt. a hint that they must not interfere with Siam.

    I have written a couple of desp. on the spirit question, wch. I hope will be approved. The position is somewhat difficult, and the only way to put matters right is to be conciliatory without sacrificing any principles. These Chinese spirit-dealers are a troublesome lot, and fully acquainted with the nature of their treaty rights. It is somewhat curious that Hopkins, who signed the petition to the Govr. of Hongkong complaining of restrictions on the spirit trade is agent there for the same line of steamers wch. Windsor, who has declared in favour of Siamese views, represents here.

32. Satow to H. Clarke Jervoise

June 12. 84.

Dear Jervoise,

My desp[atch]. 20.25 of May 5 will have shown how the spirit claims reported by Newman have been settled, & that as far as they are concerned there is no reason why the date for carrying out the convention should not be fixed; but for the stipulation in the German convention that it is not to be ratified until certain regulations for carrying it out shall have been drawn up, & agreed upon betw. the 2 Govts. of Germany & Siam, there need be no delay. I am trying to get the Siamese to hasten forward these regulations, & have now in my hands a huge draft of an Excise law framed on the model of what is in force at Singapore, wch. appears to me quite unfit for this country, & the particular circ[umstance]s. I shall endeavour to get this modified into a workable shape, but do not think it necessary to trouble you with any details at present. The fact is that the German convention transfers the seat of further negotiations to Berlin. It was done, my German colleague informs me, at his suggestion, & he is rather proud of his cleverness. As the Germans have no interest whatever in the matter, it can only be attributed to their general desire to make themselves of importance in the East. However, I suppose it is of no use resenting it, & I shall urge upon the Siamese the advisability of framing the regulations in such a manner as to render them acceptable without discussion. If this is done & they are communicated at the same time to the other consuls the execution of the agreement need not be postponed longer than the time necessary for communicating with Europe.

In acc. with your suggestion I have written a desp[atch]. on the spirit question wch. in conjunction with my previous one reporting the settle[men]t. of outstanding cases, will I hope give all the inform[atio]n. that Ld. E. Fitzmaurice requires. I am afraid that until the

PRO 30/33 14/1   Letter Book of Semi-official Letters from Siam. (March 8, 1884 – May 7, 1885)

agreement comes into force there will be cases of seizure by the spirit farmers fr. time to time, but I think it better not to make too much of them, as long as this Govt. does its best. The announcement that a date had been fixed wld. do a great deal of good. French thinks that having once got the Foreign O. to listen to them they hope to arrange matters in London without regard to the Agency. It may be so, but I feel confident of being supported by you & hope in the end to convince them that they need not depair of having their just claims considered here. Of course they are a little tricky, like all Orientals.

  y.v.t.

33. Satow to Sir Frederick Weld

Bangkok 21/6/84

Dear Sir Frederick,

 Several things that I have learnt, since last writing to you, about the pretensions of the Fr. to recover in the name of Cambodia and Annam rights over territory wch. has belonged to Siam for the last 80 or 100 years, have led me to study more closely the claim set up by the Rajah of Perak. I cannot help coming to the conclusion that there is a close parallel between the two cases, & that if the Siamese were to give the Rajah what he asks, they would have much difficulty in opposing a claim for the surrender of Battambong & Siemrap, to say nothing of other provinces wch. Fr. writers so persistently assert do not rightfully belong to Siam. I fear it might have the look of a first step in the direction of partitioning the outlying Siamese dominions, wch. I believe is not the policy wch. H.M.G. desires to pursue. I have recently laid my views before Ld. Granville in a desp. wch. I hope they will show you. At the same time I have taken care not to commit myself with the Siamese, in case the Govt. shld. decide the other way. If they do, I think the easiest way would be to give notice simply that you intend to take poss[essio]n. & let the Siamese protest. I feel now that I have discharged my conscience both towards the F.O. & yrself, & my private opinion will not stand in the way of my carrying out any instructions that may be given to me.

 I trust you are enjoying yourself in England.

  y.v.t.

PRO 30/33 14/1   Letter Book of Semi-official Letters from Siam. (March 8, 1884 – May 7, 1885)

34. Satow to Currie

25 June 1884

Dear Currie,

The Siamese have just got a telegram fr[om]. their Chargé d'Affaires in London informing them that the Spirit Agreement will come into operation on Jan. 1, & are extremely delighted. They tell me that the F[oreign].M[inisters]. of Holland, France & Portugal have promised that the provisional agreement of the consuls shall remain in force until the Convention replaces it. The new law destined to give effect to the convention will be officially communicated to us in about a month's time, after being first laid before the consuls concerned for their opinion; they do not anticipate any discussion except on the part of the German. If they give it to him in the form I suggested, he cannot well offer any objections to its provisions, as his beer is especially excepted. No additional duty is proposed to be levied on that or wines, at least for the present.

y.v.t.

35. Satow to Currie

2nd letter of same date [25 June 1884].

The Chin[ese]. have sent an official here to find out whether Siam had made a secret alliance with France, to contribute an auxiliary force in case of war breaking out. As you are aware, Harmand tried very hard to obtain even a small contingent, but unsuccessfully, so there is nothing for the Chinese emissary to learn.

We hear that the French have pensioned off the King of Cambodia, and are taking over the direct administration of the territory, but this you probably know already. It will give them a solid basis for demanding the rectification of the frontier towards Siam, but hardly strengthens the justice of their claims.

I was invited by the King to a private audience about ten days ago.[37] He said he was very pleased that matters went so smoothly now, and told me to come to him whenever I wanted anything done. He asked whether we were going to annex Upper Burmah, to wch. I replied

---

[37] See Satow's diary for June 17, 1884.

PRO 30/33 14/1   Letter Book of Semi-official Letters from Siam. (March 8, 1884 – May 7, 1885)

that we did not wish to touch it. If I saw my way to it, I should be inclined to ask him to abolish slavery for debt and make gambling debts not recoverable at law. These two things are at the bottom of everything that is bad in Siam, and it is really time that the Siamese shld. begin to put their house in order. But no one seems to have a spark of patriotism, except the King & one or two of his brothers.

    y.v.t.

36. Satow to Cecil Smith (p. 38 in notebook)
27 June 1884

Dear Smith,

I have sent you a desp. by this steamer on the case of Chia Pek I, which has been going on for the past five y[ea]rs. Capel, a clerk of Donaldson & Burkinshaw,[38] has been to me recently to ask me to take it up. After carefully going thro' the documents, I came to the conclusion that they had not a leg to stand upon, and cannot in conscience present it. They have demanded the most exorbitant sums after the usual manner of Oriental B[ritish].S[ubjects]. wch. alone is sufficient to make one disgusted with their case, even if it were a good one at bottom. I do not want to bother the F.O. with the affair, but of course if you insist I must do so. How far B.S. are entitled to our interference on their behalf, when they go money making in these out of the way places, and become quasi-officials of the native chiefs seems to me very doubtful, & every demand we make for the ingerence [intervention, interference, intrusion] of the Siamese in the affairs of those Malay states only increases their power there.

Can you oblige me with copies of the ordinances now in force in the Straits regulating the spirit trade. I want them now and then for reference.

I think I told you I intended to write a desp. opposing the claim of the Rajah of Perak; this I have done, & at the same time have informed Sir F. Weld, in order that he may not attribute it to pure 'vice'. I really do not think Low has proved his case.

    y.v.t.

---

[38] Donaldson & Burkinshaw was a law partnership in Singapore, founded in 1874.

PRO 30/33 14/1   Letter Book of Semi-official Letters from Siam. (March 8, 1884 – May 7, 1885)

37. Satow to Plunkett[39]

Plunkett Official

27 June /84

Sir,

I have the hon[our]. to acknowledge c. thanks your letter of the 7th inst. forwarding to me 6 copies of the "List of Korean Geog[raphical]. Names" printed at the cost of H.M. Legn. in Japan.

   In simple justice to Mr. W.G. Aston & Mr. B.H. Chamberlain I must take this opportunity of acknowledging the invaluable assistance recd. by me fr. those gentlemen in preparing this list, wch. was of at least equal importance with my own share of the work, & without wch. it wld. never have seen the light. For this reason it was intended that the bk. shld. appear anonymously under the title of "A Manual of Korean Geog. & other Proper Names Romanized", & I regret extremely that an alteration by wch. I am made to appear the sole author has been made fr. the M.S. title page prepared by me for the printer.

   I trust it may eventually be found possible to publish the II [Second] Part of the Manual, referred to in paragraph 4 of the Introduction, as it was designed to meet a want much felt

---

[39] Sir Francis Plunkett (1835-1907).
Secretary of Legation in Tokyo, 1873-76. Minister in Tokyo, 1884-87.

Plunkett in 1900

PRO 30/33 14/1   Letter Book of Semi-official Letters from Siam. (March 8, 1884 – May 7, 1885)

in translating fr. Japse. or Chinese writings concerning Korea.

38. Satow to Currie
11/7/84 (faint)
Dear Currie,

The story of M. Neiss' proceedings at Luang Prabang, of wch. I was at first disposed to scout [dismiss] the correctness, has now been confirmed by what I have learnt from Capt. Leonowens of the Siamese surveying party, who has temporarily returned here & by P.D. I have therefore put the chief points into a short desp[atch]. wch. I am sending home by this mail.

Colquhoun has just arrived with his party, & I have introduced them to Prince D[evawongse]. There is a good chance of the King contributing a sum of money towards the expenses of the exploration, & I am supporting this as best I can. If they succeed in starting rlwys. in Siam with foreign capital, as I hope they will do, it will afford a useful check on the acquisitive tendencies of our lively [French] neighbours in Saigon. I think this is of more importance than helping Chinese to sell cheap spirits to the Siamese, & ∴ [therefore] am disposed to do all I can to meet the wishes of the Siamese Govt. with regard to the spirit trade. If they will place in my hands officially the regulations for its conduct, of wch. I have given them a draft in substitution of what they first showed to me, I shall probably telegraph for permissions to stop the traffic until the agreement comes into force on Jan. 1 in the same way as the Dutch, Fr. & Portuguese Consuls have done. I shall take care to make such stipulations in exchange for this concession as will prevent Chinese B[ritish]. S[ubjects]. suffering any loss, & I hope that you will support me by giving permission if I ask first.

I have written a desp. announcing my intention of going to Japan about the end of Aug. but you may rely on my not leaving Bangkok if there should be any complications about the spirit traffic or any other question requiring my personal attention.

I propose to see the Govr. of Hongkong & on my way back to look in at Saigon & Singapore, wch. I can do easily without exciting attention as the Fr. mail calls at Saigon.

   y.v.t.

PRO 30/33 14/1   Letter Book of Semi-official Letters from Siam. (March 8, 1884 – May 7, 1885)

40. Satow to Currie

16 July/84

Dear Currie,

My desp. No 57 on the rlwy. project for Siam cld. not be got ready for our cover, & I am despatching it to the Acting Govr. of Singapore to be forwarded by the C.O. [Colonial Office?] Bag. The K[ing]. altho' ready to give a sum of money to carry out surveys, & secretly in his heart desirous of adopting the scheme, is too afraid of the Fr[ench]. to throw in his lot with England. What he wants is to feel assured that we have material interests at stake in the existence of Siam, & that assurance can only be given by an undertaking on the part of the Indian Govt. to make a line fr. Rangoon to the frontier of B.B. [British Burma] to join the Siamese system. The moment is propitious. France is represented only by an acting consul of no influence, & her attention is now drawn again in the direction of China. The Siamese do not expect nor ask for an alliance, but they need a material pledge that we will not leave them to be devoured by France. I know it has been said by the advocates of annexation that they wld. leave the valley of the Menam [Chao Phraya river] to Siam as a buffer between them & us, but how can they be trusted to be content with the Mekong Valley. The possession of that will bring them perilously near to Upper Burmah, & their means of being disagreeable to us will then become immense. I assume that the policy of H.M.G. is to keep Siam on her legs so that we & France may not become close neighbours, but this object will certainly not be attained if we leave Siam alone & allow her to be trampled on whenever the Fr. choose. We shld. be forced in self-defence to annex Upper Burmah, wch. I suppose no one wishes to do. These were the reasons that led me to telegraph, as I think no time os to be lost, & I hope my desp. & its enclosures will afford a satisfactory explanation. Colquhoun has gone off Hongkong today, but leaves Hallett behind, who can make all the necessary arrangements with the Siamese. I trust befpre many days are over to receive the authorization I have asked for.

    y.v.t.

41. Satow to Lee

PRO 30/33 14/1   Letter Book of Semi-official Letters from Siam. (March 8, 1884 – May 7, 1885)

16/7/84

My dear Lee,

I sincerely hope Ld. E. Fitzmaurice will have been consulted about my telegram of the 14th, asking that I may assure the Siamese that the Indian Govt. is ready to make a railway up to the frontier of B.B. [British Burma] to join a Siamese system of rlwys. I think the matter of the greatest importance, as I have endeavoured to show in my desp. Nos. 49 & 51. The French were not engaged in China, the next thing they wld. return their attention to wld. be claiming fr. Siam the provinces they have so long hankered after. We must prevent them by all means in our power from getting hold of Luang Prabang & the surrounding territory in the valley of the Mekong, wch. wld. bring them close to Upper Burma. & enable them to put pressure on us in that direction. The best & easiest means is by connecting Siam & B.B. by railway. Pray get hold of my desp[atche]s. & their encl[osures]. If Colquhoun's scheme is rejected out of mere fear of the Fr. the latter will be able to walk over the field whenever they like. Siam believes that we shld. never lift a finger to save her, unless we have joint interests such as the investment of British capital in rlwys. would create.

  y.t.

42. Satow to Currie

30 July 1884

Dear Currie,

Since I last wrote nothing further has been done with regard to Colquhoun's rlwy. scheme. Hallett is waiting to hear fr. Calcutta at what rate of guarantee a firm engaged in this sort of business wld. undertake to construct rlwys. in Siam. I have learnt that Mr. Bryce who was here a few months ago has promised the King to give him a scheme for the construction of a rlwy. fr[om]. Bangkok to Korat.[40] Meanwhile the Siamese are making their own plans for frustrating the Fr. designs on Luang Phrabang and the country to the N.E. bordering on Tonquin. They have sent full powers to the commander of their troops to take possn. of the country, & are looking about for a suitable man to appt. as resident comdr.

---

[40] The province of Nakhon Ratchasima in northeast Thailand.

PRO 30/33 14/1   Letter Book of Semi-official Letters from Siam. (March 8, 1884 – May 7, 1885)

at Luang Phrabang. They count a great deal upon the chances of rupture between France & China in consequence of the Lang Son affair,[41] but in that they are no doubt destined to be disapp[oin]t[e]d. Prince Devawong said to me yesterday that they fear they will not have time to complete their precautions, 'as the French are so hasty' to use his own words. They are quite alive to the danger wch. threatens Siam, but do not hope for any succour fr[om]. England. When they talk to me abt. their fears I tell them they must try to get European capital into the country, by giving mining concessions, leases of teak forests, rlwy. concessions, &c. to foreigners. A German firm wanted a lease of some gold mines, but the Siamese would not come to terms. Englishmen have tried to get leases of forests, but without success. I suppose like other oriental nations they fear to let foreigners of any nation get a solid footing in the interior, but it is their only possible safeguard. A rlwy. linking them on to B.B. wld. do a great deal, but I am afraid the Indian Govt. does not care to make any promise. Neiss when up at Chiengmai this spring said that 3 or 4 French exploring parties wld. traverse the Mekong valley next dry season.

I find that the C.C. of B.B. [Charles Bernard, Chief Commissioner of British Burma] has no cipher with wch. he & I can communicate. The Indian Govt. altho' possessing Cipher E have also O. The latter wld. be much more useful, & I have no doubt, if I were permitted to have a copy. I have written officially on the subject, as I think it of importance. It is also very desirable that there shld. be telegraphic communication betw. Bangkok, India & Europe, without going thro' Saigon, but the Indian Govt. have taken no notice whatever of the desp. I wrote to them early in May on the subject of the Tavoy-Bangkok line. It wld. be a very good thing if they wld. promise to join the Siamese line to Raheng. The Fr[ench]. operators here communicate every fact they can get hold of to the Fr. consulate.

I am sending an appeal <u>ad misericordiam</u> for some necessary alterations to my house. The Office of Works has done what it can, but the Treasury will not give what I ask for unless you support me. Some of the alterations, such as the erection of serv[an]ts' rooms and putting my dining room & drawing room in a fit condition for entertaining were so

---

[41] The retreat from Lang Son in Tonkin in March 1885 brought down the government of French premier Jules Ferry and brought the Sino-Japanese War (August 1884 to April 1885) to an end.

PRO 30/33 14/1   Letter Book of Semi-official Letters from Siam. (March 8, 1884 – May 7, 1885)

urgent that I have spent about £100 out of my own pocket in the hope of afterwards getting it back. The expenses of setting up housekeeping have been so great that it is money I could ill afford to lose, & I hope you will not object to giving your support to my application.

   y.v.t.

P.S. I see fr. yr. telegrams that China is to hand over Laokai to the Fr. in the extreme N.W. of Tonkquin. This is the point up to wch. the Siamese claims on the l. bank of the Mekong. It is usually put down as occupied either by indept. tribes or by Burmese Shans, but I believe the past to be that the inhabitants have hitherto paid tribute both to Luang Prabang & Annam, or more recently to the Black Flags.

   E.S.

43. Satow to Jervoise (p.45 of notebook)
31/7/84

My dear Jervoise,

 I was very glad to get the draft of the new O. in C. [Order in Council] wch. I see provides for everything I asked for. There is nothing in it about the registration of B.S. [British Subjects] With regard to this there are 2 things I shld. like to do, namely to make all B.S. register themselves here once a year for a moderate fee, say one dollar, as they do in China & Japan, & the other is to cause all Asiatics for the future to marry at the Consulate, wch. they can do without violating their religious feelings. The latter is somewhat difficult, because I do not know how far the native marriage customs wld. be recognized by Engl. law. Can a Mahommedan take four legal wives in Bangkok, as he would in India? We have frequently troublesome questions of nationality to decide owing to the habit of living with a native woman without any form of marriage. After a while she may leave the man, carry off some of the children and sell them as slaves. I do not feel quite certain whether I cld. prevent her doing this. To clear up these points I shld. like them to be legally married at the consulate, as the woman & children wld. then become B.S. Perh[aps]. when I get clearer ideas on the subject I may write officially & suggest an arrangement, but in the meantime a complete register of B.S. in Bangkok wld. be very desirable.

 I hope you will interest yourself on behalf of Archer's application for an allowance to

PRO 30/33 14/1   Letter Book of Semi-official Letters from Siam. (March 8, 1884 – May 7, 1885)

his native teacher, & my proposal for spending a little more money on wages. It can be done without increasing the vote. I asked Newman to speak to his brother abt. it, but hear that the latter was away.

The spirit trade still gives me a good deal of bother. Every now & then a Chinaman continues to get a lot of jars seized in order to have a fat compensation on the same scale as the others. I am obliged to pretend great indignation with the Siamese; they then promise to return the stuff, the Chinaman gets an order to take delivery, wch. he does by all the means in his power, & so on. Spirit continues to be imported in large quantities, & the Siamese think it is very unkind of us to let their revenue suffer, when France, Holland & Portugal are so disinterested.

They are not easy in their minds about Fr[ench]. doings in Cambodia, & I fear the same tricks will be played in the valley of the Mekong. It wld. hardly suit us if the French get hold of Luang Phrabang. Their next step wld. be to make their Treaty with Independent Burma unto a reality. We ought to do something to show them we are not asleep, & I believe a rlwy. fr. somewhere up the valley of the Menam [Chao Praya river] over to Moulmein wld. produce a wonderful effect.

y.v.t.

44. Satow to W. Gregor Taylor (p. 46 of notebook)

W. Gregor Taylor

My dear Sir,

Many thanks for the Hdbk. [Handbook] showing your lines of cable. I have replied officially to your longer letter. You will see that the Siamese have nothing further to propose, in fact Bangkok is waiting for the Co. I happen to know that pressure was put on the Siamese Govt. to accept the last draft, & I have privately informed the F.O. that the King is ready to sanction, subject to the modifications of rates that are desired. Perh[aps]. I am not wrong in inferring that the Chairman of the Co. has not been successful in his negotiations with the Fr. Govt. If so, I suppose the Co. will not proceed further in the matter, but I think it is much to be regretted that we have no direct comm[unicatio]n. except thro' Saigon, as the Tavoy line has broken down entirely, at least as far as this season is

PRO 30/33 14/1   Letter Book of Semi-official Letters from Siam. (March 8, 1884 – May 7, 1885)

concerned.

If on the contrary the Co. is ready to resume the matter where the correspondence was dropped, I shall be very glad to do all in my power to assist in the attainment of its objects.

 I am &c.

  y.v.f.

45. Satow to Prince Devawongse

9.8.84

Dear Prince D.

Before going away last week, I mentioned to you the illegal arrest by the Kalahom's gaoler of two B.S. & I regret very much now to have to bring to your notice another similar case wch. occurred during my absence. On Aug. 1 Mr. French complained to the F.M. in writing that a British subject named Tan Goh Boh had been arrested & put in irons by the officials of Bang Preng in Paklat, and he asked for the man's immediate release. Upon the ground that the amphö [district officer] who ordered the arrest had absconded, the release was refused, & the man has been kept in custody up to this moment. I shld. be much obliged if Y.R.H. wld. lay this matter before the King without delay, & I feel confident that H.M. will command that fitting redress be afforded in this as in the previous case.

 Believe me

  y.v.f.

46. Satow to Bergne (p.47 of notebook)

13 Aug.

Dear Mr. Bergne,

Since the date of my desp. no. 38 abt. the spirit question things have gone on much in the same way. Some seizures are made now & then, but on my remonstrating the spirits are usually given back. People who are not B.S. try to carry on the trade under the wing of our people, & this gives us a great deal of trouble. Besides, the loss to the Siamese revenue is very great, & the Govt. constantly complain to me. It no doubt seems hard to them that England will not do for them what Fr. Port. & Holl. have done. I confess I think it wld. be

PRO 30/33 14/1   Letter Book of Semi-official Letters from Siam. (March 8, 1884 – May 7, 1885)

politic to make whatever concessions are possible. If they wld. issue the amended regulations abolishing the monopoly & establish an excise law, there wld. be no harm in our joining the provisional agreement made with the other consuls until Jan. 1. 1855. I wld. at the same time tell them that H.M.G. consent to the agreement of April 6, 1883 being carried out on Jan. 1. The only Powers whose subjects are interested in the Trade are bound by the provisional agreement until their conventions come into force, & we shld. be in no worse position than they. If however the subjects of any power were allowed to import spirits at 3% duty, we cld. then claim the benefit of the most favoured nation clause, & we should then have shifted the odium of injuring the Siamese revenue onto the sh[ou]lders. of other people.

As far as I can see the effect of imposing an import duty equal to the excise will probably [be] the extinction of the trade in Chinese spirits, & perh. H.M.G. have no great objection to such a result. In that case, as a complete settlement of the extremely troublesome question will tend greatly to improve our relations in other respects. I trust that if I telegraph for permission to join the consular agreement, it will not be refused. I should take care to arrange that no B.S. incurs any loss. By next mail I propose to write officially in this sense.

   y.v.t.

47. Satow to Currie
Bangkok
Aug. 14th 1884
Dear Currie

The enforcement of the principle that British subjects are entitled to carry on the spirit trade until our agreement comes into force is surrounded by so many practical difficulties, that I believe it will be better to adhere to the arrangement which Palgrave refused to join, as the Siamese have repeatedly urged us to obtain permission to do so. I mentioned in a previous letter that as I was inclined to ask for the necessary authorization, and I am writing by next week's mail to request telegraphic instructions, which I hope will not be refused. When the agreement comes into force its natural effect will be to put a stop to the trade in

PRO 30/33 14/1   Letter Book of Semi-official Letters from Siam. (March 8, 1884 – May 7, 1885)

foreign spirits, whether from China or Java, as the Chinese will be handicapped to the extent of the freight of rice both ways and other charges, so that no margin of profit will be left. They are people who cannot afford to do business unless the profit is considerable. I do not know what truth there is in the Siamese statement that H.M.P. [H.M.G.?] recognized that the agreement would have this effect, but I think they must have foreseen it. I want to get the Siamese to issue their regulations doing away nominally with the monopoly, and replacing it by a system of excise. That will save the credit of the agreement and there is nothing worth fighting for after that.

I learn that Dr Néis not only offered French assistance to the Chief of Luang Prabang, but also to the Commander of the Siamese force now operating in those regions against the Chinese immigrants known as Haws, who appear to be a group of Black Flags. Also, that the French have told the Siamese that they will accept any frontier towards Annam that I can choose to mark out. This is very adroit as it leaves them a handle afterwards for disputing any assumption of suzerainty over tribes that have paid tribute to Annam, and which, they will be able to argue, have been wrongly included within Siamese boundaries. I was recently up the river Bengpe Kong which runs in the direction of Telë Sap [Tonle Sap?], and found whole villages populated by Cambodian captives, who still preserve their own language, and in some places a sprinkling of Annamites. The French will one day no doubt claim these people as French protégés. If they do, we ought to lay claim to the Peguans who are settled in many parts of Siam and particularly in the neighbourhood of Bangkok.

I have had a little trouble lately with the Kralahome, whose subordinates have in two cases arrested and kept in irons some British subjects. In one case the King has ordered the Kralahome [Kalahome] to make an apology, which he seems very reluctant to do, but he will have to give in eventually. The fact is that he is very powerful, and can often afford to disregard the orders of the King, who is far from being an absolute sovereign. Nevertheless there are signs of his gradually getting stronger. Until the authority of the great families is broken, there is little hope of any kind of improvement of this country, whoch seems to be in pretty much the same state as Japan before the revolution of 1868. I think our policy should be decidedly to support the King on every occasion.

PRO 30/33 14/1   Letter Book of Semi-official Letters from Siam. (March 8, 1884 – May 7, 1885)

Yours etc.

48. Satow to Devawongse

To Devawongse   16 Aug.

Mr. Hallett has told me the reasons wch. prevent the adoption of his railway scheme, and I fully appreciate their weight, tho' regretting their existence.

49. Satow to Currie

Bangkok

26 Aug. 1884

Dear Currie,

[Holt Samuel] Hallett has left Bangkok on the 23 for China, having failed to induce the Siamese Govt. to adopt his scheme for a rlwy. The idea [Archibald Ross] Colquhoun & he started with was a line to Chiengmai to be connected with B[ritish].B[urma]. by a branch from Raheng to Moulmein, but seeing that the Siamese were more inclined to make a rlwy. to Korat [in northeast Thailand], I advised him to be contented with that. He telegraphed to various people for terms. The lowest on wch. he cld. get any one in India to do it was a guarantee of 7 per cent, & capitalists in London asked 9. When these were laid before the King's private Secy. he said it was hopeless trying to carry the scheme thro! There were too many of the old hands in the Govt. who objected both to the construction of a rlwy & to a guarantee. The King was desirous of having the rlwy to Korat, but cld. not overcome the opposition. Besides 7 per cent was too high.

My own impression is that the real ground of refusal is the very natural one, that a concession to a foreign company would mean a great extension of extraterritorial jurisdiction, wch. they desire to limit by all means in their power. The King would be pleased to have a rlwy. to Korat if it could be made for nothing, but cannot make up his mind to incur the expense.

One good result of Hallett's long[?] stay has been that they have giving [given] up saying that the fear of the French makes them unwilling to give a concession to Englishmen and invented other excuses. They have no intention whatever of making rlwys.

43

PRO 30/33 14/1   Letter Book of Semi-official Letters from Siam. (March 8, 1884 – May 7, 1885)

There appeared in the "Times" of July 14 a telegram from Bangkok to the effect that the Siamese feared the advance of the French troops upon the capital of the country. As far as I can ascertain Colquhoun sent it in Code, but without the words underlined ["troops upon the capital of the country"], which must have been added at home. It is no wonder that its appearance shld have excited great trust of Colquhoun. Both he & Hallett are greatly devoid of tact, but I did what I could for them as Sir Owen Burne[42] asked me to help Colquhoun.

The Kalahome has made an abject apology for the imprisonment of B.S. & the King has issued a proclamation on the matter wch. only reached me late yesterday besides directing the Foreign Min. to express his regrets.

In Europe the Siamese give out that Slavery has been abolished; my desp[atch]. on the subject will show that it flourishes as much as ever, & that B.S. have dabbled in it. The decisions I have lately given in the Cons: Court will prevent the latter from supposing they may legally do so.

I hope my request for an efficient constable will be granted. It is impossible to do the office work properly without some help, as Cording has nearly all his time taken up in watching cases in the native courts. We have disposed of a large no. of old ones on the last three months. Now & then I have to send him away for several days to look after troublesome cases that have arisen in the interior, as no reliance can be placed on Siamese reports, and there are B.S. scattered all over the country either as Traders or agriculturalists. It will do good to show that we will have any eye to our people away fr[om]. Bangkok.

[Vice-Consul Edward Blencowe] Gould sends down some interesting reports [from Chiengmai], and I transmit to you copies. I hope his salary will be increased, for 6000 rupees is really much less than he is worth.

I think the Siamese without doubt are afraid of French designs on a part at least of their territory, but they are confident that the strong interest England has in their independence is a safeguard on which they may rely. In consequence they now express to me less alarm than they first did. The King's private Secy. writes to me in a private note with reference to

---

[42] Sir Owen Tudor Burne (1837-1909). Major-general. See entry in *Oxford Dictionary of National Biography*.

PRO 30/33 14/1   Letter Book of Semi-official Letters from Siam. (March 8, 1884 – May 7, 1885)

Colquhoun's alarmist telegram as follows: "And I am satisfied that all of us here know very well that no apprehension of the kind (is) contemplated (i.e. entertained) by H.M. Govt. & I have this proof in your presence in this country." Rather queer English, but he probably means that he knows England will not easily let them be swallowed up. Of course the outbreak of war in China has put them more at their ease, & the rumour of [Jules] Harmand's apptmt. to Bolivia has comforted them greatly. In consequence of this last news the French telegraph employés have made up their minds, I hear, that they will have to go when their time is up about 5 months hence.

The Indian Govt. have written that they will have the Tavoy line in working order again by next spring, & that they are ready to construct a second line fr. Moulmein to Myawadi to join a Siamese line to that place from Raheng.

The survey of the N.E. frontier is to be continued in October, & [James] McCarthy, the man who is engaged on it hopes to finish the boundary towards Tonquin during the next dry season. All that part of the country including Luang Phrabang is merely under the suzerainty of Siam, & pays no taxes to Bangkok.

y.v.t.

50. Satow to Bergne
16 Sept. 1884
D[ea]r. Mr. Bergne,

I hope we have at last got to the bottom of the mystery abt. the scale used by Mr. Gould for obtaining the results sent by him to the Govr. of Hongkong. It was not applied scientifically, & no one in the Agency cld. tell me anything abt. the matter, so at last I sent for the instrument, & a description of it goes home by this mail.

On the 13th I discussed with the King's Secty. the draft of the new Law on the spirit trade in Siam to wch. reference has been made in several of my desp. & agreed with him abt. all the points wch. concern us. It completely abolishes the monopoly, & creates an excise, wch. will be collected by farmers, as is the usual practice in Siam. It will probably be officially communicated before long, & will be sent home by Mr. French, who takes charge of the Agency during my absence on leave. He will at the same time report on the

PRO 30/33 14/1   Letter Book of Semi-official Letters from Siam. (March 8, 1884 – May 7, 1885)

arrangements for testing under Art. 2 of the Agreement, & the licensing system proposed by the Siamese, wch. appears to me to be satisfactory. The method of testing is described in the law, & the Siamese will prob. have it performed by an European chemist whom they appt. for the purpose. Under ordinary circs. I imagine the importers will raise no objection to the duties thus paid, but in cases where they dispute the accuracy of the results obtained, we shld. direct the Agency doctor to test on our side. I suppose we shall get a new doctor before long. There is no one else in the place whom we cld. appt. for the purpose without giving him a fee. It might be as well to tell the new doctor that he will have to do this sort of work; there will most likely be very little of it.

The only condition as to the issue of retail licenses that remains to be fixed is the hours of opening & closing. These I am told will be 6 a.m. & 10 p.m. as at Hongkong. In general, the law is based upon the ordinances in force at Hongkong & in the Straits.

   Believe me
    y.v.t.

51. Satow to Sir Julian Pauncefote

16 Sept. /84

Dear Sir Julian,

I trust my proposal in a desp. that goes by this mail, to make the registration of B.S. compulsory, will be favourably considered. To what I have said officially abt. the necessity there is little to be added, except that the transference of passports & certificates of nationality is a frequent thing, especially among the Burmese who swarm in the northern parts of Siam, & it leads to serious abuses. The want of a certificate of nationality is also the cause to some extent of illegal arrests of B.S. such as occurred lately & I think it wld. be well to take whatever steps are feasible to prevent them.

  Believe me y.v.f.

52. Satow to Currie (p.56 of notebook)

16 Sept. /84

Dear Currie,

PRO 30/33 14/1   Letter Book of Semi-official Letters from Siam. (March 8, 1884 – May 7, 1885)

I am starting tomorrow for Japan, & have left everything in train with regard to the arrangements required for carrying out the Spirit Convention. There is nothing else of importance on hand. The Second King complained to me a short time ago that he feared the First King was going to take away a number of the men who are bound to perform forced labour for him or to pay a commutation in money. As this wld. have seriously diminished his revenues, & thus have been contrary to the arrangement of 1874 by wch. the Second King's position was assured under a sort of guarantee from us, I thought it advisable to hint to the King thro' his private Secy. that it had better not be done. A few days later I recd. an assurance that no change wld. be made without the Second King's consent. I have not reported the matter officially, as I am inclined to think the hint will be acted upon.

I scarcely expected that my view of the Perak boundary question wld. prevail over the representations of Sir F. Weld and Sir H. Low, but I am assured that the Fr. take a lively interest in the question, & they are very thick with the Kalahôm ro whose dept. the Malay states belong. The kernel of the matter seems to be the remoteness of the encroachments wch. took place not very long after the Siamese appropriated 2 provinces of Cambodia. Whatever the King may have said to Newman on the first occasion, he quite changed his views after McCarthy's survey was recd. But I have not see[n] Newman's report, if he has made one recently.

  y.v.t.

[P.S.] I am told that the Fr. acting consul is going to suggest to his govt. the establish[men]t. of a mixed court. It would be a good thing, but not on French principles. I want the Siamese to do it on Engl. lines, if at all.

  y.v.t.

53. Satow to H.S.C. Clarke-Jervoise (outline only)

16/9/84.

Law Books

Doctor

54. Satow to Currie (p. 60)

PRO 30/33 14/1   Letter Book of Semi-official Letters from Siam. (March 8, 1884 – May 7, 1885)

Copy

Tokio, 5/11/84 (Blue notepaper, inserted)

Dear Currie,

My friend Lieut. A[lbert].G.S. Hawes,[43] whom you probably know by name, tells me that he is anxious for an apptmt. in the Consular service, & that he has applied for the vacancy at Samoa. I hope that it may be possible to give him this post, or something of the same kind, as he is a capital man of business, & has done good work here in organizing the Japanese navy & instilling English ideas into the officers. He retired from the Marines for that purpose some years ago. His age is about 41, so that there is plenty of work in him, & I hope you may be induced to use your influence on his behalf.

I have been enjoying myself here greatly, & feel that the change has done me great good. The tone towards the English Legation appears to be much improved.[44]

I expect to be back in Bangkok about the 20 Dec. On my way down in the French mail I shall call at Kelung & Saigon, & afterwds. spend a few days at Singapore in order to talk over judicial procedure with the chief justice. Hannen & I agree that the China & Japan rules will suit Bangkok with a very few unimportant alterations.

y.v.t.

55. Satow to Currie

23 Dec. 84

Private & Confidential (many crossings out!)

My dear Currie,

When I wrote to you in May, dwelling on [W.H.] Newman's personal merits & expressed the hope that some inducements might be offered to him to stay on here instead of retiring, I was entirely ignorant of circs. wch. afterwards came to my knowledge & induced me to alter my opinion.

I learnt in fact that his native woman had been in the habit of accepting large presents fr.

---

[43] Co-author with Satow of *A Handbook for Travellers in Central and Northern Japan* (Yokohama, 1881).
[44] Sir Harry Parkes had left Japan by this time.

PRO 30/33 14/1   Letter Book of Semi-official Letters from Siam. (March 8, 1884 – May 7, 1885)

native suitors to procure her favourable influence with Newman, thus confirming previous rumours which I had not credited. Not long before I came here a B.S. who had a case pending at the Agency, gave a bond for a large quantity of teak wood to a man calling himself the brother-in-law of this woman but for her account. This he disposed of to a Dutch subject for cash down and a promissory note for the bal[an]ce; & the Dutchman not paying, the brother-in-law came to me for assistance. I referred him to the Dutch Consul, who tried the case, & gave it agst. him, on the ground of fraud, as there was no teak & the bond was not worth the paper it was written on. Then the Dutchman wanted to bring an action before me to get back the money (about 2000 ticals) of wch. he had been defrauded. Luckily I discovered that the brother-in-law, who was registered in the Agency as a B.S. was not in reality a B.S. & I refused to entertain the matter, thus avoiding what would have been a disagreeable public scandal. The case was then tried by the Siamese, and the Dutchman got back his money. Newman's woman was threatened with arrest, & I was asked to protect her, wch. I declined to do. So the Dutchman recovered his money.

Of course the whole affair was talked about, and it was very unpleasant. I have thought the matter over a long time, and have resolved to lay the matter before you; only suggesting that under the circs. it might be beneficial to give Newman a change of air, as he had been recently promoted to the rank of Consul, which wld. look natural enough. In case you shld. decide not to take any such step, I hope you will look on this letter as strictly confidential.

56. Satow to Currie
23/12/84
My dear Currie,

I got back here viâ Singapore yesterday morning. Everything seems to have gone on well in my absence, & French deserves a pat on the back for the way he has managed affairs.

At Singapore I missed the Actg. Govr.[45] who had gone away to the Native States. But I cld. see that generally among the Colonial officials there is a disposition to dispute the right of Siam to the Malay peninsula, wch. they justify by the apprehension they have of Fr.

---

[45] Cecil Clementi Smith was Acting Governor of the Straits Settlements, 1884-1885.

PRO 30/33 14/1   Letter Book of Semi-official Letters from Siam. (March 8, 1884 – May 7, 1885)

encroachment there. Sir F. Weld in particular thinks the Fr. are hankering after Siam proper, & fears that when they have swallowed her up they will forestal us in the Peninsula. However fr. all I have read & heard, I think that France does not contemplate annexing the valley of the Menam. They always recognize that our interests are too strong here. What they do want is to take the valley of the Mekong wch. c. [with] its tributaries wld. bring them close to the frontier of Independent Burmah. That will be their first move, commencing no doubt with the country immediately to the West of the Annamese & Tonquinese boundary. They cannot well lay claim to Luang Phrabang as long as its chief refuses to sign a protection Treaty. Lower down the Mekong, they harp upon what they call "Siam's unjustifiable retention of the two provinces of the Tonle Repu and Melu Prey, wch. formerly belonged to Cambodia, & upon the natural tendency of Angkor & Battambang to gravitate back to Cambodia, altho' guaranteed to Siam by Treaty." I consequently believe Sir F. Weld's apprehensions to be unfounded, at least as far as the present is concerned, & that we need be in no great hurry to snatch at our share of the spoils. It is more important I venture to think that we shld. endeavour to inspire Siam with confidence in our good intentions. If the policy is to keep her as a buffer between ourselves & Asiatic France, it wld. be suicidal to nibble at her territory or weaken her prestige with her tributaries. I find Singapore disposed to contest the "suzerainty" of Siam over Kelantan & Trenganû in the Malay Peninsula, & may perh. have to write officially, if the representations I have made privately to the Acting Govr. & the Col[onia]l. Secy. have no effect.

Gould appears to have nearly got into a row at Chiengmai, by going into the chief's house at night in search of a female slave whom he claimed as the wife of a B.S. [British Subject] Luckily the matter has blown over, & the Siamese were induced by French not to make it an official matter. But I must write & caution him. It is a pity that he shld. be so indiscreet, for he is a good man. I had been projecting a tour round to Rangoon & Chiengmai, but find it wld. take too long, nearly four months; & so must postpone it till next autumn. If I were to make this journey then, I suppose I might consider it on public service.

    y.v.t.

PRO 30/33 14/1 Letter Book of Semi-official Letters from Siam. (March 8, 1884 – May 7, 1885)

<u>57. Satow to H.S.C. Clarke-Jervoise (outline only)</u>

24/12/84

No. 59 missing.

Shall probably pay for increases of wages out of my own pocket.

<u>58. Satow to Gould</u>

Bangkok

29/12/84.

My dear Gould,

I am very sorry to hear of your row with the chief as reported in your no. 17 [67?] of Oct 11, as on your own showing you did what you found it necessary, on cons[ideratio]n, to apologize for. I am afraid I shall be obliged to tell you officially what I think of the affair, but have only time today to beg you to be be more careful in future to avoid causing unpleasantness. The Convention has, it appears to me, the effect of submitting B.S. to the local law to a much greater extent than is the case down here, & I think it was intended to be an experiment in the way of diminishing the area of extraterritoriality.

Your remonstrances about the proposed expedition to the Hang valley appear to have had the good effect of inducing the Siamese to hold their hand at least for the present. I am privately informed that [Prince] Bigit has been told not to move until he receives further orders. I think you did well in the matter, but the tone of the opening paragraph of your letter in reply to the Commissioner's No. 17 of Sept. 14 is rather stronger than is usual in diplomatic communications. Let me advise you to 'mettre de l'eau dans votre vin' as the French say, under such circs.

Please send translations with any native documents you forward to me. It is not fair that the men at Bangkok should have to translate your inclosures, & I cannot read them myself.

I am told that nothing will be done about the proposed forest regulations until Bigit's return here, & that he has been called upon for a report on the subject of the arrears of timber dues.

I returned here on the 21st, too late to visit Chiengmai this season, even if business had permitted my leaving Bangkok. But I find the settlement of the spirit question still hangs

PRO 30/33 14/1   Letter Book of Semi-official Letters from Siam. (March 8, 1884 – May 7, 1885)

fire. The French have not yet ratified their convention, & ours cannot be carried out before theirs comes into force. Consequently I am compelled to my great regret to give up my plan of visiting you for this year.

59. Satow to Currie
5/1/85
Dear Currie,

Since I last wrote I have seen Pr[ince]. Devawongse, who complained very much of Gould's doings at Chiengmai, and said he was afraid he would never get on there. I smoothed the matter over as well as I cld. & told him I wld. caution Gould to be more prudent. The fact is, he writes too much, when going to talk the matter over c. the Siamese Comr. wld. be more effective. I have reported the whole affair officially, but as I have written him rather a stiff letter, I hope the matter will be allowed to rest there. If he does not take warning, it wld. be advisable to bring him down here as Acting Vice-Consul, & send up French in his place, but I do not know whether I have authority to do this without referring home first.

The King has sent instructions to Chiengmai not to take any warlike measures with regard to the territory claimed on behalf of Chiengmai up to the l. bank of the Salween, reported in French's no. 83 of Oct. 14. Gould seems to have questioned their right to move at all, & I think he shld. have contented himself with claiming that the rights already acquired by BS. be respected.

The Siamese are curious to know whether we intend to annex Upper Burmah. I always tell them that H.M.G. have no desire to interfere c. Theebaw, & that the agitation on the subject at Rangoon means nothing.

They are also very anxious to get the telegraph fr. Raheng to Rangoon, & have assured me of their readiness to construct their portion of the line. The Ch[ief]: Com[missione]r of B.B. writes to me the same thing, & I hope to arrange it before long.

I have learnt confidentially that surveyors are coming out shortly to survey the rlwy. line bet[ween]. Bangkok & Korat, wch. the King seems inclined to construct. They are sent by a firm named Tancred, Faulkener & Co. or something of that sort. Estimated cost £900,000.

PRO 30/33 14/1   Letter Book of Semi-official Letters from Siam. (March 8, 1884 – May 7, 1885)

It is not decided yet whether the capital will be provided by the King, or offered for subscription in Europe. Old Mason has something to do with it. I asked Devawongse whether the King wld. have any objection to a line from Rangoon to Chiengmai or Raheng. He said they did not want it a[t?] present. I then inquired whether the King wld. oppose it if the Indian Govt. proposed it. He replied that he wld. not. So I believe that if the Indian Govt. made the first overtures, I cld. induce the King to join.

Hallett turned up here on the 31 Dec. Colquhoun remains in China for another year as "Times" correspondent, wch. he thinks evidently will pay him better than his exploration. Hallett is not the man to conciliate the Siamese. He spends his time here in collecting stories of oppression & corruption on the part of the native officials. I have not thought it worth while trying to get the King to contribute to what Colquhoun & he call the "Exploration Fund." He wrote to Devawongse, who gave him a guarded refusal. He is now going off to Rangoon & Calcutta to see the Chief Comr. & Ld. Dufferin, & will try to persuade them to annex Upper Burmah & the Shan States away to Chiengtung. My own idea is that the money wld. be better spent on a rlwy. to Siam. We can always do the other thing whenever the French begin to quarrel with Siam abt. the Tonquin frontier, wch. they cannot do until they have settled c. China. I send you officially copies of the recent correspondence abt. this matter wch. Devawongse has given me.

I shld. very much like to ask for the apptmt. of the Att[orney]. Gen[era]l. of the Straits Settle[men]ts. to be the legal adviser of the Agency. We are not strong enough in legal matters to decide knotty points for ourselves, especially as regards the interpretation of the Treaties. If I had a lawyer to lean on, I shld. be able to take the responsibility on my own shoulders. He wld. want to have £300 a year. Do you think I may ask for this. Peking & Tokio have regular legal advice, & there are plenty of lawyers always at hand; we have not one here.

    y.v.t.

60. Satow to Bernard[46]

---

[46] (Sir) Charles Bernard (1837-1901). Chief Commissioner of British Crown Colony of Burma, 1880-83; 1886-87.

PRO 30/33 14/1   Letter Book of Semi-official Letters from Siam. (March 8, 1884 – May 7, 1885)

Confidential

5.1.85

Dear Mr. Bernard,

The King in his birthday speech in September says: "The satisfactory experience we have had of our telegraphs has decide us [illegible word] to double our lines c. the Western World by joining c. the British Indian telegraph at Myawadi." & almost the first thing Pr. Devawongse said to me after my return the other day fr. 3 mos. leave of absence was that they were anxious to know your intentions. I have ∴ [therefore] addressed an official Note to the Siamese Govt. asking by what date they cld. construct their portion to Myawadi [in southeast Burma/Myanmar], & as soon as I get their answer will communicate it to you & the Director-Genl. of Telegraphs in India. They expect their own line to Chiengmai to be completed by the end of March, & I have been told privately that they cld. construct the branch to Myawadi in 2 mo[nth]s. How long wld. the portion betw, Rangoon & Myawadi take?

Mr. Hallett has been here for a few days, & is leaving again for Rangoon. The King has not given him anything for the exploration, nor have I felt disposed to press the matter. Mr. Colquhoun has apparently decided to remain in China as "Times" correspondent for another y[ea]r at least, & I have my private doubts whether Mr. Hallett cares very much abt. it himself. He is without official credentials of any sort fr. the people at home, or fr. the Indian Govt., & consequently I have not thought it advisable to use my own official influence on his behalf. As long as the B.I. [British Indian] Govt. do not show any determination to put the matter thro', the Siamese will hesitate to declare themselves. They are anxious for that support fr. England wch. they have hitherto always been taught to think is unlikely to be given. Siam is a coy maiden who will give herself away to the most pressing suitor. If the Ind. Govt. wld. make up its mind to a rlwy. to Siam, & wld. press it on this govt. I am convinced it wld. be put thro'. The money wld. be better spent I think than on the annexation of Upper Burmah, wch. does not press. As long as the Fr[ench]. do not advance upon Luang Phrabang, we need not move in the dirction of Chieng-tung [Cheng-tung?], & France has too much on her hands at present in China & Tongking to do more than record the reservation of what she calls her rights on the N.E. frontier of Siam. I

PRO 30/33 14/1   Letter Book of Semi-official Letters from Siam. (March 8, 1884 – May 7, 1885)

am sending to the Indian Govt. copies of an interchange of Notes betw. the Fr. Actg. Cons[ul]. here & the Siamese Govt. When I was in China abt. a month ago it was the universal opinion that the Chin. Govt. wld. not abate its pretensions unless the fr. sent a corps d'armée to take Peking, & as far as one can see at the present there is no reason to change this view. The present condition of smothered hostility may go on for another year.

Gould has no doubt communicated to you his correspce. c. the Siam[es]e. Auth[orities]. at Chiengmai abt. a proposed extension of their territory up to the River Salwan, thus rounding off their frontier. I shld. like to learn your views privately. The Siamese Govt. have given me a copy of the instructions sent up to Chiengmai to the effect that no warlike measures are to be taken, & that B.S. are to be protected in the enjoyment of their acquired rights. I am engaged in a correspondence c. the F.M. [Foreign Minister] the result of wch. I shall send to the Ind. Govt. As far as I can see, all we need to do is to secure to our people any forests they are already in possession of in the coveted territory.

I had hoped to be able to visit Rangoon this spring, but am unable to get away.

Prob. I shld. be able to arrange abt. Mr. Gould being sent to Raheng to confer c. the Gov[erno]r. abt. the frontier police, as recommended by you.

    y.v.t.

61. Satow to Mackenzie Wallace[47]

5.1.85

Dear Mr. Wallace,

You will probably have forgotten my name, but may perhaps recall it when I remind you that we met at dinner at the staff mess in Cairo abt. two years ago[48] & that we talked abt. Japan. Since then I have been transferred to this country.

You have no doubt heard of the scheme advocated by Mr. A.R. Colquhoun for a rlwy. to unite B.B. [British Burma] & S.[?] Siam. He was here last summer c. Mr. Holt S. Hallett, to

---

[47] Presumably (Sir) Donald Mackenzie Wallace (1841-1919). Scottish public servant and foreign correspondent of the London *Times*.

[48] See Satow's diary for February 11, 1883. "Dined at the Headquarters staff with Sandwith... There were also Genl. Graham, Malet, Sir Henry Green, Sir Arnolf Kembal, Mackenzie Wallace, who looks like a Jew…"

PRO 30/33 14/1   Letter Book of Semi-official Letters from Siam. (March 8, 1884 – May 7, 1885)

try to induce the King of Siam to promise a contribution tow[ar]ds. the expenses of exploration. The King was shy of committing himself, chiefly I believe because he did not know that these gentlemen were supported by the Indian Govt. I wrote a desp. to Ld. Granville, of wch. a copy was sent to the Govr.-Genl. & have also urged the matter in private letters, wch. I have reason to know have been shown to Lord Kimberley. Mr. Philip Currie has probably spoken to Lord Dufferin on the subject. I shld. have been glad to press the scheme on the King of Siam, but was unable, owing to the want of official support to the project. Mr. Hallett has been here for the last few days, but has not succeeded in getting the King to promise anything. If the Indian Govt. wld. show its interest in the question by giving a contribution towards the exploration; or better still if it wld. take up the railway to Siam vigorously & empower me to push it here, I think something might be done. The Siamese want encouragement fr. India, wch. they have never yet been able to get.

Mr. Hallett leaves here tomorrow for Rangoon & Calcutta, & will before long be able to put you in possn. of a great deal more information than can be put into a letter, as he has travelled a great deal in Northern Siam.

Believe me
    y.v.f.

62. Satow to Prince Devawongse (p. 68)
7.1.85

Dear Prince Devawongse,

The Gov. Gen. of India Ld. Ripon, has sent me in acc. c. the usual custom, a Krita announcing his departure, addressed to His M[ajest]y. Wld. the King prefer that I shld. come up to the Palace to deliver it to him in person, or shall I transmit it in a note to the F.M.? I need hardly say that I shld. not consider it any trouble to myself to wait on H.M. for this purpose.

I regret to have to trouble you c. [with] the enclosed petition fr. a B.S., who complains that he has not been able to obtain pay[men]t. for some building materials supplied by him to the Palace.

Will you kindly return to me the draft I left you last Wednesday c. reference to the spirit

PRO 30/33 14/1   Letter Book of Semi-official Letters from Siam. (March 8, 1884 – May 7, 1885)

convention.

   y.v.f.

63. Satow to Prince Devawongse

9.1.85

D. P. Devawongse,

Thanks for your note of yesterday. I will send the Gov. Gen. letter thro' the F.M.

With regard to my proposed Note to the F.M. abt. the Spirit Question, let me say at once that I do not wish to take any steps that wld. have the effect of the Agreement, and that I do not propose to send it in if you communicate the draft excise law to the Consuls by the 17th inst. as you have stated to me. But after that date I can no longer postpone asking your Govt. to explain their intentions. It is necessary that I shld. be in a position to acquaint Ld. Granville with the circumstances wch. have prevented your Govt. from taking advantage of the arrangement between him & Prince Naret for putting the Agreement in force on the 1 Jan.

I have taken note of your observation as to the desirability of Mr. G. [Gould] not visiting Nan & Phrë until your instructions shall have reached their destination, & will write to him to that effect.

   y.v.f.

64. Satow to Sir Edward Hertslet[49]

Sir E. Hertslet C.B.   10/1/85

Dear Sir Edward,

Have you ever thought of printing a collection of the Treaties relating to Siam, & the O. in C. [Orders in Council] founded on our Treaties, such as you printed for Japan some years ago. Such a work would be of immense value to everyone concerned, especially if the original texts, when they are in European languages, were given, besides authorized versions in the language of the foreign contracting party. I know for a fact that of our O. in

---

[49] Sir Edward Hertslet (1824-1902) was an English librarian of the Foreign Office and author of reference works.

PRO 30/33 14/1   Letter Book of Semi-official Letters from Siam. (March 8, 1884 – May 7, 1885)

C. of 1856 there is only one copy at Singapore, & that is a MS [manuscript] belonging to a lawyer in practice there. It is really often a matter of importance, because we have a good deal of correspondence with the Straits abt. B.S. in Siam, & the Supreme Court of Singapore is our Court of Appeal. If you are disposed to take the matter up, I shall be most happy to render any assistance, either by obtaining treaties that you may not as yet have in the F.O. or by reading proofs.

If the Treaties of other countries were printed in full, a certain sale might be easily secured in Bangkok, if the book cannot be printed at the public expense. But in view of the immense utility to ourselves, I think the cost might well be defrayed by the Treasury.

Believe me

y.v.t.

65. Satow to E.B. Gould (p.70)

13.1.85

My dear Gould,

I send you a desp[atch]. abt. the Mehang valley fr. wch. you will see that the Siamese undertake not to disturb B.S. in any of their acquired rights, & have put off any armed expedition for the pres[en]t. This shelving of the expedition by Bigit was no doubt considerably due to your opposition, & is a desirable result to have obtained. I question myself whether there is any reason for our preventing their taking poss[essio]n. of this territory, & think it wld. have been quite sufficient to claim that de facto rights shld. be respected. It may be very true that ordering the people to shave their heads is a barbarity but I should not have written it to them. Y[ou]r. desp[atches]. are rendered inconveniently voluminous by the quantity of correspondence enclosed, & when you think that those long winded Siamese papers had to be translated by Cording before I could read them, you will understand why I wish you talked more to the people you have to deal with instead of writing them such staves. As a general rule writing is only useful when you want to quarrel, or when you have come to an agreement wch. it is desirable to record. The first case I am sure is not yours, & in the second you must get people to concur with your views beforehand. I abstain entirely, in writing to the Siamese, from lecturing or scolding, and

PRO 30/33 14/1   Letter Book of Semi-official Letters from Siam. (March 8, 1884 – May 7, 1885)

treat them as reasonable beings. It is the most successful in the end. You must understand that it is the desire of H.M.G. to be on friendly terms c. Siam, to win her confidence and to enable her to preserve her independence. She can only do that if the country is united under the firm rule of a strong sovereign, and a solid central power is what is needed. The party of Old Siam represented by Kalahome, Kromatah & Co. is gone, & the only hope for the future is the King. We must back him up agst. corrupt governors of provinces, encroaching people of all kinds, N.S.E. & create a more friendly feeling between Siam & England (including B.B. & India) than has hitherto existed. You and I must on our side pull together for the attainment of this end. At the immense distance you are stationed at, you can do much to make or mar & a great deal depends on your acting discretely. If my recent desp[atches]. have seemed harsh, you will I hope understand that they were inspired by a sense of duty.

 y.v.t.

66. Satow to Prince Devawongse (p. 71)
18.1.85
Dear P.D.

 With reference to the question of the importation of arms & gunpowder, & the bearing of the most favoured nation clause of the Treaties thereon, I shld. like to see any correspondence on the subject that has passed betw. the Siamese Govt. & the foreign representatives c. regard to the matter before forming an opinion on it.

 y.v.t.

67. Satow to Prince Devawongse
19.1.85
Dear Prince Devawongse

 I have been considering the subject of British men-of-war giving notice at Paknam of their intention to proceed to Bangkok, which it appears from the other treaties is all that can be required of them to do.

 It appears to me objectionable to call the notice of the British Naval Authorities to this

PRO 30/33 14/1   Letter Book of Semi-official Letters from Siam. (March 8, 1884 – May 7, 1885)

rule, wch. as you are aware, has practically been disregarded for many years past, unless a similar request is made by the Siamese Govt. to the repres'ves. of the other Treaty Powers. If therefore it is the King's desire that this shld. be done, I wld. suggest your making his wishes generally known in some official form. I shall then have great pleasure in communicating the desired enforcement of the Treaty stipulation to the Com[mande]r. in chief of the China Station. It is clearly a point wch. concerns all the powers equally.

   y.v.f.

68. Satow to Currie
22 Jan. 1885 (faint, p. 72)
Dear Currie,

The Straits Govt. contend, it appears, that Tringanu is not included in the word Siam, & have consequently refused to allow permits for the export of gunpowder to that state to be countersigned by the Siamese Consul at Singapore, as is done in the case of powder & arms exported to Siam proper. When I was at Singapore the other day, I missed [Cecil] Smith, but I begged the Col. Secy. to give way upon this point, on wch. I know the Siamese feel sore. In fact the King's Secy. said to me the other day, 'Mr. Smith & some of the members of council want to turn us out of the Malay peninsula." Smith has very candidly sent me a draft of his desp. to the C.O. [Colonial Office] in order that I might report on it, & as I think it important to lull any suspicions the Siamese might entertain as to th views of the home Govt. I have written a desp. on the subject No. 12.

There is not much to be added, but I am not far wrong when I say that Sir F. Weld looks to the ultimate absorption of Siam by France, & think it wld. be politic to forestal them in any possible designs on the Malay States of Siam; that we ought in fact to secure that part of the reversion of the inheritance. For my own part I do not believe the Fr[ench]. wld. touch Bangkok if they were not provoked; their first idea is to get hold of the Mekong valley but Siam proper they will keep their hands off, unless they want to quarrel seriously. Our trade here & that of the Germans is very large, much larger than what the Annual returns show, owing to the systematic undervaluing of imports. I see that Ld. Kimberley wrote very strongly to Singapore in former years, disapproving of attempts at further

PRO 30/33 14/1   Letter Book of Semi-official Letters from Siam. (March 8, 1884 – May 7, 1885)

extension, but desp. are easily forgotten, and they want a reminder down in the straits. Colonial people all over the world seem to be bitten with the mania of annexing at the expense of the British taxpayer, & even the Genl. at Hongkong took an opportunity the other day when Sir G. Bowen[50] was away of advising the annexation of a good slice behind Hongkong.

[Frederick] Verney[51] I see busies himself in writing to the daily papers to deny the existence of slavery in Siam. I found [E.H.] French had been employing his leisure in drawing up a report on the subject, wch. goes forward by this mail. It might be more readable if printed for the use of the F.O.

There are at last hopes of doing something abt. the Spirit Convention. By dint of hints that I would tell our people that they might freely import and sell spirits, I have induced the Siamese to communicate to the Consuls the draft law of wch. a speedy issue was promised before I went to Japan. The Colleagues are also taking an interest in it, and the Frenchman, German & Dutchman are joining with me to put the matter thro. We do not get much aid fr. the American, who because he is a minister fancies that his position as doyen is a reality. He is altogether molluscous, but we shall do without him.

The correspondence about the left bank of the Salween illustrates [Edward Blencowe] Gould's facility in inditing [composing] long letters. I have told him to arrange his business by talking, & not to write unless he wants to quarrel. However, he has stopped the Siamese effectually, & I think they are not likely to do anything at present, as the King's brother who got the thing up, is to come back to Bangkok.

The paragraphs in the papers abt. the survey for a rlwy. fr. Bangkok to Korat are confirmed by what the King's Secretary previously told me. But they have not yet made up their minds whether they will get the money from abroad or find it themselves.

[Consul Thomas] Knox's daughter [Fanny] has been here & gone again. The Siamese have given her abt. £1800 in return for the surrender of the titles to her late husband's

---

[50] Sir George Ferguson Bowen (1812-1899). Colonial administrator. Governor of Hongkong.
[51] Frederick W. Verney (1846-1913). Secretary and later Councillor to the Siamese Legation in London, 1881-1907.

PRO 30/33 14/1   Letter Book of Semi-official Letters from Siam. (March 8, 1884 – May 7, 1885)

property. She even handed over private letters from a member of the consulate who had befriended her & helped her in her troubles.

I have great hopes of the telegraph line to Tavoy being established this year. The Raheng-Moulmein duplicate line cannot be constructed before next year, as the dry season will soon be over, & there is not enough water in the rivers for the conveyance of materials. The Siamese are going ahead steadily: there is to be a line to Luang Phrabang & one down the E. coast to Chantabun & Battambong is nearly completed.

   y.v.t.

69. Satow to Prince Devawongse
5 Feb./85
Dear P. D.

I was very glad to receive your message thro' Phra Theppalu and to learn that everything has passed off satisfactorily.

Is it a fact that Prince Naret has been instructed to complain to Lord Granville about Mr. Gould?[52]

As soon as you return I think the Consuls will be ready to discuss with you the draft spirit law as far as it affects the interests of foreigners, and I hope we shall be able to arrive at an understanding without much difficulty.

The enclosed copy of a notice from the Hongkong Govt. Gazette may interest you. I learn that affairs have been settled betw. Korea & Japan, & that there is not much likelihood of the latter being induced to join France agst. China.

   y.v.f.

P.S. I will speak about the contents of your letter fr. Paknam when we meet.

70. Satow to Currie
19 Feb. 1885
Dear Currie,

---

[52] It is not clear whether this sentence has been erased or not.

PRO 30/33 14/1   Letter Book of Semi-official Letters from Siam. (March 8, 1884 – May 7, 1885)

The King has at last returned, & we have got to work again.

My proposal to do away with the flagstaff seems perh. a little revolutionary, but some of my colleagues are quite of my opinion, and would be glad to get rid of the expense. If it is thought necessary for our prestige to have one at all, it would be better to spend the £250 at once & put up as big a one as before. To cut the staff down to one half the former size would seem a greater come down than its total abolition.

My Fr. colleague does not allow that the Govr. of Saigon is coming here in March, but it may be true after all. It seems better that the Siamese & Fr. shld. try to fix their boundary, than that the public shld. have such a constant subject for gossip as the present uncertainty affords them. I twitted Prince Devawongse about the absurdity of getting Verney to deny the truth of Colquhoun's telegram about the threatening letter from the Govr. of Saigon, when we knew that there was a considerable kernel of fact at the back of it. I told him it was undiginified.

Nothing surprised me more than the telegram about the complaint prepared agst. Gould. If I had refused to give the Siamese satisfaction, they would have been justified in laying the affair before Ld. Granville. They never gave either French or myself the slightest hint that they were instructing [Prince] Naret to speak about it, as I now find they have done. They believe their Legations in London & Paris to be important engines for keeping the consuls in order, and send copies of all correspondence to Naret & Prisdang.

We are busy with the arrangements for putting the Spirit Convention into execution, but only the German & Dutch Consuls have instructions. The Frenchman has none. But we are working harmoniously and I hope may settle matters satisfactorily. The Siamese want a loophole by wch. they may keep the monopoly of the trade while appearing to establish an excise. I suppose that as long as appearances are saved we do not care much whether the Hongkong & Swatow [Shantou] Chinamen reap the profit of the trade or not. They import about 20,000 jars a month, and never have more than 10,000 in hand, so that the Siamese are not offering any very active obstruction just now.

Knox's dau[ghter]. went from Singapore to Saigon. What for? I suppose she had some Siamese secrets to sell.

Tancred & Falkener's surveyors have arrived and started for the interior to examine the

PRO 30/33 14/1   Letter Book of Semi-official Letters from Siam. (March 8, 1884 – May 7, 1885)

proposed route for a railway to Korat. I do not think much will come of it. It is only meant to throw dust in the eyes of the European public.

71. Satow to J.W. Robertson[53]
24 Feb.
Dear Sir,

Your letter of the 15 arrived here yesterday. I am in communication with the Siamese Authorities with a view to obtaining their consent to our people working on from the frontier to meet the Siamese party, but am not sanguine about success. In the meantime, I quite concur with you as to the advisability of completing the Sinbyudaing[54] line before attempting anything else, and shall telegraph to India to that effect tomorrow.

   y.v.f.

72. Satow to Chas. E. Pitman[55]
28 Feb./ 85
Chas, E. Pitman Esq.
Dear Sir,

I have communicated to the Siamese Govt. the information contained in your letter of the 10th inst. with reference to the progress made with the new telegraph line fr. Sinbyudaing to Hmoungdi, and have urged them to allow your party to push it on from the frontier to meet the Siamese working party. I have not succeeded in obtaining an unconditional consent to this proposal, but they tell me they have sent instructions to the Gov. of Petchaburi to the effect that he may ask for assistance if he thinks he requires it. Under the circs. I do not think it wld. be wise to urge them to put the old line in working order as well, as from all I can gather, it seems doubtful whether they will be able to do more than finish the new line this season. On hearing of the proposal to construct the new line, the Govr. of

---

[53] J.W. Robertson was apparently an Indian telegraph engineer.
[54] Sinbyudaing is in Myanmar/Burma near the border with Thailand/Siam.
[55] Charles E. Pitman of the Indian Telegraph Department, responsible for the Tavoy-Siam line.

PRO 30/33 14/1   Letter Book of Semi-official Letters from Siam. (March 8, 1884 – May 7, 1885)

Petchaburi caused part of the line to Amya to be taken up. The I.G's [Indian Government's] idea to have both lines is no doubt a very good one, but it was not made sufficiently clear at the outset that they desired to have the Amya pass line retained. I was under the impression that the Hmoungdi route was to be by way of substitute for it. I have telegraphed my opinion briefly to Calcutta. It would of course be useless to put a signaller into the Kanburi office, as the line is interrupted for so considerable a portion of its length. The officer intended in the last para. of Mr. French's letter of Nov. 18 is the Govr. of Petchaburi above referred to.

    Yours faithfully
    E.S.

73. Satow to Currie
2 March 1885
Dear Currie,

In a private letter from Bernard the Chief Comr. of B.B. [British Burma] he says he thinks a railway line fr. Moulmein to the Siamese frontier wld. do great good to the part of his province wch. it wld. cross, but he considers that there are many other lines wch. ought to be constructed first, & Mackenzie Wallace writes to me that they are engaged in India with a big scheme of rlwy. extension there, & that nothing is likely to be done towards carrying out Colquhoun's scheme for a rlwy. fr. Moulmein to China. I infer therefore that we shall hear nothing more of it for the present. Here the idea is to construct a rlwy. across the mountains fr. Korat to the banks of the Bangpa-Kong river near Kabine or Prakim, and from one of these points utilize the existing water communications with Bangkok. A branch line is also projected from Kabin towards the Talesap lake, and by these means the Siamese hope to divert the commerce of the Mekong valley to Bangkok. We may expect the French to oppose this: Harmand,[56] who made himself so conspicuous here two or three years ago writes to his fidus Achates [faithful friend] the Dutch Consul that he has had a conference with Ferry, & that it is almost decided that he comes here, with the rank of Chargé

---

[56] François-Jules (Jules) Harmand (1845-1921). Doctor, explorer and diplomat. Later a colleague of Satow in Japan where he was French Minister, 1894-1905.

PRO 30/33 14/1   Letter Book of Semi-official Letters from Siam. (March 8, 1884 – May 7, 1885)

d'Affaires. I suppose [this] means a 'forward policy'[57] in Siam. The American Minister[58] goes home on leave at the end of this month. It is doubtful whether he returns. The German Consul is also going on leave, his place being taken by Gabriel, the Germ. Vice-Consul at Shanghai.

I think it is well to support the Siamese in their claim to control the imprtation of arms, because it tends to restrict the supply to Upper Burma, wch. is an object with the Indian Govt. but I thought it necessary to remind them that they must stick to the Treaty, as you will see from my desp. no. 27.

The King sometimes requires a hint that his autocratic power does not extend to international matters.

y.v.t.

74. Satow to Gould
2 March 85.
My dear Gould,

Besides what I have said in my Confid'l. desp[atch]. of today's date I wish to add that it is of far more importance that you shld. be on good terms with the Laos & Siamese officials, so that you may know all that goes on & be able to inform the Indian Govt. on political matters, than that you shld. claim British protection for Burmese, who are generally well able to look after themselves, or for the women they call their wives. The Treaty of 1883 clearly does not contemplate extraterritorial jurisdiction such as it exists in the parts of Siam not affected by that Treaty, & your interference is only needed when absolute injustice is done to a B.S. With regard to slaveholding by B.S. if I can get the Siamese to make the proposed law, it will have a better effect than trying to get the English law abt. slave-trading enforced in a Siamese court. The fact is our law does not apply, except when a case has been transferred fr. the Siamese Court to yours, but such instances ought to be a

---

[57] forward policy: a set of foreign policy doctrines applicable to territorial and border disputes, in which emphasis is placed on securing control of disputed areas by invasion and annexation, or by the creation of compliant buffer states.
[58] General John A, Halderman.

PRO 30/33 14/1   Letter Book of Semi-official Letters from Siam. (March 8, 1884 – May 7, 1885)

rare occurrence.

Fanny Prapicha [nee Knox][59] is at Pnompen[?], some say in the King's palace, others say in the house of a Brit. Ind: subject.

y.v.t.

75. Satow to Currie
16 March 85

My dear Currie,

We have not made any further progress with the spirit convention. I take every opportunity of saying to Devawongse that the only way to establish the excise system wch. they have promised to the Powers is to abolish the distilling monopoly, & make the tax collectors a separate body from the distillers, but have not succeeded in bringing him round. My colleagues are lukewarm in the matter. As the French chamber has not yet satisfied the Agreement, the question does not seem to press.

The Siamese say they have learnt by telegraph that I have been apptd. Minister Resident, and I hope it will turn out to be true. They appear to be very pleased with the notion.

I have recd. a desp. from the Indian Govt. abt. apptg. Gould to be Political Agent at Chiengmai and practically telling me to decide the point. As I do not think the necessity for the step has been shown, & am opposed to it on other grounds, I have replied to that effect, & now send copies of my despp. I am convinced Siam is not at present in danger.

The Saigon semi-official newspaper is in ecstasies over the meeting of the King & the Govr. of Saigon, little suspecting that 'la perfide Albion' suggested the move.

When the German Consul went away the other day the King happened to be absent, & his application for a farewell audience was not attended to. I wrote privately to Devawongse hinting that it was not proper to let him go away without an interview, & they telegraphed for him to go up to where the King was in a steam launch, but it was too late. The German Consulate think it was intended as a slight, so I suggested that the King shld. express his regret to the Acting man, wch. has been done, and they are going to offer the

---

[59] Fanny Knox was the daughter of Consul Thomas Knox and a Siamese noblewoman named Prang Yen.

PRO 30/33 14/1 Letter Book of Semi-official Letters from Siam. (March 8, 1884 – May 7, 1885)

departed one a decoration. So I hope no bad results will ensue. The Acting man says he has instructions to be very friendly with the Siamese, and I don't think he has been told to make common cause with the Frenchman. If he has been, I shall find it out. There is a rumour that Germany will send a diplomatic repres've. to reside here.

I shld. like very much to make a trip to Rangoon and Calcutta, in order to exchange ideas personally with the Ch[ief]. Com[issione]r. of Burma and the Indian Govt. What do you think? I am sure it would be useful.

y.v.t.

76. Satow to Newman (p. 84)

1 April 1885

Extr[act]. fr. letter to Newman:

"Abt. yr own private affairs, I congratulate you heartily upon your decision to ask for a change: it cannot but be to a better post in point of emolument, & if you shld. get Manila, for wch. it is rumoured here you have applied, you will find life much less monotonous than at Bangkok. Sinclair came to me a short time ago,[60] & I gave him my opinion abt. the affair of the note for certain logs of teak, wch. he has no doubt written to you as he promised. I cld. not but come to the conclusion that the lady in question was in the habut of receiving presents à la Siamoise, but when Smith wanted to prosecute her relative in my court I took care to have nothing to do with it. How the list of Mong Goonah's creditors got into the hands of the Siamese I do not know, but as Phya Bhaskarawongse mentioned it to me one day as a bit of current gossip, I am inclined to that the hedgelawyer who drew up the list has communicated it. I am very sorry abt. the whole affair, the more so as I believe you have been betrayed by someone in whom you had placed great confidence. What can you expect, when even Fanny Knox gives to the Siamese private letters written to her by Gould, her best friend.

---

[60] "Sinclair came to talk about Newman's woman. I said I was convinced that she took bribes, & that my private opinion was that Newman wld. do well to get rid of her. Told him that I knew some of Newman's private papers had been got at, & hinted that she must have furnished them for copying to the Siamese." (Satow's diary, February 24, 1885)

PRO 30/33 14/1   Letter Book of Semi-official Letters from Siam. (March 8, 1884 – May 7, 1885)

77. Satow to Currie

15 April

My dear Currie,

I am extremely pleased to get the rank of minister, altho' I cannot attribute it to my own deserts. It has given great satisfaction to the King, whose private Secy. has more than once mentioned to me their desire to have a Min[ister]. resident, they think it amounts to according to them a higher status among the nations, and the outer public will no doubt suppose that H.M.G. is taking an increased interest in the welfare of Siam.

The last story is that Kergaradec and not Harmand is to come back here.

I think that Newman's getting another post will be a good thing on many grounds. The nature of the complaints made agst. him by the Siamese Min[ister]. I can only guess at. I presume the papers must have been despatched from here during my absence. Nevertheless, about the end of last year Prince Devawongse tried hard to get me to listen to a story about some houses wch. he said a British Indian Subject had years ago given to Knox & Newman ["as bribes" crossed out], and he wrote to me on the 22nd Jany. urging me to "put the matter in a proper light to H.M.G. in order that I may not be driven into a position wch. I would now hesitate to take on account of my trust in your just and equitable action for the mutual interests of our respective countries." I did not see him again till the 16th Feb., and then I told him I saw no sufficient grounds for reporting abt. the matter. ["and begged him to do nothing for the present." crossed out] ["(Privately, I have my doubts, but I thought it was better not to stir up these old affairs)." crossed out][61]   The affair is a good example of P. D's tricks. He tries to persuade me that he wants me to take the matter up, while he has actually sent instructions to complain to L.G. [Lord Granville, Foreign Secretary] It was the same in the case of Gould as I have pointed out in my desp. no. 35 of this mail, and with regard to the refusal of Cecil Smith to regard Kelantan and Tringganu as part of Siam. I hope you will not permit this sort of thing to go on. They had less right to complain of my subordinate until I had refused to give satisfaction. It makes [my?] position very difficult,

---

[61] There are several margin notes crossed out in this letter.

PRO 30/33 14/1   Letter Book of Semi-official Letters from Siam. (March 8, 1884 – May 7, 1885)

because the Siamese fancy they can always go behind my back to the authorities at home. [I do not think they shld. be allowed to complain home of a subordinate of mine, until they can say that they have failed to get redress from me. When the Prince spoke to French, I was expected back in less than 3 weeks, and there was no need for being in such a hurry. Besides French, being Acting Agent, had all the authority necessary to deal with the case, if he had been asked. But the Prince clearly gave Fr[ench]. the impression that he was quite satisfied with the undertaking that G[ould]. would get a wigging from me if he had acted wrongly.][62] They send everything home to Naret,[63] and then he and Verney put their heads together to turn the documents to account in showing what injured innocents the Siamese are. If Verney only knew how they impose on him.

The Times has a telegram about an important Treaty to be shortly signed betw. France & Siam. There is not a word of truth in it.

If Newman goes, I shld. recommend Gould succeeding him here, & Fr[ench]. going to Chiengmai, in the ordinary course of promotion. Each man would then be in the post for which he is best fitted.

There are no signs of the Gov. of Saigon coming here. [Indeed, he said his visit cld. not take place before the ratification of the Cambodian convention.][64]

The Siamese on their part are turning their attention diligently to the provinces wch. lie betw. this & Cambodia. Chao Sai, a cousin of the King, & one of the few sensible men in the country has been apptd. a High Com[missione]r. with unlimited powers all over the S.E. and has been at work for the past 6 mos. organizing the militia, and improving communications. He must now be at Battambong. Telegraph is being made to Chantabun, & two guardships have been placed on the frontier. I went down with him last month, and accompanied him one day's [travel?] fr. Chantabun into the interior. It is a rich country, & the people seem much pleased with the new state of things as they have been relieved from a number of petty little imposts.

The Siamese say that Norodom sympathizes with his brother[']s attempts at insurrection,

---

[62] This part has been crossed out with two vertical lines.
[63] Prince Naret Worarit (1855-1925), then Head of the Siamese Legation in London.
[64] This sentence has been partly crossed out with two diagonal lines.

PRO 30/33 14/1   Letter Book of Semi-official Letters from Siam. (March 8, 1884 – May 7, 1885)

and that the French are very unpopular in Cambodia. They have a hard task to keep order in their boasted Indo-Chinese empire.

I am very sorry to trouble you with a long desp[atch]. abt. the spirit question, but the Siamese have not been straightforward about it, & [I do not know what stories they may not write home to Europe abt. it.][65] I shld. have much preferred to be able to report that they were reasonable. Whether Chinese are able to make a profit put of the spirit trade matters little to us, but it is important to impress on the Siamese respect for treaties. The strictly personal govt. of the King is at the bottom of all our difficulties here, and I do not see how it is to be mended, except by pulling the checkstring[66] now & then to remind him that his word is not law when a treaty reads the other way.

78. Satow to Currie (p.85)

16 April.

Dear Currie,

I had a very satisfactory audience yesterday to present my credentials.[67] The Siamese wanted to make a great affair of it, & proposed a public audience, but as that involved a harangue by the Court Speaker in wch. etiquette requires that he shld. represent me as laying the Queen's letter at 'the dust of the sacred feet' of the King of Siam, I thanked them for the offer, but said I was not entitled to such an honour, wch. in Europe was reserved for ambassadors. An imitation of what usually taked place in England on such occasions was ∴ [therefore] arranged, only I had to gratify them by putting on uniform. There was a row in Knox's time abt. the use of the obnoxious phrase, but he cld. not get it altered, & the best way was to evade raising the question. I hope it is shelved for the future.

      y.v.t.

79. Satow to Prince Devawongse

---

[65] This part has been crossed out.
[66] Checkstring: a cord used by a passenger in a carriage to signal to the driver to go slower or faster.
[67] See Satow's diary for April 15, 1885.

PRO 30/33 14/1   Letter Book of Semi-official Letters from Siam. (March 8, 1884 – May 7, 1885)

21 April 1885

Dear Prince Devawongse,

I have made inquiries of the F.M. with regard to the Notes addressed to him wch. had remained unanswered, & found that you were perfectly right in your conjecture that they had been sent direct to the depts. concerned, namely the Kalahom & the Minister of the North.

I beg to enclose copies of these 2 notes, & of a 3rd dated March 14, relating the murder of a B.S. at Nongkai[68] 2 years ago, in order that you may see how little justification there can be for the delay in replying to them. And I trust that you will use yr. influence to expedite matters in these three cases.

I shld. add that the Kromatah declared that he was merely a receiver & forwarder of letters, & was utterly without power in any of these matters. My colleagues as well as myself have constantly reason to complain of the inconvenience of having to transact our official business with a Foreign Minr. who is only so in name, & I wish you wld. take an opportunity of representing this to H.M. the King, for I cannot help attributing to the present arrangements the extraordinary delays, often extending to 2 or 3 y[ea]rs. in the settle[men]t. of affairs that ought not to occupy as many months.

    y.v.f.

80. Satow to Currie

28 April 1885

Dear Currie,

I enclose a memo. on the papers contained in y[ou]r. note of the 20 Mar[ch]. It was not possible to make it shorter. The Siamese have overreached themselves by trying to prove too much. What I am not clear about is how the alleged extracts fr. the cashb[oo]k. came into existence. It is to be noted that the correctness of them is sworn to before a Siamese official, by a native clerk in the service of a Singapore lawyer named Donaldson.[69] That he

---

[68] Nong Khai is a city in northeast Thailand.
[69] Possibly Alexander Leathes Donaldson, founder and partner of the Singapore firm of Donaldson and Burkinshaw, 1873-94. However, Satow states in this letter that he is dead.

PRO 30/33 14/1   Letter Book of Semi-official Letters from Siam. (March 8, 1884 – May 7, 1885)

did so is quite clear, for his handwriting has been attested by people who knew him. He is since dead. & the truth cannot be got at. But I find no traces whatever of the sums said to have been paid to Newman, Knox & Knox's woman, & believe the story to be a fabrication, but a fabrication of old date.

In the 'Second King['] affair I think Newman was made a tool of by that old intriguer the Regent, who as far as I can gather got up the misunderstanding betw. the First & Second Kings, intending to step in & act as moderator. Beforehand he gave hints to Newman that the Second King was in danger. You know that Knox had been in the service of the Second King's father, & openly spoke of the present man's almost certain prospects of succeeding to the throne. Newman I suppose simply followed his chief's lead. It was natural enough that the First King's people shld. resent the interference of a foreign Power in Siam's internal affairs, & that resentment instead of being humoured, has always been kept alive by the ostentatious friendliness betw. the Second King & the Agency. Almost weekly presents of fruit came to me fr. him, but I take care to accept no other favours, while letting it be understood that he must not be interfered with. The position is a legacy fr. the past, wch. must be accepted, however undesirable one may think it is. For my own part I do not believe it gives us any political advantage. But lest the French shld. step in & assume the rôle of the Second King's protectors, I think it would be unwise to throw him over.

I agree with you in thinking it unnecessary to have any record of this affair of Newman's either at the F.O. or here.

  y.v.t.

81. Satow to Currie
28 April 1885

Dear Currie,

The Siamese are still obstinate abt. the excise, & I mean to leave them alone until they have had time for reflection. It is entirely their own fault. If they did not like Prisdang's arrangements with us they shld. have said so at once, instead of urging every Treaty Power in succession to conclude a similar agreement.

PRO 30/33 14/1   Letter Book of Semi-official Letters from Siam. (March 8, 1884 – May 7, 1885)

A dep. Com[missione]r. of Mergui[70] has apparently been laying claim to islands wch. belong to Siam, having I conjecture, been misled by a map. I have written abt. the matter to the C.C. of Burmah.

Thanks for yr. hint abt. the language to be adopted in speaking of possibilities in Upper B[urma].

I think it might be desirable if you take any notice of my desp. abt, the telegraph fr. Raheng to Moulmein to instruct me to express the satisfaction of H.M.G. to the King.

Prince D. referring to the article in Pall Mall of Mar. 16 abt. Colquhoun & Hallett's rlwy. scheme, said that the King did not desire to have a line fr. Raheng to BB, at any rate until there was a trunk line to Chiengmai (which may I think be referred to the Gr[eek]. Kalends).[71]

Hallett's assertion that the Siamese were willing if the Indian Govt. wld. construct the other portion fr. Moulmein is unauthorized.

Tancred & Faulkner's men [surveyors] leave by this mail. They find that the proposed line fr. Bangkok to Korat is comparatively easy, but nothing will be wettled until they return to England & make their report.

I am very grateful for my suggestion abt. a legal adviser being adopted, for there are many things in wch. we need a lawyer's help, especially in framing rules of procedure & getting our C[our]t. arrangements into order.

The Siamese have had some fighting with the Chinese immigrants known as Haws, in the country east of Luang Phrabang & claim to have been victorious.

y.v.t.

82. Satow to Currie
7 May 1885.
Dear Currie,

I send one desp. by this mail asking leave to go to Singapore to confer with the Att[orne]y. Gen[era]l. abt. the rules of procedure for the court, and requesting a reply by telegram. I have been hoping to get him up here, & considerable delay has resulted. The

---

[70] The Mergui archipelago in far southern Myanmar is in the Andaman Sea.
[71] The Greek calends: a time that is expected never to arrive or occur.

PRO 30/33 14/1   Letter Book of Semi-official Letters from Siam. (March 8, 1884 – May 7, 1885)

best plan will be to go down there. At the same time I shld. be able to talk to Cecil Smith abt. the Malay Peninsula.

With reference to my No. 37 abt. the Spirit Agreement, Prince D. told me yesterday that the Siam. Govt. Had made up their mind to accept our amendment, & I hope that there will be no more difficulties betw. them & the for[eign]: repres'ves abt. the matter.

The disturbances in Cambodia are getting serious, & have resulted in the breakdown of the telegraph on the Fr. side of the frontier. Our Tavoy line will soon be open to the public. The Siamese are keeping a watchful eye on the frontier to prevent any question arising with the Fr. abt. rebels who may take refuge in Syria.

Abt. arrang[emen]ts. to be made if Newman does not come back. I think as I said before that Gould shld. be his successor here even if he shld. prefer to stay where he is & Fr[ench]. be apptd. to Chiengmai. The latter is entitled to leave next Feb. & wld. like to go home first before going there. Cording comes next; he is in very bad health, and too irritable for Chiengmai, wch. requires a judicious man. If the matter were left to me, I shld. on the ground of Cording's health, send Archer, of whom I have a high opinion, to act at Chiengami until Fr. was ready to take up his post there.

There appeared in the Athenaeum of 14 Feb. last a notice that the Fr. had found a new route for a canal across the Malay Peninsula fr. Phanom to Bangri. I think there is some mistake, but have asked an Italian traveller named Luzzatti,[72] to whom I have rendered some services, & who is going down there, to look at the country in the region indicated. In spite of our official declaration that H.M.G. do not oppose the idea of such a canal, I am strongly of opinion we ought to do all in our power to frustrate the game of the Fr[ench]. there, if they have one.

My Germ. Colleague is very elated at having been asked to get a lawyer out for the Siamese. The fact is, I privately suggested to the King's Secy. That they wld. get an efficient man fr. Germany much cheaper than fr. England, because it seems to me that the more interest the Germans can be induced to take in this country the better for our objects.

---

[72] See F.H.H. King, 'Angelo Luzzatti and Early Mining Concessions in Siam, 1885-91,' in *Fourth PICTS* (Proceedings of the International Conference on Thai Studies), Kunming 1990, pp. 102-110.

PRO 30/33 14/1   Letter Book of Semi-official Letters from Siam. (March 8, 1884 – May 7, 1885)

Prob. however the Siamese will get a man fr. India or Burmah too. As a rule I do not believe anything gained by having Englishmen in confidential positions in eastern countries; they mostly take sides agst. us, & become more native than the natives.

The gossip at Singapore is that as soon as war is declared betw. England & Russia the Fr[ench]. will walk in here. I see no reason to expect anything of the kind.

In advance of the trade report I send an analysis showing the immense preponderance of our commercial interests in Siam, but not for publication.

    y.v.t.

83. Satow to Gould
27 May 1885

Dear Gould,

I send you my views abt. the lease registration question officially, & you will find no difficulty in acting on them. They in fact amount to this: the Siamese had no right to issue their proclamations, as they did. Still for the sake of peace go on as you have done, trying to coax or frighten B[ritish]. S[ubjects]. into having their leases registered, but if the Siamese authorities set up a claim to confiscate, then administer to them the exact legal position resulting fr. the Treaties. I have promised to give P.D. [Prince Devawongse] a copy of my desp. to you. He has already had the draft read to him, & understands the gist of the matter.

The fact is, when there is a clear Treaty stipulation neither you nor I, nor the Siamese Govt. nor any local com[missione]r. can in any way alter or depart fr. it. It is quite clear that the Treaty of 1883 does not apply to leases made before it was ratified.

I am glad to have recd. y[ou]r. desp. about taxation wch. has arrived in anticipation of my request to be furnished c. inform[atio]n. I have drawn up a memo. showing the bearing of the Treaty on the question, & have come to the conclusion that there is no power in the Chief of Chiengmai or the Siamese Govt. to levy new taxes on B.S. & that Art. IV of the Treaty of /83 refers only to the Import dues. I have shown it to Tewan, & shall send it to you by next opport[unit]y. In the meanwhile you can tell B.S. to resist any such new taxation. Art. IV is obscure but T. agrees c. me that the tariff of import duties into

PRO 30/33 14/1   Letter Book of Semi-official Letters from Siam. (March 8, 1884 – May 7, 1885)

Chiengmai must be & is the same as the tariff at Bangkok.

I have y[ou]r. private letters of April 4, 12, 15 6 16, & one <u>undated</u> relating to the capture of dacoits [robbers and murderers]. You say you "challenge any one to make anything else out of your letter" to the chief than you do. I hope this is a slip, but I must tell you that I do not consider it a proper tone for you to assume towards me. But on this matter I shall not write any more privately.

When you have reason to think that the Khahuang &c. are sending questions here instead of settling them with you, it will certainly be well to let me know either privately or officially, how the case stands e.g. as you did with respect to the clerk's gambling debt & the forged receipt, as I am then prepared to meet anything the Siamese may say to me.

If you think seriously that there are grounds for asking H.M.G. to give notice to terminate the Treaty of 1883, because of the bad working of the jurisdiction clauses, you had better write officially. There wld. be great difficulty in getting it done. We shld. then have to fall back on the Treaty of 1874, & get rid of that too. But in either case we are bound for 7 yrs. unless we can get the Siamese Govt. to consent, wch. they wld. not do except under great pressure. I am not in favour of giving up the present system until it has had a longer trial, but think that much may be done by letting the Siamese understand that their govt. in Chiengmai must be made a reality if they wish to keep the province. When the old chief dies there will be a grand opportunity.

You had better write officially about y[ou]r. need of an assistant, in such a manner that I can press the matter on the F.O.

    y.v.t.

P.S. Please have your official letters & enclosures written c. the orthodox 1/4 margin, otherwise they cannot be bound up conveniently.

END OF PRO 30/33 14/1

PRO 30/33 14/2 Semi-official Letters from Siam (May 29, 1885 – April 21, 1887)

PRO 30/33 14/2

It contains 59 letters, a few in outline or only partially quoted.

1. Satow to Currie

Bangkok, 29 May/85

My dear Currie,

You will see fr[om]. my [despatch] no. 51 of today's date that I have been obliged to interfere on behalf of the Second King, in order to prevent what was considered by him an infraction of the agreement made by Sir A. Clarke in 1875 securing to him certain revenues. In doing this I have tried to avoid hurting the feelings of the First King, wch. are naturally a little sore on this point. That the power of intervention gained by us in 1875 has ever been of any value, I do not believe, but it seems clear from Knox's & Palgrave's desp[atch]. that we are bound to exercise it whenever occasion arises.

[Dr. William] Willis, who has within the last few days been called in by the Second King, finds that he is suffering fr. Bright's disease, & I fear the poor man will not last very long. All the more reason not to set too high a value on our supposed advantages. No one but Willis, French, myself & the Second King's confidential man know of the state of his health, and it is advisable to keep it secret.

The Siamese have been told that Kergaradec is to return here shortly with the rank of Minister.

2. Satow to Gould

19.6.85

My dear Gould,

If Cox is delayed it is his own fault. He knew very well fr. me that he had to bring his case agst. Mong Shuang Gong, & I am rather surprised that you shld. have forgotten the F.O. instructions. The Siamese have been guilty of a laches[1] in not informing the Comr. of an arrangement made in London, & to make up for it have given Cox the option of going

---

[1] Laches: unreasonable delay by the plaintiff in bringing a claim. An equitable defence.

PRO 30/33 14/2 Semi-official Letters from Siam (May 29, 1885 – April 21, 1887)

agst. the chief, of wch. he will no doubt avail himself.

In your desp[atch]. No. 46 you sent me only the translation of the Comr's. reply. You shld. send Siamese originals as well as translation.

I have not seen my way in Mong Yan Gin's case to doing more than ask that the judgment of the Court be enforced agst. Mong Hla.

The Kromatah's resignation has been at last accepted, and Devan takes his place, a very satisfactory arrangement.

I think the Siamese instructions wch. I send you ought to suffice. If as Leonowens tells me has happened, any leases have been forfeited of prior date to July 1884, the foresters must be reinstated.

I do not see my way at present to interfering abt. slavery in Chiengmai. It wld. be a pity if your protection of that woman shld. cause trouble, but I trust in your discretion.

y.v.t.

3. Satow to Currie (p. 3 of notebook)

Private

25 June 1885

My dear Currie,

I send you privately a memo. on Sir F. Weld's policy of extending our influence over the Malay States & B.B. [British Burma] in wch. I have shown that this includes annexing provinces not inhabited by Malays at all. The memo. covers also part of Mr. Holt Hallett's proposals wch. I think equally [e]xtravagant. Of the question of right or wrong I have said nothing, because it probably does not count for much. But I see no reason for being in a hurry. From what Kergaradec, who came back last night, tells me it is clear that what with disturbances in Cambodia, political complications at Hué & the reduction of the hill regions of Tonquin, the French are fully occupied for the next two years at least, & lastly I don't believe in England being able to afford the men & money for such enterprises.

To tell you the truth, Hallett & Colquhoun, agreeable fellows as they are, must be regarded as adventurers. They may perhaps believe in their own honesty, but they do not stick at much. Telegrams from Hongkong to the "Times" especially, must be taken with a

PRO 30/33 14/2 Semi-official Letters from Siam (May 29, 1885 – April 21, 1887)

large allowance of salt. The correspondent at Peking, Michie[2] by name, <u>was</u> honest, but I do not know how far his trade may not have corrupted him.

If you can stick to Port Hamilton[3] I hope it will be done. It is the most valuable acquisition we have made for forty years.

  y.v.t.

4. Satow to Currie (p.4)

26 June [1885]

Dear Currie,

The Siamese have tried recently to claim that the For. repres[entati]ves are bound to enforce agst. their nationals any regulations that may be communicated to them by the F.M. I found the majority of my paid [i.e. professional] colleagues agreed with me that this pretention could not be admitted, & managed to get the new F.M. to withdraw the note in wch. it had been put forward. French tells me this is a very old game. I know that it has been never allowed in Japan, but have heard that in Turkey every govt. notification is taken as agreed to, unless a for: repres[entati]ve formally objects. I suppose that I am right in not conceding to the Siamese what the Japanese, who are far more fit to be trusted with such power, have not yet obtained.

Amongst the regulations they wanted us to publish was one about taxes on repeating firearms; I told P. Devawongse privately that I approved of it, & that if my consent were asked for officially in accordance with Art. IV of the Supple[mentar]y. Agreement of 1856 I wld. give it. But this I am told they are too proud to do. The genl. question is dealt with in a desp. Treaty No 5 of the 12 instant.

I have written officially asking sanction to a journey to Chiengmai. At present it wld. be [a] very unhealthy trip. Gould seems to think that the jurisdiction over B.S. up there ought to be taken away fr. the Siamese, but I don't see how we can upset the Treaty. It will be better for me to go and look into things myself. Under the circs. I shall not ask for

---

[2] Alexander Michie (1833-1902). Author of *The Englishman in China* (2 vols., 1900).
[3] Komundo, a small group of islands off the southern coast of the Korean peninsula. In April 1885 Port Hamilton was occupied by three Royal Navy ships. The occupation lasted until February 1887.

PRO 30/33 14/2 Semi-official Letters from Siam (May 29, 1885 – April 21, 1887)

permission to go to India & Rangoon.

The change of For: Min. is of importance & if the King could find some one to replace the Kalahome, he would displace him also. One at least of his brothers whom he has put in office is a great scoundrel, and of course they all take bribes. Still the concentration of power must preclude any reform of the administration, & I think the King is alive to the necessity of doing something if he will escape the 'civilising mission' of foreigners. He does not like however to give up the revenue he derives from vices. He is very strong & healthy, & has no signs of disease abt. him. If he lives long enough to see his sons grow up, he will try to have the oldest recognized as heir, but I fancy it is a dangerous thing to try to alter the law of succession. If on the other hand he were to die soon, one of his two whole-brothers wld. probably succeed quietly. The Second King poor man has no chance left, if Willis' diagnosis is correct. I cannot imagine the schemes of Sir F. Weld or Hallett ever being adopted, but if they were, a dispute abt. the succession wld. afford a convenient opportunity.

5. Satow to Currie (p.5)
30 June 1885
Dear Currie,

I am sending by this mail a desp[atch]. about the marriages of B.S. with Siamese women & the protection of women & illegitimate children of B.S. The Siamese Govt. have made some suggestions wch. seem quite reasonable, and propose registration to prevent disputes. I hope you will send me instructions wch. will enable me to settle these two questions. Gould's row with the Chief at Chiengmai wld. never have happened if these matters had been attended to before. I have taken this opportunity of drawing attention again to a desp[atch]. abt. the registration of B.S. in genl. wch. I sent home in Sept. last. I wrote privately to Sir J. Pauncefote about it, but he has prob. been too busy to take any notice. But it really is of importance.

My relations with the new Minr. for F.A. are satisfactory. The Siamese seem desirous of doing everything to please, & have voluntarily made a concession abt. one of the old cases at Chiengmai without my asking for it.

PRO 30/33 14/2 Semi-official Letters from Siam (May 29, 1885 – April 21, 1887)

I published the trade report for '84 in the local paper, and have heard indirectly that some of the Germans were frantic because their imitations of Engl. trade marks were spoken of. It is perfectly true. Half their trade depends upon such tricks. I have transferred the offending paragraph to my covering deps. fr. wch. it can be omitted if you think fit when it comes to be published. I mention this because the German consul is reported to have said that he would 'write to Bismarck', but to me he has not uttered a word. Perhaps it was indiscreet to say what I did, but I can prove it.

 y.v.t.

6. Satow to Gould

8.7.85

My dear Gould,

 Yesterday I took advantage of an interview I had with the King to say a few words abt. slavery in Chiengmai, and other matters of wch. you have spoken from time to time in your private letters. He said he was abt. to make a law that slaves taken in war shld. be able to redeem themselves at the rate of 50 ticals a head. The difficulty in Chiengmai was that the chiefs & officials held such a large number of such slaves but that any cases appealed to Bangkok wld. be decided acc. to Siamese law. I think you might manage to turn this to account in connection with the redemption of the fugitive who has taken refuge with you.

 I said I was much interested in the success of the system established at Chiengmai under [Chiengmai Treaty] Art. VIII,[4] & you had proved your wish to give it a fair trial by not withdrawing such cases as that of Mong Htoon fr. the court as you could easily have done.

 With regard to the elephant clause in leases at Lakhon I have suggested that I see no reason why B.S. shld. be exempted fr. the requisition to which Siamese subjects are liable, & that it seemed to me more consonant with the dignity of the Siamese Govt. to obtain what they wanted in a direct manner than by adopting the round-about course of contracting

---

[4] There were two Anglo-Siamese Chiengmai Treaties, concluded in 1873 and 1883. After the first treaty King Chulalongkorn sent a royal deputy to Chiengmai to ensure compliance with Siam's obligations (protection of the border, of British investments and concessions). After the second treaty of September 1883 Siamese control was intensified: a consular court was established for all cases involving British subjects, and Siam assumed sovereignty in fiscal and judicial matters.

PRO 30/33 14/2 Semi-official Letters from Siam (May 29, 1885 – April 21, 1887)

with individulas to render this service.

As a rule I think B.S. in Siam shld. pay tax & render services like Siamese, as long as the demands made upon them are not oppressive. Extraterritoriality was not intended to give special advantages to foreign subjects, but only as a means of protecting them from undue burdens. The imperia in imperio in a country like Siam, wch. we wish to strengthen, are a source of weakness & destroy the self-confidence of the native govt. & depend on it we shall gain our ends more easily if we can diminish the friction wch. the system causes.

It is possible that a law prohibiting slaveholding by B.S. in the Laos states may be passed.

The tax of 3% on sales of gold leaf &c. will be removed; I shall send you a copy of the instructions to Phya Montri.

The tax on finances I mean to agree to as soon as I am asked.

7. Satow to Coutts Trotter[5]
13/7/85
Dear Sir,

I have much pleasure in complying as far as lies in my power with yr. request for information to be used in the article wch. you are preparing on Siam for the Encyclopedia Britannica. My own knowledge of the country being entirely inadequate, I placed your queries in the hands of Mr. E.H. French Acting Consul who has an experience of this country extending over ten years, & I trust that the replies wch. he has furnished will be found adequate to the purpose.

With regard to the boundary of Siam towards Cambodia I may observe that it is wrongly marked in the map of Dutreuil de Rhins.[6] It ought to start fr. the point bounding the Bay of Campong Som in 101° E. Long. & runs northeast along the range of mtns. to Mt. Pangchak, wch. it follows round the acute angle, then along Mt. Tap Krebey & Mt Kréyagne, & so back to the dotted line. On the opp. side of the lake it follows the stream fr. Kiam upwards & cuts the dotted line abt. the word "Cambodge". The Siamese likewise claim the country

---

[5] Coutts Trotter (1831-1905). Geographer, Fellow of the Royal Geographical Society.
[6] Jules-Léon Dutreuil de Rhins (1846-1894). French geographer and explorer.

PRO 30/33 14/2 Semi-official Letters from Siam (May 29, 1885 – April 21, 1887)

N.E. of Luang Phrabang up to the frontier of Tonquin, marked Tran-ninh, in the inset map on Godin's map of Tonquine, & actually have forces there at the present moment engaged in resisting the incursions of certain intruders of Chinese race known as Haws.

In nearly all the books it is stated that Siam is derived fr. a Malay or Sanscrit word Sajam, meaning "brown". That this is a mere conjecture, not based on any evidence, is I think quite clear. The word Shan applied by European writers to the Lao Tribes, is Burmese for Thai, & "Siam" appears to be identical. Europeans either heard of Siam thro' the Burmese, Peguans or Malays, but most probably through one of the two former, who translated the word Thai, wch. means 'free' into the corresponding word in their own language. The Chinese word is either Siam or Sem, if we take the old pronunciation, & they prob. heard of the Thai race many centuries ago through the Burmese. The English got the name fr. the Portuguese, who in the 16th. century spelt it Siam and Sião as they now do. The theory wch. connects <u>Siam</u> with <u>Sajam</u> is no doubt due to the error of supposing the Engl. pronunciation to be normal.

As to the origin of Thai, free, there are 2 theories. One propounded by the natives is that they assumed it after they shook off the yoke of Cambodia; of this there is no proof. The other, a foreign suggestion, is that it means the ruling class, as distinguished fr. the slaves. This seems the more plausible of the two.

Probably I need hardly observe that our word Laos is the Siamese word for what we call the Shans with the English plural suffix, & that <u>ao</u> in <u>lao</u> is pronounced like ow in cow.

If you wish to know more about slavery, you might perh. be able to obtain papers on that subject fr. the F.O., & a recent report on silk-culture might also be of use. If the paper wch. I have written on the early relations of Siam & Japan is printed in time, I will take care that you have a copy. Bowring's book contains a good account of the early intercourse of Siam c. European countries, with the Exception of Engl., the materials for wch. are in the State papers Indian series 1573-1629.

Of the early writers on Siam Lalonbère is incontestably the best. Van Vliet 50 yrs. earlier (tho' published only in 1692) is trustworthy, as he had resided a long time in the country. Valentijn is a mere compiler. Of the moderns Pallegoix is to be recommended, but his statistics of population cannot be depended on. The famous ruins of Angkor (Nakhon in

PRO 30/33 14/2 Semi-official Letters from Siam (May 29, 1885 – April 21, 1887)

Siamese) Wat are, you doubtless know, in Siamese territory.

I am sorry to say that we know little of the Shans here, except that there are scattered colonies of them here & there in Siam proper, even as far south as Ratburi.

<u>8. Satow to Currie</u>
14 July 1885
My dear Currie,

I am leaving for Singapore today, & hope to see the C.C. of B.B. [Chief Commissioner of British Burma] at Rangoon without adding materially to the length of my absence from Bangkok.

My Dutch colleague, who is the universal gossip, tells me that Kergaradec speaks of having warned the Siamese to be careful with regard to the Cambodian frontier, and altogether takes a high tone. There can be no question that the public in Bangkok, & perh. elsewhere, has made up its mind that France intends to take possn. of Siam, sooner or later and the fact that H.M.G. have not announced any purpose of opposing its annexation produces the belief in their acquiescence. Of resistance on the part of Siam there can of course be no question. I have however thought it wld. do no harm to hint to the said gossip that France must not be too greedy, and that if she begins to nibble at Siam, we shall not be able to wait until everything is devoured. You can see what superior influence the French gain by the belief that they may choose their own time for plucking the pear. I do not believe the fruit is yet ripe, but since the "Times" article of Feb. 6, nothing has appeared in print at all calculated to reassure the Siamese. They profess at present to feel secure, and they fear the interference of the press on their behalf. If the condition of affairs in Europe permits of any comfort being given to them from our side, it wld. do good.

Curiously enough, they asked me ten days ago whether they shld. tell Kergaradec that a govr. of some small province in Cambodia had been driven across the frontier by the rebels to take refuge in Battambong. They said they feared consulting him might seem 'too much courtesy', and talked of bringing the fugitive & his suite to Bangkok, to hand over to Kergaradec here. I said of course that they ought to refer the matter to the Fr. Chargé d'Affaires, and not to use any language indicating an intention of putting any restraint on the governor's movements. I now learn that they have told Kergaradec, who has asked them to wait until he can get instructions from Saigon.

The Saigon paper is full of telegrams detailing movements in pursuit of rebels, of whom very little appears to be seen. I cannot resist the suspicion that much more is made of their rising than is necessary, and that we may hear before long of a violation of the frontier in pursuit. The Fr. have not given up their idea of getting a quid-pro-quo for the spirit convention, wch. they still delay to ratify, and Kergaradec says his locum tenens exceeded his powers in joining with the German, Dutchman & myself in our endeavours to settle the regulations in Feb. last. A Frenchman never gives up a point unless he gains something by it, even tho' as in the present case they pretend to want nothing. They are trying to draw the Siamese on to express great anxiety abt. the spirit convention, & I consequently do not push it.

Kergaradec is a great contrast to Harmand, quiet, gentlemanlike and slow of speech, very thorough, now and then committing himself to an explosion of rage agst. natives. He seems shy. He has been many years in Tonquin and Annam.

9. Satow to Mackenzie Wallace (p. 12)

D. Mackenzie Wallace

14 July 1885.

Dear Mr. Wallace,

I shld. esteem it a great favour if you would kindly interest yourself in the subject of a desp[atch]. wch. goes today to the For. Secy. to the Govt. of India. We are trying to establish a hospital, an institution of wch. the want is much felt, & it is suggested that a man from the Army Hospital Corps wld. be the most efficient superintendent, & if he comes fr. India, not only wld. he have experience of eastern diseases, but the expense of his passage wld. be less than if we obtained him fr. Engl. to say nothing of the saving in time. Our doctor is constantly called upon to attend Br. Indian subjects, who are mostly too poor to pay even for medicines, & tho' he practises the generosity characteristic of his profession, it will be a relief to wch. he is entitled when the hospital is able to take such people off his hands.[7] We have raised altogether abt. £400, wch. will enable us to furnish the building &

pay our current expenses for the first year, not however including food & medicines. I venture to hope that the Govt. of India may be disposed to help us with a grant of £100 a year. We might if things prosper, receive even Siamese as outpatients, wch. wld. certainly produce a good effect, in a place where there is absolutely no hospital or dispensary of any kind. The medical missionary, who has been so useful in other countries, does not exist in Bangkok, & I think it wld. be politically of value if the Indian Govt. helped to supply his place.

  Believe me
   y.v.f.

10. Satow to Currie (p.13)
Confid[entia]l.
Rangoon
8 Aug/85
My dear Currie,

The French are going ahead at a great rate in U[pper]. Burma. They are negotiating for concessions for building a r[ai]lw[a]y. establishing a bank & obtaining the administration of the frontier customs. Two days ago an envoy started for France who is to complete arrangements & to reside permanently in Paris. He also takes presents to the Emperor of Germany.

These facts are considered very serious here, & I believe also at Simla, & strong measures may become necessary in order to counteract the growing influence of France in U.B. It is a matter of course that if the French establish themselves there instead of ourselves, the uncomfortable feeling in Siam will be greatly increased, for they will then be surrounded on all sides. It is a clever design, for if successful, the whole of this vast region will become French, & our commerce will be shut out. Not only that but as B.B. is considerably dependent on the Siamese Shan States for the cattle and buffaloes used in

---

[7] Satow made a similar comment about his friend Dr. William Willis in a letter to Mrs. Aston from Bangkok dated 8 May 1885, stating he "has a large clientèle of patients who give a great deal of trouble and don't pay." (PRO 30/33 11/3)

agriculture, this province wld. suffer in the principal source of its wealth and revenue. So that the prosecution of Fr. designs in U.B. involves a great deal more than the inconvenience of having the French as an immediate neighbours [sic.] on a very long frontier. The Straits Settlements too will be isolated, & every facility gained by the French for cutting through the peninsula at leisure.

It may perh. be anticipated that if we assert ourselves at Mandalay, the Fr. will compensate themselves for their disappointment by taking Siam. I have shown the commercial value of Bangkok alone in one of my desp[atches]. this year: its value to B.B. [British Burma] is perh. not much less. The Siamese wld. be unable to offer any effective resistance.

Another question of minor urgency is the scheme of Colquhoun for an overland telegraph fr. Canton through Kwangsi and Yunnan to Esman [Esmau?] on the S.W. frontier of China, then across the Shan States wch. have revolted fr. Burma to Kiangsen on Siamese frontier, and down through Chiengmai to Raheng, where as you already know, a line is to cross over to Moulmein. The section 200 m[iles]. long across the Burmese Shan States is the principal difficulty. I have been asked by the Govt. of India to state my views, & I accordingly furnished the Ch[ief]: Com[missione]r. c. [with] the enclosed memo to the closing para. of wch. I beg your attention. It records my conviction that even in this matter of a telegraph, we shall not get Siam to join us unless we are ready to guarantee her agst. France. As to the bit across the former Burmese Shan States, I do not see any way of doing it, except by taking U.B. [Upper Burma] under our protection. If we did that, & acquired her Shan States at the same time, we shld. be independent of the cooperation of Siam, & might abandon her to her fate. If we did that France wld. have no ground of quarrel, wch. she might take if we gave her double checkmate at Mandalay & Bangkok at the same time. Still the fact that Germany has large commercial interests in Siam might render her absorption less easy than that of Tonquin.

Memo. (enclosed in above).

The telegraph fr. Bangkok to Chiengmai will hardly be finished before the end of the next dry season, & I think that some time will elapse before it is continued to Kiangsen. The

PRO 30/33 14/2 Semi-official Letters from Siam (May 29, 1885 – April 21, 1887)

Siamese are engaged in duplicating their line to Cambodia & in constructing an entirely new one to Korat. They are also under an engagement to the Indian Govt. to put up a line fr. Raheng to Miyawadi. They talk further of a line to Luang Phrabang, but I do not recollect that they had any intention of going on to Kiangsen. I cannot however assert that they will not do so. I can only say that unless urged on the subject they are not likely to undertake that extension at present.

Supposing however that a line to Kiangsen already existed, I do not see how the authority to construct the portion betw. that point & the Chin. Frontier is to be obtained, nor what certainty of its being properly protected can be looked for. The tract of country over wch. it will have to pass is under the jurisdiction of several Shan chiefs who appear to have thrown off the suzerainty of U.B. The Siamese have no desire to extend their power in that direction, nor do they possess the means. The proposed submission of Kiangtung to the suzerainty of Siam has not come to anything, & the Siamese Govt. seems to believe that nothing serious was ever intended by the chief. They are on the contrary talking of building a fort on the frontier towards Kiangtung as a measure of self-defence.

I suppose that it wld. not under present circs. be possible to utilize the influence of U.B. nor that of China for the construction of this section.

In any case, the erection of a telegraph in that region wld. appear to involve either negotiation with a number of chiefs, or the assertion of supremacy over them by the power under whose auspices the telegraph Co. is to be established.

As far as Siam is concerned, I feel sure that the King is not disposed, as matters now stand, to enter into any engagements with the Br. Govt. calculated to excite the jealousy of Fr. towards G.B. As an instance of this when the question recently arose of obtaining telegraph operators to replace the Frenchmen whose time had expired, instead of applying to the Indian Govt. who cld. have supplied their wants at a comparatively small expense, the Siamese Govt. preferred to procure the necessary staff fr. the U.S.

The only terms upon wch. it wld. be possible to induce Siam to combine with either the Br. or Indian Govts. in the establishment of the proposed overland telegraph to China are in my opinion the giving to her of such assurances with regard to the maintenance of her existing territorial limits as wld. effectually exclude the possibility of annexation by France.

She has constantly before her eyes the example of Tunis, where the pretext for Fr. action was that Italy had been endeavouring to obtain a preponderating influence. As long as we adhere to our present policy, she will do nothing for us, as the motives of fear and self-interest are alike wanting.

11. Satow to Gould

Extract to Gould.   6 Sept 85.

"Now as to yourself. The F.O. has not as yet said anything abt. the arrangements consequent on Newman's transfer to Porto Rico. I discussed the question of the Chiengmai pay being raised very fully with Bernard, & he entirely supports my view that it ought to be made 700 or 800 rupees a month. That wld. render it equal to the Bangkok £700 with the additional £400 when I am on leave. But it wld. be more convenient that the question shld. be raised by you in a desp[atch]. to me showing the cost of living & any other reasons you think necessary to mention, & I shld. then support it by stating the grounds on wch. I think the importance of the post justifies the proposal. That is quite apart fr. you coming here or remaining where you are. That may possibly be decided at home without reference to either you or me. I think the ill feeling wch. seems to exist betw. you & the King's friends might be got over by a temporary change to Bangkok, but do not quite see how a merely temporary change cld. be managed. Beyond that ill-feeling I know of nothing that could impair your utility at Chiengmai, but if it fortunately ceased to exist, your usefulness as Chargé d'Affaires here wld. in my opinion considerably outweigh the advantage to the public service of your remaining at Chiengmai. However, we can talk over these matters better when we meet.

I was very sorry to read the last para. of your desp[atch]. on the Imung affair,[8] and shld. have preferred to keep it back, but as it was written for the F.O. it must of course go. And the death of the Wangna [second king] has naturally deprived it of much of its point. The Note addressed to Ld. G[ranville]. by P[rince]. Naret was both inexact & exaggerated, & I in sending your report to Ld. S[alisbury]. have said so. You need not fear lest

---

[8] Leonowens spoke to Satow about the Imung case on June 15, 1885 (diary). "Says that in the Imung case Bigit had laid a trap for Gould into wch. he fell."

misrepresentations of the sort shld. have any weight at home or with me, & the disingenuous trick of complaining to me without saying that instructions have been sent to complain in London is not likely to be repeated.

  y.v.t.

12. Satow to Bernard
C.S. Bernard Esq. B.B.
7/9/85
My dear Bernard,

 In case you shld. not have seen it yet, I send you Colquhoun's memo. abt. his telegraph scheme wch. he laid before Ld. Dufferin at Simla. There are only 2 points in it particularly calling for notice. 1stly [Firstly] what he says as to the protection of the intervening 200 miles of Shan territory, & his suggestion to send an official to Siam to negotiate with the Siamese.

 I have not spoken to the Siamese Govt. on the subject, & shall of course not say anything to them without instructions fr. home or from the Viceroy. As to the "willingness" of Siam to protect the telegraph line beyond her present boundaries, Colquhoun's sanguine imagination has led him too far, & I adhere to what I said in the memo. I left with you. There is nothing to be gained either by inviting the Chinese to extend themselves in the direction of Chieng-tung.

 With regard to the desp[atch]. of an official to negotiate with Siam, I think it premature to talk of such a matter until the preceding question is decided.

 I was quite right in doubting as I did whether the Siamese had any present intention of extending their line fr. Zimmé to Kiangsen. But they tell me they will extend it from Raheng to Luang Phrabang viâ Pichai.

 I send also extracts from a couple of letters of Colquhoun's relative to this matter. To the letter written fr. Simla I have not yet replied, & when I do it will be to say that the project seems unrealisable under existing conditions.

 Instructions have reached me fr. home to negotiate an additional article about extradition as suggested by you, & I anticipate no difficulty in coming to an understanding with the Siamese.

    [Thanks for kindness]

P.S. Please return the enclosed memo. when you have done with it, as I have no other copy.

13. Satow to Currie

11.9.85

Dear Currie,

    The 2nd K[ing]. has departed this life, & with him all likelihood for the present of foreign interference with the succession. Kergaradec has lost what he looked upon as a trump card that was likely to slip out of my hands. The 2nd K. seems to have contemplated asking for Fr. help if in the event of any row betw. him & the First K. we had refused to help him. I have little doubt as to Newman's having put this into his head. The 1st K. & his friends are delighted, & the latter take no pains to conceal their joy. Luckily I did not try to make political capital out of the 2nd K. & have not lost my balance by his disappearance. The Siamese Govt. talk of abolishing the office, & of having the King's eldest legitimate son recognized as Crown Prince. If the K. lives as at present his health is perfectly good, the country will settle down, & progress will be possible; but in case of his sudden decease fr. any unforeseen cause, there might be a contest for the throne betw. his two legitimate brothers & the partizans of the young Prince, amongst whom the present F.M. is the best man. It might at such a time be desirable to give him a promise of our active support, ^ prevent the Fr. cutting in on the other side. I take it for granted that we do not want them to exercise paramount influence at Bangk[ok].

    The Siamese Govt. seem to be much pleased with the proposal to conclude an additional article to the Chiengmai Treaty, abt. wh. instructions were sent to me in Treaty No. 6 of June 30. I suppose "full powers" will be sent to me when I report officially that they have agreed. I shall send in a Note on the subject in a day or two.

14. Satow to Colquhoun

12.9.85

Dear Mr. Colquhoun,

PRO 30/33 14/2 Semi-official Letters from Siam (May 29, 1885 – April 21, 1887)

My absence fr. Bangkok on a visit to Singapore & Burmah has prevented me fr. answering earlier yr. letter of 12 July fr. Bombay. As regards the telegraph scheme, I fear there is one great difficulty in the way of its success, namely the want of any settled govt. betw. Esmau[?] & Kiangtsen, wch. we could induce to protect the line & Siam certainly cannot do it. Moreover, as you know, the Siamese cannot afford to join us in anything, so long as she is not guaranteed agst. the effects of Fr. jealousy. There is no intention at present on their part to extend the telegraph beyond Chiengmai.

The Indian Govt. wrote to me asking whether there was any objection to Mr. Gould's undertaking the Shan Gazetteer, & I gave my approval to the scheme. As he is on the spot & acquainted with Siamese he is in a good position to obtain information. After it was arranged, came the telegram to Mr. Bernard proposing that it shld. be placed in your hands after all, but I did not like to take it away fr. Mr. Gould to whom the proposal of the Indian Govt. had been already communicated, & said so to the Ch. Comr. [Bernard], who agreed c. me. We have everything that has been printed on the Shan States here in Bangkok. I regret however that circs. shld. have deprived you of the chance of doing a work that was your own original conception.

I am going up to Chiengmai by the Mënam abt. the middle of Novr. & shall try to do a little exploring.

The recent death of the Second King has not affected the position of England in Siam, tho' it will be thought so by those who had calculated on his being put forward as a candidate for the succession on the demise of the first K. On the other hand it has removed a constant source of soreness.

 y.v.t.

15. Satow to Currie
13.9.85
Dear Currie,

In the memo. on Sir F. Weld's policy in the Malay peninsula wch. I sent you a couple of months ago, I spoke of a practicable route for a canal that was believed to exist. I now send a confl. desp[atch]. giving information wch. seems to be reliable. It ought to be kept as

PRO 30/33 14/2 Semi-official Letters from Siam (May 29, 1885 – April 21, 1887)

close as possible. In Penang & Singapore I lately found an almost total ignorance of the country outside our own boundaries. The Colonial officials are so engrossed by administration questions, that they have no time or interest in extending their information. They have one explorer who disappears for months at a time, & then turns up again with some good work well done. It would be worth while sending him or any other competent person with a knowledge of surveying & of Malay to examine the route described by my informant.

The latter is trying to get a concession fr. the Siamese to work the coalfield he has found at & near Paklas marked in my map. He says the coal is as good or better than that of Sabuan, & more accessible. If what he says is correct, it will turn out a matter of vital importance. I shall give him what support I can, but in such a business, official interference may do more harm than good.

I have hinted in my desp[atch]. that H.M.G. might be disposed to ask for a canal concession fr. the Siamese Govt. but we shld. have to give a quid pro quo, such as an engagement to respect the Siamese possessions in the Peninsula, & that wld. interfere with Sir F. Weld's projects. The Siamese are not reticent abt. the Perak boundary question, wch. they discuss with every one who is willing. It was reported to me the other day that the F.M. said they did not fear England, but he may have meant to say that he "had no apprehensions." He probably thinks that H.M.G. is not backing up Sir H. Low & other Colonial officials very strongly. Smith the Actg. Govr. talking to me abt. the Peninsula, seemed to think it quite a matter of course that every one wld. look upon the expulsion of Siam fr. Malaya as a desirable even necessary thing in the interests of good administration, in fact as part of the 'civilizing mission' of England. Any other view appeared to him inconceivable. In fact the political horizon of Singapore is strictly limited to its vicinity. The separation in 1867 fr. India may have been a good thing for the colony, but bad for the empire. Singapore thinks only of its own hand.

 y.v.t.

<u>16. Satow to Currie</u>
26 Sept. 1885.

PRO 30/33 14/2 Semi-official Letters from Siam (May 29, 1885 – April 21, 1887)

Dear Currie,

I hope that the request of the Siamese Govt. for your good offices with Italy & Austria respecting the spirit convention will be favourably entertained. I have it in writing as well fr. the F.M. in a private note.

The Fr[ench]. ratification took place on the 12th ulto & Prisdang[9] despatched a telegram at once, wch. however did not reach Prince D's hands till the 15th. You know that the telegraph staff in Bangkok is French. In the meantime Kergeradec went to D. & proposed to obtain the ratification if the Siamese wld. consent to employ none but Frenchmen on their telegraphs throughout the country. D. refused to make this concession. A few days later he got his telegram. K. then said that the ratification was being forwarded to himself with instructions not to deliver it unless his previous proposal was agreed to. D. thereupon telegraphed in a great hurry to Prisdang, & was relieved to find that the ratification was in P's hands. The story seems not unlikely to be true; it was volunteered first to French in my absence, & now repeated to me the day before yesterday a-propos of the subject of my desp[atch]. Treaty No.9.

I propose in future to forward political desp. to India under flying seal[10] to the Chief Comr. at Rangoon, wch. is on the way to Calcutta.

The Frenchman will try to prevent the Spirit Convention coming into force by all the means in his power, but perh. he may be circumvented. There is no possibility of working with him in a straightforward manner.

y.v.t.

17. Satow to Durand[11]

26 Sept. 1885

---

[9] Prince Prisdang (1851-1935). In 1881 he established the first Siamese Legation in England, and over the next five years he became minister to eleven European countries and the United States.

[10] Under flying seal: a letter with a seal attached but not closed, so that it may be read by a person who is requested to forward it to its destination.

[11] Henry Mortimer Durand (1850-1924). Diplomat and colonial civil servant of British India. Foreign Secretary of India, 1884-94.

PRO 30/33 14/2 Semi-official Letters from Siam (May 29, 1885 – April 21, 1887)

H.M. Durand Esq. C.I.E. [Companion of the Order of the Indian Empire]
My dear Sir,

By this mail I am forwarding under flying seal to the C.C. of B.B. [Chief Commissioner of British Burma] two desp[atches]. addressed to you, & I propose to follow this course in future with all desp[atches]. to the Govt. of India, unless H.E. the Viceroy shld. prefer to have them sent direct. I venture to think that advantages may often be derived fr. the possn. of early informn. on Siamese matters by the C.C.

  I remain
    y.v.f.

18. Satow to Bergne
26.9.85
Dear Mr. Bergne.

At the last moment I think I have discovered that the Siamese Min. has made an omission in enumerating those Powers wch. have not yet signed a convention with reference to the Spirit Trade. In my desp[atch]. Treaty No. 9 of the 24th inst. I report that he mentioned only Austria & Italy. As far as I am able to ascertain Spain ought to be added to the number. Italy seems to have signed, but not to have ratified, the others have not yet concluded any Agreement.

  Will you kindly make a note of this correction, if it is really one.

  I have no copy of the Italian agree[men]t. The U.S. Minr. privately furnished me with a copy of his.

    y.v.t.

19. Satow to Currie
7 Oct. 1885
My dear Currie.

The French Chargé d'Affaires has given notice to the Siamese that he intends to place on his registers all Annamites residing in Siam, & also the Annamites or their descendants made prisoners of war in the year 1831. He quoted the Treaty with Hué wch. obliges France

PRO 30/33 14/2 Semi-official Letters from Siam (May 29, 1885 – April 21, 1887)

to give to Annamites the same protection as to Frenchmen. There are at least 5000 Annamites in Siam, & of these 1000 or more at Chantabun. I enclose a copy of a note wch. the F.M. has written me on this subject. I am not quite certain what the French treaty agreements with Siam are, but think the claim has no foundation. With regard to the prisoners of war who have been settled in Siam for at least 50 yrs. it is altogether untenable. We might as well claim all the Peguans & their descendants. I shall advise the Siamese Govt. that if they admit the Fr. claim thery must expect us to follow the Fr. example, & as regards Annamites who are not prisoners of war, to fulfil their Treaty agreements whatever they may be. But this shows that the friendly professions alluded to in one of my recent desp[atches]. by this mail are worth nothing. Kergeradec says he is instructed to 'insist on the values' of the Spirit Agreement. I asked if this meant that the Fr. Govt. required a concession in return. His reply was that at one time they had asked for the whole control of Lake Talesap to be surrendered to them as an equivalent, but the Siamese having refused to give it, France has quietly taken the necessary measures independently. Last mail I told you of the demand that all the telegraphs shld. be placed in Fr. hands, but Kergaradec has not yet confessed this to me. I am disposed to join with him ostensibly in some representations abt. the spirit trade wch. is still carried on to a small extent by French protégés as it seems useful to persuade him that I am his friend.

It is a question worth considering whether Siam shld. be induced to place herself under British protection. If I saw an opportunity for doing this, shld. I get a wigging for taking advantage of it?

Thanks for your Note of Aug. 25, wch. reached me at the same time as copy of Ld. Salisbury's Note to Naret abt. Perak. The tone of it convinces me that the Siamese Govt. had better give way with a good grace, but I will not be in a hurry to tell them so at present. I shld. like to have an indication of your wishes on this point.

20. Satow to Currie (p. 27)

21 Octr.

Dear Currie,

My last letter was written in a great hurry to catch the mail. On the 11th I saw the F.M.

PRO 30/33 14/2 Semi-official Letters from Siam (May 29, 1885 – April 21, 1887)

He produced an English lawyer's opinion obtained 2 years ago to the effect that these Annamites are properly Siamese subjects. Fortified by this he was going to reply to Kergaradec, refusing to admit that they could be registered as Fr. protégés. He seems to feel no anxiety. There are about 8000 of these people, not 5000 as I said in my last. When he asked my opinion I told him that if he conceded what this Frenchman asked, he must expect similar demands on behalf of descendants of other nationalities as Portuguese & Peguans.

On the following day he sent the draft of his reply,[12] to which I suggested a few alterations, but I fancy it has not been delivered yet. He has been away with the King, & I shall not be able to see him until after the mail goes. There can be no question that the Siamese feel great doubts about their future. In a private letter shown me lately of the F.M. in reply to one fr. a B.S. in wch. he had been advised to introduce British capital as a protection agst. France, he said that Tunis[?] had not escaped, although a British Co. was interested in a rlwy. This confirms what I said in the memo. on Colquhoun's telegraph scheme that I sent you fr. Rangoon. But I do not quite see how Fr. cld. annex Siam in the face of the commercial interests of other nations, especially Germany. It was talked abt. as a likely event 20 yrs. ago, and the danger does not appear greater now than it did then.

I propose starting for Chiengmai on the 18th Nov. and shall be away for a couple of months.

21. Satow to Currie (p. 29)
28.10.85

My dear Currie,

The news that an unconditional acceptance of the ultimatum delivered to the King of Burma is required by the 10 Nov. makes me think that it may be desirable that I shld. give up my journey to Chiengmai. If there is war, I ought to be here. But I need not make up my mind for the present.

As far as I understand the Siamese Govt. have refused to entertain Kergaradec's proposal to register as Fr. protégés the descendants of Annamite prisoners of war, but I

---

[12] This paragraph has been deleted with one vertical line and the remark in the margin: "I do not think the reply has yet been delivered."

PRO 30/33 14/2 Semi-official Letters from Siam (May 29, 1885 – April 21, 1887)

have not been able to extract a copy of their Note fr. them.

In reply to a private telegram fr. Ld. Salisbury I telegraphed that I suggest Gould coming here, & Fr[ench]. succeeding him at Chiengmai. The title of Consul might reconcile him to the position of second fiddle here, to wch. he wld. otherwise prefer his semi-independence at his present post. But I think it better for the public service that he shld. come here as being greatly French's senior in point of years, he is the fittest to take charge when I go on leave, and I want him to get accustomed to less prejudiced views.

I am sending by this mail a desp[atch]. with long enclosures abt. a new O. in C. [Order in Council] for Siam and rules of procedure wch. I hope will be adopted. Compared with the China & Japan O. in C. ours is very inefficient.

In two other desp[atches]. I have reported a step wch. I took in conjunction with the Fr. & Dutchman with reference to the everlasting Spirit Question, and the varied motives wch. influence all the parties concerned. Without appearing to go a certain way with the Frenchman I cld. not have learnt what he was up to. Cld. you not get Portuguese Govt. to instruct their man to adhere to the Arrange[men]t. of 1882, instead of following the Fr's lead.

A B.S. who prints a vernacular newspaper[13] has recently published some articles by a Siamese contributor on the Franco-Chinese war, wch. contained reflections not to the honour of France. Kergaradec went to the Siamese and urged them to put forth a press law. He then came to me, & asked me whether I shld. object to its being enforced agst. B.S. I told him what had been done in Japan some years ago by Sir H. P[arkes]. with regard to a newspaper published in Japanese by a B.S.[14] & that I was inclined personally to admit the principle that the Siamese had a right to put a stop to newspapers wch. had a tendency to excite ill-feeling. I then communicated with the editor, whom I have already had to warn once before, and hinted strongly that if this sort of thing occurred again, I shld. have to stop

---

[13] Dr. Samuel Smith published a newspaper titled *Chotmaihet Sayamsamai* from 1882 to 1885

[14] John Reddie Black launched the *Bankoku Shinbun* in 1876. Parkes was persuaded by the Japanese Government to prohibit British citizens publishing Japanese language newspapers. Black unsuccessfully contested this in the London courts. See also Satow's diary for October 22, 1885.

his paper. I have told this to K. who expressed his thanks. I shall prob. report the whole matter officially.

    y.v.t.

22. Satow to Currie
10/11/85

My dear Currie,

I have at last got fr. the Siamese a copy of their reply to Kergaradec about the Annamite inhabitants of Siam, & have sent the whole business home in a confidl. desp[atch]. I hope you think I was right in giving the amount of advice I did.

The German consul who has been winning the affections of Prince Devawongse by giving him 'private' lessons in law has been told that he is to go to Amoy, and Krencki, a very quiet fellow comes back here. The change is not altogether to be regretted, & as long as it is the German aim to put spokes in our wheel, I wld. rather have a stupid man than a clever one.

I shld. be very glad if you could back [Dr. William] Willis' application for an increase of salary, but if that cannot be done, wld. it be possible to promise that he shld. be allowed to count his service in Japan towards pension.

    y.v.t.

23. Satow to Bernard
14 Nov. 85

My dear Bernard,

Thanks for your private letter forwarding Col. Sladen's Report on the Siamese King's journey to India in 1872. There was nothing else in his cover.

Fr. the home papers & what my French colleague tells me, there is not much likelihood of [Jules] Ferry's[15] return to power, so that we need not fear further interference in the Indo-Chinese peninsula at present. The Siamese however appear to be genuinely alarmed at

---

[15] Jules Ferry was prime minister of France, February 1883 – March 1885.

PRO 30/33 14/2 Semi-official Letters from Siam (May 29, 1885 – April 21, 1887)

Lanessan's[16] report on the treaty with Burma, wch. appears to talk of the annexation of the Laos[?] of the Mekong Valley, leaving only to Siam the valley of the Menam. You no doubt will have received a copy fr. home, but I have not yet seen it.

Prince Devawongse, the King's brother & F.M. asked me last night whether the present was not a favourable conjuncture for taking possn. of those border districts wch. Gould last year prevented the man at Chiengmai fr. trying to annex. I told him that if they valued the friendship of England they had better keep their hands off.[17] In the event of Burma coming under our exclusive influence, Siam might feel assured of getting all she was entitled to.

The Fr. Ch. d'Aff. has sent in another Note abt. the Ammanites, wch. I shall forward in continuation of my previous desp[atch]. on this subject, as soon as the Siamese reply has been delivered. He tries to insist upon claiming the Annamites resident in Siam, but I think it is a weak demand, and one that can easily be rebutted.

The 'entente cordiale' with France seems to be quite a thing of the past, & I have no hesitation in opposing my Fr. colleague whenever possible, of course without doing so openly. We are on friendly terms, & I hope they will continue.

I send thro' you a desp[atch]. addressed to the Viceroy, as you may like to see it. I was very sorry the other day to give you the trouble of deciphering a long telegram for transmission to India, but it is really too bad of the F.O. to tell me they have furnished cypher X to the Indian Govt. when they apparently have not done so.

The Govr. of Singapore was expected back there yesterday. I wish he was in a position to learn what the Indian Govt. desires with regard to Siam, and wld. act in concert[?]. As things go his horizon is limited by Penang.

y.v.t.

? Price of map.

24. Satow to Currie
23 Nov. 1885

---

[16] Jean Louis de Lanessan (1843-1919). French statesman and naturalist. Governor of French Indo-China, 1891-94.
[17] See diary for November 13, 1885.

PRO 30/33 14/2 Semi-official Letters from Siam (May 29, 1885 – April 21, 1887)

My dear Currie,

I need not say that Ld. Salisbury's[18] desp[atch]. to Sir J. Walsham[19] enclosed in No. 70 of Oct. 12 interested me very greatly. In my letter of 8 Aug. I wrote to you that if we asserted ourselves at Mandalay the Fr. might seek compensation by annexing Siam. But it does not seem that they propose to come quite so far as Bangkok. The Report of Lanessan on the Franco-Burmese treaty presented to the Chambers, wch. has been shown to me by Prince Devawongse, says plainly that they ought not to pass the range of mountains wch. separate the basin of the Mekong fr. that of the Menam. Hence M. Waddington's[20] proposal to negotiate for a division of influence in the Indo-Chinese peninsula probably means that if we give them a free hand in the Mekong valley they will abstain from interfering with our proceedings in the Menam Valley & the Malay Peninsula.

I venture to think there would be serious objections to such an understanding, for the following reasons:

1stly the Laos who inhabit the most valuable portion of the Mekong valley belong to the same race as the Siamese. They speak a dialect of the same language, & their natural affinities are with the Siamese.

2ndly the Mekong valley including its tributaries on the r. & l. banks comes perilously near to the Northern Laos states included in our vice-consular district of Chiengmai, as Hallett can tell, who has explored the country, & it includes Chieng-tung anf Chieng-Hung, the former of wch. at least properly is subject to Upper Burmah; & if we annex Upper Burma or establish a protectorate, we must extend our authority over these 2 states.

3rdly the Siamese wld. not by any means thank us for such an arrangement with France, wch. wld. be sure to leak out. The Fr. Chargé d'Affaires wld. be the first to tell them.

4thly the Fr. wld. at once proceed to insist on placing a Vice-Consul at Luang Phrabang, & perh. at some of the other points recommended by Lanessan, & gradually swallow up the whole of their part. We have no such desire to be their close neighbours as wld. induce us

---

[18] Lord Salisbury became Prime Minister in June 1885.
[19] Sir John Walsham (1830-1905). In 1885 he was appointed Envoy Extraordinary and Minister Plenipotentiary to the Emperor of China and the King of Korea.
[20] William Waddington (1826-1894). French ambassador to the United Kingdom, 1883-1893.

PRO 30/33 14/2 Semi-official Letters from Siam (May 29, 1885 – April 21, 1887)

to take what was left of Siam, & consequently they would have a positive gain, agst. wch. we shld. have to set off a feeling in the Siamese mind that we had sold them to France. We shld. consequently be in a less advantageous position than we are at present. The trade of Bangkok, wch. is what we care abt, wld. be correspondingly diminished by the whole amount of produce wch. now finds its way here fr. the Mekong valley for export to Singapore.

No doubt if the Menam valley belonged to us, the improved system of administration wch. we shld. introduce wld. render it more productive, but I imagine that such an acquisition is not in contemplation, at least for the present. India will have first to organize Upper Burmah & the Shan States. She is not in a position to assimilate at the same moment such a huge additional morsel as the Menam valley, & Singapore is not ready to annex the Malay Peninsula.

All the maps are wrong. They call the Menam valley Siam, and the Mekong valley with Chiengmai, Laos: the whole is Siam; the country of the Laos is only a subdivision.

I trust therefore that no partition will be agreed to such as what the Fr. contemplate wch. wld. give the Fr. all they want & leave us with worse than nothing.

Altho' their consent to a self-denying ordinance might not be obtainable, I feel convinced that to insist upon it wld. strengthen our position. We shld. at least have the credit with the rest of the world for disinterestedness, & the Siamese wld. be thankful to us for the idea, while we shld. give breathing time to India, & keep our frontier far away fr. that of a disagreeable neighbour.

The Germans have considerable commercial interests here. They are far more numerous than the English, & show themselves keen traders. Altho' much of their business is carried on in Engl. goods & with capital derived fr. London, they absorb a large share of the middleman's profits. Is there no possibility of an understanding with them to maintain the integrity of the Siamese kingdom?

The discussion wch. Kergaradec has recently raised abt. the Annamites in Siam is an attempt to carry out part of Lanessan's programme, & he has recently returned to the charge abt. the proposed establish[men]t. of a Fr. Consular Agent at Luang Phrabang. On both matters my advice has been sought by the Siamese F.M. & I have approved the line he proposed to take. I have even assisted him with the draft of his last Note, wch. I send by this mail. It is no use giving him advice, unless one makes sure that he turns it to proper account. I send as a curiosity some marginal notes made by him on Lanessan's Report.

I have secured the agreement of the Siamese to a draft of the proposed supplementary article to the Chiengmai Treaty, & in accordance with Lord Salisbury's Treaty No. 6 have laid it before the Indian Govt. but have not yet recd. their reply. When the affair is concluded I shall report. My departure for Chiengmai is delayed partly on this account & partly by French's absence on a mission to the W. coast of the Gulf in connection with an inquiry that is being held on the homicide of a B.S. As soon as he returns I shall start, unless the Indian Govt., whom I have asked to state their wishes, tell me I had better remain here during the operations in Upper Burmah.

Is there not a slight oversight in your note to Baron Plessen of Sept. 25 enclosed to me in No. 71, as to the admission of distillers as Excise farmers. I thought I had fully reported in my No. 37 of 13 April, wch. was approved in Ld. Granville's No. 45 of June 15. What the German Acting Consul wrote to his Govt. abt. the Siamese intention to transfer the negotiations about the spirit agreements to Europe was a pure misconception. He has been rather a stumbling-block in the way of a settle[men]t. but has now promised me to use his influence to hurry up the Siamese. By dint of giving lessons in International Law to the F.M. he has made himself persona grata. He told me he was going to lecture to the Prince on the English & German Treaties, but I begged him to leave to me the interpretation of our engagements with Siam. He has been apptd. to Amoy, & will soon I hope be relieved by Krencki, who is a much better fellow.

y.v.t.

25. Satow to Currie (p. 36)

30 Nov. [1885]

My dear Currie,

The Fr. Chargé d'Aff[aires]. [Kergaradec] yesterday began to talk abt. Luang Phrabang.[21]

---

[21] See Satow's diary, November 29, 1885.

PRO 30/33 14/2 Semi-official Letters from Siam (May 29, 1885 – April 21, 1887)

He said that sooner or later they wld. put a Vice-Consul there to look after the old trade routes to Tonquin & Annam wch. will eventually be re-opened; that the Siamese had expressed their willingness to consent, provided the Fr. wld. consider a treaty similar to ours with regard to Chiengmai, 'of wch. the Prince appeared very proud.' He then proceeded to criticize our treaty & to enlarge on the danger of a British Subject being condemned unjustly on a criminal charge in the absence of a Vice-consul. He was anxious to learn whether there was any likelihood of the Treaty being abrogated.

I told him that as far as our present experience went it worked satisfactorily, & that too much reliance must not be placed upon what travelers fr. up country said abt. the matter. It did not surprise me to find that prejudices existed agst. the surrender of jurisdiction to the native authorities, as it necessarily diminished the vice-consul's importance. I explained to him that the Siamese had at first been opposed to our having a vice-consul there because they suspected a covert design to annex the Laos provinces, wch. was of course absurd, & they now began to see that it was an advantage to them, as every time we put pressure on them in order to get justice done to B.S. as agst. the Laos chiefs it strengthens their hold on the country. But I promised to tell him abt. the working of the Treaty on my return fr. Chiengmai. In short I gave him to understand that I thought such a Treaty a good thing on the whole.

The truth is, he has been pressing the Siamese to consent to a Vice-consul at Luang Phrabang, as the enclosed correspondence will show. Prince D. replied [as I advised him he was right as to Siamese views with regard to the issue of an exequatur] that they were unwilling to grant an exequatur, but that a passport wld. [be] freely given to any private person going there, & if the Fr. Govt. desire to send a temporary mission, he wld. beg to be informed beforehand of its nature. He thinks the matter is at rest for the present.

I am to sign the supplementary article to the Chiengmai Treaty this afternoon, and start for Chiengmai tomorrow.

With regard to my telegram of the 29th, the Prince told me Blowitz[22] had said to Prisdang that it was proposed Engl. & Fr. shld. delimit the frontiers of Siam, & hoped it

---

[22] Henri de Blowitz (1825-1903), foreign correspondent of *The Times*.

PRO 30/33 14/2 Semi-official Letters from Siam (May 29, 1885 – April 21, 1887)

was not the case. Evidently he thought we were going to interfere in this matter, & perh. give the Fr. what they are well known to desire, the Mekong Valley. I replied that Blowitz of course knew only just so much of the truth as his informant had chosen to impart to him, & I wld. tell him what had really happened, namely that [French ambassador] M. Waddington had suggested to Ld. S. a division of influence in the Indo-Chinese peninsula, & that Ld. Salisbury had replied by proposing a self-denying ordinance, binding both powers to leave Siam intact. At this he seemed greatly relieved.

I suppose I shall not be back in Bangkok until the end of January, but it is possible that the telegraph to Chiengmai may be open by Xmas. The journey up there takes fr. 3 wks to a month, & the journey back by river all the way somewhat less.

26. Satow to Currie

1 Decr.

My dear Currie,

The supple[mentar]y. article was signed yesterday after the mail left, and I am now starting on my journey.

The F.M. recurred again to the subject of Blowitz's information to Prisdang, wch. he professed to have obtained fr. a very high authority. B. had said the proposal was not merely to delimit the frontiers of Siam, but also to effect a partition of certain territories betw. E. & Fr., & that the Fr. & Engl. Govts. wld. communicate with P. on the matter. P. did not think there was anything in it.

I said the latter part of the story was impossible, & repeated to him Lord Salisbury's proposal to Waddington to abstain fr. acquiring Siamese territory. I was careful to say nothing abt. his reply that the idea (of a division of influence) might be a fruitful one &c. I added that if any mention had been made of delimiting the frontiers, it could only be that the French desiring to have their boundary fixed as ours already had been towards B.B. had desired our good offices with the Siamese Govt. It was possible that H.M.G. as a mark of friendship towards Siam might consent to assist in effecting an arrangement.

The Prince observed that the Fr. Govt. might probably have suggested to Ld. Salisbury that in return for them agreeing to give up Upper Burmah, it wld. only be fair to assist them

PRO 30/33 14/2 Semi-official Letters from Siam (May 29, 1885 – April 21, 1887)

in acquiring the eastern Laos states. He did not believe the Fr. had ever had serious intentions with regard to Burmah, but inly intrigued there to get an excuse for giving way to England and then requesting her to abstain from interfering with their projects with regard to the Laos.

I said that if such were really their plan, it must have been seen thro' long ago. The Fr. had no claim on G.B. in respect of U.B. because we had already done them a good turn in giving up the capitulations in Tunis, & that we were under no obligation to them.

The Prince then remarked that we had greater commercial interests in Luang Phrabang than the Fr., as the trade of that region was carried on by B.B.S. [British Burmese Subjects]

I replied that it was no doubt true, and that we had as good a right as any one else cld. have to place a vice-consul there.

He responded that the Siamese Govt. wld. not object to our having a vice-consul there, or at Battambong, or anywhere else in their territory.

It has occurred to me that it might be worth while, now that I am going to that part of the country, to extend my journey to L.P. & [I] asked him to write privately to the Siamese Comr. at Chiengmai to give me assistance if I decided to prolong my tour. He promised to do this.

It is evident that they feel considerable anxiety as to the attitude wch. H.M.G. may adopt towards the French proposals but the Prince has no belief that the French wld. consent to a self-denying ordinance.

    y.v.t.

[Satow left Bangkok on December 1, 1885 and returned on March 4, 1886. He noted his trip in three books, ref. PRO 30/33 17/13-15. They have been published by Dr. Nigel Brailey as *A Diplomat in Siam*, Bangkok: Orchid Press, 1994 revised 2000.]

27. Satow to Bernard
Chiengmai   19 Jan 1886
My dear Bernard,

You will receive by this mail a desp[atch]. fr. Gould containing the latest information as to the ideas of the Siamese Comr. here & the Chief of Chiengmai with regard to Chiengtung. The telegraph having unluckily broken down immediately after its establishment between this place & Bangkok, we are without knowledge of what has been decided upon with regard to the ultimate destiny of Upper Burmah, but as it seems undesirable in any case that either Siam or Chiengtung shld. take advantage of the overthrow of King Thebaw to make war on the other, I have impressed on the people here the necessity of their keeping their own frontier, & have sent thro' them a message to the Chief of Chiengtung advising him also to remain quiet.

I think I wrote to you fr. Bangkok that on learning of the expedition agst. Mandalay the Minr. for F.A. suggested to me that it wld. be a good opportunity for Siam to seize on the debateable land wch. she had talked of taking possn. of the year before last, & that I told him it was most undesirable that any such move shld. be made, adding that I did not doubt H.M.G. wld. see that justice was done to Siam in the matter. Notwithstanding my reply, it is possible they may still think of stealing a march upon their neighbours, & I do not feel certain that the despatch of 3000 men to Muang Fang, wch. has already taken place, is not intended as a provision to that end. Hence I have been clear in warning the Chief & the Siamese Court at Chiengmai.

Mr. Gould will hand over charge of this Vice Consulate to Mr. Archer on the 31 inst. of wch. official information will be sent to you in the ordinary course. I think it desirable to take advantage of this occasion to send Mr. Gould on a tour to Nan, Chiengsen & along the Chiengmai frontier down to the Salween, to learn all he can about the state of things. If on arriving at Chiengsen he has an opportunity of visiting Chiengtung I think it well that he shld. avail himself of it; but he will confine himself strictly to obtaining information.

I do not think that the interests of B.S. in the Laos states will suffer by Mr. Gould's removal to Bangkok. On the contrary his experience gained during the last two years will be of the greatest use in the settle[men]t. of appeal cases, which are more important than those wch. are finally disposed of here, while Mr. Archer, who will temporarily fill the post until Mr. French returns fr. leave, possesses excellent capabilities & industry.

The complete success of the expedition has produced a most salutary effect in Siam. It has greatly added to our 'prestige', while it has not diminished her confidence in our

PRO 30/33 14/2 Semi-official Letters from Siam (May 29, 1885 – April 21, 1887)

friendly intentions.

P.S. 20 Jan. Your letters of 24 & 27 Nov. have just reached me, & I am glad to think that the tour Gould is to make is approved of in principle beforehand.

28. Satow to Bernard

Chiengmai   3 Feb. 86

My dear Bernard,

With reference to your letter of Nov. 24 & the demi-official letter fr. Mr. G.S. Forbes enclosed in it, on the subject of the exploration of the Shan States, I have already written in mine of the 19th ult[im]o that Mr. Gould, after handing over charge of the Vice-consulate here on the 1st inst. wld. proceed on a 2 mos. tour, wch. is to include as much as possible of the undefined frontier of the Siamese Lao states towards the Shan states formerly subject to Upper Burma. Such observations as he is enabled to make will be at the disposal of the Surveyor-General. In addition to this, Mr. Gould is preparing fr. native sources a large map of the 5 states of Chiengmai, Lampoonchi, Lakhon, Nàn & Phrè, wch. will be completed after his arrival at Bangkok.

The Mr. McCarthy spoken of in your enclosure is now absent on a surveying expedition in the N.E. of Siam beyond Luang Phrabang, & will probably not be in Bangkok again this year; shld. he however return at the conclusion of the present dry season, I have little doubt of being able to obtain good information abt. that part of the country, & perh. even a map. I do not know enough of Mr. Collins to recommend him for the exploration.

Mr. W.J. Archer, who will be in charge of the Vice-consulate here for the next 12 mos. or so wld. be able to direct the work of native explorers in the Siamese Laos states under the advice of the Surveyor-Genl., as proposed in Mr. Forbes' letter. A native of Burma wld. of course be exposed to no danger here, & I am disposed to think that the Siamese authorities at Chiengmai wld. be glad to have work of this kind done, as they possess no trustworthy maps of the country.

I am of course unable to give any idea of the length of time that will be required to complete the work. I ought to add that the greater part of the country is mountainous &

sparsely inhabited, except in the neighbourhood of the 5 principal cities, where the population is pretty thick, but that in Chiengmai at least there are agricultural settlements in all the valleys.

29. Satow to Archer[23]

11 Feb. 86

My dear Archer,

Gould has got some of the proceedings in the Mëhongson case fr. Phra Upai, of wch. he was making a précis. I shld. like to have it, and anything else connected with that case as soon as you can manage it.

In Sataganu's case too I think Min Motoga was to furnish a copy of a power of attorney as well as of his contract with Sataganu & of certain promissory notes. If anything occurs with regard to that case, you shld. write fully, & if necessary telegraph <u>after</u> you hear of my arrival at Bangkok. It will be useless telegraphing abt. this case to French, as he knows nothing of it.

I place entire confidence in your judgment and discretion, & in return all I ask is that when you refer a case to me, you will endeavor to furnish all the documentary evidence you can obtain, as well as your own opinion abt. the facts. If there is anything wch. it wld. be inconvenient to have shown, write a private letter as well, remembering that your official despatches are not for me alone, but possibly for India or F.O. as well, & that they will remain on record in the archives for all time....

   E.S.

(fr. the first resting-place on the way to Chomtong.)

30. Satow to Jervoise[24]

12 Mar. 1886

---

[23] W.J. Archer, Vice-Consul at Chiengmai. His report 'Mr. Satow's Journey to Chiengmai' is in the National Archives, ref. FO 881/5295.

[24] Sir Harry Clarke-Jervoise (1832-1911). Head of the American and Asiatic Department, Foreign Office, 1880-1894.

PRO 30/33 14/2 Semi-official Letters from Siam (May 29, 1885 – April 21, 1887)

My dear Jervoise,

(1) French has no intention of leaving the service.

(2) Send out a second student as quickly as possible.

(3) change Sir W. Sull[?]

(4) [crossed out] I have never met a more unpractical unbusinesslike man than Gould, & unless he changes greatly I shall have to spend ½ my time in looking after him. One would like to have him for a friend, but as a colleague, no!

(5) Marriages by Newman, query illegal.

(6) Gould's salary; hope £800.

31. Satow to Currie

16 Mar. 1886

My dear Currie,

(Congratulations on KCB)

I send a desp[atch]. today abt. the question of Siam resuming tribute to China. Last night I had some talk with one of the King's brothers[25] [and] he began by saying that they had heard with great concern that there was a proposal to hand over to China the Shan States betw. the Salween and the Mekong (Cambodia River), wch. wld. include Chientung. This wld. give China a very important strategical position on the very frontier of Siam, and they did not desire to become her neighbour. The small frontier questions pending betw. Siam & the Burmese Shan States cld. be easily settled if the latter remain under the protection of England, but with China as master in that region the Siamese wld. fear encroachments.

I then led up to the suggestion of Sir R. Hart that Siam shld. resume tribute and get in return a promise of protection agst. foreign enemies.

He replied with the greatest energy that it wld. be a one sided bargain. Siam wld. be giving a great deal and receiving nothing at all, as the idea of China doing anything effectual to help her in time of need was quite impracticable. They wld. much rather be protected by an European power than by China.

---

[25] Prince Bigit, see diary for March 15, 1886.

PRO 30/33 14/2 Semi-official Letters from Siam (May 29, 1885 – April 21, 1887)

I have not put this in my desp[atch]. wch. in fact was drafted before I saw the Prince, who came to pay a call. But it is confirmatory of what I have written officially.

A country like Siam, where all the better educated officials speak & write English, is far more likely to gravitate towards us naturally than to China, whom they irreverently think of as blind & decrepit. It is just the same feeling as exists in Japan, where I see they are teaching English in all the schools throughout the country. Here the prevalence of the Engl. language, wch. we owe to the efforts of Am[erican]. missionaries, is an important element of English influence. At the present moment the French are nowhere. Kergaradec's negotiating a treaty wch. will give them the right of putting a V.C. at Luang Phrabang, & I was asked to advise abt. a counter-draft wch. the Siamese F.M. was to send him. I excused myself fr. doing so until certain matters at Chiengmai were arranged to my satisfaction. Things have not been going on at all well up there. It was very necessary that I shld. make the journey & see things with my own eyes. I have now left there as Acting V.C. a very intelligent young fellow named Archer, & started Gould off on a tour to the frontier to pick up what information he can abt. Chiengtung. The latter is an excellent, warmhearted fellow, but I am afraid his judg[men]t. is not always to be relied upon. I hope that the vacancies will speedily be filled up by the apptmt. Of new students, for French & I are alone here, & when Gould comes down French must go home on leave. G. is subject to attacks of intermittent fever, & I am afraid I have got malaria too as one result of my journey.

y.v.t.

32. Satow to Bernard

16 Mar. 86

My dear Bernard,

The enclosed letter came back fr. Dangwin[?] owing to the police post having been withdrawn, & I had to bring it down with me. Gould however will not go to Chiengtung, as the Indian Govt. have not expressed any desire to communicate thro' him. The Siamese have learnt of the proposal to hand over to China the Shan States betw. Salween & Mekong, wch. they earnestly hope will not be done. They are afraid of having China for their neighbour up there, & much prefer to have Br. authorities to deal with on the border. I am sending to you by this or next post a desp[atch]. for the Voceroy enclosing copy of one I have written to the F.O. abt. Chientung.

The Fr. Ch. d'Aff. is negotiating a Treaty c. reference to L: Phrabang similar to our Chiengmai Treaty, but containing provisions giving the V.C. a greater share of judicial authority. I rather hope he will succeed, for our arrangements have not worked well. I am going to put pressure on the Siamese to establish rules of procedure & have them adhered to by the Judge at Chiengmai.

   y.v.t.

P.S. When do you remove to Mandalay & who will be your successor at Rangoon.

33. Satow to Sir F.A. Weld

Sir F.A. Weld

20/3/86

Dear Sir Frederick,

I returned here on the 4th, & at once addressed a note to the F.M. based upon your official letter c. resp. to the outrage on Datu Makkota Alam. A copy of this I am enclosing in my official reply to you. It seems to me that the creation of trade monopolies in the Siamese Malay States or the exaction of duties exceeding three % must be contrary to Treaty, if those Malay States are, as the Siamese maintained c. regard to Kelantan & Tringanu, a part of Siam.

C. respect to Upper Perak the F.O. have simply sent me copies of the correspce. that went on at home in connexion c. the question of its rendition, but gave me no instructions to press it. In fact, my private letters point to the F.O. not desiring to press the matter, & I am obliged to reply to you that I cannot act without instructions. I shall of course send our correspce. home & ask for instructions. I hope you will not put the Perak police force in the field, or send a man-of-war to Singgora, at least for the present.

The Kralahome who was told to call on you has, I am informed, gone to Europe, & has probably been of no use c. regard to affairs in Kedah. I must see the F.M. & find out definitely what they intend doing.

   y.v.t.

PRO 30/33 14/2 Semi-official Letters from Siam (May 29, 1885 – April 21, 1887)

E.S.

34. Satow to Sir F.A. Weld

25 Mar.

Dear Sir Fr.

Mr. French has handed to me your confidential letter of 17 Mar. I do not think that the Siamese any longer confuse the 2 boundary questions, & it appears to have been owing to an oversight that in his note of the 20th Mr. Fr. omitted any reference to the complaints fr. Upper Perak.

I saw the F.M. yesterday & explained to him how the occupation of the old fort, wch. I suppose is not much more than earthw[or]k. wld. be justly regarded by Perak as a hostile demonstration, just as the action of the Afghans in regard to Penjdeh was made a casus belli. Perhaps you would think the comparison not a good one, but as G.B. condoned the Russian attack on Penjdeh, it is not impolitic to put a good face on the matter, & represent them as having acted within their rights. He promises an answer in a day or two to my Note enclosed to you a few days ago, but has admitted in principle that no higher duties than those of the genl. tariff can be levied on our traders. I am today addressing him officially on the subject of the case fr. Perak & the refusal to extradite fr. Kedah concerning wch. the papers were enclosed in your official letter of March 17.

The Kralahome has not sent any report of your conversation c. him to the King, as far as I can learn, but applied on the 20th for leave to go to Europe. There must be some confusion of dates here, I imagine, for which my informant is responsible.

y.v.t.

35. Satow to Currie

26 March 1886

My dear Currie,

As you will see from my desp[atch]. of the 22nd March (no. 21) the Govr. of the Straits Settlements has asked me to urge the Siamese Govt. c. regard to the Perak question, & that I have replied to him that I cannot comply c. his request in the absence of definite

114

instructions fr. home. The despatches which have passed betw. Sir F.W[eld]. of the Colonial Office & the correspondence betw. the F.O. & the Siamese Minr. in London have been sent out to me only for my information & I have not felt authorized to act upon them further than to give a hint now & then to the Siamese that I hoped an amicable arrangement wld. be arrived at.

If it is deemed that I shld. comply with the request contained in Sir F.W.'s letter to me of the 24 Feb. I hope the instructions sent will be clear & strong, in the form of a despatch to read & leave copy of with the F.M. But as far as my own opinion goes, it is that it wld. be unwise to press the demand of Perak, & I shld. prefer not to have any such instructions. In a private letter to me the Gov. asks whether he wld. not be justified in marching part of the Perak force of Sikhs & mtn. guns with some Malays & taking possn. of the old forts in the disputed territory & holding them until a final settlement. He asks also whether it wld. be any use his going or sending to Singgora with a man of war or otherwise & concludes by saying that he does not want to embarrass me & that we must act in concert. I replied begging him neither to march out the Perak Sikhs nor to send a man-of-war. I think I am justified in giving you these extracts that you may see exactly the spirit that prevails at Singapore.

With regard to the general question of extending our influence over the Malay States, I have good reason to believe that the merchants of Singapore are utterly indifferent, if not averse, as they do not see with satisfaction Chinamen overrunning the whole peninsula, & elbowing them out of the trade of the colony.

Seeing that Fr. colonial ambitions have lately recd. a serious check at Mandalay, & that they have lost their appetite for Tonquin & Annam, it is not likely that they will attempt further encroachments on Siam in a hurry. We ought to be the last people to disturb the present quiet by plans for taking possession of the Malay peninsula.

y.v.t.

36. Satow to Currie
29 March 1886
My dear Currie,

PRO 30/33 14/2 Semi-official Letters from Siam (May 29, 1885 – April 21, 1887)

I hope the proposals with regard to increase of Vice-consul's pay at Chiengmai, the simplification of accts. by India, paying a lump sum to the F.O. annually, & the apptmt. of a student interpreter to be stationed there will have your support. A 3rd student wld. bring the establish[men]t. up to what is provided for in the estimate. These proposals I firmly believe are necessary to rendering the Chiengmai arrangements efficient. I shall take care that the students work steadily at the language.

My further desp[atch]. abt. Hart's proposal that Siam shld. be encouraged to pay tribute to China shows I think that we ought not to move in the matter here, & I trust that I shall not receive instructions to conform myself to Sir R. Hart's policy. Perh. it might be a good thing if I were to go down to Singapore to see Sir J. Walsham on his way to Peking; it wld. give me an opportunity of seeing Sir F. Weld also.

The information abt. a German scheme for rlwys. In Siam sent in my telegram of today was given by the same prince mentioned in my letter of Mar. 16. He is named Bigit, & seems to be in high favour with the King. He wanted to know, he told me, whether the jealousy of the fr. wld. not be excited by a concession for rlwys. being given to Germans, & whether that wld. not constitute a danger for Siam. I said that considering the relative position of Germany & France in Europe, the Siamese need not be under any apprehensions. In reply to another question, I told him that the Indian Govt. did not appear disposed to support the scheme of Hallett & Colquhoun, more especially as the Siamese Govt. had given these gentlemen no encouragement. (I need not tell you that Hallett's story, so often repeated, about the assurances I gave to him, is quite untrue).

I am convinced that a rlwy. fr. here to Chiengmai, no matter by whom made, wld. consolidate Siam & be of great benefit to commerce in genl. I have seen with my own eyes the busy traffic carried on up & down the river, in spite of the obstacles created by rapids & at certain seasons of the year the lowness of the water, & I believe that a light rlwy. cld. be made to pay. The Indian Govt. however have their hands full, & are not disposed to any closer relations c. Siam than those of amicable neighbours; at least that is the impression produced upon my mind by Bernard's language & the published despatches. The trade of Siam is not altogether valueless to England, but the chief reason why we wish no change in the political position of Siam is that the Indian Govt. consider it desirable to keep her as a buffer betw. Burmah & French Indo-China. Whether the "buffer" theory is a correct one in this case is I imagine open to question. The Fr. at Saigon are far from their base, while we in Burmah & India are near. In case of difficulties in Europe betw. Engl. & France, we cld. do more to annoy them here than they cld. to injure us. But the "buffer" theory is prevalent, & I suppose is the one on wch. our calculations are to be based. India however does not feel able to give any material assistance towards the preservation of the cushion, while Singapore is endeavouring to nibble off a considerable corner. Under these circs. if Germany thinks it advantageous to wedge herself in here, it seems to me that she wld. be playing the game of India, & therefore I added to my telegram 'Strong German interest in independence of Siam seems desirable.'

P.S. The intended Fr. Vice-Consul for Luang Phrabang has arrived here – a man named [Auguste] Pavie,[26] well known as an explorer. But the negotiations for a Treaty hang fire, the Siamese not having yet presented their counter-draft.

I have given to the F.M. a memorandum complaining of the irregularities of the native court at Chiengmai, & urging reform. As soon as I am able I shall send this to the Indian Govt. with an explanatory desp[atch]., forwarding a copy to F.O. at the same time.

E.S.

37. Satow to Currie

20 April

Dear Currie,

My No. 32 contains copy of a long despatch to the Govt. of India abt. the way in wch. justice is misadministered at Chiengmai by the Siamese authorities. The Indian Govt. will prob. print it, & send you copies wch. will be more convenient reading than a long M.S. Meanwhile, I hope that when the question comes before you, you will support my views & give me the instructions wch. I have suggested shld. be sent.

In past times the Indian Govt. is said to have been rather down upon the Agency at

---

[26] Auguste Pavie (1847-1925). French colonial civil servant, explorer and diplomat who was instrumental in establishing French control over Laos in the last two decades of the 19th century.

PRO 30/33 14/2 Semi-official Letters from Siam (May 29, 1885 – April 21, 1887)

Bangkok, and to have thought the Siamese Govt. were being victimized. I hope they will do so no longer.

With regard to the Chiengmai Treaty itself, I shld. prefer trying to work it as it is, but a threat of rescission seems to me the only means by wch. we can bring the Siamese to their bearings. For a month past I have been waiting for an audience of the King in order to put the case directly before him, but have not yet been able to get access to him.

[Margin: The Fr. Treaty about Luang Phrabang is not yet signed, but will in the main follow the lines of our Chiengmai Treaty.]

Such remarks as that of Blowitz in the "Times" that Siam is of such huge political importance that if she had not existed, it wld. have been necessary to invent her do a great deal of harm to a people who are conceited enough already.

The F.M. tells me that Naret had a long conversation abt. rlwys. with Mr. Joseph Chamberlain, & that someone in England has offered to lend Siam £2,000,000 at 5%. But I do not feel persuaded that this talk will come to anything.

38. Satow to Currie

20 May 86

My dear Currie,

I wrote to you on the 26 March abt. Perak & Sir F. Weld's schemes. I hope you will have time to read my desp[atch]. No. 42 of yesterday on the same subject, & particularly his letter enclosed in it. He is determined not to let the matter rest as it is, & I cannot help thinking that he wants to get a pretext for sending the Perak Sikh force across the frontier, & so producing a fait accompli. You will see that I have induced the Siamese to agree that they will not occupy the forts in Raman as long as the Perak people do not encroach, & they want a reciprocal agreement on our side, because they suspect that now they have given the promise, it will be made use of to their disadvantage. Sir H. Low has an active agent up the Perak river named Bozzuolo,[27] who will not cease to fan the flame. If Sir F.

---

[27] See the 1886 journal of C.F. Bozzolo (Magistrate and Collector, Upper Perak) regarding the boundary dispute between Perak and Siam. FCO 141/16386 at the National Archives,

PRO 30/33 14/2 Semi-official Letters from Siam (May 29, 1885 – April 21, 1887)

Weld had such excellent information abt. the preparations being made by the Siamese, why did he not tell me where he obtained it.

For my part I cannot see the good of continually touching up this row. It naturally causes an ill-feeling towards us. The Siamese are afraid that Sir F. Weld, like some other energetic Govrs., will force the hand of H.M.G. He believes that Siam is on the point of being swallowed up by the Fr. & that Singapore must get all she can before it is too late. I do not share his alarm. The French were never further from anything of that kind than they are now. But the Siamese will never believe that we mean well towards them as long as the Singapore Govt. are allowed to carry on their present game. The "London & China Express" not long ago had a paragraph that Mr. Swettenham[28] who is now in London will carry on the negotiations begun by Sir F. Weld & Sir H. Low. All this sort of thing is very mischievous, and I wish a stop could be put to it.

I do not know whether it is to this, or to the bad advice a lawyer whom they have recently imported fr. London that I have to attribute the impertinent tone the Siamese have adopted 2 or 3 times of late in their written communications to me. Perh. Dr. Gowan the King's physician has a hand in it too. But I can manage them. I cannot manage the Gov. of Singapore.

The conclusion of a convention about Luang Phrabang will afford a safeguard agst. French designs in that quarter; but I am afraid there will be delay in exchanging the ratifications. The Siamese ought not to allow Pavie to go up, or, at any rate, give him his exequatur until the convention is ratified.

I have not yet succeeded in getting anything done towards "putting matters right" at Chiengmai but the Siamese are full of promises, & I am only waiting for Gould's arrival to press for the required reforms. I expect him in about 10 days.

y.v.t.

39. Satow to Jervoise (summary)

Kew.
[28] Sir Frank Swettenham (1850-1946) was a British colonial administrator. First Resident-General of the Federated Malay States, 1896-1901.

PRO 30/33 14/2 Semi-official Letters from Siam (May 29, 1885 – April 21, 1887)

20 May

Wrote to Jervoise that the remarks about stationery are intended for the head of that dept.; & that Beckett ought to get a rap over the knuckles for having stopped in Singapore.

40. Satow to Currie

7.6.86

My dear Currie,

The F.M. said yesterday that they had not authorized any proposal to hand over the disputed territory to be "administered" by Perak. He thought the Kalahom during his short visit to London might have said something to [Frederick] Verney; but all he knew was that the Kalahom had repeated to Verney his conversation with Sir F. Weld & that Verney appeared highly indignant. I said he wld. go off to consult the best international lawyers. This came in a private letter fr. the Siamese Ch. d'Aff. in London to Prince Naret & they had nothing official about the matter.

I told the Prince I supposed the idea was to pay to the Rajah of Raman the surplus revenue or a fixed annual sum. This he replied wld. be the case of Penang over again.

I begged him to consider what I had said as entirely unofficial, that it was worth thinking over & if the King approved of the plan he might inform Mr. Gould.

I am very much obliged for the readiness with wch. my application for leave [in Japan] has been granted & trust to come back with strength renewed.

    y.v.t.

41. Satow to Currie

25 July 1886

[Nikko, Japan][29]

My dear Currie,

I got yesterday your letter of the 28 May, in wch. you recur to the subject of the proposal that Perak shld. administer the district claimed by her fr. Raman à la Cyprus. The Siamese

---

[29] Satow's diary for this date shows he was at Nikko.

PRO 30/33 14/2 Semi-official Letters from Siam (May 29, 1885 – April 21, 1887)

F.M. as I wrote fr. Bangkok, says that Verney was not authorized to propose it, & seemed to be very adverse to the idea. As it wld. practically amount to the same thing as surrendering the territory, this is not to be wondered at. The Fr. however cld. hardly propose a similar arrangement for the former Cambodian provinces wch. now belong to Siam, as those are regularly administered by a Governor, and contain a large population.

Raman is not an integral portion of Siam, but is in much the same position as Perak itself, minus a resident. Sir F. Weld's anxiety to get the disputed bit of territory is the consequence of his general policy of extending British influence over the whole peninsula, wch. as I showed in my memo. contains, besides the Malay States, territory wch. is wholly Siamese. So that his policy if carried out wld. amount to a partition of Siam. In return for getting the peninsula, wch. is of value solely for its tin mines & the chance of finding gold, he wld. be content to abandon the rest of Siam to the French, who wld. thus get control over the teak forests wch. our people are working in the north and the outlet by wch. the timber comes to Bangkok. But the mines, besides the competition they create agst. those of Cornwall, can be worked at a profit by the Chinese alone, & the benefit England wld. reap from opening up the peninsula for the advantage of the yellow race appears to me inappreciable. Our merchants at Singapore don't want it. But it places an enormous patronage at the disposal of the Govr. of the Straits Settlements, if as I understand he makes all the apptmts. in the native states with the exception of the Residents.

Sir F.W. has invited me to join him in Perak on my way back to Bangkok to talk over affairs with him & Sir H. Low, but it wld. have a very bad effect in Siam if I went there, as the gossips wld. put on it a false interpretation, & I shall therefore return straight to Bangkok, without going viâ Singapore.

My opinion is that if it <u>must</u> be, the proposed arrange[men]t. can only be made betw. Perak & Raman without the King of Siam's sanction being asked beforehand. He would then be able to protest if he cared about doing so and tell Kergaradec that he disapproved. But still I shld. not like even that, as it wld. not increase our character[?] for straightforwardness & good faith & the Fr. wld. of course turn their attention to corrupting the Govr. of Battambang & inducing him to join Cambodia. It wld. give them some trouble, as these Asiatics do not like European interference with their internal affairs, & particularly that of Frenchmen, tho' they may yield to threats & must give way to force.

Sir F. weld wrote to me on the 30th June to say that he was sending Mr. Bozzolo to Singgura to the Siamese Govr. there ostensibly to talk about Raman & to pay compliments & give a present, but really to cross by Trang & report on [François] Deloncle's canal site quietly in accordance with your wish. He is not sending the Mr. Cameron who was proposed for this service by Sir Cecil Smith when Acting Govr. of Singapore, possibly because Cameron is known as a surveyor.

y.v.t.   E.S.

42. Satow to Sir Frederick Weld

Nikkō

26 July 1886

Dear Sir Frederick,

I have got your letters of 30 June & June 10 & 18 wch. I name in the order they reached me in. Many thanks for your kind offer to send your yacht to fetch me to Perak or Selangor. I shld. like very much to visit those places, but taken in conjunction with the subject-matter of our recent correspondence I think such a visit might be misinterpreted by the Siamese govt. & the Fr. Ch. d'Aff. at Bangkok. The latter is of course anxious that you shld. succeed with regard to the disputed territory, as it wld. help his own policy. I shall therefore return straight fr. Hong Kong to Bangkok.

I do not think there is any danger of your letters being opened at the Siamese post office, but if you fear it, anything important might be put in cypher. Mr. Gould shld. have told you that we have F.O. Cypher X, of wch. a copy has I believe also been furnished to you. Cypher E is out of date.

Of Mr. W.H. Reed's proposed concession for mines in Sai I have not heard anything except fr. yourself.

I have not learnt that Prince Naret had proposed an arrangement à la Cyprus for the disputed territory, & have every reason to believe that Mr. Verney suggested it entirely as emanating from himself. The foreign advisers of Asiatoc legations in Europe seem rather apt to be in advance of the govts. they represent.

PRO 30/33 14/2 Semi-official Letters from Siam (May 29, 1885 – April 21, 1887)

The position of Siam primarily concerns the Indian Govt. & they would not look with favour on a policy wch. wld. abandon the valley of the Mënam to France. Our principal business in Bangkok is to watch the relations between the Fr[ench]. Ch[argé]. d'Aff[aires]. & the F[oreign].M[inister]., so as to prevent a pretext being given to the Fr[ench]. for invading Siam. And if that can be done, it will not be entirely useless. As to the F.O. deciding not to protect Siam, we could hardly afford to give such a promise unless we got a quid pro quo. The sort of protection the Siamese might like wld. be impracticable. You cannot very well protect unless you establish a protectorate. The only instance of willing acceptance I can recollect is the case of Cambodia, whose King was bamboozled into signing a treaty of wch. he did not understand the meaning. The Siamese are too wideawake for that: They know that a 'protectorate' means in the first place the surrender of independence in their foreign relations & 2ndly the admission of interference in internal matters, such as taxation, slavery, judiciary, police & every other branch of administration where an European eye sees something to be reformed, finally complete subjugation without the name of conquest, the deposition of the sovereign if he proves restive & the substitution of one who is ready to be a tool, & last of all annexation. Seeing all this, the Siamese are not likely to wish for an English protectorate, and without a protectorate we cannot protect.

My own conviction is that as long as England remains what she is & keeps her eyes open, the Fr. will not attempt to cross into the valley of the Mënam. If they ever do that, I suppose they will acquire rights over those provinces in the peninsula wch. intervene between Tavoy and the Malay states. As you know, there is a belt extending right across there wch. contains no Malays. It wld. be difficult, it seems to me, to anticipate the French unless we took the valley of the Mënam, including Bangkok, as well. It is the most valuable portion of the country, well populated and fertile, besides being the outlet for the teakforests which B.B.S. are working in the north. Can we afford indeed to let these fall into French hands. You would be content with the peninsula, which can be developed only by the introduction of Chinese labour & fr. wch. little else than tin can be got. For my part, I do not think the Chinese are so much our friends that we shld. gratuitously enrich a portion of them.

My opinion has been privately asked fr. the F.O. about the proposed arrange[men]t. à la

Cyprus. In the 1st place, I feel pretty sure the King of Siam will not consent, & it seems clear that Verney had no authority to propose it. Consequently, if it must be, a direct arrangement betw. Perak & Raman is, I think, the only one that would have any chance of success. If the King knew nothing about it beforehand, it would be too late for him to do anything but protest. But I doubt whether you would like that & I do not wish to propose it. No matter how we got possession of the disputed territory, the effect wld. be the same. The French wld. then try to seduce the Govr. of Battambong from his allegiance to the King of Siam, and if he did not yield to persuasion, pick a quarrel with him abt. the fisheries on the lake and take him by force. The Siamese believe that it is your policy, as they have frequently said to me, to turn them out of the Malay States. That is why they will resist to the uttermost the first beginnings. The Perak question came on the tapis while the late Mr. Alabaster was still their adviser, & he consistently told them not to trust England's intentions. This distrust of us is the reason why I regret that the claim of the Perak rajahs has been so strongly resisted.

Excuse this long letter, wch. is meant only to show that if I do not entirely agree with your views, it is not mere perversity that causes me to differ. My instructions however relieve me from responsibility, as they tell me to do nothing while negotiations are pending in London.

  y.v.t. E.S.

43. Satow to Currie

7 Nov 86

My Dear Currie,

I have got your private letter of 29 Sept. and my instructions of the 30 about the Perak business. The King being away from Bangkok I have confined myself to telling the FM that I am instructed to make a communication abt. Perak, and will do so on the King's return; and that I hope that something satisfactory cld. be arranged.

The King will be back on the 9th. I will do my best to get Swettenham's proposals adopted; they are certainly very moderate. I have written privately to Sir F. Weld to tell him that I have instructions. In a somewhat indiscreet manner he must needs make a speech to

PRO 30/33 14/2 Semi-official Letters from Siam (May 29, 1885 – April 21, 1887)

his Legislative Council in wch. he talks of a settle[men]t. being at hand, wch. was published in the Singapore paper & read by the Siamese. That sort of thing does not help me a bit.

I hope to arrange with the Siamese for reciprocity, i.e. to let in everything free except spirits, salt, arms & ammunition, taxes on wch. Burma cannot give up. A copy of the whole correspce. has gone to India. I had been trying to arrange it without troubling you at all, but Gould having taken it up during my absence, I had no choice left.

The apptmt. of an agent at Kedah is an idea of my own, and the consent of the Siamese might perh. have been managed had not Sir Fred. inserted a para. on the subj. in the same speech and so excited their suspicions. The F.M. at once told me he did not like it. The claim of the Fr. to put a consular agent at Battambang was an unfortunate coincidence.

My trip to Japan has done me much good, and I hope to be able to tide over the next hot season, wch. is from March to May. Gould is hardly able to carry on the work with nothing but two students to help. The place is certainly undermanned, the establisht. of a Vice Consulate at Chiengmai and the copying of documents for India having greatly added to the work. The judicial business alone is quite enough for one man.

     y.v.t.

44. Satow to Currie
ca.[?] 4 Dec. 1886
My dear Currie,

This negotiation about Perak likely seems to be a long one. The Siamese say they will not give any promise until they have ascertained that (1) the Rajah of Raman will agree (2) how the free transit down the Muda river can be arranged & (3) until they have made arrangements for the rajah of Sai observing the ordinary rule of international law that one state cannot pursue its fugitive offenders into the territory of another state. This they say will take at least two months. I am trying to make them understand that it will be all the worse for them if they do not agree with their adversary while he is on the way, & have used the argument that if they hang back too long, H.M.G. may perh. disapprove of my having offered them so much with regard to the right of re-entry at the end of the 20 yrs.

PRO 30/33 14/2 Semi-official Letters from Siam (May 29, 1885 – April 21, 1887)

Swettenham in his letter of 7 Aug. 1886 to C.O. [Colonial Office] in para. 4 says: "shld. the Siamese on the expiration of the original term of agreement, refuse to continue that or a similar arrangement, then any excess of expenditure over revenue shld. be repaid to the Perak Govt. & the <u>circs. of the agreement shld. not prejudice the claims of the Perak Govt.</u>"

That is to say we shld. ask the Siamese to enter into an agreement ostensibly for 20 years, but really in perpetuity, & the consdn. offered is that the King shld. be allowed to retain the nominal sovereignty, with the addition of a small annual pension. If I had presented the scheme to the Siamese in this shape I am certain it wld. have been declined at once, & I therefore took on myself the responsibility of treating it as a lease for 20 yrs. with the reversion to the King of Siam. If the desp[atch]. containing my instructions had defined what I was to ask for, I shld. of course have not ventured to exercise any discretion, but as it merely enclosed the papers, all I cld. do was to make the best of them. It is possible that I may have asked for things not absolutely necessary, such as the addition of a slip of land over the watershed wch. Sir H. Low wishes for & the free transit down the Muda river wanted by Sir F. Weld. These requests are hardly in accordance either with the original argument that the watershed is the natural & customary boundary, or with the argument that Perak ought to have this District because the Perak river is its main artery. If the Muda river is the natural outlet, then it is not clear how it could ever have been possessed by the Perak Malays. These demands might be gracefully withdrawn of necessary.

It is important that I shld. have a map of the district, in case of my being able to arrange something.

Then there is the Krian river question. Shld. I try to settle this at the same time.

I have tried to get fr. the Kalahôm something that wld. indicate whether the King will give way or not, but without success.

To sum up, the only way to induce the King to accept a compromise is to make him feel that if he refuses, the claims of Perak will be enforced, & I am doing all I can to persuade him of this. If you think the matter shld. be settled without Raman being consulted, perh. you will telegraph me to that effect.

  y.v.t.

   E.S.

PRO 30/33 14/2 Semi-official Letters from Siam (May 29, 1885 – April 21, 1887)

45. Satow to Currie

18/12/86

I have been obliged to trouble you with a correspce. betw. a Mr. Shaw who is Belgian consul here & myself, the gist of wch. is that in consequence of my declining to lay down in writing a line dividing his responsibility as a B.S. fr. his immunity to our jurisdiction in his quality as Belgian consul, he has formally withdrawn himself fr. British jurisdiction. I have little doubt that he has been put up to it by a man named Michell[30] whom the Siamese have imported to take the place of the deceased Mr. Henry Alabaster. The said Michell had the impudence the other day tp swear an affidavit in my court in wch. he described himself as a Siamese subject, & he has also been actively engaged in an agitation agst. the new regulation about registration of B.S. Shaw has never obtained leave fr. H.M.G. to act as Belgian consul, & has no Belgian interests to protect. I wish therefore you cld. see your way to asking the Belgian Govt. to cancel his apt. for his letters to me are impertinent to say the least of them, & he seems to me to deserve something stronger than a snubbing.

Michell's chief grievance agst. me is that I do not allow him to appear in my court, but as he is the only legal practitioner here, to admit him wld. be very unfair to the suitors who have to conduct their own cases agst. his clients, & in refusing I have acted on the advice of either Rennie or Hannen, I forget which. It would please the Siamese greatly if either he or Shaw were to score against the British Legation, & your support in this matter is therefore of the greatest importance to me.

        y.v.t.

46. Satow to Currie

19.12.86

My dear Currie,

I saw the F.M. yesterday abt. Sir E. Reed's scheme, & it appears from what he said to me that the Siamese Govt. would not give a concession for a maritime canal to any one, nor

---

[30] Edward Blair Michell (1843-1926). English barrister. Legal adviser to the Siamese Government.

any exclusive concession for the other objects of the Syndicate over so large a portion of territory as it proposes to make the scene of its operations. The King wld. undoubtedly grant concessions to work mines within a limited area (as he has already done in the case of a gold mine reported by me last year) or for rlwys. but the plans of the Syndicate are too vast, & to grant exclusive rights to it wld. be to part with a large portion of sovereignty over those states.

I begged the Prince to speak to the King & let me know exactly what his views are, but I do not think that much will come of it. I of course explained that the inquiry I was making of him was quite informal.

Deloncle, the Prince said, has no promise fr. the King, nor did he ever receive any assurance whatever that cld. be construed into a promise of a concession. They carefully guarded themselves agst. that. All of value that he cld. sell to the syndicate would be his knowledge of the peninsula, wch. did not amount to much. But for the publication of Loftus' pamphlet demonstrating the impossibility of the Kra canal, Deloncle wld. no doubt have gone abt. saying it was perfectly possible, but Loftus[31] killed that schme effectually. There had been some correspce. with Lesseps, wch. the latter ended by saying he would make a canal through Kra when he had done with Panama. I asked whether he wld. show me the corrspce. & he has promised to do so. I shall write officially by next mail, but there is no time today, & by telegraph you will have already learnt the gist of the Siamese answer.

One of the inducements wch. Deloncle & Co. mentioned to the Siamese Govt. in connexion with the canal concession he asked for was that it wld. prevent Engl. encroachments! said the prince.

If my opinion was asked, I should say that under existing circs. with regard to the Perak boundary question, the patronage of the Brit. Govt. wld. be a hindrance rather than a help to the syndicate. I shld. no doubt be told that the Siamese ought not to suspect the purity of our intentions, but if they do suspect, it is not very much use saying they oughtn't to. At any rate I think it is my duty to tell H.M.G. what they do think as far as I can discover their mind.

---

[31] Captain Alfred J. Loftus, a Briton employed by the Siamese, 1871-92. Hydrographer and gunboat commander.

PRO 30/33 14/2 Semi-official Letters from Siam (May 29, 1885 – April 21, 1887)

y.v.t.

47. Satow to Currie

3 Jan. 1887

My dear Currie,

I think it is right that I shld. send you the enclosed correspce. betw. myself & the Min. for F.A. abt. the part taken by his legal adviser Mr. E.B. Michell in endeavouring to get up an opposition to the new regulation abt. Registration of B.S. The Minr. ought, it seems to me, to have stopped Michell even without my suggesting it. The argument of the Siamese & of Michell is that he is allowed to take private practice within reasonable limits, but I do not see how that can extend to his convening meetings for the purpose of telling B.S. that a reguln. issued by the authority of H.M.G. is illegal. The agitation agst. the regulation, wch. was in reality got up by Michell & Gowan (the King's physician) in the Siamese interest, has collapsed, and their public meetings have been a failure, so I do not intend to trouble you officially about that matter. The real object of these gentry was to get the support of the British community in disputing the regulation, & then to turn round & argue that Asiatic B.S. residing in the interior who did not register were under Siamese jurisdiction. The first meeting apptd. a committee consisting of Gowan, another man in the Siamese service named Marrable and an engineer named Dunlop, who in 1884 supplied Dr. Cameron with the means of asking a question in the House about Palgrave's decision in the case of Qi Baa. These three took on themselves to address to me a letter containing what I considered to be impertinent reflections upon the impartiality of the consular court, and I told them so frankly. They will perh. ask Dr. Cameron or some other person to put a question about this matter. I enclose therefore copies of the letter that passed showing what they said and what I replied to them. They have not ventured to lay the correspce. before the men whom they claimed as their constituents.

   y.v.t.

48. Satow to Currie

16 Jan. 1887

PRO 30/33 14/2 Semi-official Letters from Siam (May 29, 1885 – April 21, 1887)

My dear Currie,

The Frenchman has managed to get a desp[atch]. boat full of French colonial officials up here for the installation of the crown prince, including the commodore commanding at Saigon, the chef-de-cabinet & aide-de-camp to the Resident Genl. in Tonquin, & abt. ½ doz. others. They are lodged in the official building set apart for foreign ambassadors & entertained at the expense of the King. The Siamese did not wish the mission to come, but now it is here are obliged to be civil to it. Kergaradec however always pretended to me that it was a sort of accidental business; that a gunboat happened to be coming here, & he had suggested to several of the Saigon people that it wld. [be] a good occasion to see the sights of Bangkok. Knowing that the Siamese did not wish to have official repres'ves of Fr. Indo-China at the installation I did not think it worth while suggesting to you that Engld. shld. be represented in the same manner. The Siamese wld. have simply laughed if we had appeared to 'rivaliser' with the Fr. The telegraphic congratulations fr. the Queen wch. I formally delivered yesterday were however greatly appreciated by the King, & he made a very pretty speech in reply abt. the friendship betw. Siam & Engl. There is no time to write by this mail abt. the Crownprince business, & the fêtes are in fact not yet at an end. We are very shorthanded at the moment, one student being away up country, & the other being busily employed in registering B.S. I see that 25 years ago when there was much less work, there was a larger staff to do it.

One of my desp[atches]. by this mail encloses the papers sent to India abt. the illegal detention in prison for 7 mos. of a B.S. I have told the F.M. that I will not advise H.M.G. to accept less than £200 compensation for the man, & in my opinion he ought to get at least that sum. If possible, I will arrange the business here, but it was a flagrant case & I thought H.M.G. ought to be made acquainted with the facts. It demonstrates the necessity of providing every B.S. as far as possible with a certificate of nationality. I think you will be able to see fr. the papers I have sent what sort of persons Michell & Gowan are. They are in fine feather now, a local paper having just been started in wch. they can abuse me to their heart's content. To the abuse of B.S. in the Siamese service I am indifferent, & I have all the respectable part of the community on my side.

The Fr. are at last going to start a line of small strs. [steamers] betw. here & Saigon, with a subvention. They have not managed to get any subsidy fr. the Siamese. They also talk about Siam being in possn. of a corner of Cochinchina, wch. must be given up. If the Siamese give way abt. the Perak boundary, this claim will pretty certainly be put forward. The rajah of Raman is said to be dying, & the second man has been sent for to Bangkok. I have told the F.M. that they can take advantage of the occasion to insist upon the successor acceding to the proposal I have laid before the King for leasing the disputed district.

   y.v.t.

P.S. I have learnt on the best authority that this man Gowan has been warning the Siamese not to borrow money in England, lest they incur the fate of Egypt, & advising them to go to Germany instead.

   E.S.

49. Satow to Currie

18 Jan. 1887

My dear Currie,

I want to say a word about myself. After my illness last May I felt very strongly that my health would not stand this place much longer, & I made up my mind to ask for leave this spring, with the hope of getting a change to a more healthy post. During the cool weather of December I felt much better, & I shld. like to settle the Perak boundary question one way or the other before coming home. Another considn. is that the work here could not be done efficiently by Gould and the 2 students, so that until French's return I shld. consider myself bound to stay, except in the event of serious illness again. If I am to continue at Bangkok I ought for my health's sake, & for the purpose of renewing touch with European ideas, to get a run home as early as possible this year. If on the other hand I could look forward to another post, I wld. endeavour to stay here some months longer, & seek refuge fr. the heat of March – May at the house[32] I have on an island in the gulf, & then come to England on the earliest opportunity.

---

[32] The house was on an island named Koh Si Chang ('Koh' meaning island in Thai). Satow was there as follows: September 17 – 19, 1884; May 29 – June 2, 1885; October 8-10, 1885; April 10-15, 1886; April 29 – May 6, 1886, December 5-7, 1886.

I shld. be very much obliged if you would kindly take this into considn. & let me know whether you think I shld. take leave early in the spring with the intention of returning to Bangkok, or delay till the autumn & then quit the place for good.

When Fr[ench]. comes out I think it would be desirable to station him in the first place at Bangkok as acting consul during my absence, Gould at the same time becoming Ch. d'Aff. & Acting Consul-Genl. Archer wld. continue to act as vice-consul at Chiengmai.

I enclose a letter Willis has written me on the subject of my health.

y.v.t.

50. Satow to Currie

4 Feb. 1887

My dear Currie,

In order to be quite sure abt. the legality of the new Registration regulations, I privately asked the Attorney-Genl. at Singapore, who is legal adviser to the legation, for his opinion. He has given it to me in a letter of wch. I enclose an extract, & you will see the gist of it to be that he thinks it wld. have been safer to proceed by O. in C. [Order in Council] This seems to be a point of some importance & worth referring to the law Officers, but I abstain fr. writing officially on the subject as owing to the part taken by employés of the Siamese Govt. in disputing the legality of the regulations, I do not wish any one here to suppose that I doubt the validity of a regulation wch. has been approved by the Sec. of State. I have my own doubts however whether the regulation can be applied in the Chiengmai district, seeing that by the Treaty of 1883 we have surrendered to the Siamese Govt. jurisdiction over B.S. resident there.

One of the three persons mentioned in my private letter of 3 Jany. registered himself a few days ago, & paid the fee. He has now presented a petition in the consular court, agst. myself & the student interpreter who recd. the fee; I have refused to receive it, & I suppose they will now try to carry it to the Supreme Court at Singapore. They have put a para. in the papers saying that they have collected £240 for legal expenses to enable them to carry on the several actions they are going to bring.

I have not summoned or fined any of the ½ doz. British born B.S. who have hitherto

PRO 30/33 14/2 Semi-official Letters from Siam (May 29, 1885 – April 21, 1887)

omitted to register, because I am informed that they propose to bring an action agst. me to recover the fine, & tho' I shld. plead the sanction of the Secy. of State to the Regulation, I do not think any good wld. be done by affording these people an opportunity of publicly disputing the authority of H.M.G. in a court of law, to say nothing of the cost to the public of defending the action thro' all its stages fr. Singapore to the Privy Council.

Moreover the prime object of the regulation being to secure the registration of Asiatic B.S. who by having no certificate of nationality frequently get laid by the legs in a Siamese prison, & thus cause trouble & inconvenience. I do not propose to be very strict in enforcing it agst. the British-born. They carry a certificate of nationality in their countenances, & run no risk of arrest.

The Asiatic B.S. on the other hand is only too glad to have a paper to show, & during the month of January there presented themselves for registration 750, who being all males over 21 prob. represent a population of B.S. of thrice that no. in Bangkok alone. There are at the sapphire mines four or five days journey from here a larger no. of British Burmans, estimated at fr. 500 to 800. At or in the neighbourhood of Rahëng I am told there are perh. 2000 of the same race working in the teak forests, & there may be another 500 or so in teak forests further to the East. In the native states on the West coast of the Malay peninsula there are a vast crowd of B.S. chiefly Chinese naturalized in Singapore & Penang, whose numbers I have no means whatever of estimating, & who will prob. never present themselves for registration. But I am still of opinion that it is desirable to make every Asiatic B.S. as far as possible provide himself with a paper of nationality, & I cannot devise any more effectual method than that enacted for China and Japan by the O. in C. of 1865. And if there are any doubts abt. the strict legality of the regulation framed under §1 of the Siam O. in C. of 1856, then I wld. submit the desirability of making an O. in C. for the purpose.

The penalty for non-registration originally provided by §29 of the O. in C. of 1856 never has been enforced, nor could be. I entirely agree with the language of Sir Ed. Hornby in his instructions to consular offices in China & Japan, wch. has recently been repeated by Sir R. rennie, when he says "It is difficult to carry out the remainder of the penalty (i.e. non recognition & refusal of protection as a B.S.) as motives of humanity forbid us to leave our fellow subjects, simply because they have not registered themselves, to the tender mercies of the native authorities." How the Siamese auth: wld. treat B.S. if they had jurisdiction over them is exemplified by the case I reported in my deps. No. 2 of Jan. 4 of this year.

I shld. be very glad if you could send me a cypher telegram to say whether the regulations may be enforced, or whether they will be replaced by our O. in C.

y.v.t.

51. Satow to Currie
28/2/87

My dear Currie,

I hope my desp[atch]. No. 18 of Feb. 22 will be found to contain all the information you require abt. the scheme for a consular officer in Kedah. I consulted Sir F. Weld privately before writing it, & am sending him a copy of this desp[atch]. so that he may comment on it to the C.O. [Colonial Office] if he thinks fit.

The Siamese are beginning to cry out for a revision of the treaties and an increase of the import duties from 3 to 10 per cent ad valorem. The medium thro' wch. they make their wishes known to the public is the local newspaper "Bangkok Times", wch. was started at the New Year. It is supposed to be supported by them.

My desp[atches]. Nos. 13 & 20 will show you what sort of person the Siamese Min. for F.A. has taken to his bosom. I suspect that the Perak business has put the Minister's back up, for he has not been friendly since I put the Swettenham proposal before him & the King. Therefore they try to make all sorts of difficulties for me, & put this man Michell up to offer me provocation in the hope that I shall lose my temper. It was hoped that all the B.S. would turn against me on the registration question, but there they have been disappointed, and the writer of the memorial enclosed in my no. 15 told me that its principal object was to show that they did not approve of the other letter signed by Gowan, Dunlop & Marrable, wch. I sent you privately. Michell & Gowan have now taken to abusing me in the Singapore & Hongkong papers, but I do not care for that one atom as long as I have your support.

y.v.t.

PRO 30/33 14/2 Semi-official Letters from Siam (May 29, 1885 – April 21, 1887)

52. Satow to Currie

14 Mar/87

My dear Currie

You will have seen fr. my desp[atch]. of the 5th inst. that the opponents of annual registration have got an opinion in their favour fr. Mr. R.S. Wright, & are bent upon taking legal proceedings agst. me in the Supreme Court at Singapore.

It appears to me not altogether desirable to admit that the Chief Justice of the Straits Settlements has power to pronounce upon the validity of a regulation issued under the O. in C. & approved by the Secretary of State & if I am liable to be sued in the Singapore Court for one action, the malcontents will be continually disputing may acts & trying to get the Chief Justice to pronounce on them. It is the Attorney General's advice that I shld. allow an appearance to be entered for me if Mr. Marrable brings an action to recover the registration fee, but I do not think the Singapore Courts have any jurisdiction over me with respect to any acts done in my consular capacity. The malcontents are really no more than 4 in no. but as they have a lawyer among them (Michell) they can give a good deal of trouble. Two others are like him in the Siamese service, & to use their own language "great interest in the result of the contest is taken in Court circles at Bangkok".

The Perak business hangs fire. I am still without instructions as to the points submitted in my nos. 82 & 85 of last year, & hope that your desp[atch]. No. 2 of this year, wch. has not yet reached me, may contain them. The F.M. in reply to a question put to him unofficially said a couple of days ago that he thought it likely that the proposals wld. be accepted, but I do not build much on that. But he said at the same time that the King was going to discuss them shortly with his council of Ministers.

     y.v.t.

53. Satow to Currie

23.3.87

My dear Currie,

I was away at the seaside when your telegram of the 16th about Perak arrived, but immediately on my return I went to see the F.M. with the result recorded in my desp[atch]. of yesterday. I have spoken abt. this business 5 times since the beginning of the year, [margin: 9 Jan, 13 Jan (Kalahôm), 12 Feb., 9 Mar., 12 Mar.] but it was always a put-off. The Siamese in my opinion are merely trying to delay as long as possible. They think I may go on leave, & possibly, if the efforts of their allies among the B.S. are successful, not return. Then they wld. have a new man to deal with, & so gain another year or two. I mean to do what I can to force them to say yes or no, as I conjecture that your telegram means that. My speaking to 2 or 3 of the council is unlikely to be of much use. Gould's opinion is that the council merely registers what the King & For: Minr. have previously made up their minds to, but I am not certain that he is right. I have been careful never to put anything relating to the proposals in writing, so that they may not have anything to quote afterwards. But that wld. not prevent them from trying to hoodwink a possible successor, & I think it is desirable, if H.M.G. wish it, to settle the business while I am still here.

  y.v.t

54. Satow to Currie

25 Mar. 87

My dear Currie,

 You will see from the desp[atch]. abt. registration that goes forward today that Gowan & his friends do not cease fr. badgering me about the assumed illegality of the regulation & especially of the fee. I wish you could do something, either in the shape of an authoritative declaration that the regulation is legal, so that I may enforce it agst. the halfdozen agitators, or get it legalized by a short Act of Parliament, as was done in the case of the O. in C. [Order in Council] of 1856. These men being Siamese employés, their triumph will make my position here extremely difficult.

  y.v.t.

55. Satow to Currie

10/4/87

My dear Currie,

PRO 30/33 14/2 Semi-official Letters from Siam (May 29, 1885 – April 21, 1887)

Very many thanks for your prompt answer to my request for leave of absence. I cld. not get away earlier than the beginning of May, as I want to leave the field clear for Gould. I am extremely pleased to find that you are satisfied with what I have done, & I shall be quite contented to continue here as long as I can be useful, if my health holds out. It is not an agreeable place to live in, & the Siamese are often very tricky & troublesome. But a few months in England ought to set me up again, & compensate for a good many annoyances that I have had lately.

    y.v.t.

56. Satow to Currie

10.4.87

My dear Currie,

In my desp[atch]. of today I have contented myself with saying that if the Siamese proposals about Perak are accepted they will render all improvement of the leased district impossible. But in a few days I shall tell the F[oreign]. M[inister]. that I am certain they will not be entertained, & that if his instructions do not enable him to make considerable modifications, it will be no use trying to negotiate. They accept the principles, they say, but wish to render the concession utterly useless. Still it is something to have got so far. I have talked to one or two of the King's brothers, who were pointed out to me as opponents of any concession, & the majority of the council wch. was at first hostile, has turned the other way. It will be advantageous to negotiate in London, for here the Frenchman knows everything that is done, I suspect thro' the Kalahome.

57. Satow to Currie

10.4.87

My dear Currie,

A week ago I went up to the Palace & told the F.M. that I was going home. I also reminded him that there were a great many questions still pending, wch. I hoped he wld. settle before I left, adding that I did not wish to tell H.M.G. that I had exhausted all the means of persuasion. He promised that everything shld. be arranged. Two days afterwards the King & he determined that he shld. go to England to congratulate the Queen on the completion of the 50th year of her reign. I heard this thro' a third party, & it was impossible not to conjecture that my own departure had something to do with this sudden resolution. However, when he came down a couple of days later to announce his selection for this mission, he put it on the ground that the Japanese & Persians are also sending Princes to the celebration of the Jubilee. He expressed a great desire to travel home with me, & as I of course said I shld. be greatly pleased, it has been so settled. We shall be in London by the 14th June, where he will remain for a fortnight. He is to bring the Royal Family Order for the Queen & the Grand Cross of the Crown of Siam for Prince Edward. Afterwards he is to make the round of all the Treaty Powers, staying 4 or 5 days at each capital. He takes with him the new Ministers for England & France, neither of them men of much importance. The man destined for London has been until recently commissioner at Chiengmai, a good-natured sort of fellow, but very ugly. My French colleague of course looks upon this journey of the Foreign Minister & myself in company with great jealousy, but I am afraid it cannot be helped. The urgency of my departure has already enabled me to settle a very trifling question of compensation to a B.S. who had been kept in prison for some days without my being informed, wch. had been hanging fire for more than 2 mos., & has produced a general improvement, so that I have hopes of being able to dispose of all outstanding questions of any importance. The Siamese are naturally of a dilatory disposition, & when they get sulky, as they do every now & then, it becomes impossible to move them. They are like a pack of naughty, spoilt children.

The Prince wants me to come back with him through America & Japan, & in the latter country he hopes to arrange for the reestablish[men]t. of the relations wch. a couple of centuries ago existed betw. the two countries. It is possible that if he carries out this part of his plan, it might be useful for me to be on the spot, but that wld. involve my leaving England after a stay of only 6 months. However you will decide that. His fortnight in London, with the addition of a week in the beginning of September, will scarcely suffice for the settle[men]t. of the Perak business, I am afraid, but perhaps he can be made to alter his programme & lengthen his sojourn in England.

Archer is doing well as Acting Vice-consul at Chiengmai, & I shld. like him to be kept there as long as possible.

    y.v.t.

58. Satow to Jervoise (p.78)
11.4.87

My dear Jervoise,

One of the King's halfbrothers Prince Devawongse, is coming home by the same steamer as myself to represent the King at the Jubilee festivities, & will be accompanied by Phrya Montri the new E[nvoy]. E[xtraordinary]. & M[inister]. P[lenipotentiary]. I shld. be immensely obliged if you wld. do what you can towards ensuring the Prince a good reception, & especially see that he gets his proper place as a R.A.[Royal ?] representing the King at all the functions. He is known personally to Prince Albert Victor & Prince Geo. of Wales, having been sent to see them at Singapore in Jan. 1882. Phya Montri wld. I suppose get the same invitations as any other diplomatist of his rank. Please do whatever you can for me in the same line, as it will give me weight with the people here. We are due in London on the 14th June.

    y.v.t.

P.S. Prince Devawongse is the most important man in Siam after the King.

59. Satow to Currie
21 April 1887

My dear Currie,

I trust my desp[atches]. Nos. 45 & 46 will show that I had some good grounds for acting as I did with regard to Mitchell in his action agst. Bush, & that the Law Officers, who prob. had not the other Treaties before them may be disposed to modify their opinion. The shares of [Edward Blair] Michell & [Dr. Peter] Gowan have been bought by Bush, it was not necessary for me to communicate to the former the instructions contained in your telegram of the 16th.

I see that various distorted accounts of this affair & the registration question have got into the home papers.

PRO 30/33 14/2 Semi-official Letters from Siam (May 29, 1885 – April 21, 1887)

My desp[atch]. No. 48 will show you how far this man Michell is going, & proves conclusively that he is acting with the approval of the Siamese Govt., who always put forward one of their employés to do what they dare not do for themselves. Their neglect to answer my Note asking for assistance is tantamount to refusing it, & I hope some notice will be taken of their attempt to undermine the authority of the Consular Court over B.S.

Mr. [James] Marrable [telegraph engineer] whose bogus action agst. me in the Consular Court to recover his registration fee was reported at his request in my desp[atch]. no. 31 of 25 Mar. is going down to Singapore ahead of me, prob. to institute an action agst. me in the Supreme Court, & will no doubt try to get me detained, so that his Siamese employers may reach home first.

I have settled some of the arrears of business with the Siamese, but the imprisonment case of the B.S. Ibrahim Khan reported in my No. 2 is as yet in statu quo. I want if possible to make the proposal come fr. them, instead of presenting a demand.

Dr. Gowan sent me a copy of his letter to Lord Salisbury three or four days after it had been despatched. If my previous despatches have not already anticipated all he says, I trust to be able to give a complete explanation on reaching England. He is wo[e]fully disappointed at my not firing him for non-registration, and thus depriving him of the opportunity of posing as a public-spirited pltf. [plaintiff] in some court of his own selection, hence his abuse of those who did register.

 y.v.t.

END OF PRO 30/33 14/2

PRO 30/33 14/3   Semi-official Letters from Uruguay (August 4, 1890 – March 30, 1893)

PRO 30/33 14/3
The notebook is labelled
"Letters from Montevideo
1889 – 1893 March".
It contains 86 letters.

1. Satow to Sanderson
Private
4 Aug. 1890
Dear Sanderson,[1]

You will of course have had full acc[oun]ts. fr[om]. Bland of the attempted revolution at B.A. The outbreak was telegraphed over abt. 10 o'c. on the morning of the 26th & Capt. Musgrave was the 1st person to tell me of it. I at once advised him to send over the "Beagle" & the "Bramble" wch. are small enough to get into the new port, & to take his own ship "Cleopatra" as near as possible, so as to be at hand in case his intervention was needed. He went off to see the 2 captains, & I felt pretty sure that at least he would send them. Then came in the Man[age]r. of the Lond[on]. & R[iver]. P[late]. Bank c. telegrams, one of wch. reported that the Argentine Pres[iden]t.[2] had gone off in the "Isabel" to Rosario. I was glad to be able to tell him that probably a couple of ships wld. go over. Later on in the day I learnt for certain that Musgrave was sending "Beagle" & "Bramble" that afternoon, & then despatched my T[elegram]. to you. After the orders had been given, I got a telegram fr. Bland inquiring whether there were any ships here, & telegraphed back that he wld. see a couple next morning. It is abt. 12 hrs. steaming for ships drawing as much as they do. Musgrave decided to stop here until he heard further, being apparently under the impression that he cld. easily learn by telegraph whether his ship were wanted or not. He wld. however have been in a much better position to know what was going on if he had taken the "Cleo."

---

[1] Thomas Henry Sanderson (1841-1923). Assistant Permanent Under-Secretary of State for Foreign Affairs, 1889-1894. Permanent Under-Secretary, 1894-1906.
[2] Miguel Juárez Celman (1844-1909) was Argentine President from October 12, 1886 to August 6, 1890. He was succeeded by Carlos Pellegrini (1846-1906) from August 6, 1890 to October 12, 1892.

PRO 30/33 14/3 Semi-official Letters from Uruguay (August 4, 1890 – March 30, 1893)

across. Even if, as he said, she cld. not get within 10 miles, that distance cld. easily have been covered by the "Bramble" or by a steam launch in less time than a telegram cld. have been sent & delivered to him. Besides, it produces a good effect all round on these occasions, if British naval officers are seen to be on the 'qui vive'. On the 27th another telegram reached me fr. Bland to say that the ships had arrived at B.A., no immediate danger to B.S. & the Cleopatra not wanted at present. This, tho' nominally fr. Bland, was as I have since learnt, a telegram fr. Humpage of the "Beagle" intended for Musgrave. I went off at once to the Club, & finding him there, showed it to him. Abt. an hour later on in the same afternoon a teleg. addressed to M. was delivered at my house, & an officer of the "Cleo." happening to be with me at that moment, I begged him to take it on to M. at once. The latter then telegraphed to "Bramble" to come over & fetch him. I rather think this T[elegram]. to M. said that the Argentine squadron was bombarding the city. M's T. was misdirected, & did not reach the "Beagle" till abt. midday on the 28th. Humpage at once sent off the "Bramble", but she did not get here till midday on the 29th. M. on hearing the acct. brought by her, determined to go over in the Cleo. Taking the Bramble c. him, & left abt. 4 in the afternoon. In the meantime the terms of the surrender had been arranged c. the revolutionary party, & at ¼ to 6 I got a T. fr. Humpage, to say that the whole business was over, too late of course to stop M. So he arrived then when his presence could no longer be of any use. I consider that Humpage behaved very judiciously in suggesting that the Argentine squadron shld. be invited to cease bombarding the city, & I have no doubt that had it been necessary to use force to put a stop to the bombardment our 2 ships with the Spaniard in the "Infanta Isabel" wld. have been able to apply it effectively, & they wld. in all probability have been joined by the Uruguayan gunboat that was also lying at B.A. to say nothing of the Brazilian "Trajano" [Srajano?].

Musgrave came back in the "Cleo." on the afternoon of the 1st, leaving the Bramble at B.A. The feeling of nearly everyone here, native as well as foreigner, except those who belong to the ring that surrounds the President, is that the failure of this attempt to overthrow Juarez Celman is a great misfortune. The excitement when the first news came was immense, as was the gloom produced by the certainty that the revolution had been unsuccessful. People said to me they had hoped Juarez Celman's downfall wld. have been a

PRO 30/33 14/3   Semi-official Letters from Uruguay (August 4, 1890 – March 30, 1893)

lesson to Julio Herrera, as his triumph will on the contrary encourage him to continue in his present courses. There is said to be a party forming agst. him, but as long as he is supported by ex-Prest. Tajes he need not fear. Anyhow, I don't at present see any reason to anticipate a row.

   y.v.t.

2. Satow to Sanderson (stamped p.3)
18 August 1890.
Dear Sanderson,

 The situation here seems rapidly to be growing worse. 3 days ago there was a report that the Ministry had resigned in a body, or talked of doing so, but the Prest. Had persuaded them to remain. This at once sent gold up to 136, & it has since gone up further. Fresh legislation is contemplated with the object of saving the National Bank, but all confidence in the ability of the Minr. of Finance & of the President to weather the crisis is at an end. People are beginning to talk of an approaching military pronunciamento. The downfall of Juarez Celman has been a serious blow for Herrera, Casey & all the others who were trying to bring abt. 'curso forzoso', & the obstinate refusal of the banks & wholesale merchants to recognize any but a gold basis has rendered it all but impossible.

 In the present uncertainty of politics I shall have much difficulty in proposing the extension of the period of provisional arrest, as instructed in Treaty No. 9 of July 2, but I will sound the Minr.

 The "Times" correspondent Thomson came to see me yesterday, & told me a long tale abt. his doings in Buenos Aires. Quorum pars magna fui [In which I played a great part] was the burden of his tale. He is now on his way to Chile, whence he will visit Peru & Bolivia, & cross the continent back to Buenos Aires.

 His one idea is to make things look better than they really are, in order not to frighten European capitalists: to give the Argentines time to tide over their present difficulties. This country he regards as of hardly any importance at all, in wch. he is doubtless right.

   y.v.t.

PRO 30/33 14/3   Semi-official Letters from Uruguay (August 4, 1890 – March 30, 1893)

3. Satow to Sanderson (stamped p.4)

21 August 1890.

Dear Sanderson,

Today's papers announce the resignation of the Mins. of Finance & War, the former because he & the Pres. disagree abt. the means to be adopted to meet the financial crisis, the latter on acct. of some changes in the command of regiments, wch. the public consider ominous of coming trouble. 2 men in particular whose apptmts. were published yesterday have the reputation of unscrupulous ruffians. Herrera wants either to resuscitate the National Bank with the aid of foreign capital, or to establish another & bigger concern of the kind on its foundations (the superstructure being a complete ruin), in order to have a milch cow[3] as the phrase is fr. wch. to draw supplies for his own amusement & to satisfy the needs of his adherents. It seems that this is the only method of governing in this country. And as the Uruguayans themselves have no cash that can be squeezed out of them, the European capitalist is persuaded to become the victim. I look on the greater part of what is said abt. the great 'progress' of Uruguay as dust thrown in the eyes of the public.

Ex-President Tajes ever since his term came to an end has kept away fr. Montevideo: but he is a very sphynx and no one seems to have much idea of what his plans may be. De Leon, who was minister of war under Tajes, & Herrera's 'competitor' for the Presidency is rather a dangerous man. I think it is certain that there is great discontent among military men, wch. Herrera is trying to crush by calling to his side men who will stick at nothing, and it is very doubtful whether he will be able to carry out his plans for remaining in power. Thomson of the Times seems to have produced a serious fall in Unifieds by his telegram. I do not venture to say there will not be a serious row here.

  y.v.t.

4. Satow to Sanderson (stamped p.5)

4/9/90

Dr. Sanderson,

---

[3] Milch cow: a person or organization that is a source of easy profit.

PRO 30/33 14/3   Semi-official Letters from Uruguay (August 4, 1890 – March 30, 1893)

Since last mail went things seem to have gradually quieted down. The President has got his own men in as Colonels of the regiments, & people think his position stronger than ever. He is negotiating with Barings for more money, they say £3,000,000 to put the National Bank on its legs again, but there seems to be some hitch. Barings want to have a more effective control than Herrera is willing to concede.

I shall shortly send home my trade report, wch. has been read by Davie the Vice Consul, who is a man of business, & one of the bankers. They have not disapproved of it, so I imagine the statements contained in it are not far from correct. I find the general opinion among merchants & bankers to be that such reports are perhaps interesting to read, but not of the slightest practical value.

      y.v.t.

5. Satow to Villiers (stamped p.6)
Copy
Confidential
Montevideo.
26 June 1889.
Dear Sir Villiers,[4]

I write in haste to catch the mail, abt. the consular accounts & fee accts. of the quarters ended 31 Decr. & 31 Mar.

Your telegram of 16, wch. was delivered to Mr. Ayre a week after my arrival, was not mentioned by him. A fortnight ago the recorder arrived, wch. I handed to him, supposing that it was a matter that concerned him alone. Yesterday evening I recd. your telegram, wch. this morning I showed to Mr. Ayre, asking him when the accts. were despatched. He answered that the Dec. accts. had been sent off in March, the March accts. later, he cld. not remember when. I asked him to ascertain the precise dates, & show me the covering despatches, adding that I wld. come down to the Consulate at one o'clock to see them. I came down here at one o'clock, & found that he was absent. I am informed by the clerk that

---

[4] Sir Thomas Villiers Lister (1832-1902). Assistant Under-Secretary of State for Foreign Affairs, 1873-94.

PRO 30/33 14/3   Semi-official Letters from Uruguay (August 4, 1890 – March 30, 1893)

the accts. have never been sent & in fact I have them now in my possession, all made out ready for signature but still unsigned, & the bills wch. shld. accompany them are not with them. The balances to be remitted are £134.12.3 & £156.7.9 respectively. These accts. have been made out by my clerk. There is evidently something amiss here, & a glaring contradiction betw. Mr. Ayre's statements to me, & the actual state of the papers. But until I have seen him I cannot say more.

  y.v.t.

6. Satow to Ayre

same date

Dear Ayre,

I came down to the office at one o'clock expecting to find you here to give me the dates on wch. you had despatched the accts. referred to in the telegram wch. I showed you this morning. You were not here, altho' you cannot have failed to understand that I wished to see you at the office at that hour.[5]

I must request you to call on me tomorrow morning as early as possible to give me the explanations wch. you must yourself feel are very necessary.

  y.f.

7. Satow to Currie (stamped p.7)

Copy

[no date given]

Dear Currie,

In a desp[atch]. wch. goes home by this mail I have reported as briefly as possible on Ayre's irregularities with respect to the accts. But this is not all. He is a confirmed drunkard, & neglects his duties in a serious manner, leaving his work to be done by the clerks. He loses papers I entrust to him & as far as I can see is altogether useless. I trust his resignation will be accepted.

---

[5] See also diary for May 16, 1889. Ayre's reputation was not good.

PRO 30/33 14/3   Semi-official Letters from Uruguay (August 4, 1890 – March 30, 1893)

I am unable to offer any suggestion as to the choice of his successor. My clerk, a decent young fellow enough, is too young (only nineteen) while the other clerk has not sufficient education. What is required is a man sufficient of a gentleman to command the respect of the Engl. residents, and of the native officials. But the salary assigned is altogether inadequate – only £400 a year. For houserent & servants a man wld. require at least £300, and I do not think £800 a year wld. be too much to give. Ayre's salary was eked out by his wife & sister giving lessons. Wld. it not be possible to send me a man fr. Europe?

At last I have found a house & am moving in this week. The Consulate office will be underneath, the most convenient arrangement under the circs. I have to pay £500 a year for the whole, but it wld. be impossible to get anything cheaper; other things are in proportion. The climate is delightful, & the people, both English & native, very friendly, so I am quite contented – If only I had a competent consul.   [End of letter]

8. Satow to Villiers

July 8. 1889

Dear Sir Villiers,

My desp[atch]. of the 6th contains all that seems necessary to report officially abt. the delay in sending home the accounts. When Ayre came to me on the morning after my hurried letter to you, he tried at first to mislead me by showing entries on the debit side of the cash b[oo]k. apparently to his credit, but in further examination they turned out to be payments made by him to cover previous deficits. He pretended not to know what had become of the money, but it is evident fr. the cash book that it has all gone into his pocket, & he does not even suggest that the money had been made away with by the clerk. I gave him a few days law[?] in order to see whether he cld. obtain a loan to meet the remittances, which he did at last. I am not sure that he ought not to have been suspended at once, but as he offered to send in his resignation I thought that wld. be sufficient. There was no need to have a scandalous exposure. Of course it is well known here that he drinks, & I had even heard it before I left England fr. Wyndham. I noticed fr. the beginning that his manner was odd, & not clear-headed, & that he seemed to be absent fr. the office very frequently. His resignation will I trust be accepted.

PRO 30/33 14/3 Semi-official Letters from Uruguay (August 4, 1890 – March 30, 1893)

Then comes the question of whom to appt. as his successor. The system. [Letter ends here.]

9. Satow to Ayre (stamped p.17)
C.J. Ayre Esq.
H.M. Legation
7 August 1889.
Sir,

On examining the book containing the cemetery accounts & comparing it with the Consulate Cash book, I find that in the year 1888 cemetery fees to the amount of $609 20 cents more or less were received by you. Of these fees I can find no entry in the cemetery cash.

I must request you therefore to be as good as to furnish me with an explanation of the omission of this sum from the cemetery accts.

I am & c.   y.v.s.
E.S.

10. Satow to Ayre
D[ra]ft.
B.L. Montevideo.
12 Aug./89
Dear Mr. Ayre,

I hear that you have left M.V. & are with Mr. Ricketts, to whose care therefore I have addressed this cover.

Mrs. Lanny has been in today with the receipt for Lanny's wages for July, & she informs me that $35 is still owing, for wch. he gave you a receipt in full. This makes $35 additional to the amount wch. you owe to the cemetery fund.

I am somewhat surprised that you have left this place without settling your accts. It was a voluntary promise on your part, & I expected you wld. observe it. On Friday the 15th inst. there will be a meeting at my house to elect a Cemetery Committee, & it will not be

PRO 30/33 14/3 Semi-official Letters from Uruguay (August 4, 1890 – March 30, 1893)

possible much longer to keep the real state of things fr. the public. The Committee's first meeting may perhaps be delayed until the 22nd, & unless I receive from you before that date the whole amount that you owe to the Chest, whether on acct. of Cemetery Fees, or on acct. of the mate of the "Trojan", I shall be compelled to make the facts public.

  y.f. E.S.

This never reached Ayre. Mrs. Ayre called one morning, & I told her the whole story. She said it wld. be useless to write a telegraph to Ayre, as he cld. not get back in time. I gave her a note of the amount due to the cemetery and said I wld. not lay the accts. before the committee before Friday the 23rd.

11. Satow to Ayre (stamped p.10)
D[ra]ft.
C.J. Ayre Esq.
Aug. 16. 1889
Sir,

When I saw you last you expressed the hope of being able to place in my hands in three days time the amount you owe to the cemetery for the balance of fees collected since Jan. 1888. You have not done so, but I learn that you have left Montevideo contrary to the promise voluntarily made by you; not to quit this place until you had settled that acct. by the sale of a piece of land in your possn.

I am informed that you retained $35 out of Lanny's wages for June, altho' in the cemetery accts. You put down the whole sum due to him as paid. That amount of $35 must be added to what you have to hand to me for the Cemetery. On the same occasion you purposely conveyed to me the impression that you had drawn out of the consulate chest since the 1st July only $40, whereas you well knew that since that date you had obtained over $760 from the chest. Part of this you might perhaps imagine to be your own money, inasmuch as after providing for the remittance of the 6 months consular fees up to Mar. 31 and the Board of Trade balance for the first quarter of the year, there remained in the chest $140.73 out of the $1800 you borrowed in order to provide for the bills. But a little

PRO 30/33 14/3   Semi-official Letters from Uruguay (August 4, 1890 – March 30, 1893)

reflection wld. have shown you that as you were bound to replace in the chest a sum of $510 deposited in there for the benefit of the mate of the "Trojan", wch. you had little by little appropriated for your own purposes, there was not in reality a single cent of your money in the chest.

During the present quarter, fr. the 1st July up to the day you were informed by me that you were suspended fr. your official duties, there had been received in Consular fees $517.82 & there were actually remaining on that day in the chest only $30.83. Consequently you have since the 1st of July last appropriated $486.99 of public money.

You have also appropriated a bill for $70.14 sent fr. Paysandú as a remittance on acct. of a deceased British seaman, & have employed it in paying to the sexton Carlos Lanny wages wch. you have debited to the cemetery account. You have therefore to make that sum good also.

In your capacity as Acting Consul-Genl. you administered the est[at]e. of the late Mr. Palgrave, & there was a balance in your hands of $265.53 wch. money is not in the chest. It is evident that you have appropriated this also.

In addition to these sums you have to replace in the chest $570 deposited for the benefit of the mate of the "Trojan", making in all $1392.66 besides what you owe to the cemetery acct.

Unless you return forthwith to Montevideo, and settle all these accts. I shall take such steps as may appear necessary under the circs.

y.v.s.

E.S.

Note. I think I showed this also to Mrs. Ayre. She paid me $851 odd cents for cemetery fees alluded to. The rest was deducted fr. what Ayre was entitled to as Acting Consul-Genl. and for office expenses fr. date of Palgrave's death until my arrival. Ayre also was shown the draft of the foregoing.

12. Satow to Pakenham[6] (stamped p.12)

---

[6] (Sir) Francis Pakenham (1832-1905). Envoy Extraordinary and Minister Plenipotentiary to Argentina, 1885-1896.

PRO 30/33 14/3   Semi-official Letters from Uruguay (August 4, 1890 – March 30, 1893)

25 Sept. 1889

Dear Mr. Pakenham,

The reasons for my telegraphing to you were these:

At the beginning of the week an officer of the "Richmond" came down here, & said that he had been told on what he regarded as excellent & trustworthy authority that you had telegraphed for the squadron in consequence of the alarm felt by the English mercantile community of B.A. in connexion with the financial position. I said I could not believe it, but he replied that his informant said he had fr. a man who had never been mistaken before.

Yesterday I recd, a visit fr. Mr. R.A. Thurburn the manager of the Lond. & River Plate Bank, who said he had just returned fr. B.A. That he considered the state of things very alarming, strikes multiplying among the working population, great want of confidence in the govt. hints that a knife or a bullet might perh. be put into the president and a financial crash was pending wch. might lead to serious disturbance; & that the presence of the squadron in the River Plate wld. tend to have a reassuring effect.

Of course I told him that it wld. not do for me to interfere in a matter that came within your province solely, and that as long as there was no apprehension of rows in M.V. I could not summon the squadron. But at his request, I undertook to tell you what he had said. If you shld. feel disposed to ask the opinion of Mr. Anderson of the same bank, who lives I believe at Belgrano, he wld. very likely tell you the same sort of thing. Many thanks for your prompt reply.

The telegrams in your local papers abt. the impending arrival of the squadron are, as far as I know, without foundation. They very possibly originated in the report brought down by the American officer above-mentioned. If you think it desirable I will have it contradicted in the two local English papers. [End of letter]

<u>13. Satow to Sanderson (stamped p.13)</u>

4 March 1890

My dear Sanderson,

As was pretty generally expected, Julio Herrera y Obes[7] has been elected president.

PRO 30/33 14/3   Semi-official Letters from Uruguay (August 4, 1890 – March 30, 1893)

Nominally the ex-president has exercised no influence over the chambers, but it was clear to every one that Herrera was his candidate. A newspaper says rightly that the President of a S.A. Republic possesses greater power than any European constitutional monarch; he is almost an absolute sovereign, whose reign is limited, but who has the right of nominating his successor. So here Tajes, Herrera and one Leonidas Barreto who held no official post, ruled the country during the last term, & Herrera, Tajes and Barreto will rule it now. It is merely the nominal repres've that has been changed of this triumvirate. Tajes is said to be worth 6 or 7 millions of dollars, while Herrera is rather poor having spent so much in bribing the electoral body. So at least it is said. I suppose it means that he is not so well off as his partners. However three years ago he could not pay his bill at the Restaurant, so he has done something for himself.

What is really to be feared is that he will steer the country in such a manner that 'curso forzoso' will result. His promises in this regard are not worth the paper they are written upon. President Roca it is remembered declared that he wld. cut off his right hand before he would sign a decree suspending cash payments; but he did it nevertheless a few months later. The class of people who wished for Herrera to come into power are a sufficient criterion of what he is likely to do; they are such as casey, Bowen and one or two more acute speculators. Probably he will try to keep on good terms with European Powers. He is no longer as young and hotheaded as when he broke off relations with England. Yesterday the diplomatic body was received by him, the colleagues who are accredited to B.A. as well having come over for the purpose. It was a purely formal ceremony. Afterwds. we went to call on the ex-President, who made a little speech to thank us for the honour paid to him in his quality of private citizen. The general verdict is that whatever his faults may have been, he has conferred an immense benefit on the country by putting an end to militarism. Herrera has not yet nominated his ministry. It is supposed that Blas Vidal who until recently [was] minister at Rio will take F.A.

I am going the day after tomorrow to Maldonado for a fortnight's seabathing. [End of letter]

---

[7] Julio Herrera y Obes (1841-1912) assumed office as 16th President of Uruguay on March 1, 1890 and left it on March 1, 1894.

PRO 30/33 14/3   Semi-official Letters from Uruguay (August 4, 1890 – March 30, 1893)

14. Satow to Cecil Hertslet

21 Nov. 1890.

Dear Mr. Hertslet,

In answer to your inquiry of the 16th October about the Extradition Treaties with Peru and Spain, the ratifications of the former have never been exchanged, though the Treaty was approved by the Uruguayan Chambers. That with Spain was approved by the Chambers on the 18th January 1886 and the ratifications were exchanged on the 11th October 1886 at Montevideo.

I do not gather from your letter that it is desired that I should place this on record officially, but of course I will do this if it is required.

Believe me,

y.v.t.

E.S.

15. Satow to Sanderson (stamped p.15)

24 Nov. 1890

Dear Sanderson,

The telegrams fr. London announcing the failure of Baring Bros. have produced something like a crisis here, and there has been a considerable fall in the shares of the National Bank, and a corresponding rise in gold.

The customs duties have diminished from $1000,000 a month to 500,000 & the Govt. is so hard up that its payments to the army, police and officials of all classes are 3 months in arrear. They have also made default in the payment of the guarantees due on the Central & Midland railways. People begin again to talk of the President being turned out & replaced by a military man. The Blanco party are said to be negotiating with Latorre, who is popular in the country districts, & who is beginning to have adherents in Montevideo itself. Trade is quite at a standstill. There are no buyers for wool, wch. is the principal export, and altogether the outlook is a gloomy one.

On the other hand, I think Herrera will hold out as long as he can. He is busily occupied

PRO 30/33 14/3   Semi-official Letters from Uruguay (August 4, 1890 – March 30, 1893)

with the elections to the new chambers, wch. will be packed entirely with his creatures. Moderate men think it is better to let him stay where he is than to replace him by Agustin de Castro, the Pres. of the Senate, who wld. be his legal successor, or to fall back upon a military man. The English are mostly in favour of having a soldier as president, but they have little or no influence on the course of political events. There has been a severe drought & the locusts have invaded the northern department. The Govt. cannot hope to obtain funds wherewith to revive the National Bank. There is no doubt that the general discontent is very serious, and nothing wld. surprise me less than the sudden overthrow of the president & the proclamation of a dictator.

   y.v.t.

   E.S.

16. Satow to Sanderson (p.16)

11 Dec. 1890.

Dear Sanderson,

On the 9th inst. the Minr. for F.A. (Blas Vidal) Interior (A. Capurro) & Justice (C. Berro) sent in their joint resignations &c. to the Prest. Their motives have not been made public, but I have little doubt that they are unwilling any longer to be associated with the President's financial failures, & with a Finance Minister who is a commercial bankrupt. Callorda, the Minr. of War, remains in. I do not yet know for certain whether Montero the finance minister will resign.

18 months ago I was told that an annual deficit of a million or so was the normal condition of things in the country. When Tajes went out, the new Minr. of finance pena speedily found out that it wld. be necessary to borrow abt. that sum to make both ends meet. And they got it from Barings. As the revenue still decreases, there is every prospect of the deficit next June being at least a million st[erlin]g. As they can no longer borrow in Europe, they must either economize or default. The latter expedient seems most in accordance with their character.

I recd. a circular asking what measures wld. be taken in respect of §3 of the McKinley tariff. I think that this country will do nothing.

PRO 30/33 14/3   Semi-official Letters from Uruguay (August 4, 1890 – March 30, 1893)

Dr. Krauel is to be presented today. Uruguay is altogether unwilling to send delegates to the intercontinental rlwy. commission.

   y.v.t.

17. Satow to Sanderson

24 Dec. 90

Dear Sanderson,

 Things are still as they were. I hear nothing abt. new ministers, & it is possible that the President will go on for some time without making nominations unless he can get some respectable nonentities to accept office. He is of an arbitrary disposition, & no minister with views of his own can long remain in his cabinet.

 A brother in law of Santos whom I occasionally consult, assures me that Herrera has all the army with him, & that as revolution is impossible what he fears is as attempt may be made on Herrera's life, by one of those who attribute to him the present depression. Herrera is now trying to borrow gold from the Brazilian Govt. to resuscitate the Banco Nacional, & it is his only hope. The general opinion is that the bank will have to liquidate. The chambers have been induced to pass a scheme for its reorganization, wch. depends entirely on the success of the proposed loan. A bill has also been presented to them for the reduction of the budget by abt. ½ a million of dollars, & the increase of import duties on various articles of luxury such as tobacco, spirits & silk goods. Trade is almost at a standstill, & people tell me that there has not been such depression for 25 years. I don't see much prospect of its terminating until some one else is found foolish enough to make a loan.

 I shld. like to come home on leave next May or June, if Grenfell is able to take up his apptmt. as vice consul. Neither of my clerks is fit to be left in charge. Bédouret, the acting Consul, is a person who can't even spell.

   y.v.t.

18. Satow to Sanderson (p.18)

Jan. 22. 1891.

Dear Sanderson,

PRO 30/33 14/3 Semi-official Letters from Uruguay (August 4, 1890 – March 30, 1893)

Everything is going on here pretty much in the same manner as when I last wrote. The President with only two ministers instead of five, is trying to get a loan to put the National Bank (his milch cow) on its legs again, & having failed to get what he wants fr. Europe & the U.S. is negotiating with Brazil. In the meantime, the govt. of the country is carried on on tick; none of the salaries & pensions, except to a few favoured individuals, having been paid since September last. And yet I am certain that with ordinarily honest administration the country cld. perfectly well pay its way. The President has surrounded himself with the men who at the head of the troops upset Ellauri in 1875, a gang of cutthroats ready for anything, & there seems little likelihood of any attempt made in the direction of a revolution.

The sensible men in the country are convinced that armed disturbances wld. be worse even than having Herrera for President. The Chilean Govt. have sent a Secy. of Legation here to stop the "Almirante Condell" a new torpedo boat just out fr. England, & he is trying to persuade the Prest. to issue an order that no coals are to be supplied to her. But I think that if the Captain wishes to continue his voyage & join the Chilian Squadron, he will find an enterprising business man to give him coals somehow. [End of letter]

19. Satow to Sanderson

Feb. 5. 1891.

Dear Sanderson,

There is nothing new here. The talk abt. a loan fr. Brazil has entirely died down. During the last fortnight confidence has revived among financial people, because they see the Bank of England rate has gone down. But the revenue is declining, and trade suffering severely. Most Englishmen think that this country as well as the Argentine Repub. will before long have to make default.

The Chili Secy. has gone away, having failed in his mission. Balmaceda[8] despatched a number of officers & men fr. Santiago overland to supersede those who brought the "Almirante Condell" out fr. Europe. The news came ahead of them by telegraph, so the

---

[8] Jose Manuel Balmaceda (1840-1891). President of Chile, 1886-91. Shot and killed himself at the end of the 1891 Chilean Civil War.

PRO 30/33 14/3   Semi-official Letters from Uruguay (August 4, 1890 – March 30, 1893)

captain got warning in time. He promptly obtained coals fr. an English firm, and sailed at once. The American flagship is expected to get to Valparaiso the 22nd of this month. She is an old wooden tub.

All our ships except the "Bramble" are down at the Falkland Islands.

      y.v.t.

20. Satow to Sanderson (p.19)

Feb. 19. 1891

Dear Sanderson,

The only thing of interest that has occurred since I last wrote is the return here of the "Almirante Condell" together with the "Almirante Lynch" & another Chilian vessel. As far as I can learn the two latter, which were manned by no very warlike crews, were captured at Sandy Point in the Straits of Magellan: they proceeded then to sea with other crews & took the Condell, wch. they brought up here to get a crew from Chili across the Andes. The three vessels are now at Buenos Aires.

Herrera's speech to the chambers is in the opinion of most people a cynical attempt to throw the responsibility for the present financial crisis that attaches to himself on other shoulders. To blame Barings for it is particularly ungrateful & I imagine will not produce a good effect in Europe. What he says abt. gold having been taken out of the country to pay for the excess of imports over exports is no doubt all wrong; the excess has been paid for in Unified Bonds. Several men of standing among the Engl. community have said to me lately that they fear Uruguay (as well as the Argentine) will default. I suppose the Uruguayans will begin as they have in fact already done, with the railway guarantees, the cedulas, the interest on Unified payable here, & finally the unified payable in London.

With honesty, they could pay everything, but unluckily honesty is precisely what is lacking.

Politically Herrera's position is unshaken. He has just elected a chamber full of his own adherents, with just enough admixture of opposition members to keep the pond from putrifying, and in the Senate he has a majority. He can do just as he likes.

      y.v.t.

PRO 30/33 14/3   Semi-official Letters from Uruguay (August 4, 1890 – March 30, 1893)

21. Satow to Sanderson (p.20)

Mar. 6. 1891

Dear Sanderson,

The new ministry was installed yesterday, & this afternoon I am going to make the acquaintance of the Min. for F.A. The Finance Min. is the most intelligent of the whole lot & there is some fear that he may be ambitious of distinguishing himself, instead of working quietly & steadily in the direction of economy.

The President has managed at last to make a loan with Brazil, thro' an Engl. Bank here, the "English Bank of the Rio de la Plata'. It is kept very dark at present, no doubt with a view to speculations on the Bourse. I shall try to find out more abt. this loan. The Uruguayans already owe a very large amount to the Brazilian Govt. & it wld. not surprise me to find that Marshal Fonseca[9] has had a finger in the present negotiations.

   y.v.t.
    E.S.

22. Satow to Sanderson (p. 21)

April 1. 1891

Dear Sanderson,

As far as can be seen at present Herrera's new ministry is giving satisfaction & is likely to work well. Herrero y Espinosa endeavours to make himself agreeable; he is young & energetic, & in these points a great improvement on the amiable Blas Vidal.

If it shld. be thought advisable to remove from Article I of the Extradition Treaty the exception in favour of subjects & citizens, I think it wld. be well that I shld. be instructed to take no steps until the Chambers, by ratifying the Treaties of the South American Congress, have shown that they accept the principle.

I hope to shortly arrange for compensation to the master of the Argentine barque "Catalina", wch. was wrecked here over a year ago in conseq. of the Port Authorities

---

[9] Deodoro da Fonseca (1827-1892), first President of Brazil, 1889-1891.

PRO 30/33 14/3 Semi-official Letters from Uruguay (August 4, 1890 – March 30, 1893)

having illegally seized and removed her to an unsafe anchorage. The master, who is also owner, is a Scotchman named Wallace. As he chose to have his property under the flag of a foreign country, I told him that he must look to the Repres've of that country to obtain redress. But I have at the same time continually spooned on the Argentine minister [Enrique] Moreno (a grandnephew of the man who corresponded with Ld. Palmerston about the Falkland Isl.) to do what was required. I mention this case because I have heard that Admiral Henry Grant, who was out here about various salvage cases for Lloyds is going to publish the story in London, & it may be convenient for you to know that I have been pushing Wallace's claim as far as was possible officially.

I have exchanged visits with the new Bishop, who was enthroned the other day with great pomp. The President, though not a paragon of piety and virtue does all he can to win the goodwill of the clerical party. His minr. in Brazil belongs to it, & he is abt. to appt. another strong Catholic to Madrid. The loan fr. a Bank in Brazil is an accomplished fact, but I do not see any evidence that politics have had to do with it. Financially, things are mending slightly, but the monthly payments for difft. Depts.. are still a whole quarter behindhand.

y.v.t.

23. Satow to Bergne (p.22)
April 4. 1891.
My dear Bergne,[10]

With reference to my desp[atch]. Treaty No. 8 of yesterday, abt. the duty of the Uruguayan Govt. to give notices of changes in the Tariff, the desp[atch]. from F.O. to wch. it is a reply speaks of Art. 3 of the Commercial Treaty. Perhaps that was an error made in copying the draft, or it may have originated on this side. My draft, however, of Jan. 14th is correct.

It seems strange that the Uruguayan Govt. shld. have been induced to agree that notice shld. be given of changes in "Uruguayan laws", & I think it probable that if we were to

---

[10] Sir John Henry Bergne (1842-1908). Superintendent of the treaty department at the Foreign Office, 1881-94.

PRO 30/33 14/3 Semi-official Letters from Uruguay (August 4, 1890 – March 30, 1893)

insist on their observation of any part of the last para. of Art. II they wld. laugh in our faces.

You will see fr. my Treaty No. 5 that they desire a further amendment of the Extradition Treaty. I have suggested to Sanderson that I shld. be instructed to do nothing until the Chambers have ratified the Treaties of the South American Congress of Montevideo, wch. wld. establish a precedent for the extradition of citizens. I am told (semi-officially) that all Extradition Treaties are held by native lawyers to be violations of the Constitution, but that on acct. of their utility this inherent vice is ignored.

  y.v.t.
  E.S.

24. Satow to Sanderson (p.23)
April 30, 1891.
Dear Sanderson,

I have done everything in my power to secure the payt. of the Midland Rlwy. debenture coupon, & I am told on good authority that if the repres'ves in London will accept £40,000 by telegraph, that sum will be deposited here today in the Engl. Bank of the River Plate. The Govt. after all has had to rely mainly on its own resources, & has scraped together £30,000. The said bank will lend the odd £10,000. I am told that the local manager said he wld. be content with £20,000, the repres'ves of the rlwy. in England wanted £40,000 & Gibbs asked for £80,000. What is owing to the other two lines abt. wch. you telegraphed, the Northern & Northwestern, is not at present forthcoming. The foreign bank managers here do not care to lend money to the Govt., as it is outside their usual line of business. There is a rich bank, the Banco de Comercio, the shares of wch. are held by well to do Uruguayans, wch. one wld. think shld. be the first to offer funds to its own govt. but it is less disposed to help them than the managers of English banks.

The Midland rlwy. was one of those in wch. the late Santos was interested, & the present people consequently care very little abt. it. I observe that the chairman at the last meeting of shareholders, on being brought to book about the want of a dividend, quoted Palgrave's trade report as the authority for a statement made in the prospectus as to the exceptional richness of the country thro' wch. the line was to be constructed. The fact is, most of the

PRO 30/33 14/3   Semi-official Letters from Uruguay (August 4, 1890 – March 30, 1893)

rlwys. out here are contractors' jobs, who agree with govts. for huge guarantees wch. everyone knows they neither can nor ought to pay.

The Protocol abt. extradition has been sanctioned by the chambers, & a notice to that effect, of the usual kind, was published yesterday in the official gazette. I shall try to send it by the mail wch. closes this afternoon.

My desp[atch]. No. 9 Treaty encloses a memo. on the attitude to be assumed by Uruguay at the Postal Congress. The Minister tells me that this document does not represent the views of the govt., & that its publication was a piece of indiscretion on the part of the Postmaster-Genl. But no 'démenti' [official denial of a published statement] published, & I think there is no doubt it represents what Uruguay will ask for. The fact is, the internal post office is administered in an extravagant manner, with abt. 5 times as many officials as are necessary; and newspapers are forwarded all over the republic free of charge. The cost of this free transmission ought to be borne by the Education Dept. not by the foreign posts. Also Uruguay pockets all the charges on unpaid letters wch. are considerable in amount, especially on letters from Italy. And she does not pay a cent for the transport of the mail sacks, not even for landing or shipping them.

Politically everything seems perfectly quiet here. No one wants to imitate the example of the Chilians.

      y.v.t.

25. Satow to Barrington[11]

May 14. 1891.

D[ea]r. Mr. Barrington,

I have written officially asking for leave of absence, & add a few lines privately by way of explanation. Family affairs partly and partly the state of my health make it desirable for me to come to England as soon as possible. Owing to my having had no vice consul to whom the consulate cld. be entrusted, I have been able to get but little change from Montevideo. From what has reached me indirectly I fear Mr. Grenfell is not likely to take

---

[11] Sir Eric Barrington (1847-1918) was Principal Private Secretary to Lord Salisbury (in his role as Foreign Secretary), 1886-92.

PRO 30/33 14/3 Semi-official Letters from Uruguay (August 4, 1890 – March 30, 1893)

up his appointment at present. Neither of my clerks has sufficient experience or judgment to be placed in charge as Acting consul-general, and such an apptmt. would be very distasteful to the native Authorities. I have therefore suggested that a secretary from the diplomatic service should be sent here during my absence. If that arrangement were made he could have the use of my house rent free (unless I should be able to let it furnished during my absence, wch. is hardly likely). Probably he would dine at a hotel as some of the bachelor diplomats do. He wld. then have to bring only such plate and linen as he required for himself. I should expect to be away fr. Montevideo for not more than six mos. the length of my accumulated leave.

  y.v.t.
   E.S.

26. Satow to Bergne
May 14, 1891.
My dear Bergne,

 These ingenious Orientals [Uruguayans] have started another hare. They insist upon it that in addition to exchanging ratifications of the protocol I signed a short time ago, I must be provided with a separate Full Power for the mere exchanging:- unless, they add, the Power I already have includes this. I have looked at it, & find that it does not contain the word "exchange". I am going to show them a copy & ask them whether the words "do & transact all such other matters as may appertain to the finishing of the aforesaid work", are sufficient.

 If therefore I should telegraph that a Power for exchanging is needed you will understand what it all means.

   y.v.t.

27. Satow to Sanderson (p.26)
May 14. 1891
Dear Sanderson,

 The £40,000 required for the Midland rlwy. coupon was paid in to the Montevideo

PRO 30/33 14/3   Semi-official Letters from Uruguay (August 4, 1890 – March 30, 1893)

agents of the Co. on the 5th. Immediately afterwards on the 7th a sort of ministerial crisis was produced, by the Minr. for Education & Public Works tendering his resignation on the ground that the military estimates were excessive. It was supposed that this wld. drag down the whole cabinet. I went to see the Minr. for F.A. on the 8th & found him very despondent. I urged on him that he and the other two, Finance & Interior, shld. stick to their posts. Then he brightened up after a bit, & said that in his own opinion there was no reason for resigning & that the Budget for 1891-2 showed an estimate & surplus of over $1,000,000. They remained in, & a substitute for the makebate [a person who causes contention or discord] was immediately found. I hope therefore that we shall go on comfortably again for a while.

I have written officially & privately also to Mr. Barrington asking for leave of absence. My health needs a change & for family reasons I want to get home. [End of letter]

28. Satow to Sanderson
May 28. 1891.
Dear Sanderson,

I received the telegram of the 14th on the following morning, & sent for the local agent of the Northwestern rlwy, who is a certain Téofilo Dias, well in with all the official people. It was agreed betw. us that he shld. go to the Min. of Finance & try to frighten him with the idea of my having recd. telegraphic instructions, for if there is anything these people particularly dread, it is diplomatic intervention. I also took an opportunity of speaking to the Minr. for F.A. abt. 10 days ago when he was here one evening. Up to the present date nothing has been done towards satisfying the Northwestern claim, wch. as far as I can learn amounts to $115,000 or £24,500 for the year ending 30 Apr. 1890, besides a probably similar amount for the succeeding 12 mo[nth]s, the accts. of wch. have not yet been passed. The Minr. of Finance has promised to pay down £16,000 & to telegraph to Baring Bros. in liquidation undertaking to be responsible for £14,000 advanced by the latter to the rlwy. Dias says he expects this to be done in the first week in June. I have not been able to see the Min. of Finance myself, being practically confined to the sofa by a temporary lameness, but I shld. prob. not have been able to get any more than this out of him in a personal interview,

PRO 30/33 14/3 Semi-official Letters from Uruguay (August 4, 1890 – March 30, 1893)

as he is the throes of producing his Budget.

On the 26th & for a day or two before rumours of a conspiracy agst. the President were flying abt. As far as I can learn, one of the 5 colonels in command named Estevan, had sounded a brother colonel as to the side he wld. take in the event of a military outbreak, but he was promptly denounced to the President, who had them all to his house and explanations were given. He will no doubt be removed fr. his command, but there was no danger, I believe, of any trouble, nor can I see any.

  y.v.t.
    E.S.

P.S. The financial condition seems to be improving, & on the 1st June the National bank will revert to specie payments as far as the lesser notes ($5, $2 & under) are concerned.

29. Satow to Bergne

28.5.91

My dear Bergne,

I have succeeded in convincing the Min. for F.A. that a Full Power is not needed for the exchange of ratifications.

In a book much relied on here, the Guia práctica del diplomatico Español of de Castro Casaleiz, vol. 1 p. 406 there is a form of Full Power for the exchange of ratifications, wch. had prob. misled him. I had prepared a crushing memo. on the subject, with the aid of Calvo, but it seems to be no longer required.

  y.v.t.

30. Satow to Sanderson (p.28)

2 June 1891.

Dear Sanderson,

I enclose a memorandum of what I know abt. Barne's case, regretting its great length. As far as I recollect I never heard he was <u>adjudicated</u> a Bankrupt, but he had run away fr. his creditors & had committed an act of bankruptcy. That was quite enough reason I thought for withdrawing the few words I had said on his behalf. Prince Devan is quite accurate in

PRO 30/33 14/3   Semi-official Letters from Uruguay (August 4, 1890 – March 30, 1893)

saying that I refused to give any reason. He omits however to say that all this occurred months before the sudden termination of negotiations with Barne. He went into the business, I shld. say, with his eyes open. I never knew why he cried off at the last moment, for Barne's "rudeness" was evidently only a fortunate pretext.

    y.v.t.

      E.S.

31. Satow to Sanderson

June 11. 1891.

Dear Sanderson,

As soon as I was able to get about again, I went to work to stir the Min. of Finance up about the Northwestern guarantee, but without success. What I had been told of the promise to pay £16,000 during the 1st week in June must have been untrue. The day before yesterday & again yesterday I spoke to the Minr. of Finance, and he tells me that the offer he made to the Co's representative here was of 10 square leagues of pasture land (as I wrote in my official no. 9 of April 20), but this had been refused.

Both he & the Minr. for F.A. openly spoke of the other railway, the Midland, as a "clavo", which seems to be a combination of job and swindle. Still to save it from bankruptcy they had made an effort to pay the guarantee; but the Northwestern was not in the same urgent position & moreover having been the recipient of great favours in former times, ought to be willing to do a service in their turn to the Oriental Govt.

I suppose it is natural that the men now in power, who did not share in the sums given for these concessions, should be irritated at the idea of being now obliged to pay the piper.

They are sending a Dr. Ellauri (a former president) to London on a miscellaneous financial mission, to endeavour to obtain a reduction of the rlwy. guarantees; the further unification of the debt, and a modification of the scheme for its extension; at present the bonds are paid off at par & by annual drawings. They want the bondholders to give this up, and to allow them to buy bonds in the open market with the money destined for the drawings. In that way, they say, the capital of the debt wld. be reduced twice as fast as at present. One may well doubt however whether the money wld. be so applied.

PRO 30/33 14/3   Semi-official Letters from Uruguay (August 4, 1890 – March 30, 1893)

The new Venezuelan Minister here, after presenting his credentials in Paraguay is going to Washington, where I am told by the Min. for F.A. there is to be a meeting of Venezuelan representatives in all America, to discuss the questions in dispute between Venezuela & G.B. & what they expect to get by it is the aid of the United States.
   y.v.t.
     E.S.

Memorandum referred to in letter [dated 2 June 1891, no. 30 above] on p.55[12]

The first mention I find of Captain Barne amongst my papers is an entry in my journal [diary] under date April 7, 1886. "Devan told me that Barne had applied for an appointment, dating fr. the British Consulate-General. I said it was incredible."[13]

Capt. Barne had been some time in Bangkok, & was staying at the house of his friend Mr. Peter Hamel, the Netherlands consul-general. He had more than once been to see me abt. a promised concession of the Kabin gold mines, & had asked me to use my influence on his behalf. So on the 24th April, while waiting for our audience of the King, I said to Prince Devan that I hoped the authorities wld. regard Capt. Barne's application with favour, or words to that effect.

A few days afterwards in reading a law report, I came upon Capt. Barne's name. Whether it was in the "Times" as Mr. French suggests I cannot say. I am certain however that either then or afterwards I saw a report of the matter in the official "Law Reports", wch. are furnished to H.M. Legation in Bangkok; & wch. I generally read soon after their arrival. It appeared that some one had taken proceedings in bankruptcy agst. Capt. Barne, & that his solicitor had put in an affidavit in which some explanation was offered of Capt. Barne's not appearing in court.

---

[12] Satow appears to have numbered each single page, just as a book is numbered. The stamped numbers – apparently added later at the Public Record Office in accordance with usual practice – appear on the top right corner only, and refer to two pages. Thus the Memorandum here appears on p.59 (Satow's numbering) and p.30 (stamped number).
[13] The diary entry actually reads: "Barne. He says B. has applied for our apptmt. & dates fr. the British Consulate-Genl. I said it was incredible."

PRO 30/33 14/3   Semi-official Letters from Uruguay (August 4, 1890 – March 30, 1893)

I took an early opportunity of asking Capt. Barne abt. the matter. He was in the habit of using visiting cards with the name of a Club (I think the Junior United Service) and "Ham House" on them. I said to him that I had seen this report of proceedings, wch. in my opinion implied that he was a bankrupt, & that in consequence he cld. hardly be any longer entitled to call himself a member of the club; & that he was certainly not residing at Ham House. I therefore thought he ought not to use such cards in Bangkok, & inquired whether he had heard of these proceedings. He replied that he had not. I expressed my suspicion that his solicitor had not communicated with him. He answered that at the time of the proceedings he was in Brussels, & had forgotten when leaving for the east to send any directions to his solicitor for letters to be forwarded to him. I do not recollect whether I said I shld. withdraw what I had said abt. his application to Prince Devan, but I made him understand that I looked on him as a doubtful character. For, a day or two afterwards Mr. Hamel came to ask me for an explanation. I told him exactly how the matter stood, & probably showed him the law report. He informed me that he had made Capt. Barne's acquaintance on the west coast of Africa, & that they had been very intimate there. Barne a short time ago had written to him that he had got into difficulties in connection with some glass works, & had lost everything. Mr. hamel had lent him £500 & invited him to come out to Bangkok to try his fortune. I told Mr. Hamel that to all appearance Barne had run away from his creditors.

Under the date 15th May I find the following entry in my diary: "Barne. Said I wished him [Prince Devan] to consider as unsaid what I had said to him about Barne before seeing the King on the 24th ult[im]o. He replied that Barne had offered £1000 down for the sapphire mines [of Phailin] and various other advantages, but he had declined. They did not wish any concession to fall into the hands of Frenchmen on that side and they were afraid of Barne."

"I said I knew nothing of Barne; he had dined with me once and that was all. But I should not have liked to see the sapphire mines given to him over the heads of the [Asiatic] British Subjects, who were working there and paying their dues."

I was absent from Bangkok on sick leave between June 7 and Sept. 28. After my return I heard that Capt. Barne had been prospecting in the interior, & that he was carrying on

PRO 30/33 14/3   Semi-official Letters from Uruguay (August 4, 1890 – March 30, 1893)

negotiations with Prince Devan for a concession of gold mines.

Under date of Jan. 27, 1887 I find another entry recording a conversation with the Prince: "Barne has written him [Devan] rather a rude & threatening letter abt. his desired concession. I repeated what I had said before, that I did not wish to be understood as in any way favouring Barne's application, & that I withdrew what I had once said in his behalf."

My impression is that Capt. Barne was at the date referred to living as a free patient at the Bangkok Hospital under Dr. [William] Willis' care. He came to see me one day and showed me the correspondence. I told him, as far as I can recollect, that he had no legal claim agst. the Siamese Govt, but I thought they had not behaved well to him.

Again on Feb. 12 I find an entry of another conversation: "<u>Barne</u>. Why did he [Prince Devan] go out of his way with his eyes open to promise a concession to Barne & then put him off until the invalid became impatient & wrote a peevish letter. I thought he had treated Barne very badly, & was very sorry for it. He would not appear in a very favourable light if Barne were to publish his letters. I did not intend to take up Barne's case, but as one gentleman speaking to another, I felt that he had gratuitously made a promise which he had no intention of fulfilling."

"He [Prince Devan] spoke very vehemently abt. the 'rudeness' of Barne's letter. Barne had apparently adopted Hamel's "rude straightforwardness" on which he prided himself. He said Hamel had gone abt. Bangkok saying what Barne wld. get out of them, etc. I begged him not to believe in or listen too much to the stories carried to him. If he listened to gossip, he could not prevent his judgment being warped."

"He [Devan] tried to make out that in his note promising to fix a day for signature he had mentioned the necessity of consulting the other departments. I reminded him however that I had read his note, & knew that it contained nothing of the sort. I had also seen Michell's letter & that of Phra: Phairat. He said it would be a warning to him not again to do anything for people he knew nothing of. I said my conscience was clear: six months after I had said to him that I withdrew whatever I had said in Barne's favour, he chose to promise a concession. He said that Gowan had also applied for the same concession, & he had to treat all the applicants equally."

That is the last entry I have been able to find. I have an impression that Capt. Barne went

PRO 30/33 14/3   Semi-official Letters from Uruguay (August 4, 1890 – March 30, 1893)

down to Singapore, & tried to induce Sir F. Weld, who was then Govr. of the Straits Settlements, to take up his case, but I forget the results.

The report of Barne's case referred to will I think be found in the Law Reports publ. in the last quarter of 1885 or first quarter of 1886.

It will be seen from a comparison of dates that Prince Devan was not prevented by what I said to him in April & May from negotiating with Capt. Barne for the grant of a concession some months later. That then everything was settled except the date for the signature of the agreement. Various delays were made, which drew from Barne an angry & peremptory letter, & the negotiations were then broken off.

(signed) Ernest Satow
Montevideo
June 2, 1891

32. Satow to Sanderson (stamped p.34)
July 9, 1891
Dear Sanderson,

I learn on excellent authority that the Brit. st[eame]r. SS "Wandle" which passed thro' Montevideo on the 3rd inst. bound to Pensacola in the U.S. has just transshipped a cargo of arms to the Chilian insurgent transport Maipó, making use of the Falkland islands for the purpose. The transfer was effected in a bay close to Port Stanley. What the newspapers say abt. its having taken place in the Straits of Magellan is therefore incorrect. The Maipó arr[ived]. first, & told the Port Stanley Authorities that she was going to Madeira, & under that pretext obtained 75 tons of coal. Despatches fr. the Govr. to the Col. Office wch. are forwarded in my bag doubtless tell the whole story.

The "Times" correspondent in Chile [Maurice H. Hervey] passed thro' yesterday in the "Liguria" homewards; he maintains that he is right & the rest of the English in Chile wrong about the merits of the contest. I did not see him. We get very little trustworthy news here

PRO 30/33 14/3   Semi-official Letters from Uruguay (August 4, 1890 – March 30, 1893)

about Chilian affairs. Balmaceda has an agent here, one Luis Cardozo, formerly Chilian Consul-genl. in Madrid. He told me the other day that he had forwarded from here viâ Buenos Aires and the pass over the Andes a cargo of Winchester rifles from the United States, wch. were transshipped from an U.S. steamer into a local one at Rio, & so conveyed to Montevideo.

The Venezuelan envoy is still here, but shortly proceeds to Paraguay, & then home again. Several people have told me that the object of this mission, the first ever sent to the River Plate, is to create sympathy for Venezuela in her dispute with us. He disseminates a pamphlet entitled "Venezuela y la Gran Bretaña, cuestion limites de Guayana" and various maps illustrative of the progress of negotiations. As it was printed at Caracas, I have no doubt you have recd. copies. I called on him on the 5th July wch. is the Venezuelan anniversary; we had previously exchanged cards.

Many thanks for your telegram abt. Grenfell's departure from England & my leave. I hope to get away on the 3rd Septr. & to arrive in London about the 26th.

y.v.t.

E.S.

33. Satow to Pakenham
Private
21 July 1891
Dear Mr. Pakenham,

Many thanks for sending me a copy of your letter to F.O. abt. charges on vessels in distress. I had recd. a similar instruction to cooperate with my U.S. Colleague, but I do not find him disposed to take up the question, & hitherto scarcely have thought any more abt. it. I went very fully into the matter a couple of years ago, & when Admiral Grant was here discussed it frequently with him. It does not appear that anything can be done. Everybody is in league to make as much out of the underwriters as possible. The Capt. of the port shares with the tug owners in the enormous amounts claimed for salvage. If a case were brought into court things wld. go no better.

The only possibly [possible] remedy, wch. I suggested two years ago, would be for

PRO 30/33 14/3   Semi-official Letters from Uruguay (August 4, 1890 – March 30, 1893)

Lloyds to appoint <u>an honest man</u> here as their agent on a fixed salary, and they wld. probably have to change him every two years at least.

The F.O. people probably know as well as we do that nothing can be done, but it suits them to appear obliging, and so they pass the Lloyds letter on to us to see what reply can be made.

I suppose you have recd. as I have, an instruction to negotiate with the Argentine Govt. for the exemption of sons & grandsons of English parents from service in the army or national guard. I have sounded the Oriental Minr. on the subject, & he won't hear of it. The majority of Englishmen's sons have become Orientals voluntarily, & would not care to be exempted. The likelihood of their being called on to serve in the National Guard is extremely small, and as for the army, that is recruited by voluntary enlistment.

There has been much excitement here abt. a rumoured official note of Krauel to the Argentine Govt. abt. the provincial loans & cédulas; it has also been stated that van Bruyssel would follow suit, & that you were presenting a claim for the murders of British subjects in Corrientes years ago.

There was reprinted here yesterday an article signed Sarandé from La Prensa, about the threatened separation of Rio Grande from Brazil, & its union with Uruguay to form a Cisplatine Republic. Whatever the designs of Rio Grandenses may be, I feel persuaded that the Uruguayans would never willingly combine with them, & that they would rather join the Argentine Confederation. They hate everything that is Brazilian as a Dutchman does a German.

  y.v.t.

<u>34. Satow to Sanderson (p. 37)</u>
July 24/91
Dear Sanderson,
 Concerning my desp[atch]. Commercial no. 15 of yesterday
 The mail has been delayed for 24 hrs. & I have at last managed to get hold of the Min. of Finance. He showed me a letter from Matthew B. Hale & Co. of Buenos Aires, written as Barings agents, & assuring him that they had never pressed the Northwestern of Uruguay

171

PRO 30/33 14/3   Semi-official Letters from Uruguay (August 4, 1890 – March 30, 1893)

for repayment of the £14,000, and that they were willing to let it stand over for the present, not wishing to be hard on the Uruguayan Govt. That they (the Govt.) were plunged into tremendous difficulties by the suspension of the English Bank of the River Plate, whose bills they hold to the amount of £95,000. This was destined to meet the coupon. They hope to get a further loan of $2,000,000 fr. Rio bankers & their minister there assures them it can be done, but up to the present moment they have not got the money.   As to Barings saying that "they have not recd. instructions for transfer to Oriental Bank of liability for £14,000" he had not negotiated directly with Barings, but with a Mr. German Colladon, who is the agent of Matthew B. Hale & Co. who are Baring's agents. There is evidently a mistake somewhere, and I conjecture that in my desp[atch]. No. 11 of June 10 I must have written Oriental Bank instead of Oriental Govt.

The financial position is really very serious. The English Bank that has just failed holds about $700,000 in notes of the National Bank, wch. it could not possibly pay. To save it from a run, the Govt. decreed at first 3 days holiday until yesterday, and then extended it to tomorrow. Whether on the 27th they will be any better off seems to me doubtful. Anyhow, it would not be of the slightest use to press for the payt. of the Northwestern of Uruguay Rlwy. guarantee. I am afraid that they may even have to suspend paying interest on their debt. The payt. of all their officials, & the army is now between 4 & 5 months in arrear. Mr. Allan Darton the manager of the N.W.R. of Uruguay thinks with me that it is of no use to press them, & he has advised his directors agst. diplomatic intervention, wch. only creates a hostile feeling to them. The Central of Uruguay refused to join the other three minor railways in their representations to the F.O. & of course have been making capital out of their abstention.

   y.v.t.

35. Satow to Sanderson (p.38)
Aug. 20. 1891.
Dear Sanderson,
 Grenfell arr[ived]. on the 9th and I am leaving by the "Magdalena" on the 3rd Sept.
 The "Espiègle" came in from Chile on the 15th with 25 tons of silver sent by Balmaceda

PRO 30/33 14/3   Semi-official Letters from Uruguay (August 4, 1890 – March 30, 1893)

to pay for the "Aquila". It was landed & lodged in the London & River Plate Bank wch. has purchased it from the Chilian Govt. agents. On the 17th the Congressional Agent at B.A. telegraphed at great length to the manager of the bank, protesting agst. the whole transaction, & trying to frighten him with hints that when the Congress party came into power they wld. bring an action. The manager came to me, & I told him that in my opinion he was perfectly safe in purchasing silver from any de facto govt. The telegrams from Santiago of yesterday seem to indicate that the congressionalists are beginning to move, but as the telegraphs are in Balmaceda's hands we learn only what he chooses to make known. Govt. people here insist that the 'revolution' must fail. The Comr. of the Espiegle on the other hand says there is no doubt of its ultimate triumph.

   y.v.t.

36. Satow to C.M. Kennedy[14] (p.39)

[Note: This letter has been cancelled by Satow with two vertical lines and the word "Cancelled" written at the top.]

Private.

M.V.

Feb. 22. 1892.

Dear Mr. Kennedy,

In his Commercial No. 1 of Jany. 25 last Grenfell wrote that he could not find the circular of July 30, 1891 containing the report of the Rule of the Road Committee, but in fact we have received it. In the register however it is described as "Collisions at Sea" & so he must have overlooked it.

I spoke to the Minr. for F.A. about it on the 20th, & found that he referred the matter to the War dept. abt. 2 months ago, & had not yet recd. their answer. I will write officially when I hear from him that they agree.

   y.v.t.   E.S.

PS. I had to pass ten days in quarantine on my arrival here, in violation, as it seems to me,

---

[14] (Sir) Charles M. Kennedy (1831-1908). Senior Clerk, Commercial and Sanitary Department, Foreign Office, 1872-1894.

PRO 30/33 14/3   Semi-official Letters from Uruguay (August 4, 1890 – March 30, 1893)

of the provisions of the Sanitary Convention of Rio. It is a serious hindrance to trade that steamers should have to refuse cargo & passengers from Rio to the River Plate, & yet on arriving here find that they are subjected to as rigorous quarantine as if they had not observed the convention. I hope to work on my Argentine colleague here and get the matter arranged.

   E.S.

37. Satow to Sanderson

Mar. 3. 1892.

Dr. Sanderson,

 Owing to the yellow fever at Rio I had to undergo quarantine on my arrival here, but managed to pass the time on board the "Magdalena" instead of going to the lazaretto. The few people I saw & the local newspapers were full of the uneasy political situation, discontent of the Colonels, approaching downfall[l] of Julio Herrera. I landed on the 19th February. The next evening after dinner I was disturbed by news that a regiment had revolted & the President had taken refuge in the Cabildo. So I put on my hat & walked out to see what had taken place. There was no revolution after all. But some overzealous policeman had telephoned to the President that the Regt. of Light Artillery was coming in the direction of Montevideo, and he, for a moment perh. , thought there was a row on. But by the time I got to the Square, he had gone back quietly to his own house. The Col. of Artillery was one of the men employed by the President to get up the comedy of a revolutionary movement in October last, & every one was rather surprised on the 23rd to find that he had been removed fr. his command on the pretext that his regiment, by going out to exercise at an unusual hour, had "infused alarm into the bosom of the govt." Some people think that the Col. was trying it on, & that if no notice had been taken he wld. a few days later, after people had got accustomed to these nocturnal promenades of troops, have marched into town & taken possession of the govt. house. This is quite possible in a country where every soldier is ready to make himself dictator if opportunity offers. Herrera had I think been preparing this coup agst. the Colonels, for he was ready to reorganize his cabinet at a moment's notice, when the Minr. of War resigned, and on the afternoon

PRO 30/33 14/3 Semi-official Letters from Uruguay (August 4, 1890 – March 30, 1893)

previous I had been semi officially told that the ex-minister for F.A. wld. shortly come back to office. Instead of the alarmed countenances I met with on the 19th, now I find restored confidence on every side. People who were before among the worst croakers[15] now assure me that the President may securely hope to complete his other two years of office.

With regard to finance I find the Govt. punctually paying 45% of the Customs revenue daily into the Lond. & R.P. Bank, and I do not share the forebodings of those who shake their heads and ask 'how long will it last'.

If the President were kicked out and a military dictatorship set-up, doubtless the first thing wld. be to repudiate all his financial arrangements. But there seems no likelihood of such an upset, and it is to his interest to pay the reduced coupon if he can.

I am sorry I was not able to say goodbye before I left, but I did not know that you were away until the last day or two.

Things seem to be quiet in Rio Grande. I do not in the least believe in the province separating from Brazil in order to set up in partnership with Uruguay.

   y.v.t.

38. Satow to Pakenham (p.41)

4/3/92

Dr. Mr. Pakenham,

My French Colleague has sent a note, of which the enclosed is a copy, to the Oriental [Uruguayan] Govt. protesting agst. the quarantine now imposed on ships that touch at Rio, no matter how rigidly they may have observed the regulations of the Sanitary Convention as far as in them lies.

He is very anxious that Mr. Rouvier, yourself & I shld. join him in this step.

It appears that the Messageries boats actually observe the rule abt. discharging fr. one side of the ship only, & during the day only. Like the Royal Mail & other Engl. steamers they have not been able to procure Sanitary Inspectors, & there is no properly isolated pontoon. They too, discharge their cargo into lighters procured by their local agents.

---

[15] Croaker: a person who talks dismally.

PRO 30/33 14/3   Semi-official Letters from Uruguay (August 4, 1890 – March 30, 1893)

I had thought it might be possible to do something by working with Moreno, who being one of the signatories of the convention, considers it in some manner his own child with wch. he can deal, but St. Chaffray seems to have had a passage of words with him on the subject last Friday, and I fear he may be less amenable.

If you shld. be disposed however to address to the Argentine Govt. a Note, based on the representations of the Royal Mail Co's agent at Rio, & will kindly give me a copy of what you write, I am quite ready to follow suit. Especially as the Company's agents both here and at Buenos Aires, having interests of their own to cherish, do not trouble themselves about those of the Company.

I have taken an opportunity of speaking to the President and to the Min. for F.A., so that as far as I am concerned they are probably prepared for some kind of official remonstrance.

This morning's telegrams announce that you are probably destined to succeed Plunkett[16] at Stockholm. If there is any foundation for the report, let me offer you my congratulations. Can it be that Plunkett is going to Lisbon? It wld. probably suit his wife's health better than Stockholm.

   y.v.t.

39. Satow to ? (p.42)
7 Mar. 1892
Sir,

In reply to your letter of the 1st Feby. with reference to my subscription, I beg to state that I left England on the 14th January last, and regret very much any inconvenience that may have been caused by my not having officially communicated to you the fact of my departure from the United K[in]gdom.

As it is impossible that this letter shld. be in your hands by the 1st of April, seeing that there will be no English mail steamer from M.V. before the 10th instant, I infer that by the strict letter of Rule XIII I have made myself liable to a fine as well as to the loss of membership. The best thing I can do under the circumstances is to enclose a blank cheque

---

[16] (Sir) Francis Richard Plunkett (1835-1907).

PRO 30/33 14/3   Semi-official Letters from Uruguay (August 4, 1890 – March 30, 1893)

for you to insert the amount of my pecuniary liability, and I shall be much obliged if you will be so good as to acquaint me with the decision wch. the Committee may see fit to take in my case.

 I am &c.
  E.S.

P.S. I left Engl. by the Royal Mail Str. "Magdalena".

40. Satow to E. Cecil Hertslet

B.L. [British Legation]   M.V. [Monte Video]

7 Mar. 1892.

Dear Mr. Hertslet,

In ans[wer] to yr. note of the 4th ulto. addressed to Mr. Grenfell, requesting him to report the date & place of ratification of the Consular Convention betw. this country & Peru, the conclusion of wch. was reported by Mr. Palgrave in his desp[atch]. no. 6 commercial of Feb. 13, 1886 I beg to say that on applying for information to the Min. for F.A. here, I was told the convention in question never has been ratified.

 I remain
  y.v.t.

E. Cecil Hertslet Esq.

41. Satow to Sanderson (p.43)

April 13. 1892

Dear Sanderson,

The "Times" correspondent at B.A. [Buenos Aires] has been telegraphing home a story abt. the American Admiral having obtained from the Uruguayan Govt. a site for a coal depôt at M.V.

I think he is a little overexcited about the doings of the Americans in S.A. The facts are simply these: when it was thought that the U.S. might go to war with Chile they sent down two colliers here, (three others having got as far as the West Indies were stopped by orders from Washington) and after the squadron had filled up, the remainder of the coal was

177

PRO 30/33 14/3   Semi-official Letters from Uruguay (August 4, 1890 – March 30, 1893)

handed over to one Evans who is our naval contractor too, to dispose of, and he deposited a part in his own yard, & a part on Rat Island (also called Isla de la Libertad) in the bay of M.V. This island is rented by a syndicate of merchants from the Uruguayan Govt. The "Times" story is a maresnest. Herbert tells me he saw the letter fr. M.V. in wch. this information was conveyed to the "Times Correspondent", & he afterwards saw the writer (whom I know), who contradicted what he had himself written. My informants are the Senior Naval officer Captain Lang [and] Humphreys the Agent of the Royal mail. The Min. for F.A. laughed at the whole business. The jealousy of these people is far too lively to permit of any island or other site being given up to any foreign Power. They have just made a great row merely because the American Ad[miral]. thro' our vice Consul at Maldonado had obtained permission from the local authorities there to put a wire fence around the graves of half a dozen American and English sailors on Garrito island. Moreover they look with great suspicion on the attempts that are apparently being made to bring about an intimate understanding betw. the U.S. and the Argentines, and are not at all disposed to follow suit.

I have been unable to learn anything certain abt. the movements of the American squadron. But Herrero y Espinosa told me yesterday he believed Admiral was hanging on here until instructions should be recd. from Washington about some proposals made either by or to the Argentines when the squadron was recently at La Plata.

There has been some talk here about a bill being introduced into the Chambers providing for giving to resident foreigners the quality of citizens, without depriving them of their original nationality, but the govt. does not view it with favour, and it seems to have been dropped.

   y.v.t.

42. Satow to Sanderson
April 28. 1892
Dear Sanderson,

There is still some talk about the bill for compulsory naturalization of foreigners, but I doubt its being brought in, much less its being passed. Two of the Ministers to whom I have

PRO 30/33 14/3   Semi-official Letters from Uruguay (August 4, 1890 – March 30, 1893)

spoken on the subject are adverse to the project, and I have reason to believe that the others are also. Of course I have pointed out to them the uselessness to say the least of it of a measure wch. could only add a number of unwilling and therefore unfriendly citizens to the electorate. I shall report officially if it ever comes to a head, & in the meantime Wyndham has told me what was done in Brazil, wch. I suppose will be sufficient guide for me.

The Min. for F.A. has laid before the Fr. Ital & Germ. represves. a draft Convention recognizing the Uruguayan nationality of sons of Fr. Ital & Germs. respectively born in this country, the object being their exemption fr. military service if they visit the countries wch. at present claim their allegiance. The Germ. replied to him he wld. not injure his reputation by sending it home. The Italian I am told returned a similar answer. The Fr. is going to lay it before his govt.

The latter is also negotiating a treaty of commerce of the usual character. I cannot quite reconcile this with what Dr. Krauel told me had been said to him by the Min. for F.A. namely that they are looking forward to the year 1895 when out Treaty expires, in order that they may be free from all arrangements with regard to their tariff. The Uruguayans are trying to get Liebig's Extract admitted into France at something less than the minimum tariff rate, & would like to have some equivalent to offer.

The American Admiral in the "Chicago" left this morning for Barbadoes (to coal) & the U.S. The "Atlanta" follows in a few days. The third & last of the new vessels, the "Bennington" remains for the present as senior officer's ship, with two wooden sloops. This is the normal force which the U.S. usually have on this station.

43. Satow to Sir Roger Goldsworthy[17]

27 April 1892.

Dear Sir Roger,

I have just received another despatch from you addressed to "E. Grenfell Esq. H. Majesty's Minister", a clerical error of your copyist, I suppose. Mr. Grenfell's name is <u>Alfred</u> and during my absence on leave he was merely Acting Consul-genl. A reference to

---

[17] Sir Roger Tuckfield Goldsworthy (1839-1900) was Governor of the Falkland Islands from 1891 to 1897.

PRO 30/33 14/3   Semi-official Letters from Uruguay (August 4, 1890 – March 30, 1893)

Whitaker's almanac would enable your scribe to address your despatches correctly.

    Believe me

    yours very faithfully

        E.S.

44. Satow to Armstrong[18] (p.46)

28 April 1892

Dear Mr. Armstrong,

I have just received your private letter of the 26th inst. enclosing the £3 worth of surplus stamps. In order however that we may have an official record, I think that it will be better if you write to me an official dispatch, stating that on balancing the accounts of your vice consulate on the 31 March, you found yourself in possession of £3 of stamps more than you shld. have according to the entries in the fee book, and that you enclose them to me in a sealed packet.

I shld. be very glad to pay a visit to Salto, but at the present moment am laid up on the sofa with a bad knee, and see no prospect of being able to move abt. freely for a month or two to come.

    y.v.t.   E.S.

45. Satow to Matthews

Secy. Brit. & For. Sailors' Society

Mercer Street, Shadwell

Ap. 29. 1892.

Dear Mr. Matthews

I have been much gratified by the contents of your letter of the 22nd Mar. as it shows that we have been acting in full accord with the wishes of the Board of the British & Foreign Sailors' Society, & even anticipated them. One of the first steps I took after landing here was to see Mr. Williams abt. continuing the work of the Mission & Home, & to

---

[18] Vice-consul at Salto, north of Paysandú.

PRO 30/33 14/3   Semi-official Letters from Uruguay (August 4, 1890 – March 30, 1893)

organize a committee of workers. But we thought it desirable to carry on under the same superintendence & for the present under the same roof the relief of the indigent English speaking persons who from time to time present themselves, & at first Mr. Williams expressed his willingness to fall in with this arrangement. We started a "United Charities" committee and issued the enclosed circular. The salient feature of our plan is the collection of monthly subscriptions, wch. have been promised to the extent of $115 a month, instead of living on capital, as the former committee did. Out of these funds we shall try to do the purely charitable work of the Home & Mission, the Night Shelter, general relief of the poor, & providing passages to England now & then for people who are unable to work their way home by reason of infirmity.

It may perhaps be difficult to keep the accts. so far separate as to show exactly what is spent under each of these headings, but I think there is no doubt that we shall have to a certain extent to supplement the grant we get from you and from New York, & under the circumstances I hope the two societies will continue those grants as long as we keep the Home & Mission going. I found the general state of opinion to be such that it wld. have been quite impossible to maintain the mission & home in existence without combining with it other local charities.

Williams has however resigned, without stating any reasons in his letter of resignation. We are on the point I believe of engaging a man who will be at least as efficient.

    Believe me,

      y.v.t.

46. Satow to Bishop Stirling[19]

May 4. 1892

My dear Bishop,

I am much obliged for your two letters of April 29 and 30. The slip you enclose (and wch. I return herewith) is conclusive as to the necessity of the chaplain obtaining your license, and at the meeting of pewrenters yesterday I took an opportunity of saying very clearly that

---

[19] Waite Hockin Stirling (1829-1923). First Anglican Bishop of the Falkland Islands, 1869-1900.

PRO 30/33 14/3   Semi-official Letters from Uruguay (August 4, 1890 – March 30, 1893)

this was so by virtue of an arrangement betw. the Archbishop and the F.O. And I also said, in reply to a question abt. the form wch. Mr. Chamberlain's resignation had taken that in addition to addressing the Secy. of State officially, he wld. naturally inform yourself. I have not been able to find any trace of Lord Derby's circular in my archives, but that may be because in Octr. 1874 the F.O. decided (for a time) to cease its contributions in aid of the church at M.V.

At the meeting yesterday the only result arrived at was the carrying of a resolution to invite Mr. [Cecil] Luckman through Mr. Chamberlain, to come over for a Sunday or two, as very few of the subscribers present seemed to know him. When they have seen & heard him they will make up their minds. Perh. this was the best thing to arrange under the circumstances. Very few seemed to know anything of Mr. Shemield,[20] and I do not quite see how his name could be brought forward, unless the subscribers agreed to put the matter in your hands. But I imagine that what passed on a previous occasion with regard to Mr. Allen might possibly be a reason why you would not care to accept an invitation to nominate the chaplain. As far as I am personally concerned, I shld. be quite willing to leave the matter in your hands, but I conceive that having suggested to the Committee first Mr. Prichard and then on his refusal Mr. Luckman, I am pledged not to oppose the candidature of the latter. If the subscribers could possibly unite upon a choice, I should for many reasons think that person the preferable candidate.

47. Satow to Sanderson
May 12. 1892.
Dear Sanderson,

The bill conferring citizenship upon resident foreigners was after all read a first time in the Chamber of Deputies the day I last wrote to you. But two days later the originator published a letter in one of the papers saying that for the present he thought the project inopportune, & for that reason he had taken his name off the back of the bill. The idea was to get hold of the Italian population, all of whom are republican and anti-clerical in feeling.

---

[20] Rev. William Henry Shimield, Anglican chaplain at Salto, 1874-82.

PRO 30/33 14/3   Semi-official Letters from Uruguay (August 4, 1890 – March 30, 1893)

Consequently it was opposed by both the clericals & the genuine Uruguayans, who have no intention of being swamped by foreigners or sons of foreigners either, if they can help it. I conclude that for the present we shall hear no more of the matter.

When Genl. [George] Maney told me abt. his instructions to negotiate a reciprocity treaty[21] he had already been imbibing & he took two stiff tumblers of whiskey & soda while he was with me. <u>In vino veritas,</u> I think.

   y.v.t

48. Satow to Bishop Stirling

May 17, 1892.

My dear Bishop,

I have your two letters of the 6th & 13th, the latter enclosing four F.O. documents, wch. I now return. They most completely prove that your license is necessary in the case of the chaplain of M.V.

As to Mr. Luckman's leaving Córdoba it wld. be out of place for me to pretend to an opinion. But as it seemed very likely that he wld. be the choice of the pewrenters, I assumed as right to give him my advice, & particularly that he shld. abstain from trying to justify his having left that place, by putting a strained interpretation on the wording of his license "to Córdoba, Tucuman & any other place where no church work was provided for." I trust he has been to see you, & made his due submission. My presuming to advise him on this matter was of course solely based on the expectation of his being nominated here, & I was anxious that he shld. put himself right with you before he came to us.

Mr. Handcock seems to have greatly pleased a portion of the congregation last Sunday, & I hear unofficially that his chances are very good. If I hear anything more definite I will let you know.

One word of explanation I shld. like to offer you with regard to the omission of the Committee & myself to consult yourself from the first with regard to the choice of a chaplain. The Committee of course are elected merely to administer the church property, &

---

[21] On May 1, 1892 (diary).

PRO 30/33 14/3 Semi-official Letters from Uruguay (August 4, 1890 – March 30, 1893)

are not represves of the pewrenters in any matter of an extraordinary character. So that they cld. not have initiated any negotiation. On my part, having studied the past history of the church here, & found that on a previous occasion, after putting themselves in your hands, they had actually rejected the incumbent nominated by you, & chosen one for themselves, I did not like to run the risk of your being treated a second time with such discourtesy. I do not know of course, how far my predecessor's action in the matter contributed to this unfortunate step on the part of the subscribers, but I feared to suggest that the new chaplain shld. be nominated by you. Still, I hope that as soon as the choice is made, the trustees will communicate with you in proper terms, with a view to obtaining your sanction by the issue of a license. This wld. naturally be a more or less unofficial step on their part, as they have not <u>legally</u> anything to do with the apptmt. of the chaplain.

It is possible that some may wish to agree with the new chaplain for a short term of years; but this again could not be more that [than] a private understanding between the parties.

  Believe me,
   y.v.s.

<u>49. Satow to Luckman (p. 51)</u>
May 21, 1892.
Dear Mr. Luckman,

In answer to your letter of the day before yesterday, asking me to decide for you whether your candidature for the M.V. chaplaincy shld. be maintained or not, I regret very much to tell you that after consulting the trustees & one or two of those who had originally intended to support you, I have come to the conclusion that it wld. not be desirable to persevere with it. I shld. add that this consultation has been a private one. It is not that there is any feeling agst. you, but that Mr. Handcock seems to have interested a large number directly in his favour, & that he is as far as we can see the choice of the majority.

Let me add that I shall be very sorry if the withdrawal of your name shld. cause you more than a passing regret. I shall then feel that I have been the cause, by mentioning your name to the trustees in the first instance.

PRO 30/33 14/3   Semi-official Letters from Uruguay (August 4, 1890 – March 30, 1893)

Believe me

y.v.t.

50. Satow to Barrington (p. 52)

Dear Mr. Barrington,

By the last mail but one I recd. an official informing me that Grenfell had not passed his examination, & the Civil Service Comrs. have sent him a notice to say that a fresh nomination will be necessary in order that he may present himself a second time for examn. For the past six yrs. there has been only an acting consul or Vice-Cons. here, an arranget. wch. is very inconvenient, & I am anxious to see it come to an end. An acting man on half salary cannot be expected to be as zealous in the performance of his work as one who has the definitive apptmt. Grenfell is just over 49 so that before long he will have passed the limit of age. That he is likely to be a useful public servt. is sufficiently attested by the desp[atch]. written approving of his conduct of business here while he was acting consul-genl. the other day. It must be further to his credit that he had had absolutely no previous experience. He knows Spanish perfectly, and is persona grata with the native officials. If he is not apptd. I think it will prove very difficult to get the right sort of man for the very low salary of £400. For these reasons I shld. be glad to see an exception made in his favour, exempting him from the necessity of passing an examination, if feasible.

y.v.t.   E.S.

51. Satow to Cockerell

6 June 1892

My dear Cockerell,

Will you kindly send me a copy for my archives of the Annex to Circular Consular of Dec, 28. 1881. Owing to the Archives at this place not having been bound, papers are constantly going astray. We shld. also like a copy of the volume of consular instructions, the edition we have being very ancient.

My B.S. here are beginning to ask when the transfer of the cemetery Funds is to take place. I have to hold a general meeting of subscribers this month, & I shld. have been glad

PRO 30/33 14/3   Semi-official Letters from Uruguay (August 4, 1890 – March 30, 1893)

to be able to make an announcement on the subject.

I hope you are flourishing & not overwhelmed c. work.

   y.v.t.

52. Satow to Jervoise (p.53)

June 8. 1892.

My dear Jervoise,

I see from the newspapers that a blue book on Chile has come out recently.

Is there any objection to a copy of this being sent me from F.O. In fact I never get any F.O. parliamentary papers to speak of, though they wld. be much more useful & entertaining reading than the enormous packages of trade reports that reach me from time to time. You were so good as to promise me a copy of the blue bk. on China that you were editing abt. the time I left, but I am afraid it has slipped your memory.

This part of the world is famous for 'canards', thou' perh. in the absence of Mr. Thomson of the "Times" you may not get so many of them telegraphed. The last on hand is a rumour that the Argentines were going to annex Paraguay, wch. brought forth an indignant protest fr. the patriots of Asuncion.

I am told by my Brazilian colleague that the career of the "South Atlantic Republic" in Matto Grosso has come to an end.

   y.v.t.

53. Satow to Sanderson (p.54)

June 23, 1892.

Dear Sanderson,

Dr. Krauel [the German Minister] signed on the 20th his commercial treaty, and I expect shortly to be able to send home a copy. I imagine that it will be found to contain nothing new or special. Saint Chaffray is still negotiating.   The other trety proposed by Dr. Herrero y Espinosa to the Fr. Germ. & Ital. ministers, providing for the mutual recognition of nationality acc. to country of birth is "dead", as he recently told me with great frankness.

The latest topic of conversation is the breakdown of Mr. Noetzlin's negotiations with

PRO 30/33 14/3   Semi-official Letters from Uruguay (August 4, 1890 – March 30, 1893)

native capitalists for a combination to found the new Bank of Uruguay. The Senate refused to eliminate the clause providing for the nomination by the Govt. of the president of the board of directors. Various compromises were proposed, but none were acceptable to the capitalists. They wld. not consent to the Govt. having any handle for interfering with any bank in wch. they were to put their money. All sensible people approve of their attitude. Others say that 'capital is odiously unpatriotic'. For the moment therefore the govt. has no prospect of getting any money except from ordinary revenue. The Minr. of Finance Ramirez on the failure of what had been his pet scheme, resigned in a fit. This is much to be regretted, as his presence in the cabinet was a guarantee for honest endeavour to pay the foreign creditors. However, as his two allies Herrero y Espinosa & Genl. Perez remain, I think that things may continue to go smoothly. At the first symptom of any financial dishonesty Herrero will, I am pretty sure, send in his resignation.

The 'revolution' in Rio Grande does not affect this country at all. Matto Grosso is quiet again, and the Brazilian Govt. have now a naval force in the Upper Paraná sufficient for every purpose, including the prevention of any plans of annexation of Paraguay to the Argentine republic.

Adolfo Guerrero [the Chilean Minister] in presenting his credentials yesterday gushed greatly about the unblemished friendly relations betw. Chile & this country, but if one may judge by the language of the govt. people during the Chilian civil war, <u>they</u> at least have no love for the party at present in power at Santiago. That the Chilians are enemies of the Argentines &, still more, friends of Brazil, is sufficient ground to determine the feeling [of] Uruguayans against Chile.

<u>54. Satow to Lang</u>

July 6. 1892.

Dear Capt. Lang,

Thanks for your note of the 29 June wch. reached me yesterday. It gives me very great satisfaction to find that you are in agreement with me with respect to the incident of the 24th of June. I enclose for your perusal a copy of the desp[atch]. wch. I have written to Lord Salisbury, at the end of wch. I have suggested that as long as Prest. Herrera y Obes remains at Govt. House, that is till the end of Feby. 1894 no naval officer shld. ever call on him, & that on my part I shld. not go near him except on official occasions. The attitude we shall adopt we can now leave to H.M. Govt. to decide upon. If you can send Dr. Herrero y Espinosa's letter to the Admiralty without its losing its character as a private letter from him to me, I shall have no objections. You will see that I have sent a copy to the F.O. but then I have marked my desp[atch]. 'confidential'. It wld. not be convenient nor desirable for the correspce. to be made public in any way, and the word 'confidential' is intended to indicate that such is my opinion. It was Dr. H. y E who put the word 'particular', wch. corresponds to our 'private', on his letter.

I have been laid up with a mild attack of influenza, but am now better, the only results so far being a cold in the head and a temperature lower than the normal. There is still a good deal of it about in this country.

    y.v.t.
      E.S.

55. Satow to Sanderson
July 7. 1892.

Dear Sanderson,

The incident with the President reported in my desp[atch]. no. 23 of June 29th has not fortunately given rise to any further unpleasantness, and the only newspaper that reported it, gave him a proper measure of blame. It was simply a piece of bad manners. When a little lawyer suddenly finds himself exalted to a pinnacle of despotism, he loses his head, & fancies that he may treat everybody, foreign officials as well as his own ministers, as if they were his lacqueys. Lang behaved extremely well & left the matter entirely in my hands. I shld. have preferred to have an apology delivered on board the "Sirius" to Lang himself, but he had left before it was possible to arrange anything.

I have had to dismiss the consular clerk for peculation. Altho' I had established a rule that the fees shld. be paid into a bank weekly, he managed to evade this by receiving fees without putting on the stamps. He also made away with money received for seamen's wages that had to be remitted to the B. of T. [Board of Trade], altogether I suppose abt.

PRO 30/33 14/3   Semi-official Letters from Uruguay (August 4, 1890 – March 30, 1893)

£100. I am told that he was originally a son of Major Munro's washerwoman. I have put my legation clerk into his place, & have telegraphed for a nephew of mine named Reginald Allen, who has been out here before and whom I can trust.

My experience in Montevideo with subordinates picked up on the spot has not been fortunate. There was Mr. Ayre[22] who had to be sent about his business directly after my arrival, for having embezzled about £800. His predecessor Mr. Levum[?] died suddenly, in default to the British Hospital & owing money right & left. I wish the system could be altered.

56. Satow to Sanderson

14 July 1892

Dear Sanderson,

The German commercial treaty was published yesterday, and I expect to send it home next week. The French treaty was signed on the 5th but has not yet been printed. I believe it chiefly differs fr. the Germ. in the form of the 'most favoured nation clause'.

Saint Chaffray left for France on leave of absence the day before yesterday, his place being temporarily filled by Frédéric Mercier, a Secy. of Legation, who has just been transferred here fr. Mexico. St. Chaffray was not liked here, and managed to quarrel abt. questions of etiquette with the Brazilian & Argentine colleagues. He absolutely cut the former on several occasions.

I am told by the Min. for F.A. that in the recent fighting in Rio Grande between the Old Republicans & the Federalists, in wch. the latter got the worst of it, there were a good many Uruguayan mercenaries engaged. In one skirmish out of 30 killed 18 were Uruguayans. He also says that the so-called Federalists secretly aim at independence, and hinted that some day or other Rio Grande wld. become part of Uruguay. I told him that Rio Grande has still much to do before achieving its separation from Brazil. There is a very popular Spanish proverb wch. recommends fishing in troubled waters, these people no doubt have in their mind. Threats were uttered the other day by the victors in Rio Grande of crossing the

---

[22] See letters 5 through 11 above.

PRO 30/33 14/3   Semi-official Letters from Uruguay (August 4, 1890 – March 30, 1893)

frontier & seizing some of their opponents who had taken refuge at Rivera, but they thought better of it. The Uruguayans have sent a regiment of 300 cavalry to the spot.

One of the Argentine torpedo boats belonging to the squadron recently despatched to Spain for the Columbus celebration at Palos foundered at sea a few days ago, the captain & most of the crew being saved. The papers say that after leaving Spain, the squadron will be invited to visit France, and two of the ships will later on @roceed to England for new armaments.

I have paid the amounts wch. the consulate clerk had embezzled, in all some £166, including hospital fees collected from the shipping and collections for local charities. But I have given the Hospital Treasurer to understand that my doing so is not to be construed as a precedent of, and that H.M.G. are in no way responsible.

y.v.t.

57. Satow to Sanderson

4 Aug. 92

Dear Sanderson,

The alarm on the frontier has completely subsided, and so has the talk of Rio Grande separating from Brazil. The party to wch. designs of re-establishing the monarchy were attributed, of wch. Silveira Martins[23] was the reputed head, is entirely discredited. This is the man whom the Brazilian republicans, at the time of the revolution agst. Don Pedro took so much trouble to keep away from the province.

The President has not filled up the post of Minr. of Finance. H. y E. told me the other day that he expected C.M. Ramirez, on his return fr. Paraguay whither he has gone for his asthma, will reoccupy that post. If he does, there will be hope of Uruguay paying interest on its bonds. But the monthly salaries are again 3 months in arrear, & amongst foreigners there is talk of prob. repudiation. There is a bill before the chambers for the coining of $3,000,000 of silver & the issue of the same amount of convertible notes, wch. finds no favour with the outside public. Noetzlin, the agent or partner of Cassels, who has been here

---

[23] Gaspar de Silveira Martins (1834-1901). Brazilian politician.

PRO 30/33 14/3 Semi-official Letters from Uruguay (August 4, 1890 – March 30, 1893)

more than 2 months, has entirely failed in his negotiations for the establishment of the new National Bank on wch. so much was thought to depend; and also in making arrangements abt. the Western Railway for wch. Barings contracted to take about £1,500,000 of bonds at 85.

[crossed out: The Fr. commercial treaty does not amount to much; the export of Liebig's Extract to France is at present non-existent.]

In spite of the despondent tone in the press amongst commercial people, the customs revenue shows hardly any signs of decrease, and I do not myself see any good grounds for these people defaulting.

    y.v.t.

58. Satow to Lang
M.V.
4/8/92.
Dr. Capt. Lang,

I was much interested in reading the account of the "Sirius" performances at sea, and congratulate you on having such a fine vessel under your command. You have of course seen how the Argentines managed to lose their torpedo boat [though] the Capt. & most of the officers were saved; it seems curious that the commodore of the squadron shld. have gone on ahead without bothering himself abt. her. Many thanks for the programme of your movements. There is nothing stirring down here. The little row on the frontier towards Rio Grande seems to have been of no importance after all, but it is the habit of the people here to make a great cry about nothing at all.

    y.v.t.
     E.S.

59. Satow to Sanderson (p.60)
Aug. 18. 1892.
Dear Sanderson,

There has been no more talk of frontier troubles with the Rio Grande, but a story has

PRO 30/33 14/3   Semi-official Letters from Uruguay (August 4, 1890 – March 30, 1893)

been set in circulation abt. the unprovoked murder of Oriental Stockfarmers in that state by a Col. Elias, wch. however still lacks confirmation. A large number of Rio Grande fugitives have crossed over into the Uruguayan dept. of Cerro Largo, & are interned at the town of Melo. They are said to number betw. 5000 & 6000, but this sounds like an exaggeration. They gave up their arms, wch. consisted of old-fashioned firearms and lances hastily improvised out of blades of sheep shear. The principal man among them is a Dr. Barros Cassal,[24] who is the author of the talk abt. Independence & joining Uruguay. Herrero y Espinosa says that of annexation except as the result of a war there is no possibility, & that he looks upon the idea as an unrealizable utopia.

The Brazilian Govt. is putting off negotiations for a commercial treaty with this country, because they fear to offend Rio Grande by giving favourable terms in respect of jerked beef, the principal product of both Uruguay and the former.

Herrero y Esp. has some doubts whether he will be able to get his French Treaty through the legislature, on account of the dislike entertained here to the most-favoured-nation clause in any form. Ramirez the ex-finance Minr. is expected here in a few days, & I am almost certain that he will re-enter the cabinet in his former capacity. Every effort is being made to pay the interest on the debt, & the remittances go forward to Glyns with regularity. Reductions in the budget are promised, & as far as I can see at present, there is no danger of defaulting to be apprehended.

Grenfell is busy with a Trade Report wch. will be ready I hope for next mail. He is very delighted with his apptmt., news of wch. was telegraphed to him by his sister Mrs. Pascoe Grenfell.   y.v.t.   E.S.

60. Satow to Jervoise (p.61)
Aug. 18. 1892
My dear Jervoise,

Very many thanks for the bluebook[s] on China & Chile.

I have given a card of introduction to a Mr. F.B. Hill, who will bring to you a tin case

---

[24] Joao de Barros Cassal (1858-1903). Brazilian journalist and politician.

PRO 30/33 14/3   Semi-official Letters from Uruguay (August 4, 1890 – March 30, 1893)

containing the diplomas of our Hospital Doctor, wch. have to be revalidated by the Uruguayan Consul-Genl. in London, in order to enable him to take a degree here & practice. I shld. be very much obliged if you would allow these diplomas, wch. are not very big, to come out to me by bag, as I want to help Dr. Jamieson and the hospital.

So you have got your new chief. There is a telegram to say that the French are already talking abt. calling upon Mr. Gladstone to fulfill his pledges with regard to the evacuation of Egypt. The last thing my French colleague said to the Uruguayan Minr. before going on leave was: "I hope Mr. Gladstone will get in because then the English will have to clear out of Egypt."

   y.v.t. E.S.

61. Satow to Jervoise

1 Sept.

My dear Jervoise,

I am keeping back my desp[atch]. no. 28 of the General Series for next mail, as the enclosures are not yet ready.

Your despatch No 6 of the General series has not reached me.

   y.v.t.
    E.S.

62. Satow to Sanderson (p.62)

8 Oct. [1892]

Dear Sanderson,

I have sent you a short despatch recounting the main features of a little dispute these people had recently with the Argentines about dredging a channel leading to the Rivers Uruguay & Paraná, wch. happens to lie entirely within the jurisdictional waters of Uruguay. I tell it just as Herrero y Espinosa told it to me, and I think it is a bit of swagger on his part to represent that it might have led to a serious complication. I shall send a copy to [British Legation Secretary in Buenos Aires George] Welby,[25] so that he can give you a correct

193

PRO 30/33 14/3 Semi-official Letters from Uruguay (August 4, 1890 – March 30, 1893)

version if necessary from the Argentine point of view.

During the last five or six weeks the inhabitants of M.V. have had dangled before their eyes by President Herrera the prospect of a loan of $5,000,000 at 85%, the money to be found by Baron Reinach[26] of Paris. But now it seems to have fallen thro'. People talked as if the failure of this loan wld. endanger the position of the President, but I cannot see any signs of such a result. The country is suffering from prolonged drought, the crops may all be ruined, and cattle & sheep are dying for want of pasture. That ought to impoverish the republic still more, & increase the financial difficulties of the Govt. yet I see Uruguayan Unified Bonds are creeping upwards in London.

The Dutch are proposing to negotiate a commercial treaty, but their trade is of hardly sufficient importance to make it worthwhile.

 y.v.t.

63. Satow to Kennedy (p.63)
18/10/92

Dear Mr. Kennedy,

Will you kindly send me for my archives a second copy of the Report on fishing vessel lights enclosed in the Circular of 3 Sept. last. There came only one copy, & that I am sending to the Uruguayan Minr. In order to induce them to make up their minds with more clarity than on the previous occasion, I am having the whole thing put into Spanish.

 y.v.t.

64. Satow to Sanderson
M.V.

20/10/92

Dear Sanderson,

Last time I saw Dr. Herrera y Espinosa he began to speak again about Zeballos,[27] the

---

[25] Satow met Welby again on April 9, 1915 (diary).
[26] Probably the Jewish German banker Baron Jacques de Reinach (1840-92), though he died in 1892.

PRO 30/33 14/3   Semi-official Letters from Uruguay (August 4, 1890 – March 30, 1893)

late Argentine Min. for F.A. and to say that if he & Pellegrini had continued in office another year, there wld. have been a war in South America. He thinks that this continent has had a lucky escape from falling into the European condition, in wch. every state is armed agst. its neighbour. The duel of the future for wch. Central & South America ought to prepare wld. be with the U.S., and the former ought to cultivate close friendship that they may be able to act in union when the time comes. Then he alluded to the Chilian project of Genl. Körner for an army of 80,000 men, and added that the Argentines could easily raise 200,000 good soldiers in a fortnight, besides 25,000 Italian volunteers in B.A. All that the Argentine Repub. had to do was to sit still, and in 10 yrs. time by mere growth of population she wld. become the preponderant power in South America.

The cholera fright here seems to be abating & the Uruguayans have carried out what they promised, namely not to quarantine ships from English ports only, - notwithstanding the great pressure put upon them by the Argentines to quarantine everything & everybody.

y.v.t.

65. Satow to Bergne (p.64)

M.V.   25.10.92

My dear Bergne,

I hope you won't think I am boring you too much with despp. [despatches] abt. this absurd flag question. The Chilians it seems originated it, in order to find an excuse for annoying the U.S. by ceasing to celebrate the 4th July, & when they communicated the idea to the other S.A. Repubbs. [Republics] the latter all jumped at it, to show their determination to be treated on a footing of equality by la vieja y carcenida[?] Europa. ["the old and caring Europe"] The fact is the practice of hoisting flags &c. arose in old days, when these Republics were less populous & less self-important; the foreign consuls hoisted flags on the local anniversaries and the foreign men-of-war fired salutes. Then the local people reciprocated the compliment by hoisting flags & firing salutes on each consul's national day. It grew up spontaneously, without any thought of what was done in Europe.

---

[27] Estanislao Zeballos (1854-1923) was Argentine Minister for Foreign Affairs three times.

PRO 30/33 14/3   Semi-official Letters from Uruguay (August 4, 1890 – March 30, 1893)

Salutes came to an end some years ago, but flags remained. Suddenly out comes a decree in Chili, then in Buenos Aires & lastly here, insinuating that European govts. were not properly reciprocating these courtesies, and if they did not do so in future, S.A. wld. take no more notice of their anniversaries. This without a word to any of the corps dipl. [This part crossed out: "I found most of my colleagues disposed to regard the issue of this decree as an intended piece of impertinence, & we took no notice of it. At last after a fortnight's interval the Min. for F.A. sent us a copy, enclosed in a Note of the same date as the decree, in order to make it appear that there had been no delay on his part in communicating it. Our first idea was to say that if a change was desired this at any rate was not the way to bring it about, by proclaiming in the face of the world (of S.A.) that if Europe did not reciprocate in the matter of flags, they wld. cease to recognize her festivities and occasions of mourning."]

It never occurred to me, I confess, that the demand was for the Uruguayan anniversary to be celebrated in Engl. by hoisting the Union Jack on all our public buildings, but it seems this was H. y E's idea. I told him that it was impossible; if we did it for one we shld. have to do it for all, & that exact reciprocity was impossible; that courtesy ought to be spontaneous, and not a matter of bargain. Mr. Ribot[?] on the 25 Aug. last sent the Introducteur des Ambassadeurs to congratulate the Uruguayan Ch. d'Aff. who has accordingly reported the fact with great pride to his govt. & they have published his desp[atch]. in the papers, & they are going to reciprocate with an aide-de-camp. What is the exact equivalent of a Presidential aide de camp expressed in terms of F.O. functionaries? Here the custom is to send the band of one of the battalions to play God Save the Queen, Hail Columbia &c. before the respective legation; I suppose they will withdraw that too, unless the same thing were done in London for the Uruguayan Legation there. It may have been necessary in earlier times to stipulate with Chinese about forms and ceremonies, but if we begin to bargain with people of Spanish race about such things, we shall only be laying a foundation for eternal disputes.

We had a great todo early in the month abt. Columbus, and most of us after the fêtes were over heartily regretted that he had ever existed. But I suppose America was a useful outlet for the energies of the Spaniards of those days, and who knows whether they might

PRO 30/33 14/3   Semi-official Letters from Uruguay (August 4, 1890 – March 30, 1893)

not have made things very much more uncomfortable for England & France if they had not been so much occupied elsewhere picking up gold & silver. I have heard a Spaniard attribute the decadence of his country to the constant drain of the best fighting men that then took place to Mexico & Peru.

  y.v.t.

66. Satow to Sanderson (p.66)

2 Nov. 1892

Dr. Sanderson,

 I am going over to Buenos Aires today to see some friends, & expect to get back here on the 8th. There is nothing new here. The proposed loan of five million dollars of wch. there has been so much talk for the past two months is, as far as one can judge, to turn out a fiasco. Some people go as far as to say that there never were any proposals at all, but that the whole thing was got up by the President for political purposes. There had been some endeavours on the part of the Blanco party, who are the only people here with money, to gain over a few of the military leaders, in order to turn out the President. In order to counteract the machinations of his opponents he devised this proposed loan, wch. if obtained, wld. have gone far to satisfy the greed of his own supporters, who by this time must be very discontented. But I do not think there is any danger of such a conspiracy coming to a head: Herrera is a match for them all in intrigue.

  y.v.t.

67. Satow to Sanderson

24 Novr. 1892

Dear Sanderson,

 I have sent you a desp[atch]. abt. the state of things on the Rio Grande frontier. It appears that the man Vieira, mentioned in it as a secret agent, is a knave who does not scruple to forward all manner of groundless rumours as if they were facts, in order to prove his utility to his employers.

 The other day he reported also to Rio [de] Janeiro that Alvim,[28] the newly arrived

PRO 30/33 14/3   Semi-official Letters from Uruguay (August 4, 1890 – March 30, 1893)

Brazilian Minr. had been seen walking in the streets with Silveira Martins, and plotting agst. the Republican régime with him. S Martins used to be suspected of monarchical preferences, and Alvim I know from his conversation detests the republic. So the accusation produced a profound effect, and it was rumoured that Alvim was to be recalled. The Uruguayan Govt. has however telegraphed to Blas Vidal at Rio to say they hope he won't be removed, as he is agreeable to them. It is a fact that he walked with Martins, who is a college friend. I should be very sorry to lose Alvim, for he is one of the few civilized men in the place, and I see a good deal of him. He is an immense improvement on his predecessor Carvalho who has just gone to Lima.

This Govt. is well furnished with information as to what goes on at Rivera, because there is rlwy. communication all the way to the frontier. But in the other direction namely of Bagé, the rlwy. goes no further than Nico Perez [in Florida, central Uruguay], only abt. halfway; & the general in command of the frontier, Casimiro Garcia, who ought to be constantly at or beyond Melo, spends his time chiefly in M.V. So it is quite possible that things may not be so quiet on that part of the frontier.

It seems as if Chili, Brazil & the Argentine Republic were by no means satisfied of each other's pacific intentions. There is still much talk of an alliance betw. the two first, obviously agst. the third. The Argentines are said to have a contract with [Ludwig] Loewe [& Co.] for 150,000 perfected Mauser rifles, of what they call the Argentine pattern, & that until this quantity is delivered, the other two can get none. 50,000 with 1000 rounds each have already been delivered in B.A. The Argentines also asked the Lond. & River Plate Bank to advance them £150,000 towards payt. for an ironclad they are to get fr. Engl. I do not think the Argentines will break the peace, but they are afraid of the Chilians.

There is a proposal before the Chambers to authorize the conclusion of a convention with the Argentine Republic for the dredging of the Limetas channel at the mouth of the Uruguay & Paraná, in Uruguayan territorial waters, towards wch. this govt. is to contribute $15,000. This I expect will speedily be arranged, but it is said that the dredging will take several months to complete, and the consequence additional cost of freight on corn to

---

[28] Julio Henrique de Melo e Alvim

PRO 30/33 14/3   Semi-official Letters from Uruguay (August 4, 1890 – March 30, 1893)

exporters, will be about $3,000,000 in paper I suppose, or about £200,000. y.v.t.

68. Satow to Sanderson

Dec. 8 [1892]

Dear Sanderson,

[T]he Manager of the Lond: & R.P. Bank, who receives the 45% of Customs Duties for payt. of interest on the Consolidated Debt came to see me yesterday & told me confidentially that he thought this country wld. default before long. There was considerable difficulty in paying the last coupon. The next will be paid, but with increasing difficulty. After that, unless trade revives greatly, or reductions are made in the expenditure, the Govt. must stop pay[men]t. The Council of Foreign Bondholders, Glyns, the L. & R.P.B. people in London, & Noetzlin know this. Noetzlin is the agent of a Mr. Cassels, and arranged the reduction of interest last year for the Uruguayans. They are not at all grateful to him, & accuse him of having pocketed an enormous sum for commission, while their agent Ellauri got only about £16000.

Genl. Maney the U.S. colleague has come back, having left N. York before the election of the new President. He seems to have some hope of being allowed to stay on here. He is generally half intoxicated by dinner time.

The agitation on the frontier of Rio Grande continues, and there seems good reason to suppose that the Argentines are supplying arms for the "Federales" (Rio Grande émigrés). On the 2nd there was a slight outbreak at San Boyà, a Brazilian vill. Opp. to San Tomé in Corrientes. It is very diff[icult]. to get at the truth here. But the papers allege that all along the frontier of Rio Grande & Uruguay there are bands of émigrés, armed, & preparing to move on the 15th of this month.

H. y E. the day before yesterday said to me "grave complications are impending in South America, in a day or two I shall have all the data & proofs in my hands, & after laying a plan before the President, I will come to you one evening. I must tell you all about it," & then he hinted that Uruguay wld. ask for the support in some way of H.M.G.

I pressed him to tell me what it was all abt, but he wld. only say that it concerned Brazil,

PRO 30/33 14/3 Semi-official Letters from Uruguay (August 4, 1890 – March 30, 1893)

Chili & the Argentines. I suppose that what Uruguay wants is to have her neutrality guaranteed in the event of war betw. these three. I expect H y E will say that they are strong enough on land, & that they cld. put 45000 men into the field in self-defence, but that they want help to maintain the neutrality of their ports. Of course the necessity of maintaining an armed neutrality wld. be an excellent excuse for defaulting. I shall know more in a few days. Wld. it be possible to get Argentina & Brazil to sign a convention to respect the neutrality of Uruguay?

The vessel I spoke of in my last wch. the Argentines are about to buy or order is to be obtained fr. Armstrongs, at the price of £350,000 & is called an ironclad.

y.v.t.

69. Satow to Herrero y Espinosa (p.70)

Dec. 10

Dear Dr. Herrero y Espinosa,

Enclosed you will find a Spanish translation of the observations on the laws of the Republic relating to nationality & naturalization wch. I propose to send to my Govt. together c. copies of the laws themselves that you have kindly furnished to me.

I shall be very much obliged if you will read my memorandum & indicate to me any points in wch. you think the subject requires further elucidation.

y.v.s.

70. Satow to Welby (p.70)

13.12.92

My dear Welby,

I send you copies of 2 desp[atches]. to F.O. wch. will go in my bag by the "Potosí" on Thursday, but if you have anything to add in the way of information you will almost overtake her by the "Clyde". The 15th is supposed to be a critical day, as the "Federales" have given out that it is their intention to have a row then in Rio Grande. If they shld. attack Rivera, I imagine the Uruguayans will easily get the better of them, but I trust nothing will happen of that kind. I telegraphed yesterday the substance of No. 33 to Lord Rosebery.[29]

PRO 30/33 14/3   Semi-official Letters from Uruguay (August 4, 1890 – March 30, 1893)

Herrero y Espinosa tells me that Assis Brazil[30] has had an "incidente" at B.A. with somebody, and that he will have to leave. Also that my Brazilian colleague here has heard fr. Rio that he is to be recalled; in that case one of those violent Rio Grandenses may be sent.

? is the story of a secret treaty betw. Bolivia & the Argentines the same sort of pretext that the wolf used towards the lamb.

I shall be glad to hear if you have any information either confirmatory or destructive of mine.

Assis Brazil said to me that the Rio de la Plata was the natural frontier of Brazil, but it must be obtained by pacific means. Zeballos' idea was to give them down to the Rio Negro, & take the rest for the Argentine. The Urug[uayans]. however object to being either swallowed whole or divided into 2 mouthfuls.

y.v.t.

71. Satow to Greville[31] (p.71)

14 Dec. 1892.

Dear Mr. Greville,

Please do not let anyone know that you have recd. any information fr. M.V. on the subj[ec]t. of the accompanying despp. [despatches] & especially the appeal for assistance of wch. the 1st speaks. I have telegraphed to London, but have recd. no ans[wer]. yet.

Acc. to all accts. the state of affairs in Rio Grande is deplorable. Murder, rape, destruction of property of opponents is the order of the day. The sympathies of the Uruguayans are undoubtedly with the "Federales", but for all that they are too much alarmed for their own safety not to do all in their power to observe their neutrality. This is naturally difficult, as the estancuros in the north of Uruguay are mostly of Brazilian origin,

---

[29] Archibald Primrose, Lord Rosebery (1847-1929). British Liberal politician. Prime Minister 1894-5. Foreign Secretary 1886; 1892-94.
[30] Joaquim Francisco de Assis Brasil (1857-1938). Brazilian advocate, politician and diplomat. Governor of Rio Grande do Sul, 1891-92.
[31] (Sir) George Greville (1851-1937). Secretary of Legation, Rio de Janeiro, 1892. Minister Resident at Bangkok, 1896-1900.

PRO 30/33 14/3   Semi-official Letters from Uruguay (August 4, 1890 – March 30, 1893)

& the "émigrés" naturally look to them for harbourage & succour.

I shall be very glad to know whether you have any information confirmatory of what I have been told abt. alliances &c.

      y.v.t.

      E.S.

P.S. I think I once had the pleasure of meeting you at diner at Philip Currie's rooms in the F.O. but it is so long ago, 1875 or 1876, that you have prob. forgotten it.[32]

72. Satow to Sanderson

Dec. 14. 1892

Dear Sanderson,

Things are apparently going from bad to worse in Rio Grande, and threats are uttered agst. Uruguay for alleged assistance to the "Federales" wch. one hopes there will be no attempt to carry into execution. Alvim dining here last night said that the Uruguayan Govt. was doing all that could be expected of it, and that the Rio Grandenses are unreasonable. The fact is the north of Uruguay is very largely populated by Brazilians. In the five northern departments of Paysandú, Salto, Artigas, Rivera & Cerro Largo they hold twice as much property as the Uruguayans. It is natural therefore that the émigrés fr. Rio Grande shld. easily find a refuge on Uruguayan territory, and be able to form plans for subverting the people in power at Porto Alegre. The arms wch. the "Federales" possess have chiefly come from Buenos Ayres. The Argentines displayed great activity in disarming & interning the few men who crossed the Uruguay river to San Tomé after the abortive ourbreak at San Boja wch. I mentioned in my last, but there seems reason to believe that they are secretly fomenting the troubles in Rio Grande. When the time comes they will show themselves actively friendly to the "Federales". The Uruguayan Govt. also sympathize with the "Federales", but nevertheless do all they can to maintain their neutrality. At Santa Ana the Brazilians had a fortnight ago 110 infantry, 140 cavalry & 30 artillery, 280 in all, while the Uruguayan town of Rivera is occupied by a regiment of Uruguayan cavalry 300 strong. I

---

[32] It was September 13, 1876 according to Satow's diary.

PRO 30/33 14/3   Semi-official Letters from Uruguay (August 4, 1890 – March 30, 1893)

hope these sanguinary Republicanos who rule Rio Grande will not lose their heads, but only last night there was a rumour that they were going to make a raid from Yaguaron on the Uruguayan town of Artigas, and cut the throats of all the émigrés there. But the latter have now moved inland.

I am told that in former times it was always Rio Grande that was the cause of war betw. Brazil and the Argentines.

The "Federales" are no doubt separatists & this accounts in a large measure for their possessing the sympathies of the Uruguayan Govt. For the latter argue that shld. the Federales succeed in getting back into power & making Rio Grande independent, then the province wld. gravitate towards Uruguay, on acct. of their identical economic condition; and instead of Uruguay suffering by the competition of Rio Grande in the jerked beef trade, both wld. be subjected to the same customs duties by Brazil; and at the same time Rio Grande not having a decent port, wld. receive her foreign supplies thro' M.V.

The Rio govt. being afraid of Rio Grande declaring itself independent always supports whatever party is in power there, and the "Republicanos" trade on this fear to secure a large share of influence in the cabinet. If they make a move agst. Uruguay, they can drag Peixoto[33] with them. I rather think Vice-Admiral Mello is a Rio-Grandense. The govt. of Rio Grande telegraphs to Alvim as if he were their represve. and not the represve. of the Central govt. to complain of the disorder that is permitted on the frontier. The poor man does not know wch. way to turn, as he thinks the Uruguayans are making every effort to prevent their territory being made a basis of operations. It seems to be the general feeling here that a row with Rio Grande is imminent and that wld. mean war with the whole of Brazil.

H. y E. told me that just before the fall of Marshall Deodoro[34] he had made up his mind to send an ultimatum to Uruguay about the $11,000,000 owed by the latter to Brazil.

He says they are extremely afraid of any attack on them by Rio Grande, because that wld. bring upon them the protection of the Argentines and the country wld. become, as it has been before, the battlefield of its two powerful neighbours.

Brazil cannot get at the Argentines by land, and her first step wld. be to send a squadron

---

[33] Floriano Peixoto (1839-1895). Second President of Brazil, 1891-1894.
[34] Deodoro da Fonseca (1827-1892). First President of Brazil, 1889-1891.

PRO 30/33 14/3   Semi-official Letters from Uruguay (August 4, 1890 – March 30, 1893)

to the River Plate to blockade Buenos Ayres. They wld. try to obtain possession of M.V.

If Chile, as we must expect from what Dr. Lira has been saying at Rio, and acc. to the terms of the alliance believed to be on the point of being concluded joins Brazil, the attempt to make M.V. the base of naval operations becomes a certainty.

That means the ruin of Uruguay and the probable loss of her independence. She will not go with either party if she can help it. She wld. be as reluctant to join the Argentines as the Brazilians.

After H. y E. had said what I have told you, I suggested that his object might be attained by getting Brazil, Chile & the Argentines to enter into conventions to respect the neutrality of Uruguay, on the principle of the conventions we made in 1870 with Fr[ance]. & Ger[man]y. as to Belgium. He replied most decidedly that he considered it wld. be useless. I am inclined to the same opinion myself. A suggestion to that effect by an European power wld. probably be recd. with very bad grace by all three.

He then said something about waiting till the 15th of Feb. when a Senator named Angel Floro Costa, whom they look on as a traitor, will retire, and then in a secret session to get authority fr. the Senate to conclude a convention. I infer from this that what they want is to enter into a treaty of guarantee with G.B. He added that he was convinced that Zeballos (the late Argentine Min. for F.A.) had made some approaches to Mr. Pitkin for an alliance but without result. It was generally supposed that when Admiral Walker[35] was waiting here with the "White Squadron" for developments in Chile, he made some overtures to the Argentines wch. came to nothing because Chile gave way.

It is popularly believed here that Engl. & France are joint guarantors of the independence of Uruguay. I have always told people that no such undertaking has ever been put on paper.

I have confidentially told all this to Lang and shown him my despatch no. 33. He had intended to go down to Tierra del Fuego, but will remain here until after Christmas, and if necessary I shall make arrangements for keeping in touch with him after he leaves for the south. He says the Uruguayan gunboats are utterly useless, and the Brazilian ironclads can do 12, not merely 8, knots, as H y E told me.

---

[35] John Grimes Walker (1835-1907), admiral in the U.S. Navy. Commander of the Squadron of Evolution (White Squadron).

PRO 30/33 14/3   Semi-official Letters from Uruguay (August 4, 1890 – March 30, 1893)

I have kept Greville & Welby fully informed.

73. Satow to Sanderson

M.V.

22 Dec. 1892.

Dear Sanderson,

There is very little to be added on the subject of the supposed alliance betw. Brazil and Chile to what I have said in my official No. 35. I let Herrero y Espinosa understand that H.M.G. wld. in appreciating the value [of] his communication prob. be influenced by what had happened in 1884 betw. Santos & Palgrave, and reminded him of the children crying wolf: the point of wch. he declined to see, replying that the wolf comes at last. He said that on Blas Vidal's arrival he wld. bring him to see me. That their Min. at Santiago said there was nothing in the rumour, no matter of surprise; Arrieta is a great deal mixed up with the local politics of Chile, and is not of much use, so they are going to send him a secretary who will be specially charged to find out about this matter of the alliance.

Altho' the newspapers say that things are quieter in Rio Grande, my colleague Alvim tells me it is not so, & cannot be, so long as there are 16,000 émigrés on this side of the frontier, longing to upset the govt. of Dr. Castilhos[36] and get back to their homes & farms. He is repeatedly disturbed by telegrams from Rio Grande wch. he has to communicate without a moment's delay to the Urug. Govt.

It appears that the Rio Grandenses had for a long time been trying to get one of their men into the Cabinet, but the appt. of Paulo Sousa to F.A. and of another man to the 2nd vacant post in the Miny. at Rio has dashed their hopes to the ground. I was wrong in saying that Vice Ad. Mello is fr. Rio Grande: he is of Rio Janeiro.

      y.v.t.

        E.S.

74. Satow to Sanderson

---

[36] Júlio de Castilhos (1860-1903). Brazilian Governor of Rio Grande do Sul, 1891, 1893 - 1898.

PRO 30/33 14/3   Semi-official Letters from Uruguay (August 4, 1890 – March 30, 1893)

M.V.

Dec. 26. 1892.

Dear Sanderson,

There have been paragraphs in the papers of late alleging that Chile had supplied Paraguay with 10,000 rifles, or the means of purchasing them, & that an alliance had been concluded betw. the 2 countries. J.S. Decoud[37] who is accredited to Rio as well as here, came to see me today as he usually does when in M.V., & said he wanted to deny categorically all these reports, in wch. his name had been mixed up, without the shadow of a justification. Paraguay had no alliances, & was determined to hold aloof fr. all conflicts betw. Brazil & the Argentine Repub. or betw. the latter & Chile. Ever since the conclusion of the Paraguayan war of 1865 the policy of his country has been clear & simple, namely the maintenance of a strict neutrality. Therefore the rumours that had been set afloat about an alliance with Chile were absolutely without foundation.

He then proceeded to say that he thought certain European Powers might be disposed to assist Paraguay in maintaining her neutrality.

I said that judging fr. what Carlos Calvo[38] had said on the subject of European intervention in this part of the world, S.A. wld. be disposed to look very unfavourably on any action of a European Power tending to support Paraguay, as that support must of necessity in the end be of a material character.

To this he answered that he still thought it not impossible, as he understood that Great Britain had on one occasion expressed her readiness to guarantee the independence of Uruguay.

I admitted that there had been something of the kind.

He then said that he was speaking to me quite confidentially, & he wld. not ask me to bring this matter to the notice of H.M.G., but at the same time, shld. I have an opportunity of doing so, he hoped I wld. if I saw fit, etc., report it.

I told him that as my colleague in B.A. was accredited to Paraguay, it was through him that any such communication ought to be made, & asked whether thre Paraguayan minister

---

[37] José Segundo Decoud (1848-1909). Paraguayan politician and journalist.
[38] Carlos Calvo (1824-1906). Argentine lawyer and diplomat.

PRO 30/33 14/3 Semi-official Letters from Uruguay (August 4, 1890 – March 30, 1893)

there had spoken to Welby. Decoud replied that he rather thought there had been no conversation betw. them.

I said that I could not write officially abt. Paraguay, as that country was out of my province, but that I wld. acquaint you privately with what he had said.

Some visitors came in, & our conversation was interrupted, but I may perhaps have an opportunity of recurring to the subject with him tomorrow evening.

When Decoud was in Rio the other day he approached the Brazilian acting Minr. for F.A. upon the subject of the remission of the war indemnity, wch. amounts to an almost fabulous sum. Mello said "Yes, with great pleasure, but what political combination can you offer us in return?" To which Decoud replied "Nothing." About three weeks ago, this question of the indemnity was discussed by a leading Buenos Aires paper the "Prensa", & Assis Brazil immediately rushed into print with a long explanation, showing why Brazil had not yet remitted this indemnity. I imagine that under these circs., if for no other reasons, it may be safely concluded that Paraguay will be no party to an alliance that wld. bring her into line with Brazil. The Uruguayans have remitted their portion of the indemnity, wch. was only $3,690,000, as far back as 1883.

Decoud is a man who I think may be trusted, & that he is telling the truth in this particular instance I have no doubt. He has been more than once Paraguayan Min. for F.A., & being also a near relation of the present President is able to speak with authority about his own country.

 y.v.t.
  E.S.

75. Satow to Sanderson
Dec. 29. 1892.
Dear Sanderson,

I have not had an opportunity of extracting anything more from [J.S.] Decoud abt. South American complications.

Yesterday afternoon the "Siglo" published telegrams, purporting to come from Valparaiso and Rio viâ New York, announcing the signature of an "offensive & defensive

PRO 30/33 14/3   Semi-official Letters from Uruguay (August 4, 1890 – March 30, 1893)

alliance betw. Chile & Brazil" on the 23rd inst.

H. y. E. on the 27th said that he shld. come to see me yesterday afternoon with Blas Vidal, to supply further information, but he did not keep his engagement. Vidal arrived the day before yesterday, and must have left Rio after the 23rd. I am therefore curious to know what he has to say about the matter.

Alvim, my Brazilian colleague, jeers at the idea of Brazil doing anything so foolish as allying herself with Chile, to pull the chestnuts out of the fire for her. But he says that [Adolfo] Guerrero and Assis Brasil tried to patch up something of the kind with Dr. Lira, when the latter was in Buenos Aires (as I wrote in my No. 33 of Dec. 12).   Alvim's denial of course proves nothing, except that he has no instructions to speak. He seems reassured as to his own position here, his proceedings having been approved by the Govt. at Rio.

What seems quite certain is that the Uruguayan Govt. are abt. to buy 20,000 repeating rifles, wch. will cost them £100,000 wch. they can ill afford, besides the price of sufficient ammunition.

  y.v.t.

   E.S.

76. Satow to Sanderson (p. 79)

Jan. 5. 1893

Dear Sanderson,

I have not seen either Herrero y Espinosa or Blas Vidal since I last wrote. They did not fulfil their promise to come and tell me all about the "alliance", and I infer that they have nothing to offer by way of confirmation. In Buenos Aires on the 1st or 2nd was published an exchange of telegrams between Assis Brazil and the Director-Genl. of the Min. for F.A. at Rio as follows'

    B.A. 28 Dec. 1892

H.E. the Vice president of the Republic, Rio Janeiro. "The press publishes telegram fr. Santiago saying that on the 23 of this month an offensive & defensive alliance was signed betw. Brazil & Chile. Desirable to know the truth. Signed Assis Brazil.

PRO 30/33 14/3   Semi-official Letters from Uruguay (August 4, 1890 – March 30, 1893)

Rio de Janeiro 31 Dec. 1892 To Brazilian Minr. B.A. In the absence of the minister and by order of the V.P. of the Republic I declare to you that Brazil has no treaty of alliance of any kind with Chile (signed) Cabo Frio, Director-Genl. of the Min. for F.A.

This has been republished here. The genl. impression seems to be that the rumour is not altogether without foundation, tho' the actual signature on the 23rd Dec. may not be a fact. Decoud says he does not believe in any "anticipatory alliance" among the South American nations.

I am going to see Herrero y Espinosa this afternoon to try & arrange abt. the presentation of some medals sent out by the B. of Trade for gallantry in saving life that will afford him an opportunity if he wishes to say anything further abt. Brazil & Chile.

The Commissioners for taking evidence about the Balmaceda silver will be over here shortly, & I have had private notice that the L. & R.P. Bank intend to call me as a witness.

My defaulting clerk, of whom I told you, appropriated about £180 of seamens' wages, wch. I have just had to make good to the Board of Trade. He has signed an undertaking to repay it by monthly instalments, but I am not sure he will do this. The bulk of it was recd. just before I returned, while Grenfell was in charge, but as I did not look into the state of the chest, I fancy the loss must be mine.

The responsibility for Consular business ought to rest with the Vice consul, who can personally superintend, and not with the minister.

   y.v.t.

PRO 30/33 14/3   Semi-official Letters from Uruguay (August 4, 1890 – March 30, 1893)

La alianza chileno-brasilera no exis[te]

DIGNA ACTITUD DEL MINISTRO ASSIS BRAZIL—LA DIPLOMACIA DE LA VERDAD—Buenos Aires, Enero 1.º—
El lector recordará el telegrama trasmitido al *New York Herald* por su corresponsal de Rio Janeiro, comunicándole haberse firmado un tratado de alianza ofensiva y defensiva entre el Brasil y Chile. El asunto es fresco todavia, pues ayer mismo nos ocupábamos de él.

La prensa de Chile publicó tambien ese despacho, y desde Valparaiso fué trasmitido á esta capital.

Como alguna alarma habia despertado aquella noticia, tomando en cierto modo de sorpresa á la opinion general, el digno ministro plenipotenciario del Brasil entre nosotros, doctor Assis Brazil, que con tanto celo mantiene y estrecha las amistosas relaciones entre ambas repúblicas, se ha dirigido, en seguida de divulgarse esa noticia, al presidente de la República de los Estados Unidos del Brasil, obteniendo una contestacion que desautoriza terminantemente la noticia de la alianza con Chile, como era de esperarse.

Al publicar con todo placer tan importante noticia para la gran causa de la paz y de la union fraternal de los pueblos sud-americanos, muy grato nos es recomendar como el colaborador mas decidido y eficaz de esa misma causa, á la diplomacia de la verdad y de la franqueza, si no iniciada, dignamente representada entre nosotros de parte del Brasil, por el ilustrado republicano Assis Brazil, que ha dado nobles y leales pruebas de su respeto sincero por esa politica, por esa diplomacia, única destinada á conservar y hacer grandes y felices á estos pueblos, en todos los tiempos.

Hé aquí los importantes telegramas á que nos referíamos.

«Buenos Aires, 28 de Dezembro de 1892 - Excmo. señor vice-presidente da Republica.—Rio de Janeiro.—Impresa publica telegramma de Santiago, dizendo foi assignado a 23 de deste mez alliança offensiva e defensiva entre Brazil e Chile. - Convem se saiba verdade. - (Assignado): *Assis Brazil.*»

«Rio ñe Janeiro, 31 de Dezembro de 1892.—Ministro Brazileiro - Buenos Aires —Na ausencia do senhor ministro y de ordem do senhor Vice Presidente da República declarovos que o Brazil não tem Tratado de Allianca de cualquer natureza com o Chile.

210

PRO 30/33 14/3   Semi-official Letters from Uruguay (August 4, 1890 – March 30, 1893)

77. Satow to Sanderson

Jan. 5. 1893

Dear S.,

As I anticipated, H. y E. beg[an]. to talk abt. the alliance of Brazil & Chile as soon as the nominal occasion of our meeting was disposed of. It seems that he had expected me to go to him on the 28th; but prob. the difficulty was in persuading Vidal to come to the Legation.

He began by producing a translation of Lord Granville's confidential desp[atch]. no 4 of Mar. 12, 1885 relative to Santos' wish for a guarantee of neutrality, certified by Palgrave as a correct version in wch. the words 'good offices' are rendered by 'apoyo efective', effective support. It had been in the possession of P's widow, whose son in fact brought it in while I was there. The handwriting of document I recognized as that of Ayre, formerly clerk & acting consul.

He then called in Blas Vidal fr. the next room, & began by saying to him that I was evidently inclined to regard it all as a false alarm.

I replied that from the telegrams I had recd. fr. Ld. Rosebery I gathered that such was the opinion of H.M.G.

Blas Vidal then commenced by saying that towards the end of the year the ten years stipulated betw. Chile & Peru for the temporary occupation of Arica & Tacna wld. come to an end. It was clear the Chilians wld. retain possession; they have already paid to Peru several million dollars (in the form of a loan) & all they have to do is to get a plebiscite, & say to Peru 'Here's the balce." The secret treaty betw. Argentina & Bolivia mentioned in my No. 34, wch. stipulates for the 21° parallel (not 20° as I wrote by a slip) pretends to hand over to the former the 'hinterland' of Atacama to wch. Chile lays claim. The treaty has been approved in secret session both at La Paz & in B.A. (while Pelligrini was still in power). And as soon as Arg. tries to get the said treaty executed, there will be a casus belli. On the other hand the Brazilians have an idea that compensation has been promised to Bolivia at the expense of their province of Matto Grosso. With regard to the Misiones boundary question that cld. not originate any complication, as it has been submitted to arbitration.

PRO 30/33 14/3   Semi-official Letters from Uruguay (August 4, 1890 – March 30, 1893)

Mello, who was till lately the acting Minr. for F.A. constantly referred to the Chileans as "our allies", & that he is certain they are pretty well agreed.   (Nothing has been signed; the telegram of the New York Herald that a treaty was signed on the 23rd Dec. was untrue.) Influential Brazilians are in favour of our alliance, & amongst these are the V. President Peixoto & Mello. While Chile desires an alliance offensive & defensive, Brazil wishes it to be defensive while stipulating for joint action in certain cases. To the Brazilians it is of importance to secure safety fr. attack, & also agst. the machinations of the Argentines stirring up civil war in Rio Grande. They 'must do something' as Mello said to him.

Then he recurred to the policy of Engl[and]. in former times, & quoted a joint note addressed by Sir E. Thornton[39] & the Fr. Ch. d'aff. Maillefer to the Brazilian Ch. d'Aff. Amaral at Montevideo on 23 Jan. 1858, in wch. they contest the right of Brazil to interfere alone, since the protocol of Sept. 3. 1857 (State papers Vol. 49, p. 1231) revising the previous Treaty of alliance of 1851 had placed Brazil in the same relation to Uruguay as any other power, & speaking of Engl. & France as "guarantors" of the independence of Uruguay. (I have not been able to find this in my archives wch. are very imperfect, but they showed me a Brazilian version in a Brazil blue bk). He also cited a note of Sir J. Hudson of 8 Nov. 1851 to the Brazilian Minr. for F.A. in wch. similar language was used.   And then he proceeded to say that the desp[atch]. of Ld. Granville, tho' speaking only of 'good offices' was based on the same policy of maintaining the independence of Uruguay and the freedom of commerce in the River Plate. It was necessary to provide beforehand for the eventualities that might spring out of the present understanding betw. Chile & Brazil. Would G.B. in the event of war breaking out in the River Plate act in continuity with her former policy and maintain the neutrality & independence of this country. A mere declaration of her intention wld. be quite sufficient to prevent any idea of seizing M.V. or the island of Flores as a basis [base for operations], or the entry of Brazilian troops into the Republic & marching down to Colonia.

H. y E. added that it was scarcely possible for the present year to pass over without war, & it was more likely in the spring (i.e. March-April) than in the autumn, because by the

---

[39] Sir Edward Thornton (1817-1906). Chargé d'affaires to Uruguay in 1854-8.

PRO 30/33 14/3   Semi-official Letters from Uruguay (August 4, 1890 – March 30, 1893)

latter date the Argentines wld. be fully armed, while the others wld. not. That with their domestic divisions it was natural that Chile & the Argentines shld. seek in foreign complications a means of internal reunion, & while Brazil wld. repeat [reap?] the benefit of foreign war in consolidation of her loosely compacted provinces. What else cld. the Argentine cabinet have been consulting abt. for a whole week in secret with the aid of Roca, the general-designate in the coming war, Mitre[?], & Zeballos?

I said very little in reply, except that they cld. not expect that in London the situation shld. be appreciated in precisely the same manner as by themselves. As H. y E. already possessed a Spanish translation of Ld. G's desp[atch]. I promised him a copy of the Engl. text.

They sais they wld. come & renew the conversation next week.

    y.v.t.

78. Satow to Bergne
Jan. 12. 1893.
My Dear Bergne

I hope that this time I have delivered the medals awarded by the Board of Trade in proper form. These people very much prefer to make a great business of such a matter.

I shld. like to suggest that on any future occasion there should be no **money** rewards. They are not appreciated nor understood. A piece of emblazoned parchment wld. be much better. If you have an opportunity will you try & have this adopted.

    y.v.t.
       E.S.

79. Satow to Sanderson
Jan. 18. 1893
Dear Sanderson,

I have heard nothing more abt. possibilities of trouble in South America, from either Herrero y Espinosa, or Blas Vidal. The latter came yesterday to return a call I had made on his wife, and did not allude to the subject, tho' he sat here for nearly an hour. But they are making trials of Mauser rifles, & talk of buying 10,000.

PRO 30/33 14/3   Semi-official Letters from Uruguay (August 4, 1890 – March 30, 1893)

Mercier, the Fr. Ch. d'Aff., accidentally let out last night that he has recd. instructions from Paris to try to find out what truth there may be in rumours of Brazilian designs on Uruguay, wch. had been reported from Rio by Gerard.

At the present moment what chiefly occupies attention here is the curious difficulty into wch. Saenz Peña has got himself, unable to find any one to accept the Ministry of the Interior. No one likes to prophecy what may be the result. Rio Grande seems quiet for the moment.

y.v.t.

80. Satow to Sanderson

Jan. 26. 1893.

Dear Sanderson,

It seems as if the Govt. of Rio Grande expects an attempt at revolution, for they have given orders to concentrate the troops at Porto Alegre. I cannot discover that the émigrés here are disposed to make a move.

H. y E. discovers great anxiety to know what H.M. Govt. will say to his application for the protection of Uruguayan neutrality. I have told him that according to my calculations my despatches on the subj. cld. not have reached home before the 12th inst.

The Urug. Minr. at Santiago telegraphed recently to inquire whether it was true that Uruguay was going to make an alliance with the Argentine Republ. & was told to contradict emphatically any rumour to that effect.

My own feeling is that there is no danger of war, but then I am without the means of knowing what the feeling in Chile and Brazil may be. If H. y E. is to be believed, Roca's dictature in the Argentine Republ. is imminent, and with it war. But I have not much confidence in his foresight. In this case too my feeling is that Saenz Peña will last longer than his critics think, or say.

The Espiègle silver commission sat here on the 23rd. I was asked to corroborate the evidence of Mr. Thuburn of the L. & R.P. Bank as to the advice wch. I gave him on the matter in Aug. 1891. Then the Bank's lawyer Dr. Pena was examined; he had given the same advice as myself. I have asked Mr. Merivale, who is on the commission as counsel for

PRO 30/33 14/3   Semi-official Letters from Uruguay (August 4, 1890 – March 30, 1893)

the Bank, to give me a copy of my evidence. Mr. Walter, the barrister on the other side, says that if the Chilian Govt. lose the action, they will make it a diplomatic question, & propose to refer it to arbitration.

My nephew R.S. Allen[40] who has been my clerk for the past four months, and wrote a neat hand, has gone home. I have had to take a boy of 17 named Maurice Vignolles, whom after training I shall hand over to Grenfell for the consular work, and take back Wilson. The latter tho' bearing an English name is an Uruguayan, who has been at the legation since Palgrave's time.

I have asked for sanction to an expenditure on binding the old archives; they are in a deplorable condition. I hope you will approve this.

81. Satow to Kennedy

C.M. Kennedy C.B.

Jan. 27. 1893

Dear Mr. Kennedy,

In ans. to your letter of Dec. 26 inquiring what "headlands" are those meant in the Uruguayan-Argentine Pilot convention (enclosed in my No. 8 treaty of last year), I have ascertained that by "outside the headlands" is meant oversea navigation, & that the "Headlands" are Cabo Santa Maria in Uruguay & Cabo San Antonio in the Argentine Republic.

Many thanks for your kind wishes for the New Yr. wch. I heartily reciprocate.

   y.v.s.

P.S. Jan. 30

Just recd. Commercial No. 1 calling for a report on this subject. I hope to have it ready for the Royal Mail Steamer a fortnight hence.

   E.S.

82. Satow to Sanderson

---

[40] Reginald Satow Allen (b. 1864). Son of Arthur John Allen and Ernest's eldest sister Margaret Agneta.

PRO 30/33 14/3 Semi-official Letters from Uruguay (August 4, 1890 – March 30, 1893)

Feb. 16. 1893.

Dear Sanderson,

The Fr[ench]. also have a question with the Uruguayan Post Office like our own, but coupled with a claim on the part of the Fr. Govt. to be reimbursed for the conveyance of mails to Europe by their subsidized steamers. Mercier tells me that he had instructions to speak on the subject to the Min. for F.A. who referred him to the Director general of Posts. The latter was extremely uncivil, and said the Govts. had nothing to do with the question, wch. was solely for the Post offices to settle internationally. M. told him he believed B.A. had already given way on this point & had promised to pay what was claimed, only asking for time, which annoyed him considerably. M. also says that recently the M.V. post office required the post office agent on board a Fr. mail str. to hand over to them the mails addressed to B.A., on the pretext that Urug. was responsible for their transmission thro' her territory. Of course the agent refused.

The question is one of much more than a few thousand dollars profit to be made by the Urug. Post Office, and it hardly seems correct that this country shld. be able to get it decided in her favour by a side wind. It is one in wch. international law is involved. I have not mentioned the subj. to the Min. for F.A. It is best to let sleeping dogs lie, and the resident plumes himself on his vigour in dealing with foreign powers abt. P.O. questions.

I shld. like to suggest that my memo. shld. not be communicated to the General Post Office in extenso, but that (if Lord Rosebery approves) they shld. be told that H.M.G. does not admit the claim advanced by the Urug. post office to have the Rio de la Plata recognized as Urug. territory. If the two post offices get to discussing the point on its merits, they will be trespassing on the functions of the Foreign Offices, wch. the Urug. P.O. at least is only too ready to do.

Monson's desp[atch]. and West's memo. referred to in my covering desp[atch]. give the diplomatic aspect very fully, and I have therefore avoided going over the ground a second time.

  y.v.t.

83. Satow to Sanderson

PRO 30/33 14/3   Semi-official Letters from Uruguay (August 4, 1890 – March 30, 1893)

Mar. 3. 1893.

Dear Sanderson,

I have sent you a short desp[atch]. abt. the affairs of the Rio Grande, because as we have rlwy. communication with the scene of the disturbances, information comes here more rapidly than to Rio Janeiro. I shall send a copy to Greville.

Alvim is constantly receiving telegrams both fr. Rio Grande & Rio Janeiro complaining of the want of energy of the Uruguayan govt. He is a monarchist himself, & wld. be glad to see the Federals triumph, so that I do not attach full value to his assurances that Uruguay is trying to preserve a strict neutrality.   It was rather an unlucky circ. that Herrero y Espinosa returning from Paysandu the week before last found himself in the same train with Silveira Martins, & dined with him halfway. The newspapers took notice of it at once. Still it is so clearly to the interest of Uruguay not to give umbrage to the dominant party in Brazil, that they must wish they had the power to prevent their territory being made a basis of operations.

I think H. y E. has given up his idea of a war betw. Chile & the Argentine republ[ic]. for this year at least. He talked of coming to spend an evening and tell me more abt. South American politics, but a week has elapsed, so there is evidently nothing very pressing to be said.

Mr. John Jones has been at me lately to ask whether I have recd. instructions about the claim of the late Mr. Littlejohn agst. the Uruguayan Govt. reported in my No. 26 of Sept. 1 last year.

[End of letter]

84. Satow to Cockerell

6 Mar. 1893

My dear Cockerell,

A single copy of the New Consular instructions reached me by bag the day before yesterday, but in a lamentable condition, owing to its having been baked in the process of fumigation of the mails.

I suppose you are sending out copies to the Vice consulates in this countries [country?].

PRO 30/33 14/3 Semi-official Letters from Uruguay (August 4, 1890 – March 30, 1893)

There are 4 in number, Salto, Colonia, Paysandú & Maldonado. I want a couple of copies here, one for Grenfell & one for myself. Then I shall send you back the baked copy.

These ½ doz. copies shld. be sent as a parcel not by post.

  y.v.s.
   E.S.

85. Satow to Bergne (p.89)

22 March 1893.

My Dr. Bergne,

The Danish Govt. have offered the "Dannebrog" (chevalier) to my friend Chas. S. Lockie, Danish Consul-genl. at Bangkok, & he is very anxious to get leave to accept it, & wear it.

He is a very good fellow & has always been a most loyal supporter of the British Legn. in Bangkok, besides, wch. is here perh. beside the mark, discharging his duties as Danish Consul-genl. in a most exemplary manner.

  y.v.t.

86. Satow to Villiers[41]

30 Mar. 1893

Dear Mr. Villiers,

I hear a rumour that before long there will be some moves in the diplomatic service, & that the legation at B.A. is in consequence likely to become vacant. If that event shld. happen, I hope Ld. Rosebery may be disposed to take my name into consideration in filling up the vacancy. I am induced to apply for the post by the belief that the acquaintance I have gained with R.P. [River Plate] affairs during my four years residence here wld. assist me in discharging its duties efficiently, & at the same time I venture to think that the interests of the public service have not sustained any detriment during my tenure of the M.V. [Monte Video] mission.

---

[41] Sir Francis Hyde Villiers (1852-1925). Civil servant and diplomat. Private Secretary to Lord Rosebery in 1886 and 1892-4. Minister to Portugal from 1906, and Belgium from 1911.

PRO 30/33 14/3   Semi-official Letters from Uruguay (August 4, 1890 – March 30, 1893)

yours very faithfully,

Hon. F. Villiers
F.O.

END OF PRO 30/33 14/3.

PRO 30/33 14/4 Semi-official Letters from Uruguay (March 31 – June 9, 1893) and Morocco (September 4 – December 18, 1893)

PRO 30/33 14/4

1. Satow to Sanderson

March 31, 1893

Dear Sanderson,

Many thanks for your letter of the 15th Feb[ruar]y with enclosures. I think I now quite understand the line to take if Herrero y Espinosa makes any further appeals. I did not show him Ld. Rosebery's No. 1 of Jan. 17 much less give him a copy; but merely copied out the latter part on a slip of paper, wch. I held in my hand while talking to him & translated freely into Spanish. So he has no written record of the ans[wer]. of H.M.G.

He has gone off till Easter Monday, to meditate upon his reply to Alvim, I imagine. These people love a war of words, a tournament of gallant phrases. I shall not fear any result until I hear of a Brazilian man of war coming here. They withdrew abt. two years ago the "stationnaire" they used to have here, as a sign of deference to their Sister Republic. As far as I can learn nothing decisive has occurred in the Rio Grande. The Federales retreat whenever they find themselves outnumbered by the govt. forces. There is no doubt that Saraiva, a sort of guerilla chief from this country on whom great hopes were placed, has been beaten badly. Hearn is anxious to have a man-of-war sent to his port, but the bar of Rio Grande is a nasty place to cross, & naval men don't care to go there. At present I do not think a ship is likely to be wanted. Very alarming reports seem to reach Rio Grande from the interior of the province, but in most instances they have been exaggerated. At any rate I believe Lang is disinclined to send a ship unless he gets a requisition from Greville direct. He has been away down south for the last three months & I expect him back in a day or two.

Lira the Chilian Min. at Rio, a short time ago wrote to Blas Vidal, who had been Uruguayan envoy there, to tell him that <u>he</u> had obtained fr. the Brazilian Govt. the concession (namely the remission of the Paraguayan war indemnity) wch. Decoud asked for a few months back; he added that he did not know D's address, & begged him to transmit this information. The object no doubt is to maintain Vidal in the belief that there is a close understanding betw. Chile & Brazil. To judge from the row wch. has just happened betw. the Braz. Minr. at Asuncion & the Parag. Govt. there is no love lost betw. Br. &

PRO 30/33 14/4 Semi-official Letters from Uruguay (March 31 – June 9, 1893) and Morocco (September 4 – December 18, 1893)

Parag. H y E. maintains that the friendly language interchanged between Chile & the Args. is merely to gain time. That does not seem very likely; it wld. be a piece of treachery that even Chilians wld. hardly be capable of.

 y.v.t.

2. Satow to Sanderson

May 11. 1893

Dear Sanderson,

 There has been nothing special to tell you lately. But last week a fight took place in the Western part of Rio Grande on the River Inhamduhu[?] betw. the people in power & the Federales, in wch. the latter seem to have had the worst of it. The revolutionary troubles seem to be almost entirely confined to that district, & the Porto Alegre & Rio Grande are quite safe. There has been a little frontier trouble but Urug. is anxious to keep the peace. No signs are visible of the general rising on wch. Silveira M. & his friends counted. The Presidt. has obtained from the Chambers authority to add 50 men to each cavalry regiment, wch. means only 200 altogether, & to buy 20,000 stand of arms,[1] the perfected Mauser. They were negotiating for some time with Grenfell's cousin Hubert, but could not pay cash, nor give good enough security, so the business fell through. People outside say that the sole object of the President is to increase his hold over the military men, so as to ensure the elections going in his favour. But there is no need for that. As far as one can judge, he is all powerful and will have no difficulty in nominating his successor. Probably he will go to the Senate directly, after he hands over, and will be elected President of that body, consequently next successor to the Presidency, in case of its becoming vacant by resignation or death. There is at present no candidate in the field for the next Presidency in March 1894.

 I think they are quite right in buying Mausers, as every other country in S.A. is getting them. Some excitement was created the other day by a telegram, purporting to come fr. New York, that the Brazilian squadron had been suddenly ordered to return to Rio

---

[1] stand: (British) a complete set of arms or accoutrements for one soldier.

PRO 30/33 14/4 Semi-official Letters from Uruguay (March 31 – June 9, 1893) and Morocco (September 4 – December 18, 1893)

forthwith. But on the whole, since the signature of the limits protocol at Santiago,[2] the fear of an upset in this part of the world seems to have blown over.

    y.v.t.

      E.S.

3. Satow to Cockerell

22 May 1893.

My dear Cockerell,

In my desp[atch]. Cons. No. 24 of Oct. 14 last year, I explained at some length how I had been led by a blunder of an overzealous clerk into paying to H.M.G. £7.17.0 on account of fees more than was due, and I asked permission to credit myself with this amount in my next account. But I have not recd. any answer. It is possible that I ought to have labelled the despatch with some other designation, but to save time I shld. be greatly obliged if you wld. move the proper authority to favour me with a reply.

    y.v.t.

4. Satow to Sanderson

May 24.

Dear Sanderson,

Altho' Herrero y Esp. talks of their having shown 'benevolent neutrality' towards the de facto Govt. of Rio Grande, there is no doubt whatever that both he & Alvim desire ardently the triumph of the revolutionists, and this is also the disposition of the Uruguayan govt. & people in general. No wonder that they are disquieted at the idea of Alvim's recall & the despatch of Montero hither on a special mission. While he was acting Govr. he allowed the Rio G. press to utter very bold threats, but my impression is that he will not effect much by trying to bully these people.

At the dinner given to Quirno Costa[3] & [the Chilean minister] Guerrero last week the

---

[2] The protocol signed on May 1, 1893 between Chile and Argentina to settle their frontier dispute.
[3] Norberto Quirno Costa (1844-1915). Argentine Ambassador to Chile, 1892.

PRO 30/33 14/4 Semi-official Letters from Uruguay (March 31 – June 9, 1893) and Morocco (September 4 – December 18, 1893)

president in his speech said that "all danger of war between these sister republics had disappeared with the signature of the protocol,' wch. amounts to saying, somewhat indiscreetly, that up to that moment there was danger.

A more extraordinary thing however was Herrero y Espinosa telling me in a burst of confidence that he was the originator of the telegram published in N.Y. about the 27th of Dec. last stating that the alliance betw. Chile & Brazil had been signed on the 23rd of that month. He induced the manager of a telegraph office here whom I think I can identify to get it arranged with the N.Y. people. I remarked that in future I shld. suspect every sensational telegram of having him for its author. [Margin: It is humiliating to have to confess it but I am afraid I took the whole business too seriously.]

I have seen the instructions given to the new Uruguayan Minr. in Rio, Vasquez Sagastume,[4] & they do not indicate the slightest inclination to fall in with Brazilian ideas abt. the interning of fugitives.

We have no positive news about the state of things in Rio Grande, but in any case the Federales do not seem to be making any headway.

    y.v.t.

5. Satow to Philip Currie[5]

June 9. 93

My dear Currie,

I was exceedingly gratified to receive Ld. R's telegram offering me Tangier, all the more because it was so entirely unexpected. I am quite sure that I owe this to your recommendation, & am heartily obliged to you. There is no other appointment that cld. more completely meet my wishes. I feel that it will be something of a responsibility, but I hope I may be able to bear it with serenity. There are one or two things I shld. like to settle before leaving M.V. but I hope to be ready to start homewards this day four weeks.

    With renewed thanks, I am, y.v.t.

        E.S.

---

[4] Jose Vasquez Sagastume (1828-1897).
[5] Philip Currie (1834-1906). Permanent Under-secretary of state, 1888-93.

PRO 30/33 14/4   Semi-official Letters from Uruguay (March 31 – June 9, 1893) and Morocco (September 4 – December 18, 1893)

6. Satow to Sanderson

[Last letter from Uruguay]

June 9. 93

Dear Sanderson,

There is nothing new since I last wrote abt. Things in Rio Grande, or the relations betw. Brazil & this country. [Vitoriano] Monteiro[6] has not yet arrived. I am told that [José] Vasquez Sagastume was instructed to ask confidentially that he shld. not be sent.

Licignano[7] who was here the day before yesterday fr. B.A. had a long talk with H y E, in wch. the latter drew an alarming picture of the situation as regards Brazil. But when I went to him the next day he hardly mentioned the subject, so I infer that what he said to L. was a rhetorical recapitulation of all that he has communicated to me since the beginning of the year.

With regard to the Littlejohn claim, concerning wch. instructions were sent to me in No. 11 of April 4, the Govt. have given a promise, as yet only verbal, to settle it. I drafted a Note a month ago, & gave a copy to the Min. for F.A. who brought it before the President in Council. For some 3 weeks the Prest. held out. The Min. then advised me to send a signed copy, & in a couple of days I heard thro' a third party that it was to be settled. Licignano has had a precisely similar claim pending for a long time past, and we have worked together.

I am very pleased at the prospect of going to Tangier. It is the realization of a dream to be so near home. If I can get Littlejohn's claim arranged, & one or two other pending matters, I shall be ready to start this day four weeks.

The map of Rio Grande I am sending is said to be very correct.

    y.v.t.

    E.S.

---

[6] Vitoriano Ribeiro Carneiro Monteiro (1859-1920). Brazilian lawyer, diplomat and politician.

[7] Giuseppe Anfora di Licignano (1828-1894). Italian diplomat. Minister in Buenos Aires and Montevideo, 1883-92. Minister in Asunción (Paraguay), 1892-94.

PRO 30/33 14/4 Semi-official Letters from Uruguay (March 31 – June 9, 1893) and Morocco (September 4 – December 18, 1893)

Morocco

For the diplomatic background see Frederick V. Parsons, *The origins of the Morocco Question, 1880-1900*, Duckworth, 1976.

7. Satow to Currie

Sept. 4, 1893

Dear Currie,

Since my arrival we have been busy about quarantine, & I have sat for 6 hrs. with my colleagues at the Sanitary Board. The Fr. Ch. d'Aff. [Chargé d'Affaires] appears to rule the roost, Souhart,[8] a sort of Fr[ench]. Parkes. He tells me he has some expectations of succeeding Balloy at Teheran: I devoutly wish they may be realized.

[Karl von] Boleslawski the Austrian manifests great desire to be a friend, and says I may "speak quite plainly" to him. Volunteered the information that "Sir Charles [Euan-Smith][9] was a great misfortune" and that the Sultan looks on the Fr. as his saviours. Naturally, I had nothing to tell him but that I was trying to understand the situation.

I earnestly hope [Sir West] Ridgeway's[10] proposals for the reorganization of the consular service will be adopted.[11] If Morocco is of any value to us, it is worth spending a little money to improve our position. I take it this country is more important to us politically than even commercially. In all matters a trading V.C. [Vice-Consul] will always be at a disadvantage as compared with Fr. & Sp. V-Consuls de carrière.

---

[8] Fernand-Arthur Souhart, First Secretary at the French Legation, 1892-94.
[9] Sir Charles Euan-Smith (1842-1910) preceded Satow as Envoy Extraordinary and Minister Plenipotentiary at Tangier. Appointed in 1891, he travelled to Fez, the capital of Morocco, in 1892, in the hope of concluding a commercial treaty and an agreement to end slavery. After disagreements with the Sultan, his mission failed and no treaty or agreement was signed. He was relieved of his post in 1893.
[10] Col. Rt. Hon. Sir Joseph West Ridgeway (1844-1930) was the head of a special mission sent to Morocco in January 1893 to restore good relations after Euan-Smith's failure in 1892.
[11] On August 22, 1893 Currie had told Satow he thought Ridgeway's proposals were impossible because he (Currie) could not get the money. (Satow's diary)

PRO 30/33 14/4   Semi-official Letters from Uruguay (March 31 – June 9, 1893) and Morocco (September 4 – December 18, 1893)

Besides Ridgeway's proposals, there is one which I think of making shortly namely, the apptmt. of a consular assistant here in place of the present consular clerk, who gets £100 a year out of the office allowance as salary, & is besides Reuter's agent and a banker alias money-lender! De Vismes is the only man we have who can read & write Moorish, and we ought to have a man growing up to take his place.

I want to give up the office allowance and give vouchers for the expenditure, which it does not cover.

 y.v.t.
  E.S.

8. Satow to Currie
17.9.93
Dear Currie,

I don't think much importance is to be attached to the row at Fez betw. the Sultan's gatekeeper and the "Jews and Christians" of Gharnit's letter. Macleod has written privately that he thinks the B.Ss. shld. be fined, but A. Maclean, who has read the correspce. thinks a reprimand ought to be sufficient. His view is that our people were imprudent & therefore to blame for being where they were, that they ought to have gone away when the gatekeepers first objected to their presence; & that the gatekeepers then put themselves in the wrong by using force.

In any other eastern country I shld. have thought the affair too trivial to report, & shld. in fact not have troubled Ld. R. with it, had not Gh. asked that it might be sent home.

I have also not written abt. the robbery of the couriers on the road fr. here to Rabat. In this case the Fr[ench]. were equally interested, so I arranged with Souhart to write similar notes complaining to the Sultan.

I am told that some of the interpreters of the foreign legations have an interest in the free export of grain being discontinued, especially the German dragoman [professional interpreter] & Sicsu the Belgian; because they can then carry on a nice little trade by means of free passes granted to the legations. It is unlikely that the Sultan will pay any heed to the joint note of the colleagues, but to have got two months more is something gained. The

PRO 30/33 14/4 Semi-official Letters from Uruguay (March 31 – June 9, 1893) and Morocco (September 4 – December 18, 1893)

merchants thought they had only till Oct. 12; it now turns out that the concession ends on Dec. 9.

Kaid Maclean[12] has come down here. He tells me the Sultan is to be at Talifelt on the 22nd instant, and that he is afterwards going to Figuig [on the Algerian border]. Then he will return to Rabat.

As to Figuig, it seems unwise of him to go there, provoking Fr. susceptibilities, but if he will, I don't see how it can be helped. Offering our advice to him when he does not ask for it seems worse than useless.

There is an Austrian at Rabat named Gayling, who tells people confidentially that he is employed by the Br. Govt., & that he is waiting for instructions fr. Ld. R.: he will then go to Figuig to put a spoke in the Fr. wheel. He seems well provided with Engl. banknotes, & has changed £170. This is Harry Maclean's report.

Shall I disavow this man?

y.v.f.

P.S. I have got a journal kept by the interpreter of Kerdec, the Frenchman who was at Fez during Sir Ch. Euan Smith's mission. It is very curious. K. & the interpreter have quarrelled. Souhart was in the business. Devismes obtained it, & will make a précis, wch. I shall send you privately with the original papers. E.S.

9. Satow to Currie

25/9/93

My dear Currie

Many thanks for your two notes abt. drawing for money if needed.

The article on the Pall Mall is attributed here to Meakin. He is also thought to be O'Conor's inform[an]t. with regard to Bubeker.

You know there is a great deal of difficulty in getting the Sultan's sanction to any purchase of land by a foreigner. I do not propose to write officially, but this is what I think of doing. In any case where a B.S. bonâ fide purchases or is already in possn., to back him

---

[12] General (Kaid) Sir Harry Maclean (1848-1920). He went to Morocco in 1877. Instructor to the Moroccan army. British political agent at the Sultan's court.

PRO 30/33 14/4   Semi-official Letters from Uruguay (March 31 – June 9, 1893) and Morocco (September 4 – December 18, 1893)

up by every means per fas et nefas [by all means, permitted or not] and if the native Auth. protest, I shld. then tell them the clause in the Madrid convention was not intended to give the Sultan the right of making arbitrary objections.

K. Maclean says the Sultan will be at Morocco city fr. Nov. till May. Both he & White think it wld. not be advisable to hold back fr. going to present credentials. I am waiting to see what ans[wer]. they write to my letter announcing arrival, & then shall be better able to form an opinion.

   y.v.t.

10. Satow to Currie
29.9.93
My dear Currie,

Kaid Maclean left again for Rabat the day before yesterday. At his request, I have written a letter to Gharnit sounding his praises, as has been done before.

He introduced the subject of his position as our confid[ential]. agent. He agrees with me that it wld. not be desirable to make him Consul with an office allowance. That we shld. wait until I see the Sultan, & then I shld. say that I have found Mc. a straightforward man, a good servt. of his and at the same time an Englishman in whom I trust; and that whenever he makes any state[men]t. to him on my behalf, he is to regard it as coming straight from me. In short that he shld. recognize that K. Maclean is a confidential go-between.

Maclean informs me he is not in the least anxious to give up his present position with the Sultan, but that he is a poor man, who finds it difficult to make money in the way Moorish officials do.

I did not discuss with him the amount he looks for from us; but I suppose he expects something more than he has recd. in times past. He says that as soon as the proposed arrange[men]t. about his position is made, he wld. take as his private secretary a young fellow named S.W. Bewicke (the St. Stephens Club) who knows Arabic, and has been here abt. two years.[13] Then there would always be some one with the Sultan, even if he were

---

[13] Satow later mentions William Standert Bewicke's death in Gibraltar and that he got him appointed vice-consul at Tetuan in 1895. (Diary, August 16, 1912)

PRO 30/33 14/4   Semi-official Letters from Uruguay (March 31 – June 9, 1893) and Morocco (September 4 – December 18, 1893)

away on leave in Engl.

I shld. be glad to know what I may promise to Maclean.

y.v.t.

11. Satow to Currie

29.9.93

My dear Currie

I had several talks with K.M. during his stay here, and gave him a short memo. abt. what he might say to the Sultan when he next sees him.[14] That will prob. be at Rabat in about two months time. Fr[om]. there the court will go to Morocco.

He says that the Sultan feels himself helpless about Tuat, and that if the Fr[ench]. choose, they must have it. As to Figuig, he is inclined to go there from Tafilet, but fears the F[rench]. might not like it!

I told him that in case the Sultan gave him an opportunity, he shld. say the advice of the British Govt. was "to keep quite quiet, and not seek to get any stronger hold than he has had hitherto." Maclean was also to warn him agst. allowing any harm [to] come to a Frenchman named Deschanel who is just starting for a journey to Tuat.

Cape Juby.   M. says the Sultan feels this business very much. I told him in case the Sultan spoke to him abt. it to say "Who do you prefer to have for your neighbour on the other side of the Wad Draa?" Nothing more; as a text for meditation.

Mellah at Mogador. I said that "plans were reported to have been prepared by a govt. engineer, & the only question is abt. the funds for building: if the Sultan cannot find the money, let him hand over the ground to the Jewish Sheikhs. It wld. produce a good effect if the Sultan were to do this off his own bat."

M. replied that it was the fault of the richer Jews of Mogador, who owned the houses in the present Mellah, and were so opposed to the cheapening of rents by its extension, that they had presented a petition protesting that no extension was needed.

I told him that the Sultan shld. disregard that, and simply give the ground wch. had been

---

[14] See diary for September 26, 1893.

PRO 30/33 14/4   Semi-official Letters from Uruguay (March 31 – June 9, 1893) and Morocco (September 4 – December 18, 1893)

asked for. By that we shld. know whether he wished to please H.M.G.

With regard to my going to see the Sultan much depended on the ans. to my letter announcing my arrival. He might say to the Sultan that "H.M.G. were much hurt at the way Sir Ch. E-S. mission had terminated. They are in no hurry to make any approaches to H.S.M. [His Sultanic Majesty] unless they see some tokens of good will on his part." At Maclean's request I added "The emperor knows whether the friendship of Engl. is of any value to him. Engl. of course is quite able to take care of her own interests without help."

Maclean said that it wld. be difficult to get the Sultan to write a letter inviting me to Court, as this wld. establish an inconvenient precedent, but wld. it suffice if the Sultan sent him a message thro' me. I said it wld. be enough for myself, but I wanted some visible token wch. others might see, and that wld. be the immediate release of the Agents of B.S. who had been imprisoned & the settlement in favour of Grace Bros. of a question relating to the tenancy of a house at Mogador.

Protection. Mc. says the Fr. & It. are every day giving protection to Moors, to any one who asked for it. That the Sultan cares nothing for our disinterested attitude of abstention, so long as we cannot make the others give up the practice.

Isn't it rather Quixotic to allow persons who wld. willingly come under our aegis [to] place themselves faute de mieux under Fr. or It. influence. It may sound very well to offer to the Sultan in exch: for commercial concessions, our good offices with other Powers for the abolition of protection, but we ought to know that we shall have no faithful allies in this anti-protection crusade.

I propose therefore to give a protection-paper now and then to a deserving object, without making any official matter of it. Besides, under the Madrid Convention we are entitled to twelve protégés, & we only have half a dozen.

 y.v.t.

12. Satow to Kaid Maclean

2/10/93.

Dear Maclean (Kaid H.)

I enclose the Fr[ench]. newspaper & transl[atio]n. The latter however does not come

PRO 30/33 14/4 Semi-official Letters from Uruguay (March 31 – June 9, 1893) and Morocco (September 4 – December 18, 1893)

quite to the end of the article. It seemed advisable to omit from "M. Privat-Deschanel est un partisan convaincu de l'annexion militaire de Touat" and the following two paras.

Can you tell me anything of Mulai el Hadj of Tamshlot or Tanieslet near Marrakesh. I have a sort of vague impression that you told me he had been taken under fr. protection lately. I have a special reason for wishing to know whether this is the case or not.

y.v.t.

13. Satow to Currie

2/10/93

My dear Currie,

With reference to my desp[atch]. Cons[ular]. No 19 of today abt. Macleod's office allowance I want to say that I have written in the belief that Ridgeway's proposal for turning Kaid M. into a Consul or V-C. to go abt. the Court will not be adopted, & that Euan-Smith's arrange[men]t. of keeping an unpaid VC. at Fez is to be preferred. Abt. K.M.'s future position I wrote privately a few days ago. I think he can be most usefully employed as an unofficial agent, much in the same way as Linares,[15] who goes abt. c. the Sultan & has apparently gained a good deal of obstructive influence. Macleod will do better when he has a little more experience, & as the step has once been taken of putting him at Fez, I shld. be sorry to see any change – unless, of course, a V.C. de carrière were sent there, wch. I presume is at present out of the question. If there is no financial difficulty in the way of his allowance being granted, I hope it may shortly be settled.

If paid Vice-consuls are to be apptd. to Saffi, Laraiche & Mogador, as I hope will be done in accordance with Ridgeway's scheme, they cld. only be obtained I suppose fr. the Levant Assistants.

y.v.t.

14. Satow to Lord Rosebery

8 Oct. 1893

---

[15] Dr. Ferdinand Linares (1850-1938). French political agent at the Sultan's court.

PRO 30/33 14/4   Semi-official Letters from Uruguay (March 31 – June 9, 1893) and Morocco (September 4 – December 18, 1893)

Dr. Ld. Rosebery,

When Kaid Maclean was down here I had some talk with him abt. protection & looking at the print I saw that the Sultan had hinted to Sir Ch. Euan-Smith that our refraining fr. giving protection did not do him the least good, as long as we cld. not induce others to abandon the practice. I came to the conclusion that the system pursued by France and Italy will not be given up, & that many a good opportunity of acquiring influence may be lost to us owing to refusal to entertain the applications that Moors wld. make. There seems to be little doubt that many of the people are well disposed towards us, & wld. prefer to be under the aegis of Engl. When Mr. Harris,[16] whom I knew only by report called on me[17] & said that he had corresponded with you about Mulai el Hadj of Tamshlot, I saw that the suggestion was a good one, but hardly liked to do anything unless he cld. show me your letter. That he was not able to do, but as he seemed to be speaking in perfect good faith I telegraphed. I was very glad to receive your ans[wer]. in the affirmative. Of course I do not intend to inform the Moorish Govt., at least not at present.

Miss Herdman[18] who came to see me today,[19] spoke of a Sherif near Fez who is desirous of coming under British protection. He is an important man among some tribes round the site of Volubilis[20] marked in Bianconi's map. She seems a discreet & sensible woman, & deserves encouragement. It is very plucky of her companion Miss [J.L.] Read to go & live at Sifro [Sefrou] by herself. They seem to be getting a hold over some of the Berbers.

The Fr. Germ. Ital. & Belg. Ministers are away still. Potestad[21] said to me the other day that Spain wld. at all risks put an army on shore to resist a Fr. advance to the Muluya, & asked what I thought England wld. do. I replied that I felt certain she wld. stand by any power in resisting an attempt to seize Tangier, but that I cld. say nothing abt. the Muluya.

---

[16] Walter Burton Harris (1866-1933). Journalist, traveler and socialite. Special correspondent for *The Times* in Morocco, permanent correspondent from 1906.
[17] See diary for September 29, 1893.
[18] Miss Emma Herdman was part of the Mission to the Berbers at Fez, and the North Africa Mission, which had a majority of women members. She directed the N.A.M. from 1888 until her death in 1899.
[19] See diary for October 8, 1893.
[20] A partly excavated Berber and Roman city near the city of Meknes.
[21] Marquis de Potestad-Fornari (1828-1917) was the Spanish Minister in Morocco in 1893.

PRO 30/33 14/4   Semi-official Letters from Uruguay (March 31 – June 9, 1893) and Morocco (September 4 – December 18, 1893)

He was very pleased at being supported in the Melilla affair, as neither the Italian nor the Germ. Ch. d'Aff. had been near him. As for Souhart, he believed him to have been closeted with Torres[22] pretty frequently, & to have been consulted abt. the answers to his notes demanding reparation. I find that Souhart is greatly detested by the Austrian German, as well as by the Spaniard, and it wld. be a general relief to everybody if he got his promotion to a better post.

It is believed that the Sultan is still encamped outside the centre of Tafilet, and that he has difficulties with his brother there. His next move seems uncertain, but Kaid Maclean expected him to be at Morocco abt. Xmas. I have told him to take an opportunity of saying to the Sultan that I shall not go to Court unless he shows signs of a better disposition towards England. Personally I have no desire to go there until I feel assured of a good reception. I have seen Torres once only since my arrival, when we exchanged visits [on August 30th and 31st in diary] but I hear he expressed some curiosity about my going to see the Sultan.

I hope my request for an assistant at the Consulate will be granted, & a man picked out who has special ability in <u>talking</u> Arabic. The question of oral interpretation with the Sultan seems fr. all I have heard to be of the greatest importance. De Vismes is an admirable scholar, but every one tells me he is not fluent nor elegant in colloquial Arabic.

    Y. m. t. [Yours most truly?]

15. Satow to Lord Rosebery

9 Octr. 1893

Dear Lord Rosebery,

In continuation of my letter of yesterday, I learn that both the Germ. & Italian Ch. d'Aff. have spoken to Torres in support of the Spanish Minr. [Potestad]   The latter intends to content himself with his representations to Torres, and will not address the Court; the "advice" given him by those he has consulted is to the effect that if he wrote in strong terms to the Sultan the latter wld. be angry, if he wrote in moderate style, the Sultan wld. fancy

---

[22] Si Hadj Mohammed Torres was the Moorish Minister for Foreign Affairs, resident in Tangier. A descendant of an Andalusian Muslim family.

PRO 30/33 14/4 Semi-official Letters from Uruguay (March 31 – June 9, 1893) and Morocco (September 4 – December 18, 1893)

that Spain was afraid of him. He prefers therefore to wait & see the result of the report made by Torres.

I had suggested to him that he shld. send Major Cañizares from Morocco to the Sultan, with instructions to urge him to take speedy steps, & I offered to instruct Kaid Maclean to go with him. We are both convinced that Souhart is offering advice to the Sultan & it seemed to me not unlikely that these two officers wld. be able to produce a counter effect. At first Potestad inclined to accept this proposal: but after some reflection, & consulting the former Sp. dragoman Rinaldi, drew back. It may be that he does not wish to commit himself openly to any kind of joint action with Engl.: in fact he said that Spain had by supporting Sir Ch. Euan-Smith been involved in his failure, meaning no doubt that Engl. could not be relied on to put her foot down. Or perhaps he does not venture to imperil the position of the Sp. Military Mission by sending to the Sultan one of its members, after H.M. had expressly desired that the Missions shld. not accompany him to Tafilelt. At the same time Potestad tells me that the Dr. of the M.M. was much pressed to go with the court, as he is the ordinary medical attendant of the ladies of the harem, but Cañizares refused to give him permission. Had he gone, Dr. Linares wld. prob. have been left behind. The Sultan has recently sent for two Ulema[?] from each of the ports, Sadiker Hadan & Temsemani (the latter is a nickname fr. his birthplace or place of residence) that he may consult with them on matters of importance. One rumour is that the question to be submitted to them is an arranget. with France abt. frontier matters but P. says he has heard that there is a suspicion of a protectorate being on the tapis [under consideration]. If that be the case he does not see how the accomplish[men]t. of the project is to be prevented, for tho' Spain wld. be willing to resist by placing a force on the Mediterranean boundary, she lacks the necessary naval force to cover a disembarkment.

I am not able to judge what chance of success such a project may have, but I am disposed to think Souhart's object will be to lead the Moorish Govt. to treat the affair with insouciant[?] attention, in the confidence that Sp. will not venture on very active measures of reprisal agst. the Riffians. Potestad thinks the existence of the Sp. Govt. depends on their showing that they are acting with formness, but hints that they are in no position to undertake a campaign agst. the tribes, who he says can turn out 60,000 men armed with

PRO 30/33 14/4   Semi-official Letters from Uruguay (March 31 – June 9, 1893) and Morocco (September 4 – December 18, 1893)

Remingtons made in Spain, whence they are smuggled to the Riff.[23]

Added a p.s. to say that Henckel did not send or write or speak to Torres.

16. Satow to K. Hy. Maclean
13.10.93
My dear Maclean,

Many thanks for your letters of Sept. 29 & Oct. 5, with the description of the road fr. Fez to the Sultan's camp. Your idea of going in person to the Sultan, with a letter abt. the arrest of the Agents is excellent, & I am sending you a letter to Gharnit abt. the matter, explaining that I think it of such extreme importance that instead of trusting to correspce. or other means, I am despatching you to express my feelings orally. This will render the other letters to him wch. you sent me to look at unnecessary, and so we will put them in the fire. I am very anxious that the Sultan's people shld. treat the Fr. traveller Deschanel with every attention & watch over his safety as if he were the apple of an eye.

In case they shld. talk about Melilla to you, I am sure you will counsel them wisely. You know by this time that on the 2nd the Riff people attacked a party engaged in constructing a fort near the Sanctuary of Sidi Guariach, & there was a serious engagement in wch. the Spaniards lost 18 killed & 13 wounded, the Moors we suppose suffering more heavily. The Spaniards of course were entirely within their rights, & the Riff people behaved abominably. It behoves the Sultan to bestir himself, if he does not wish to see a conflagration arise the extent of wch. & its ultimate consequences would be difficult to foresee. I have recd. special instructions fr. London to support the Sp. Min. The Sultan must stop the Riff people from attacking.

   y.v.t.
    E.S.

P.S. I enclose copy of an unsigned note wch. I sent to Torres. Speak to Gharnit in the same strain. E.S.

---

[23] The Riff is a mainly mountainous cultural region in the northern part of Morocco.

PRO 30/33 14/4   Semi-official Letters from Uruguay (March 31 – June 9, 1893) and Morocco (September 4 – December 18, 1893)

17. Satow to Currie

16 Oct. 1893

My dear C.

I heard fr. Kaid Maclean the other day that he had recd. fr. Gharnit a temporising ans[wer]. abt. the arrested agents, & at his suggestion I have written a rather stiffer letter to Gharnit than before, & despatched it to Maclean to be taken by him to the Sultan's camp. I told Potestad that I was going to send off Maclean, in order that if he liked he might profit by the opport[unit]y. He merely asked that I wld. tell Macl. to speak to the Sultan in the sense of my Note verbale to Torres.

The Sultan's principal wives passed thro' Rabat the other day on the way to Morocco, wch. seems to show that he is on his way thither. His favourite son M Abdul Aziz is in the neighbourhood of Casablanca to settle the disturbances that have occurred there, & the eldest son Mulai Mahomèd is to go to the Beni Hassan & put them in order. These are the people that have lately been robbing the postal couriers, Engl. Fr. & Moorish without much distinction.

The Sultan will have a pretty bill to pay for the Melilla business. It has been suggested to me [Margin: (this was by Anspach)][24] that the Spaniards wld. be justified in seizing Mogador as a material guarantee for pay[men]t., but I don't think this idea emanated fr. the brain of Potestad. It was more likely intended as a draw. I professed the greatest horror at the bare notion.

Mr. or Capt. Gayling[25] is here, & brings credential fr. the "African & Gold Coast Trading Corpn. Ltd".   He says he is to meet another agent of the said Co. & to travel to Timbuctoo. I hope they'll eat him.

    y.v.t.

P.S. The Spanish Military Mission will shortly be withdrawn. I hear that this was decided

---

[24] Edward Anspach was the Belgian envoy in Morocco.
[25] Geyling was an Austrian imposter, pretending to be consul for a nonexistent state, Araucania-Patagonia. (Douglas Porch, *The Conquest of Morocco*, Farrar, 2nd edition 2005, p. 19).

on 3 mos. ago, as a measure of economy. Whether France & Italy will follow suit I don't know.

18. Satow to Currie

25 Oct. 1893

My dear Currie,

Tattenbach[26] came back on the 21st & on the 23rd Henckel, who was sent here fr. Madrid to be in charge during his absence, went off. The latter is a very charming fellow.

We have news fr. the Sultan up to the 7th inst. At that time he had not yet heard of the Melilla affair, & Potestad does not expect an ans[wer]. before the 29th. I almost doubt whether he will get it then. The Sultan is hardly the man to reply by return of post. Italy, France, Germany, Portugal & England have now all spoken to the Moorish Govt. in support of the Spaniards. Somehow people do not appear to confide [i.e. have faith] in the Sultan's power to control the Riff tribes. Even Potestad, who is very outspoken, blames the Spanish Govt. for having acted so precipitately in ordering the construction of the fort. This part of the country, round Tangier, is largely populated by people fr. the Riff, & there is, I am told, a great deal of enthusiasm expressed about the supposed defeat of the Spaniards. The Sultan will prob. not reach Tafilelt, & they expect him at Morocco before long, perh. by the middle of Nov. Maclean left Rabat for the camp on the morning of the 16th, & must be almost there by this time. On his arrival he will send me an express.

Fr. the telegram abt. Bub[e]ker wch. came today I am afraid that my proceedings with regard to that gentleman are considered hard. I send a copy of the letter I drafted to be sent to him by De Vismes. If anyone else but himself shld. come to know of it, that wld. be thro' Bub[e]ker's own fault. I have not had any direct correspce. with him since my arrival, because altho' he won his case in the Gib[raltar]. court, & he is well spoken of in the correspce. I cannot help fearing that a strict investigation may reveal some black spots. I am certain that to the men in the legation it wld. be a great relief if we had no more dealings with him. As a political newsmonger he is of very little use, and many of the things he

---

[26] Count Christian von Tattenbach, German Minister Resident in Morocco.

PRO 30/33 14/4 Semi-official Letters from Uruguay (March 31 – June 9, 1893) and Morocco (September 4 – December 18, 1893)

wrote to my predecessors were incorrect. His letters to me since my arrival here have done little but prophesy smooth things abt. the Sultan's intention of returning to his ancient friendship with England. But I see no proofs of that. The messenger sent fr. Fez to the camp with my letters announcing my arrival and urging the release of the imprisoned agents of B.Ss. was kept waiting 22 days, & then dismissed with a short note to Macleod that answers were in preparation. That does not show any very great eagerness to be friendly. So I incline to mistrust Bubeker.

I am afraid the inquiry I have been instructed to institute will be a difficult business. Clearly I must conduct it myself, and hear all the evidence thro' an interpreter, wch. is an imperfect manner of arriving at the truth. I shld. therefore be heartily glad if his resignation were accepted as a final windup of the whole business.

  y.v.t.
   E.S.

P.S. A circular fr. Gharnit to the F.RR. [Foreign Representatives] has just come dated 4 Oct. & stating that the Sultan is about to proceed to the Gharb to punish tribes who have taken advantage of his absence to carry off the public treasure to Tafilelt, & to rob the couriers of the Govt. & the FRR. Various alarmist reports were going abt. a week ago of his being surrounded & hemmed in by Berber troops, in fact in dire straits, & a telegram to that effect was sent to London & Madrid by the telegraphic agents; but I have not seen that it has been published.

26 Oct.   E.S.

19. Satow to Currie

30 Oct. 1893

My dear Currie,

People here are beginning to gossip abt. the meeting of the Channel & Mediterranean squadrons at Gib., & saying that Engl. is prepared for eventualities. I have explained to those who have spoken to me on the subject that last year, in order to avoid hurting some people's susceptibilities the Channel squadron was kept away fr. Gib. but that this year it has come there in the normal course of things.

PRO 30/33 14/4   Semi-official Letters from Uruguay (March 31 – June 9, 1893) and Morocco (September 4 – December 18, 1893)

Potestad suggested to me that a naval demonstration of the Powers off Tangier wld. make a wholesome impression on the Sultan's mind. I said that was possible, but on condition that it was not after the style suggested by M. Ribot.[27]

If it shld. ever come to that, I am inclined to think that a visit of men of war of some size to Mogador & Mazagan wld. produce a more immediate effect on the Sultan than a demonstration at Tangier.

I have reported in my No. 153 of 23 Oct. that Souhart had informed Potestad that he had received instructions to support him thoroughly. Tattenbach having more than once expressed to me his doubts whether the Fr. Legation was acting on the square, I asked P. yesterday afternoon what he thought. P. replied that before he left Madrid Vega de Armijo[28] had told him there was an agreement betw. Spain & Engl. not to take any step in Morocco without informing each other. That he might consequently consult quite unreservedly with the Engl. represve., as also with the Italian and German. But with the Frenchman he was to be on his guard. After the offer of support I made to him by Ld. Rosebery's instructions, Moret[29] had written or telegraphed to him in the same sense. Since the frank language held to him by Souhart, he was of opinion that he had no reason to misbelieve him. Personally Souhart was no favourite of his, but in the present instance he thought he was acting straightforwardly. He wld. have been less inclined to trust d'Aubigny[30] who has played him a trick or two.

I said to Potestad that for my part I thought Souhart had spoken honestly. If he were working agst. Spain, he wld. have kept away and said nothing.

Tattenbach seems to be preternaturally suspicious, also a little inclined to be obstructive for the pleasure of the thing.

It appears that Linares, who left Fez with the Sultan, quitted the camp recently for

---

[27] Alexandre Ribot (1842-1923). French prime minister five times: 1892-93; 1893; 1895; 1914 and 1917.
[28] Don Antonio, Marquis of Vega de Armijo (1824-1908). Spanish Minister of State, 1892-3.
[29] Segismundo Moret y Prendergast (1833-1913). Spanish Foreign Minister, April 1893-November 1894.
[30] Jules Henrys, Comte d'Aubigny (1844-1922). French Envoy Extraordinary and Minister Plenipotentiary at Tangier, 1892-94. Replaced by Monbel.

PRO 30/33 14/4   Semi-official Letters from Uruguay (March 31 – June 9, 1893) and Morocco (September 4 – December 18, 1893)

Morocco, where he is supposed to have arrived by this time.

It is extremely difficult, almost impossible indeed, to find out anything with certainty. Even the Fr[ench]. with Dr. Linares constantly by the Sultan's side, are not correctly informed. Bubeker in that matter is of very little use, & of what he knows we have not the monopoly. He writes also to the interpreter of the Austrian legation, who is his Tangier man of business.

 Yours very truly
  Ernest Satow

<u>20. Satow to Currie</u>

1 Nov.

My dear Currie,

As soon as I got your reply to my telegram that I might comply with Potestad's request to write to the Moorish govt. in support of the Spaniards, I sent notes to d'Aubigny, Tattenbach & Gentile proposing to combine in concocting something that wld. serve as a common basis of what we had been asked to write to Gharnit. Tattenbach came first (I am confined to the sofa, & so cld. not go to see them), & undertook to telegraph to Berlin for leave to join. Then d'Aubigny, who expressed his regret at having already the previous day, immediately after Potestad left him, sat down & written a Note in the required sense, which he despatched the same courier by the evening for Fez. He told me what he had said, wch. was in so many words that the Sultan shld. at once return fr. the road to Tafilelt & proceed in person to the Riff. He added that he was no friend of joint notes, or common action, because when they came together, first one colleague and then another, offered objections and amendments, so that valuable time was lost. Gentile came last, and readily agreed. This afternoon I have also seen the Portuguese, whom Potestad asked might be invited to join. The two latter have agreed to a rough draft wch. I have prepared. They will make their own translations, and send them thro' us. Tattenbach has not yet got authorisation. I hope however that we may get our Notes off by the 4th or 5th, if not earlier. There is a government courier fr. Fez. Noone here seems to have any definite information abt. the Sultan's movements. Potestad believes him to be on his way to Morocco having already

240

PRO 30/33 14/4   Semi-official Letters from Uruguay (March 31 – June 9, 1893) and Morocco (September 4 – December 18, 1893)

recrossed the Atlas. d'Aubigny believes him to be halfway between the Atlas and Tafilelt. It does not at all suit the French book that he shld. go to the latter place, hence d'Aubigny's hurry to ask him to come away at once to attend to affairs at Melilla. Gentile thinks he is close upon Tafilelt. I am afraid that he will not hurry himself abt. the Spaniards, & that his first ans. when it comes will be of an evasive character. There are these people abt. Rabat & Laraiche whom he has got to reduce to obedience before he takes proceedings agst. the Riff. I hope however a good deal from Maclean's representations, when he reaches the Sultan. I hope to hear from him before very long. Anyhow the Spaniards have got into a nice mess in Melilla.[31]

I don't think there is any danger here. A suggestion has been made by the Belgian, no doubt prompted by the Fr.man, to ask Russia to subscribe to the Cape Spartel lighthouse. But I do not think it is the business of the lighthouse commission to invite any Power to subscribe, unless they get instructions. At present Russia is represented by Spain. If the Russians offered to subscribe, I suppose they wld. be admitted. Otherwise, we may as well leave it alone.

Arthur Herbert[32] arr. this afternoon, he is going to be Master of the Hounds this season.

y.v.t.   E.S.

21. Satow to Maclean

3rd Nov. 1893.

My dear Maclean,

I was very glad to get your letter of the 24th; it has relieved me of much anxiety. You seem to have gone very quickly.

The Fr. & German Ministers have at the request of the Sp. Min. already written to the

---

[31] The Melilla War was a conflict between Spain and 39 of the Riff tribes of Northern Morocco. It began in October 1893, was openly declared on November 9th, and was resolved by the Treaty of Fez in 1894 by which Morocco paid war reparations and pledged to pacify the tribes.

[32] Probably Arthur James Herbert (1855-1921). Diplomat and later first British envoy to Norway, 1905-11. Satow had known him when he was in Uruguay and Herbert was at Buenos Aires.

PRO 30/33 14/4 Semi-official Letters from Uruguay (March 31 – June 9, 1893) and Morocco (September 4 – December 18, 1893)

Sultan urging him to at once turn back & proceed to the seat of disturbance, on the ground that he cannot trust any Khalifa to do things properly at Melilla. Colaço, Gentile & I are writing today in somewhat similar sense, but not actually recommending him to come back fr. Tafilelt in so many words, but we express the concern of our govts. at his being at such a distant part of his dominions when his immediate attention is required by a serious event. But that you may better understand I send you the rough draft of my note to Gharnit.

Genl. Magallo was killed in a big fight that took place on the 27 & 28. Then on the 1st there was more fighting & again on the 2nd. The Sp. are increasing their garrison & have now 7000 men there. But what I now hear on good authority is that the Beni Snassen have made up their minds to join the Riff people. Yesterday the Riffians of the surrounding country attacked in force, nearly reaching the forts. The Span. sent a ship to bombard the vill[ages]. of the coast of Kebdana, opp. the Chafarinas isl[and]s. & destroyed the dwellings. You shld. only tell such parts of this as you think expedient.

But I want you to impress upon the Sultan's mind that the little cloud I spoke of in my note to Gharnit is rapidly increasing in size, & that the safety of his dominions is threatened unless he makes very great exertions to bring the Riff back to order. It is useless for him to suppose that the conflict will be confined to Melilla, or that by doing nothing he can save himself. Engl. Fr. & Italy are supporting the Sp. govt. in their action, at present only with their openly expressed sympathy, but later they may each of them find it necessary to take actual measures by the side of Sp. to ensure that the rights of Sp. are recognized. If that shld. come to pass because H.S.M. persists in going to Tafilelt instead of coming down to this part of the country he will have only himself to blame for the downfall of the Empire of Morocco.

I repeat the situation is one of the greatest peril, & nothing but the personal presence of the Sultan can save it. [End of letter]

22. Satow to Currie

6/11/93

My dear Currie,

Tattenbach after all did not join the Italian & myself, but wrote direct to the Sultan, &

PRO 30/33 14/4   Semi-official Letters from Uruguay (March 31 – June 9, 1893) and Morocco (September 4 – December 18, 1893)

then came to tell me he had done so, because having had instructions fr. Berlin he cld. not delay a moment.

He also suggested to Torres that if the Sultan's first ans[wer]. is unsatisfactory he shld. conceal it fr. P. in order to avoid the unfavourable impression it wld. make on the Sp. Govt. Then he went to P. & took credit to himself for a piece of friendly advice given to Torres.

When P. told me this curious story. I advised him not to countenance any such proceeding for it wld. be sure to get out, & other people wld. get the credit of being better informed than himself.

P. talked to me with great frankness. He says the head of the Span. mil. mission who is now in Tangier, wishes to call together all the Spaniards in Tangier who are liable to military service, & they have been considering how these men might be armed. There must be a few hundreds. I have no doubt that the idea at the bottom of this is to be ready, in case of necessity to anticipate anyone else in occupying Tangier. He has also spoken of the necessity of having a few ships ready at Algeciras, & asked me whether I cld. bring ships here. I told him I had no instructions, & rather than hastily take any such step wld. run some risk of danger to the foreign community.

There is no fear however of these schemes coming to fruition unless the Sultan shld. refuse or hesitate to give satisfaction. Then the Span[iar]ds. wld. probably propose a joint occupation of some sort, perh. themselves at Tangier, the Fr. up to the Muluya [River] & ourselves somewhere else.

The information I telegraphed on the 3rd as coming fr. Morocco was Bubeker's. White thinks it is mere bazaar gossip.

   y.v.t.

23. Satow to W.B. Harris
Confid.
T[angier].
8/11/93.
My dear Harris,

Thank you very much for your letters of the 22nd, 26th & 29th Oct. I hope the letter wch.

PRO 30/33 14/4 Semi-official Letters from Uruguay (March 31 – June 9, 1893) and Morocco (September 4 – December 18, 1893)

de Vismes is writing to B[ubeker]. will put his mind at rest as regards protection. There has never been any idea of withdrawing it fr. him. Notice was given to him of an inquiry in consequence of instructions recd. fr. home, where there seems to have been an expectation of further awkward questions being asked in the House [of Commons]. I don't know yet, but I shld. not be surprised if B's letter of resignation were held to render inquiry into the past unnecessary. As I cld. not employ a man into whose character I had been directed to inquire until that inquiry was terminated, I said that B. shld. place his letter of apptmt. in my hands. But he has besides that a protection paper given him in 1886. I need not tell you that for my own part I have no desire to have an inquiry, & am doing all I can to stop it.

Our other friend[33] has written a letter in wch. he specially desires you shld. be allowed to accept the horse. You know I don't read Arabic, & it is rather a pity he shld. have written abt. the matter. But I don't see any reason why you shld. not accept the animal. Only don't tell people where you got it from. If there is one thing to be avoided it is giving people excuses for chattering. We have not yet heard what the Sultan means to do about Melilla; it is time he made up his mind, because things are getting serious.

Much luck on your journey fr. wch. I hope you will return safely.

y.v.t.

24. Satow to Currie

14.11.93

My dear C.,

I think that in my No. 166 I have managed to give you pretty nearly the text of Torres' note to P. It certainly does not admit that the Sultan will have to pay an indemnity, the word 'pay' being used only of the Riffians, & that in a metaphorical sense. P. says Moret has written to him that the Sp. Govt. desires to act with moderation, but that the newspapers give them no peace. He seems to suspect the Fr. of some underhand play & is not quite at ease abt. Tattenbach. The latter is perh. the origin of the rumour that the Sultan wld. propose arbitration, but as you will see fr. my desp[atch]. No. 167 the French legation

---

[33] The Sherif of Tamshlot (diary, November 3, 1893).

PRO 30/33 14/4   Semi-official Letters from Uruguay (March 31 – June 9, 1893) and Morocco (September 4 – December 18, 1893)

seems to be scheming for something of the kind. P. changes fr. day to day. At one time he was all for the status quo, then for joint pressure by Engl. France & Spain & any one else who wld. join. The last visit he paid me was the day before yesterday, when he discussed the share each of us wld. have in the partition of Morocco wch. he thinks imminent. He said that of course Sp. wld. get the least valuable portion. I did not allow him to suppose that this idea tempted me at all, & all along, to all the colleagues I have uniformly said that Engl. wld. not encourage any alteration of the status quo, & that she does not desire to put her hand into the hornet's nest. Everything is perfectly quiet at Tangier & at Tetuan. Macleod however writes that there is an uncomfortable feeling at Fez. Of the Sultan we have no certain news. Cañizares, the head of the Sp. military mission with the Sultan, who arr. here the day before yesterday, says the report at Morocco city was that the Sultan was not to be expected there till the mid. of Xber. [October] It turns out that Linares has been with the Sultan all the time. The latter had not on the 21st VIIber [September] reached the tomb of his ancestors, wch. app[ears]. to be a couple of m. S.E. of the prin. place in Tafilelt, but his brother Mulai u-Reschid had come out to meet him. I have not had any ans[wer]. to the letter I wrote to Gharnit announcing my arrival, & no notice has been taken of the Notes demanding the release of the arrested agents of BSs. But I expect to extract something out of the Sultan by Maclean. The Tangier town talk is that the Fr. are egging on the Sp. to make a great row over the Melilla business, & that we are trying to have it arranged à l'amiable [in a friendly way].

W.B. Harris started fr. Morocco city abt. end of Oct. disguised as a Moor, bound for Tafilet. I hope he will come to no harm. Bub[eke]r. has written several letters abt. my request that he shld. give up the paper of apptmt. given him by Sir J. Hay, wch. he has done; he seemed at first to think that his protection was to go too, but I have had a letter written by De Vismes reassuring him on this point. He still continues to send letters containing the gossip of the bazaar, wch. does not as a rule prove to be true. I have not had time yet to send you the correspce. on this subj. but it is for you to decide whether his resignation is to be accepted. If I may have an opinion it wld. be in favour of accepting it, saying something courteous to him abt. his past services and making him a present. The F.O. wld. then be able to say that he was no longer in any sense an agent of the legation, &

PRO 30/33 14/4 Semi-official Letters from Uruguay (March 31 – June 9, 1893) and Morocco (September 4 – December 18, 1893)

you could add that you had given instructions to have his past conduct inquired into, if you thought so much shld. be conceded to Meakin, who is O'Conor's source of information. The more I think of it, the more I am astonished at the impertinence of the Germans speaking to H.M.G. abt. the unfitness &c. of Bub[eke]r. They employ as their own dragoman quite as great a knave.

White has gone to Gib. abt. the trial of Alvarez who will prob. escape conviction, for want of witnesses. The Basha of Tetuan refuses to send his, & P. who was duly requested to give instructions, forgot. I have apptd. De Vismes to act pro. tem., wch. I hope will be approved.

y.v.t.

25. Satow to Hervey
Tangier Nov. 14/93
Dear Mr. Hervey,

I sent your telegram a short time ago asking to whom the office allowance for last quarter was paid, but I suppose it has been overlooked, as I have recd. no ans[wer].

The practice was formerly to pay the wages of the jailer, consulate clerk, cavass [armed police officer, guard, courier] &c. out of the fees, & when the acc[oun]ts. were made up the head of the mission repaid the amounts out of the office allowance, or rather I shld. say with the aid of it. Acc[ordingl]y. the wages for J[uly], Aug. & Sept. were so paid. I have of course no difficulty, as regards the pay[men]ts. for the period since I took charge, but to whom am I to look for reimbursement for the period ending 29 Aug.

My present idea is to send you the accts., with such of the fees as I can, leaving it to your dept. to settle with White & Ridgeway. As the office allowance shows a loss to the man who draws it, you can understand that no one is particularly anxious to have it paid to him.

Do you see any objection to the Consular accts. being sent to you direct from Casablanca for that port & subordinate vice consulates, & from the Tangier consulate for itself & subordinates in like manner. It wld. relieve me of some labour, & not throw any upon yr. department.

PRO 30/33 14/4 Semi-official Letters from Uruguay (March 31 – June 9, 1893) and Morocco (September 4 – December 18, 1893)

y.v.t.

26. Satow to Currie

17 Nov.

My dear C.

Many thanks for your private letter of the 8th. I am quite ready to admit that I acted with precipitation as regards Bubeker. The genl. approval by Ld. R & yourself is very encouraging & I appreciate it highly.

Applications have already been made to me for good offices in obtaining the contract for a loan wch. the applicants anticipate the Sultan will need to raise to pay the Sp. indemnity. One is fr. Isaac Abensur[34] who wants to go in for it with his cousin [Abraham] Pariente, the other fr. Forde[35] on behalf of himself & Fernan. I am telling them that I can give no promises abt. a matter wch. is yet in nubibus. [lit. 'in the clouds']

Nothing yet fr. Maclean; the Fr. paper has it that he has been turned back by the mtn. chiefs of the Atlas, & has returned to Morocco, but I have no news. Bubeker writing on the 7th did not mention his return. The same paper has also made an outcry abt. 4 ironclads of the Mediterranean squadron performing evolutions off Tetuan. Ad. Fairfax it seems thought of doing the same, but White told Lake it wld. be indiscreet, & we got a telegram yesterday to say the ships wld. not go near the African coast.   Potestad spoke to d'Aub. abt. the malicious article in the "Reveil du Maroc" wch. I sent by last bag, & he promised that the tone shld. be changed.

As far as I can learn the Sultan will have great difficulty in recrossing the Atlas, even if he wishes to do so. At the time the last couriers left he was engaged in composing a quarrel of some standing betw. the people of Tafilet & the Ait Atta a neighbouring tribe, & geny. in establishing his influence in that region. He prob. has no intention of going to the Riff, & I cannot help thinking he means to pass the winter where he is. Unless indeed the novelty of

---

[34] Isaac A. Abensur (1869-1937) was British delegate to the legislative assembly of Tangier and for years president of the Tangier Jewish community. A banker by profession and an interpreter (dragoman) to the Austrian legation. President of the Hygiene Commission. British national by virtue of a special law of the British parliament.
[35] Lewis Forde, Vice-consul at Laraiche.

PRO 30/33 14/4   Semi-official Letters from Uruguay (March 31 – June 9, 1893) and Morocco (September 4 – December 18, 1893)

½ doz. FRR [Foreign Representatives] acting in concert shld. frighten him into more active measures. It may have the contrary effect of suggestong to him that he had better keep out of the way of such disagreeable Mentors as long as possible.

d'Aubigny tells me he thinks the Melilla affair is going to be arranged quite comfortably, without its spreading any further. But at present this seems rather an optimistic view to take.

Benani is I think likely to be very useful. He is going off today to Marseilles to put off his Fr. nationality.

y.v.t.

27. Satow to Currie
Conf[idential].
22 Nov. 1893
My dear Currie,

P[otestad]. came to me just now & read to me a letter fr. Moret, dated 17 Nov. wch. begins by telling him that the nature of his communications to some of his colleagues as reported by them seem to have given rise to the idea that he is pursuing a policy wch. [could?] excite mistrust of Spain on the part of various Powers. I looked at the passage in Moret's letter, wch. seemed to suggest, as P. said, that he was suspected of aiming at a rapprochement with France. So I said that such an idea had never entered my head, as indeed it never has. I reminded him that we had once discussed the question whether Souhart was acting in good faith, and that we had both come to the conclusion that there was no ground for distrusting him; also that he had expressed to me the hope that out of this common anxiety might spring a common diplomatic action in the future. He added that it was true that he had expressed a personal opinion to Souhart that Fr. might for aught he cared take that & that Cantagalli had said pretty much the same. But that was not a reason for suspicion. I shld. be very sorry if anything I had said shld. be supposed to bear the meaning that Potestad was not perfectly frank and outspoken.

He read to me the rest of Moret's letter in wch. the latter directs him to point out to Torres that things are going on very slowly, that the 2nd ans. of the Sultan is not generally regarded as altogether satisfactory, that it contains nothing new & in particular that it does

PRO 30/33 14/4 Semi-official Letters from Uruguay (March 31 – June 9, 1893) and Morocco (September 4 – December 18, 1893)

not mention the subject of the indemnity. M. thinks the Sultan ought to give T. full powers to discuss this and other questions. P. is to tell him that Melilla is full of Sp. troops & they must strike a blow, unless the Sultan bestirs himself more actively. It is evident that Moret is getting impatient, not being alive to the fact that the Sultan is practically inaccessible at the present moment, & that it takes at least 12 days for a letter to reach him. [End of letter]

28. Satow to Currie

Secret.

Nov. 23. 1893.

My dear Currie,

Altogether I have given Benani $165, wch. at the current rate is £26.9.0. He has gone to Marseilles, to put off his French nationality, in wch. it seems he ought to be able to succeed.

Fr. what De Vismes tells me, it seems rather doubtful whether he will be a safe man to make use of. He has let out to various people that he gave documents to Devismes, & the Fr[ench]. Legation must know it. It appears too that he has an idea of going to see E-S. [Euan-Smith]

However, I don't think the money has been thrown away, only one must be cautious in the future in dealing with him.

   y.v.t.

29. Satow to Currie

Nov. 27. 93

My dear Currie,

I send you copy of a letter fr. Miss Herdman, a missionary lady at Fez, about a curious application to her to forward a letter to H.M.G. from a Sherif in the Sous. I think she now rather regrets having refused, but I have given he an opportunity of sending the letter to me if she likes to change her mind. The Shereef in question may either be a son of Mulai Mohammed Ben Hussein who was formerly said to be in correspce. with the Fr. (North Africa Print Pt. XVII p. 50) or a chief of the Ait Bu Amran with whom Curtis had doings in 1883 (North Africa Print Pt. IV p.43) or thirdly of the tribe with whom the Kirby syndicate

249

PRO 30/33 14/4   Semi-official Letters from Uruguay (March 31 – June 9, 1893) and Morocco (September 4 – December 18, 1893)

have been negotiating.

Potestad certainly seems to suspect me of having had a hand in his being called over the coals for talking indiscreetly to colleagues, tho' he does not say it right out. I shld. be very glad to know whether anything has been said at Madrid on this matter, for he has been much less cordial since he got that letter fr. Moret.

We are without news of the Sultan, & I have not had a line fr. Maclean since Oct. 25. I shld. not be surprised to hear that the former was marching to Morocco by way of Tarudant.

  y.v.t.

30. Satow to Currie

27 Nov. 1893

My dear Currie,

I have consulted White about the present for Boobeker, & he thinks that a silver gilt coffee service would be greatly appreciated. I propose to keep back my letter to him until the present arrives. In the meanwhile I enclose a copy of the draft for your approval.

  y.v.t.

31. Satow to Dallas

28.11.93

My dear Dallas,

Can you tell me whether any decision has been taken about my No. 139 of 5 Sept. asking that Quaritch[36] might be instructed to send us an Arabic Dicty. & a book on Mohammedan law. It is scarcely necessary to add that they are required for the Chancery, not for my private delectation.

I hope the silence with regard to my proposals for increasing wages of scribes & soldiers & for the apptmt. of an assistant to the Tangier Consulate means that these matters are being favourably considered. I am sadly in want of an unmarried man with a gift for colloquial & for making himself acceptable to natives.   [End of letter]

---

[36] Bernard Quaritch (1819-99), London bookseller.

PRO 30/33 14/4 Semi-official Letters from Uruguay (March 31 – June 9, 1893) and Morocco (September 4 – December 18, 1893)

32. Satow to Sir H.D. Wolff (part of letter)

Sir H.D. Wolff[37]

4 Dec.

I see a great deal of Potestad, wch. is natural under the circs. & we frequently consult together. The Sp. Govt. seems not to be aware of the great difficulty & uncertainty there is in communicating with the Sultan. They have telegraphed to P. that they must be placed in "immediate contact" with the Sultan. We none of us know for certain where he is at present, but conjecture him to be on the other side of the Atlas, somewhere near Tafilelt. So we send letters to Fez & the people there forward them on acc[ording]. to the best of their judg[men]t. The lowest estimate of time wch. a letter takes to reach him is twelve days. If you had an opportunity of saying something abt. this to Mr. Moret it might help him to understand the difficulties of P's position.

33. Satow to Currie

5/12/93.

My dear C.

Miss Henderson has sent me the mysterious letter, wch. purports to come fr. the Sherif formerly said to be in communication c. the Fr. It is obscurely expressed & De V. is not quite sure of its meaning. But apparently the idea is that the Sultan's seal shld. be surreptitiously affixed to some kind of charter empowering the Sherif to trade with the English, wch. wld. be handed to us to produce in case the Sultan made objections! It looks rather like a plant.

I telegraphed that Gaiffe professes to have a written promise of a concession to raise a loan, wch. in itself is not improbable. The information comes fr. [the Italian Minister] Cantagalli, who is most anxious to give check to the Fr[ench]. on every possible occasion. I told you of the application for countenance made to me by Forde & Fernan: the father of the former had to do with the former loan. If you approved, I shld. be inclined to give

---

[37] Sir Henry Drummond Wolff (1830-1908). British Ambassador to Madrid, 1892-1900.

PRO 30/33 14/4 Semi-official Letters from Uruguay (March 31 – June 9, 1893) and Morocco (September 4 – December 18, 1893)

Fernan a letter to the Court recommending him in general terms, for I imagine that the open support of this legation wld. at present be without value. All the Jews of Tangier are on the 'qui vive', & I daresay that Tattenb. will have a candidate for the loan. I suppose one need not mind who gets the business provided it is not a Fr.

P[otestad]. came to consult me yesterday morning abt. a note he was going to send to Torres. He had recd. a telegr. fr. Moret demanding to be placed in "immediate contact" with the Sultan in spite of his repeated explanations to Madrid that the Sult. is at least a fortnight's postal dist[ance]. fr. Tangier & that they must have patience. He is much inclined to say to Moret: "If you do not trust me, send some one else," but C. & I have urged him to say nothing of the kind. I have, at P's request, written to Sir H. Wolff [see previous letter] begging him if he sees an opportunity to explain to the Minr. for F.A. [Moret] the great difficulty there is in communicating with the Sultan, & I have sent him privately a copy of my No. 171, for even if it were opened by the Spanish Post, it contains nothing that might not be published in the market place.

To return to P's note reproducing the language of Moret's teleg: "The construction of the fort is proceeding peaceably, but as long as the Sultan does not himself take direct measures agst. the Riffians, it is the presence of a large Sp. army alone wch. restrains them, & the least collision might strike a spark wch. would light up a conflagration & perh. lead to war." Both C. & I objected to this phrase, wch. cld. only be interpreted as meaning war with the Sultan, & I hope P. will modify it, though it is an exact transcription, he says, of the teleg.

We have had some talk, that is C[antagalli]. & myself, with T[attenbach]. abt. the advisability of our sending in a note in support of Potestad. C. initiated it, by talking to T. but the latter is not easily to be induced to act in concert with anyone else, because he wishes to preserve the position of Sultan's confidential adviser wch. he imagines himself to enjoy. C. does not wish he says to separate himself fr. T. & wld. only act alone with me in the event of our getting special instructions to stir up the Sultan again.

What is curious is that Kerdec is evidently inspired by some one at Court, or perh. by the Fr. legation to poohpooh the Spaniards, & to insinuate in his paper that as the outbreak in the first instance was the fault of Spanish negligence, they will have to content themselves

PRO 30/33 14/4   Semi-official Letters from Uruguay (March 31 – June 9, 1893) and Morocco (September 4 – December 18, 1893)

with a very moderate indemnity, & I have no doubt myself that the Fr. are minimizing the importance of the affair in their confidential communications with the Sultan. One thing seems clear, that H.S.M. is in no hurry to leave his Tafilelt business to come to Fez or even to Morocco.

Young Carleton who was at Fez c. Euan-Smith & has recently married a certain Mrs. Leared, who is old enough to be his grandmother, is now the bosom intimate of Kerdec, after having been the confidant of Benani; & that even the sums of money wch. he got for his revelations to us are known to the other side.

Bubeker writes from Morocco that Maclean had reached the Sultan's camp. But it is strange that no letters shld. have come fr. him. Harris has reached Dades travelling towards Tafilelt.

y.v.t.

34. Satow to Currie
11 Dec. 1893
My dear Currie,

I heard on the 5th fr. Maclean. He reached the Sultan's camp on the 7 Nov. & wrote on the 10th that H.S.M. was going that day to pray at the Tomb of Mulai Al Sherif. & would shortly start for Marrakesh, where with good weather he might arr. by the end of this month. But more recent news makes it highly doubtful whether he will get there before the middle or end of January.

He writes that he had told Gharnit "all his grievances", i.e. the things I had said to him for the Sultan, & had been promised satisfactory answers; but nothing has come yet. He found them under the impression that the Spaniards have no money to make war with. Of course he said to Gharnit that Melilla was a serious business, but the latter seemed to think the Sultan had done enough in sending his brother to pacify the Riffians & in writing letters of regret for the Sp. Minr. At the time Maclean wrote the news of Margallo's death[38] had not reached him.

---

[38] General Juan Garcia y Margallo was the Spanish governor of Melilla, 1891-93.

PRO 30/33 14/4 Semi-official Letters from Uruguay (March 31 – June 9, 1893) and Morocco (September 4 – December 18, 1893)

Kerdec's paper continues in the same tone abt. Spain, ascribing the blame of the whole business to the imprevision of the Sp. Govt. I shld. not be surprised if what B. writes fr. Morocco be true, that the Sultan will behave towards Sp. as he did to England last year, and one can guess pretty well who is putting him up to this. Potestad does not feel confident that the Fr. are acting in good faith. Cantagalli thinks they are working to make the Sp. feel that their present friends cannot help them, officially in order then to step in and offer their good offices with the Sultan. He complained to me yesterday of the Sultan not having taken any notice of the representations of foreign powers abt. Melilla: the Sultan has not deigned to ans[wer]. any one of us; & I daresay he resents our interference. What will happen if the Sultan continues to stay away, & the Sp. lose patience. I tell him that threats of war are intended for public consumption, or may be to act as a stimulus to P. whom the Sp. Govt. evidently think is not active enough. But they do not see the difficulties he is surrounded by. For me, it is Kerdec who to fill his pockets offers bad advice to the Sultan.

In a confidential desp[atch]. about a missionary at Fez, I have suggested what seems to me to be a practicable line to adopt towards them. I shld. be very glad if you would consider this. For their missionary work they ought to depend on their own resources & their own means of conciliating opposition, & the request of Mr. Badger for a "Sultan's letter" seemed altogether injudicious.

As regards the postage on private correspce. it seems that Euan-Smith extended the practice to the staff, and wrote a very large number of letters himself. But allowing the Gib. P.O. to charge on official correspce., in order that then branch post offices here may show a surplus of course has far more than doubled the normal charge. We shall see next Qr. what it comes to. For the present I have stopped all franking of private correspce. But the postage on all my letters wld. not come nearly to what I am out of pocket on the office allowance.

I have been looking into some of the so-called "claims", and am inclined to think that there are not many that can be pressed on the Sultan, not even all those on wch. Ridgeway reported. It is a very laborious matter, however, for the documents are rather voluminous, & have to be sought out & got together in dossiers. Mr. Hunot having reported that the Sultan was coming back by Tamdant, I have written to him to take the opportunity of going there as originally proposed, to get his claim investigated. I don't think much of either of his

PRO 30/33 14/4   Semi-official Letters from Uruguay (March 31 – June 9, 1893) and Morocco (September 4 – December 18, 1893)

claims.

Stoke the Sultan's elephant died on the 2nd. His skin & tusks were preserved, & his body was cut up in pieces & buried. Macleod reports that Fez is plunged in grief by the event. y.v.t.

35. Satow to Currie

11 Dec. 1893

My dear C,

Cantagalli says he expects to get hold of a copy of the letter given by the Sultan to Gaiffe, promising that in the case of his wanting to borrow money the contract shld. be given to Gaiffe. He says however that the Crédit Lyonnais is to arrange the loan, their agent here being the Fr. protégé Benehimol. The other day d'Aubigny had B. to lunch, a most unusual circ., to talk over the business. This explains d'Au's recent anxiety to know the amount of the indemnity. P. has told me that the troops at Melilla cost $25,000 a day: that is $750,000 a month, or say 3 millions fr. October 2 to the end of Jany. That is only 185 million pesetas. I don't see therefore where the 50,000,000 fr[ancs]. Of Cantagalli is got from, but P. says the Sultan will have to pay everything that Spain is out of pocket by this business, wch. may be anything up to a 100 million pesetas.

Pariente came & showed me a letter fr. Louis Emanuel saying that he had talked to S. Montagu[39] about raising a million £ & urging him to send definite news abt. the indemnity: he said that M. had seen Sir E. Grey abt. the matter. P. wants a letter to the Sultan fr. me, but as Forde the V-C [Vice-Consul] at Laraiche has also asked me to back him, I thought better to refer the matter to Ld. R.

Abraham Sicsu the Belg. Consul who is partner with Mansur the Germ. dragoman in that piece of land on the straits that Pyke & Minchin (North Africa XVIII, p.51) tried to sell to H.M.G. in 1888 has been to tell me that he is negotiating a sale to Donald Mackenzie of Cape Juby, & asked if I had any objection. I told him it did not concern me; that if his titles were in good order he could sell to any one he liked. It seems that there is an idea abroad in

---

[39] Samuel Montagu, 1st Baron Swaythling (1832-1911). Banker who founded S. Montagu & Co.

PRO 30/33 14/4   Semi-official Letters from Uruguay (March 31 – June 9, 1893) and Morocco (September 4 – December 18, 1893)

Tangier that the legation tries to put obstacles in the way of B.S. buying land, wch. seems absurd. If a B.S. chooses to invest his money in that way, & gives the necessary tips to the Kaid & Basha to get their sanction, I don't see what the legation has to say to it.

36. Satow to Currie
Dec. 17. 1893
Secret.
My dear C

Maclean came back fr. the camp a couple of days ago bringing satisfactory letters, abt. wch. I am writing separately.

His expenses, there & back for fodder, men's wages & food, and three mules wch. died on the way amounted to $536 or abt. £86. Considering the cost of travelling in this country, this seems moderate. I shld. be glad if [you] will sanction my repaying it to him.

With regard to the arrangement mentioned in yr. Secret of Oct 13, he tells me that hitherto he has nearly always managed to avoid accompanying the Sultan on his annual expeditions, because it costs him so much in food for men & animals, & the work proposed that he shld. do wld. necessitate his going abt. always with the Sultan. As long as the Fr. have Linares always at the Sultan's elbow it wld. certainly be advisable that we shld. have our man there also. If you did not think it too much I shld. like to be in a position to promise him £400 a year for himself & Secretary beginning fr. (March next) as you propose.

He has brought me a man from Tafilelt, who undertakes to keep me informed of Fr. doings in Figuig, Ain Shair, & Tuat, and I proposed to give this man a small present to begin with, say £8 or so ($50), & I am going to give Cid Mohammed Torres 50 bags of wheat, wch. will cost abt. £20 ($120 or so). In all £114.

  Yours very truly
    E.S.
Postscript see further.

37. Satow to Currie

PRO 30/33 14/4 Semi-official Letters from Uruguay (March 31 – June 9, 1893) and Morocco (September 4 – December 18, 1893)

Private

17 Dec.

My dear Currie,

Maclean arr. on the 14. bringing letters from Gharnit in reply, (1) abt. courier robberies, of no great importance, (2) to my note announcing arrival wch. seems very civil, (3) abt. arrest of agents. This he was told to keep back until he recd. by a courier whom he left behind him in camp some Sherifian letters ordering release. But he gave it to me all the same. They release two men unconditionally, the other two who are alleged to be Sheikhs cannot be given up if upon examination the allegation is found to be true, otherwise they will be released. I propose, before treating this note as officially in my hands, to wait & see what Maclean's courier brings. He assures me that Gharnit promised him that all four shld. be given up, and that it will be done. [Margin: But Gharnit has before now broken promises made thro' M.] I have asked him to again explain that the unconditional release of all four is a <u>sine qua non</u> for I don't want on the first occasion of seeing the Sultan to have complaints to make, & we may be quite sure that if I go to Court without first obtaining the release, it will be much more troublesome to get out of them afterwards.

Arthur Herbert & his wife who are here at present want me to take them up, but I am not sure that it wld. be convenient to have any sightseers with me.

Maclean did not see the Sultan. At first Gharnit & the others were very cordial, but then Linares told them d'Aubigny wld. be very angry, and tried to make things as uncomfortable as possible. In the camp there was also a French engineer who professes to be a renegade, but very thick with Linares, and at least a dozen Fr. subjects turned Mussulmen. Then Harris arr[ived]. on a donkey disguised as a Moor, & with a very bad throat, quinsy I think. Maclean induced Linares to go & see him, but L. reported to Gharnit that H[arris]. was only shamming in order to be taken into camp. Then he was called in a second time & lanced the swelling for him. Maclean brought back H. to Morocco where he left him to recruit. H. wrote to me that he got scanty courtesy fr. the Moorish govt. but I don't know what else a man can expect when he travels in disguise.

[H. wrote to me that he had been offered a horse by the Sherif of Tameshlot as a token of gratitude for having procured him B[ritish]. Protection, & asked whether there was any

PRO 30/33 14/4 Semi-official Letters from Uruguay (March 31 – June 9, 1893) and Morocco (September 4 – December 18, 1893)

objection. I replied that I saw none. I hear that the horse has arrived at Tangier.][40]

On Maclean reaching Tafilelt he found the Sultan's people talking abt. proclaiming a Holy War. They had been told by Linares that the Sp. were too hard up to be able to fight & imagined that in this way they wld. be able to make mincemeat of them. They were also anxious to know whether it was possible to square members of the Sp. Govt. & I am afraid M's ans. was not exactly a decided negative. He told them they were fools to imagine that the Holy War wld. help them, it wld. only bring all the other Powers upon them as well. I am inclined to think fr. what he has said that he has helped them with suggestions as to what they shld. put in the letters to the Sp. Min., & Queen Regent wch. are said to have arrived here, making out as good a case for themselves as possible. Gharnit strongly asserted to him that the Span. Min. here had been officially warned not to let the fort be begun during the Sultan's absence. That any such warning was ever given has been denied, as you already know. In any case M. says the Sultan wishes to do all he can to satisfy Spain. As regards executing the ringleaders, that will be difficult, but H.S.M. will eventually achieve it by stratagem. He does not know anything about an indemnity having been asked for. When he left Court, the letters written by the FRR after Margallo's death had not arrived.   The Sultan started fr. Tafilelt on the 25th Novr. for Morocco by way of the Glaoni pass, and it was officially given out that he wld. arrive there on the 25 Decr. But as he intended to stop a few days <u>en route</u> to punish a vill[age]. where the sword & clothing had been found of a brother of his who was murdered a couple of yrs. ago he wld. prob. not get to Morocco before the end of the month.

On the whole I think fr. what they have written & fr. Maclean's reports that I might safely propose to pay the Sultan a visit. That the Moors are very much in the hands of the Fr. yet not quite willingly & that they will be glad to be on friendly terms again with us, provided we do not demand too much fr. them.   I am inclined to think that it wld. be unwise to aim at our exclusive influence, (wch. is the natural ideal of Englishmen in this country), unless it shld. be shown by experience that the Moors cannot do without a Mentor. But I am sure that after what happened last year nothing very brilliant or striking is

---

[40] Satow's parentheses, beside which he has written 'Omit'.

PRO 30/33 14/4 Semi-official Letters from Uruguay (March 31 – June 9, 1893) and Morocco (September 4 – December 18, 1893)

expected from me, and that in all my proceedings I shld. rather imitate the tortoise than the hare. Meanwhile I am trying thro' Maclean to establish relations with one Sid Larbi Zubdi, who is the Sultan's steward, and is said to be a rising man.

I am sending thro' this man to the Sultan a letter recommending Pariente for the loan business, but if what I have been told is true the Fr. have forestalled us thro' the Gaiffe and the Crédit Lyonnais.

Potestad told me that fr. his private letters he is led to believe that the safety not only of the Sp. cabinet but even of the dynasty depends upon Martinez Campos[41] obtaining some sort of satisfaction from the Sultan's brother. He has spoken more than once in this rather alarming way. I have no means of judging of its exactness. But under the circs. I thought I cld. do no harm by frightening Torres a bit, and I believe that he was impressed. I have acted in conjunction with Cantagalli, whose instructions are to act in concert with Tattenbach and myself; but Tattenbach has twice declined to join. He prefers to act independently, following I suppose his instructions.

Maclean says that the Sultan undertook, as I had suggested to him, to send orders at once to Mogador to build the Mellah, and Gharnit even offered to give him the letter to be forwarded thro' me, but he told them the Sultan had better do it as his own act.

He also advised them not to meddle with Tuat or Figuig, but just leave them as they are. Fr. what the Tafilelt man he brought with him says the people of all those posts, including Ain Shair pay no attention to the Sultan in political or administrative matters, recognizing him solely by praying for him publicly in the mosques.

About Juby nothing was said, and he thinks the Sultan's resentment has cooled down, now that he finds the trade of Mogador is not interfered with.

P.S. to first letter of 17 Decr. [to Currie].
I enclose an acct. of Maclean's showing various sums spent by him on couriers, out of money given him by Ridgeway. It shows a balce. in his favour of $36. to 12, and I have given him $50 in addition to the $536 already mentioned, wch. I am not paying till I hear fr.

---

[41] General Arsenio Martinez Campos (1831-1900). Named general-in-chief of the African army in 1893. Negotiated for Spain in the peace treaty of Melilla in 1894.

PRO 30/33 14/4 Semi-official Letters from Uruguay (March 31 – June 9, 1893) and Morocco (September 4 – December 18, 1893)

you.

38. Satow to Currie

18 Dec.

My dear C.

I am reporting by this mail that I have written to Boobeker [Bubeker] in the name of H.M.G. thanking him for his services. He has sent me copious & numerous letters of late protesting his devotion to England & his desire to continue to be of service, & there is absolutely no danger of his desiring to enter the employ of any other legation, or to give up the protection wch. has been his glory & honour for so many years past.

I am afraid that the Missionaries at Fez may cause us some trouble. It arises fr. the new schools that were started by the Edwards'. I am doing what I can to calm their perturbed spirits, & hope the thing may blow over. It wld. be a serious matter if any Xtian converts were to be thrown into prison or otherwise maltreated, & I suppose that in such a case I shld. have to make official remonstrances. It wld. be useless to expect any assistance fr. one's colleagues on behalf of the Prot. converts.

    y.v.s.

P.S. 18 Dec.

I shld. of course ask for instructions before taking any official steps on behalf of converts.

END OF PRO 30/33 14/4

PRO 30/33 14/5 Semi-official Letters from Morocco (December 25, 1893 – March 9, 1894)

PRO 30/33 14/5

1. Satow to Kaid Maclean[1]

1893   Dec. 25

My dear Maclean,

I hope you had a comf[ortable]. voyage to Casabl[anca]. & have quite got rid of your cold.

Things are going on quietly but slowly at Melilla.[2] The point at pres[en]t. being debated is the evacuation & delimitation of the neutral zone 500 metres broad round the Sp[anish]. lines.   M.A. [Mulai Arafa] declares he has not force suffic[ien]t. to arrange these matters. The Sp. Govt. have offered to supply the force. It will have to be done sooner or later, & the Sultan wld. do well to express his acceptance of the offer.

Besides the indemnity, the fig[ure]s. of wch. cannot be named until there is a definite prospect of Spain being able to withdraw her army, I have reason to believe that a slight extension of territory will be looked for, just enough to secure Melilla from easy attack. I imagine also that the punish[men]t. of the ringleaders will be urged. Maimon [Mohatar] wld. be one of these.

It is important that you shld. impress upon the Sultan the desirability of coming to terms quickly, otherwise it is impossible to say what an extension the affair may take. If, by declining to accede to the just demands of Sp[ain]. he gave her any justification for the occupation of a port as a material guarantee, other Powers might think it incumbent upon them to follow suit. That is altogether opposed to the traditional policy of England, wch. above all desires the integrity of the Moorish empire to be preserved.

As soon as the Sultan reaches Marraksh, wch. cannot be delayed much longer, one wld. think, it wld. produce an excellent effect if the Sultan were to make an advance the Sp.

---

[1] General (Kaïd) Sir Harry Aubrey de Vere Maclean (1848-1920). British political agent at the Sultan's Court.
2 Melilla is a Spanish autonomous city and port located on the north coast of Africa, sharing a border with Morocco. Its area is 12.3 square kilometres. In 1893 the Riff Berbers launched the First Melillan campaign (Margallo War). It began in earnest on 3 October 1893, was openly declared on November 9th and resolved by the Treaty of Fez in 1894.

PRO 30/33 14/5   Semi-official Letters from Morocco (December 25, 1893 – March 9, 1894)

Govt. by writing to say that he has returned there & will lose no time in preparing to meet the wishes of Spain.

With regard to the release of the four agents, whether they be sheikhs or not, the Br. Govt. will take no denial; it is a right based on Treaty, wch. admits of no discussion, & they have instructed me to insist on these men being set at liberty unconditionally.

Will you please say to Gharnit privately that it is a mistaken policy to forbid Mr. Edwards to teach such things as arithmetic, mathematics and the English language. The latter knowledge they ought particularly to desire to see diffused, if they are disposed to be friendly with England.

   y.v.t.

P.S. I shall of course not make any approaches to them on the matter of going to Court until I hear of the four men having been released. That is the token by which H.M.G. will judge of the disposition of H.S.M. [His Sultanic Majesty] towards them. If you have a convenient opportunity & you find Gharnit obstinate or dilatory, please slip this into the Sultan's ear – not otherwise.

   E.S.

2. Satow to Currie

25 Dec. 93

My dear C.,

 My sincerest congratulations &c.[3]

Things don't seem to make much progress here. My last desp[atch]. abt. Melilla is based on what I know to be the feeling among the colleagues. They are surprised at the Sp. Govt. not having long ago instructed P[otestad]. to proceed to Morocco City & they do not see the wisdom or justice of passing over P. to send a special envoy. With [Martinez] Campos at Melilla & their plenipo[tentiary]. at Morocco they do not need anyone here above the rank of a Sec. of Legn.

There has been a good deal of correspce. betw. this & Melilla abt. the neutral zone wch.

---

[3] Currie was made Ambassador to the Ottoman Empire from 1893 to 1898.

PRO 30/33 14/5   Semi-official Letters from Morocco (December 25, 1893 – March 9, 1894)

Campos wants to have cleared. It has abt. 30 Moorish dwellings on it, & some gardens. Mulai Arafa says he has not force enough to turn the people out. Campos offered to provide the force. Mulai Arafa consulted Torres, who says to P. that glad as he might privately be to see it done he does not for the life of him dare to put it in writing. On the 22nd P. giving us to understand that all he wanted fr. Torres was to write to Arafa to agree abt. <u>marking out</u> the neutral zone got T[attenbach]., d'Aub[igny]., C[antagalli]. & myself to speak to Torres. I contented myself with saying to the latter that he ought to show his good will by writing the letter, & he more than ½ consented. But next day P. not content with this, or not conceiving that Moret[4] wld. be content, revised the proposal to clear the ground by force wch. he had dropped for a day or two, & T. then became recalcitrant again. I cannot understand why the Sp. Govt. does not let things be at Melilla & send their man straight to the Sultan who is certainly by this time at Morocco.

Wolff[5] telegd. yesterday that Moret says d'Aub[igny]. is trying to influence the Sultan not to yield to the Sp. demands. I asked P. what he thought, & found him to believe that d'Aub. is acting squarely. Cantagalli thinks P. believes too much. For my own part I see no evidence, & so telegd. back that the presence of a Sp. negotiator at Morocco wld. counteract any such machination & that Maclean wld. be instructed to support him. I enclose a copy of what I have written to Maclean, after consultation with P. His idea is that [French political agent at Court Dr. F.] Linares' policy is to make the Sultan quarrel c. every Power, in order that he may have no friend left but Fr[ance]. Now that the Sultan is back at Morocco the exclusive influence of Linares is at an end. But the Sp[aniards]. ought to lose no time in sending some one there.

The Sp. Cons[ul]. at Tetuan has hinted that old notion the B.C.G. [British Consul General?] there is concerned in smuggling arms there. I called on him for a report in the particular case complained of, but his explanations seem not to bear out the Spaniard's assertions. I have asked Pd. to furnish me with any definite information that he may receive. In case there were real[?] ground for suspicion, the best thing to do wld. be to send some

---

[4] Segismundo Moret y Prendergast (1833-1913). Spanish foreign minister, April 1893 – November 1894.
[5] Sir Henry Drummond Wolff (1830-1908). British ambassador at Madrid, 1892-1900.

PRO 30/33 14/5   Semi-official Letters from Morocco (December 25, 1893 – March 9, 1894)

one, say De Vismes, over to Tetuan to make an enquiry.

    y.v.t.

3. Satow to Maclean (stamped p.4)

Dec. 26. 1893.

My dear Maclean,

 It is believed at Madrid that the Fr. Min. is trying to egg the Sultan on to refusing to comply with the demands of Spain. I have no special reason to believe this of him in person, but it is quite possible that the doctor [Dr. Linares], out of pure cussedness, may be putting such notions into H.S.M. ears. Of course you will do your best to counteract any such machinations, if you have anything that causes you to believe that they are going on.

 I have just recd. your note of the 21st, & am glad you got safely to DAB.

    y.v.t.

4. Satow to Sanderson

Sanderson 4/1/94

Tangier

4 Jan. 1894

My dear Sanderson,

 Best wishes for the new year & hearty congratulations on your apptmt. [as Permanent Under-Secretary of State for Foreign Affairs] I do not forget that you gave me some very valuable advice abt. this place before I came, & now that, as I suppose, it comes directly under your supervision, I hope you will give me a hint now & then as to the line to be pursued.

 In my last I told Currie that Wolff had telegr. that Moret suspected intrigues to prevent the Sultan acceding to the Sp. demands, & Potestad's belief that d'Aubigny is acting on the Sq[uare, i.e. honestly] Cantagalli suspects the Fr. are trying to make the Sultan fancy that he need not take much notice of the Sp. demands, in order that in the end the indemnity may be all the larger, & the Fr. bankers have the more to lend. T. thinks that d'Aubigny's cue is rather to persuade the Sultan that he ought not to give more than 20 milln. Pesetas, &

PRO 30/33 14/5   Semi-official Letters from Morocco (December 25, 1893 – March 9, 1894)

to support him in resisting any larger demands, so that he may later on claim the credit of having helped the Sultan out of a difficulty, as he did in the case of Euan-Smith's mission. Either way the Fr. influence wld. grow. But T. is a great intriguer himself, & all that can be said is that these suggestions are but surmises.

Montagu[6] arr. here on the 27 Wed. & left on the 31 Sunday: so he had not given himself much time to work on behalf of the Jews or for the loan negotiation. I told him that until I went to Court I cld. not hope to interfere effectively on behalf of the Jews of Morocco. He has written a letter to the Sultan, wch. I am going to send on in the usual way thro' Gharnit. As for the loan business, he does not seem to be very anxious abt. it, & when I told him he ought to send a negotiator to Court with funds to administer in the shape of tips, he declared that neither he nor Rothschild wld. have anything to do with bribing. But in this country it is absurd to expect concessions without expending a little palm-oil. Engl. business methods don't suit here. He has left with me a letter to be forwarded to Kaid Maclean abt. the loan. It is scarcely possible that he shld. get it.

E[rnest].H[arrison]. Forwood[7] has also offered to Torres to negotiate a loan. He came to see me last night, & talked abt. various matters connected with shipping business along the coast. He says we ought to have a paid consul at Mogador, wch. I think is very likely. However, I suppose it is no good to say anything abt. that at present. Forwood will write to me abt. various things when he gets home. I asked him to give the F.O. the information he has abt. Ratto's so-called concession to trade with the Azafat tribe.

Potestad has sent a couple of his Sp. doctors to Mazagan to prepare for Martines Campos' journey to Morocco. He is entirely put in the negotiation for the final settle[men]t. It is rumoured that the French idea is an extension of territory round Melilla in place of an indemnity, but the Sultan cld. not give it without fighting the Riffians or buying it fr. them, so the suggestion is not likely to come to much.

I have not yet heard of the release of the other two agents of B.S., & have instructed Kaid Maclean to say that they must be unconditionally released.

---

[6] Samuel Montagu (1832-1911). Jewish banker who founded Samuel Montagu & Co.
[7] Forwood was Chairman of the London Shipping Exchange in1898.

PRO 30/33 14/5 Semi-official Letters from Morocco (December 25, 1893 – March 9, 1894)

P.S. It is said that there was an attempt made to assassinate the Sultan a day or two before he entered Morocco. He was at a place 3 marches away, & suddenly he started early in the morning & did the 3 marches in one day.

5. Satow to Maclean
4 Jan. 1894
conf[idential]. 1
My dear Maclean,

    Thanks for your two letters of the 29th Dec, Nos 8 & 9.

    I send you a letter fr. Mr. S. Montagu who came here on the 27 & left again on the 31. He had a two fold mission, one to try & do something for the Jews of Morocco City, the other to express his readiness to arrange a loan for the Sultan, wch. wld. be brought out by the Rothschilds.

    On the subject of the Jews he has addressed a letter to the Sultan, wch. I am forwarding in a letter to Gharnit. I merely speak in genl. terms, & have not mentioned either Kaid Wida nor the word persecution, so you need have no hesitation abt. handing over the two letters.

    He has said nothing about the loan to the Sultan, nor have I spoken of it in my letter to Gharnit. [Abraham] Pariente will in fact act as Montagu's agent, & I have already written on his behalf the letters wch. you have recd.

    Mr. E.H. Forwood has been to see Torres & offered him to provide the money, if they like. I imagine he said to Torres that it wld. be money in his pocket if the loan was given to Forwood Bros.

    The last rumour here is that the French will suggest to the Sultan that instead of paying money to the Sp[aniards]. he shld. offer them a bit of territory, say the peninsula of Tres Forcas [Cape Three Forks]. But that wld. be disastrous, for the French wld. then say they must rectify their frontier & advance to the Mouluya. It wld. be much better for the Sultan to make up his mind to pay the Spaniards a good round sum, wch. he will get back in three or four yrs. fr. the customs, especially if he allows the export of grain.

        y.v.t.
           E.S.

PRO 30/33 14/5   Semi-official Letters from Morocco (December 25, 1893 – March 9, 1894)

P.S. Martinez Campos will leave for Mazagan by the 15th I think. Troops are already leaving Melilla for Spain.

6. Satow to Sanderson (stamped p.7)

Private

Tangier

6.1.94.

My dear Sanderson,

Our bosoms have been agitated by a question of etiquette. The day before yesterday Moret telegraphed to Potestad "We want to know whether the Diplomatic Body at Tangier wld. go to call on the Ambassador Extraordy. on his arrival with the squadron, and what wld. be their attitude in case the Ambassador landed."

P. communicated this to Colaço the doyen who advised him to see the rest of the colleagues. Cantigalli objected strongly to the idea of paying the first call, on the ground that it wld. lower the prestige of the Body in the eyes of the Moors. Tattenbach said he must ask for instructions. D'Aubigny talked big, & said he wld. treat him like any ordinary colleague, that is if he recd. notice of his landing early enough he wld. send a secretary to meet him, but he wld. not make the 1st call. Bolesl. & myself saw no objection to making the first call, since he is to have the rank of Ambassador.

Thereupon we held a meeting yesterday at wch. everyone was of opinion that to go on board to visit Genl. Campos was, for various reasons, quite impossible. And with regard to the calling on him first when he comes ashore, we came to the conclusion – in order to avoid an open disagreement – to wait for such instructions as our govts. might send to us. D'Aubigny spoke very moderately, said he had no objection to go to a reception at wh. P. might introduce us to Campos, & ended by saying that if the colleagues got instructions to pay the first call he wld. follow suit. Cantag. was the only one who wld. have refused.

Before the meeting I had a second talk c. P. who acknowledged that it was absurd to ask us to go on board, & that rather than have any unpleasantness, he wld. urge on Moret not to let Campos some here, & propose himself to go over & see the latter at Algeciras. He was to write to that effect by this morning's post. So I suppose the storm will be laid.

PRO 30/33 14/5   Semi-official Letters from Morocco (December 25, 1893 – March 9, 1894)

The new American Barclay[8] will be an acquisition; he seems to be honest, wch. his predecessor certainly was not.

I am sending a memo. about one of Hunot's so-called claims, wch. appears to me preposterous. As his story was inserted in the print, I hope this answer to it will be given a place there too.

It seems incredible that there shld. be 1047 claims of B.Ss. [British Subjects], as reported by Ridgeway, & I hope before long to show good reason for rejecting the majority of them. The practice here has been to forward anything that a B.S. declared was a claim to the Moorish Auth. without at all investigating its nature or looking into the proofs. The result has been that the Legn. has been made to appear as a supporter of claims that had not a leg to stand on.

The rule I propose to adopt in every new case is that the V-C who sends it to the legation shall personally inquire into it, & obtain at least such evidence as is sufficient to establish a prima facie case. He is practically the pltf's [plaintiff's] lawyer as the legation is the counsel for the prosecution, & neither ought to take any step in relation to a case until he has acquainted himself with all the facts. I hope, if I have time, to make a thorough examin[atio]n. of the papers in the legation & to repost at length in a few months' time.

I hear fr. Redman[9] that one of the imprisoned agents for whom Kaid Maclean brought me a letter ordering his release, is still detained in prison, so that up to the present only one has been let out. I am going to write a stiffish letter to Gharnit abt. it.

  y.v.t

  E.S.

P.S. Cantagalli got telegraphic instructions this morning to act with me in the matter of calling on Campos, & T. has instructions to act in concert c. C, B & myself. But as I hope Campos will not come here after all, I have not asked for instructions. The Germ. Govt. sees no objection to our paying the first call.   E.S.

---

[8] John Judson Barclay (1834-1910).
[9] Alfred Redman was Vice-Consul at Mazagan (El-Jadida) from 1873 to 1896. (See Table of British Consuls and Vice-Consuls in Moroccan Ports during the second half of the nineteenth century, in Khalid Ben-Srhir, *Britain and Morocco During the Embassy of John Drummond Hay,* Routledge, 2004, p. 283)

PRO 30/33 14/5   Semi-official Letters from Morocco (December 25, 1893 – March 9, 1894)

7. Satow to Maclean
No. 2 conf.
9/1/94
My dear Maclean,

I am adopting your excellent plan of numbering letters, & this is the 2nd I have written since the beginning of the year. My most sincere regrets to hear that you have been so ill. When the housekeeper heard of it she said "the poor gentleman was not fit to go away fr. here, but he was so brave that he refused to take care of himself." I trust however that you are now better, & will soon be able to proceed on your journey.

You are aware that there is a Fr. syndicate working for a loan to the Sultan for the purpose of paying the Sp. indemnity. The man Gaiffe who furnished all that silver coin has a hand in it; he is believed to have got a written promise from the Sultan to give him the contract for any loan H.S.M. might need: the promise I believe was made when Gaiffe was last at Fez. You see, the Sultan need not consider himself bound even to Gaiffe, if he can find any one else ready to lend him the money on more favourable terms. But in any case H.S.M shld. beware of giving to a Fr. syndicate any hold over the Customs revenue, by pledging it as security for a loan, or allowing him any control, or to collect the duties. And one reason of this is that they wld. then have a powerful grip over a very important source of revenue. It is possible too that it might give rise to difficulties with other PP [Powers], who wld. not like to see a Fr. agent at every Customhouse exercising control over the foreign trade, able to screw every penny out of other merchants & favouring their own at the expense of the Sherifian treasury. Use either of these reasons as may seem to you best. Besides [Samuel] Montagu, there is also Forwood Bros. who are willing to arrange for a loan if required. If a loan becomes absolutely necessary it is best to send an agent down here to negotiate with the various financial agents. Abensur tells me it is of little use making presents beforehand, but that for work actually done the usual douceurs will be given. He tells me however that he does not think any loan will be made, because Spain talks of receiving the indemnity in ten annual instalments. There seems to be good reason to believe that the amount demanded will be 25 million pesetas.

PRO 30/33 14/5   Semi-official Letters from Morocco (December 25, 1893 – March 9, 1894)

I regret to tell you that Redman reports fr. Mazagan under date Jan. 5 that he forwarded the letter you gave me thro' the Gov[ernor]. to the Khalifa Hadj Abdalla Brazizi, who replied acknowledging the receipt of his brother's letter, & simply saying in answer "I have now to inform you that I have applied to my Brother as concerns his letter to me." The agent has not been released. I shall have to make a row about this, in a letter to Gharnit.

Please give the advice abt. not allowing a Fr. syndicate to have any control over the customs as <u>coming from yourself</u>.

But as regards the agent you may tell the Sultan from me that I consider an unworthy trick has been played on me by Gharnit handing you that letter of Kaid Hamed Boazizi wch. was evidently not intended to bring about the release. I wrote on the 23rd September, & this is the sort of answer I get. I value the fine words of Gharnit in his letter to me at their true value. Actions speak louder than words. If at the time the Vizier uses all this fine language, he still persists in sanctioning a violation of Treaty (the Madrid Convention), I put one agst. the other & conclude that U.E. [H.E.?] is not to be believed.

      y.v.t.

      E.S.

P.S. Ld. Rosebery would object very strongly to anything but an international control of the Customs, whether it be for interest on a loan from French syndicate or for collecting the instalments of an indemnity. He will not here [hear?] of any single Power having sole intervention therein & thinks it shld. be carried out by the Ministers of the Great Power.

8. Satow to Maclean

No. 3

12/1/94

My dear M,

Thanks for your No. 11. By this post I am sending to you for delivery to Gharnit a sharpish letter abt. the refusal of the Khalifa Hadj Abdalla to release Ansado's man & the two others, respecting whom I say in my letter that you <u>told</u> me there was an allegation that they were sheikhs; whereas they were in the lists for 1892 & before, & yet no objection was taken. I have added that H.M.G. values deals more than words & that polite speeches are

PRO 30/33 14/5 Semi-official Letters from Morocco (December 25, 1893 – March 9, 1894)

like froth upon the surface of a shallow stream with other bits of oriental imagery.

The accompanying letter in a thin square envelope is from [Lloyds agent at Tangier Eugene] Chappory to Gharnit, on behalf of E.H. Forwood, offering to make a loan if necessary. Please give it to Gharnit fr. me. I have no time today to write to him abt. the matter. But he very likely knows who Forwood Bros. are, & that they wld. do as agents for a loan just as well as any one else, if the Sultan shld. need to raise money in that way.

I will send on yr. letter to S. Montagu. As my letter to Cid Fedoul goes into the matter of the Jews at Morocco city quite fully enough, I do not think you need say anything to the Sultan, except that I have (or rather HMG [has]) no desire to interfere, & that we are merely anxious that his reputation as a wise & humane sovereign shld. be maintained.

Thanks very much for the offer of the horses; at present Friar is as much as I can manage, & I think it will be better to wait until I come up to court to try the two you speak of.

Now to business. I am authorized to repay to you the $536 your journey to Tafilelt cost, & the balance of your acct. c. Ridgeway. As regards your allowance I am authorized for 2 yrs. from Mar. 31 next to give you fr. time to time in the form of an occasional present at the rate of £400 a year, & I suppose this implies that at the end of the time they wld. talk the matter over again. I hope this will be agreeable to you.

Will you let me know to whom I shall pay the $536 & $36.12.

I wrote very fully to the F.O. abt. the friendly letter that had reached me fr. the Court & the promise to release the 4 men. The opinion at home is that we must wait & consider further before settling anything abt. a visit to the Sultan. I am told here that H.S.M. does not care whether I go to see him or not. That is perhaps true. The B.Ss.[?] are at least equally indifferent, & so until they are convinced by his <u>actions</u> that the Sultan is disposed to be friendly they will not make any advances to him. Please manage somehow to let H.S.M. get an inkling of this.

  y.v.s.

   E.S.

P.S. I hear Petri has gone to Morocco abt. a contract for exporting grain for the Sultan. I don't want at all to interfere, but I shld. like to know particulars of what he is doing.

The Sp. Mission headed by M.C. [Martinez Campos] will probably reach Mazagan in

PRO 30/33 14/5 Semi-official Letters from Morocco (December 25, 1893 – March 9, 1894)

less than a week's time. I have as yet no information abt. the terms he is going to propose to the Sultan. But in any case, I shld. wish to say to the Sultan that he shld. not listen to the counsels of those who wish to embroil him with Spain. E.S.

9. Satow to Sanderson (stamped p.13)

14. Jan. 94

My dear S.

On the 8th Cantagalli got instructions fr. Rome that in London it was considered that Martinez Campos was entitled to the first call, & that he was to act with me. On learning this I went to see the Fr.man & the German, whom I found ready to follow suit. So I told Potestad that he might teleg. to Madrid that the instructions of the colleagues enabled them to make the first visit.

P. seemed inclined to think Campos had better not come, & was the slightest bit huffy, not towards myself, but in speaking of the colleagues. The fact is that he & Cantag. don't hit it off, the latter having taken it into his head that P. neglects him. Anspach whom I saw the next day had no doubts abt. our making the first visit, & in uniform if necessary. He in fact wrote a letter to Cantag. to be read at the meeting of the 5th saying as much, wch. Cantag. suppressed. Now however I hear that Camp. is not likely to touch at Tangier, so the question of etiquette has been needlessly raised.

E.H. Forwood's agent here has written to Gharnit offering to negotiate a loan, and at his request I have forwarded it thro' Maclean. But Montagu's agent tells me he thinks there will be no loan, because the Spaniards will receive the indemnity by instalments.

Tattenbach came to see me a few days ago, & asked me abt. my going to Morocco. I told him that nothing was settled, that I had no idea when it wld. be, that personally I was in no hurry; that when the time comes I shall be greatly disinclined to undertake anything on behalf of my colleagues unless certain of their active support & cooperation, & I gave him generally to understand that my visit wld. be only for the purpose of presenting my credentials.

He told me that he sent his credentials immediately on arrival, & had a separate letter when he went to court; Boleslawski who has not been to the court, also sent his credentials

PRO 30/33 14/5 Semi-official Letters from Morocco (December 25, 1893 – March 9, 1894)

by letter. But I do not know whether this is a general practice.

Gharnit sent me a message thro' Maclean asking me when I go to Court to announce my visit thro' Torres, in the usual way. I gather fr. this that there is some expectation at Court of my shortly proposing to go up. But I have not authorized Maclean to make any state[men]t. abt. the matter except this[:] that HMG were not in a hurry to make any advances to the Sultan, after the way in wch. E-Smith's mission had terminated, & that a tangible proof of good will was an antecedent condition; e.g. the unconditional release of the 4 agents.

As I wrote on the 6th, only one of the four has been let out. The promises made to Maclean at Tafilelt were broken, as I rather expected they would be. I have written a letter to Gharnit saying that the 3 remaining men must be released, & that H.M.G. attaches value to deeds, not to polite speeches. I do not propose to trouble you with a copy of it at present; the correspce. as yet entirely onesided is becoming voluminous. So also in the case of courier robberies.

I wrote a long letter to Maclean abt. the proposed French loan, warning the Sultan not to give any exclusive control over the Customs to the Fr. Syndicate, & saying that the other PP. wld. be sure to object on the ground that their people were made to pay duties on less favourable terms than Fr. merchants. I added in a postscript that Ld. Rosebery wld. not hear of anything but an international control of the customs.

Currie told me privately the other day that Ld. R. thinks it will be better not to settle anything about the visit to the Sultan without further cons[ideratio]n. I shld. like to say that for my own part I shld. be very unwilling to go until these three men are let out of prison, & that I am in no hurry to go even then. Of course I have been told by both White & Maclean that as long as I do not go to Court the Fr. will continue to have it all their own way, & that we shall not get our business attended to. But that is a local opinion. They tell me the Sultan does not care a bit, & that he wld. rather I stayed away. I have written again to Maclean that H.M.G. are equally indifferent, & that until the Sultan shows by his actions that he is disposed to be friendly they will not make any advances to him, & I have asked Maclean to let him have an inkling of this.

Anyhow until Campos' mission is over we ought not, it seems to me, to think of my

PRO 30/33 14/5   Semi-official Letters from Morocco (December 25, 1893 – March 9, 1894)

going; for we don't quite know how it will turn out. Doubtless the Fr. will do all they can to make it turn out badly.

Morant arrived yesterday. He seems a nice boy. De Vismes is laid up with scarlatina, & will not be allowed out for another five weeks. Meanwhile White does his best to supply his place, & with the best will in the world. I wish I had that Arabising assistant for whom I am told it is useless to hope.

      y.v.t.   E.S.

P.S.   [W.B.] Harris told me the other day that he had recd. a call fr. d'Aubigny, who came to express the concern of the Fr. Govt. that Linares shld. have made any observation to the Sultan's people abt. Harris' visit to Tafilelt; that the promise made by the Sultan had no reference to travellers, but only to foreigners who might sow the seeds of dislike to France among the Arabs of that oasis, & so cause unnecessary bloodshed when Fr. eventually claims possn. of Tafilet. Harris thinks Maclean was hinted at & that d'Aub. wished the information to be conveyed to me.

H. also told me that Malet[10] had written to him inquiring abt. Bubeker, and saying that the only reason wch. prevented Germany fr. working with us in Morocco was the employment of this man as our confidential agent at the Court. I told H. that mallet wld. prob. learn all abt. the matter fr. the print, & that I thought the pretence of our employing B. preventing the Germans from working with us was a great deal "too thin". Of course H. knows a great deal abt. the B. business.

10. Satow to Sanderson (stamped p.16)

15 Jan. 1894.

My dear Sanderson,

Torres I learn is much disturbed at the idea of this special mission of Martinez Campos. He cannot understand why any special mission shld. be sent at all, much less why Campos shld. have been chosen.   He thinks this portends some exaggerated demands on the part of Spain, wch. the Sultan may not be able to concede, & then says T. it will be necessary to

---

[10] Sir Edward Malet (1837-1908). British Ambassador to the German Empire, 1894-95.

PRO 30/33 14/5 Semi-official Letters from Morocco (December 25, 1893 – March 9, 1894)

have recourse to arbitration.

This idea of arbitration has been no doubt suggested to him. We have heard of it before, & it has usually been attributed to a Fr. source. I am not sure however that it has not also been dwelt on by Tattenbach, who poses as the Sultan's friend. He is much given to ridiculing the Sp. proceedings in this affair. I shld. not be at all surprised if it was to turn out that he is playing a game of his own.

P. has several times assured me that Spain will not demand more than her expenses. I am inclined to think fr. what he says that the sum asked for will be 30,000,000 of ps. [pesetas]
  y.v.t.

No. 4 to Maclean. Jan. 17 telling him that Campos wld. arr. at Mazagan on the 21st Jan.

11. Satow to Sanderson (stamped p. 17)
18.1.94

My dear Sanderson

I have had a talk with Pot[estad]. abt. the complaint of del Mayo enclosed in Lord R's No. 2 of 9 Jany. It appears fr. the draft of his desp[atch]. to Madrid, that he had sent it off before communicating the Consul's report to me. He does not appear to have written since to say that I had given him every possible kind of satisfaction. These reports fr. Consuls he tells me are mere routine business wch. are forwarded to Madrid as a matter of course. Such things he leaves to his very officious Secy. Galicia (with whom moreover he is not on good terms) & it was Galicia who wrote the dft. Pot. promises to set the matter right. I thought the thing was at an end when I showed him our consular agent's report, & never dreamt that it had already been sent officially to Madrid.

Today Nahon writes asking for unlimited leave in order to attend to his health. He told me on the 20th Novr. that he was thinking of resigning, but hoped that protection wld. be given him. He is a Jew of Morocco. It is quite possible that he may have business connexions or family relations with people who smuggle arms, & being of a timorous character dare not interfere. What B.Ss. [British Subjects] there are at Tetuan are Gibraltar people I fancy. y.v.t.

PRO 30/33 14/5   Semi-official Letters from Morocco (December 25, 1893 – March 9, 1894)

12. Satow to Sanderson

Private.

22 Jan. 1894

My dear Sanderson,

I am thinking of writing a line to Bubeker for his information telling him that the amount of the indemnity has been reduced at our instance & saying that the Sultan had better pay it, lest worse shld. come upon him. This dressed up with a sauce composed of 7 Sp. men of war that passed here yesterday steering for Mazagan & Ordega's article wld. make a dainty dish for H.S.M.

Maclean was to have left Rabat the day before yesterday for Morocco, so he will be there as soon as Martinez Campos. P. did not behave nicely in the matter of Navarro's complaint agst. Nahon, for he signed his desp[atch]. to Madrid without thinking of it, & then came to me with the original.

I have had Rev. Ch. Gore[11] & Shaw Lefevre[12] staying here. The latter was in Tangier for a little over 24 hrs, so he will know all abt. Morocco on his return. I lent him Ridgeway's report to read.

Bubeker writes that the people at the Court discuss affairs constantly with [French political agent Dr. F.] Linares, who is like Kerdec. B. thinks Campos' mission will turn out like Euan-Smith's. He reports that the Sultan is determined to say that he will not accept a settlement on the basis of an indemnity, particularly if the amt. demanded be large. I send you an opinion by de Vismes, who writes to me from scarlatina quarantine.

        y.v.t.   E.S.

13. Satow to Maclean

No. 5

22.1.94

My dear Maclean,

---

[11] Reverend Charles Gore (1853-1932). Principal of Pusey House, Oxford, 1884-93.
[12] George Shaw-Lefevre (1831-1928). Liberal party politician.

PRO 30/33 14/5   Semi-official Letters from Morocco (December 25, 1893 – March 9, 1894)

Your No. 1 recd. & very glad I am to hear you are on your way. By way of Mazagan, I sent you a letter of the 12th telling you abt. the arrange[men]ts. to be made with regard to yourself & [W.S.] Bewicke, & Redman despatched it from there on the 17th, so the courier will be on the lookout for you with it. There is another letter on its way to you dated 9 Jany., wch. I had told Lyons to send by sea to Rabat, & I suppose he has had no good opportunity.

I am not surprised at Kaid l'Arbi having to leave without the letters, & as I told you in my letter of the 12th I have spoken to Gharnit pretty plainly abt. his shuffling, & said that H.M. Govt. will lose their patience some day if this sort of thing goes on. And now I have sent all the correspce. to Ld. R. The letter fr. Cid Fedoul that we exchanged an undertaking abt. I have treated as not in existence, in accordance with what was agreed on betw. us. So please tell Gharnit that you did not deliver the letter, & ask him for the letters he promised ordering the release.

I am told that Ansado's man was badly treated, & have called for an accurate report on his physical condition.

Seven Sp[anish]. men of war conveying Marshal Campos passed here yesterday forenoon. I think you may safely tell the Sultan that it is owing to the friendly advice of England that the indemnity claimed is reduced by 1/5, i.e. fr. £1,000,000 to £800,000, & that he wld. be wise to pay it, because if he refuses, the Sp. have the means of making themselves disagreeably felt. Certain of the <u>Sultan's</u> friends had advised the Spanish Govt. to occupy Tetuan (this was Roustan[13] the Fr[ench]. ambassador at Madrid) & when that was not assented to M. Ordega, whom H.S.M. doubtless remembers, wrote an article in the Révue Bleue in Paris suggesting that the whole of the Riff shld. be given over to Spain, as Fr. had no objection to seeing Spain occupying the coast betw. the Muluya & Tetuan. But if the Sultan reflects he will see that the way to force a man to agree to something he does not like is, not to tread on his toes, wch. are far from the seat of Intelligence, but to seize hold of the throat & compress it, & prevent the circulation, &c. In this affair the British & other Govts. have taken the side of Spain because she had right on her side, & moreover there was fear that she might be provoked into undertaking military operations on a large scale. It

---

[13] Theodore Roustan (1833-1906). French Ambassador to Spain, 1891-94.

PRO 30/33 14/5   Semi-official Letters from Morocco (December 25, 1893 – March 9, 1894)

is not necessary to have much money in order to make war, for the Russians in 1877 invaded Turkey & nearly took Constantinople when they were nearly bankrupt; but in time of war every one is full of zeal, & people will lend money to a Govt. or let it have arms & provisions on tick. So that to side with Spain is the part of a true friend to the Sultan, because that gives the friendly powers a position with regard to her in wch. they offer counsels of moderation.

The expenses of the Melilla affair were undoubtedly betw. 28,000,000 & 30,000,000 of pesetas, so the Spaniards have not presented an exorbitant bill.

I want you to do all you can to further the objects of Marshal Campos' mission, and to say to him that it will give you the greatest pleasure to be of use to him.

I understand that the Sp. Govt. accept the idea of an undertaking to pay fixed instalments out of customs revenue, giving to the Sp. the right to supervise or control the Customhouses in the event of delay in pay[men]t. at the fixed time. This seems very reasonable, & is quite approved by the Br. Govt.

They are altogether opposed to the idea of a loan for paying off the indemnity secured upon the Customs duties, because that wld. mean invidious interference.

I shall be very glad to see your friend Bewicke if he passes thro' here.

De Vismes is writing a letter to B.B. [Bubeker?] setting him right as to our policy in respect of Spain, and giving him the tips contained in this letter abt. the insidious advice of the Fr. &c. I enclose it to you, that you may keep it, until you have yourself had an opportunity of first speaking to the Sultan in this sense.   y.v.t.

       E.S.

14. Satow to Maclean

No. 6

Jan. 26. 1894

My dear Maclean,

Thanks for yr. 2 letters of the 21 & 22. My no. 1 was the letter of Jan. 4 wch. you have already acknowledged. No. 2 was sent to Morocco thro' Redman & 3 & 5 will I hope reach you thro' the same channel. I am sending you a letter to the Sultan wch. I beg you to deliver

PRO 30/33 14/5   Semi-official Letters from Morocco (December 25, 1893 – March 9, 1894)

into his own hands, written in consequence of instructions I have recd. to support the Spanish demands as to indemnity & to promote the settlement of the other points. The Germ. Minr. spoke much in the same sense to Torres abt. 4 days ago. What the Fr. line is I cannot discover; you will prob. find out at court. All I know is that they have promised the Sp. Govt. to support them, & the Spaniards believe them to be acting loyally. The Italian is acting with myself, & I may possibly transmit his letter with this. In my no. 5 I told you pretty much what I am now writing to the Sultan, namely that the Sp. are acting very moderately in asking the sum they demand, wch. is less than what the expedition has cost them, & that a failure to come to an understanding with Spain may provoke a war. I have added a short recapitulation of preceding events & of my previous representations to them.

I am very sorry to hear that you are still troubled with influenza, but hope the change of air to Morocco will cure you.

y.s.

E.S.

15. Satow to Maclean

No. 7

Jan. 27. 94.

My dear Maclean,

I enclose to you also the Ital. Min's letter for the Sultan, & beg you to deliver it along with mine.

It is said that the Sultan wants to give territorial compensation to Spain instead of money, but I think this is a Fr. notion, who put it forward either that if accepted by Spain they may thereby get a handle for demanding Figuig and Tafilelt on the next occasion of a row wch. they wld. provoke for the purpose, or in order to make the negotiation fail, that they may fish in troubled waters. This idea is to be urgently combatted.

I hope you will not find any of the instructions I have sent you too contradictory to be carried out. But they amount to this: Back up Campos as to the indemnity, & pay[men]t. by instalments, with the right of supervising the collection of the Customs in the event of delay in pay[men]t. of the instalments & generally to support him in the other demands, wch. I

PRO 30/33 14/5   Semi-official Letters from Morocco (December 25, 1893 – March 9, 1894)

suppose comprise the clearance of the neutral zone, the punishment of the Gelaya tribe, & preventive measures for the future.

 y.v.t.

  E.S.

P.S. Altho' in a previous letter I said that England had brought about the diminution of the am[oun]t. to be claimed as indemnity, I think it would be more exact to say that the joint influence of England & Italy had induced Spain to moderate her demand.   E.S.

16. Satow to Sanderson

1 30 1894

My dear Sanderson,

 Your teleg. of the 25th reached me when it was too late to overtake Martinez Campos, who started fr. Mazagan to Morocco on the morning of the 23rd. But I had already in private letters to Maclean provided him c. instructions as to the support he shld. give to the Sp. embassy. Maclean left Rabat on the 22nd, & I calculate that he wld. reach the Court the same day as M.C. & is in time to give him any assistance that may be required.

 On the 25th I was able only to see Cantagalli, who agreed that the most effectual way of reaching the Sultan was to write to him direct, for Gharnit being in Fr. pay is not a safe intermediary. The Ital. Govt. had instructed him to do whatever I did. I tried to see d'Aubigny but he was out, & it was too late to do any more. On the morning of the 26th I saw Tattenb. who told me he had already acted on his instructions, wch. were to speak to T[orres]. who is as you know a mere figure-head. It is a curious thing that the Germ. shld. not have told even P. that he had done this. Altogether his way of doing things is unusual, & leads to the suspicion that while appearing to back up Sp. he is secretly advising the Sultan agst. them, pointing out the weak places in the Sp. case. Anyhow, instead of being frank abt. his action, he speaks or writes & then days after the Spaniard hears of it, as it were by chance. I made another attempt to see d'Aubigny, who was out for his ride. Then Cantagalli went to see him, & was most certainly denied. Later in the day, abt. half past 3 I met him coming leisurely up to see me, after having doubtless despatched his instructions to Linares by a steamer that left at 3. His assertion that he had recd. no instructions

PRO 30/33 14/5   Semi-official Letters from Morocco (December 25, 1893 – March 9, 1894)

whatever c. regard to Campos' mission is strangely in disagree[men]t. with what Moret told Wolff abt. Fr[ance]. having sent instructions & acting loyally. For the essence of loyal action here is that the Fr. RR.[Foreign Representatives] shld. act in combination. So if Campos gets his demands it will in my opinion not be thanks to Fr. & Germ. support.

There is a rumour that the Sultan will refuse to go beyond 25,000 pesetas for each Sp. killed, wch. wld. come to abt. 1 million doll. altogether, but I think this is a Fr. ballon d'essai, & merely indicates the advice they have been giving. They have also suggested quite recently to the Sultan that he shld. offer territorial compensation. I have told Maclean to try & counteract this advice. I have also told him to say to the Sultan that the diminution of the am[oun]t. asked for is due to Italy as well as G.B.

My reason for writing to the Sultan was that at the outset I delivered only a memo. to Torres. After Magallo's death I wrote to Gharnit, & a letter to the Sultan ∴ [therefore] marks the importance of the present moment.

   y.v.t.

17. Satow to Sanderson (stamped p.24)
6 Feb. 1894
My dear Sanderson,

It is reported here that H.R.H. the Duke of Cambridge[14] will visit Gib[raltar]. abt. the end of March, & that it is his intention to cross over to Ceuta. There has been a good deal of talk lately in the papers about a supposed desire of England to exchange Gib. for Ceuta, wch. does more credit to the ingenuity than to the good sense of those who started the report. I don't know what the Duke's object may be, but I cannot help thinking that his going there will merely serve to resuscitate the rumour and to give fresh occasion for the enemies of Engl[and]. to blaspheme. On similar grounds I shld. deprecate a visit to Tangier.

Potestad told me Moret had written to him privately to the effect that "these miserable matters of money" wld. not stand in the way of an arrange[men]t. with the Sultan, wch. looks as if he were not going to insist on the full amt. of the indemnity.   Tattenbach says

---

[14] Prince George, Duke of Cambridge (1819-1904). Commander-in-Chief of the Forces (British Army) from 1856 to 1895.

PRO 30/33 14/5   Semi-official Letters from Morocco (December 25, 1893 – March 9, 1894)

the two parties will certainly arrive at a settlement, but it will be much less. Cantagalli, who is always pessimistic, thinks whatever comes to pass will be by permission of the Fr. He hopes however that the news of Timbuctoo[15] will have a great effect on the Sultan's mind by disposing him agst. the French & he has taken care that it reaches his ears.   I find Cantagalli very careful not to do or say anything that cld. give offence to the Sultan; he is almost pusillanimous in his desire to conciliate. Tattenbach much in the same way. The Fr. on the contrary don't mind in the least what they say, and talk as if they were in the habit of bullying him, regardless of the result. d'Aubigny talks of going on leave in March, so that altho' Souhart has him[?] in his pocket, it seems likely that he will stay on.

I have no news yet fr. Morocco of the result of the negotiations. Maclean, who had been detained at Rabat by illness, cannot well have got there before the 29th or 30th. Cantagalli tells me his advices are that up to the 21st the prevailing feeling was that Fr. wishes & counsels wld. have great weight in the settlement arrived at, & that Ovilo[16] & [Dr.] Cortés who preceded the embassy were uttering very big threats of invasion of Morocco & so on.

   y.v.t. E.S.

18. Satow to Sanderson

10 Feb. 1894.

[No. 8?]

My dear Maclean,

An impression has reached the Sp. Govt. fr. Marraksh that some agent or agents in the entourage of the Sultan have led him to believe in the possibility of support being given to him by Engl. & Italy, so as to be able to resist the demands of Spain with respect to the indemnity.

I cannot discover where this utterly absurd story originated. Neither Italy nor England has the slightest intention of interfering betw. Spain & the Sultan, except to reiterate the

---

[15] On December 15, 1893, Timbuktu was annexed by a small group of French soldiers, led by Lieutenant Gaston Boiteux. It became part of French Sudan, a colony of France, now Mali.

[16] Felipe Ovilo Canales (1850-1909). Military attaché at the Spanish legation in Tangier.

PRO 30/33 14/5   Semi-official Letters from Morocco (December 25, 1893 – March 9, 1894)

advice they have already given him, to admit the Sp. demands, wch. they consider moderate in the extreme, being greatly less than their expenditure. It was telegraphed lately that Engl. & Italy had combined to recommend moderation, but to infer fr. that that they will countenance the Sultan in refusing to pay the amount demanded is ridiculous. I have only to repeat to you the injunction I have already given to back up Genl. Campos as to the indemnity & payt. by instalments with the right of supervising the collection of Customs in the event of delay in payt. of the instalments; & generally to support him in the other demands, wch. I suppose comprise the clearance of the neutral zone, the punish[men]t. of the Gelaya tribe, & preventive measures for the future.

   y.v.t.
   E.S.

19. Satow to Sanderson

Feb. 10. 1894

My dear Sanderson,

On getting Ld. R's teleg. No. 6 abt. attempts to persuade the Sultan that Engl & Italy were taking steps to procure the withdrawal of the Sp. demands, I went to see P[otesta]d., who showed me a telegr. he had recd. fr. Moret saying: "The ensemble of news fr. Morocco makes me suspect that in spite of the unanimity of the European cabinets, certain agents in the entourage of the Sultan make him believe in the possibility of some offensive (? mistake for 'decisive') support on the part of Italy & Engl. wch. permits him to resist the demands of Spain with respect to the indemnity. In view of this & in order to dissipate all doubts, please go & see Mohd. Torres, & reminding him of my last note, let him see that troops are ready to embark in Andalusia & a squadron to sail for the Moorish coast in case of a rebuff (desaire [Spanish]) to the Genl. Communicate the substance of this to your colleagues, not omitting those of Italy & England."

P. went off to Torres & spoke the menacing words, & then proceeded on around among the colleagues, luckily beginning c. Cantagalli, who tells me that he spoke rather strongly to him abt. the readiness of the Spanish Govt. to believe ill of their best friends, & pointed out that to circulate this telegram wld. be simply to play into the hands of France. He persuaded

PRO 30/33 14/5   Semi-official Letters from Morocco (December 25, 1893 – March 9, 1894)

him to promise that he wld. not forward any letter for Torres to the Sultan containing this threatening language. So P. instead of going on to d'Aub. & then the rest of us stopped in his wild career, & telegraphed to Moret that there was nothing in the rumour, & that he thought it premature to threaten, so wld. not forward any letter for Torres. (At prest. the Spaniards alone can get letters to Morocco, by their own boats). He also wrote a long private letter to Moret, in wch. he expressed his utter disbelief in any such intrigues, so at variance with the repeated assurances given to him by Cantagalli & myself, & adding that if opposition to the negotiations of Campos came from anywhere, it must be from one of the other legations. (It is not diff[icult]. of course to see whom he was pointing at. The notion of an arbitration to fix the amount of the indemnity is certainly of Fr[ench]. origin, & was first started in the Diario de Tangier, in wch. Kerdec has a hand. K on the contrary accuses Tattenbach of being the villain of the piece). He also read to me the last note he had addressed to Torres by Moret's instructions, saying that if the Spanish terms were refused, war wld. result, ending in the dissolution of the Moorish empire. He suggested to me that "that villain Bubeker" as he called him might have been playing off his own bat, but I hardly think that likely. Maclean it appears got to Morocco on the 2nd or 3rd (this I have heard only indirectly) & left again the following day. I conjecture that when the messenger fr. Casablanca overtook him with the letters fr. Cantagalli & myself to the Sultan, he left his wife & family on the road, & pushed on to Morocco to deliver then, & then went back to pick up his wife. I do not think it possible that he can have said anything to the Sultan wch. wld. put the idea into his head that England & Italy wld. assist in any further reduction of the indemnity.

Still I think it is just within the bounds of possibility that the teleg. fr. Rome that the original am[oun]t. was reduced at the instance of the two countries may have had a false interpretation put on it. I do not think anything in my letter to the Sultan cld. have been misunderstood. The most prob. origin of the story to my mind is Galicia, the 1st Secy. of the Sp. legation. Just before he left to join M.C. he went to say goodbye to Cantag. who wished success to the mission, whereupon he sneered & replied: "We know what value to put on the friendly assistance of foreign powers." [17] G. is mischievous, & quite capable of

PRO 30/33 14/5   Semi-official Letters from Morocco (December 25, 1893 – March 9, 1894)

inventing a malicious lie.

To satisfy Potestad I have written the enclosed letter to Maclean, & showed it to both Cantag. & Pd.; the latter asked permission to take a copy for Moret. So I trouble you with a copy too. Cantag. is writing in a similar sense to a hanger-on of his named Petri, who is now at Morocco city.

P. got a teleg. this morning directing him to ensure the menace of warlike measures reaching the Sultan without delay: this is lest any one shld. base dilatory counsels to the Sultan on a theory that Spain does not mean business.

M.C.'s last letter to him said: I see signs "of resistance, & mention has been made of arbitration". This I do not think there is any chance of the Sp. Govt. accepting.

y.v.t.

P.S. I have (12 Feb.) since writing the above heard that Martinez Campos, instead of adhering to the sum agreed upon by the Sp. Gov. c. Ld. R, boldly asked the Sultan for 40,000,000 pesetas, but that subsequently he reduced it to 25,000,000 down or 30,000,000 spread over a term of years. My informant is P. himself.

Maclean undoubtedly reached Morocco on the 3rd, but I have heard nothing fr. him. I think it is possible that he may have delivered to the Sultan the letters addressed to him by Cantagalli & myself, & that he may have added that acting on the friendly advice of Engl. & Italy the amount Sp. wld. demand wld. be reduced fr. £1,000,000 to £800,000. If he did say this, he wld. also urge the Sultan to agree to the latter fig[ure]. I have no letter fr. him & ∴ [therefore] can but conjecture outside possibilities.

Bubeker told Cantagalli's agent that the am[oun]t. of the indemnity wld. be submitted to arbitration, so it may easily come to be said that we made the suggestion.

Tattenbach is much upset at what has been said of him in the "Liberal", that he was counselling the Sultan to refuse the indemnity demanded. He accuses Cantagalli, who he says is allied with Tangier Jews who supply the Sultan; if the latter has to pay a large sum to the Spaniards, he will have less to spend with the Jews. "I, on the other hand, he said, have no interest at all in the Sultan paying 10,000,000 pesetas more or less".

---

[17] See Satow's diary for January 24, 1894.

PRO 30/33 14/5   Semi-official Letters from Morocco (December 25, 1893 – March 9, 1894)

Cantagalli on the other hand loses no opportunity of telling me that Tattenbach is playing the same game with the Spaniards as he did with Euan-Smith, of ostensibly supporting, while secretly undermining, & that he has advised the Sultan, thro' Torres' Secretary who went from here to Morocco, not to admit the whole of the Spanish demands.

Potestad read to me a letter fr. Martinez-Campos wch. arrived today, in wch. he says things were going on satisfactorily, the Sultan & Gharnit getting accustomed to the idea of an indemnity, until the Moor in question reached Morocco, when they suddenly relapsed into their previous attitude of <u>non possumus</u>, basing their refusal on some precept of the Koran. Still, the letter did not speak in a tone of discouragement. I gather that the Spaniards are not disposed to insist on the whole of the demands in relation to the indemnity, but they waver so much that it is impossible to say with certainty what they really wish.

   y.v.t.
   E.S.

20. <u>Satow to Sanderson (stamped p. 30)</u>
13 Feb. 1894.
My dear Sanderson,

A short time ago[18] I went to see the Engl[ish]. widow of the Sherif of Wazan,[19] who told me something of her plans.

She contests the legality of a document wch. bears the seal of the late Sherif, purporting to make his eldest son by a Mohammedan wife Grand Sherif – on the ground that it is not properly witnessed & also because the dignity is one that cannot be bequeathed, but must go acc. to popularity.

She is leaving in a few days for Algeria to visit some property belonging to the Sherifs of Wazan, ostensibly, but her real object is to test the popularity of her sons, whom she is taking with her.

Her plan is to wait until her sons come of age, & then let them choose their destiny for

---

[18] See Satow's diary for January 31, 1894.
[19] Emily Keene (1849-1944). She went to Morocco in 1872 as a governess to Mrs. Ellen Varley's children. Married the Sherif of Wazan in 1873.

PRO 30/33 14/5 Semi-official Letters from Morocco (December 25, 1893 – March 9, 1894)

themselves, i.e. whether they will remain under Fr. protection, or be reconciled to the Sultan. She did not hint at Engl. protection. The principal object she has in view is to make her eldest boy Grand Sherif, by ousting the man whom the Fr. have recognized.

Wld. there be any harm in saying that she might on occasions of difficulty count on the sympathy & support of this legation?

   y.v.t.

21. Satow to Maclean
Tangier
15 Feb. 94
No.9
My dear Maclean,

I hear that you got to Morocco on the 3rd inst., & am wondering why I have not heard from you. But letters are probably on their way, and in this country one must learn to be patient.

You will have recd. my letter of the 10th forwarded thro' the Sp. Minister. I don't think there is anything to be added to what I said on that occasion, but I hope that the negotiations of Genl. Campos will terminate to the satisfaction of the Sp. Govt.

I reported on the refusal of the Sultan's Govt. to release the agents, as I told you in my No.5 of the 22nd Jan. And now I have recd. very stringent instructions with regard to the matter. I am only waiting to hear the result of my last Note to Gharnit dated 12 Jan. before acting on them. G's letter, wch. you brought me, I have treated as not having been delivered, acc. to the agreement betw. us. If when you receive this the two men are still in prison, please say fr. me that I shall address to the Moorish Govt. only one more letter on this question, wch. will be a letter that they will not like. What I say & do they may be confident is based on positive instructions fr. home.

   y.v.t.
    E.S.

22. Satow to Maclean

PRO 30/33 14/5 Semi-official Letters from Morocco (December 25, 1893 – March 9, 1894)

No. 11

17.2.94

My dear Maclean,

Yr. letters of the 9th & 10th reached me yesterday. I am glad to hear that Cid Fedoul promises officially that the two remaining agents shall be released.

Their names are

Bushaib bel Hadj Amar Uld Sultana, confined by Bershed, and

Mohamd. Benschum Ziani held in confinement by Kaid Hadj Hamet bel Arbi Mediuni.

Mohd. Ben Attar was released by Hadj Abdalla Ben Dahman Bouzizi shortly after the refusal reported by Redman & complained of in the letter to Gharnit wch. you delivered for me, dated Jan. 12.

As you suggest, I return to you that letter you brought down, & wch. we have treated as non-existent. It had been registered by de Vismes, so I have cut off those parts of the paper. I don't know that you need return it to Gharnit, unless he expresses an earnest desire to have it back.

My going to Court to present my compliments to the Sultan entirely depends on their doing what is right in this matter.

   y.v.t.

   E.S.

23. Satow to Maclean

No. 12

17. Feb. 94

My dear Maclean,

You will have seen in the papers that the French have at last taken Timbuctoo & intend to remain there. Col. [Eugène] Bonnier who took possession then started in pursuit of some Touaregs who were in the neighbourhood: he was surprised during the night & had to beat a retreat, during that operation, he, 9 other officers & abt. 70 men fell [on January 15, 1894]. The Fr. Govt. says it had intended to recall him, because he had taken this step prematurely, but now that they have experienced this reverse, they are resolved to act with energy,

PRO 30/33 14/5   Semi-official Letters from Morocco (December 25, 1893 – March 9, 1894)

sending more troops there, with cannon, etc. Timbuctoo is to become the centre of the French domination in that part of the Soudan, & thence they will no doubt spread in all directions. Tendouf [Tindouf in Algeria] is one of the places wch. they think will be necessary as a stage in the construction of their rlwy. fr. Algeria to Senegal. The "Figaro" says now is the time to take possn. of Tuat.

Perh. you can make use of this information, & if you can tell me what impression the taking of Timbuctoo has produced on the Sultan's mind, it wld. be very interesting.

y.v.t.

24. Satow to Maclean

13 (no No. 10)

I am writing to catch post. Yrs. of 10th. I telegd. to London & Madrid & informed Sp. & Ital. Mins. who have also telegd. for instructions, wch. we have not yet recd. directly. But I learn fr. another source that the Sp. Govt. will insist on 25,000,000 or 20,000,000 in gold.

The additional million was for interest or its equivalent on the deferred instalments.

Fr. Min. has informed Sp. that the Fr. Govt. will give the most unreserved support to Sp. & that all he wants to know is the am[oun]t. Sp. will insist upon. That will prob. be teleg. to us in a day or two & we shall all follow suit. The Great Powers are unanimous on this question, & my advice to the Sultan will be to accept the recommendation that will be made to him in support of the Sp. demands.

25. Satow to Sanderson

18 Feb. 1894

My dear S.

It was the German who told Potestad that the Frenchman had advised the Moorish Govt. to grant the Sp. demands "if they were acceptable". P. wrote or telegraphed this to Moret, who appears to have been much struck by it, & in order not to make invidious distinctions, said that Foreign PP [Powers] in general had used that language.

Macl. reached Morocco on the 2nd Feb., & delivered the Notes to the Sultan fr[om]. Cantag[alli]. & myself on the following day. It was the day on wch. Campos had his 1st

PRO 30/33 14/5   Semi-official Letters from Morocco (December 25, 1893 – March 9, 1894)

business interview with the Sultan & so upset H.M. equanimity by saying that the "indemnity <u>ought</u> to be $8000,000" (<u>deberiaser</u>). But whether Maclean saw the Sultan & delivered our letters before or after Campos' interview I do not know. Prob[abl]y. before, because that seems the only explanation of the Sultan telling Campos that England & Italy wld. prevail on Spain to withdraw her demands. Then Maclean had an hr's talk with the Sultan on the 7th, & told him I most strongly advised him to settle with Sp. & to pay them the sum they asked, wch. thro' the joint influence of Engl. & Italy had been reduced by 1/5. That I advised him to try to induce Spain to accept it in instalments, but if they wanted it all at once, to let it be known that he wanted money, & to ask for tenders for a loan. The Sultan was very civil to him, & told him to say that he & all his people like England & the English better than anybody else. Everybody was much nicer to him than they have been for a long time. He also called on Campos & told him that I had instructed him to be of use to him in every possible way. Maclean's opinion was that the Fr. doctor Linares was helping the Sultan as much as he could without being really agst. Spain. He was told at the Court that Campos had demanded six million dols. & that the Sultan had offered 3 mil[lio]n. Then on the 10th he was sent for by the Sultan, who told him he wanted to give four million, & that he was to write to me for advice.

As you know, I at once communicated the offer to P. & told Cantag. Later in the day I got Gharnit's letter, dated 6 days earlier than Maclean's. These 2 communications coming together seem to have got mixed up in Moret's mind.

Maclean writes also that he had it out with Gharnit abt. the imprisoned agents. The old knave made all sorts of excuses, & asked him to write & tell me officially that letters ordering the release of the two men shld. be given him in a few days. I have not yet acted on Ld R's No. 15 Very Conf. but I wrote to Maclean on its receipt that something disagreeable was in prospect for the Moorish Govt. if the men were not speedily let out.

He says he is sure the Sultan means to settle with the Spaniards, as he is quite happy & got married to a pretty young woman only the other day.

Our business relations with the Sultan are carried on under circs. of such great difficulty that more than one of the colleagues begin to talk abt. the necessity of our going to reside at the Court, at least for a great portion of the year. And this has been brought home to us in a

PRO 30/33 14/5 Semi-official Letters from Morocco (December 25, 1893 – March 9, 1894)

very marked manner on the present occasion. We none of us know except in a very fragmentary manner & after a lapse of several days what goes on at Morocco, & by the time answers can reach Morocco with the instructions of our govts. the situation is pretty certain to have changed so greatly that they will be scarcely applicable. We are the prey of every lie or exaggeration or travesty of the truth that any stupid or malevolent fellow likes to place in circulation. The situation is something like that of the Foreign PP [Powers] in China while their repres'ves lived in Macao & Hongkong. If it cld. be managed we ought to spend a great part of the year at Fez or Morocco, at wch.ever the Sultan happens to be. Such a system wld. do more to introduce civilized ideas into Morocco than all the preaching of all the philanthropists, & to break down the existing wall of exclusion. If one Power took this step all the others wld. have to follow suit.

   y.v.t.

P.S. The personal relations betw. Cantag. & Tattenbach are not very cordial. Cantag. has for some weeks absented himself fr. the whist party that meets nearly every day at the German legation. T. got his instructions abt. the am[oun]t. of the indemnity the day before yesterday. C. met him yesterday morning early & asked him whether he had instructions. T. said No! & then went off straight to P. to reads him the draft of a Note to the Sultan, wch. he had already got translated & had put in Torres' hands. When he heard this C. was very angry. They had previously accused each other to me of suggesting to the Sultan to pay as little as possible. E.S.

26. Satow to Sanderson (stamped p.36)

Secret

Tangier

20 Feb. 1894

My dear Sanderson,

 In a letter "private & secret" of Dec. 29 Currie informed me that I might make a payment of £86 to Kaid Maclean, & £8 & £20 respectively to a man fr. Tafilelt & to Torres.

 The 50 bags of wheat I gave to Torres cost £22.10.9, so I have drawn on the Sec. of State at thirty days sight for £116.10.9.

PRO 30/33 14/5   Semi-official Letters from Morocco (December 25, 1893 – March 9, 1894)

I have not yet drawn for the $36.12 owing to Maclean on Ridgeway's acct. for couriers, as I have paid him rather more than that, & it will be more convenient to send in the whole acct. later.

y.v.t.

E.S.

27. Satow to Maclean

No. 14

20 Feb. 1894

My dear Maclean,

As I expected we have all been instructed to urge the Sultan to agree to the 25,000,000 pesetas ($5 000 000) demanded by Spain, & letters to this effect fr. d'Aubigny, Tattenbach, Cantagalli & myself have gone this afternoon by Sp. steamer to Mazagan. There is no help for it. The Spanish Govt. in reply to all that was said to it, insisted on that sum, and the Govts. were not able to influence their decision. That seems to show that it is animated by great determination.

I am sending Coutts & Co. a cheque for £86 to be placed to your acct. As to the other point you mention, namely the £400 being regarded as a salary instead of a present, I will see what I can do when I next see Sanderson,- you may rely on my doing what I can to meet your wishes.

Can you say anything to the Sultan abt. the difficulty betw. Kaid Wida & the Jews of Morocco abt. the convert's wife. I hear he has again insisted that they shld. produce the woman or swear on the Sefer that they don't know where she is. I wrote a very conciliatory letter to Gharnit as a coverer to Saml. Montagu's letter, but I shld. like the Sultan to know privately that Lord Rosebery takes a great interest in the Jews.

The Fr. newspapers in Algeria are now crying out that they must of course at once take possession of Tuat, but that neither that place nor Timbuctoo will be of any use without the Sus. Truly l'appetit vient en mangeant. You may tell H.M. this if you have an opportunity. I know of a colleague who will prob. send him some translations of these articles.

y.v.t.

PRO 30/33 14/5 Semi-official Letters from Morocco (December 25, 1893 – March 9, 1894)

28. Satow to Maclean

No. 15

Tangier

22/2/94.

My dear M.

Your No. 7 reached me yesterday morning by the "Mogador", & No. 6 fr. Casablanca yesterday. I am greatly pleased with the way you have cleared up the suspicions cast upon the good faith of the Engl. & Ital. Govts.

The sum of £800,000 in gold was understood by H.M.G. to be equal to 4 million fr. or 25 000 000 pesetas, i.e. 5 million dollars. There seems to have been a little confusion, owing to the idea that pesetas & francs are the same thing, as indeed they were before the depreciation of silver.

The Fr. Minr. has also recd. instructions to support the demand for $5 000 000. I think it prob[able]. that if the Sultan agrees to this, the terms & dates of pay[men]t. will be made easy to him.

I will consult F.O. abt. the cypher. I quite agree that it wld. be useful.

      y.v.t.

      E.S.

29. Satow to Sanderson (stamped p. 38)

Confid.

23 Feb. 1894

My dear Sanderson,

I see that in Lord Rosebery's No. 2 Consular of Feb. 7 a consular allowance for a man at Morocco city is spoken of as obtained fr. the Treasury. Nothing has yet been done abt. making the app[oin]tm[en]t. since Ld. S's [Salisbury's][20] No 8 of Aug. 5, 1892 to Euan-Smith, instructing him that the apptmt. shld. be deferred. And as far as I see at present there

---

[20] Lord Salisbury was Foreign Secretary until August 11, 1892.

PRO 30/33 14/5   Semi-official Letters from Morocco (December 25, 1893 – March 9, 1894)

is no pressing need of it. But since the Treasury has given the money, I shld. like to suggest another application of it, if it cld. be arranged, namely in increasing De Vismes' salary. Shld. our policy here in support of the Spaniards prove successful, it wld. be in a great measure owing to the fact of my being able to get my letters put into Arabic by de Vismes without the aid of a Moorish scribe. De Vismes gets only £400 a year, and it is a very small salary for the services he renders. He has 11 yrs. service. I shld. be very glad if something cld. be done for him, so that he may not lose heart, or fancy that his abilities are not duly appreciated.

   y.v.t.

30. Satow to Maclean
No. 16
24 Feb. 1894
My dear Macl.

 Your news of the 17th (i.e. No 8) is of great importance.

 Please say to the Sultan fr. me that I have heard that the Fr. Govt. have offered to lend him money to pay the Sp. indemnity. That this will put him in the hands of the Fr. Gov. who will be a most unrelenting creditor, & like Shylock will exact from him the pound of flesh without mercy. It is much better to trust to the generosity of Spain than to false friends who offer him what seem to be most advantageous terms of low interest & no security. It reminds one of the profligate who deludes a girl by promises of marriage to yield up her person & then when he has got her into his power, refuses to carry out his promise.

 In the last resort, if you do not find the Sultan yields to reasoning like this please take a firmer tone, & say fr. me that Engld. will, in case he accepts this loan fr. the Fr. Govt. take measures to protect herself & her interests agst. the obvious consequences namely his falling into Fr. hands. In short, that if he cares to be on any kind of terms with us, he had better refuse the offer.

31. Satow to Maclean
No. 17

PRO 30/33 14/5   Semi-official Letters from Morocco (December 25, 1893 – March 9, 1894)

Mar. 1

My dear Maclean,

I entirely approve all you have done & said up to the last date reported by you in No. 9 of the 19th. Do not for anything in the world give advice to the Sultan contrary to the wishes or interests of the Sp. Ambassador. Certainly not to follow the line of Petri in letting Ci Fedul to give as little as possible.

You may give your confidential informant any sum you think fit.

<u>Private</u>   The Fr. Govt. have promised to recall Linares, & he is to come at once to Tangier. But there may be delay.

It will perh. not be necessary to say anything to the Sultan abt. the proposed Fr. loan, but you will judge.

Insist on the <u>unconditional</u> release of the remaining 2 men. Please speak to the Sultan if you can abt. this point. Tell him that the Brit. Govt. will not be friends with him if he does not do it.

    y.v.t.

32. Satow to Sanderson

Tangier 25.2.94

My dear Sanderson,

It seems clear that 2 days after [he] recd. offer of loan of three millions from Linares, the Sultan saw M.C. [Martinez Campos], & proposed to him that he shld. accept exactly that sum, but it is pretty clear that he was disposed to give way. I enclose copy of Maclean's letter of the 17th as well as of confidential instructions wch. I have sent him today. It wld. be disastrous if Linares succeeds in getting the credit with the Sultan of having lowered the indemnity by 2 millions & also gets for France that hold over him wch. a creditor has over a debtor. He has been now some 17 years or so at the Court & has a great influence over the Sultan, increased no doubt in 1892. I therefore have tried to counteract this move [and] taken on myself the responsibility of telling Maclean to use some strong language if necessary.

Things vary from day to day. One thing has resulted from the most recent reports to

PRO 30/33 14/5   Semi-official Letters from Morocco (December 25, 1893 – March 9, 1894)

Madrid & Tangier that Sr. Moret & Potestad are convinced that whatever fair assurances may be given by the Fr. Govt. & by d'Aubigny, Linares is playing a purely Fr. game. Campos spoke & wrote the other day in gratifying terms of the help that he had been given by G.B. & Italians, while opining that the conduct of France was inevitably bringing Spain nearer to Engl. & the Triple Alliance.

In my last desp[atch]. I have drawn attention to the diversity of proceedings of the various colleagues, wch. is much to be deplored. The Fr. man one does not expect to be very open, but the Germ. ought to be more ready to consult. He has, as he thinks a personal influence with the Sultan, of wch. he is very proud, & does not like to sacrifice it. But nothing can be done here – except to go from bad to worse – unless the Powers who usually work together will give up pursuing exclusive objects & make their repres'ves follow suit. The impulse must come from Europe, for Tangier air is too laden with the ideas and prejudices of the past for any of us to be able to adopt the remedy spontaneously. My desp[atch]. is in no way meant as a complaint agst. [the Austro-Hungarian Minister Karl von] Boleslawski, who is an excellent fellow, but his 'note verbale' to Torres will be of no use whatever. I am greatly pleased with the hearty cooperation of Cantagalli.

I have delayed taking any further official steps with regard to the 2 imprisoned agents, as I think the moment is not opportune.

  y.v.t.
   E.S.

33. Satow to Maclean (stamped p.42)
No. 17
1 March 1894
My dear Macl[ean].

My no. 16 was handed to the Sp. Min. for desp[atch]. with his own this afternoon viâ Mazagan.

I have recd. your No. 8 of 17 Feb. (it was marked 7 by mistake) thro' the Sp. Mission, 8 2nd edition, a second copy of No. 8 by post, your Nos. 9 & 10, all right, intact.

No. 8 I have already replied to. No. 8 2nd edit. You are certainly quite right in having an

PRO 30/33 14/5 Semi-official Letters from Morocco (December 25, 1893 – March 9, 1894)

explanation with Martinez Campos & assuring him that he may rely on us.

Petri after all cld. not stand the strain of a little adversity, & when he saw that there was a possibility of the Ambassador accepting less than Cantagalli had urged on the Sultan, he thought it wld. be a clever trick to hedge, so did what you told me. But we must not follow the example of such people.

Your No. 10 Gharnit has replied to my Note in an altogether unsatisfactory way that as to the remaining 2 men, their Governors having stated that they were <u>sheikhs</u>, he is beginning to attend to the matter of their release & he will reply to me very soon.

I sincerely hope the men will be released without further ado. If after a few days more waiting I do not receive the orders for their release, I shall have to write the letter spoken of in my no. 9, & after that no friendly relations will be able to exist betw. the two govts. As to the question of the men being <u>sheikhs</u> I will myself have an inquiry held by someone whom I can trust, as soon as the men have been released, but their release must come first.

    y.v.t.

P.S. I believe, tho' I am not officially sure, that the 3 millions offered by the Sultan will be accepted, the decrease in the amount being accorded to H.S.M. on the responsibility of the Queen Regent & Marshal C. If so, we need not press for anything more.

34. Satow to Sanderson (stamped p. 43)

<u>Secret</u>

Tangier

Mar 1. 1894

My dear Sanderson,

 I have recd. the coffee service for Bubeker, & have handed it over to his agent here, J. Abensur, accompanying it with an official letter of delivery. He has duly acknowledged it, & promises to send it on by the 1st opportunity.

 One or two of the local papers immediately had a para. alluding to B's resignation & the present given him by H.M.G. I suppose the information to have been given by Bubeker's agent.

    y.v.t.

PRO 30/33 14/5   Semi-official Letters from Morocco (December 25, 1893 – March 9, 1894)

35. Satow to Sanderson
Secret
Tangier
1 Mar. 94
My dear Sanderson,

I enclose a list showing exactly what presents I have in stock & how the rest were disposed of. The gold chains are with the watches.

I am under the impression that I have already sent you a list of desiderata in the way of presents in view of the possibility of my going to Court. If it has not reached you, would you mind telegraphing.

y.v.t.

PS. The fire-escape is still at Fez; being too bulky to bring away it was left behind by Euan-Smith.

36. Satow to Sanderson
1 Mar.
Dear S.
[Asking for a cipher for K. Maclean]

37. Satow to Villiers (stamped p. 44)
Tangier
5/3/94
My dear Villiers,

A[rthur]. Herbert has asked me to take him with me when I go to see the Sultan, & I believe he has already written to you on the subject.

I have told him that I am quite willing, but that the time is not yet fixed, & that if he goes with me it ought to be as a member of the mission, if it cld. be arranged to attach him to me for that purpose. I shld. be very glad if this can be done consistently with your rules.

It is not proposed that Mrs. H. shld. go.

PRO 30/33 14/5   Semi-official Letters from Morocco (December 25, 1893 – March 9, 1894)

38. Satow to Maclean

No.18

Tangier. 9/3/94

My dear Maclean,

I have your No. 11 of 24 Feb. No. 12 of 26 & No. 2 of Mar. 1. The latter I recd. the day before yesterday. Is there a No.1 on the road?

It was a great satisfaction to hear that the indemnity was settled for 4 millions. You may now be told that when the Sultan's offer of that sum reached me thro' you, I at once communicated it to the Sp[anish]. & Ital[ian]. Min[ister]s, & that all three of us telegraphed, to London Madrid & Rome resp[ectively]., urging its acceptance. I have good reason to know that Ld. R[osebery]. pressed it on the Sp. Govt., who declined it, & declared they wld. insist on 5 mill[io]ns. Consequently the Italian Min. & myself recd. instructions to return that ans[wer]. to Gharnit's letter asking for an expression of opinion as to how much of the six millns. asked for originally the Sultan shld. pay. We are told that Cts. T & d'Aub[igny].[21] got precisely the same instructions fr. their Govts. I think you may perh. be able to make use of this inform[atio]n.

I had just got so far when yr. letter No.1 of the 27 Feb. was put into my hands.

Wld. it be safe, without more evidence than Gharnit's word, to write to F.O. that a letter has been sent to Mogador abt. the Jews' Q[uarte]r. & that the Sultan will pay for the building?

As to the decoration offered you by the Marshall, you wld. not be allowed by the Queen to accept it, because permission is given only in cases where the recipient has been in the exclusive service of the Govt. wch. gives the decoration, & to receive such a thing without being able to wear it wld. scarcely be worthwhile.

It won't do to have those two agents sent to the Court to be employed with the Sultan. They must be released & allowed to go back to their employers. After that, if the govt. like,

---

21 Jules-Ludovic Henrys, Comte d'Aubigny (1844-1922). French Envoy Extraordinary and Minister Plenipotentiary at Tangier, 1892-94. Replaced by Joseph-Raymond Baylin de Monbel.

PRO 30/33 14/5   Semi-official Letters from Morocco (December 25, 1893 – March 9, 1894)

I will have the question of Sheikh or no Sheikh inquired into.

   Will you kindly tell them this, if when you receive this letter, the orders for release have not been given.

>   y.v.t.
>   E.S.

Enclose Coutt's & Co's receipt for £86.

END OF PRO 30/33 14/5

PRO 30/33 14/6   Semi-official Letters from Morocco (March 8, 1894 – July 10, 1894)

PRO 30/33 14/6   Satow's Semi-Official Correspondence

1. Satow to Sanderson

8 Mar. 94

My dear S.

I got last night a letter fr[om]. Maclean dated 3 Mar., saying that the Sultan & Campos have agreed on 4 mill[io]n $, but nothing abt. the details. One of the conditions was that the Sultan sh[ou]ld. not borrow fr[om]. any one, another is that he may pay in the Isabel $ [Isabelinos] of w[hi]ch. there are a large quantity in this country, but are no longer current in Spain. At present they are at a discount of 5 or 6%. The Sultan has quite recently issued decrees prohibiting their being used as currency, with the intention of depressing the price so that he may buy them up cheaply for the indemnity. He had in reality plenty of treasure, & c[ou]ld. easily pay ready money, but like all misers pretends to be poor.

P[otestad]'s news confirms Maclean's ab[ou]t. the am[oun]t. accepted. It is possible, I think, that the agree[men]t. may say that the proper am[oun]t. of the indemnity is 5 miln. but that out of cons[ideratio]n. for the Sultan the 2[nd] Regent consents to take less.

Last week when Wolff's teleg. of the 24[th] to the effect that the indem[nit]y. w[ou]ld. be largely reduced reached me Cantag[alli, the Italian Minister] & I felt that we had given ourselves away, & I went on the 27th to give P. a bit of my mind abt. them urging us to say 5 [million dollars] to the Sult[an]. & then taking 3, as was then rumoured that they were going to do. I reminded him of the offer of it[?] w[hi]ch. came fr. the Sultan thro' Maclean, w[hi]ch. had been recommended by Cantag[alli] & myself. But the Sp[anish]. Govt. had treated the offer c. contempt & said they w[ou]ld. not take a penny less than 5. It w[ou]ld. not be fair to those who had supported the demand for 5 if Sp. were now to take less than 4.

There is no doubt fr. what Linares[1] said to Maclean & Petri that he had urged the Sultan not to give more than three millions, & I am pretty certain that d'Aub[igny]. & Souhart[2] had on their own acct. been speaking & writing in the same sense. Then they got very precise instructions fr. Paris to support the larger demand. Petri (who is Cantagalli's

---

[1] Dr. Ferdinand Linarès (1850-1938) was the French political agent at the Sultan's court.
[2] Fernand-Arthur Souhart was First Secretary at the French Legation, 1892-94.

301

PRO 30/33 14/6   Semi-official Letters from Morocco (March 8, 1894 – July 10, 1894)

temporary agent at Morocco) fancying that Fr[ench]. counsels w[ou]ld. prevail went to Gharnit & told him Italy did not care what the Sultan did, & that he sh[ou]ld. pay as little as he c[ou]ld. I told this to P. c. the addition that I was convinced Cantag[alli]. had not authorized this. Maclean stuck to his text & preached 5 & lest there sh[ou]ld. be any doubt I wrote to him on the 1st that he must on no acct. follow P's example. The effect has been good, & Campos is so pleased with Maclean that he offered him a decoration. The Germ[an]. I have no doubt had also been recommending to the Sultan a lower sum, till he got definite instructions to back the 5. It was a bitter pill for him, & a still bitterer when it got abt. last week that Campos had accepted 3. He tried then to make out that he had only recommended the Sp. demand in general terms. The Sult[an]. apparently wrote to him thro' Gh. that the am[oun]t. was to be 3 after all, & he is now again himself for the moment until he hears what has been finally settled.

The only thing that seems to me regrettable is that the Sp. sh[ou]ld. think we were trying to make capital out of the indemnity by forwarding the offers of Montagu & Forwood[3] But it seemed necessary to do that in order that the Sultan might not get the money from France. I have carefully avoided this subj[ect]. with P. except to the extent of telling him that multitudes of B[ritish]. S[ubjects]. had besieged me with offers.

M[aclean] writes that the Sultan proposes to release the two remaining agents, & to give them employ[men]t. at the Court. I am waiting to hear further before I write to Gh. again, & in any case I think that it will be better to defer acting on Ld. R[osebery]'s last instructions till Campos is safely away fr. Morocco.

The Art[icle] in the Epoca of [February?] 28 caused a good deal of annoyance amongst the colleagues. There is too much truth in what is said of the Fr[ench]. & Germ[an]. legations, & perh. of the Ital[ian]. also. Who the author is I have not been able to find out.

H[erbert]. & his wife & E[smé]. Howard[4] off to Fez on the 5 [March]. Lord & Lady Meath [Reginald Brabazon] here; she is going to get out a lady doctor.

    y.v.t.

---

[3] Montagu v. Forwood was an 1893 legal case concerning agency and set-off. (Law Reports 2, Queen's Bench 350).
[4] Esmé Howard, 1st Baron Howard of Penrith (1863-1939).

PRO 30/33 14/6   Semi-official Letters from Morocco (March 8, 1894 – July 10, 1894)

2. Satow to Kaid Maclean

No. 19

12. 3. 94

My dear Maclean,

I think it is getting time to bring this affair of the Agents to an end, & have therefore written the enclosed Note to Gharnît, containing the <u>ipsissima verba</u> [exact words] of Lord R's instructions to me. I send it to you open that you may know its contents, & if you like have copies made, in case Gharnit sh[ou]ld. put it in a pigeon hole instead of showing it to the Sultan. You w[ou]ld. then be able to provide Zibdi with a copy to inform H.S.M.

In case the orders for the release of the two agents have been given please [send] the letter back to me without taking any further steps.

I am also told to "intimate privately that, even if the friendship of G.B. were not at the present time of peculiar value to Morocco in other ways, it is only out of consideration for the Sultan that H.M.G. resist the constant appeals that they sh[ou]ld. give active support to British enterprise in the vicinity of Cape Juby in a manner w[hi]ch. w[ou]ld. certainly be far fr. agreeable to H.M."

In short if they prefer keeping these men in prison to being on friendly terms with us, why they can take their choice. Each party can then go its own way. They will have had the pleasure of refusing to observe a stipulation of a treaty (the Madrid convention) by w[hi]ch. they are bound to us; & they will not be surprised if we, finding it impossible to obtain from them by repeated remonstrance the redress of a wrong committed by two of the Sultan's Governors, come to the conclusion that he prefers a quarrel.

Lord R. is a man who does what he says. He will not as Prime Minr. forget the words he uttered as Foreign Sec. & his power to execute them is ten-fold greater than before.

I don't want this to be said to Gharnit, but to the Sultan direct, if you can find a good opportunity, & of course you will put it in your own words.

I am tired of this business.

   y.v.t.

PRO 30/33 14/6   Semi-official Letters from Morocco (March 8, 1894 – July 10, 1894)

3. Satow to Sanderson

14 Mar. 1894

My dear Sanderson,

The Sp. business being arranged, Tangier has returned to its normal condition of repose, & the colleagues will be able to devote their attention to municipal matters. The supply of water is becoming an urgent question. Very little rain has fallen this winter, less than ¼ the average, & we are threatened with a famine as well as dying of thirst. I have assured d'Aubigny who had to do with the creation of the municipality of Alexandria that I am desirous of cooperating actively with him in these questions. He observed that little by little Tangier w[ou]ld. become internationalized, w[hi]ch. w[ou]ld. be the best guarantee for things remaining as they are. France does not wish for Morocco, but as little desires to see any one else here. I said that I entirely shared those views.

The V.C. at Fez who trades as Mcleod & Co. reports the arrest of one of his agents, a Jew, by the Basha of Mequinez, who extorted $150 fr. him as the price of his liberty. I have written to Torres on the subject, by way of a commence[men]t. but am not reporting it officially as yet. There will be time enough for that when all our efforts here to get the $150 refunded have failed. A Moor, naturalized B.S., to whom I had told Macleod to give good offices, was assaulted & badly hurt the other day. He complained that he had been robbed of a large quantity of banknotes, jewelry &c. worth £200, but subsequently confessed that this part of his story was a fabrication. He was however badly hurt. I have told Macleod to continue his good offices, with the object of getting the assailants arrested & punished.

I have recd. nothing of later date than the 3rd fr. Kaid Maclean, & do not know for certain that Campos has signed his convention.

d'Aubigny leaves on the 20th for 3 wks to change his rooms at Paris, going by a st[eame]r. w[hi]ch. touches at Melilla & lands him at Oran. He says that on his return here Souhart will go on a long leave. The local Fr. paper had been publishing a string[?] of articles, w[hi]ch. people suppose were inspired by Souhart, urging the necessity of keeping the same staff at the Legation instead of changing them so constantly, & suggesting that Souhart w[ou]ld. be the proper man to succeed d'Aubigny.

y.v..t.

PRO 30/33 14/6   Semi-official Letters from Morocco (March 8, 1894 – July 10, 1894)

P.S. I am going to Gib. today till the 17th.[5]

4. Satow to Sanderson

Tangier

20.3.94

My dear Sanderson,

At last I have got the last two agents liberated, at least I hope so, unless the Sherifian letters sent me thro' Maclean are shams. It was necessary to use a little stronger language than actually appears in my desp[atch]. I told Maclean to say that I sh[ou]ld. address the Moorish govt. only one more letter on the subj[ec]t. w[hi]ch. w[ou]ld. be in terms they w[ou]ld. not like. After that no friendly relations w[ou]ld. be able to exist betw, the 2 govts. As I wrote to you before, I have not acted on Ld. R's No. 15 Very Conf. of Feb. 7, because I wished to try every expedient first. However on the 12th, as I was beginning to get sick of these delays, I wrote a note to Gharnit, putting in the strong language of the desp[atch]. & sent it to Maclean, with instructions to deliver it only in case the orders to release the men had not been given. As a matter of fact the very day before Maclean's letter enclosing the orders had started from Morocco, so the bolt I had prepared will be returned into the quiver.

As far as I can judge there seems to be no reason why I sh[ou]ld. not go & present my credentials. If the presents were ready, I might start a month hence & reach Morocco by the end of April. I suppose that I shall merely deliver my letter & leave again after a fortnight's stay. It w[ou]ld. be a good thing for me to return to Tangier by way of the coast as far as Rabat & Fez, just to gain knowledge of the country. You w[ou]ld. I hope send me to Mogador in a corvette (there is no sleeping accommodation on board the "Bramble") & I sh[ou]ld. propose to do the return journey on horseback.

Is it absolutely necessary that I sh[ou]ld. deliver Euan-Smith's letter of recall, w[hi]ch. was furnished to me? If possible, it might be discreet to burke [get rid of] it altogether.

The party w[ou]ld. consist of self, De Vismes, Reader, Morant, a doctor & Arthur Herbert, if my proposal that he sh[ou]ld. be officially attached to the Mission, made in a

---

[5] Satow inspected the dockyard at Gibraltar and went up the Rock on March 16, 1894. (Diary)

305

PRO 30/33 14/6   Semi-official Letters from Morocco (March 8, 1894 – July 10, 1894)

private letter to Villiers, be sanctioned. I do not want to take a numerous company with me, & sh[ou]ld. prefer having strict instructions to limit the number to members of the legation.

Maclean says he has heard from a reliable quarter (I fancy this is some man about the Court whom he calls T.A. [Abdul Wahed][6]) that the Sultan will not leave Morocco this year.

Gharnit hinted to Maclean that he sh[ou]ld. like a present for getting the letters releasing the agents; this seems an impudent pretension, but I suppose is the way of things in this country.

I have not heard of Linares having actually left Morocco, but there seems no doubt that he got a sharp reprimand fr. the Fr. Govt. for his excessive zeal agst. the Spaniards. Kerdec, the editor of the Diario de Tanger, has gone there, to present the Sultan with an album of photos. Cantag's agent Petri (a Tangier merchant) who came to call today, tells me that there was a talk at Morocco of my shortly going there. As far as my own utterances are concerned, I have always told people that it is still in the dim future, that perh. I would go to Engl. before visiting the Sultan & so forth. Cantagalli wants to go to Court, as he can get nothing done; he has claims for plunder of certificated agents for w[hi]ch. he can get no redress.

d'Aub. went on leave on the 16th by direct boat to Marseille. Potestad goes early in April.

y.v.t.

P.S. Mar. 22   I ought to have said that it'll take fr. 1 mon[th]. to 6 wks fr. the time when I despatch a Note to the Court to say that I am going up, before the Sultan's people w[ou]ld. be able to get the tents, mules, etc. ready at Mogador. So I hope you'll teleg. to me instructions as soon as it is decided, that I may lose no time. The presents I think sh[ou]ld. be sent direct to Mogador by one of Forwood's boats, so that I c[ou]ld. pick (cont. p. 23) them up there.

As to presents, the military balloon, like most of the other things, were suggestions of H[arr]y. Maclean's; for my own part I have no particular wishes abt. any of the items in the

---

[6] "Abdul Wahed (T.A.) is going down the coast to examine what has been done by the Umana with the arms & ammunition that have been supplied to them. He is an engineer." (Satow's diary, March 21, 1895)

PRO 30/33 14/6   Semi-official Letters from Morocco (March 8, 1894 – July 10, 1894)

list. Capt. Delmé Ratcliffe of the Sappers A.D.C. [Aide De Camp] to Genl. Hopton at Gib. came to me today to say that he wished to go c. me whenever the mission takes place, to take surveys & so on. I told him that I had refused all applications of the sort. He is a perfect stranger to me, & brought no sort of recommendations. He says he is going to Engld. in a week & will ask the Intelligence Dept. & the F.O. for permission. I threw as much cold water on him as possible, & I hope you will not hear of his being attached to me.

As to a Dr., if Greig, my own medical man here, sh[ou]ld. wish to go, may I take him. I understand there is an allowance of £1 a day, & he w[ou]ld. like to go if he got it.   E.S.

5. Satow to Kaid Maclean
No. 20
Tangier
20 March 1894
My dear Maclean,

I can hardly tell you with what satisfaction I recd. your No. 3 with the 2 letters abt. the agents. I am despatching them to y[ou]r. br[other, Allan Maclean].[7] c. instructions to send a soldier to bring the 2 men to him, or else go himself to the places where they are confined. I have also requested him to ascertain what am[oun]t. of truth there is in the allegation that they are <u>sheikhs</u>. I am much amused at Gh.'s idea that he ought to get some money for releasing these men. Of course I c[ou]ld. not think of such a thing on the present occasion, but if he acts the part of a friend, & he spoke as a friend in his letter of 3rd Shaaban,[8] he will find that I shall not be ungrateful. You might tell him this. And also say that I am glad the letters were sent direct to me, for the Br. Govt. attached great importance to this request of theirs being complied with. As I have always told them, their complying with this demand, w[hi]ch. was the very first I had to put forward after my arrival, was to be the criterion whether they intended to be friendly to Engl. & nothing in the world w[ou]ld. have induced me ever to go near the Court as long as these agents were not released. Now, if H.M.G. instruct me to go to Court I am confident that they will treat me in a friendly

---

[7] Allan Maclean was Consul at Dar al Baida.
[8] Shaaban is the eighth month of the Islamic (lunar) calendar.

manner. With regard to Gh's wish that I sh[ou]ld. send these 2 men to the Court to be under your care for the Sultan to investigate whether they are <u>sheikhs</u> or not, I must think over that.

Can you tell me whether, when you were here in Sept. or Dec. last you took away any rifles of yours that had been deposited in the Consulate. I seem to have a recollection of having heard something abt. it at the time. How many were there? I have a particular reason for wanting to know.

y.v.t.

<u>6. Satow to Sanderson</u>

Tangier

21/3/94

My dear Sanderson,

You perh. may have seen my name at the bottom of a letter in the "Times" of the 14th appealing for support to the Engl. school here. Of course the letter is Ernest Hart's,[9] who being a Jew is interested in the promotion of the interests of this school, frequented largely by Moorish Jews. I do not know what measure of support we are likely to get from the public at home, but in the meantime it has occurred to me that we have here a means of substantially helping the school without coming to the Treasury. Of the $10,000 w[hi]ch. Euan-Smith got fr. the Basha of Fez there still remains a sum of over $2200. De Vismes tells me he has sent to Hervey an acct. of the disbursements made up to the present. Out of the balance if you see no objection I sh[ou]ld. like to make a donation in the name of H.M.G. say $500 (rather less than £80) to the school and a similar sum to the Engl. hospital at Tangier maintained by the N.A. [North African] mission for the treatment chiefly of Moors. Both Sp. & Fr. have hospitals here, w[hi]ch. are mainly supported by their govts. I w[ou]ld. of course not say where the money came from but the announcement of such gifts c[ou]ld. not fail to produce a good effect.

y.v.t.

---

[9] Ernest Abraham Hart (1835-1898). English medical journalist.

PRO 30/33 14/6   Semi-official Letters from Morocco (March 8, 1894 – July 10, 1894)

E.S.

7. Satow to Kaid Maclean

No. 21

22.3.94

My dear Maclean,

Will you please take an opportunity of stirring up Gharnit abt. the repayment to the Sanitary Board at Tangier of certain sums of money expended by them last year on quarantine at Mogador. The Sanitary Bd. have written to the Sultan direct, 1ce. [once] last year & again in Feb. The 2nd letter was sent thro' Redman, and I think was handed in by you on the 22nd of last month. As the money to meet the expenditure had to be borrowed, & we are responsible for interest on it to the bankers who advanced it, we are anxious that the Sultan sh[ou]ld. give orders to the Umana to repay it to us. In connexion with this subject I want to suggest to the Sultan the desirability of building a proper lazaretto[10] somewhere on the coast: for preference I w[ou]ld. say at Tangier. That w[ou]ld. be much better than agreeing to let all Moorish pilgrims perform their quarantine at the Algerian lazaretto of Matifou, for 2 reasons (1) it w[ou]ld. cost much less in the end, if we may judge fr. the fact that the quarantine charge for a single vessel w[hi]ch. took pilgrims there last year was nearly 5000 francs, say over $1000; (2) I think other Powers might object to their vessels having to undergo quarantine ar a Fr. lazaret. It is of great importance that we sh[ou]ld. keep out cholera as far as we can by adopting proper precautions, & the construction of a lazaret seems to be absolutely necessary.

I am sending by you for delivery to Gharnit a letter about some debts owed by a Moor of Fez, named Benzelum, to some Br. Ss. in Scotland. Braunschweig a Fr. subj. is another of the creditors, & there is a Germ. creditor. I am anxious to prevent the Fr. or the Germ. fr. getting priority, as they are evidently trying to do. Sh[ou]ld. this be done the responsibility w[ou]ld. fall on the Moorish Govt.

The theory of the development of an ordinary commercial debt into a claim agst. the

---

[10] (here) A building for quarantine purposes

PRO 30/33 14/6   Semi-official Letters from Morocco (March 8, 1894 – July 10, 1894)

Sultan is this: every govt. is bound to see justice done by the Courts, & to make solvent debtors pay their creditors. When the debtor cannot pay in full, then on the application of the creditors the property of the debtor must be sold & divided amongst the creditors pro ratâ, care being taken that none of the creditors be left out.

If thro' the neglect of the Sultan's officers, Kaids, Bashas or what not, a creditor does not get justice, then he appeals to his govt. for aid, & the claim becomes one on the Sultan. This is why it is so necessary to impress on local people, like the Basha of Fez for instance, that they must deal fairly & promptly with the claims of foreigners.

I have recd. a cypher for you fr. the F.O. & am keeping it here for another fortnight in order to send it to Mazagan by an Engl. st[eame]r. Please calculate the prob. time & send a trustworthy man to Redman for it. Redm. will not know anything but that he is to deliver it only to the man you send.

   y.v.t.

    E.S.

P.S. The amount claimed by the Conseil Sanitaire is $7290 and svn [sovereign?] 12

8. Satow to Kaid Maclean

No. 22

23.3.94

My dear Maclean,

I am sending the cypher to you by the hands of Mr. H. Gurney, who is leaving for Morocco city, so you will not have to despatch a messenger to Mazagan to fetch it. I recommend this gentleman to your good offices during his stay.

I have just recd. your No. 4.

There is one very important letter I want answered, abt. Forde's[11] claim [illegible phrase] inquired into. Sir West [Ridgeway] wrote 8 Muharram last year informing Gh[arnit]. of the result of the investigation, & stating that the am[oun]t. demanded was $2000. In 7ber (Rebia I.10) I wrote again, urging a settlement, but have recd. no reply. I do not want to

---

[11] Lewis Forde, Vice-Consul at Laraiche. Below the claim is referred to as "Forde's Habassi claim".

PRO 30/33 14/6   Semi-official Letters from Morocco (March 8, 1894 – July 10, 1894)

have to discuss affairs of this kind when I come to Court. So please remind Gh. & tell him also that I want answers to all the letters in the enclosed list. You will see that some of them are already several months old.

You can charge expenses of Tafilelt man to HMG & when he goes, tell him to be exact in writing to you anything he can find out for certain abt. the doings of the Fr[ench]. in those parts. You can then send the letters to us. If T.A. c[ou]ld. get me a copy of the Treaty, it w[ou]ld. be worth $20, but not if it is delayed too long. It has not been made known here. Abt. [John] Bonich I will write on another occasion.

I telegd. home news of the letters of release & hope soon to get instructions to go to Court. I know the presents are being prepared. They struck at the idea of a balloon, w[hi]ch. they tell me w[ou]ld. cost £1200. Many thanks for the dates w[hi]ch. are excellent.

Don't say anything at pres[en]t. abt. my coming to Court. But you might say to Gh. that I am pleased at having recd. the letters, & that I am disposed to be their friend.   y.v.t.

9. Satow to Sanderson

Tangier

27.3.94

My dear Sanderson,

Many thanks for your letters of the 20th & 21st.

When I sent you that list of presents I had not the least idea of their cost, & I don't suppose Kaid Maclean had either. Some of the presents Euan-Smith bought, especially the firearms, seem extravagantly dear – they don't look the money they cost. And the fire escape will be useless to give as a present, if I go to Morocco. I think the shire stallion will do better than the phaeton & ponies, as the Sultan is fond of big horses. Please let me have hall clocks. And if there is anything over, pray let me have some pieces of handsome curtain stuffs, w[hi]ch. these people are sure to appreciate.

When I hear fr. Allan Maclean that the 2 men have actually been set at liberty I will send you a telegram, & then I hope you will reply authorizing me to write to the Court that I propose to pay them a visit. I have consulted White abt. Ld. K[imberley]'s suggestion that it might be politic to let some interval lapse betw. Campos' visit & mine. He thinks that if I

PRO 30/33 14/6   Semi-official Letters from Morocco (March 8, 1894 – July 10, 1894)

go on a merely complimentary mission the Sultan's attitude will not be at all affected by what has passed. Morocco is hot during the summer, & travelling later than June w[ou]ld. be very trying. If therefore Ld. K.[12] sh[ou]ld. decide not to send me at present, the mission w[ou]ld. have to be put off till the autumn. The Spanish business being now quite settled, it w[ou]ld. not occur to the Colleagues that I was trying to spoil the Spanish game. In any case they are pretty sure to suspect something. If one does nothing, they will fancy one is lying low like brer rabbit. My own idea w[ou]ld. be to avoid business topics as much as possible, & to tell the Sultan that I w[ou]ld. come up later to discuss outstanding claims. Possibly I might be able to get a few small things settled, such as getting leave for people at the coast to repair their houses & so on, mere routine matters. Unless Ld. K. has some special instructions to give me I do not at present know of any important affairs that require to be broached.

One of Forwood's steamers will be leaving London abt. the 30th April, w[hi]ch. w[ou]ld. afford a convenient opportunity for despatching the stallion & the clocks. She w[ou]ld. reach Mogador abt. May 15th. That date w[ou]ld. suit very well for my starting on the journey to Morocco.

As marching all the way back to Tangier w[ou]ld. cost a good deal both to H.M.G. & the Sultan, I think it might be advisable to visit the ports by sea in the corvette w[hi]ch. I sh[ou]ld. ask for. To do that on the way to Court w[ou]ld. have one great advantage, that I sh[ou]ld. be able to converse with the Sultan avec connaissance de cause, [in full possession of the facts] and it w[ou]ld. also conciliate the British merchants on the coast, who fancy that their wishes & requirements are systematically disregarded. I w[ou]ld. give a couple of days to each port, so that the trip would take about a fortnight.

      y.v.t.

P.S. Estimated time for mission

Tangier to Mogador by ports	14 days
Mogador to Morocco	6 "
Stay at Morocco (outside)	21 "

---

[12] Lord Kimberley succeeded Lord Rosebery as Foreign Secretary on March 10, 1894. He was succeeded by Lord Salisbury on June 21, 1895.

PRO 30/33 14/6   Semi-official Letters from Morocco (March 8, 1894 – July 10, 1894)

Morocco to Mazagan	5	"
Mazagan to Tangier	1	"
	48	

10. Satow to Kaid Maclean

No. 23

30.3.94

My dear Maclean,

I hear fr. your brother [Allan] of a big packet fr. the interior addressed to me, w[hi]ch. I conjecture contains letters fr. you. It will prob[ably]. arrive in a day or two, as he has kept it for a steamer.

In the meanwhile I send you for delivery to Gharnit a Note abt. Moh'd el Kûsh, the Capt. of the Port at Laraiche, who has lately been degraded and imprisoned. All the merchants are strongly in favour of this man, & the F.RR [Foreign Representatives] were asked to intercede for him. We, most of us, spoke to Torres, who replied that it was a matter that concerned the Sultan alone, as el Kush was his officer, & that we had no business to interfere. I told him that it was very much my concern, because owing to the ability & diligence of this man, the business of Br. merchants my countrymen is greatly facilitated. The colleagues say they will do no more, & that the Sultan w[ou]ld. be annoyed! That is a view that it does not behove me to take, & I shall never be deterred I hope fr. doing my duty by any consideration of the kind. In order that you may know what I am writing, I send you a copy of the Engl[ish]. of my letter to Gharnit, & a copy of the Arabic to show the Sultan in case you sh[ou]ld. have reason to think Gharnit has burked it. I want H.S.M. to believe that by listening to reasonable representations from a foreign Minister (myself) he is likely to make a friend, but a friend who will always say frankly what he thinks, believing that a wise sovereign prefers to hear the truth.   y.v.t.

11. Satow to Sir Percy Anderson[13] (stamped p. 16)

---

[13] "Sir Percy Anderson was the most famous African expert of his day. He had been senior clerk in the Consular and African Department throughout its existence (1883-93) and then

PRO 30/33 14/6   Semi-official Letters from Morocco (March 8, 1894 – July 10, 1894)

31.3.94

Dear Sir Percy,

I have felt obliged to write an official desp[atch]. abt. the scheme outlined in Ld. Kimberley's No. 4 Consular of the 20th inst. w[hi]ch. I am afraid may appear somewhat of a controversial nature. But as the responsibility for its efficient working will in a great measure be thrown on myself, I wished to point out the defects w[hi]ch. it appears to me to present.

In the desp[atch]. mention is made of my "own recommendation with regard to certain posts". This must be an allusion to what I said in a private letter to Currie abt. paid V-Cs at Laraiche, Saffi and Mogador. My only other proposal was that a Levant assistant sh[ou]ld. be sent here to learn Moorish Arabic, but I was told that c[ou]ld. not be. I suppose that an application for a student interpreter w[ou]ld. have been equally unsuccessful. Yet to obtain capable speakers & writers of Arabic is an essential condition of any improvement in the efficiency of the consular establish[men]t. in this country. I hope Capt. Comrie[?] is an Arabic scholar.

I am afraid that the scheme will be unpalatable to more than one. [Allan] Maclean is an excellent fellow, but has no experience of consular work, is ignorant of law, not very fluent in Arabic, & can neither read nor write it, speaks neither Fr[ench]. nor Sp[anish]. Yet his post is going to be made more important than that of White, who has nearly 12 yrs. service, 9 of them as Consul at Tangier, is thoroughly conversant with every detail of judicial & other consular business, & speaks Arabic fluently, besides Fr. & Sp. And while the salary is the same at each post, the Consul at DaB [Dar al Baida] has a house rent free, granted a long time ago by the Moorish Govt. I have no doubt that if the post of DaB with the importance it is proposed to give it had been offered to White, he w[ou]ld. have accepted it.

When Payton was apptd. to Genoa De Vismes very naturally applied for the vacancy at Mogador, before it was known that there was in contemplation the transfer of the Consulate

---

supervising under-secretary of the African Department until his death in 1896. He ruled a vast empire; his suggestions were rarely vetoed and his political chiefs took an active interest in his affairs only in moments of crisis." Zara S. Steiner, *The Foreign Office and Foreign Policy, 1898-1914*, Cambridge University Press, 1969, p. 44.

PRO 30/33 14/6   Semi-official Letters from Morocco (March 8, 1894 – July 10, 1894)

to DaB & the reduction of the salary to £400. He was told, when Maclean recd. the apptmt. that he was in reality better off with his £400 a year at the legation & house rent allow[an]ce. of £50. But there being a house rent free at DaB, De Vismes w[ou]ld. have been at least as well off there, to say nothing of the higher rank and the comparative independence of the post. Now however he sees the DaB consulate raised to £600, & he feels a little sore that after 7 yrs service in Morocco he sh[ou]ld. have been practically passed over in favour of a man who has worked for a few months only.[14]

I do not say anything abt. Reader, because glad as I sh[ou]ld. have been to see him drawing a larger salary than £150 a year, w[hi]ch. is hardly enough to live on when a man has no private means, he has not at present any claims to promotion derived from length of service.

The Consulate was removed fr. Mogador to DaB on the ground that the trade of the latter place had become the more important. So it no doubt had, if the figures of the total trade alone are regarded. The returns of British trade however show that Mogador is slightly superior. The local merchants & their principals at home who protested had consequently reason on their side, when they remarked that Consuls are not appointed to look after foreign trade. You can have no conception of the feeling that has been aroused. These people not unnaturally say, if you can afford money for a paid V-C, why not station him at Mog[ador]. instead of putting him at DaB where there is already a paid consul.

The theory of superintending consuls is excellent, on paper, but it does not work here. Every matter has to come to the Legation in the end, & it is much better that the V-Cs sh[ou]ld. report direct to me than that they sh[ou]ld. send them reports thro' DaB, by w[hi]ch. arrange[men]t. time is lost. The other day the V.C. at Mog. sent a desp[atch]. to Maclean abt. a matter that had to be reported to me; the steamer was not able to put into DaB on acct. of the weather. So the desp[atch]. went on to Gib. & thence back to DaB, & I recd. it after an interval of 6 w[ee]ks! instead of in a couple of days.

I am convinced that to leave the Consular districts as they are & to station the new V-C.

---

[14] Satow himself had felt passed over in January 1868 when John Lowder was appointed Acting Consul at Hyogo, and he was kept at the Legation by Parkes as Japanese Secretary on a slightly lower salary.

PRO 30/33 14/6 Semi-official Letters from Morocco (March 8, 1894 – July 10, 1894)

at Mog, w[ou]ld. be the best solution. The latter arrange[men]t. w[ou]ld. at any rate satisfy the public.

 y.v.t.
  E.S.

12. Satow to Sanderson

Tangier

Apr. 4. 94

My dear Sanderson,

I have written a desp[atch]. abt. the proposal to put all the coast ports under DaB [Dar al Baida] w[hi]ch. I hope will be considered. It is not as if I had no experience of extraterritoriality countries, & Japan in my early days in many ways resembled modern Morocco.

This country is in reality split up into two by a great wedge of unsubmissive tribes whose base is on the Atlas & the apex at Rabat, so much so that the Sultan himself has to go round by that place in order to pass fr. Morocco to Fez, & couriers fr. Morocco to Tangier come viâ Mazagan, & all up the coast. To cut across straight being absolutely impossible. Thus, in addition to the other considerations urged in my desp[atch]. there is this, that the Cons[ul]. at DaB attends to the affairs of BSs [British Subjects] in the Kingdom of Morocco, the Cons. at Tangier to those of the Kingdom of Fez. It does not in the least facilitate business for correspce. to go betw. the V-Cs & the legation tho' the Consul at DaB, & delay must always occur, for the strs. do not stop long enough for a desp[atch]. u.f.s. [under flying seal][15] to be read by him and sent on the same day. It w[ou]ld. be more convenient for all concerned if the V.C. wrote direct to the legation on all matters except the quarterly accounts.

We have had rather a stormy meeting of the Colleagues yesterday. Souhart in Dec. last contrived to get himself elected chairman of the Commission d'hygiène, w[hi]ch. is a committee of subscribers to a fund for cleansing the streets. He then persuaded the

---

[15] despatch under flying seal: a despatch with a seal attached but not closed, so that it may be read by a person requested to forward it to its destination.

PRO 30/33 14/6 Semi-official Letters from Morocco (March 8, 1894 – July 10, 1894)

colleagues to give the Commission a quasi-legal status, based on d'Aubigny's concession for cleaning the streets, & finally has taken on himself to frame regulations fixing a date for their coming into force, & then writing in peremptory terms to the RR. [Representatives] & consuls requiring them to enforce said regulations. He was however completely sat upon by Tattenbach, who used the rough edge of his tongue in a way that rather scandalized most of us.

[Margin: I have drafted a municipal constitution for Tangier based on that of Alexandria with the necessary modifications, & I am submitting it privately to the Colleagues. I don't feel sanguine abt. an agree[men]t. being come to to recommend it or anything else to the Govts. but at any rate I shall have shown my goodwill. The proposed taxes on cattle fowls & eggs to Gib. has been dropped by common accord.]

Souhart is leaving on the 25th so that one disturbing element will be removed.

Tattenbach is a difficult person to deal with. He has taken offence at not having been consulted by Ridgeway & d'Aubigny abt. the recommendations they made to the Sultan for the improvement of the ports, and declines to concur in the removal of the steam tug fr. Rabat to Laraiche. The Sultan has promised that one for Laraiche sh[ou]ld. be purchased thro' him, but Tattenb. refuses to move in the matter, & so the Fr. & Eng. Recommendations have no effect. I have not written abt. it, hoping to bring him to reason, but I fear he is incorrigible.

Potestad went on leave yesterday, & will try to get another post. He has made himself rather remarkable here by carrying on a violent flirtation with a Miss Graham, one of the visitors. He used to deny himself to the colleagues for the sake of this amusement w[hi]ch. made them furious. Galicia the Secy. is left in charge. I have no reason myself to complain of Potestad. During the Melilla affair he was very open & straightforw[ar]d., but he affects to despise all our small local affairs, like quarantine, lighthouses, street cleaning, water supply & so on. I wish Moret w[ou]ld. app[oin]t. Dupuy de Lôme[16] here; he is a firstrate man for all such things, & an excellent colleague.

Sultan's letters ordering release of 2 agents have not had desired effect. I still hope the

---

[16] Enrique Dupuy de Lôme (1851-1904). He had been a colleague of Satow in Montevideo.

men may be let out, as governors have a way of refusing to comply, & afterwds. submitting to the inevitable. I think we ought to insist on their being released, before making any approach to the Sultan. A. Maclean writes to me privately that Bershid had imprisoned another Br. Agt. [British Agent] but that he hoped to arrange his release without making an official matter of it. But I hear that he has not been successful.

K[ai]d. Macl[ean]. writes that the belief at Court is that the Sultan will remove fr. Morocco at the end of May, & he thinks it likely to turn out so. The Sultan he says has given orders for the construction of the New Mellah[17] at Mog[ador]. out of his own funds, but a site has yet to be found. The old story in fact over again.

One of my reasons for wishing to pay my visit to the Sultan at Morocco is that I may look into these Jewish matters both here & at Mog[ador].

13. Satow to Sanderson

5 April 1895 [1894?]

My dear Sanderson,

I got your letter of Mar. 26 yesterday evening after the bag had left. I am very sorry that Ld. R. sh[ou]ld. think I had disregarded the intimation conveyed to me abt. writing to him. But the fact is he became Prime Min[ister]. almost immediately after I got his letter of the 17 Feb. w[hi]ch. reached me by bag on the 28th.[18] There was nothing of any interest to write abt. till the mail of the 8th by w[hi]ch. time it was settled that he w[ou]ld. leave the F.O. I had made a note on the envelope of yr. letter on purpose that I might not omit writing. I concluded that under the circs. it was not intended that I sh[ou]ld. write. I have written direct to him giving this explanation.

14. Satow to Lord Rosebery

5 April 94

Dear Ld. Rosebery,

---

[17] A mellah is a walled Jewish quarter of a city in Morocco.
[18] Rosebery officially became Prime Minister on March 5th. As Foreign Secretary he was officially in office until March 10th.

PRO 30/33 14/6   Semi-official Letters from Morocco (March 8, 1894 – July 10, 1894)

I have just heard fr. Sanderson that you had expressed your surprise at my not having complied with your request that I sh[ou]ld. write to you. I regret very much that I sh[ou]ld. appear to have disregarded Y.L. [Your Lordship's] wishes in the slightest, but the fact is that the instruction did not reach me until Feb. 28[th]. Just at that moment I was without news of Marshal Campos' proceedings & had nothing of interest to communicate by the mail of Mar. 1. By the 8th we had telegraphic news of your having accepted the Premiership & I conclude[d] that under the altered circs. the request no longer held good. If this was a mistake, I trust it will be excused, & if I may still write I shall be very glad.

My efforts to get the imprisoned agents released have not yet been successful. Gharnit sent me letters ordering their release, w[hi]ch. I forwarded to DaB [Dar al Baida], & they were transmitted to Kaid Bershid & the Kaid of Medinna. Their replies to Allan Maclean were evasive, & the men had not, up to the day before yesterday, been let out. But it is possible that, as happened on a previous occasion, these two Kaids may after all comply with the Sultan's orders, & that we shall hear indirectly that the men have been released. I hope that this will prove to be the case, for I do not think I ought to go to Court till this question is settled. Bershid seems to have given trouble for years past, & it is very important that he sh[ou]ld. be checked. He quite lately arrested another agent of a B.S. [British Subject] but this case has not yet come before me officially, as A. Maclean hoped to get the man set at liberty by friendly representations. But the necessary delay in my going to Court, on acct. of these matters, is very unfortunate. Until I have made the personal acquaintance of the Sultan & his Min[ister]s. & have visited the ports I am working more or less in the dark. It is difficult to weigh accurately the value of reports that reach one without knowing the people who send them, & the local circs. There is the question of the Jews' quarter at Mogador & the alleged ill-treatment of the Jews by the Kaid of Morocco w[hi]ch. I sh[ou]ld. like to look into on the spot. As to the former, I have recd. promises thro' Kaid Maclean, but cannot rely on their being fulfilled. There is also the question of homes & stores for B.Ss. at the coast ports, w[hi]ch. I want to take up. It is a source of much heartburning, & the Legation is accused, wrongly no doubt, of not taking sufficient trouble on behalf of the coast people. Something I might perh. do to conciliate them. I have taken the liberty of suggesting in a desp[atch]. that the transfer of the new paid

PRO 30/33 14/6   Semi-official Letters from Morocco (March 8, 1894 – July 10, 1894)

V-C at DaB to Mog. if feasible, w[ou]ld. be hailed with satisfaction by the merchants there, who do not believe that a trading V-C. can be altogether disinterested, & maintain that their trade is as important as that of DaB. What they had wished for was for Mr. Johnston to be apptd. but I doubt whether a salary w[ou]ld. have enabled him to shake off the habit of mind into w[hi]ch. all the trading V-Cs. seem to have fallen, & tho' there c[ou]ld. be no question now of his being apptd. they w[ou]ld. be made very happy by having Capt. Comrie to look after their interests.

   y.v.t.

15. Satow to Kaid Maclean (stamped p. 23)

No. 24

6 Mar 94

My dear Maclean,

I sent on the two Sherifian letters to your brother, & he transmitted them to the Kaids of Medinna & Ulad Haris[?]. I am sorry to tell you that he got for answers that they were replying to the Sultan, & the men have not been released. This shows that the letters were not peremptory orders for the release, but merely given in order to temporize & keep us in play.

I am writing again to Gharnit as stiff a letter as possible, without actually breaking off with the Moorish Govt. And I am sending you a copy, w[hi]ch. I beg you to personally hand to the Sultan, if you can manage that.

Some of the papers have it that I am coming up to Court shortly to worry the Sultan with a repetition of Euan Smith's commercial treaty.[19] There is not a word of truth in this. H.M.G. wish me to present my credentials, as a mark of friendliness, but nothing more, & as I have always said, I am not going to both[er] H.S.M. with claims or any other matters. It will be simply a complimentary mission. But I cannot take any steps towards this, until the the two agents are released, for on a complimentary mission it w[ou]ld. not be fitting that I sh[ou]ld. begin by complaining of a matter of this kind. The European public naturally

---

[19] See Bonsal, Stephen, *Morocco as it is, with an Account of Sir Charles Euan Smith's recent mission to Fez*, Harper, 1893.

PRO 30/33 14/6 Semi-official Letters from Morocco (March 8, 1894 – July 10, 1894)

expect that my mission will take place shortly. It will surprise them very much when they come to know that I do not go to Court & learn that the reason is because the Moorish Govt. will not do what is a simple act of justice.

For my own part, you might add, that convinced as I am of the Sultan's desire to be on terms of friendship & cordiality with Engld. it is clear to me that some flatterer & designing person abt. the court is trying, by keeping the facts from him, to make a breach betw. H.S.M. & the Queen.

Yr. letters up to No. 5 & one without a number, dated Mar. 30, have reached me. If you are able, by a little present of money, to induce that renegade Jew to divorce his wife, I shall entirely approve, & you may charge it to H.M.G.

I have explained to the Marquis de Potestad the reason why you c[ou]ld. not accept a decoration.

What you write abt. the new Mellah buildings at Mogador is satisfactory as far as promises go, but we must not be content with that. I shall not be contented till I hear that a beginning has been made with the buildings.

Fr. what De Vismes tells me, I conclude that T.A's map is not made to scale, & is therefore not of very great use to geographers.

Yr. brother & his wife were here the day before yesterday in the "Mequinez", but he did not land. I expect to see him back tomorrow on his way to Daralbaida.

We really must have the two agents released, they block the way very inconveniently.

   y.v.t.

16. Satow to Sanderson (stamped p.25)

11 Apr.

My dear Sands,

Not only did the 2 Kaids reply to Allan Maclean in the evasive manner reported in my desp[atch]. but one of them wrote to him a day or two previously, thro' the Kaid of DaB to warn all B.Ss. agst. employing any Moors of Oolad Haris, M'dabhra or Oolad Ali as "agents", as he, Kaid Bushid, w[ou]ld. not recognize them. As soon as I get Maclean's official report I shall write to the Court and protest.

PRO 30/33 14/6   Semi-official Letters from Morocco (March 8, 1894 – July 10, 1894)

On receiving yr. teleg. abt. the "Arethusa" I telegd. to the Admiral at Malta that I sh[ou]ld. not want her for another month, & that I w[ou]ld. let him know as soon as anything was settled.

You will approve I hope of my not having gone quite as far in the direction of strong language as I was authorised by Ld. R. my reason being that it w[ou]ld. not be in harmony c. the Note I shall have to write as soon as the men are let out, proposing to pay the Sultan a friendly visit. I have therefore merely said that I am instructed to demand the immediate release of 2 agents, & I have given H. Maclean a duplicate of my note that he may show it to the Sultan.

Some of the local papers have it that I am going to renew E[uan]-S[mith]'s proposals for a commer[cial] treaty, & the "Imparcial" of Madrid, quoting the "Heraldo", says that this information comes fr. a Tangier paper that "defends Engl. interests & maintains the best relations with the legation." That abt. relations betw. the legation & a newspaper is the merest bosh, for I have not had any kind of communication direct or indirect with it since the editor paid me a formal call a few days after my arrival. But as colleagues are suspicious, & the rumour has very likely been made use of to prejudice the Sultan, I have told one or two of them that there is not a word of truth in it, & I have also written to Harry Maclean to quiet the mind of H.M. Sultan on the point. Kerdec is still at Morocco, but the Fr. legation will not admit it; they pretend that he is at Malaga getting married. De la Martinière is at Wazan again; probably[?] to get some assistance fr. the Sherif with regard to Tuat.

I have given Cantagalli, Tattenbach, Boleslawski, Anspach & Souhart my draft scheme for the organization of a sort of municipal council here, to utilize d'Aub[igny]'s 3 concessions abt. w[hi]ch. there has been so much correspce. Fr. the first 3 I have had very favourable opinions. I mean to show it to the others privately in turn & then ask Colaço to call a meeting to ascertain the genl. opinion on the subject. If nothing comes of it, I shall at least have demonstrated to the Fr. & everybody else that I am not disposed to put obstacles in the way of their praiseworthy efforts to endow Tangier c. waterworks, drains & well-paved streets. Tattenb. said he was disposed to send the draft home & ask leave to discuss it. He says that the result of the scheme will be not only to take Tangier out of the Sultan's hands, but to stimulate the people at the coast ports to demand similar powers, so that in the end all these places w[ou]ld. be in a certain sense internationalized. I replied that I saw no objection to this, & that I sh[ou]ld. be glad if he w[ou]ld. send the draft to Berlin. I may shortly report on the question - , but at present it seems better to wait a week or two until I can sound all the colleagues.

As d'Aub. & Cantag., who are both in favour of some such scheme have also made remarks to me abt. the effect being to internationalize Tangier, it seems possible that we have here the germ of an 'entente' abt. this part of Morocco at least.

Maclean is here waiting for a steamer to carry him back to his post. He seems a little inclined to think that he is the only man whose opinions abt. Morocco are worth listening to, & is jealous of my asking White's advice. I hope in time he will smooth down. The Herberts & Esme Howard are leaving today, but the former may be detained, as a local hotel keeper has just at the last moment sued him for the hire of tents &c. w[hi]ch. he never had. I consider it a rascally attempt at extortion.

There is a little difficulty again at Tetuan. Nahon reports that the Captain of the Gibraltar "falucho" Herminia wounded one of the Basha's soldiers in a smuggling affray, but got away before he c[ou]ld. be arrested. I teleg. to Biddulph to ask him to have the man taken up and sent over here, but he naturally replied that it was out of his power. Nahon is again appealing to be relieved of his duties, on the ground of ill health, but as I have no one to put there even temporarily he must go on until he drops.

   y.v.t.

17. Satow to Bergne

12 April 1894

My dear Bergne,

Have you any objection to the Trade Reports for the 2 consular districts of this country being sent to the legation & then to F.O. instead of direct. I c[ou]ld. then prefix a summary, w[hi]ch. w[ou]ld. be useful for annual comparison of the trade of the whole of Morocco, & the 2 consular reports might be printed together, instead of separately as at present. I cannot give instructions however to have this done, unless I know that it will be approved.

PRO 30/33 14/6   Semi-official Letters from Morocco (March 8, 1894 – July 10, 1894)

y.v.t.

18. Satow to Sanderson (stamped p.28)

12 Apr. 1894

My dear Sanderson,

Abt. 10 yrs. ago, when there was a scheme on foot for building a church here some corresp[onden]ce., noted on the other side, took place betw[een]. Sir J.H. [John Hay] & the F.O. abt. a contrib[utio]n. fr. H.M.G. & £100 was promised.

Subsequently it was found impossible to raise funds for a stone structure, an iron ch. was substituted & H.M.G. was not asked for the promised £100.

The original scheme has now been revised, with good prospect of starting with a subscription amounting in all to £1000, the total cost being estimated at £2600 or £2700.

The ch. wardens have come & asked me whether H.M.G. w[ou]ld. be still disposed to contribute, & whether the sum c[ou]ld. not be made larger say £250. But before writing officially, I thought I had better ask yr. opinion as to this point, & I shall be much obliged if you will kindly tell me what prospect there [is] of such an application being acceded to.

y.v.t.

Correspce. concerning Engl. church at Tangier.

No. 28 to F.O. of April 7, 1883

No. 20 fr. F.O. of May 3, 1883

Separate fr. Sir J.H. dated 19 Oct/84 fr. London.

19. Satow to Kaid Maclean

No. 25

13 Apr. 1894

My dear Maclean,

Your three letters 6, 7 & 8 reached me yesterday by sea fr[om]. Casablanca. If the agents are let out, & the Sultan remains at Morocco till after the Aid el Kebir, I sh[ou]ld. be able to pay my visit to him, w[hi]ch. w[ou]ld. be one of ceremony only. As for commercial negotiations, that is not to be thought of. Gharnit's promises to reply to letters and to send

PRO 30/33 14/6 Semi-official Letters from Morocco (March 8, 1894 – July 10, 1894)

soldiers to collect Forde's $2000 are very agreeable to the ear, and I trust he will fulfil them expeditiously. Forde's case certainly sh[ou]ld. be settled at once, so that there may be nothing to disturb the harmony of our relations when I come to the Court.

I quite agree with you that if I am not able to visit the Sultan at Morocco it w[ou]ld. be better to wait till he goes to Fez. But if some of the colleagues were to go to Rabat, I think I ought to go too. The future is so uncertain here that it seems to be little use making plans.

You suggest that I sh[ou]ld. give the renegade Jew's wife protection, as he will not consent to divorce her. Can you help me to find out her name and address. The idea seems a good one, but it must be arranged warily.

I return Emanuel's letter. Your reply to him was closed, but as you requested me to read it, I opened the envelope, & put it in another. Yr. ans. seemed to me perfectly judicious. The suggestion that the Jews in London sh[ou]ld. ascertain for themselves what is the truth of all these stories appears to me excellent.

I will settle with White the acct. you sent me.

W[ou]ld. it not be possible to get copies of the Sherifian letters given to you, so that in sending them on we may always know what we are doing. It w[ou]ld. greatly facilitate business. You will know best what arguments to use c. Gharnit to persuade him that this is a good plan.

I will try to get a Kodak [camera] for Bonich with plates, and send it on viâ Mazagan. No one I have asked seems to know anything abt. such matters.

    y.v.t.

P.S. The note to Gharnit w[hi]ch. accompanies this is in support of what the Germ. Minister [Tattenbach] has written urging that coals, oil, paint etc. be supplied to the steamtug at Rabat, & that he be empowered to order one for Laraiche.

I sh[ou]ld. be much obliged if you could expedite the issue of orders for the pay[men]t. of the Cape Juby instalment of £10,000 that became due on the 10th. I have written twice to Torres reminding him, but have got no ans[wer].

    E.S.

20. Satow to Sanderson (stamped p.30)

PRO 30/33 14/6   Semi-official Letters from Morocco (March 8, 1894 – July 10, 1894)

Secret

13 Apr. 1894

My dear Sanderson,

I enclose an acc[oun]t. of K. Maclean for couriers & 2 pay[men]ts. in connexion c. the Sherif fr[om]. Talifelt, who is going to keep us informed as to Fr[ench]. doings when he gets back to his oasis. May I draw on you for the am[oun]t. w[hi]ch. at the present rate of exchange w[ou]ld. be equivalent to about £24.

 y.v.t.

 E.S.

21. Satow to Sanderson

Secret

14 Apr. 1894

My dear Sanderson,

Before Ridgeway left he arranged with Kaid Maclean to send a man to Figuig, & he informs me that he has found one who will do. He has bought him a mule, and he is ready to start at any moment. Maclean wants to furnish him with a <u>Kodak</u> to take views of the road & Figuig itself, but I cannot obtain one here, nor do I know anything abt. such articles. Could you have one sent to me, with a supply of dry plates? I could then send it down to Morocco City.

Maclean arranged with Ridgeway to give the explorer $40 a month and $1 a day expenses. But he now writes that the man he has selected, a Gibraltarian who looks like a Moor, will not go for less than $3½ a day, besides the loan of a tent and a second mule. Part of the arrangement is that he shall engage a newswriter at Figuig and perh. one at Tuat.

At present Kaid Maclean is my only source of information abt. what goes on in the country. I wish I had a second string to my bow besides De Vismes. Then there w[ou]ld. be some one to go about and find out what is happening, e.g. at Wazan where de la Martinière is now staying.

22. Satow to Sanderson (stamped p.31)

326

PRO 30/33 14/6   Semi-official Letters from Morocco (March 8, 1894 – July 10, 1894)

16 April 1894

My dear Sanderson,

My draft scheme for organization of Commission d'hygiène into a sort of municipality without the name has now been read by everyone but the Portug. & Amer. Bole[slawski] is sending it to Vienna, because he thinks that Tattenbach will send it to Berlin, & he tells me that he has written in its favour. That being the case, I will send you a copy next week, just to report progress, but otherwise I sh[ou]ld. have waited until I c[ou]ld. get the colleagues to express some kind of opinion at a meeting. Fr[om]. Souhart I have not heard a word. He prob. will not like the idea of anything that emanates fr. our side being successful. Anspach is favourable, but thinks there will be objections to the proposed taxation. The Sp. Ch. d'Aff. Galicia has the draft in his hands, & I hope he will support it.

Me. Souhart tells me that there has been some talk of her husband being sent either to Siam or Madagascar. I tried to frighten her with accts. of the cholera, typhoid etc. at Bangkok. He w[ou]ld. be a great nuisance there; indefatigable, violent & unscrupulous as he is, he w[ou]ld. be a thorn in the side of our man there.

I have reported that as T. has moved the Sultan to provide a steam tug for Laraiche Souhart & I agreed to recommend that arrange[men]t. It is very curious that Tattenb[ach]. after refusing repeatedly to stir in the matter, nevertheless adopted the suggestion I had made to him, but kept it secret fr. me till the other day, when I extracted the information fr. him by a casual question. To get either the Fr. man or the Germ. to take any step in concert is very difficult, but I mean to go on trying. Even in the matter of debts to be recovered fr. Moorish subjects, where we have interests in common, they refuse to combine. Very possibly they think that to act in concert with a Power whose influence has fallen so low (in the genl. opinion) w[ou]ld. be to their disadvantage.

K. is at Morocco City, & sends articles down here for the Diario de Tanger. His last one is devoted to proving that Cantag. sent up Petri to intrigue agst. the Sp. & when his proceedings began to appear suspicious, he endeavoured to cloak his manoeuvres by accusing Linares. And then he goes on to point out how loyally the Fr. legation & he had acted, the former in begging him not to go to Morocco while negotiations were pending, & he by remaining in Tangier, to the detriment of his interests & those of his principals the

PRO 30/33 14/6   Semi-official Letters from Morocco (March 8, 1894 – July 10, 1894)

"Forges et Chantiers". I believe never the less that with the exception of one moment of weakness when he was inclined to recommend the Sultan not to pay more than he c[ou]ld. help, Cantagalli acted on the square throughout.

I have dunned [made insistent demands on] Torres again within the last few days for the Cape Juby indemnity & have also written to Maclean. Torres wrote to the Sultan more than a month ago, but has got no ans[wer]. Ramadan & the feasts w[hi]ch. succeed it always cause an unusual hitch in business.

H[enry]. Marsham, who is a director of some cable manufacturing Co. that has its headquarters at Silvertown [in the Port of London] came over last week with the object of finding out whether he c[ou]ld. land a cable. I told him the thing c[ou]ld. not be done without the strong backing of H.M.G. and that the Moors w[ou]ld. throw all sorts of difficulties in the way. Our having already laid a cable did not at all mean that we c[ou]ld. get leave to lay a second. His idea now seems to be that the Fr. w[ou]ld. have the best chance of succeeding, because they c[ou]ld. point to the Engl. & Sp. cables, & claim the same privilege.

Ld. Mt. Edgcumbe & Valletort have also been here; they made the usual excursion to Cape Spartel lighthouse[?] & left for Spain yesterday.

Herbert was completely victorious in his case, & left on the 14th for Madrid. The pltf. had not a leg to stand on.

I expect the Biddulphs tomorrow for a few days stay.

y.v.t.

23. Secret   21 April 94
To Sanderson informing him that Maclean has acknowledged receipt of Cypher Z.

24 Sanderson   21 Apr. 94
Asking for reply to White's No. 8 of 26 Feb. abt. receiving English silver in pay[men]t. of fee.

25. Satow to Sanderson

PRO 30/33 14/6   Semi-official Letters from Morocco (March 8, 1894 – July 10, 1894)

April 21. 94

My dear Sanderson,

K.M. [Kaid Maclean] writes that he is "informed on good authority" that it was the Fr. Govt. that offered the Sultan a loan of $3,000,000 to pay the Spaniards with. I suppose M. was afraid of writing this to me until he c[ou]ld. send it in cypher.

E.H. Forwood writes to me that he is again addressing Gharnit abt. a loan, & his agent here has asked me to forwd. his letter to Court. But De Vismes who has examined it, finds it so blurred as to be illegible, & I am going to return it. What I did on a previous occasion was to send the letter to Maclean, & ask him to deliver it, but no ans. ever came. As the Sultan has undertaken not to pledge the Customs until the 4 million are paid off, I don't see how Forwood or any one else c[ou]ld. put a security that loanmongers w[ou]ld. look at.

Something has been said abt. establishing a lighthouse at Mogador. Souhart was very anxious that the Cape Spartel Commission sh[ou]ld. undertake its construction out of the surplus of abt. 10,000 fr[ancs]. but the rest of us told him we had no powers under the lighthouse convention to occupy ourselves with anything but Cape Spartel. Then the Mogador agents of the Steamship Companies wrote me a letter as President of the Cape Spartel Commission asking us to take the matter up. Forwood's agent however did not join. I persuaded the colleagues that as it was a question that did not concern the lighthouse commission as such, the letter sh[ou]ld. be passed to the Doyen for him to answer, & to inquire of the steamship agents how much their companies w[ou]ld. contribute towards the cost of construction. There the matter rests for the present. But E.H. Forwood has an idea in his head of inducing the Sultan to pay for the construction & maintenance out of his own pocket & to entrust the execution of the work to his firm, Forwood Bros. & Co. He promised, when he was here, to send me some information abt. the kind of light that c[ou]ld. be suitable, the cost &c, but for some reason or other now declines to give it. He is under the impression, I believe, that when I go to the Sultan I shall be able to apply for this concession for him, as well as for one to construct a landing pier at Tangier, but I think that at present it w[ou]ld. be wise not to undertake anything of the kind. I sh[ou]ld. prefer to try whether by acting fairly by one's colleagues in such matters one might not gradually bring about a better feeling than had prevailed in past times, when the principal object of the FRR

PRO 30/33 14/6 Semi-official Letters from Morocco (March 8, 1894 – July 10, 1894)

[Foreign Representatives] seems to have been to dish each other with the Moors. Any proposition Forwood might have to make I sh[ou]ld. be willing to lay before the colleagues, and if it were advantageous I think they w[ou]ld. be disposed to recommend it. But official support on my part to direct negotiations of Forwood's with the Sultan w[ou]ld. not be desirable.

I have learnt today that d'Aubigny is nominated to Bucharest and that Monbel is to succeed him here. Souhart goes on 1st May for 6 mos. leave. I am giving him and his wife a little friendly dinner before they go. I have had the Biddulphs here, and they left today.

Many thanks for the great trouble you have taken abt. the stallion for me. But until the agents are actually released I don't think we can be certain of anything. I hope to hear in a day or two from Maclean, & that the answer will be satisfactory, but if not, what am I to do next? I seems to have wellnigh exhausted all means of persuasion. Linares is still at Court, and I hear he is not coming away. Perhaps he advises them to resist. But supposing the men are let out, then I am confronted with the possibility of the Sultan moving northward very soon. Kaid Maclean's last news was that he w[ou]ld. not leave Morocco till the latter part of June, but the general rumour is that preparations are being made for him to reach Rabat by that time.

y.v.t.

P.S. My teleg. answer to the Eastern Teleg. Co's inquiry abt. the possibilities of a cable being laid at present was meant to express what I believe is the case, that no representations of the kind from us have any chance of being listened to. The experience of everyone is that nothing can be got out of the Sultan by writing. Personal intercourse with him is necessary, and that at this moment is impossible. There are other things that in my opinion w[ou]ld. precede asking for leave to land a cable, - as, e.g. the question of foreigners holding land & building houses, the old claims; and lastly the certainty of opposition fr. certain colleagues unless they got specific instructions to give a hearty support.

E.S.

26. Satow to Sanderson

21 April 94

PRO 30/33 14/6   Semi-official Letters from Morocco (March 8, 1894 – July 10, 1894)

My dear Sanderson,

I have been obliged to write to you officially [margin: See p.53] sending home Nahon's application for leave, and I am in desperation about Tetuan. The man himself is utterly incompetent, and is now laid up with a bad ulcer, so that he is physically incapacitated as well.

Abt. 2 mo[nth]s. hence a Mr. Mensink a Dutch missionary who has on one occasion temporarily acted as a Consular agent there will return to Tetuan, & I understand that he will undertake it again tho' mala voluntate. [unwillingly] He is of course not a competent person either.

I w[ou]ld. propose detaching Reader, but then a salary w[ou]ld. have to be found for him, and I sh[ou]ld. be left without anyone to copy.

Pisani, who was suggested by some other Rockscorpion is a rogue, & c[ou]ld. not possibly be employed: £45 a year, the amt. of the fee-allowance, w[ou]ld. not tempt any honest man to go there.

y.v.t.

27. Satow to Kaid Maclean

No. 26

Tangier

April 25, 1894

My dear Maclean,

I have recd. your letters 00, 10 & 11. The idea of having the 2 agents br[ough]t. up to Court does not please me. I have telegd. home for instructions, but in the meantime try all you can to have them at once sent down to Darelbaida to your bro[ther]'s care to be handed over to me. If you will refer to yr. No. 3 & to my letters on this subject you will see that I never consented to their going to the Court. They were to be released – not put in honourable confine[men]t. as sending them to the Court means.

y.v.t.

Enclosing copies of old letters to the Court abt. Levy's claim &c.

PRO 30/33 14/6   Semi-official Letters from Morocco (March 8, 1894 – July 10, 1894)

28. Satow to Sanderson

Tangier

Ap. 25/94

My dear Sanderson,

These Moors are very vexatious with their shuffling ways, but I suppose one must be philosophic & make the best of the position.

The understanding betw. Maclean & Gharnit was that the 2 men sh[ou]ld. be released & that the ? [question] of whether they sh[ou]ld. be sent up to the Court or not sh[ou]ld. be left to me to decide. Gharnit read the letters of release to Maclean, who believed that they were all right. But as literary Arabic is very different fr. colloquial, & Maclean does not understand the former, this was no use as a check. Fr. the construction of the letters now sent, of w[hi]ch. Gharnit has sent me a copy thro' Maclean, it is clear, so De Vismes tells me, that the original orders for release added that the Kaids were to send them up to the Court. It is evident therefore that Maclean was taken in by Gharnit. As I have from the beginning said that the release of these men must precede the presentation of my credentials, I think it is important that I sh[ou]ld. hold on, in spite of the inconvenience involved in my being still kept fr. making the acquaintance of the Sultan & his ministers.

I sh[ou]ld. propose to remain at Tangier until the autumn, by w[hi]ch. time I hope to have got the agents out, and to be able to propose to the Sultan to pay him a visit. In the meantime, if Lord Kimberley sees no objection I sh[ou]ld. like to go down the coast in a man-of-war & see the ports. My doing this without taking any notice of the Sultan than to inform Gh. that I was abt. to visit the ports w[ou]ld. probably be felt by the Sultan as a snub, & w[ou]ld. have a wholesome effect.

My idea is to write to the Court that the agents must be handed over to me thro' H.M. Consul at DaB, & when they get there, to tell them they may go abt. their business. If there was any danger of them being further molested, I w[ou]ld. give them protection under Art. XVI of the Madrid Convention, for a "motif tout-à-fait exceptionnel."

I am sending you a desp[atch]. abt. the Jews at Morocco, containing a memorandum furnished by Mr. [Henry] Gurney, who has just returned fr. there. I fancy his information may be relied on, & it is confirmed by what I hear fr. Kaid Maclean.

PRO 30/33 14/6 Semi-official Letters from Morocco (March 8, 1894 – July 10, 1894)

There was a rumour at Morocco that some Fr. companies had appeared at Tuat, & wanted to build a fort there, but the people were collecting to oppose it. This sounds very vague.

Maclean writes that some of the cartridges made at the Italian gun factory at Fez had been sent up to Morocco to be tried. Maclean & the Fr[ench]. chief of the Military Mission Schlumberger fired off ten in the presence of the Sultan. They were bad in every way & were unanimously condemned. Then at the Sultan's request Schlumberger & Macl. drew up a report giving their reasons for condemning the cartridges, & orders were sent to Fez to stop their manufacture. Cantagalli will be furious when he hears it, & fancy that it portends a 'rapprochement' betw. Engl. & France on the affairs of Morocco. Maclean was told that for the future only Engl. made cartridges are to be used, w[hi]ch. no doubt will mean an addition to his income. He says that he has recd. orders to recommence drills again. This, he tells me, the procuring of cartridges fr. England & the Sultan's manner towards himself are sure indications of the favourable turn the wind is taking towards England. But I can quite understand his anxiety that we sh[ou]ld. be on good terms with the Sultan. It improves his own position. And so he gives a favourable interpretation to every straw that he sees floating abt. The Sultan & H.M.G. are two peevish children who have fallen out, & he is the judicious old nurse who is trying to coax them into making it up again.

   y.v.t.

29. Satow to Sir Percy Anderson (stamped p. 39)
Apr. 26, 1894
My dear Anderson,

Thanks for your letter of the 10th abt. my remarks on the reorganization scheme. I did not in the least desire to slight the conclusions at w[hi]ch. Ld. Rosebery had arrived, but rather to represent what seems likely to prove inconveniences in the working, & the views of British merch[an]ts. abt. the concentration of paid officials at one port. I confess that I sh[ou]ld. like to keep the consular districts as they are, for it is more convenient to have Rabat & Laraiche in direct communication with Tangier than that the V-C [Vice-Consuls] there sh[ou]ld. have to send despatches down the coast to Darelbaida & up to me. That

PRO 30/33 14/6 Semi-official Letters from Morocco (March 8, 1894 – July 10, 1894)

w[ou]ld. avoid the severance of those ports from Fez & Alcazar. I think it is easier to manage Fez business direct from here. Then in giving instructions to Maclean c. regard to the superintendence of the V-C south of him, I sh[ou]ld. like to be authorized to tell him that despp. fr. those officers are to be sent under flying seal, in order that he may know what is going on, & that they are not to be unnecessarily delayed. You may rest assured that whatever is decided I shall cheerfully try to carry it out, & to make the best use of the means placed at my disposal for the conduct of public business. I quite see that the paid V-C at DaB is an essential part of Ld. R's plan.

The personal feelings of White & De Vismes abt. Maclean's elevation are only of importance as far as supposing himself to have a grievance is an impediment to a man's usefulness. However, both White & De. V. are extremely willing workers, the latter spending 8 hours a day at the Chancery. It seemed only fair to them to let you know what they thought. I have no complaint to make of Maclean's doings at all. But I saw a great deal of him during the 3 mos. he was at the legation last autumn, & do not think very highly of his abilities. There is no doubt of his zeal & desire to be useful.

The perennial difficulty of Nahon's wishing to have leave of absence & of finding a substitute has again cropped up. I have a sort of promise fr. Mr. Mensink to take the consular agency sometime in June, & in the meantime Morant seems to think it might amuse him; I am telegraphing for leave to appt. him till Mensink goes back to Tetuan.

One word more about my desp[atch]. If you think there are any portions of it w[hi]ch. might be usefully admitted, I am quite willing to be guided by your advice.

    y.v.t.

30. Satow to Kaid Maclean

No. 27

Tangier 27/4/94

My dear Maclean,

I have got teleg. instructions to protest agst. the 2 agents being taken to Court & to insist on their being sent to me at once. I have ∴ [therefore] written a peremptory note to that effect, & I enclose as before for yourself a copy & translation for yr. information & to make

PRO 30/33 14/6   Semi-official Letters from Morocco (March 8, 1894 – July 10, 1894)

use of if necessary with the Sultan.

It is very much to be regretted that the Moorish Govt. sh[ou]ld. shilly-shally in this manner. They will have to bear the consequences, for insulting the B[ritish]. S[ubjects]. in this way, their oldest friend. Pray use y[ou]r. utmost effort to get this matter arranged, because everything depends on it. Indications of a friendly disposition towards Engl[and]., such as you have recently mentioned, do not impress me in the least, as long as this wrong remains unredressed.

As for these men being Sheikhs, that is all a pretence. They have been in the service of foreigners for any number of years. But they might be Sheikhs ten times over, & yet the Moorish Govt. w[ou]ld. have no right to touch them.

y.v.t.

31. Satow to Sanderson (stamped p.41)

Tangier

1 May 94

My dear Sanderson,

I have heard nothing fr. the Court since last w[ee]k. My last note abt. the imprisoned agents ought to have reached them a day or two ago. A. Maclean writes to me that the Kaids quite recently offered to release them if it were made worth their while, but the employers thought it better to refuse under the circs.

As far as I can gather other legations have similar difficulties fr. time to time, notably the Sp. & the Ital. Reg[ardin]g. the Fr[ench]., it is impossible to learn anything, but from what they say, now & then they have great trouble in getting answers to the letters they write to the Court.

d'Aubigny came back yesterday; he says he will remain for 5 or 6 wks. Souhart left today. We all went down to the landing place to wish him & his wife goodbye in an affectionate manner. He will not be regretted by any of the coll[eague]s.

Galician came to ask me the other day whether the Moorish Govt. had said anything to me abt. smuggling arms. It seems the Spaniards are very anxious abt. the matter, & I am ∴ [therefore] very glad to be able to send Morant to Tetuan for a time, where he will be able

PRO 30/33 14/6   Semi-official Letters from Morocco (March 8, 1894 – July 10, 1894)

to tranquillize the somewhat feverous temperament of the Sp. Consul Navarro. I see the "Débats" talks of a "Conférence" to deal with this question in Morocco, but it is impossible to deal with it except by taking the coast under a sort of joint tutelgae [tutelage]. It w[ou]ld. be rather a bore if in addition to lighthouses, quarantine & street scavenging in Tangier we had to sit on an International Anti-smuggling commission. I do not think there is much done here in arms; if there were the Spaniards ought to be able to find it out.

I am sorry to send you such a long story abt. Hunot's Tarudant claim. I imagine the real truth to be this. Hunot had for some years ceased to entrust any goods to this man. Up to 1873 a little money came in by dribbles & then ceased altogether. On the whole it had been a good business, & he did not bother about an unimportant balance. Then in 1879 came the man's death. That seemed a good opportunity for making a little money. So he made a claim, not only for what this man owed him, but also for the debts of two others; charged the total to the dead man, described him as his agent, & asserted that 'property' of theirs in his hands had been robbed. Nothing further was asked fr. him than this, & he furnished neither details nor proofs. The theory was that the burden of disproof sh[ou]ld. be thrown on the Moorish Govt. K.S.[?] evidently thought the claim c[ou]ld. not be pressed; there was nothing to go upon. I am informed that among the "expenses" incurred by Hunot in prosecuting this claim was a payt. of $600 to a high official, very possibly Gharnit. That may be the explanation of the promises held out to him that the claim sh[ou]ld. be settled.

The Admiral has telegraphed to me that he w[ou]ld. like to know when I shall want the "Arethusa". I have replied that I can't tell him for another ten days. If Lord K. approves of my suggestion abt. visiting the ports independently of going to see the Sultan, will you kindly telegraph to me. In a week's time I ought to know what effect my last Note abt. the imprisoned agents has produced. As to the Sultan's movements nothing can be affirmed. It is quite on the cards that he might remain there at Morocco till late in the year. The suggestion of the Debats (22 April) that he is leaving Morocco in order to avoid my visit seems absurd. It only indicates the animus of the writer.

   y.v.t.
    E.S.

PRO 30/33 14/6 Semi-official Letters from Morocco (March 8, 1894 – July 10, 1894)

32. Satow to Kaid Maclean (stamped p.43)

No. 28

May 3, 1894

My dear Maclean,

I have just recd. your Nos. 12 & 13. Many thanks for procuring the orders for the payment of the Juby indemnity.

A story has reached the F.O. that the Sultan lately called on the Morocco Jews to pay tribute, after having let them alone for 18 years or so. I enclose a copy of [Reuben] Elmaleh's report, & beg you to let me know what amt. of truth there is in it.

The Spanish Ambassador in London officially informed Ld. K. that the Queen Reg[en]t. wished to give you a decoration, but was told that permission c[ou]ld. not be granted, as you had not been employed abroad exclusively in her service. But Ld. Kimb. added that he was glad to hear you had been of such signal service to the Sp. Ambr.

        y.v.t.

added in cypher.   I shall send you a camera in two or three wks. time. You may agree to give Bonich $3½ a day besides loan of a tent and the two mules.

4 May. I have recd. letter dated 22 April fr. Vizir stating that for reasons of economy Sultan wishes HMG to instruct their officers to return home at the time w[hi]ch. he will fix, & that he is writing to the Fr. & Sp. mins. in the same sense. You are not mentioned by name. Sh[ou]ld. you hear anything abt. it please report. You need not feel any anxiety. The only thing HMG c[ou]ld. reply w[ou]ld. be that they have no officers, but I shall advise them to return no answer.

33. Satow to Sanderson (stamped p.44)

May 5. 1894

My dear Sanderson,

Maclean writes to me that the Fr[ench]. emissaries mentioned in my letter of April 25 as having appeared in Tuat are now reported to have actually begun to build a fort at Timmimoun, in the very centre of that district, long[itude]. 45" E of Greenwich 29° N. lat. That the people have not resisted but have asked the Sultan what they are to do. There has

PRO 30/33 14/6   Semi-official Letters from Morocco (March 8, 1894 – July 10, 1894)

been a fight betw. a Moorish tribe & the Hameen (?) a tribe under Fr. jurisdiction, the former taking 70 camels & killing 14 men.

Macl. has ∴ [therefore] despatched his Tafilet man to Timmimoun to find out what truth there is in this story. It will take him a couple of months to go there & back. The people round the Sultan confirm the report, & say that the Fr. are claiming the whole of Tuat.

Fr[om]. what Potestad & Cantagalli have said to me at different times, I gather that as far as their personal opinion goes they do not see any advantage in further opposing the Fr[ench]. acquisition of Tuat. If we c[ou]ld. suppose they w[ou]ld. go no further then I sh[ou]ld. be of the same opinion, but as they w[ou]ld. never rest contented with Tuat, Sourara[?] & Tidikelt, it seems that we may just as well continue to object to Tuat, as give it up & then find ourselves shortly afterwards confronted with a Tafilelt question.

I have recd. orders on the Customs of four of the ports for the payt. of the Cape Juby indemnity, w[hi]ch. ought not to be long delayed. I hear that money for the Sp. indemnity was to leave Morocco on the 25th April.

Maclean says Gharnit has expressed a hope that my visit to the Sultan will be deferred till he reaches Fez, from which I conclude that they have neither the wish nor the expectation of seeing me at Morocco. He has been asked to get an Englishman to go there to superintend a cartridge factory w[hi]ch. he [the?] Sultan owns, & has recd. various other orders. The tide has turned he thinks, & he regards himself as being high in the Sultan's favour at present. Nothing seems to have been said to him abt. the proposal to dismiss military instructors, so I have told him what Gharnit has written on the subject, adding that he need be under no apprehension for himself. Sh[ou]ld. there be a Fr. intrigue on foot for his being dismissed & Linares left in possn. of the field at Court, it w[ou]ld. be easy to defeat it by giving Maclean an official apptmt. ; but at present I think we need say nothing. I have not ventured to mention the subject to either the Fr. Italian or Spanish colleagues, preferring to let them be the first to broach it.

There really seems to be signs of something being done at last abt. the new Mellah at Mogador. With regard to the recent letter of the joint committee abt. ill-treatment of the Jews at Morocco on the occasion of the tribute being paid, the Portuguese colleague has recd. no complaints. One was made to Cantagalli, who wrote to remonstrate with Gharnit,

PRO 30/33 14/6   Semi-official Letters from Morocco (March 8, 1894 – July 10, 1894)

but the latter treated the matter in a light and airy manner, w[hi]ch. will lead to more correspce. I am writing to Maclean for details of what happened, & will report as soon as I get them. Elmaleh the man at Mogador has the reputation of being always in a great hurry to publish whatever he hears without stopping to investigate.

The Fr. having recently had a couple of men-of-war here, the Senior officer at Gib. inspired by a spirit of imitation, wrote to inquire whether there was any objection to three torpedo boats coming over on the 15th. I replied that in my opinion there was none.

Foolish people fr. time to time talk to me abt. Tangier eventually becoming Engl[ish]. Boleslawski's wife for instance the other day. The doctor of the Sp. Leg. [Cenarro] told me yesterday that a majority of Spaniards believe we have designs, but added confidentially that if my draft scheme for the Commission d'hygiène were adopted, it w[ou]ld. go far to relieve everybody's apprehensions. I told him he had hit the bullseye.

y.v.t.

34. Satow to Kaid Maclean (stamped p.46)

No. 29

Tangier

16 May 94

My dear Maclean,

I have your Nos 14, 15 & 16. Many thanks for all the information they contain. Your letters are never too long, & the more I learn abt. what goes on at Court the better I shall be able to form an idea of the people there. Abt. Bonich's journey I wrote in my no. 28. C. [With] regard to Mr. [William S.] Bewicke I have no reason at all to make any objection to your using him confidentially, & ask [as] we had spoken together abt. him when we last met I did not think it necessary to say anything more. But if I omitted to reply to a direct question respecting your employing him, pray put it down to my being in a hurry, as I often have to be when writing for the coast. We seldom get more than a couple of hours notice of the departure of steamers, & then I have your bro[ther]. [Allan] to write to as well, & I must necessarily keep copies of what I write.

I cannot tell you anything special abt. d'Aub[igny]'s change of post, but I believe that it

PRO 30/33 14/6   Semi-official Letters from Morocco (March 8, 1894 – July 10, 1894)

is promotion for him, at least in grade if not in pay as well. He remains here till the beg[innin]g. of July when [Joseph Raymond Baylin de] Monbel comes. The latter is a great sportsman: I used to know him in Japan a good many years ago. P[otestad]. is expected back this week; his pay has been raised and his grade as Envoy. Souhart has gone on leave; he is not expected to return.

I send you a letter to be delivered to Gharnit in case the 2 agents sh[ou]ld. not have started when you receive this, w[hi]ch. I think will be what you wish me to write. I have up to the present refrained from employing the strong language w[hi]ch. Ld. R[osebery]. authorized me to use, & I think that as he is a man of his word, it will be dangerous for the Sultan & his Mins. to provoke him too far about this matter. On the other hand, if they had given way with good grace in the beginning it w[ou]ld. have produced an excellent effect on the mind of the Br. Govt. who w[ou]ld. then have stood their friends as before.

If they hold out abt. these agents much longer, it will come in the end to the application of force, & then they will have to give way on other matters as well. For when a Govt. is forced to have recourse to the ultima ratio regum [armed force, war] it indemnifies itself for the trouble it is put to by settling all its grievances at once, tacking on to its original demand everything else that it has been asking for during many years past. All this I beg you to say to Gharnit, & much more, in case the men have not yet started for DaB [Dar-al-Baida].

I am going down the coast in the "Arethusa", a 2nd class cruiser of 5000 tons, to visit the ports, & expect to start on the 18th. I shall begin with Laraiche & go fr. one to the other, calling however at Casabl[anca]. on the return journey as well. I expect to get to Mogador on the 29th or 30th. The enclosed letter to Gh. acquaints him with my intended voyage. I send you a copy of only the Engl. as it is scarcely necessary to provide you with an Arabic [copy] to show to the Sultan. Gh. is hardly likely to keep it back.

White will go on leave when I return fr. the coast & will be away till 7ber [September]. As far as I can at present see there is no likelihood of my leaving Tangier either then or before. This is my present feeling abt. the matter, but you know how the unforeseen sometimes upsets one's calculations. If for instance the Sultan were to suggest that my being on the coast w[ou]ld. make it convenient for me to present my credentials, I w[ou]ld. visit Morocco at no matter what inconvenience. At the same time pray do not hint at such a thing, for I sh[ou]ld. not be provided with presents, & sh[ou]ld. have to hire tents & camp equipage at whatever place I happened then to be. I have not mentioned this idea to any one here.

       y.v.t.

35. Satow to Sanderson (stamped p.48)

17 May 94

My dear Sanderson,

There was a good opportunity for going over to Tetuan, so I went on the 11th, & returned the day before yesterday. It is a delightful placed [place] compared to Tangier, quite Moorish, & lies in fine mountn. scenery. Morant is working hard at Arabic. His chief colleagues are the Span[iar]d. Navarro & the Fr. consular agent, a very active Algerian, who is credited with having taken abt. 1000 mtneers [mountaineers? mutineers?] under his protection. That is prob. an exaggeration. The Sp. have a church & schools beside the consulate & make a great fig. So does the Fr. agent. They both flaunt their flags in the eyes of the natives, while ours is conspicuous by its absence. I am going to send one to Morant to hoist over his office. Nahon is a wretched old creature. His brother in law inhabits the consular house at the port, & winks at the smuggling. I frightened the latter by telling him in the presence of the halfdozen inhabitants of the port that the Br. & Sp. Govts. were agreed upon putting a stop to the smuggling of arms. If we & the Span. were to start a joint exam[ination]. of the faluchos [small boats, feluccas] that go there perh. it might lead in time to a foreign customs inspectorate. I hear that the Gib[raltar]. Auth[orities]. are much worried by the smuggling business, & in addition to my desp[atch]. abt. Tetuan I am going to send you a memo. on what takes place here. The Span. went to Cantag. the other day & asked him to make a search in the house of an Italian protégé, whom with a Portug. & somebody else of that sort he accused of having smuggled arms on his premises. Cantag. took time to consider.

My last letter fr. the Court is dated the 6th. Maclean writes that he had recd. promise that the 2 agents sh[ou]ld. be released & sent to DaB as I had demanded. In case the prom[ise]. sh[ou]ld. not be carried out I have sent him a peremptory little note to make use of or not

PRO 30/33 14/6   Semi-official Letters from Morocco (March 8, 1894 – July 10, 1894)

acc. to circs. One of the men was clapped into prison the moment he reached Morocco, so it was merely a transfer fr. one jailer to another.

The Sultan sent for Maclean the other day & asked if he knew why d'Aub. was leaving ([ ] fr. Maclean's cyphered letter of 29 April). I sh[ou]ld. not be surprised if either Cantag. or Tattenbach had tried to persuade the Sultan that d'Aub. was removed because the Fr. Govt. was dissatisfied c. him. They are both cap[able]. of making a little capital that way.

Linares passed thro' Tangier the day before yesterday on his way to Fr. on leave.

The Forwoods' agent at Morocco abt. contract for lighthouse & removal of Verité wreck; also I suppose to offer loan. Have sent thro' Maclean E. Forwood's letter on the latter subject.

Ad[miral]. has telegd. that he will send the "Arethusa" to be here today. I propose to take De Vismes, necessity of interpreter & Reader. Giving couple of days on average to each port, sh[ou]ld. get thro' the whole business in a fortnight. Have asked for permission to go to Juby to see whether D. Mackenzie's idea of a port is feasible. Have simply told Gharnit I am going, without making mention of Sultan. Sh[ou]ld. H.M. ask me up to the Court [I] sh[ou]ld. take the opportunity, but H.M. not likely to do this. Good effect of man-of-war on Moors; it is a proof of support from home that they can appreciate. The Austrian when I told him said he was heartily glad; I think Cantag. a little jealous.

y.v.t.

P.S. Cantag. is going on leave in a few days to find out whether Antonelli is coming, & also to see Dr. [I] believe he has kidney disease, with other complications.

36. Satow to Maclean (stamped p. 50)

[No. 30]

Mazagan   27 5 94

My dear Maclean,

I have recd. your Nos. 17 to 22. It was a great satisfaction to me on arriving at DaB to find the two agents already there. So that affair is settled as betw. the Moorish Govt. & ourselves. I propose however to give these 2 men protection either under the Madrid convention or as semsars,[20] as was done in a previous case, in order to mark the gravity of

PRO 30/33 14/6   Semi-official Letters from Morocco (March 8, 1894 – July 10, 1894)

these seizures, & as a hint to all whom it may concern that the only effect of arresting 2 B. S's agents will be to withdraw the agents fr. the future fr. their power. On our side however we shall be increasingly careful to avoid giving certificates to men who have had difficulties with their Kaids. I want to be quite fair to the Moorish Govt. in this as in all other things [matters?].

I hope the man implicated in the murder of the Jew mentioned in your no. 17 will be duly punished. There will otherwise be a great row abt. it, & I may perh. get instructions to speak strongly to the Sultan on the matter. If you have an opportunity please hint to the Sultan that it is quite on the cards that if complaints continue to be made abt. the treatment of the Jews at Morocco City by Kaid Wida & by the Kadi Mustapha, some Foreign Power desirous of acquiring a position of infl[uence]. in this country may sooner or later take all the Jews under its protection. Of course he knows that Engl. is very desirous to avoid anything of the kind, & I think it w[ou]ld. produce a very good effect if H.S.M. were to instruct Gharnit to answer the letter I wrote to him last year covering one fr. Mr. S[amue]l. Montagu to the Sultan abt. the position of the Jews. When I get to Mog[ador] I shall be able to see how much reliance can be placed on the promise as to the extension of the Mellah there.

Gharnit's letter to me abt. protection &c. I can't ans[wer]. till I get to Tangier, w[hi]ch. will be abt. the beginning of June 1 or 2. But of one thing he may be assured – the F.RR. [Foreign Representatives] will not agree to limit the no. of <u>mokh[alata]</u>.[21] On the other hand I will promise him to do my best to keep it within bounds.

[Sanction for tips &c. in case of 2 released men.

Fernan told me Linares not to come back.

Thanks for cushion & hopes of Tafilelt carpets.

At Mog. will try to see Elmaleh his letter to Emmanuel sent off.

Cantag. went on leave, ill, but hope will come back.

---

[20] semsar: native commercial agent, or broker enjoying consular protection. (Khalid Ben Shrir, *Britain and Morocco During the Embassy of John Drummond Hay, 1845-1866*, Routledge, 2005. Glossary, p. 285)

[21] mokhalata: employees of commercial houses. See Sir E. Satow, *Guide to Diplomatic Practice*, 2nd edn., 1922, Vol. 1, p. 180, §199.

PRO 30/33 14/6 Semi-official Letters from Morocco (March 8, 1894 – July 10, 1894)

Please urge Gh. abt. Forde's Habassi claim.

Have sent off Kodak & letter fr. Sp. Govt. abt. decoration.]²²

Quite appreciate Gh's advice abt. not presenting credentials at Rabat, personally am disposed to follow it. Only in case of Monbel going there for that purpose.

37 Satow to missionary Cuthbert Nairn (stamped p.52 of notebook)

Conf[i]d[ential]

Cuthbert Nairn

Mogador.

31. 5. 94

My dear Sir,

Reports have been recently published in the Jewish Chronicle & forwarded to the leaders of the Jewish community in London of humiliations & grossly rough treatment inflicted on the Jews of Morocco City by Kaid Widah & the Cadi Mustapha in connection c. the recent pay[men]t. of the tribute to the Sultan. In the course of conversation c. young Mr. [Moses?] Corcos of Mog[ador]. on this subject, I observed to him that I thought exaggerated acc[oun]ts. had been given to the public, but he assured me in reply that he had the information from a trustworthy source, & that some of the missionaries had been present on the occasion, & witnessed the rough treatment complained of.

Instructions have reached me fr. Lord K[imberley]. to inquire into this matter, & report on it. I sh[ou]ld. be greatly obliged ∴ [therefore] if any of the missionaries of the Socy. to w[hi]ch. you belong w[ou]ld. be so good as to furnish me with a State[men]t. of what they have seen. If desired, I w[ou]ld. treat this communication as confid[ential]. but it might be better perh. that in any report to the F.O. I sh[ou]ld. give the names of my informants, as I often find that anonymity lessens the value of testimony.

There is another p[oin]t. on w[hi]ch. I sh[ou]ld. like to ask your advice. HMG. wish to have a Consular agent at Morocco, who w[ou]ld. furnish regular reports of matters of public interest, act as intermediary betw. H.M. Legn. & the Moorish Auth: & look after the

---

²² These square parentheses are Satow's, perhaps indicating that this part was sent by cypher.

PRO 30/33 14/6   Semi-official Letters from Morocco (March 8, 1894 – July 10, 1894)

interests of B.Ss. For these services, w[hi]ch. need not interfere with the ordinary profession or calling of the gentleman apptd, the allowance given w[ou]ld. be £100. It might be made for a year or two, if thought preferable.

W[ou]ld. you be disposed to undertake the duties w[hi]ch. I have thus briefly sketched? And if your time is too much occupied to accept, may I ask you to be so good as to tell me of any gentleman whom you think might be likely to accept the app[oin]tm[en]t.

I leave today for Tangier, where I beg you will be so good as to address me an ans[wer].

Believe me

y.v.f. [yours very faithfully]

38. Satow to Maclean (stamped p.53)

No. 31

D.a.b.

1 6 94

My dear Maclean,

I have yr. 3 letters 23, 24 & 25. The last one was delivered to me at Mogador by a brother of Pepe Ratto. Many thanks for the information contained in them.

You ask abt. the new U.S. Cons-Genl. Mr. Barclay.[23] He gives me the impression of being an honest man, anxious to rectify abuses. But, as I told him fr. the beginning, to undo the illegitimate protections granted by his predecessors is a very diff[icult]. thing, & doubtless he has found it so. He has changed several of the U.S. consular agents, not very wisely, but I do not for a moment believe that he has sold the apptmts.

I am very sorry not to have been able to visit the Sultan at Morocco, chiefly on acct. of the Jewish question, w[hi]ch. I had hoped to sift[?] thoroughly. I have made inquiries at Mogador & find your report of Kaid Wida fully confirmed, but the Kaid Mustafa is said to have been an imperious brute. I have some hopes of getting further confirmation fr. Nairn, & have also asked him whether he or any of his people w[ou]ld. accept the proposed consular agency at Morocco. Zerbib[24] gave me his ideas abt. the Jews, w[hi]ch. I thought

---

[23] Barclay first called on Satow on December 12, 1893. (Diary)
[24] Zerbib was agent of the London Jewish Evangelization Society based in Mogador. See

PRO 30/33 14/6   Semi-official Letters from Morocco (March 8, 1894 – July 10, 1894)

were very judicious. The Sultan may be assured that all his efforts to see that the Jews have just treatment will receive due recognition at the hands of H.M.G.

If you have an opportunity please tell the Sultan that I have recd. great courtesy at the hands of the various gov[ernor]s. of the ports, & am altogether pleased with the treatment I have experienced. My visit to the Coast has enabled me to understand the various questions that are pending much better than if I had remained at Tangier & read reams of reports.

As to claims, we have looked into nearly all, & if Gharnit asks you again abt. the subject you might tell him that the only cases in w[hi]ch. they will be urged agst. the Sultan, & pay[men]t. demanded of him, will be those where it is quite evident that the Moorish officials by their apathy, indifference or obstructiveness have prevented justice being done. What you tell me you said to him abt. my views on this subject is exactly a copy of my mind. [All claims that, owing to insufficient investigation in the past, have been presented will be withdrawn fr. the lists, & the total will thus be considerably reduced.][25]

If you wish to go home I will not offer any opposition, but I hope you will be back again before I go to Court. That I trust may be in 9 or 10th [September or October] next. Thank goodness, the great diminution in the claims list will enable the mission to be one of little more than friendly talk. I hope therefore that you will have no difficulty in getting leave fr[om]. the Sultan.

The instructions you have given to B. [Bonich] seem to be very full, & I have nothing to add to them. I hope the camera &c. will have reached you safely, but they will hardly have got to Morocco before you left there.

As soon as I get to Tangier I will place to yr. acct. the amt. you mention, & if in any other way I can aid you I shall be most willing.

We go on this evening at six, & I hope to be in Tangier early tomorrow morning. y.v.t.

        E.S.

P.S. I found fr[om]. Kaid Kagregy that tho' he was kept at Morocco City abt. the Mellah extension, no instructions were given him to have the work commenced. The only thing he

---

diary for May 31, 1894.
[25] Satow's parentheses.

PRO 30/33 14/6 Semi-official Letters from Morocco (March 8, 1894 – July 10, 1894)

knows is that plans were made. Please tell Gharnit that I was greatly disappointed at this, especially after the messages he had sent me thro' you that everything was settled, & that if nothing is done, after all the promises made, Ld. R. will be greatly displeased.

I went thro' the Mellah & convinced myself that it is greatly overcrowded, & a new Mellah, of at least equal dimensions to the two existing ones combined, is necessary. I find also that many of the Jews who have houses fr. the Sultan, or rooms, sublet them to poorer Jews at very much higher rents than they themselves pay. It w[ou]ld. be desirable if possible to prevent this for the future, especially in the new Mellah.

The only practicable way of doing this would be to place this matter in the hands of a commission who c[ou]ld. be trusted to carry out the rule that no sub-letting sh[ou]ld. be permitted at higher rents than those paid to the Sultan. The members of the commission sh[ou]ld. be men who hold no property in the Mellah & men of standing & recognized probity. It w[ou]ld. be a very good plan to name Johnston (not in his official capacity[26] but as an old & respected resident of Mog.), Reuben Elmaleh, Zerbib & 2 more of the same sort as members of this commission. In this way the Sultan's benevolent intentions towards the poor Jews w[ou]ld. be fully realized.

Will you tell me whether this idea c[ou]ld. be carried out. It is similar to that of the land Courts in Ireland who fix 'fair rents' of agricultural holdings, the only difference being that in one case it is rent of lands, in the other that of houseroom, w[hi]ch. it is sought to regulate.

y.v.t.

39. Satow to Sanderson

5 June 94

My dear Sanderson,

I returned on the 2nd fr[om]. what has proved a most satisfactory expedition fr[om]. every point of view. The local auth[orities]: were extremely obliging & polite, & the BSS [British Subjects] jubilant. I also made the acquaintance of all the foreign consular officers,

---

[26] Johnston was Vice-Consul at Mogador.

PRO 30/33 14/6   Semi-official Letters from Morocco (March 8, 1894 – July 10, 1894)

who with the exception of the Sp. & Fr. are mostly a very shady lot. Of our own men there is not much to be said. Poor old Redman at Magazan 76 yrs. of age & very deaf is quite incompetent. The idea that he ought to have an independent opinion & express it to the Min. at Tangier seemed quite new to him. Hunot was away fr. Saffi, but the man who acts for him young D. Reid seems intelligent & active. Frost at Rabat is a good man, honest & intelligent. Forde at Laraiche does not inspire me with confidence, & Johnston at Mogador is too clever by half.

The result of the exam[ination]. of the claims has been to greatly reduce their amount, & I begin to have my doubts whether there will be any large demand to present to the Sultan. The plan in the past seems to have been to let people make whatever claims they liked, & send these into the M[oorish]. Govt. without exam. & without making any distinction betw. cases in w[hi]ch. the Govt. was responsible for a failure to collect the money & those where the debtors were insolvent.

The Sultan left Morocco C[ity]. on the 21st, proceeding towards Rabat by way of Tadla. He is not likely to reach Rabat before the end of this month. I hear Tattenb[ach]. was much exercised on learning fr[om]. a gossip that I had taken my uniform with me, but as I came back on the exact day that I had told everybody, he has said no more.

P[otestad]. is back, but will go again on leave early in July. Moret wants him to go & see the Sultan at Rabat, & suggested that he & I might go together. But I have told him that the Sultan does not care for informal visits of this kind, & that he had better postpone presenting his credentials till the autumn, when if he likes one might be at Fez together. I do not know what Monbel will do, but if all three went up abt. the same time it w[ou]ld. [be a] variation fr. the usual arrangement by w[hi]ch. while one man is at the Court the rest remain at Tangier devoured by curiosity & jealousy.

I think of sending Allan Maclean to greet the Sultan as he passes near DaB, & perh. the Sp. & Fr. colls. may send their consuls too.

The new American Consul-genl. Barclay is generally reported to be selling consular apptmts. & protections, but I am not quite sure that the rumours have any other foundation than the spite of the Matthews party.

The Sultan's favourite son Abdul Aziz[27] passed by Casablanca the day before I returned there to land Maclean. This boy of 14 is to be made the Sultan's lieut[enant]. for the whole country, thus completely supplanting Mulai Mohammed.

Morant wants to remain at Tetuan till the end of Sept. & w[ou]ld. like to be apptd. Cons. Agent at Morocco City in Jan. next. He is working industriously at Arabic, & I have no doubt w[ou]ld. do for the post. Before receiving his application I had written to one of the missionaries, Cuthbert Nairn, to ask if he or one of his people w[ou]ld. undertake it.[28] But it w[ou]ld. be preferable to have Morant. I will write to Anderson on this matter, but I wished to tell you my ideas.

If Capt. [Francis Charles] Cromie had been on the spot Maclean w[ou]ld. have liked to act for White, who goes on leave today, w[hi]ch. in some ways w[ou]ld. have been a convenient arrange[men]t., but under present circs. it c[ou]ld. not be. It is however a great bore to have to give up De Vismes for the greater part of the day to Consular work. The separation of the Legation fr. the Consulate, w[hi]ch. were formerly in one building, was altogether a mistake.

Kaid Maclean writes that the Sultan wants him to go home to get H.M. a war balloon. He seems to have plenty of money to gratify his whims.

   y.v.t.

40. Satow to Sir Percy Anderson (stamped p.58)
5 June 94

My dear Anderson,

Your private letter of May 9 reached me just before I started on my tour down the coast.

The conclusion I have come to is that Rabat might conveniently be joined on to Maclean's district for every kind of business except legal. My reason for this exception is that if the V-C. at Rabat wanted a legal difficulty solved he c[ou]ld. obtain a result much more rapidly by writing to the consul at Tangier – White – who understands such questions – than by applying to Maclean – who for lack of experience will for a long time to come have to refer here for advice. The principal object of enunciating the places in a Consul's

---

[27] Abdul Aziz (1878-1943) was Sultan after his father's death, 1894-1908.
[28] See Letter no. 37 above.

district is for the purpose of Sect. 4 IX of the Morocco O. in C. [Order in Council] chiefly for legal purposes, & therefore I w[ou]ld. suggest leaving the enumeration as it is. On the other hand Rabat is only 50 m[iles]. fr[om]. DaB a distance w[hi]ch. can easily be got over in a day & a half by land. It is a place not conveniently reached by sea, as the bar is often impassable. Laraiche presents similar difficulties. But it is only 60 m. fr[om]. Tangier, while the distance fr[om]. Laraiche to DaB is ab[ou]t. 130. For this reason as well as for the others urged in my desp[atch]. as to the political and commercial divisions of Morocco, I still think Laraiche sh[ou]ld. remain under Tangier for all purposes.

I propose however to write a desp[atch]. on the subject in a few days.

As regards Mogador, if the Treasury c[ou]ld. be induced to give another £300 & restore the office allowance to £115 I sh[ou]ld. still be in favour of a paid V-C. there. The Spaniards have consuls de carrière at all the ports. The Fr. at DaB have Colomb, who is an excellent Arabic scholar, & at Mog. Pellegrini as V-C, besides young Leriche as dragoman, who is really learned. As I showed in my desp[atch]. the British Trade of the place is within a few pounds of that of DaB. Apart fr[om]. this, it is a great stronghold of the Jews, among whom the Engl[ish]. lang[uage]. & ideas are spreading. The place ought not to be neglected. Johnston is a fair Arabist, speaks Fr. & Sp. fluently, but has a shifty eye. I sh[ou]ld. prefer that the post if created, sh[ou]ld. be given to a gentleman, who must also be an Arabic scholar. Unless a man knows Arabic, he may have all the other requisite qualifications, but he will not do for a consular officer.

<u>Tetuan</u> & <u>Morocco</u>. Morant writes to me that he w[ou]ld. like to remain in charge of the Cons[ular]. agency at Tetuan till the end of Sept. or beg[innin]g. of Oct. Nahon I suppose is strictly entitled to go back as soon as he likes, but I shall do my best to keep him away, as he asked for 'unlimited' leave. Morant, who is working hard at Arabic, offers himself for the Consular agency at Morocco in Jan. next. Before his letter reached me I had written to ask Mr. Cuthbert Nairn, one of the missionaries, whether he or any of his staff w[ou]ld. accept the apptmt. But I do not feel bound to recommend any of the missionaries, & sh[ou]ld. prefer to send Morant. Will you let me know what you think of these two matters.

   y.v.t.

P.S. Can you give me an idea when Cromie is likely to come out. Maclean talks of asking

PRO 30/33 14/6   Semi-official Letters from Morocco (March 8, 1894 – July 10, 1894)

for 6 w. leave before long, to fetch his wife back.

41. Satow to Sanderson (stamped p.60)

6 June 1894

My dear Sanderson,

I have drawn today on the Secy. of State at 30 days sight for £50 w[hi]ch. I have paid to Kaid Maclean on acct. of expenses incurred by him for starting Bonich and for couriers, etc. His acct. I will forward when I receive it.

      y.v.t.

42. Satow to Maclean (stamped p.60)

No. 32

6 June

My D[ea]r. Maclean,

[£50 sent to Coutts. Return Emanuel's letter. Enclose one fr. Moret.][29]

We have recd. a circular fr. Torres written by the Sultan's direction, warning us of an expedition to be sent agst. the Gharb, & requesting that our people will withdraw their interests in time. Can you find out what the Sultan's real intentions are c. regard to the Gharb. It is of the greatest importance that I shld. know as soon as possible.

The colls: are somewhat divided in opinion: some want to ans[wer]. "tell us first whom you want to punish among our m[okhalata] & s[emsar] & then we will act." To reply in this way seems to me to be equiv[alen]t. to telling the Sultan that he must not send an expedition to the Gh[arb]. & practically to withdraw that region fr[om]. his authority; thus giving it over to anarchy. I am inclined to be more fair. At the same time I do not want BSs. [British Subjects] to suffer, & am going to propose that the expedition is not sent until the end of harvest, i.e. Sept. to give our people time to realize, & that places shall be assigned where they may place their herds & flocks in safety.

We have only 39 m. & 6 s. in the Gh[arb]: The Itals: have somewhat over 50, the Belg.

---

[29] Satow's parentheses.

PRO 30/33 14/6   Semi-official Letters from Morocco (March 8, 1894 – July 10, 1894)

betw[een]. 30 & 35 besides 6 <u>s</u>. The statistics of the others I do not know. Can you get at them. Lists are supposed to be furnished to the Moorish Govt., but not all do it.

Why does the M[oorish]. Govt. recognize Brazilian protégés &c. They have no Treaty, & no Brazilian ought to have either <u>s</u>[emsar] or <u>m</u>[okhalata]. The row at Rabat the other day was all abt. a Brazilian protégé. Colaço being in charge of Brazil. interests is provided thus with a double engine for selling protections.

All here say Barclay sells protections & apptmts, but I am at present inclined to think it is only his entourage, interpreter & Stalker.

   y.v.t.

43. Satow to Sanderson

Tangier

June 7. 94

My dear Sanderson,

The M[oorish]. Govt. seems disposed to raise the question of protection & we are confronted with a serious dilemma by the announced expedition into the Gharb. The choice seems to be betw. refusing to allow the Sultan to exercise his authority in the only fashion known to Moors, or of giving up the present system of agricultural partnerships, wch. are a sort of second class protection. The Fr[ench]. I think will hold out for protection, but most of the colls: wld. be willing to give it up, except the Port[ugue]s[e]. & Yankee who make a revenue out of it. In the draft Note to Torres wch. I submit for approval I have tried to steer a middle course.

There are only three Br. firms of importance in this country, namely Murdoch Butler & Co, Fernan, & Lamb Bros. who are established at DaB [Dar al Baida] & Saffi. The latter have a great no. of agents. At Tangier & Laraiche the people who are interested chiefly are Forde the V-C [Vice-Consul], Lady Kirby Green & her son Jack, the rest being Gib[raltar]. Jews & Spaniards of no acc[oun]t. I have troubled you with despp. [despatches] abt. this matter, as it may possibly become important, & I am not sure that I know the mind of HMG. Rumour has it that the Sultan will send an Envoy to Madrid, c. instructions to revive the negotiations of 1886-87.

PRO 30/33 14/6   Semi-official Letters from Morocco (March 8, 1894 – July 10, 1894)

Allan Maclean seems to be of opinion that protection is a good thing for the Sultan as well as for foreign trade; that the fields of the "agents" are better cultivated & that the taxes are more regularly paid; while Gharnit & others round the Sultan secretly like it, because they now & then get handsome tips fr. the Gov[ernor]s. for winking at their putting agents in prison. This however seems to me a partial view of the question. If every nationality committed as few irregularities as we do, the system wld. not be a bad one, but I have no doubt myself that the number of protégés of all classes wld. be found to be in the inverse ratio of the commercial interests of various countries.

   y.v.t.

44. Satow to Sir Percy Anderson (p.63 in notebook)
June 8. 94

My dear Anderson,

 When I came to look into the question of re-arranging the consular districts, I found that it w[ou]ld. not do to give the judicial supervision of Rabat to one consul & the administrative to the other, & therefore in the desp[atch]. on this subject w[hi]ch. I am now sending you I have simply included Rabat in Maclean's district giving him also Salli & Mahdia. If you do not approve of this, then you will find in the enclosure to my No. 7 a distribution in exact accordance with the scheme by w[hi]ch. all the Atlantic ports are to be placed under Maclean's supervision.

 Looking again at Ld. K[imberley]'s No. 4 I perceive that part of Maclean's duties is to be advising the Vice Consuls as to their duties under the Morocco O. in C. [Order in Council] I trust that in time he may become qualified for this task; for the present I think it will be found better to instruct him to refer all such questions to the Leg[atio]n. It w[ou]ld. hardly be fair to expect a man who has been a soldier all his life suddenly to become a lawyer.

 My present desp[atch]. will by itself be sufficient, I think, in reply to y[ou]r No. 4 Consular, & my No 7 can be treated as non-existent. But at the same time I do not wish to withdraw it, because it represents my views on the subject, w[hi]ch. a visit to the coast & personal knowledge of all the men has not altered.

   y.v.t.

PRO 30/33 14/6 Semi-official Letters from Morocco (March 8, 1894 – July 10, 1894)

E.S.

45. Satow to Maclean

No. 33

June 9, 1894

My Dr. Maclean

I am sending 3 letters to Gharnit: 1 expressing satisfaction at reception on the coast, a 2nd abt. Juby indemnity, wch. they don't pay, & 3rdly complaining of Sid Ali Eneshdi [Erreshdi?] Basha of Fez for his unfriendliness, particularly in shielding the Benani brothers in evading pay[men]t. of their debts to Br. creditors, when they have plenty of money, & lastly in imprisoning an Agent of a Br. semsar without giving notice to Macleod. I shld. prob. have taken no notice of it, but that the Basha had the old fellow flogged unmercifully, & that too on the ground that he had referred to Macleod some question abt. taxation.

The colleagues are not yet agreed abt. the ans. to be given to the circular of Torres mentioned in my last, & I am still waiting for instructions from home.

y.v.t.

46. Satow to Sanderson (stamped p.64)

June 10. 94

My dear Sanderson,

The Sultan's death was altogether unexpected.[30] A previous letter fr. K. Maclean seems to have gone astray, wch. may have announced his illness. None of the colleagues recd. the news till late this afternoon. I thought it best after consulting with Potestad, to tell the Frenchman, & then there was no reason for not giving the news to the rest.

It is desirable that we shld. get the colleagues to act in concert, if possible, so I have persuaded [the doyen] Colaço to call a meeting for ten o'clock tomorrow, but I doubt whether d'Aub. will be disposed to attend. 1 or 2 seem to think that a rival candidate may

---

[30] Hassan I of Morocco (1836 – 7 June 1894).

PRO 30/33 14/6   Semi-official Letters from Morocco (March 8, 1894 – July 10, 1894)

be put forward in the person of the late Sultan's eldest brother (or uncle) Mulai Ismail. Gentile, who of course knows Morocco well, thinks we might do ourselves harm by recognizing Abdul Aziz [Abdel Aziz] before we are certain that he will be accepted by the people of Fez, and that if the people in general fancied we were trying to put our influence into the scale, they wld. turn agst. him. All these cons[ideratio]ns. have their weight. On the other hand, Abd. Aziz is only 16, & there is more chance of our being able to exercise a good influence over him than over M[ulai]. Moh[amed]. the elder son of the late Shogun, who is described in the memo. enclosed in E[uan]-S[mith]'s No. 207 of April 16, 1892 (That memo. I think is from information furnished by Kaid Maclean). Furthermore, if we gave him a helping hand, to however slight an extent, it wld. give us reason to expect something in return hereafter.

However, even supposing that a ship is placed at my disposal, I shld. be very cautious as to my proceedings. In a week I shall get messengers back fr. both Fez & Rabat, if not sooner, & so learn what is the outlook at those two places.

I am anxious that at any rate the ground on wch. ships are sent shall not be "for the protection of foreigners' lives & property". I do not think either are in danger, except perh. at Fez & Rabat; but there is no record of foreigners as such having been in danger in 1873 when Mulai Hassan succeeded, at Rabat (there were no foreigners at Fez in those days as far as I know), & I don't want to raise an alarm. Allan Maclean writes privately "I have made arrangements for the safety of Europeans here", apparently in concert with the Govr. & I have complete confidence in him and the Engl. men at DaB. [Dar al Baida] On the former occasion the only town on the coast that was threatened was Mogador, & nothing serious happened.

Fr. the symptoms described by Maclean I am disposed to think the Sultan had a fever. One or two colleagues have however suggested poison.

    y.v.t.

P.S. I have told Frost in a private letter to congratulate A.A. for me, if he can manage to see him. But this may be difficult. Anyhow it will not commit H.M.G. E.S.

47. Satow to Maclean

PRO 30/33 14/6 Semi-official Letters from Morocco (March 8, 1894 – July 10, 1894)

34.

10 June.

[In reply to No. 2 abt. Sultan's death][31]

48. Satow to Sanderson

13 June 94

My d[ea]r. Sanderson,

My despp. will put you in possn. of nearly all the information that has reached me. I hear fr. Tattenbach that the consuls at DaB are talking of provisioning & arming a house for the foreigners to retreat to in case of need, wch. if true shows that they are not quite as cool as one wld. wish them to be.

d'Aub[igny]. came to the meeting after all, but I have not seen him since. He has not heard fr. his military mission since the 26 May. One of the local papers says he [the Sultan] died on the 4th. It is possible, like anything else, but I have a letter fr. Gharnit dated the 6th enclosing Sultan's letter fr. the Govrs. & Admors[32] of the ports, instructing them to treat me well, & it wld. have been curious if he shld. have taken the trouble to write a dozen letters & seal them with the Sultan's seal if he had been dead already 2 days.

My latest fr. Kaid Maclean is the 10th. At first he & Allen [Allan] Maclean were desirous that I shld. go at once to congratulate AA. [Abel Aziz] but the former seems now to think his chances are diminishing, & that they depend on Cid Hamed Ben Moosa not being assassinated. He had heard that they wanted to assass[inate]. Cid H. on the night of the 9th, as they fear he will exercise a paramount influence over AA. So until we hear that AA has got safely to Rabat with C.H. we cannot feel sure of anything.

W. B. H[arris]. came to me the day before yesterday & said he was going to Rabat. [See diary for June 11, 1894.] I replied that he cld. be of much more use if he wld. go to Wazan & Fez, find out the feeling there & pull the strings in favour of AA. He is fond of adventure & readily agreed to what I wanted. So I gave him letters to Gharnit & the Amin Mukhri ( )[33] and a little money. I hope you will approve of this, & that if he does well I may make

---

[31] Satow's parentheses.
[32] Admor: Jewish scholar or rabbi.

PRO 30/33 14/6   Semi-official Letters from Morocco (March 8, 1894 – July 10, 1894)

him a present afterwds. He went off yesterday morning sans attracting notice (a story or two abt. Hadj Abdullah). Maclean paid £50 for Zeus. Now I have the "Bramble" this will not happen again. I suppose I had better pay this out of Secret.   [End of letter]

49. Satow to Maclean (stamped p. 67)

No. 35

June 13, 1894

My dear Maclean,

I have your Nos. 2 & 4 & the unnumbered one dated 6 June fr. Borj Miskinu. Many thanks for all the information they contain. I am sending the "Bramble" to get news, & she has orders to wait for you, letters & Frosts, & then return at once to Tangier.

Will you let me know whether in yr. opinion the chances are agst. A A remaining on the throne. At the present moment the foreign PP [Powers] are not disposed to hurry to recognize him officially, but I wrote to Frost to congratulate him privately if he cld. contrive to do so. I am doing all I can in this neighbourhood to keep the people quiet & prevent them fighting among themselves. Here everything is peacable.

In a letter I sent via DaB I said that the best place wld. be a council consisting of Gharnit, the Hazhib, Hadj el Mati[?] & a couple more so as to have a majority, unless the Ch[inese]. expedient of making the mother Regent can be adopted. With a young sovereign perh. something cld. be done in the way of reforming the system of taxation, wch. seems the crying evil. I am not asking for men-of-war to protect us, & I think we shall manage to do without. I cld. not come to Rabat unless the colls: did also, & we must wait for more certain news that A.A. will maintain himself before doing anything openly. But I do not think any power wishes to set up a rival candidate. The important thing is that the Moors settle it, quietly, without such an amount of disturbance as wld. give any power the right, or even a pretext for interfering.   y.v.t.

50. Satow to Maclean (stamped p. 68)

---

[33] Left blank by Satow.

PRO 30/33 14/6   Semi-official Letters from Morocco (March 8, 1894 – July 10, 1894)

No. 36

16 June

My d[ea]r. Macl[ean].

The Fr. Engl. & Sp. Govts. are working together on the present occasion, in a way that has never been done before, & I think if we can manage to agree it will be all the better for Morocco & for the Sultan. We (d'Aub., P. & self) have today agreed to teleg. to our respective govts. recommending to reply to Gharnit's circular letter fr. Dar Uld Zidon[?], congratulating Abdul [Abdel] Aziz on his accession, & saying that we are prepared to present our felicitations in person if that wld. be agreeable to H.M.

I hope that our govts. will agree to this, & then the replies wld. be despatched by the 1st opportunity, as the Fr. have the "Lalande" & we the "Bramble" besides a Sp. vessel the "Venadito" we can always communicate.

We do not wish to say or do anything that Abdul Aziz, this is his Mins. wld. not wish or think might do them harm in the eyes of their countrymen. But it seems to me, as to you, that the attitude taken by the Powers may considerably affect the result, & that a little backing fr. them will strengthen the position of the new Sultan.

It wld. be unwise for any Power to take the lead in offering material assistance of any kind. A throne established by foreign bayonets wld. have to be maintained thereby, & the end wld. be the independence of Morocco wld. be at an end.

If I might offer a word of encouragement to the desponding, I shld. say to them, no cause was ever won except by taking a sanguine view of it. To the Mins. especially I wld. give the advice to sink differences & pull together for their own sakes. For I suppose that if a rival candidate were set up & was successful, their heads wld. not be worth much.

The Fr[ench]. are going to have 2 ironclads & a cruiser at Oran. We shall have the Howe, Sanspareil & Spartan at Gib[raltar]. by the 20th & the Arethusa before, I hope. So there is force enough at hand to protect the most timorous of the foreign population if need be. Luckily everything is going quietly at present, & we have recd. the news that A.A. was proclaimed at Fez on the 12th. Here he was proclaimed last night. [End of letter]

51. Satow to Sanderson

PRO 30/33 14/6   Semi-official Letters from Morocco (March 8, 1894 – July 10, 1894)

17 June

My dr. Sanderson,

The last day or two the great ? [question] has been whether we shld. say to Abdul Aziz that we wld. go to see him at Rabat, if he liked. Now it seems to be decided betw. P[otestad]. d'Aub[igny]. & myself that we shall not mention Rab[at], but only say that we are ready to go & see him when & where it may be agreeable to him. This formula will, we think, enable the others to act with us.

If we were to persist in going to Rabat agst. the opinion expressed by Torres to 2 or 3 of the dragomans that it wld. not be convenient, our doing so wld. have been a beginning of putting pressure on the Moorish Govt. by a junta so to speak, of the 3 PP, & wld. gradually, if they pursued the same line, have led to intervention. Then Spain wld. have been the earthen pot swimming with the iron & brazen. She wld. have dropped into the background, as in Tonquin & Mexico, & then we shld. be left alone with the Fr[ench].   How long cld. we pull together?

At prest. P. d'Aub. & myself get on very well. T[attenbach]. whose position of 'Sultan's adviser' has come to the ground is naturally jealous.

There was another reason for not insisting on Rabat being mentioned, & that is that acc. to all probability A.A. will start fr. Fez as soon as he hears that he has been proclaimed at the great mosque there, wch. was done on the evening of the 12th. We shld. look rather foolish if we proposed to visit him at Radat, & found that he had left meanwhile for the capital.

I have just recd. a letter fr. [W.B.] Harris dated Wazan, 14th. in wch. he reports having arr. there, & induced the Shereefs to keep things quiet. He also got them to announce to the town the accession of A.A. & to confirm it. They will give every support to the young Sultan. The argument he used was that F.PP [Foreign Powers] wld. possibly invade the country if things do not remain quiet. The Shereefs announced their intention to a crowded court of supporting the claims of A.A.

Official letter fr. Macleod at Fez reports that all the local Shereefs & Ulema had given in their adhesion.

Kaid Maclean is rather pessimistic. He tells me things said to him by the Ministers wch.

PRO 30/33 14/6   Semi-official Letters from Morocco (March 8, 1894 – July 10, 1894)

imply great jealousy of each other, & especially of Cid Hamad Ben Morsa. The letters read in the mosque here yesterday were signed by the 5 min[ister]s, so they will apparently form a sort of council. Whether a regent will be apptd. I do not know.

Nothing that the papers say is in the least degree trustworthy.

E.S.

52. Satow to Maclean (stamped p.71)

No. 37

18 June 1894

My dear Maclean,

There is doubtless a letter on its way to me by courier fr. you abt. the 16th inst. I have suggested to Frost not to use the land route at present, as we can arrange I think to communicate by sea every 2 or 3 days: each of the 3 powers having a desp[atch]. boat.

Identical notes of reply to Gharnit offering the felicitations of our Govts. & adding that we are instructed to present ourselves to H.S.M. as soon as it may be convenient to him & at the place of his choice are being sent by this st[eame]r. the Sp. cruiser "Venadito", by Engl., Fr. Sp. & Ital. & Port. The others say nothing abt. a visit. Not having men-of-war at hand they do not like to commit themselves to the chance of being invited to Rabat.

If as I hear there is a probability of the Sultan remaining long enough at Rabat for the F. Mins. to visit him there, say 10 days or a fortnight fr. now, I strongly advise Gh. to invite all the Mins. to go there. If he does not, it will not seem a friendly way of responding to the amicable expressions in our note. It is very important that at the present juncture the Moorish Govt. shld. avoid giving any offence to any Foreign Power. I hear that the "Legazpi"[?] did not obtain the money that was lying at Mazagan. If your advice is asked on this point, you shld. advise them not to delay the payt. Punctual performance of its obligations will create a favourable impression on the minds of European nations.

The policy of Morocco has always been to try to create divisions & jealousies among the PP [Powers]. That is unwise, for it has not in it the demerits[?] of permanent success. A far better policy, looking to the future of the country wld. be to treat all European Powers with equal confidence & courtesy.   [End of letter]

PRO 30/33 14/6   Semi-official Letters from Morocco (March 8, 1894 – July 10, 1894)

53. Satow to Sanderson (stamped p.72)

June 20

My dr. S.

I have very little doubt that Tattenbach told Torres we were going to Rabat, & inspired him with the objection to our doing so. He of course disliked the idea because he wld. have had to seek hospitality on board an Engl. Sp. or a Fr. ship. Besides he seeks to maintain the position of Sultan's adviser wch. he had with M.H. [Mulai Hassan]

Kaid Macl[ean]. writes fr. Rabat on the 17th that he had mentioned to Gharnit the possibility of the F.Ms. visiting the Sultan, to wch. he replied that he hoped we shld. not do so at present, & that he had been informed by the Fr. interpreter that d'Aub. wld. not go there. On the other hand Cid Hamad ben Moosa said to Macl. that he wld. be delighted to see the FMs at Rabat.

M. says C.H. is practically the ruler & will be so, unless he is put out of the way. The young Sult[an]. is reported to have said

[three blank lines]

This has been repeated, & the jealousy of the Vizier & Min. of War is very lively. The last news was that the Sult[an]. wld. start fr. Fez on the 23rd. Things continue to look well. The most turbulent tribe near Rabat, namely the Zem[mours] & Yaris[?] have sent in their alleg[iance]s & offer of safe conduct. Foreign opinion tranquil[?] chiefly the [ ] crops not got in, & a row predicted 3 mos. hence. But I don't wish to prophesy. Good reports fr. Morocco & all V-C. [Vice-Consuls] except Mogador who has not written. Am not at present thinking of teleg.ing for Arethusa, as Tage is here only in pursuance of Fr. announcement.

54. Satow to Maclean (stamped p.73)

38.

June 20. 1894

PRO 30/33 14/6   Semi-official Letters from Morocco (March 8, 1894 – July 10, 1894)

My dear Maclean,

Your Nos. 6 & 7 have reached me safely. The name of the Fr. Khalifa is Malpertuy, the dragoman to the Fr. legation.[34] I have not been able to discover anything abt. his doings at Rabat, but I suppose the object was to replace for a moment Linares. We must hope to preserve an outward cordiality with the French, but I do not feel sanguine abt. obtaining more. Still it is something to have broken the ice with them.

I highly appreciate the service rendered by your man in bringing the news to DaB, & beg you to be so good as to give him a present of $20 on my behalf. And if I have not done so before let me here express my great sense of the obligation under wch. we are to you for having hastened to communicate the news, & for enabling us to in a manner lead the way in determining the course to be taken by the powers.

I have passed your letter to the Marshal on to the Sp. Min. to be forwarded, after having read it. Nothing cld. have been better expressed.

Cid Fedool's letter is to the effect that the Sultan will not pay those $7000 to the Sanitary Board. This is altogether wrong. The Board were acting as repres'ves of the Sultan for the good of the people of Morocco. On the faith of his having conferred the sanitary authority on them they borrowed this money fr. Nahon & Benshimol. But you need not trouble to speak about this at present, for the Sanitary Board will have to write abt. the matter, & we have no call to put ourselves out for them. Today we dressed ship and fired salutes in honour of the Queen's accession, the Moors also joining.

The Fr. have the "Tage" here, a big cruiser of 7000 tons, besides the "Lalande". The Italians have the "Lombardia" at Gib. & the "Arethusa" is there too, but we are of opinion that it is unnecessary to have them brought over at present, as there is no danger to anybody.

    y.v.t. E.S.

55. Satow to Maclean (stamped p.74)

No. 39

21 June

---

[34] Jean-Claude-Lazare Malpertuy was First Dragoman at the French legation in Tangier in 1894, later Consul at Mogador (1899-1900) and Casablanca from 1902.

PRO 30/33 14/6   Semi-official Letters from Morocco (March 8, 1894 – July 10, 1894)

My D[ea]r. Maclean,

Thanks for your No. 8. The advice you have given to the Govt. is excellent, & the Sp. Min. having got the order for the delivery of the specie at Mazagan, & a promise to pay the balance as soon as they get to Fez is satisfied. You know what a just & straightforward man he is; the Moorish Govt. will receive every cons[i]d[eratio]n. fr. him, & yet they will not be successful if they try any tricks.

Gh[arnit]. writes that the Sultan will not be able to receive us at Rabat, a very civil letter, & I am quite satisfied that the matter is so arranged; it had to be decided one way or the other.

What is of particular interest to know is the prob. date of the Sultan's arrival at Fez. It wld. be imprudent to delay long on the way, as his father did, at Mequinez.

[illegible line in Satow's parentheses]   E.S.

56. Satow to Maclean
No. 40.
22 June 94.
My d[ea]r. Macl[ean].

With regard to B. [Bonich] whose interesting letter you have sent me, I think he had better not undertake the journey that had been proposed if there is any danger, but that you shld. employ him as you think he can best be turned to acct. in travelling abt. giving good counsels whenever they are likely to be useful & in reporting the feelings of the tribes & their prob. movements.   y.v.t.

P.S. The Principal point to impress upon all Moors, whether members of the Govt. or tribesmen, is that to have fighting among themselves is the best way to invite foreign intervention. Let them ponder over this carefully. My advice to Bu [Ba] Hamed is to remove all the unpopular governors who have made themselves obnoxious by extortion, & to try what can be done in the way of regular taxation. To allow the free export of wheat & barley wld. keep all the people quiet. This year there has been a magnificent harvest, & if the farmers are allowed to sell them barley for export, they will be so busy that no one will think of fighting. When you get to Fez you will see [Walter] Harris, & will learn fr. him

PRO 30/33 14/6   Semi-official Letters from Morocco (March 8, 1894 – July 10, 1894)

what has been done by the Engl. legation to counsel the people to be quiet. You will tell Bu [Ba] Hamed as much as you consider desirable. E.S.

p.s. p. 155.

To H. Maclean

fr. p. 155

[Death of Carnot]35   25th June

I hear most satisfactory acc[oun]ts. of the feeling among the tribes near Tangier, Jibel Habib & Beni Harosh Angera & Beni Hanzmar. They have agreed among themselves to keep order, & all they ask is that the Basha may be changed.

If you have a good opportunity, please tell this to the Hajib for the Sultan. That I am very pleased for his sake that the people are conducting themselves well, & I hope he will appt. them a pair of good Bashas here in place of M. Kishid & the present Basha of Tangier, so that peace may be kept. Also that all the Powers are much pleased that things are so quiet on the coast.   E.S.

57. Satow to Sanderson

June 23/94

My dear Sanderson,

I saw d'Aub[igny]. on the 20th, after the mail had left, & told him that I had no present intention of bringing the "Arethusa" here, as I did not wish to give other people a pretext for crowding the bay c. [with] their ships, & that I understood his having the "Tage" here besides the "Lalande" was a sort of counterbalance to our superior advantage in having ships lying at Gib[raltar]. wch. is so much nearer than Oran. He of course replied that he had no objection to the "Arethusa" appearing here, but as I do not see any real need, I shall not send for her without instructions fr. Ld. K. There is absolutely no danger to Europeans here that one cannot conjure away by talking to the country people thro' our protected Moors.

What occurred at Arzila36 was this. The Isla de Luzon went there & exchanged salutes

---

35 Marie François Sadi Carnot (1837-94). Fifth president of the Third Republic of France. President from 1887 until his assassination in Lyon on June 25, 1894 (aged 56).

PRO 30/33 14/6 Semi-official Letters from Morocco (March 8, 1894 – July 10, 1894)

with the fort: then a party landed to walk abt., perh. to buy provisions. The captain is one of those sailors who are never happy but when they are on shore. Then a report was spread that the Xtians [Christians] were coming to take Morocco, & the tribesmen came flocking down to repel the invader. The townspeople on their side took the alarm, & shut the gates. After a while the real state of the case was explained to the tribesmen, & they began to disperse. There is a Jew at Arzila who is consular agent for halfadozen foreign powers (I don't know what they want with one at a place wch. is not open to trade); he took the infection very badly, & despatched a courier to Tangier with letters calling for protection by all means in the power of the Dipl. Body, but I don't suppose anyone will treat him seriously.

Still the affair might have had untoward consequences. All the Moors abt. here got very excited, & began driving their herds into a place of safety, & shouldering their guns to go off & see what was up. I saw Pot[estad]. & remonstrated with him abt. his ship having gone to Arzila in that heedless way. He says the capt. is not under his orders. If that is the case the Sp. Govt. is not acting fairly by us. They ought not to send ships to prowl abt. the coast & excite alarms. The Sp. flag to a Moor is like a red rag to be[?] a bull, unfortunately.

When the "Lalande" went to Rabat with despp. on the 15th d'Aubigny sent down his dragoman Malpertuy, without telling any one. Of course the colleagues were very inquisitive abt. the nature of his errand. Maclean writes to me that he told Gharnit that d'Aub. did not want to go there to see the Sultan, & I daresay that was the main purpose. Linares being in Europe, it was natural enough that d'Aub. wanted some one to communicate his ideas on the situation, as a sort of counterpoise to our advantage in having Maclean there. I told Maclean to try & persuade the Mins. to invite us to Rabat, but Gharnit being on the negative side, he was not able to carry the point. No doubt the Fr. legation is anxious to prevent the others fr. seeing too much of the court people. When the time comes for me to visit the Sultan it will be necessary to say that I am starting on such-and-such a date, & to take no refusal.

If it were ever proposed to transfer the Foreign Legs. to Fez, wch. several of the colls:

---

[36] Arzila is a fortified town on the Atlantic coast of Morocco, about 31 kilometres south of Tangier.

PRO 30/33 14/6   Semi-official Letters from Morocco (March 8, 1894 – July 10, 1894)

consider absolutely necessary if we are to keep this country from going to pieces, I venture to prognosticate that the Fr. wld. oppose the move.

Their new Fez V-C. Marsilli [Marcilly] arrived fr. France 4 or 5 days ago. He is a young fellow who knows a little Arabic, & for the present does not look likely to be dangerous.

[Walter] Harris fr. Fez on the 17th. His arrival there was opportune, the day before a deputation was to start for Rabat to offer homage to the Sultan. I had given him a letter to the Amin Mukhri, who recd. him very well, & insisted on putting him up. Directly after he got in, the Basha & a no. of Sherifs of Mulai Edris came to the house to have a feed, wch. gave him an opportunity of speaking words of wisdom. They were all very civil. There is no doubt, he says, that M.A.A. [Mohamed Abdel Aziz] is securely on the throne. Mulai Ismail is practically a prisoner, but he has acknowledged A A.

D'Aub. has told me of the recognition of the Sultan by the Sherifs of Wazan, & the papers attach great importance to this. I have very little doubt that Harris talking to them had a good deal to do with influencing them to decide upon the line they wld. take, & in writing letters to all the tribes to the same effect.

I have asked Harris to remain at Fez until M.A.A. arrives there, so that he may be able to report on his reception.

Bonich the man who was to have gone to Figuig wld. I think be better employed in travelling abt. the country & gathering information as to the feeling of the tribes, & I have sent instructions to K. Maclean accordingly. However if you consider Figuig more important he can easily be shunted in that direction. He supposes himself to be gathering news for some Lond[on]. editor in league with Bewicke, K. Maclean's Secretary.

The Italian "Maisilia"[?] is at Gib[raltar]. but Gentile tells me he will not bring her over unless the safety of Europeans requires it. I find Gentile an excellent man to work with. Cantagalli of late was very excitable & Gallophobe.

   y.v.t.

58. Satow to Sanderson (stamped p.79)
Tangier
1 July

PRO 30/33 14/6   Semi-official Letters from Morocco (March 8, 1894 – July 10, 1894)

My dear Sanderson,

Kaid Maclean wrote me a rather alarming letter fr. Rabat, saying that he & the ministers of the Sultan thought that place wld. not be safe after the departure for Fez, so I thought it advisable to send down the "Bramble" with a letter to Frost to ask his opinion. Fr. was quite strong that nothing was to be feared, & that there was no need for a man-of-war being stationed there. So my anxiety was relieved.

I think K. Maclean is a bit of an alarmist; the fact is, he reflects the feelings of the people around him, & fear & uncertainty seem to pervade the minds of both Moors & Jews in this country.

Harris writes to me that the officials at Fez had heard that serious trouble had occurred at Melilla, & were apprehending war with Spain; they implored him to write at once & beg me not to support Spain until they had had time to write & tell me all abt. it. There is nothing whatever at Melilla, but some wild rumour has reached them from Oujda, a place on the Algerian frontier, where canards [hoaxes] are very likely to be hatched. When that pother [commotion] occurred at Aizila the other day many of the Moors, who knew of the hitch abt. the indemnity, fancied that the Sp. were trying to obtain 'a material guarantee'.

There have been a few rows here & there, one or two unpopular officials in country districts have been put out of the way, & no debts are paid for the moment. The Chamberlain Bin Hamed & the Vizier Hadj el Maati are at daggers-drawn, & people say one of them will get rid of the other; but as long as there is no rival Sultan to set up, that prob. will not matter.

Things are quiet at present. What we are anxious to hear is that the Sultan has safely arrived at Fez. Acc. to the best inf[ormation]. I have he ought to get there on the 4th or 5th, in wch. case I shld. hear of it on the 7th or 8th.

d'Aub[igny]. says he shall leave 48 hrs. after the news arrives, & he is keeping the "Tage" in order to return home with more éclat. P[otestad]. is anxious to send away the Conde de Venadito because she is wanted to be in attendance on the Queen-Regent at San Sebastian. The "Lalande", I am told by Souhart, is to go down the coast to Mazagan & Mog[ador]. to obtain news; a tribe a little way inland fr. the former place has murdered its vice-govr. & elected a man in his place. Souhart goes in her. Since I have heard this I think it will be better to keep the "Bramble" a few days longer.

The "Lalande" easily does 18 knots; the "Bramble's" bottom is so foul that 9 is the utmost that can be screwed out of her.

I wonder what the coll[eague]s: will say when they see the Mediterranean squadron coming to Gib[raltar]. on the 7th. Nothing I am afraid will convince them that we have no desire at all to possess ourselves of Tangier. And perh[aps]. that is not to be wondered at, when it is a common topic of conversation among the men at Gib. that we shall come here one day or other.

That sort of talk seems to me on a par with the suggestion that we shld. give up Gib. in exchange for Ceuta.

I am keeping Harris at Fez till the Sultan arrives there, after wch. event I shall have no further need for him. He has done very well, I think, especially in influencing the Wazan people. May I give him £100? He ran a considerable personal risk, & it wld. have been difficult to find any other European willing at such a moment of uncertainty to undertake such a service.

   y.v.t. E.S.

59. Satow to Sanderson (stamped p.81)

Tangier

6 July 94

My dear Sanderson,

Potestad is doubtful whether he will come back here. He was to have got an increase of pay, but the Cortes[37] refused it. Now there is a talk of his being apptd. to Mexico, but he vows he wld. rather retire. What he really chafes at is that tho' everyone attached to M[artinez]. C[ampos]'s mission, & even 3 of his own subordinates got decorations, the Sp. Govt. has not vouchsafed any recognition of his labours during the Melilla business. I shall be very sorry if he goes. He is perfectly straight & we are on the very friendliest terms. That of course makes some of the others jealous but that does no harm.

---

[37] Cortes Generales: The legislative chambers of Spain.

PRO 30/33 14/6 Semi-official Letters from Morocco (March 8, 1894 – July 10, 1894)

B[oleslawski]. came to me the other day[38] bent on instilling into my head the notion that I was giving myself away to the Fr[ench]. & ought to be more on my guard ag[ain]st. their wicked machinations. In return I deplored the line taken up by Tat[tenbach], with whom I was most anxious to work in concert, but he made it impossible. Then Tat. came a day or two after [on July 4th] to lament over the intimate relations betw. the Fr. legn. & Pot. who had actually recd. a banquet on board the "Tage" (wch. never took place at all). Then he discovered great uneasiness at the visit of Souhart to Mogador in the "Lalande", & suggested that some dark design lay at the bottom of it. Lastly Gentile came to hint that Souhart's trip was connected with the intrigues formerly carried on by the Fr. consul with a leading chieftain in the Sus.

Tat: lately took upon himself to write an official letter to the Portuguese in support of a B.S's [British Subject's] claim agst. a Portug[uese]. Jew. I have got him to apologize for his officiousness, & have into the bargain convicted him of equivocating. He is not to be believed on his word, I am afraid.

Cantag[alli]. I hear is better in health, & has hopes of coming back in the autumn.

y.v.t.

P.S. The "Lalande" returned this morning, having spent only two hours at Mog[ador]. I suspect Souhart was very glad to get back to Tangier, for she is most uncomfortable.

60. Satow to Sanderson

7 July 94

My dear Sanderson,

The proposal of Señor Moret for joint action for the suppression of contraband trade in arms, to be limited to "the three Powers, who," d'Aub[igny]. said the other day rather indiscreetly at a meeting of the coll[eague]s: "are principally interested in Morocco", is I think certain to excite jealousy. Already the notion that Eng. Fr. & Spain are working in concert has aroused the suspicions of the legations of the triple alliance,[39] & Tat.

---

[38] On July 2, 1894 – see Satow's diary.
[39] The Triple Alliance of 1882 was an agreement between Germany, Austria-Hungary and Italy. It expired in 1915.

particularly seems to feel that he is being left out in the cold. Yet he is a man who never can be got to work in accord with others. The Italians are easier to deal with, for they wish to go with us. So if in some way Moret's plans can be enlarged so as to take in the Triple Alliance, I think there will be more chance of success.

I don't much believe in the practicability of a preventive service carried on by Spaniards. They seem to have smuggling in their blood.

My own idea wld. be, if the thing is to be done at all, to get the Sultan to transfer his powers to the Dipl. Body, as he has already done in quarantine, & to give them his steamer the "Hassani" to be a revenue cruiser. They must have funds to pay a proper staff of inspectors & coast guards. Prob. 2 vessels wld. be needed, one for the Atlantic coast, 1 for Tetuan & the Riff coast.

It seems that during Morant's absence fr. Tetuan last week the local British smugglers took the opportunity of running a cargo.

There seem to be some indications that Fr. is prepared to accord to Spain the lead in Morocco, tho' the local legation wld. oppose any such idea. But as d'Aub. & Souhart are both going away, perh. that does not matter, & Monbel will come out properly primed. As Spain cannot keep the lead, then at some future day Fr. will come in to help her. We shall not be able to stand aloof, & shall prob. be able to assert our claim to an equal share of influence. The next phase wld. be a sort of triple control, if we succeeded in beating the others out of the field, wch. I think wld. be diff[icult]. The Ital. legation has its agents everywhere, & the Germ. wld. lose no opportunity of making difficulties. In spite ∴ [therefore] of personal peculiarities of colleagues, I hold that it is better to induce the triple alliance, or at any rate Germany & Italy, to take a leading share in the affairs of this country. I observe that these two countries are inclined to turn the cold shoulder to Spain just now, in revenge for the non-ratification of the commercial treaties; but Italy has political interests of importance & Germany commercial interests of value. They cannot afford, I shld. think, to forego the chance of saving the <u>status quo</u>, wch. it is prob. wld. go fast downhill if Fr. Spain & Engl. jointly hold the reins to the exclusion of others.

P[otestad]. talks of going on leave next week, & will make a report on the question bef. he goes. He will tell Moret that he has done all that is feasible with his colleagues, & that it

PRO 30/33 14/6   Semi-official Letters from Morocco (March 8, 1894 – July 10, 1894)

is now necessary to address the resp[ective]. Govts.

      y.v.t.

P.S. The legation hinted at by d'Aub. as taking a benevolent view of smuggling is the Portuguese. Colaço is no better than a Moor. How shld. he be, having been born & brought up here. E.S.

61. Satow to Sanderson

Tangier

8.7.94

My dear Sanderson,

 I ought to have told you that when the question of recognizing A A [Abdel Aziz] was being debated, Moret almost at the beginning wrote or telegraphed, I think the latter, to P[otestad]. to at once offer all moral and <u>material</u> support to him. He told me of it at the time, but said he shld. not do anything so compromising, & begged me not to repeat it. But his interpreter Saavedra, who had read the telegram, told Torres without his chief's authority. P. related to me how it had slipped out, but added that he thought Torres wld. take no notice of it, & that he himself shld. not allude to it further. It seems however to have leaked out, for the triple alliance legations know it, & they think Fr. capped the offer, coupling it with a warning not to interfere with Tuat.

 This incident & one or two other little things seem to show that Moret is ambitious of playing a leading part in this country. His proposal that Spain shld. patrol the coast is another instance. I suppose he is egged on by the Fr. Amb. Everyone says he is a vain & weak man, to whom this idea wld. appeal strongly. But it is altogether a mistake for him to suppose that the Moors will fall in with it. They hate Spaniards, & can gauge the value of their support.

     y.v.t

      E.S.

62. Satow to Maclean

41.

PRO 30/33 14/6   Semi-official Letters from Morocco (March 8, 1894 – July 10, 1894)

My d[ea]r. Maclean   10.7.94

Yr. letter of 28 June was delivered here day before yesterday.

My own personal feeling abt. visiting the Court is to leave here abt. middle of 9 ber [November], but I have not yet officially informed the F.O. & therefore I think it will be better not to say anything to the M[ooris]h. Govt. at pres[en]t. But I shall write home & at once abt. the matter. In the meantime, can you let me know what w[ou]ld. be a good present to make to the young Sultan. For his father I was going to get a shire stallion, but the y[ou]ng. man may have other preferences. Also tell me whether you think Sept[ember]. w[ou]ld. be a good time for my visit.

[Dr.] Cortes is now waiting at Rabat for a st[eame]r. to bring him on here, & he will take his time abt. going to Fez. At least that is the pres[en]t. idea.

Russi told me a few days ago that the roads were quite quiet betw[een]. Morocco City & Saffi. Round DaB [Dar al Baida] there are some signs of unrest, & it wld. be an excellent thing if the various Kaids [tribal chiefs] cld. go back to their provinces, or if the Govt. are going to make any changes in the personnel, that it shld. be done without delay. For I imagine that until the tribes get some one to rule them, there will not be entire tranquility.

We must not let Gharnit forget [Lewis] Forde's Habassi claim. Now that the Court is in the vicinity, it will be easy for him to have that money collected. I do not wish to have it supposed that because a Sultan dies all business is to be at an end. To carry on as usual is the best proof that they can give us that they are a govt.

Of course the proposed exped[itio]n. agst. the Gharb of wch. we were told is at an end, but I shld, be glad if you wld. find out for certain whether this is so.

I wrote on June 29 to Gharnit abt. the necessity of making the proclamation agst. Isabelinos [coin] effective everywhere. Now I am told that at Mazagan the Admors [Jewish scholars] have not been vigilant, & that a large quantity have been smuggled in there by Ansado who is agent for Nahon of Tangier. I wish a stop cld. be put to this in the gen[era]l. interest, not only of our trade, but in that of the Moors themselves, who are being flooded by this demonetized coin wch. always drives out the good coin. I am going to write to Torres on the subj. Perh[aps]. if you had a talk with the Amin Mukri you cld. get him to see the importance of the matter.

PRO 30/33 14/6   Semi-official Letters from Morocco (March 8, 1894 – July 10, 1894)

The French still have the Tage & Lalande here, & I keep on the Bramble for company. The Spaniards have no ship. There was a Portuguese iron-clad here for a while, & as it was reported to me that she was going down the coast & wld. prob. visit Arzila, I telegraphed to Lisbon. The result was that she was ordered over to Cadiz nominally to take in coals & water, & I rather hope she will not return to these shores. There is a Brazilian here, who loafed in on his way fr. Toulon to Rio, without any special object.

   y.v.t.

Satow's list of letters is at the end of the notebook.

PRO 30/33 14/6 Semi-official Letters from Morocco (March 8, 1894 – July 10, 1894)

No.	date	to whom	p.	No.	date	to whom
	8 Mar	Sanderson	1		Apr. 21	Sanderson
19	12 "	Maclean	6	26	" 25	Maclean
	14 "	Sanderson	9		" 25	Sanderson
	20 "	Sanderson	12		" 26	Anderson
20	20 "	Maclean	16	27	" 27	Maclean
	21 "	Sanderson	18		May 1	Sanderson
21	22 "	Maclean	20	28	" 3	Maclean
22	23 "	Maclean	24		" 5	Sanderson
	27 "	Sanderson	26	29	" 16	Maclean
23	30 "	Maclean	29		" 17	Sanderson
	31 "	P. Anderson	31		" 27	Maclean
	4 Apr.	Sanderson	35		" 31	C. Nairn
	5 "	"	41	31	June 1	Maclean
	5 "	Ld. Rosebery	42		" 5	Sanderson
24	6 "	Maclean	45		" 5	Anderson
	11 "	Sanderson	49	S	" 6	Sanderson
	12 "	Bergne	54		" 7	"
	12 "	Sanderson	55		" 8	Anderson
25	13 "	Maclean	56	33	" 9	Maclean
S	13 "	Sanderson	59		" 10	Sanderson
S	14 "	Sanderson	60		" 13	"
	16 "	Sanderson	61	35	" 13	Maclean
	21 "	Sanderson	{65a, 66}	36	" 15	"

PRO 30/33 14/6   Semi-official Letters from Morocco (March 8, 1894 – July 10, 1894)

to whom	p.				
Sanderson	70		17 June	Sanderson	138
Maclean	72	37	18 "	Maclean	141
Sanderson	73		20 "	Sanderson	143
Anderson	76	38	20 "	Maclean	145
Maclean	80	39	21 "	"	147
Sanderson	81	40	22 "	"	148
Maclean	85		23 "	Sanderson	150
Sanderson	87		July 1	"	157
Maclean	91		" 6	"	161
Sanderson	95		" 7	"	164
Maclean	99		" 8	"	168
C. Nairn	103	41	" 10	Maclean	169
Maclean	105				
Sanderson	110				
Anderson	115				
Sanderson	119				
"	122				
Anderson	124				
Maclean	126				
Sanderson	127				
"	131				
Maclean	133				
"	135				

PRO 30/33 14/6   Semi-official Letters from Morocco (March 8, 1894 – July 10, 1894)

Photograph of the list.

END OF PRO 30/33 14/6

PRO 30/33 14/7   Semi-official Letters from Morocco (July 10, 1894 to November 22, 1894)

PRO 30/33 14/7   Satow's Semi-Official Correspondence

1. Satow to Sanderson

Tangier

10 July 1894

My d[ea]r. Sanderson,

H. Maclean writes to me fr[om]. Mequinez that Gharnit had consulted him ab[ou]t. the visits of the F.M.M. [Foreign Ministers] to the Sultan at Fez. As the accommodation is limited there, & the Moorish Gov[ernmen]t. w[ou]ld. be unable to house them all at once, Macl[ean]. suggested that they sh[ou]ld. be invited to go in couples, & he thinks that advice will be acted upon. He adds that if I want to go up independently without waiting for the M[oorish]. Govt. he c[ou]ld. find animals & tents, & manage to put me up.

This plan will I am sure annoy all the colleagues, as there are none who w[ou]ld. like travelling together. Even if the chiefs were friendly, their staffs w[ou]ld. fall out. I c[ou]ld. get along with [the Spanish minister] Potestad, but not with all the men who w[ou]ld. go with him. Besides it seems likely that he w[ou]ld. be transferred to Constantinople.

I think the best plan w[ou]ld. be for me to say that I will go ab[ou]t. the middle of September, & that I sh[ou]ld. travel alone with my own staff.

If you approve of this I will send an official estimate of the expenditure & a list of presents for the young Sultan, who I understand confidentially is still of an age to appreciate toys. Those w[ou]ld. take the place of the shire stallion we were going to give the late Sultan. I have written to Kaid Maclean to let me know what will be wanted.

Things are going quietly enough at Mequinez but the Chamber[lai]n. B. H. [Bu Hamed]¹ is gradually concentrating all the power in his hands. The Sultan's mother takes a leading part. The Vizier Hadj El Mati & Cid Ali Misfiwi also are influential, but in a lesser degree. Hadj el Mati is losing ground. There is also an idea of getting rid of Gharnit & making Torres F.M. at Tangier, with powers on the scale exercised by Bargash. That w[ou]ld. mean perh[aps]. greater celerity in the settlement of claims, & local matters of small import, but it

---

¹ Bu (Ba) Hamed (1840-1900). Grand Vizier and de facto ruler of Morocco, 1894-1900.

PRO 30/33 14/7   Semi-official Letters from Morocco (July 10, 1894 to November 22, 1894)

w[ou]ld. be a bar to any kind of progress.

Maclean says that as soon as the Sultan reaches Fez, say ab[ou]t. the 15th, the greater part of his army will disperse, the governors going off to their provinces with their followers. Then there will be a critical time, as some of the tribes round Fez are disaffected. Maclean's courage is undoubted but I think he is a little pessimist. After I have been to Fez I shall be better able to gauge the situation, and the exact signification of what he writes me.

The "Tage" left today. Tomorrow I am going over to Gib[raltar]. with Pot[estad], privately to have a look at the fleet, in the "Bramble",[2] & on Friday the Admiral pays me a private visit here. After that I think the "Bramble" may as well go away. I have kept her here as a pendant to the "Tage" & "Lalande".

y.v.t.

E.S.

2. Satow to Kaid Harry Maclean (p. 2 stamped in notebook)

No. 42

July 13, 1894

My dear Maclean,

Your 3 letters of July 3, 6 & 7 reached me on the 10th, & that of the 10th this morning. Much obliged for the various items of news. Owing to a misunderstanding, I have kept your first courier waiting these 3 days, & now send him c. this note. I will desp[atch]. Kaid el Arbi tomorrow with the football & lawn tennis balls, as soon as I receive them fr. Gib[raltar]. & I will also write a letter to Bu Hamed.

With regard to shunting Gharnit & making [Cid Mohammed] Torres really F.M. [Foreign Minister] I sh[ou]ld. have no reason to regret the first part of the plan, for he has not been a friend of ours at all. I consider that the long delay in my getting those 2 men given up was owing to him, & it was a bad beginning of our relations. But I am not sure that I sh[ou]ld. wish to see Torres endowed with greater powers, as that w[ou]ld. mean that the business of the F.RR. [Foreign Representatives] w[ou]ld. be relegated to Tangier. I

---

[2] HMS Bramble was a Bramble-class gunboat. The class consisted of four gunboats with six 4-inch guns and four machine guns, built for the Royal Navy in 1886.

PRO 30/33 14/7   Semi-official Letters from Morocco (July 10, 1894 to November 22, 1894)

sh[ou]ld. prefer to transact all business of importance direct with the Court, & Torres is not our friend. I am told he has not forgiven us for getting him reprimanded ab[ou]t. the Juan Trinidad affair. But the question is too important to make up one's mind on in a hurry, & I sh[ou]ld. prefer to wait until my visit to Court before I can say wch. w[ou]ld. best suit us. I do not mean by this that I expect the Moorish Govt. to be guided in this matter by what I say, or what the Coll[eague]s: might say, only that I am not ready to express an opinion.

With reg[ard]. to my coming to Court, I have written privately to F.O. that I think it w[ou]ld. be well for me to make a start ab[ou]t. the middle of Sept[ember]. & that I wish to go up by myself, not with any colleagues, that I will accept your offer to lend me some tents & animals: that I sh[ou]ld. not mind being at Fez with other colleagues, but I c[ou]ld. not travel with them or their staffs.

When I come it will be, as we have always said, a visit of courtesy, to make acquaintance with the leading people, not to ask for commercial concessions or to present a host of claims. I shall not want to stay long, as I must get home on leave before the winter sets in. But until I get a reply fr[om]. the F.O. it will be best not to say anything definite to the Court people. There is no objection to your telling Bu Hamed what you <u>suppose</u> my ideas are.

I read the pencil letter you sent me: it is the composition of some harmless enthusiast, very amusing.

Hadj el Mati's fall does not appear to have been long delayed. If it is the case that he & his brother were for setting up Mulai Mohammed, are they likely to attempt anything of the kind now they have been turned out? I am told that the Jamai family is very powerful in Fez.

With respect to Gharnit, I have frequently heard it rumoured that the Amin Abdersalam Mukri w[ou]ld. probably be his successor. Betw[een]. you & me, I sh[ou]ld. be pleased to see this, for I have heard excellent reports of his honesty & capacity for business.

I sh[ou]ld. be very glad if the reports ab[ou]t. Egypt brought by the man you mention sh[ou]ld. suggest to the leading Moors that something might be done to reform their own administration. What you say ab[ou]t. candidates for governorships having to pay for their posts is of course very true, & the idea of getting things improved sounds Utopian. On the other hand, it w[ou]ld. not be possible for me to tell the Tangier & Angera people to put

PRO 30/33 14/7   Semi-official Letters from Morocco (July 10, 1894 to November 22, 1894)

forward a candidate & make up a purse. But since Bu Hamed has been good enough to say that these two Kaids shall be changed, I sh[ou]ld. like to mention the name of a man who is very well spoken of here. Cid Abdersalam Ahardan. I do not know him personally, but I understand that he is not likely to rob the people & so make trouble for the Govt. If you think it w[ou]ld. be safe to suggest him, pray do so on my acc[oun]t. Formerly Tangier & Angera were one govr.ship, & I believe it w[ou]ld. conduce greatly to good gov[ernmen]t. if the two were re-united.

I am very pleased to hear of B.H's language ab[ou]t. y[ou]r. services, & I hope you may prosper & that your friends will keep in power.

There is no foundation as far as I know for the report that I am going to Japan.[3] My own belief is that it will not be offered to me, & I have no intention of asking for it. I like Morocco, & it interests me greatly.

   y.v.t.

P[otestad]. is perh[aps]. going to Constantinople. He will go on leave in a few days. d'Aub[igny]. only awaits news of the Sultan's arr[ival]. at Fez to start likewise. Tat[tenbach]. remains here all the summer. Cantagalli I hear is better.

   E.S.

3. Satow to Kaid Maclean
[No.] 43
July 14.
My dr. Macl.

Yr. acc[oun]t. for couriers etc. wch. you sent me the other day was $328.25 & the £50 I paid in to Coutt's on yr. behalf at the rate of exchange of yesterday was equiv[alen]t. to $307.50. So I still owe you $20.75 on that acc[oun]t. I enclose Coutts & Co's receipt for the £50. If you want anything more, please let me know.

---

[3] Power Henry Le Poer Trench arrived in Tokyo as Minister to Japan on August 20, 1894. He succeeded Hugh Fraser who died en poste on June 4, 1894. Trench suffered an attack of 'aphasia and paralysis' in late February 1895. Then Satow arrived in Tokyo as Minister on July 28, 1895.

PRO 30/33 14/7   Semi-official Letters from Morocco (July 10, 1894 to November 22, 1894)

y.v.t.   E.S.

4. Satow to Kaid Maclean (stamped p.5)

[No.] 44

July 14.

My Dr. Macl[ean].

Here is a letter for Cid Hmet ben Morsa, & a copy of the Engl[ish]. for your edification. One of these days I will write to him ab[ou]t. smuggling arms & ammunition, wch. is carried on at various places, esp. Tetuan, Tangier & I am told, the coast near DaB. It is to the interest of the Moors that this sh[ou]ld. be restricted as much as possible, & also to that of the Fr[ench]. & Sp[anish]. Therefore any proposals that sh[ou]ld. come fr[om]. them for the suppression of contraband sh[ou]ld. not lightly be put aside, but be carefully considered. Nothing in this direction can be achieved, I believe, without joint action of the Moorish Govt. & the foreign leg[ation]s.

y.v.t.

Sunday (15)   Recd. yr. no.15 yesterday afternoon. Many thanks for the correction. The other letter for Gharnit is ab[ou]t. some Benani at Fez who owe money to various Bss. [British subjects]. We have been urging these cases both at Fez & here for some time past, but unsuccessfully. The debtors are able to pay, as they have property, but will not sell them. If Gh[arnit]. is out of office, please hand the letter to B.H. c. if necessary explanations.

E.S.

5. Satow to Kaid Maclean

[No.] 45

19.7.94.

My dr. Maclean,

Your no.16 reached me on the 15[th] at 7 p.m. & No 17 on the 17th ab[ou]t. 4 or 5 o'cl.

I sh[ou]ld. be glad to hear whether there is any confirmation of the story of the yr. [younger?] Jamai having written a letter asking for foreign backing for their party. Also

381

PRO 30/33 14/7   Semi-official Letters from Morocco (July 10, 1894 to November 22, 1894)

whether the Sultan has sent for the Beni Warein & Ulad el Hadj to guard the neighbourhood of Fez. This latter piece of news came to us thro' Gentile, & seems to have some connection with what was said in y[ou]r. No.17 of the Sultan having let out the 100 men of the Isheroughan, who seem to be neighbours of the other two tribes mentioned.

[Sent his man to Terry to have his finger attended to.

Glad to find story ab[ou]t. [Walter B.] Harris untrue. To get the propagator of the lie punished if advisable.

To thank Harris for letter of 13th.][4]

6. Satow to Sanderson
July 20. 94.
My d[ea]r. Sanderson,

After all the Ad[miral]. did not come here. He only wanted to know fr[om]. me whether ships were needed for Morocco, & I was able to tell him, when I went over to Gib[raltar]. that for protecting life & property of Bss. [British subjects] they were not in my opinion necessary. With political reasons for having ships there I had nothing to do. I sent "Bramble" away yesterday, the "Lalande" having left the bay. D'Aub[igny]. tells me however that she only went to Gib. to coal, but he thinks there is no reason for retaining her any longer. The Port[uguese]. ironclad came back here yesterday.

Moret's project of getting a mandate fr[om]. the PP. [Powers] to overhaul foreign vessels in Moorish waters & search for contraband arms was disclosed by d'Aub. to the German & the Belgian. Then they all came down on me in succession for information. I listened, & told them they must be cautious abt. accepting the story in the way it had been told them, but I refused to satisfy their curiosity abt. a communication that had been made to me confidentially. At the same time I showed them the instructions I had recd. fr. Ld. Kimberley, & convinced them that as far as H.M. Govt. were concerned they wished to act in concert with all the PP. The coll[eague]s of course saw in Moret's plan of consulting only c. Engl[and]. & Fr[ance]. only another proof of the disposition to settle the affairs of

---

[4] Satow's square parentheses

PRO 30/33 14/7   Semi-official Letters from Morocco (July 10, 1894 to November 22, 1894)

Morocco betw[een]. the 3 PP. & this made the German & the Italian particularly furious.

The dismissal of the 2 Jamai fr[om]. office was bound to come. They had been plotting to put Cid H'med ben Musa out of the way fr[om]. the 1st moment after the proclamation of A[bdel]. A[ziz]. Whether it was M[ulai]. M[ohammed]. or M[ohammed]. J[amai]. that they wished to have seems not quite clear: Maclean says the latter, other people the former. If Cid H'med manages to hold his own, I think it will be to our advantage. He sent me very friendly messages thro' Maclean, & I have written him a letter thanking him for his expressions of good will. Maclean says his mother was a Jewess, & if so we may expect him to treat the Jews with fairness. The changes that have taken place were predicted to Allan Maclean by a C[our]t. Eunuch who was passing thro' DaB [Dar al Baida] on the 1st, so they do not strike one as being of the hasty character they seem to have to people like Gentile, who did not know what was passing. His information comes fr. one of the Ulema at Fez, & natives are not as trustworthy informants as Europeans who can gain the confidence of the Govt. people. Macleod has done very well on the present occasion; he stands well with Mukri, the chief Amin at Fez, & from him learnt a great deal of what is going on. Harris has gone on to Mequinez.   [report abt. his visiting mosques untrue. His teleg[ram]s. thro' me to Times Reuter diff[icult]. to manage – his disguise as Moor necessary to reach Fez. Colls: expected movements.

Am not convinced that story of Mohd. Seghir writing to ask for Fr. support is true. Gharnit supposed to have a foreign protection paper. Hope Mukri may succeed him.][5]
E.M.S.

7. Satow to Kaid Maclean (stamped p.8)

[No.] 46

July 21. 1894

My d[ea]r. Maclean,

In my No. 41 I wrote to you ab[ou]t. the importation of Isabeline coins into Mazagan, & said I sh[ou]ld. address Torres on the subject. I now enclose a copy of the letter I sent to

---

[5] Satow's parentheses

PRO 30/33 14/7 Semi-official Letters from Morocco (July 10, 1894 to November 22, 1894)

Torres, requesting him to lay the matter before the Sultan.

I sh[ou]ld. be much obliged if you w[ou]ld. urge the matter upon the attention of the Grand Vizier, & if necessary show him the enclosed copy of my letter to Torres.

        y.v.t.

8. Satow to Sanderson
Secret.   21.7.94.
To Sanderson advising bill on Sec[retar]y. of State for £50, & enclosing receipts of A. Maclean & Capt. of "Zeus".

9. Satow to Kaid Maclean
[No.] 47
Tangier
23.7.94
My dear Maclean,

Something that has reached me lately produced on me the impression that the Moorish Authorities as a whole don't treat Macleod properly, as an agent of the Br. Govt. charged c. the protection of B.Ss. [British subjects] I took therefore the opportunity of informing Gh. that M. is a person in my confidence, & requesting him to listen to any representations M. may make to him on behalf of the BSs. at Fez. As the Fr[ench]. are abt. to send to Fez a V-C. de carrière [a professional Vice-Consul], I am particularly anxious to give Macleod all due support, & I am sure I can rely on you to second my efforts in this matter.

        y.v.t.

10. Satow to Sanderson (stamped p.9)
24.7.94.
My dear Sanderson,

The Sultan entered Fez safely on the 21st, & so the 1st act of the drama is over. He looked pale & nervous, I am told. The poor boy seems to appreciate the perils of his position. When he had his 1st interview with the Grand Sherif of Wazan he burst into tears

PRO 30/33 14/7   Semi-official Letters from Morocco (July 10, 1894 to November 22, 1894)

& hid his face in the cushions on wch. he was seated. Bu H'med does everything, & his brother the Min[ister]. of War cannot move a step without referring to him. It seems that no further changes are in immediate contemplation, & that Gharnit will remain. So that the idea of giving Torres the same powers as Bargash formerly had seems to have been dropped, if it was ever seriously entertained.

There may perh[aps]. be some trouble among the tribes of Rahamna near Morocco, who have written to the Govt. to say that they will rule themselves. But there is a great deal more talk than action ab[ou]t. these people, & it does not seem likely, as far as I can judge, that the country is forthwith going to be torn in pieces by anarchy, any more than in the lifetime of the late Sultan. The fear of giving a foreign Power a pretext for interference seems to be pretty widespread.

Maclean writes now that there was no truth in the Fr[ench]. military mission having promised to ask the Fr. Govt. to assist the party of the fallen Viziers.

Fr[om]. what Pot[estad]. tells me it w[ou]ld. seem that the Sp. Govt. are not quite at their ease ab[ou]t. Melilla, & have some apprehensions of an outbreak there later on in the year. But at Tangier we know absolutely nothing of what passes in the Riff. The only thing that seems pretty certain is that no expedition will be sent against the Riff this year by the Sultan, & the neutral zone will not be marked out until after the Sp[anish]. Min[ister]. has been to Fez & made fresh arrangements. I think it w[ou]ld. be very imprudent to leave this matter to be dealt with by the Commandant of Melilla & Mulai Arafa.

Pot[estad]. goes on leave today. The probabilities are in favour of his coming back here. Moret, he says, told [Spanish politician Antonio] Vega de Armijo, that he w[ou]ld. not move him. He is very anxious to go to Fez with me, & I do not very well see how I can get out of it, tho' I am not by any means anxious to be thought to have him in my pocket.

[presents – end of Sept. for arrival in Fez][6]

      y.v.t.   E.S.

11. Satow to Kaid Maclean

---

[6] Satow's parentheses

PRO 30/33 14/7   Semi-official Letters from Morocco (July 10, 1894 to November 22, 1894)

Maclean No. 48
Conf[identia]l.
Tangier
26.7.94
My dr. M.,

Pr[ince]. Philip de Borbon y Braganza & one Schomerus (who represents himself as the son of a former Gov. of Elmina & of an African princess) are ab[ou]t. to proceed to Fez to offer to establish a Bank of Morocco, for wch. they will ask the Sultan to give them a concession, as well as for rlwys, mines, telegraphs, & a host of other things. They will also offer him a loan of £2 000 000 on the security of the Customhouses!

I believe these people to be mere penniless adventurers. The Prince, who is rather too-well known in Tangier, has been giving out in London that he is in a position to obtain concessions, that he is well-known at Court &c. He gets £400 & Schom. £100 for coming here, & if they are successful these sums are to be doubled. Their principal is a Mr. Allport, said to be the son of a late Rlwy. manager in England.

Sch[omerus]. asked me for a letter of introduction to Gh[arnit]. for a soldier to travel & for a house at Fez. As I look on him as little better than a knave, I refused to do anything for him, & said he must go under the aegis of Ph[ilip]. the Pr[ince]. The latter I believe has a letter fr. the Sp. Legn. Moret in his usual gushing manner gave Pr. Philip a letter of recommendation to the Sp[anish]. Chargé d'Affaires, but I don't think he w[ou]ld. have done this had he known the plans of these gentry.

I have told Macleod to be very reserved in his attitude towards them, & if questioned by the Moorish officials to say that he knows nothing ab[ou]t. them. I have not given him all the above details, wch. please keep to yourself. But I sh[ou]ld. be glad to hear what sort of reception they meet with at Court, & what progress they make with their negotiations.

   y.v.t.

12. Satow to Kaid Maclean
[No.] 49
30.7.94

PRO 30/33 14/7   Semi-official Letters from Morocco (July 10, 1894 to November 22, 1894)

My dr. Macl.

The accompanying letters to Gh[arnit]. are to request him to have certain debtors to British subjects sent into Mogador & to give orders for the settlement of a robbery claim on Seràghna. The sums are all of them some what trifling, & I think the Moorish Govt. is bound to do all in its power to get them settled.

I am going carefully thro' all the claims & sifting out all those wch. are not properly substantiated. I have no intention of presenting any that are not well-founded. If the M.G. [Moorish Government] is negligent, I suppose the responsibility will in the end be cast on them.

Thanks for your No. 20. I agree with you that it was a shame to punish a man for obeying orders, but I suppose B.H. wanted to make an example.

I hear the no. of <u>askars</u> [soldiers] has greatly diminished, & that not more than half the usual number were present on the occasion of the Sultan's entry into Fez. Is there any attempt being made to recruit the army. Without it I fear it will be difficult to maintain, or rather to restore, the authority of the Sultan.

What likelihood is there of his making a move to Morocco before the winter? I want particularly to know this, as my visit to Court must depend on H.S.M. arrangements. And can you tell me why Gharnit is so particular in asking that I sh[ou]ld. write ab[ou]t. my mission thro' Torres. It has by no means been the uniform practice in the past to announce it thro' him.

y.v.t.   E.S.

<u>13. Satow to Kaid Maclean</u>

[No.] 50

30.7.94

My dr. Ml.

When I was at Mazagan in May last I despatched a letter to Gharnit ab[ou]t. some money due fr[om]. the Moorish Govt. on acc[oun]t. of claims settled by Sir John Hay, & fr. Darel beida I wrote him another saying that I was going to give protection under Art. XVI of the Madrid convention to the 2 released agents. I wrote this partly with the hope that he

PRO 30/33 14/7   Semi-official Letters from Morocco (July 10, 1894 to November 22, 1894)

w[ou]ld. reply to me that the Sultan undertook they sh[ou]ld. not be touched, for if I had an assurance of that kind I sh[ou]ld. be quite satisfied & sh[ou]ld. not give any protection papers. But I did not wish to suggest this. If these two letters ever reached Gh[arnit]. it must have been at the moment of the Sultan's death.

I therefore enclose duplicates, wch. I beg you to hand to Gharnit, explaining that my reason for sending them is that having recd. no ans[wer]. I am afraid the originals have not reached his hands.

y.v.t.

14. Satow to Sanderson (stamped p.13)

1.8.94.

My dr. Sanderson,

Harris returned fr. Fez a couple of days ago, & has furnished me c. the enclosed notes of recent events & their bearing on the genl. situation. He takes a more hopeful view of the future than Allan Maclean, who has recently given me his ideas, wch. you will also find enclosed. My own disposition is to believe that he is a little too gloomy in his prognostications.

The Sultan's brother Mulai Omar who was Viceroy at Fez until the other day has been placed under arrest in his own house: he seems to have indulged in some feeble projects of setting up for himself, but he has been snuffed out, & I don't think we shall hear much more of him. He had ordered one of his men to cut the heads of all the drums,[7] to prevent their being beaten for the proclamation of A.A. [Abdul Aziz] When the latter got to Fez, the G.V. [Grand Vizier] had the man punished [in the] well-known Moorish manner by scoring his palms with a knife, & after filling the wounds with salt, sewing them up in wet leather.

There is perhaps some foundation for the story that the fallen ministers tried to get the Fr[ench]. to back them. The Gr[and]. Sherif Wazan, Mulai el Arbi, told Harris that the Fr[ench]. military mission knew more abt. the conspiracy than was at all proper. Maclean was asked by a friend of the ex-min[iste]r. to write to me & ask me to intercede for them, &

---

[7] A drumhead (drum skin) is a membrane stretched over one or both of the open ends of a drum.

PRO 30/33 14/7   Semi-official Letters from Morocco (July 10, 1894 to November 22, 1894)

it is very likely that the Fr. officers were also appealed to. It is not possible to find out anything abt. the doings of d'Aub[igny]. He keeps entirely aloof, & when one does get hold of him evades all conversation on political matters. He was to have left Tangier immediately after the Sultan's arrival at Fez, but there are no signs of his doing so, & it seems to be on the cards that after all he may remain, instead of going to Bucharest.

I know nothing more abt. the piratical attack on a British ship by Moors of the Riff than what I telegraphed last night.

Our friend Mukri the Treasurer of Fez has sent a message to me thro' Macleod that it is of no use my writing to Gharnit, that I had better address Bu Hamed, & send my letters thro' himself, he undertaking to have my business put thro'. Macleod replied very discreetly that he doubted whether official custom wld. allow of this. I think for the present it is better to go on writing to Gharnit. There are some debts due to Br[itish]. firms at Manchester fr. Moors at Fez, wch. I am trying to recover, & I am also trying to put a little life into some of the so-called "claims" in [Sir West] Ridgeway's list, by asking to have instructions sent to Mogador & elsewhere to attend to these somewhat mouldy affairs; namely in order to put on record that they have not been dropped altogether. Later on I shall be able to refer to these letters, if nothing is done.

I do not think it worth while to engage in the intrigue suggested by Mukri for the overthrow of Gharnit, whom he wishes to succeed. An attempt was made a few days ago to upset Mukri himself, but he succeeded in getting the Sultan's mother to take his part, & maintained his position.

The person who called himself Dr. Schomerus struck me as being a liar. He says he is the son of a late Govr. of Elmina and of an African princess, & that he had letters from Ld. K[imberley]. regretting that he had not chosen to enter the consular service. Then he produced to me an unattested copy of an agreement betw. one Allport & Prince Philip de Borbon y Braganza & himself to proceed to Morocco & obtain concessions for rlwys, telegraphs, a bank & a loan of £2 000 000. Moret gave Pr[ince]. Ph[ilip]. a letter of recommendation to the Sp[anish]. legation, wch. rather annoyed Pot[estad]. as he felt obliged to help the man after that. I have told both Macl[eod] & Macl[ea]n. to be very reserved towards these people on their arrival at Fez, & I declined to give Schomerus any

PRO 30/33 14/7   Semi-official Letters from Morocco (July 10, 1894 to November 22, 1894)

introductions to the Court.

[Marsilli [Marcilly?] gone to Fez 27 July. Souhart bringing wife out.][8]

Secret   Aug. 1. 94.
Harris' expenses   £28.18.4 &
                                    100
                              £128.18.4

I gave him £5 in cash when he left & now £123.18.4 in a cheque on my banker. Have drawn for the total

E.S.

15. Satow to Kaid Maclean

[No. 51]

2.8.94

My dr. Maclean

I have heard fr. the F.O. approving my plan of paying a visit to Fez in 9ber [September, the 9th month]. What I shld. propose to do is to leave here abt. the 28th, & if the Sultan does not furnish me c. tents & baggage animals, I will profit by y[ou]r. offer, only I think H.M.G. ought to pay for them.

I do not want to travel along with any coll[eague]:, & so please tell the M. Govt. so. Of course I have no objection to being at Fez at the same time as any or all of my coll[eague]s: but I must travel alone.

My party will consist of 5 in all, Morant, De Vismes, Reader, a doctor & myself.

Of course I shall write a proper official Note to the M. Govt. but cannot get it off by today's post. I have recd. all y[ou]r. letters up to no. 21. Many thanks for the information they contain.

y.v.t.

---

[8] Satow's parentheses

PRO 30/33 14/7   Semi-official Letters from Morocco (July 10, 1894 to November 22, 1894)

16. Satow to Kaid Maclean (stamped p.16)

[No.] 52

Tangier

6 Aug. 1894

My dear Maclean,

I send a couple of letters for Gharnit. One is to inform him that Rabat, Sali & Mehdia have been taken out of White's Consular district & placed in your brother's. All that is necessary is for Gharnit to get a letter to the Govr. of Rabat informing him that your brother [Allan Maclean] is Consul for that district in addition to the V-C. The other letter informs Gh. that I propose to leave here on the 28 Sept. to present my credentials. His suggestion that I shld. write abt. this matter to Torres I have not attended to, because I find on inquiry that the rule on these occasions has been to write direct to the Vizier for F.A. at the Court.

I shld. be much obliged if you wld. tell Bu Hamed that very disquieting reports reach me fr. Mazagan. The tribe of Boazizi has risen & expelled its Khalifa, who has taken refuge within the walls of the town with his brother-in-law the Govr. The Kaid of Oolad Furj is also at Mazagan, having had to fly fr. his people. I hope that nothing will happen at Mazagan to make it necessary to send men-of-war there for the protection of foreigners & their property. Such an incident at the present juncture wld. completely destroy the good impression produced on the Powers by the tranquility that has attended the succession of the present Sultan.

y.v.t.

P.S. very confidential

I have recd. a letter fr. the Sherif of Tamshlot (written for him by Bubeker's scribe) in wch. he tells me that the Sultan before leaving Morocco went to Tamshlot to sacrifice, & that there was some conversation abt. the Fr[ench]. people who have an oil press at Morocco, & who buy olives fr. the Sherif, & then the Sultan asked him whether he had Fr. protection, to wch. he ans[were]d. No! but I have English protection. The Sultan was silent & then observed, you did right: the Engl[ish]. are my good friends. The letter then goes on to state that he wants me to write to Torres(!) and ask him to give letters to Hadj Wida & Ben Daoud, informing them that he is under Br. protection.

PRO 30/33 14/7   Semi-official Letters from Morocco (July 10, 1894 to November 22, 1894)

This seems to me like a plant of Boobeker's, & I cannot understand what he is up to. I shld. never think of telling Torres, much less of writing to him. But I shld. be glad if you can find out anything abt. the way in wch. the Court people regard this Sherif, & whether he is in any danger, or exposed to enmity on the part of the govt. For I am certain Ld. Rosebery will not allow him to come to any harm. If you thought it desirable, I shld. be glad that you shld. drop a word to B.H. to this effect I do not like the intervention of Bub[eke]r. whom I greatly mistrust, but as the grant of protection was arranged thro' him, it is quite possible the Sherif may place confidence in him.

    y.v.t.

17. Satow to Sanderson
Aug. 7. 1894
My Dr. Sanderson,
 Sending copy of Maclean's acc[oun]t. see my letter S. of 6 June [in previous file]
$328.25 of wch. I have paid him
$307.50
 <u>9.85</u> footballs
$317.35

18. Satow to Sanderson (stamped p.18)
Private
7.8.94
My dr. Sanderson,
 At the beginning of Oct. last with Ld. R[osebery]'s approval, I gave Br. protection to the Sherif of Tamshlot near Morocco City rather than let him fall into the hands of the Fr[ench]. Now I receive a letter of wch. De Vismes has made me a translation, asking me to inform Torres of his having protection, & to get letters to the 2 Gov[ernor]s. of Morocco City informing them of his being under Br[itish]. protection. This letter was written by Bubker's scribe, & I am asked to send the letters that Torres is to write thro' him. I have not complied with this request, for I am not quite certain of Bubker's good faith or honesty, but

PRO 30/33 14/7   Semi-official Letters from Morocco (July 10, 1894 to November 22, 1894)

I have written to Kaid Maclean to try and find out how the Court people regard this Sherif, and whether he is in any danger; & in case he thinks it desirable, to hint to the Grand Vizier that the British Govt. will not allow him to come to any harm.

If you think it better I will write a conf[idential]. desp[atch]. abt. the whole affair. I enclose a copy of the letter, so that you may see exactly what the Sherif says, or is represented as saying.

y.v.t.

P.S. I wrote to Ld. R. at the time informing him of what I had done.

19. Satow to Sanderson

9.8.94

My d[ea]r. Sanders[o]n.

The "Epoca" has it that I have presented an "energetic claim" to Torres respecting the piratical attack on the sch[oone]r. "Mayer." There is not a word of truth in this, for I have not even mentioned the subject to Torres, & propose to say nothing unless I receive instructions.[9]

The same paper talks of an attempt to poison the Sultan. H. Maclean [or Harry Kaid Maclean?] writing on the 2nd says that for several days he had been unwell, & for the last 2 had not appeared outside his apartments. He had been asked by Bu Hamed for guidance wch. he supposed was for the Sultan, who was reported to have a good deal of fever. The boy overeats himself & does not take exercise. He used to enjoy playing football, but the court people consider it undignified, & have put a stop to it.

There is a curious state of things in the country S. of DaB [Dar al Baida]. All the governors being absent at court, the principal tribes refuse to recognize the authority of their substitutes, & are living under a sort of federal régime of their own, but keeping order on the roads by the enactment of severe regulations agst. plunder of caravans etc. In 1 or 2

---

[9] This is true at the time of writing. However, see Satow's diary for August 23, 1894 (Ruxton, p.438) and his letter No. 31 below to Kaid Maclean. He mentions the piratical attack on the Mayer to Torres, and indicates that he will "present the definite demands of H.M.G." later. These included an indemnity. On January 16, 1895 Maclean took a note from Satow to Gharnit about the piracy.

PRO 30/33 14/7   Semi-official Letters from Morocco (July 10, 1894 to November 22, 1894)

cases they have killed the governor's substitutes, whom I am told well deserved their fate. A couple of these worthies, who had made their escape, took refuge at Mazagan, & old Redman was in a fright lest the tribes shld. attack the town in order to obtain poss[essio]n. of them. But finally yielding to the representations of the consular body, the gov[ernor]. sent them off under a strong escort to DaB, & Mazagan is tranquil again. As the southern govrs. have now started fr. Fez for their provinces, under the leadership of Mohd.-el-Amrani, brother-in-law of the late Sultan, it is prob[able]. that the auth[ority]. of the govt. will be shortly re-established.

Precisely the same sort of things occurred in 1874 when Mulai el Hassan came to the throne.

d'Aub[igny]. left on the 6th, & I hear that Monbel is expected in 3 or 4 weeks time.

y.v.t.

W.B. Harris leaves today for London.

20. Satow to Kaid Maclean (stamped p.20)

[No.] 53

9.8.94.

My dr. Maclean,

Thanks for your Nos. 23 & 24. It is a great pity they don't let the young Sultan amuse himself at football or anything else that he likes. There is a teleg. in the "Epoca" saying that private teleg[ram]s. had been recd. in Lond[on]. on the 4th speaking of an attempt to poison(!) the Sultan!

Also that I had presented an "energetic reclamation" to Torres regarding the piratical attack of the 26th ulto. [last month, i.e. July] on a Gib[raltar]. sch[oone]r. near Alhucemas. I have not even mentioned the matter to Torres, as no instructions have reached me from the F.O.

I enclose Macleod's bill for the tennis balls &c. [Margin: $9.85] wch. I have deducted fr. the balance I owe you for couriers, etc.

The Khalifa of Buaziz & the Kaid of Ooled Furj were sent under a strong escort to DaB by the Govr. of Magazan, to whom the consular body at that port had represented the

PRO 30/33 14/7   Semi-official Letters from Morocco (July 10, 1894 to November 22, 1894)

danger of keeping them in the town. Fr[om]. what I hear these two tribes had much provocation fr. their Kaids [chiefs].

Who were the 2 Englishmen who came to Fez & wanted to see the Sultan? You do not mention their names.

It is sickening to hear that Gharnit again puts me off with pretences abt. fighting in Habassi.

He seems to have had a talk with [Jules] Huret the correspondent of the "Figaro", and to have told him that Engl[and]. had offered to buy Tangier, but that the Sultan had refused. What an unconscionable old liar it [Gharnit] is. Huret publ[ishe]d. the whole of his conversation; among other things he said that the influence of Engl. had come to nought some yrs. before the late Sultan's death. That may be true, but for a minister for F.A. to say these things is indiscreet.

Pray don't let him escape settling the affair of Murdoch Butler & Co. It ought to have been seen to by us long ago.

y.v.t.

21. Satow to Sanderson - Letter summary

13 Aug. Wrote to Sanderson the chief contents of Maclean's no. 25 of Aug. 6, & reported tenor of Galicia's conversation yesterday.[10]

22. Satow to Kaid Maclean (stamped p.21)

[No.] 54

13 Aug. 1894.

My dr. Maclean,

The Diario de Tanger's M[ooris]h. corresp[onden]t. (who I believe is a Benani, cousin of the man who was c. Kerdec in 1892, the ex-interpreter to the forces in Egypt) says that Marsilli [Marcilly?] had a private audience of B.H. If that is true, I hope you will be able to

---

[10] See Satow's diary for August 12, 1894. "Galicia came, complaining that d'Aubigny had contradicted him in his priv[ate]. letter to Pot[estad]. abt. the Moret proposals for combating contraband…"

PRO 30/33 14/7   Semi-official Letters from Morocco (July 10, 1894 to November 22, 1894)

arrange for Macleod to be recd. also. I shall write to Macleod that he is not to have business relations with the Gr[and]. Vizier, or go to him on any matter without special instructions. He is to settle his affairs with the Basha or with anyone whom the Sultan may app[oin]t. to attend to Viceconsular affairs at Fez, & he may go to Gharnit unofficially, if he thinks his aid likely to be of any use.

[Hadj Abdulkerim] Brisha, who was formerly at DaB & lives now at Tetuan, wld. be a good man for Basha of Tangier & Angera. But I am told there is something agst. him, that he treated badly the Circassian woman who was one of the four, the Sultan's mother being another. So perhaps he is not in favour at Court. If however this is more gossip without foundation, there is no man I shld. be better pleased to have here, for he has sometimes been serviceable to us.

   y.v.t.

23. Satow to Kaid Maclean (stamped p.22)

[No.] 55

Aug. 15, 1894

My dr. Maclean,

Many thanks for y[ou]r. No. 26. As soon as I receive Gharnit's official letter of reply saying that the Sultan will be able to receive me, I will write about tents & transport.

Thank you for your efforts to make B.H. look on the consular ? [question] in the right light. It is of course very unwise to make diff[iculties]. abt. Marsilli[11] or Macleod. The latter I am sure they have no reason to complain of, & it is useless their objecting to Marsilli. Much better take the matter with a good grace, since it is inevitable. I am writing to Gharnit a letter on the subject of language used to Macleod by him the other day in the presence of a Sherif, and enclose a copy of the Engl. wch. please show to Macleod. It is all over the place that the M[ooris]h. Govt. have made difficulties abt. Marsilli's arrival.

I read in one paper that Sid Taher Simra[?] Benani has been apptd. to the charge of matters relating to Consular protection, in another that he is to have charge of the claims of

---

[11] In Satow's diary he appears as 'Marcilly'.

PRO 30/33 14/7 Semi-official Letters from Morocco (July 10, 1894 to November 22, 1894)

foreigners & foreign protégés at Fez agst. Moorish subjects. Which is it?

The two Jamai arrived at Tetuan on the evening of the 12th.

y.v.t.

24. Satow to Kaid Maclean

[No.] 56

17.8.94.

My dr. Macl.

c. ref. [With reference] to my no. 55 of the 15th I enclose you a copy of the Arabic version of my note to Gharnit, & I sh[ou]ld. be very glad if you would show it to B.H. as my reply to Gh's language to Macleod concerning consular officers at Fez.

I want Macleod to be on friendly terms c. [with] both Gh[arnit]. & the Gr[and]. Viz[ier]., tho' he is not in official relations with them. Consequently I am very much annoyed at Gh's. using such inconsiderate language.

y.v.t.

25. Satow to Sanderson (stamped p.23)

Sanderson

20.8.94

In my let[ter]. of the 9th I mentioned that the country to the S. of DaB was very disturbed, but that the Gov[ernor]s. having started for Fez it was prob[able]. that things w[ou]ld. shortly be settled. Perh[aps]. what is now goin[g] on is the crisis of the fever, but the position of affairs at Mazagan does not seem very satisfactory; & there is a sort of state of siege there. If it were only fr[om]. Redman that I had the request for a gunboat, I sh[ou]ld. have thought little of it, but I have seen letters fr[om]. a man named Spinney, who knows all that goes on, & is not nervous [by nature]. Then I also had urgent private letters fr. Madden to the same effect. Both of them asked for the "Bramble". These letters, full of details, reached me yesterday morning, & I at once went off to see Souhart, Galicia & Gentile. I found they had recd. the same news, & that things looked grave. I told Souhart my opinion that the "B[ramble]" wld. reassure foreign residents & stop the stampede that is

397

PRO 30/33 14/7 Semi-official Letters from Morocco (July 10, 1894 to November 22, 1894)

beginning. He assured me that he saw no objection to her going down, & that a week ago he had written to Hanotaux warning him that things were in a critical state at Mazagan. I found G. & G. both of the opinion that the presence of a ship wld. do good & I informed them that I proposed to send the "B". Then I went to the German, but cld. not find him. When I did later on, he tried to throw cold water on my proposal hinting that the Fr[ench]. wld. at once find an excuse to bring back their ships, & so on. I am always ready to consult T[attenbach]. & to tell him what happens, but he is never pleased c. any but his own suggestions.

If anything were to happen at Maz[agan] as for instance the destruction of Br[itish]. property in the houses & stores outside the walls of the town, it wld. be a heavy responsibility. I have therefore taken the alternative, wch. seems to me the safer, & no one will be able to say or suppose that there is any dark design under the desp[atch]. of the B[ramble].

A very quiet & decent miss[ionar]y named E. was assaulted outside DaB by some c[oun]try. Moors a few days ago & Madden may perh. have some difficulty in obtaining redress. I have therefore authorized him to detain the Bramble on her way back, if he thinks it wld. help him to have a ship there, but I have privately warned him not to employ her as a menace. I think he is prudent & cool.

The two disgraced Vs. reached Tetuan on 12th [Maclean's story of intercession of Sherif of Wazan. Perh, not true.][12]

Have informed Souhart of what I have written to Gharnit abt. his language on the subject of V-Cs. T[attenbach]. & G[entile]. have both spoken to Torres in similar sense & T. says he will tell his govt. that a Germ.V-C. at Fez is necessary for Germ. commerce.

P.S. I have not told any of the colls: that the B[ramble]. may perh. be used as a scarecrow at DaB.

26. Satow to Kaid Maclean
[No.] 57

---

[12] Satow's parentheses.

PRO 30/33 14/7 Semi-official Letters from Morocco (July 10, 1894 to November 22, 1894)

T[angier].

Aug. 20. 1894.

My dr. Maclean,

I wrote to you in my No. 52 of this [these?] disquieting rumours from Mazagan, & asked you to tell B.H. that I hoped nothing w[ou]ld. happen to make it necessary to send men-of-war there for the protection of foreigners. A fortnight has elapsed, & things are worse rather than better. The town is practically in a state of siege, according to the news of the 17th wch. reached me yesterday. I have therefore despatched the "Bramble" this morning with instructions to take Madden down to Mazagan & find out what is going on. The commdr. has instructions to afford protection to B. Ss. [British Subjects] & their property. I have written a note to Gharniy informing him of this, & I send you a copy of the Engl[ish]. for your information. Please take an early opportunity of explaining this to B.H. & tell him that before taking this step, I consulted with my Fr. Sp. & Italian coll[eague]s:, who quite agreed to the necessity.

I hope very sincerely that the insurgents round Mazagan will be quieted, & that they will not carry out their threat of attacking Hadj Mohd. Ben Hamdunia's house, for they wld. not stop there, & the next thing would be the plunder of the streets & houses outside the town. In that case he will see we shld. not be able to stand by with our hands folded.

I don't think it will be of the slightest use for the Court to write letters to us abt. the V-Cs. at Fez. The thing is done, & I daresay other Powers who have commercial interests, as for instance Germany, will follow suit. I hope they will be reasonable abt. the matter.

I am told that so far fr. Cid Ali er-Rushdi, the late Basha of Fez, having been told that he was a state prisoner on his arrival at Laraiche [Larache], he has been actually installed there as governor.

Before telling B. [Bonich] that you do not want him for his expedition, please let me know. By his next reports I shall be able to judge whether he is likely to be of further use.

   y.v.t.

27. Satow to Maclean

[No.] 58

PRO 30/33 14/7   Semi-official Letters from Morocco (July 10, 1894 to November 22, 1894)

Tangier
24.8.94
My dear Maclean,

Torres delivered yesterday to all the F.RR. [Foreign Representatives] the letters ab[ou]t. the V-Cs. [Vice-Consuls] addressed to the sovereigns. I think it an unwise step to have taken, but as I informed Torres yesterday when one sovereign writes to another all a Min[ister]. can do is transmit it. I daresay some colls. may try to make out that they wld. be quite disposed to comply with the wishes of the M[ooris]h Govt. & if they do, you will doubtless hear of it. I do not think any row will be made about the watermelon. Nor have the Fr[ench]. sent any man-of-war here, as yet. The Sp[anish]. have the "Reina Regente" lying here since yesterday & we shall have the "Amphion" at Gib[raltar]. The Italians are also sending a ship.

It was not at Rabat but Azemour, as you doubtless have already heard, that A-Amrani halted. On the 18th he was still there. Kaid Aisa of Abda had reached his <u>kasbah</u> on the 17th. The Kaid of Shiadma with him [Hunot's news of 17.][13]

The letter in yr. no. 25 contained a letter fr a man names Guessus at Mazagan abt. some debt or other that Macleod must have spoken to Gharnit abt. It is a ridiculous way of going on. If they are not reasonable abt. Mac[leod]'s apptmt. wch. is purely for local matters, perh. something more disagreeable to them may happen. Only do not tell them this.

28. Satow to Kaid Maclean

[No.] 59
Tangier.
Aug. 27. 1894.
My dear Maclean,

Many thanks for Bonich's reports wch. are very interesting. I quite agree with the arrange[men]t. you have made with him, & will at once put the necessary funds at your disposition, as soon as you let me know what is wanted. Later on we may perh[aps]. be able

---

[13] Satow's parentheses

PRO 30/33 14/7   Semi-official Letters from Morocco (July 10, 1894 to November 22, 1894)

to send him to his original destination.

Very alarming reports reach me fr. the S[outh]. & by this time B.H. must have recd. them also, of a league among the tribes round Morocco, with a leaning towards Mulai Moh[ame]d. All my informants appear to think that El-Amrani can do nothing unless he is accompanied by a strong force.

The Fr[ench]. are holding their hand. They have not sent any ships to Mazagan, tho' the Sp[anish]. & Italians have each a good sized cruiser. The "Reina Regente" sailed for Mazagan on Saty. afternoon, & the Ital. "Etruria" arr[ived]. here yesterday. She will remain at Tangier for the present.

An anarchical state of things will suit Fr[ench]. policy very well, I dare say, & if it spreads towards the Algerian frontier will give them good justification for interfering. I have written to the Sherif of Tamshloht to do all he can to keep the tribes faithful to A.A. [Abdul Aziz] I do not mind the uprising agst. the Kaids so much, provided they do not rebel agst. the Sultan & adopt a rival candidate.

Wld. it be possible to send among them a discreet man who wld. talk to the leading men of the tribes, & impress upon them the danger of foreign interference (by wch. I mean of one particular nation [France] wch. has an army of 20,000 men mobilized close to the frontier) if they continue to fight among themselves. To abstain fr. attacking the towns on the coast where foreigners reside is prudent conduct, but it is not enough, they must keep the peace among themselves. B[onich]. wld. hardly be the man for such an errand, I suppose?, & he wld. at once suspect that he was being employed by a foreign govt. I shld. like to know what you think of despatching such a messenger, & is there anyone who cld. do such an errand?

Last week it was rumoured here that the Sultan was dead, & I am sure some of the telegr. agents will have reported it. Gharnit's retention of the letters on the ground of his sickness seems to be token anxiety, or is it only a pretext for enjoying delay a little longer.

y.v.t.

P.S. I have just learnt that the Fr. Govt. are sending a man-of-war, wch. is shortly expected.

29. Satow to Sanderson (stamped p.28)

PRO 30/33 14/7   Semi-official Letters from Morocco (July 10, 1894 to November 22, 1894)

Aug. 28. 94.

[My dear] Sanderson,

You will think that I am at last deluging you with reports on Mazagan, but I will keep them within bounds in future. The gen[era]l. conclusion seems to be that Europeans are in no danger. The Gov[erno]r. himself w[ou]ld. not have come into the town but for the persuasion of some of the foreigners, who did not think themselves safe as long as he was outside. Poor old Redman is quite useless, & his reports cannot be relied on at all. The best man at Mazagan for information & judgment is Spinney: I believe that in past years he has not been on very good terms c. the Legation.

Both Madden & Currey seem to have done very well, & I hope you will give them a word of approval. I enclose a letter fr[om]. a Jew of Mazagan to another at DaB describing what happened.

The Ital[ian]. cruiser seems inclined to remain for the present, but Souhart told me yesterday that he wld. send his down the coast, especially to Saffi. She came in the morning. I had a talk with him over the situation, wch. he considers is become [becoming] worse daily, & indeed that seems to be the genl. opinion of foreigners.

[Extracts fr. Maclean's no.30 abt. tribes in the South. Optimistic views of B.H. No ans. to letters written to the Court, & no constituted authority to enforce pay[men]t. of debts due to foreign merchants.][14]

[V-Cs at Fez seems likely to cause trouble. Long extract fr. Maclean.][15]

I confess that for my own part I do not like to propose a step backwards. No doubt E-S's [Euan-Smith's] way of establishing V-C at Fez was very offensive, & when he wrote in a desp[atch]. that it was done "with the Sultan's concurrence", he said the thing that is not. Still, there Macleod is, & has been for the past 2 yrs. The Treas[ur]y. has given money for the post, & M. whether officially recognized or not has been treated as a Br[itish]. Agent.

If I might make a suggestion it wld. be that the Moorish Govt. shld. be told that I shall be instructed to discuss the matter when I go to Fez & endeavour to arrive at a solution acceptable to both parties. One special reason for my desiring this is that altho' at first the

---

[14] Satow's parentheses
[15] Satow's parentheses

PRO 30/33 14/7   Semi-official Letters from Morocco (July 10, 1894 to November 22, 1894)

Court was disposed to welcome me, & a letter to that effect had actually been written, it has not been delivered to Maclean. Gh[arnit]. says now that B.H. is detaining it, because some at the Court want to put off my visit. I do not get any ans[wers]. to my letters to Gh., a dozen of wch. are apparently pigeonholed. I am not able to find out the cause of this unwillingness, but it may be that some kind friend has been suggesting to them that the new Br[itish]. Bashador ['ambassador', i.e. minister] will make them pay for the treatment of his predecessor.

Have spoken to Torres in a genl. way abt. the Mayer piracy, preliminary to presenting a claim later on.

y.v.t.

30. Satow to Sanderson?
Secret.
Aug. 29. 1894
£8.18.8 for expenses of having Fernan up to Tangier in 93, also £20 for hire of "Empresa" to come up fr. Rabat with letters direct in June.

31. Satow to Kaid Maclean (stamped p.30)
[No.] 60
30.8.94.
My d[ea]r. Maclean,

By an oversight of my own, my no. 59 was not despatched last Monday. Since then the Fr. cruiser Forbin has arrived.

Pot[estad]. writes to me that he is to have Constantinople, & so I imagine his successor will be apptd. before long. He is Don. E. Ojeda,[16] an old acquaintance of mine, married to an Engl[ish]. wife. Monbel too is expected shortly.

Y[ou]r. No. 30 reached me on Monday evening. I have told Sanderson privately everything you say abt. the M[ooris]h. feeling on the subject of V-Cs. H.M.G. I do not

---

[16] Emilio de Ojeda (1840-1911). Formerly Secretary of Spanish Legation at Tokyo (1869-77) and later Minister at Morocco (1894-1902). His wife was Julia Brooke.

PRO 30/33 14/7   Semi-official Letters from Morocco (July 10, 1894 to November 22, 1894)

doubt will take it all into cons[ideratio]n. but I have much doubt whether they will be pleased to receive such a request fr[om]. the very people who neglect every communication made to them by the Queen's repres've in this country. I have not recd. a single ans[wer]. to any of my letters abt. affairs of B.Ss. The claim of Forde in Habbasi still remains unsettled, & the M[ooris]h. Govt. have taken no steps. I wrote a polite letter to B.H. & another to Gh[arnit]. Neither has deigned to reply. There must be something like ordinary civility shown to the rr. [representatives] of F.PP [Foreign Powers] if the Moors wish to remain on friendly terms.

I have recd. instructions abt. the "Mayer" piracy off the Riff coast at the end of July, & on the 23rd I spoke to Torres abt. it. She was bound to Melilla & Oran with a miscellaneous cargo, & got becalmed abt. 6 m[iles]. fr. shore. The Moors of Bocoya, near Peñon de la Gomera, came off in considerable numbers (armed of course), maltreated the master, tried to kidnap the boy (you can guess with what object), plundered nearly all the cargo & insulted the flag by tearing it up & trampling upon it. I said to Torres that H.M.G. expected the M[ooris]h. Gov[ernmen]t. wld. be ready to make full reparation & to express their regret in a suitable manner, also to take whatever steps may seem practicable for the punish[men]t. of the offenders.

I have not yet presented the claim in writing, as the am[oun]t. of the pecuniary compensation to be paid to those who suffered injury has not yet been fixed by H.M.G.

Torres promised to write to the Court abt. the affair.

I am sending the "Bramble" back to Gib. on the 7 Sept.

   y.v.t.

32. Satow to Kaid Maclean (stamped p.31)

[No.] 61

31 Aug.

My dr. Maclean,

I see I have omitted to tell you of the "Bramble's" return here on the 25th with better news as to the safety of Mazagan, but the tribes were still effervescent. By the last news it appears that the Oulad Buaziz are still undecided as to the choice of a Kaid, while Shtooka

PRO 30/33 14/7   Semi-official Letters from Morocco (July 10, 1894 to November 22, 1894)

& Hanzia have gone under the Kaid of Azemour. Fr[om]. Maraksh, dated 23rd Nairn writes that the Rehamna people are encamped outside the Ducala Gate, & parade the city in numbers. Hadj Wida is alarmed & keeps the Kasbah gates strictly watched. Abt. this there can be no doubt, for he can see it with his own eyes. He adds that rumour speaks of the R. men demanding the release of M M. & that B. Dawad is favourable to the proposal, but I suspect his source of information to be Bubekir, & B. cannot be trusted either for his facts or the inferences he draws from them.

I have just recd. your Nos. 31 & 31, together with the camera, & letter to be forwarded in case I wish to use B.

I shld. be glad if you wld. make the proposed present to T.A. & give a tip to Gh[arnit's]. scribe for any letters or copies you may get fr. him for me.

It wld. certainly be regarded as a sign of the Govt. feeling its position uncertain if they put me off till the spring. I am not sure that certain of my colleagues might not prefer this, as they think very likely that I shld. forestal them. But my only object is to see the people at the Court, talk to them abt. gen[eral]. 'subjects', & I have no intention of asking for any commercial or other concessions.

Yr. letter no. 32 makes me think that possibly the Govt. consider their position so insecure that the roads are not safe, & that they are going to ask that my mission be deferred on that acc[oun]t. For my own part I wld. not mind running a little personal risk, because it seems to me of importance that the Court shld. without delay enter into personal relations with all the foreign mins. The advice you have given to B.H. on this as on all other matters is admirable.

Up to the present he seems to have been living in a fool's paradise.

    y.v.t.

If anything of a pressing nature occurs please let me know by special courier. They must ans[wer]. me abt. my mission without delay, because if the presents arrive, I must necessarily start for Fez. I cannot keep a pair of cobs[17] &c. here waiting until B.H. is

---

[17] A cob is a small horse of stout build with strong bones, large joints and steady disposition. It is a body type of horse rather than a specific breed, and is used for driving carts.

405

PRO 30/33 14/7   Semi-official Letters from Morocco (July 10, 1894 to November 22, 1894)

graciously pleased to receive me.

33. Satow to Kaid Maclean

[No. 62]

1 Sept.

Sending him "Akbar" of Aug. 22 containing article stating 10 Fr[ench]. & 80 other European prisoners at Tafilelt.

Ojeda arrives today, Monbel it is said, next Thursday.

34. Satow to Sanderson (stamped p.33)

2.9.1894

My dr. S.

I wrote to Gharnit that the "Bramble" was going to Mazagan, & I now hear fr. Maclean that Bu Hamed & the rest of them were much put out. They maintain that it was unnecessary. Other nations w[ou]ld. follow suit, & it w[ou]ld. produce a bad effect.

But I had given notice to Bu Hamed a fortnight before that if nothing was done to restore order, a vessel of war wld. be sent. Of that friendly hint he took no notice.

Gh[arnit]. has written a funny reply to the effect that turbulence is usual among the tribes of Morocco during the lifetime of the Sultan, & much more so when they die. That this behaviour was much worse on former occasions of the kind, & yet rebellion was put down. So it will be on the pres[en]t. occasion.

The "Reina Regente" has not yet returned fr. Mazagan, & the Italian is here. The Frenchman has gone to Cadiz to coal. I have written to the Senior Officer at Gib[raltar]. to say that in my opinion the "Amphion" ought to be kept at Gib. as long as the ships of the other powers stop here. It is all the more necessary as I hear that the "Bramble" has been ordered home. She left here for Gib. yesterday.

The Italians & Fr. captns. have been brought to call by their respective Ch[argé]. d'Aff[aires]. The Italian has with much stress informed me that his instructions are to act in accord with all the other commanders, but especially with the Engl. I have suggested that the next time a ship goes down the coast, it shld. be his.

PRO 30/33 14/7   Semi-official Letters from Morocco (July 10, 1894 to November 22, 1894)

Ojeda arr[ived]. yesterday, but I have not yet seen him. P. goes to Constantinople. Both these appointments have been on the cards for a long time, & I am therefore convinced that when Moret told Bonham that he was going to remove P. because of his hav[ing] bungled the suppression of contraband of arms business, it was said in order to throw the blame of his own blunder on somebody else.

Monbel is expected in a few days in the "Tage". Ojeda came in the "Reina Mercedes".

Maclean says he had found on the morning of the 25th Aug. that the Govt. were going to ask me to defer my visit to the Spring. He told them that this wld. have a very bad effect, & be a sure sign of weakness. He strongly advised them to receive me, & thought they were now inclined to do so. He wrote again 2 days later, but there were no signs of their having made up their minds.

I am convinced for my own part that when the Spring comes the Sultan will go to Morocco to settle things there, so that if we were to accept a put-off now, we shld. receive it again 6 mos. hence.

Short of their absolutely writing to me that they cannot guarantee my safety by the road, I think I ought to go whether they like it or not, & I would hire the necessary tents and animals here. Fr[om]. people under our protection I could get a sufficient escort, if necessary.

The men now in power have sufficiently shown the spirit that animates them by the attitude they have taken up abt. the Vice-consuls. If F.Ms. [Foreign Ministers] also are only to be allowed at Fez on sufferance, they will never get there at all. I shld. be very glad, if you approve of my idea, to have a telegram authorizing me to proceed to Court without waiting for the Sultan's consent.

There has been some bad feeling at Fez abt. the Italian arms factory. The late Sultan thought it rather an expensive toy. A great deal of money has been spent & no return. The Court wld. like to get rid of the Italian officers, & Bu Hamed asked [Colonel] Bregoli for the accounts, wch. he refused to give. But I have been told that Gentile got a promise fr. the late Sultan that he wld. never dismiss the Italians. Hence, when a circular was written to Engl[and]. Fr[ance]. & Sp[ain]. a few months back asking for the withdrawal of Military Missions, it was not sent to the Ital[ian]. Min[ister]. However that may be, Maclean writes

PRO 30/33 14/7   Semi-official Letters from Morocco (July 10, 1894 to November 22, 1894)

that Bregoli has made a fresh contract, & that the factory, wch. had been closed for some time past, is to be reopened.

Maxse[18] has just sent me an Algerian paper, making an outcry abt. an insult to the Fr. V-C., & suggesting that the Fr[ench]. squadrons shld. be sent here to occupy the Customhouse till redress is given & all the Europeans alleged to be detained at Tafilelt, Figuig & In-Salah released.

The so-called insult was that some children threw some melon-husk at him, I believe not even intentionally, for wch. he at once obtained redress by having the father put in prison. Marcilly fr[om]. all I hear & read seems to be doing very well, & the M[ooris]h. Auth[orities]. however much they may say behind his back, always end by giving way. The prison was recently opened in the dead of night to let out a Fr[ench]. protégé whom the Basha had imprisoned.

In Maclean's mind there is a certain bias agst. consuls, trading or otherwise, for he is aware of Ridgeway's proposal to make <u>him</u> Brit. Cons[ul]. at Fez. Macleod is naturally biased in favour of their retention, & writes to me acc[oun]ts. of the popular feeling, wch. don't at all tally with Bu Hamed's notions of what the Fez people think.

A letter of Maclean's dated the 27th begins: "I do not wish you to be alarmed, as I think there is every probability of things righting themselves." He goes on to say that the gen[eral]. opinion, both of the Court and in the town, is that the situation is critical & the least spark wld. upset the govt. & cause a gen[era]l. rebellion. Bu H., he says, is a weak Vizier & his brother the Min[ister]. of War no good as commander. The Govt. is therefore very weak. They try to curry favour by making presents, wch. does not answer with the Moors, who only get cheeky & "ask for more". The Sultan gave $12000 to be distributed among the poor, very little of wch. Maclean thinks will reach those for whom it is destined.

Maclean had it out with B.H. about things in genl. At first he did not quite like it, & asked who were the people who thought things were in such a critical state. M. told [him] 'everybody, including yr. own br[other]. the Min. for War'. Then he became interested & began to ask advice. M. suggested that the Sultan shld. show himself to the people more,

---

[18] Ernest George Berkeley Maxse (1863-1943). Vice-Consul in Algiers, 1891-4.

PRO 30/33 14/7   Semi-official Letters from Morocco (July 10, 1894 to November 22, 1894)

that he shld. try to get all the F[oreign]. Min[isters]. to come & see him. And he gave him also a plan for enlisting an army of 10,000 men, paying them regularly, & giving privileges to their families. M. thinks that something will be done, & that nothing is required beyond a little firmness & energy on the part of the Govt.

Gentile has talked to me a good deal abt. B.H. & his friends belonging to the Bokhari, descendants of a body of black soldiers imported fr[om]. the Soudan 200 yrs. ago, very much more fanatical than the Arabs, to whom the imprisoned Viziers belong. That we may look therefore for a retrograde movement at the Court. This has certainly been verified by the recent events, & by the language of the Basha of Mequinez to some Jews, whom he ordered to go barefoot. When they expostulated on the ground of the hardship, & urged that they were foreign protégés he answered that M.H. who was a friend of the Xtians was dead, & now they had nothing to do with protection.

A couple of days ago Reader was attacked by some fanatics, & if he had not been protected by some saner Moors, wld. have been badly hurt. As it was, he came off with a scratch on the nose and the loss of a ring wch. was dragged off his finger. As soon as I heard of it, I sent De Vismes to Torres and the Basha to insist on the men being arrested. One is in prison, but there were 5 or 6 concerned, & I shall do my best to have them [imprisoned?]. If not I shall ash the colleagues to second my efforts.

Maclean writes abt. the Sherif of Tamshloht that he is in good odour at the court, & advises that nothing shld. be said to B.H. abt. our having protected him. I have sent him a message that he is in no danger.

The last news fr[om]. the coast up to yesterday was that all was quiet at Saffi & Mazagan, but there was a small civil war going on among the tribes east of Mogador. Both Johnston & Hunot are well-informed, but Redman knows nothing of what goes on. I have asked Spinney (a merch[an]t.) to write to me. Nairn the man whom I recommended for consular agent at Morocco, writes that he thinks perh. a consul may be sent there, but no matter what is decided abt. the apptmt. he will send me news. He is I think to be trusted.

    y.v.t.

P.S. Morocco City is threatened by the powerful tribe of Rahanma, with whom one of the Govrs. Ben Dawud is said to be in league. The other, Hadj Wida, who has Mulai

PRO 30/33 14/7   Semi-official Letters from Morocco (July 10, 1894 to November 22, 1894)

Moh[ame]d. in his charge, has made preparations for defence by mounting canon on the walls of the citadel. The latest news fr. Mogador (telegram via Canary Islands) of the 30th Aug. is that great alarm prevailed. But we don't know who sent the telegram; if a Jew, it is not of importance.

Tattenbach's ideas abt. the way to settle the Fez Vice Consul question are of the wildest. I don't believe the German Govt. wld. give a penny towards the salary of a Germ[an]. cons[ul]. there. All he wishes is that Macleod be driven out of the place, because he can trade under more advantageous conditions than German merchants.

      E.S.

35. Satow to Kaid Maclean (stamped p.38)

[No.] 63

7.9.94

My dr. Maclean,

The news contained in your ciphered sheet of the 31st was so grave that I teleg[raphe]d. to stop preparation of present & am now expecting to hear further fr[om]. you this evening. As you have not sent a courier, I hope the cloud has passed off.

Very big rumours have reached us fr[om]. a Jewish source of massacres at Demnat, Zania Wlkla(?) Sidi Rahal, & Temunlelt[?], mellahs plundered & Jewesses sold by auction at fr[om]. $20 to $25. But I believe these are mostly inventions, at least so Spinney says writing fr[om]. Mazagan on the 4th inst. while the events themselves are said to have occurred before the 20th[?] August.

I have your 2 letters 33 & 34, the latter of wch. arr[ive]d. a few minutes ago. It is very satisfactory to hear that the news of the Sultan's health is better. But I am vexed at not getting any reply to my letter offering to proceed to Fez. Nor do I receive answers to any of my other letters. I wrote to them abt. Your brother's district being extended so as to include Rabat, & asking them to notify the Gov[ernor]s. of that town, Salé & Mehdia; but Gharnit has not replied to that either. It is very uncivil on his part.

The new Fr. Min. [Monbel] arr[ived]. yesterday in the "Tage". He is an old acquaintance of mine, as is also the new Sp. Min. [Ojeda]

PRO 30/33 14/7   Semi-official Letters from Morocco (July 10, 1894 to November 22, 1894)

Can you find out who is Gentile's correspondent at the Court. He is some one who knows a good deal of what is going on.

Linares came back with Monbel yesterday.

        y.v.t.

Bonich came to see me today.[19] I did not allude to his employ[men]t. He returns to Saffi tomorrow.

36. Satow to Kaid Maclean (stamped p.39)

[No.] 64

10.9.94.

My dear Maclean,

Many thanks for your No. 34. Gentile leaves for Fez today or tomorrow. He <u>says</u> he is going ab[ou]t. the position of his military mission & the man-of-war wch. is being constructed in Italy for the Sultan. As far as I am concerned he may have as many factories ships & other semi-commercial jobs as he likes, and I hope that as far as you can you will maintain a neutral attitude in respect of such things. But I shall be interested to hear all about his doings, & especially with regard to what you tell me Gharnit said, that the Italians had written & agreed with the M[ooris]h. Gov[ernmen]t. abt. Consular apptmts. at Fez & promised to do all they can to help them.

His sudden journey to Fez, wch. was announced by him only yesterday, has taken the colleagues by surprise, tho' it has doubtless been hatching for some time past.

The Fr[ench]. legation say, with some appearance of truth, that they had not told the Sherif of Wazan to intercede on behalf of the Jamais, & that as soon as they heard of it, they wrote & told him to "stop that", as his action wld. be supposed to be inspired by them. You may safely say, if you think it worth while, that it was an independent action of the Sherif's, & that the Fr. have no desire to interfere. It is as much their interest to see the govt.

---

[19] "John Bonich came in the morning, dressed like a Moor, & looking like one. Thinks the Sultan made a mistake in making Abdul Aziz his successor instead of Mulai Moh[ame]d. who is a man of energy. He wld. have begun by cutting off a few heads, and then things wld. have been quiet." (Satow's diary, September 7, 1894)

PRO 30/33 14/7   Semi-official Letters from Morocco (July 10, 1894 to November 22, 1894)

strong & the country quiet as it is any one's.

I think it possible that Sp[ain]. Fr[ance]. & Engl[and]. may continue to pull together for the maintenance of the status quo, in the same manner as they did in the recognition of the Sultan by the letters we sent to Rabat. If we had not acted together, & so dragged the others along with us, no recognition wld. have been made then, & perh. not even now. So if you see indications of joint action, don't be alarmed, & I hope you will keep on good, and as intimate terms as possible with the Fr[ench]. I admit that Souhart & his confederates played E[uan]-S[mith] a scurvy trick, but it would be impolitic to bear malice, especially as we marked our disapproval of his doings by recalling him & giving him no further employ[men]t.

I see that Gh[arnit]. wants we [me?] to talk with Torres abt. the sayings & doings of the Fr. V-C. If our friend Gh. thinks I am going to back him in these matters, he is reckoning without his host. The other day I asked him to tell me the melon-story, wch. he did, as I think, quite correctly. But I do not yet see my advantage in siding with Moors agst. Europeans. So long as they treat representations of the Br. Govt. with silent neglect, they will get nothing from us.

y.v.t.

37. Satow to Sanderson
10.9.94.

My dr. Sanderson,

The Sp[anish]. "Reina Regente" came back fr[om]. Mazagan on the 5th, bringing better news of the state of things round Morocco city, & a flat contradiction fr[om]. Mr. Spinney of the alleged "atrocities" committed ag[ain]st. Jews at Demnat & other places, wch. I had teleg[raphe]d. to Ld. K[imberley]. as a rumour. She went away almost at once to Algeciras. On the following day the Italian "Etruria" went off to Mazagan in such a hurry that no one cld. send any letters by her. Today the [French cruiser] "Forbin" is starting to visit all the ports on the coast, the idea being that all the flags shld. be seen in turn.

Maclean writing on the 3rd says that the Sultan has been suffering fr[om]. bad boils on the neck; he is better, but cannot get back his strength. Gh[arnit]. sent me a message that he

PRO 30/33 14/7   Semi-official Letters from Morocco (July 10, 1894 to November 22, 1894)

is ashamed of the delay in answering my letter, but that they had been waiting for the Sultan to recover. Maclean however thinks they have not confidence in their people, or in other words that they do not feel sure of their position.

I teleg[raphe]d. this, & then in reply to y[ou]r. priv[ate]. teleg[ram]. said that I thought the cobs had better be bought & desp[atche]d. to Tangier. A few minutes later came in Gentile with the announce[men]t. that his govt. had instructed him to proceed to Fez, & that Aspromonte an attaché just arr[ive]d. wld. take charge during his absence. In reply to a question he said there was the position of their military mission wch. required regulating & various other matters, such as the bringing out of the cruiser that is being built for the Sultan. But Maclean says Gh. told him the Italians (i.e. Gentile) had written & agreed with the M[ooris]h. Gov[ernmen]t. abt. consular apptmts. at Fez & promised to do all they cld. to help them. This does not sound altogether incredible. The Italians certainly do not intend to find more for a consular officer at Fez, therefore they can easily renounce the exercise of the right, & Gentile's own personal ambition is to reside at Fez himself as a member of the Italian legation. The keeping open of the Arms Factory at Fez is a matter of amour propre agst. wch. nothing can be said, & the pay[men]t. for the cruiser is a thing wch. prob. wld. be inconvenient to have delayed.

Monbel & Ojeda are both greatly vexed at this sudden move of Gentile, who in past times has frequently contrived to be on the scene when there was a special mission at Fez, & part of his vocation is to intrigue agst. the Fr[ench].

I have written to both Maclean & Macleod to keep me informed of his doings, but not to put spokes in his wheel, as I don't care how many arms factories they may have or how many cruisers the Sultan may choose to order. So I hope they will take the hint. And I have also said to them that they shld. keep on as friendly terms as possible with both the Fr. & Sp. officers. As regards the latter there never has been much difficulty.

I returned Monbel's visit yesterday.[20] He is an old acquaintance of mine in Japan abt. 16 yrs. ago [i.e. 1878]. He seems disposed to be friendly, & said that his instructions were to act in accord with all his coll[eague]s: & especially the Engl[ish]. one. He certainly will do

---

[20] See diary for September 9, 1894.

PRO 30/33 14/7   Semi-official Letters from Morocco (July 10, 1894 to November 22, 1894)

all he can to gain Ojeda, whom I am told he went to see the night of his arrival, but old acquaintance might acc[oun]t. for that. With Ojeda I had some talk last night, à propos of a visit wch. he is shortly to make to Melilla, in fact he expected his instructions fr[om]. Moret today. They want him to see M. Arafa to begin with, so as to form an idea as to the possibilities of carrying out Martinez Campos' convention. If the delimitation of the neutral zone is not begun by Nov. 1 there will be an outcry in Spain. The PP [Powers] that said last y[ea]r. to Spain don't make war but negotiate instead, & we will back you up, are he thinks bound to see her thro' with the business. Fr[ance]. & Engl[and]. & Spain together cld. overcome any obstacles. He thought it wld. be a good thing if he, Monbel & I were to pay our visit to the Sultan abt. the same time, not travelling together, but starting one behind the other c. a couple of days interval, say abt. the middle of Oct.

I said that for myself personally I had no objection to the proposal, & if the three Govts. had an understanding, the effect on the Moors wld. be considerable.

Ojeda also mentioned the status quo several times. I rejoined yes, the status quo political & territorial, but not stagnation in other matters.

Next time I have an opportunity I shall try to make him see that it will not do to leave the Triple Alliance out, & that at all events we must always invite the cooperation of Italy & Germ[an]y. Tho' c. Tattenbach & Gentile we shall never get it. With Cantagalli it wld. prob. be different, as he does not need like Gentile to fill his pockets by means of jobs shared with influential Moors.

It appears that the Fr[ench]. V[ice].C[onsul]. at Fez is showing a great deal of "energy". Not content with the Fr. Algerians & Jewish protégés, he claims the descendants of the people who emigrated fr. Tiemcen[21] when Algeria was conquered. Some of these Tiemcenys did not like his claim. Gh[arnit]. asked Maclean to tell me that a fat Fr. Moor came to him fr[om]. Marcilly, & rudely said that if he & the M[ooris]h. Govt. did not do what Marcilly desired, the result wld. be the arrival of a Fr. fleet & the establish[men]t. of a protectorate; & Gh. added that he had written to Torres to talk the matter over with me! I am afraid Torres wld. find but cold comfort on this point.

---

[21] Tiemcen is a city in north-western Algeria.

PRO 30/33 14/7 Semi-official Letters from Morocco (July 10, 1894 to November 22, 1894)

I see Reuter's agent has industriously informed the world of the scuffle of half a dozen Moors with Reader, so I suppose it will become necessary to write abt. it officially. The Basha has put half a dozen in jail, & being urged by me, despatched messengers to capture an equal number who were on their way to Mequinez. Doubtless some of the captives are suffering vicariously, but that is the usual way here; they clap the first comer into prison in the meantime, & afterwards when the real culprit is caught, they let the other go, on pay[men]t. of his dues. I am quite satisfied with the way the matter is proceeding, & hope before long to have it settled.

   y.v.t.
   E.S.

38. Satow to Kaid Maclean (stamped p.44)
[No.] 65
Tangier
13.9.94
My dr. M.

Many thanks for your Nos. 35, 36, 37. The latter two I recd. ab[ou]t. ½ p[ast]. 7 a.m. day bef[ore]. yesterday & No. 35 later in the day by the post. C. [With] this goes a reply to Gh[arnit]. to say that I propose to start not later than the 5th Oct. & that no doubt the M[ooris]h. Gov[ernmen]t. will take measures to ensure that due attention be paid to me by the Auth[orities]: on the way, & asking him to send the necessary tents & escort & baggage animals at once.

In the pres[en]t. condition of things I am sure you are more usefully engaged at Fez than in travelling here to bring me to the Court, & I hope you will arrange to remain where you are. I enclose lists showing what we require in the way of tents & animals. The carriage & cobs with most of the other presents will be here abt. the 25th. The Mags. rife [rifle?] for B.H. a little later. The only bulky present will be the carriage. The enclosed list of presents will show you what I have & what is coming fr[om]. home. Can you give me a notion how much coin I may have to disburse in tips to official people? And can I get money in Fez if I want it, say fr. Macleod. [End of letter]

PRO 30/33 14/7   Semi-official Letters from Morocco (July 10, 1894 to November 22, 1894)

39. Satow to Sanderson

15.9.94

My dr. S.

[French Minister Joseph-Raymond] Monbel tells me his news fr[om]. Fez is that on the 12th there w[ou]ld. prob[ably]. by [be] a great row, including an attempt on the life of Bu Hamed. If the prophecy is fulfilled you will hear of it by telegraph before you receive this. I suspect his source of information to be the Sherif of Wazan, who is a great partisan of the Jamais, & not not [long?] ago sacrificed a bull before the Palace gate to propitiate the Sultan in their favour. While [Walter B.] Harris was at Fez I cld. find out what the Sherif thought & did, but now the channel is closed.

Fr[om]. a source wch. is quite new, but seems quite trustworthy, I learn that the Sultan's illness is secondary syphilis. One wld. have thought that sufficient care wld. have been taken by the old women abt. the court to ensure the girls whom he marries fr. time to time being clean. Bu Hamed does not like to employ a Fr. or Sp. doctor, but perh[aps]. a man may be procured fr. Gibraltar.

A fellow named Molinary fr[om]. here went up to Fez with the Brazilian Prince. I have seen a letter of his in wh[ich]. he boasts that he has been heaping fuel on the fire of agitation agst. the Fr. V-C. in revenge for what the Fr. did at the time of Euan-Smith's mission. I told the man who showed me this to lose no time in informing Mr. M. that he is at the same time playing an anti-Engl[ish]. game.

Monbel evidently regrets very much that Marcilly was sent to Fez at a moment so unpropitious. If it were only a question of <u>amour propre</u> he wld. willingly agree to take Marcilly away. I said to him that as far as my personal opinion went it was not desirable to withdraw the 2 V-Cs. Whether they were formally recognized or not, they are always looked upon as rr. [representatives] and are able to effect a great deal. But I knew that H.M.G. wld. consult the govts. of Fr. & Sp., & that to arrive at an understanding betw. the 3 PP. [Powers] I thought was of more importance than any particular line of policy wch. might eventually be adopted in this matter.

I have had 2 or 3 talks with him and Ojeda separately. The latter as I have told you, is

PRO 30/33 14/7   Semi-official Letters from Morocco (July 10, 1894 to November 22, 1894)

very desirous that we three shld. be in Fez together, acting in accord. Monbel says he personally wld. like nothing better, but there are certain practical difficulties, 1stly transport for so many people, 2nd the tradition that when a Fr. Min. goes up he must try to settle 1001 affairs that have been dragging along since the last mission, & he cld. not possibly inform himself on all these in so short an interval. I suggested to him that perh. he might leave those for a 2nd visit in the spring, & told him that my instructions were to discuss no claims on the occasion of my first visit. I thought there wld. be matters of much greater importance to discuss at the present moment. For my own part, I thought that our presence at Fez, particularly if our govts. gave us instructions of similar tenour,[22] wld. be likely to do good. There the conversation ended. He says he has acquainted the Fr. Govt. with the proposition (put forward by Ojeda & approved by myself) to go to Fez at the same time.

You may have seen a teleg. to the effect that Italy wld. send a Cons-genl. to Fez. I am pretty certain this is not true. But I said to Monbel that I had little doubt someone had said to the Mh. Govt. that after the commercial VC a VC de carrière had come, that he wld. be followed by a V-C & so on, until one fine day the legn. wld. be transferred to Fez. As to the advisability of such a measure I shld. not form an opinion till I had seen the place & the people. I repeat this in case anything shld. be reported to you on the subject.

M[onbel]. shows much greater desire to be communicative than d'Aub[igny]. but takes advantage of his recent arrival to avoid expressing an opinion as much as possible.

Ojeda starts for Melilla this afternoon in the Isla de Luzon to see what possibility there is of getting M.C's [Martinez Campos's] convention carried out as regards the neutral zone & it is quite evident that his idea is to get very active support fr. both Engl. & Fr. M. says he does not believe the Riff peoples will consent to clear out of the neutral zone, even if they were compensated by the Sultan, & that the latter is utterly unable to face them. The Sp. Govt[']s. existence he thinks depends on their satisfying the national point of honour by taking some kind of action. They will not do that at Melilla, where fighting is impossible, but at some point on the Atlantic coast, say Mazagan. That is Monbel's own opinion. Ojeda has not gone beyond trying to impress on me the need of energetic support fr. Engl. &

---

[22] 'tenour' is an archaic spelling of 'tenor'.

PRO 30/33 14/7   Semi-official Letters from Morocco (July 10, 1894 to November 22, 1894)

France.

Tatt[enbach]: tries to pooh-pooh Ojeda's idea that the Sp. nation will get excited if nothing is done to mark out the zone, & I partly think he is right. Ojeda produces on me the impression that he is trying to frighten us with a bug bear, which Moret has instructed him to make as ugly as possible.

Two of the men concerned in the assault on Reader were arrested at Alcazar, & are to be brought here in a few days. When I have got all the culprits & had them punished, I propose to report briefly.

Yesterday morning news reached here of highway robbery in the immediate neighbourhood of DaB [Dar al Baida] by mounted Moors of some ½ doz. Europ[ean]s. of whom Madden is said to be one. But strangely enough I have no inform[atio]n. The Danish V-C was another of the party & there were a couple of Germ[an]s.

I have written to Gh[arnit]. that I am starting for Fez abt. Oct. 5 & asking him to send escort & baggage animals. My orig[inal]. instructions were that my visit to the Sultan was to be one of mere ceremony, & I have been in the practice of telling people that it wld. be so. I mean colls: & for the information of the Court. But I suppose that under present circumstances it may be wished that I shld. do more than present my credentials. There will perh. be the V-C. question to be discussed, & the indemnity for the piratical attack on the "Mayer" to be obtained. I am told the Court wld. think I harboured some sinister design if I did not ask for something in the way of claims to be settled. There is one of Forde's that Ridgeway wrote abt. & there are a few others which I think the Mh. Govt. shld. pay. In my own opinion $10,000 wld. cover everything wch. they could justly be called on for at the present moment. If a favourable opportunity shld. present itself might I do this? Or would you like to see the report on claims that I am preparing? I want White to see it before I send it off, & he will not be back before the 28th inst. [End of letter]

40. Satow to Sanderson (stamped p.48)
16.9.94
My d[ea]r. Sanderson,

Since writing yesterday I have had an official report fr[om]. Madden of the occurrence at

PRO 30/33 14/7   Semi-official Letters from Morocco (July 10, 1894 to November 22, 1894)

DaB, & am sending an official desp[atch].

Tatt[enbach]. & I have agreed to address a Note to Torres in similar terms demanding that the M[ooris]h. Govt. take every means to secure the apprehension of the offenders & the restoration of the property taken fr[om]. the persons of the six German & Br[itish]. subjects & that the Gov[erno]r. of the town write to each of the consuls concerned (Madden & Butler) expressing his regret at the occurrence. We do not propose to demand an indemnity, considering that the punish[men]t. of the offenders & restoration of the property ought to be sufficient satisfaction.

We will then go to Torres, to deliver our letters, & ascertain what temper he is in. If I find him reasonable I shld. reconsider the desirability of sending a man of war to Casabl[anca]. But it may prove necessary in any case, to get Torres' letter to the Govr. carried down without loss of time. In that case, if there is no merchant st[eame]r. going I shld. still think it necessary to send the "Amphion" or whatever other vessel is placed at my disposal.

The "Forbin" has left DaB for Mogador & the "Etruria" has returned here. It wld. be a partial satisfaction I think for the humiliation of the Br[itish]. Act[in]g. Cons[ul] if a man-of-war were to appear on the scene.

Tatt: tells me he has debated much with himself whether he wld. ask for a man of war, & has decided that he will not, as the Emperor wld. not 'militarily speaking' like the com[man]d[e]r. of one of his ships to be placed in the possible position of having to look on it [as] an outrage upon Europeans without having sufficient means for repression.

y.v.t.

P.S.   I have heard fr[om]. Fez morning of the 13th that the festival went off splendidly, & Monbel's news turns out bad. From Morocco City Nairn writes dated 6th that things are quiet there, the tribesmen having cleared out. They were sending a deputation to the Sultan & wld. await his ans[wer]. before doing anything more.

Peace is also secured for the moment round DaB, but a fortnight hence there may be the beginnings of a row, unless the conspirators are forestalled.

E.S.

PRO 30/33 14/7 Semi-official Letters from Morocco (July 10, 1894 to November 22, 1894)

41. Satow to Kaid Maclean

[No.] 66

17 Sept. 1894

My dear M.

Many thanks for your Nos. 38 & 39. I am very pleased that everything passed off so well on the day of the feast. My Fr[ench]. coll[eague]: had heard fr. Fez, from a M[ooris]h. correspondent, that there was likely to be an attempt on B.H's life.

I enclose you a spare copy of an acc[oun]t. sent me by Madden of what occurred to him & some others close to DaB on the 9th. The official report only reached me the day before yesterday. The Germ[an]. Min[ister]. & I are acting in concert, & have addressed a Note to Torres calling on him to give proper instructions to Bargash to effect the arrest & imprisonment of the offenders & restoration of the property of wch. they were robbed. This there ought to be no difficulty abt., for the men are known, & the Zuata Kaid must be induced to give them up. If this is not done, on the ground that the Sultan has no authority over the Zuata tribe, it will simply am[oun]t. to England having a Melilla-Riff business too. I think, fr[om]. what I hear, that the Kaid of Mediuna[23] is exerting himself to help Bargash. The latter is a weak impotent creature, quite unfit to be gov[ernor]. of a town in these times, and instead of attending to his duties as Gov. he is all day long at the Custom house dutying goods & receiving the dollars. I think it wld. be proper for B.H. to send instructions of the most peremptory kind to the Kaids round there to join together for the common good.

A very serious report has reached me that the Mediuna people were on the p[oin]t. of rising ag[ain]st. their Kaid the other day, but have put it off for 20 days fr. the feast. If B.H. wishes to prevent the revolt, wch. will be sure to spread over the whole of Shaonia, now is the time for him to act.

Fr[om]. Morocco City I hear, dated 9 Sept. that the tribes had left, & had put off till the day after their feast their final decision.

The cry of all my correspondents is that unless the Sultan shows himself down there c. a strong force, the Hanz will get hold of M.M. [Mulai Mohamed] & make him their Sultan,

---

[23] Mediuna is a province in the region of Casablanca-Settat.

PRO 30/33 14/7   Semi-official Letters from Morocco (July 10, 1894 to November 22, 1894)

the result of wch. wld. I suppose be civil war. You are better able to judge than I how far these prognostications are to be relied on.

I have got the "Amphion" here & shall desp[atch]. her to DaB with the result of Torres' ans[wer]. as soon as I rec[eive]. the letter for Barg[ash].

[End of letter]

42. Satow to Kaid Maclean (stamped p.51)
[No.] 67
22.9.94
My dr. Maclean,

I have yr. Nos. 40, 41 & 42 for wch. many thanks.

The "Amphion" returned this morning fr[om]. DaB. She reports that Bargash had expressed his regret for the attack on Madden & his friends, but that the Kaid of Zuata pretended to know nothing ab[ou]t. the brigands, tho' their names were furnished to him. I am therefore writing to Gharnit abt. the affair, & the Germ. Min. will also do so, but his letter will go thro' Torres. I enclose a copy of the Engl. in order that you may know [that the] Germ. Min. & I agreed not to ask for any indemnity. Hope Sultan will do his best.

[News of fighting at Mediuna. Ulad Zian & Ziarda agst. Zuata. Saffi warning[?] of Gov. Ziltery agst. Eda O Ziungen & 50 Mloogas. Cantag[alli]. expected back.][24]

43. Satow to Sanderson
24.9.94
My dr. Sanderson,

[arr[ival]. of cobs &c.][25]

Have heard again fr[om]. Gharnit that the Sultan bids me welcome, & will send the necessary transport animals & so forth.

Ojeda has come back fr. Melilla, without having, apparently, learnt much ab[ou]t. the chances of the neutral zone being marked out. That makes me think that the state of things

---

[24] Satow's parentheses
[25] Satow's parentheses

PRO 30/33 14/7   Semi-official Letters from Morocco (July 10, 1894 to November 22, 1894)

there is not very hopeful. At the same time he says the matter is in the hands of the Military Gov[erno]r.

I hope the Sp[anish]. Gov[ernmen]t. will be prudent, & abstain, at least till Ojeda has been to Court, fr[om]. taking any steps to enforce their rights. He is on the point of going down the coast in the "Reina Regente" to visit the ports, but I do not see the precise advantage of his doing this just now. Perh[aps]. Moret's idea is to postpone his journey to Fez until my return, as Monbel is not going thither for the present. M. explains to me that he cld. not possibly proceed to Fez without at the same time presenting the various demands of Frenchmen, to acquaint himself with wch. must take him a considerable time.

Cantag[alli]. arr[ived] today & came up to see me; unfortunately I missed him.

Maclean writes to me (extr[act]. fr. his No. 44 marked therein).

B.H. said he heard the Fr[ench]. papers were writing agst. him, & Maclean advised him not to mind that, but to keep friends with the Fr[ench]. B.H. said the reason of these attacks was that he wld. not entertain their projects for supplying all sorts of things the Sultan does not want.

B.H. is having all the Kaids arrested who have been kicked out by their people, & is sending men to reinforce El-Amrani, who is still at Azemour. He is afraid to send a large expedition at present, as he does not know friends fr. foes, & the men sent might perh. assist the insurgents instead of helping to put them down.

On the whole things seem to be quieting down in the South and quite recently one of the missionaries traveled safely fr[om]. Mazagan to Morocco. At DaB there was fighting on the 21st betw. the neighbouring tribes of Mediuna, Ulad Zian & part of Ziaida agst. Zenata and another portion of Zimida; & it was to be renewed, on the 23rd. After that, I am told, a truce may be expected.

Monb[el]. is of opinion that the whole country is in a state of anarchy, & that the outlook is serious. For myself I am not anxious abt. the final result, as fighting is the normal condition of M[ooris]h. tribes, & it seems unlikely that they will hold together long. Unofficial Englishmen like Hunter & Russi of Saffi disbelieve in the desire attributed to the Rahanma tribe of setting up M.M. as a rival Sultan. Hunot on the contrary believes they will try it. I am disposed to trust Hunter's judgment more than Hunot's.

PRO 30/33 14/7   Semi-official Letters from Morocco (July 10, 1894 to November 22, 1894)

I am afraid there is not much chance of our getting those Zenata brigands arrested or the property recovered, in spite of the Mediuna Kaid's promises. Madden & Pattisson acted with great judgment I think, & the latter has done very well, considering his want of experience, & the very diff[icul]t. position he has been placed in. I hope there will be no more trouble at DaB.

The Ital[ian]: capt[ain]. proposed to me that a vessel of war of each of the 4 powers shld. alternately visit the ports. I put him off till all the ships shld. be back at Tangier & Ojeda returned fr. Melilla. I have spoken to Monbel, who does not like the idea, because it seems to him that Italy ought not to claim as active a part as Engl. France & Spain. The Capt. of the "Etruria" very unnecessarily offered refuge on board his ship to the foreign residents at both DaB & Saffi, wch. offer was declined with thanks. Not being myself in favour of this plan of patrolling the coast, I have said to Monbel that I prefer the ships remaining here, & that we shld. let the Italian's suggestion drop.

I have sent you a short desp[atch]. abt. Jewish atrocities containing all the exact information I have been able to obtain fr. Nairn, wch. is partly corroborated by what Maclean writes fr. Fez.

B. Ss. [British Subjects] at Mogador are said to be selling ammunition to insurgents, & Monbel declares that Johnston is cognizant of it, but cannot put a stop to the sale. I have written to Johnston to inquire the facts, & have told Monbel that if all the colls: agree to do the same, I wld. under the exceptional circs. take upon myself to prohibit our people fr. dealing in arms & ammunition. Of course I wld. teleg[raph]. for instructions before giving such an order, & I doubt the colls: even agreeing to such a measure, still less their carrying it out.

   y.v.t.

44. Satow to Kaid Maclean (stamped p.54)

[No.] 68

25.9.94

My dr. Maclean,

Many thanks for your Nos. 43 to 46. As to G[entile?]. I understand he is bearer of a letter

PRO 30/33 14/7   Semi-official Letters from Morocco (July 10, 1894 to November 22, 1894)

fr[om]. the King[26] to the Sultan in reply to the announce[men]t. of his accession; and of course there is the question of paying for the man-of-war. I don't think the transfer to Spaniards as part of the indemnity is likely to be very successful.

The presents have nearly all arrived. The pair of cobs is first rate. But the carriage is in a huge packing case. I really don't know how it is to be transported, it is so big & heavy. Will it be possible to put it on 4 camels I wonder. The distance fr. Rabat is less, but how cld. it be got fr. there in time? Perh. you can give me a suggestion.

It is quite true that people have been going abt. & saying that the pres[en]t. govt. is very fanatical & anti-foreign; & of course the line taken abt. the vice-consuls strengthened that impression. On this point however I have no instructions as yet, & can say nothing. B.H. must not mind what newspaper people say.

You advised me once to keep an acc[oun]t. of all the articles recd. as muna on the way, & I think it an excellent idea. We will see if it cannot be carried out in conjunction with the Ameen[?] who is coming fr[om]. the Court.

Cantag[alli]. arr[ive]d. yesterday; he looks very thin & I do not think he has altogether recovered.

I hope the DaB affair will be promptly dealt with by the Sultan, & that Gharnit's promises will be fulfilled. Your letter of the 21st arrived very conveniently, & I at once telegraphed its contents. I am very pleased to hear of the Ducala people & their deputation.

   y.v.t.

45. Satow to Kaid Maclean (stamped p.55)
[No.] 69
1 Oct. 1894
My dear Maclean,

Many thanks for your Nos. 47 & 48, the former containing a letter to the Oomana. I am sending the carriage to Laraiche [Larache], in order to avoid the Akbar el Hamra, & shall travel that way, probably, in order to pick it up.

---

[26] At this time the King of Italy was Umberto I.

PRO 30/33 14/7   Semi-official Letters from Morocco (July 10, 1894 to November 22, 1894)

If the Sultan likes to fine the Zuata tribe, I have no objection, but the Germ. Min. & myself are opposed to the practice of substituting a pecuniary indemnity for the punish[men]t. of aggressors. What we want is therefore that the 6 men concerned shld. be (whipped &) imprisoned, & the stolen goods returned. That is sufficient satisfaction for them. If a fine in addition to go into the coffers of the State is thought advisable, there will be no objection raised on our part.

My latest news fr. Morocco City as of the 20th (see letter of Nairn to Madden).

Reports were current of the Sultan's death, also of a massacre of Azenour[?] Shllah by the advanced guard of the Sultan's army.

Marakesh is evidently as great a nest of 'canards' [false rumours] as Tangier, & I have no[t] attached any importance to this news.

The general impression here is that things are quieting down [movement of ships][27] If the Mh. Govt. do not like to see vessels of war on the coast, they shld. exert themselves to prevent Moors committing outrages on foreigners.

   y.v.t.

46. Satow to Sanderson (stamped p.56)

2 Oct. 1894.

My dr. Sanderson,

All obstacles to my journey to Fez seem to have been removed and I count on being able to start on the 9th or 10th.

Ojeda read to me a translation of Lord K's note to Del Mago of the 15th, & I gather that it is decided to inform the Sultan that I shall receive instructions to discuss the V-C question at Fez with a view to arriving at a solution satisfactory to both sides.

I have suggested to Ojeda & Monbel that we shld. try to agree upon the line I shall take when there, and I expect we shall meet for that purpose tomorrow evening. By that time my bag will have arrived, probably with instructions.

Monbel has said to me that were it not for the difficult position of the Mh. Govt. he wld.

---

[27] Satow's parentheses

PRO 30/33 14/7   Semi-official Letters from Morocco (July 10, 1894 to November 22, 1894)

certainly not permit them to ignore the Vice Consul's authority over French subjects as they daily endeavour to do, e.g. in ordering an Algerian to close a smoking shop without having first asked the French Vice Consul, as part of a general order to close such establishments. Then he went on to say that he believed the real remedy lay in the powers having none but consuls de carrière throughout Morocco. I said that even supposing we went to that expense I was certain neither Italy nor Germany, much less other countries would. He remarked that surely the status quo was worth a thousand or so a year to Great Britain. With regard to the others, he supported their right to appoint consular agents depended not on any express stipulation, but on the most favoured nation clause in the English French and Spanish treaties. That if we consented to abrogate the article allowing the appointment of merchant-consuls, the right of the others who depend on the most favoured nation clause would vanish, there being no longer any stipulation to which it could apply.

I said this was a novel suggestion, and I did not know whether international lawyers would admit that it was feasible. Any how, it would be necessary to examine the text of the various treaties.

The argument is this: The Moors chiefly object to the presence of vice-consuls because of protection. Commercial consuls are those who commit irregularities. The only way out of the difficulty therefore is to do away with merchant consuls. As long as they exist the illegitimate protections will continue to increase, until the Sultan's authority will vanish into thin air.

I agree very much with all this. Wealthy Moors as well as poor ones take protection to escape ordinary taxation as well as extortion. It seems altogether unjust that protégés should not pay the ordinary taxes. Macleod's Arabic scribe was called on to pay his share towards an indemnity given to a man who had been beaten, the share being assessed on a piece of ground he possessed. There is no justice in his being exempted. Miss Herdman's landlord, who has a protection paper, refuses to pay the excise on slippers he deals in. But as long as he is not taxed at a higher rate than others, why should he not pay?

The telegrams from Rome about the object of Gentile's visit are very curious. And if Cantagalli is instructed not to join into any Anglo-French concert, and that he is to act in concert with me when I act alone or along with Tattenbach, I shall have to fight shy of him

PRO 30/33 14/7 Semi-official Letters from Morocco (July 10, 1894 to November 22, 1894)

for the most part. No one here knows the real object of Gentile's mission, and I have kept it entirely to myself, with the exception of Reader, who may be trusted. The report has got about that he is up there to prepare things for me, and that England and Italy are engaged in some secret negotiation. I have told Ojeda and Monbel that if the British Govts. advice had been asked, Gentile would probably not have gone to Fez. It seems that Moret was greatly disturbed by this notion.

Crispi's idea is the maddest thing I ever heard of, unless he wishes to provoke a row.

Things are rather quieter, but down south there is still talk of the insurgent tribes desiring to make Mulai Mohammed Sultan. A short time ago Maclean wrote to me privately that if any serious attempt to set him up as a rival Sultan were made, he would at once "disappear"; now he has suggested to Ba Hamed to bring Mulai Mohammed to Fez. If they could safely do this, it would be a wise move, as there would then be no nucleus for disaffection to gather round in the south. Troops are being enrolled at Fez, orders have been given for barracks to be built, and small detachments are on their way to the coast. One of these has orders to try and arrest the Zuata men who attacked Madden and his friends. The fighting between the tribes at Daralbaida is at an end, and the Zuata have promised to give up the stolen property, but Madden seems to think the promise is unlikely to be fulfilled.

When I return from Fez, if things remain quiet, I should like to come on leave for a couple of months. I have to get a game knee looked to, and feel that a change of thoughts and surroundings would do me good. I will write to the private secretary about it.

y.v.t.

47. Satow to Wodehouse

Oct. 3. 1894.

Dr. Mr. Woodhouse, [sic][28]

I telegd. a day or two ago that Reader had resigned, & suggesting Madden as a successor in the post of legation clerk. He is well-known I believe in the Lib[rarians]. Dept. F.O. & as acting consul at DaB [Dar al Baida] has done very well. I think he w[ou]ld. do excellently

---

[28] This is the Hon. Armine Wodehouse, Lord Kimberley's son and private secretary.

PRO 30/33 14/7 Semi-official Letters from Morocco (July 10, 1894 to November 22, 1894)

well for the post of clerk here.

On the mission I shall have De V[ismes]. for interpreting & translating & Morant for copying. Perh. I may also be able to get some work out of the doctor. Even if Reader had not said that he wished to go at once, he is not well enough to travel, being down with fever.

Perh. Ld. K. may wish to make other arrange[men]ts. here, but if there is to be a legation clerk, it wld. be a great convenience that he shld. arrive at Tangier as soon as possible.

    y.v.f.

48. Satow to Sanderson (stamped p.60)
3 Oct. 94

Sand[erso]n

Cantag[alli]. told me a day or two ago that Gen[tile]. was to see the S[ultan]. & in fact that he supposed him to have already done so. But up to the 27th his audience had not come off, tho' he had a long conference with B.H. The latter says he wld. like the Sultan not to ans[wer]. the letters brought by G. I am afraid he is badly advised. Gh. I am told said that G. looked crestfallen, & fr. Macl[ean]. I hear he was in a very bad humour. Prob[ably]. he has not made any way with the business he was sent up about. I have abstained fr. any interference as I think the Moors are certain to refuse what Italy asks. Something however must have leaked out, for the Diario de Tanger says that there is some arrange[men]t. betw. Italy & England by wch. the former is to do the work & the latter find the money.

Tatt: has got hold of a foolish story that Johnston c. the Fr. & Sp. consuls at Mog[ado]r. had suggested to the Basha to land men fr. the "Forbin" for the protection of the town it is absolutely untrue.

It seems that Oj[eda]. went to Cantag[alli]. to propose that the Italian & Sp. men of war shld. go down the coast together. Cantag. told me he had instructions not to act with Sp., but only with myself, & that he had recd. the proposal coldly. I don't know whether Oj. meant it seriously or only as a draw.

Moret after desiring that Oj[eda]. shld. go to Fez without delay, changed his mind & told him to pay a visit to the coast ports to inspect consulates & inquire into abuses of the

PRO 30/33 14/7   Semi-official Letters from Morocco (July 10, 1894 to November 22, 1894)

protection system. Then he veered back again & wrote that he had better go to the Ct. Oj[eda's]. opinion is that he had better stay where he is, as the Sultan can do nothing at present to carry our M[artinez]. C[ampos]'s convention, & for him to go there without achieving a success wld. be disastrous to the position of the Sp. Govt. I think Oj. who at first wanted to conciliate the Sultan by taking the Mh. view of the V-C. question is beginning to think it will be better to put a man at Fez. Their difficulty wld. be to find a suitable person.

 y.v.t.

49. Satow to Kaid Maclean (stamped p.62)

[No.] 70

Tangier

2 Oct. 1894

My dr. Maclean,

 Certainly if they can bring M.M. thro' all that excited crowd of tribesmen & bestow him in a secure place of confine[men]t. they will do well, but I imagine he will need a very strong escort.

 Here is my last fr[om]. Hunot (29 Sept.). Many thanks for no. 49. y[ou]r. suggestion ab[ou]t. addressing the Court regarding the DaB [Dar al Baida] affair exactly coincides with my instructions. I have telegraphed for the best set of lawn tennis things I can get, and hope they will arr[ive]. in time. The gunstock went over to Gib[raltar]. today to be repaired, & I have also written for the drill books.

 y.v.t.

50. Satow to Kaid Maclean (stamped p.62)

[No.] 71

Oct. 5. 1894.

My dr. Maclean,

 The Sp[anish]. Govt. have addressed a very urgent representation to the Sultan thro' Torres, reminding H.S.M. of the necessity of carrying out the convention signed at

PRO 30/33 14/7   Semi-official Letters from Morocco (July 10, 1894 to November 22, 1894)

Marrakesh with Marshal Campos. Letters addressed to the Court (28 August) by the Sp. legation have remained unanswered & the Sp. Govt. is greatly annoyed at this neglect, as well as at the inaction of the M[ooris]h. Comr. [Commissioner?] Mulai Arafa at Melilla. If the M[ooris]h. Gov[ernmen]t. do not speedily carry out the stipulations of the convention, the Sp. Govt. will be driven by public opinion into making war on Morocco.

I have recd. telegraphic instruction fr. Ld. K. to support the Sp. demands, & this morning I delivered a note verbale to T[orres]. warning the Mh. Govt. of the consequences of a continual disregard of their obligations towards Spain. In the present condition of things it is unlikely that if Spain entered the field, certain other PP. [Powers] wld. hold aloof. My advice to B.H. is to proceed at once to the delimitation of the neutral zone. All the force that M.A. needs for this purpose is 500 horsemen, but certainly not less. If the Sultan were to have a civil note written at once in reply to the Sp. ultimatum, promising to begin this work before the end of the month, I think I cld. undertake to induce the Sp. Govt. to grant a respite. But above all things it is necessary that B.H. shld. realize that a Foreign Power like Sp. must be treated with proper courtesy, & that she will not stand being perpetually put off with excuses.

Please urge this on B.H. Everything possible must be done to keep Spain quiet, & the only means of doing it is to give her satisfaction.

Thanks for your 50, 51, 52. Glad Gentile called, also that he has been recd. by Sultan.

I have had instructions from home to urge that satisfaction in accordance with my demands is given in the DaB affair, so if I don't get a letter shortly from Gh. I shall address him again.

My most recent piece of news is that the Kaid Ombarek of Ait Zilten fled to Mogador, but was refused admittance, & had to take refuge at Sidi Mogdul on the shore of the bay. Of the arrival of the new Kaid of Zemran at his seat of govt. I have heard nothing yet.

As to Bubker, I think the truth is that he & Bu Daoud are old foes, & they are prob. traducing [speaking ill of] each other to their respective superiors. O that I had an intelligent Br. Agent in Morocco City.

I have not been able to get [illegible word].

    y.v.t.

PRO 30/33 14/7 Semi-official Letters from Morocco (July 10, 1894 to November 22, 1894)

51. Satow to Sanderson

Oct. 7. 1894.

My dr. Sanderson,

Many thanks for your letter of the 22nd Sept. giving me hints about the line to take at Fez abt. the V-C. ? [question] & claims.

In a conf. desp[atch]. I have sent home notes of a talk on the former subject wch. I had with Monbel & Ojeda. The financial difficulty in the way of substituting paid consuls for merchants is, I know, very great, & I have not given them to understand that H.M.G. will take any steps towards it. Still, my own opinion is that the merchant (unpaid) consuls are mostly inefficient. An old man like Redman is quite useless for any purpose. Forde is too much engaged in business to be any help to us. Johnston I think is clever but shifty. His great ambition is to become a paid consul, but I do not think his training under Payton has done him any good. Frost is a good man, but very delicate in health, & it is very inconvenient that he shld. be annually away from his post for a couple of months. If I could have a student interpreter or assistant to train here under my own eye, with a prospect of being able to station him later on at one of the ports, that wld. be a beginning of a better state of things. The old-fashioned unpaid V-C has been an obstacle rather than a help. Examining the so-called claims has shown this. The claims were never properly looked into by them or my predecessors. The theory seems to have been that to examine them was a 'trespass on the Sultan's authority'. Hence they were thrown at the Sultan's head in the form in wch. they came from the coast, & the burden of examination thus cast on the moors, who are quite unable to draw inferences even from facts, much less to clear up misstatements. With regard to the claims I am carefully analyzing each, and as far as possible ascertaining the exact amount due in each separate case, & I have nearly got thro' the whole list. Perh. I may be able to complete the investigation before leaving for Fez, & then the results can be sent home by White. You may be quite certain that I shall not press them unduly, & that I shall avoid mentioning them except as a matter that must be discussed on a future mission. But about 3 or 4 I have already written to the Court & recd. civil answers, promising future action when quiet is restored.

PRO 30/33 14/7   Semi-official Letters from Morocco (July 10, 1894 to November 22, 1894)

Gentile was recd. by the Sultan on the 1st. & has written to Cantag[alli]. that it will take some time to arrange the business on wch. he went up. Cantag. has said nothing abt. Crispi's scheme, & I have not told him that I know of it. But G's remaining at Fez during my stay may perh. lead the Moors to think this scheme is supported by H.M.G., wch. will be awkward. It wld. be a convenience if he cld. be withdrawn for a while. Of course I have not breathed a word abt. this scheme to either Ojeda or Monbel. A local paper has said that Italy is to do the work, England to supply the money. France to look on & say nothing; wch. looks as if there were some suspicions abroad.

Monbel thinks the strong language of Ojeda is for parliamentary consumption, & that there is no intention of taking warlike measures. It certainly looks as if his conjecture were correct.

There are no men of war here now. The "Faucon" [29] is somewhere on the coast. The "Etruria" has gone to Gib. to meet the Italian Admiral, who is there in the "Morosini", with one smaller vessel. Cantag. asked if I knew the object of his presence there, & when I replied in the negative said "You know exactly as much as I do". Tattenbach suspects me of knowing the real object of G's mission. I told him I had heard fr. Fez that G. had letters to present, on wch. he said they were prob. fr. Crispi, adding that there had been letters fr. him before. With Monbel & Ojeda I am on good terms, but with Cantag. not as confidential as formerly. I think I must contrive to let B.H. know in some roundabout way that H.M.G. do not support Crispi's scheme.

I am sorry to lose Reader,[30] who is a very good honest boy, but he fancies he can better himself by going into business with a man named Gordon-Miller, who has lately appeared on the scene. I am very glad however to get Madden in his place.

Prince Philip de Borbon y Braganza has returned here having done nothing; he is a mere adventurer.

The men who assaulted Madden & his friends have not yet been arrested. I think I must talk seriously abt. this affair when I reach Fez. Of those who assaulted Reader I have 3 in prison, & propose to let them remain there for the present. Such occurrences ought not to be

---

[29] The French warship *Faucon* replaced the *Forbin* (Satow's diary, September 24, 1894).
[30] Reader told Satow of his intention to resign on September 30, 1894. (Satow's diary)

PRO 30/33 14/7   Semi-official Letters from Morocco (July 10, 1894 to November 22, 1894)

passed over lightly as if they were common assaults.

I expect to start for Fez on the 11th inst. That will enable me to get the Queen's letter abt. the V-C. translated & sent on ahead, so that it will arrive about a week before me.

   y.v.t.

52. Satow to Kaid Maclean (stamped p.66)

[No.] 72

Tangier

9 October 1894

My dr. Maclean,

My last news fr. DaB, dated 5th, is that none of the gov[erno]rs. summoned there to receive Sultan's letters had turned up. They were 2 of Ziaida, 1 fr. Zuata, & Bersheed. Hamid Bel Arbi is at DaB. He at first gave a good supply of muna[?] to the Sultan's 100 men, but is gradually reducing it. Ulad Haris & M'zab have been fighting again & some of the former killed, but Madden hoped things wld. be settled betw. them.

Thanks for yr. letters up to no. 53, arr[ive]d. last might. Your man Kaid el Arbi arrived yesterday, with the pony you kindly sent for my use. I am sorry to say that it has hurt its near hind foot, just above the hoof, & it looks as if it had been cut with a cord. If it is not well enough by the time I start I shall leave it behind in good care. I am making my preparations for starting on the 11th, but rain began yesterday, & I am afraid there may perhaps be some delay. Of that I will let you know in time, if it happens. The Oomana chartered a Sp. schooner to convey the carriage to Larache, & it left yesterday. So I hope that difficulty is surmounted.

The escort arrd. yesterday, & I had a short interview with the Kaid.

I do not think Bubker is inciting the people agst. the present Sultan & govt. & what B.H. hears agst. him of course comes fr. Ben Dawud his old enemy. I have particularly told B. that H.M.G. are on the side of Abdul Aziz & that he must do all in his power to keep the tribes quiet. I don't know that he has much influence, but what he has is sure to be exerted on behalf of law & order.

   y.v.t.

PRO 30/33 14/7   Semi-official Letters from Morocco (July 10, 1894 to November 22, 1894)

53. Satow to Sanderson (stamped p.67)

Tangier

11 Oct. 94

My dear Sanderson,

Both Cantag[alli]. & Monbel seem to have exaggerated to their gov[ernmen]ts. the character of the steps that Ojeda & I had taken in pressing the M[ooris]h. Gov[ernmen]t. to carry out the Marakesh convention.[31] The former telegraphed that Oj[eda]. had delivered an ultimatum, demanding an ans[wer]. within 10 days, & that I had written to the Sultan. The latter also confused the notes verbales wch. Ojeda & I had communicated to Torres with official notes. After they had thus misinformed Paris & Rome they came to ask me what I had recently done, & as I told them exactly what had happened, I hope the flutter is by this time over. Then Oj[eda]. got instructions fr. Moret to go round to his colls: & offer tranquillizing assurances. He thinks Cantagalli purposely misunderstood him, & Monbel's misapprehension he attributes, doubtless correctly, to his deafness.

The idea of the German is that Oj[eda]. shld. simply have written to the Court that Sp[ain]. wld. give them 6 months grace, & that if the Treaty were not then carried out, Sp[ain]. shld. have recourse to stronger measures! But no one thinks of following Tattenbach's advice.

Fr[om]. Fez I hear that energy is being shown in various directions, & some people say that reinforcements have been sent in the direction of the Riff, presumably to carry out the delimitation of the neutral zone. In the same way, the tribes round DaB have been ordered to fall upon the Zuata, & "eat them up", if they do not give up the men who attacked Madden & his companions. It is necessary to make an example of these people, as otherwise the position of Europeans in the coast towns wld. become intolerable.

When I went to say goodbye to Monbel yesterday & introduce White as taking charge of the legation during my absence, he drew me apart and said that Kerdec is going to start for Fez today, but he added "he goes on his private affairs, without any mission fr[om]. me". I

---

[31] The peace treaty dated January 29, 1894 negotiated by Arsenio Martinez Campos.

PRO 30/33 14/7   Semi-official Letters from Morocco (July 10, 1894 to November 22, 1894)

replied that I was quite sure of that. This is the man who made so much mischief at the time of E[uan]-S[mith]'s mission. Souhart, who as Ch[argé]. d'Aff[aires]. worked the machine fr[om]. this end, says that he is leaving on the 28th. Otherwise I have little doubt that he and Kerdec together wld. play the same game as in 1892. I am afraid the colls: will not get out of their heads that we are working secretly with the Italians, & if anything leaks out abt. Crispi's scheme the effect will not be nice.

I teleg[raphe]d. asking leave to give $150 to the widow of the man who was injured by a pellet of powder fr. one of the "Bramble's" saluting guns, & died in consequence. I did not write or send Madden's desp[atch]. on the subject, because he suggested $100 in it while writing to me privately that $150 wld. be the proper sum to give. I think £25 is very little to give under the circ[umstance]s. & hope there will be no difficulty.

[Am starting this afternoon.]³²

54. Satow to Kaid Maclean
[No.] 73
Camp n[ea]r. Had el Gharbia
12.10.94
My dr. Maclean,

We met the postal courier with y[ou]r. no. 55 this morning on the other side of the Akbat el Hamra, and your no. 56 was delivered to me a little after 11 by yr. special courier.

What the Sp[anish]. Min[ister]. has told me is that a letter was written to the M[ooris]h. Govt. abt. the 28 Aug. in wch. they were reminded of the Maraksh convention, & the necessity of its stipulations being carried out, & at the same time they were told that Sp. wld. take into friendly consideration their representations abt. the question of V.C. at Fez. It was in fact only 5 or 6 days after the Sultan's letter to the sovereigns had been delivered to the foreign legations by Torres. To that letter the Sp. Min. says they have not recd. any reply.

He went to see Torres on the morning of the 4th & read to him a note verbale. The

---

³² Satow's parentheses. He was starting for Fez.

PRO 30/33 14/7   Semi-official Letters from Morocco (July 10, 1894 to November 22, 1894)

interpreter also showed Torres an Arabic translation, fr. wch. T. took notes: very likely copied it all. That was to be despatched the following day to Fez. It is quite possible that his courier did not travel as fast as our post, & so you got the news in my letter before Torres' report arr[ive]d. But by this time you will have heard of its having reached Gh. My note verbale, wch. was delivered on the morn[in]g. of the 5th, may perh. be a day later on arriving.

I am much obliged to you for having spoken to B.H. abt. it as you did. You know what the Spaniards are. Civil words will go a long way with them. Telling them there are $400,000 packed in Morocco but that they cannot bring them down is not of much use; in fact I think it is a mistake for the Mh. Govt. to confess its weakness. If it cannot get those $400,000 out of Morocco, let them take them out of the Treasury at Fez. Anything rather than tell the PP. [Powers] they are weak. It only encourages those who count upon that weakness for the eventual fulfilment of their designs.

In Tangier the report has been spread that Mulai Ismail had gone towards the Riff with 400 horsemen. I have said that as far as I know this was merely an expedition to the Hiyaina [?] country. The Diario de Tanger's Fez correspondent had this in, but Torres told me that no men had been sent to the Riff, & that nothing cld. be done unless the Sultan went there in person. At the same time he said that Mulai Arafa was buying the land in the neutral zone. Seeing that it is a width of only 500 metres, and a few miles along the Melilla frontier, the difficulty ought to be very little. Torres said that all the people were willing but the inhabitants of three villages. That cld. be got over easily if, once the Mh. Govt. made up their minds.

Fr. Ojeda I know nothing about the Sp. doctor, & I don't think he makes much use of him. Pot. used to make all his communications to Torres, & the new Minister has always followed his example. It seems to me incredible that he shld. have kept back letters entrusted to him for delivery. I am very glad however that you have induced B.H. to receive him.

I shall not write anything of the contents of yr. letter to the Sp. Min. until I hear again from you.

Gh[arnit's]. letter abt. the DaB affair is satisfactory as far as it goes, and I quite approved

PRO 30/33 14/7 Semi-official Letters from Morocco (July 10, 1894 to November 22, 1894)

of the dismissal of Bargash. But I expect the Mh. Govt. to persist in its efforts to have the offenders given up, and the stolen property restored, including of course Dr. Kracke's horse. [End of letter]

55. Satow to Ojeda[33]
Confidential
15 Oct. 1894
[Place not specified, en route to Fez]
Ojeda
My d[ea]r. coll[eague]:

Two letters have reached me fr. my corresp[onden]t. at Fez of the 9th & 11th, & I think you may like to hear their contents, tho' the news is scarcely of sufficient importance to be used officially. Your note verbale, or T's notes on it had not reached the Moorish Govt. on the former date. The seriousness of the situation was however fully explained to B. Hd. & he was urged to send 500 horsemen at once to Mulai Arafa, answer all the letters of the Sp. Govt. and pay up the indemnity.

The G.V. [Grand Vizier] promised everything, & said the money for the 2nd instalment is being counted & that $400,000 are ready packed in Morocco. But speaking confidentially he said he did not know where to find so many as 500 soldiers. To this my correspt. replied that he must hire men for this service & pay them well.

In the 2nd letter he says your note verbale had been recd. fr. Torres, and Gh. had told him it wld. be answered at once, & that full satisfaction wld. be given to Spain. Gh. was confident everything wld. be amicably arranged, as all previous letters had been answered, and they hoped to send a friendly mission to Madrid. Dr. Cortes [the Spanish Agent at Fez] had an interview with B.H. on the 10th and was to see him again the day before yesterday.

Both Gh. & B.H. declare that all previous letters have been answered. In that case the letter of Aug. 28 of wch. you have spoken to me must have gone astray – unless, wch. is

---

[33] Emilio de Ojeda y Perpiñán (1845-1911) succeeded Potestad as Spanish Minister. He arrived on September 1, 1894 (Satow's diary). He was Minister in Morocco from 1894 to 1902.

437

PRO 30/33 14/7 Semi-official Letters from Morocco (July 10, 1894 to November 22, 1894)

quite likely – they recd. it & did not think it required immediate attention. That is their way of doing business, and has been from time immemorial. I suppose it was signed by Galicia, for if my memory serves me right, you did not arrive in Tangier till the beginning of Sept. Anyhow, if they send a satisfactory reply now, the point will hardly seem to you to be of any further importance.

The weather is magnificent, the heat not excessive and the nights cool. I am delighted with the country, but feel that I must come up here another time in the spring, for the landscape would be greatly more attractive when fresh and green.

There is a great dearth of drinking water on the march.

When I get to Fez I will write again. In the meantime, believe me, yours very sincerely.

E.M.S.

56. Satow to Ojeda (stamped p.72)

Fez, 27 Oct. 94.

My dear Colleague,

Your letter of the 17th reached me a couple of days before I got here (wch. was on the morning of the 25th). Dr. Cortes came to see me that afternoon, and afterwards I asked Maclean to see B.H. and tell him that the position was serious, that an Embassy must be sent immediately to Spain, to explain the situation & to deliver the indemnity money wch. is now due, & that he must inform Cortes & write to you that this wld. be done.

B.H. replied Oh, but you know Europe will never allow Spain to make war on us, to wch. he answered that if the Sultan put himself in the wrong the PP. [Powers] wld. certainly not think of interfering. Then he said, "But it requires 2 to make a war; we shall not fight, & where will the Spaniards be then?", to wch. the natural response was that they would get a beating & have to pay a great deal more money. What children in intelligence, at the same time as cunning as the serpent.

Of course, I know that the Spanish feeling is averse from saying anything about money, but alas it is the only argument these people understand. May I offer a suggestion of my own? It is that your corresp[onden]ce. wld. produce a much greater effect if it were addressed to Gharnit instead of Torres, and sent here by special courier or thro' the post to

PRO 30/33 14/7   Semi-official Letters from Morocco (July 10, 1894 to November 22, 1894)

Cortes to deliver. It wld. arrive more quickly, and be answered sooner. Above all, I believe that your presence here wld. accelerate the arrangement of these matters. But if they sent an embassy, as B.H. has promised, you wld. I suppose not come to Fez until its return fr. Madrid. Our position at Tangier, so far fr. the Court that there is a constant risk of correspce. crossing, is very disadvantageous for the transaction of business.

I am to be recd. by the Sultan on the 29th. Today he went as usual to his garden outside, tomorrow is Sunday, so it had to be deferred. I have seen Gharnit since, but have not talked business. After my audience I shall speak to them as a matter of course about the DaB. affair in wch. Madden and others were attacked by tribesmen who have not yet been imprisoned as T. & I had demanded. The question of the V-C I shall leave for them to open.

Of Fez I have seen nothing, as etiquette keeps me indoors until my audience, but fr. the gallery upstairs there is a very fine view, reminding one of backgrounds such as one sees in old pictures, for instance Lorenzo da Credi's[34] Natalizio in the Accademia at Florence.

Remember me to Monbel, and tell him I have had the pleasure of making the acquaintance of the Military Mission & of Dr. Linares,[35] also of a visit fr. M. Marcilly. The weather is now splendid. [End of letter]

57. Satow to Lord Kimberley (undated)
Dr. Ld. K.

I reached Fez the day before yesterday [October 25, 1894][36] after a somewhat longer journey that usual, having been delayed on the road by the difficulty of transporting over the bad roads a carriage wch. forms one of the presents for the young Sultan. There were no signs anywhere of disaffection, and the whole of this part of the country appears perfectly quiet. My reception at Fez was on the usual scale, all the troops & a large no. of the townspeople having turned out. The soldiers may be very brave, but they looked as if they

---

[34] Lorenzo di Credi (c. 1459 – 1537). Italian Renaissance painter and sculptor, known for his paintings on religious subjects.
[35] Dr. Ferdinand Linarès (1850-1938) was the French political agent at the Sultan's court.
[36] Satow entered Fez on October 25, 1894. Hence this letter must be dated October 27th. On the entry into the capital see Bernard M. Allen's *The Rt. Hon. Sir Ernest Satow: A Memoir*, (Kegan, Paul et al. 1933), p.98 et seq.

PRO 30/33 14/7 Semi-official Letters from Morocco (July 10, 1894 to November 22, 1894)

had never been drilled.

I am sending a short desp[atch]. reporting the steps I have taken to support the representations of the Sp[anish]. Agent. The G[rand]. V[izier]'s. first reply to [Kaid] Maclean whom I sent to him with an urgent message was that it takes two to make a war, & that as Morocco was peaceably disposed, Sp[ain]. wld. not think of attacking her. Macl[ean]. then said that anyhow the Sp[aniar]ds. wld. make them pay a great deal more money, if they did not come to terms abt. the delay in executing the convention of Morocco. The G.V. rejoined that Europe wld. never let Sp[ain]. go to war. Finally however he gave way, & promised to do what was asked in the way of sending an embassy & paying $600 000. The latter he can easily do, as there is plenty of money in the Sultan's Treasury.

It is entirely owing to Kaid Maclean that the Sp[anish]. Agent Dr. Cortes has been recd. by the Vizier. He had been here 2 mo[nth]s. & cld. not obtain an audience. Ojeda instead of addressing himself directly to Gh[arnit]. speaks to Torres at Tangier, the result being that the force of what he says is considerably toned down by the time it reaches BH. The phrase abt. Europe not allowing Spain to use coercive measures sounds as if it had originated in a Fr[ench]. mouth, but one cannot be certain.

The Sp. Govt. having now obtained a promise wch. they can dangle before the Cortes[37] & so escape uncomfortable questions fr. the opposition, will prob. relax their energy, & I expect the definitive desp[atch]. of the Embassy will be delayed for a while. Brisha, who was formerly govr. of DaB has been suggested by [Dr.] Cortes as an acceptable person: he is a personal friend of Cortes.

My audience has been fixed for Monday the 29th, & I am told the Sultan intends to make me a very cordial reply, that is to say B.H. means him to do so. A hitch has arisen with regard to B.H. himself. He wants me to go & see him, on wch. occasion I shld. take with me the presents that are intended for him, and has let me know thro' Maclean that his importance as G.V. surpasses that of any previous holder of the post; consequently he cannot return my call. This seems an inadmissible pretension. He pressed for an immediate ans[wer]. but I have said I must consider. If he had the title of Regent, the difficulty wld. be

---

[37] Cortes Generales are the bicameral legislative chambers of Spain, consisting of the Congress of Deputies and the Senate.

PRO 30/33 14/7   Semi-official Letters from Morocco (July 10, 1894 to November 22, 1894)

less, but as it is, I do not feel inclined to give way, especially as I have had no opportunity of consulting my coll[eagues]: & do not wish to commit them.

The Fr. Mil. Mission, Dr. Linares & the Fr. V.C. have been to call on me as well as the 2nd in Command at the Italian factory & Gentile. The latter wanted to come out to meet me the day before my arrival, but I managed to put him off. However he rode out the morning of my entry into Fez, & Col. Ferrara in full uniform accompanied me the greater part of the way. At the Court the Moors say Gentile told them Engl. was prepared to back Italy in everything; & that she had allowed the Italian men of war to lie at Gib. in readiness. They made him some promises abt. paying the arrears on the man of war building at Leghorn [Livorno], & then he said he wld. send the "Morosini" & her consort back to Italy. I shall arrange so that the M. Govt. know that we are not supporting Italy in my schemes. G. has a window fr. wch. he watches those who go in & out of my gate.

Dr. Lin[ares]. said to me that the situation in Morocco was very dangerous, that no one cld. say how things will turn out, etc. He seems a little inclined [to] act independently of Monbel, who being only a newcomer has no prestige. The genl. tone of the Fr. seems to be that the country is going to the dogs.

As far as I can judge I shld. be inclined to say that time is on the Sultan's side, & there is no risk of a rival being set up. He will almost certainly visit the South next spring, & the tribes will then be in a more submissive frame of mind.

P.S. The Brisha mentioned above has been a member of several embassies to Europe.

E.S.

58. Satow to Sanderson (stamped p.76)

27.10.94

My dr. S.

A Sp[anish]. courier is just starting with the M[ooris]h. ans[wer]., & I have just had time to write a letter to Ld. K, giving an acct. of things here. I am afraid B.H. is inclined to give himself airs, as if he were something more than G[ran]d. Vizier. It is rather foolish, & will make enemies for him.

The Italian Gentile is still here, having as yet not managed to settle his affairs. Col.

PRO 30/33 14/7   Semi-official Letters from Morocco (July 10, 1894 to November 22, 1894)

Bregoli of the arms factory wants to go home, but they refuse to let him unless he admits in writing that he is unable to produce so many rifles a month, as he has contracted for. I am afraid I shall hardly get away in ten days as I had proposed to myself, but I shall make every effort to stick to what I told the Sp. & Fr. colls: abt. my plans & intended proceedings.

      y.v.t.

59. Satow to Ojeda
Ojeda
Fez, 8 Nov. 1894
My dear Colleague,

Your letter of the 2nd reached me the day before yesterday, and after consulting with Cortes, who had also heard fr. you I sent a message to Gharnit (who was laid up with fever) that the Sp. Govt. had made all preparations for the conveyance and reception of the embassy, and it wld. look discourteous & produce a bad effect if they did not despatch it at once. Gharnit sent his priv. Secy. to me, who said they had been hesitating between the Basha of Mequinez and a couple of merchants, prob. it wld. be the first named. He was certain a letter wld. at once be written to Torres telling him to acquaint you with the nomination.

This morning Gharnit came to see me fr. B.H. to say that they had apptd. Hadj Abdulkerim Brisha envoy and Cid Abdulkerim Bensliman secretary. That instructions wld. at once be sent to the former, who is at Tetuan, to be ready to start, and that the embassy will embark as soon as the presents, wch. are in course of preparation are ready.

I have said nothing abt. the money, as I understand fr. Cortes that the Sp. Govt. have practically consented to wait for the $400,000 until they can be sent fr. Marakesh to Mazagan, & there seems to be no question but that the envoy will take with him the $200,000 now due.

Yesterday I recd. the papers with news of the Cabinet crisis and of Sr. Moret's resignation. I trust this is merely provisional, in order to facilitate reconstruction. We have also heard of the Emperor of Russia's death.[38] I am curious to see whether the predictions

PRO 30/33 14/7   Semi-official Letters from Morocco (July 10, 1894 to November 22, 1894)

made of great changes in international politics following this event are going to be realized.

There is not much to tell you of. The latest news from Morocco, recd. viâ Casablanca, that the Rehamna had sued for peace, has greatly relieved the govt. But they are sending a nominal force of 2000 men southward, to secure the fruits of their pacific victory. I have seen Ba H but once: he returns my official call today. Nothing has been yet said betw. [us?] on the subj[ect]. of the vice consuls, and I have done no business of any kind, preferring to put off speaking on official matters until the exchange of visits with the G.V. shld. be accomplished.

    y.v.t.

60. Satow to Lord Kimberley

Fez, 8/11/94.

Dear Ld. K,

My public audience of the Sultan went off very satisfactorily, and he made me a very cordial reply. The day after I was told thro' Maclean that the G[rand].V[izier]. wld. exchange calls with me, so the hitch was got over. He had at first flatly refused to return my visit, & I had let him know that in that case I shld. be to my regret unable to call on him. I went to his house on the 1st, & he comes to me today. The conversation was general, abt. the state of things in the South, wch. he said was what always happened on the death of a Sultan, & that it wld. come right in the end. Altho' this sounds optimistic, I expect events will justify him. On the subject of Melilla I failed to get anything out of him. Linares is credited with having told him that Fr. will assist Morocco with men & money agst. any European Power that may attack her, & that they need not mind the Spaniards, as they cannot afford to go to war.

After the first alarm on the subject of paying up the indemnity and sending an embassy to explain the situation, B.H. relapsed into indifference, & the Sp. Agent Cortes was unsuccessful in obtaining the nomination of the Envoy. Yesterday, having recd. a priv[ate]. letter from Ojeda & after consultation with Cortes, I sent a message to B.H. the result of

---

[38] Alexander III of Russia died on November 1, 1894.

PRO 30/33 14/7   Semi-official Letters from Morocco (July 10, 1894 to November 22, 1894)

wch. was the app[oin]t[men]t. of envoy & secretary & promise that as soon as the presents are ready the embassy shld. start.

Beyond this I have done nothing, preparing to leave all business until after the Grand Vizier returns my call. The fact that he has been induced to go back upon his original refusal is I think of great importance to our future relations, & a point has been gained that wld. have caused much friction betw. him & the foreign RR. [Representatives] After calling on him, I went to see all the other ministers, who had previously called on me but informally, and to every one I brought a present. They have without exception been extremely polite, anxious to forget what happened during Euan-Smith's mission. But they are beginning to wonder what there may be in store, and as the Moorish phrase goes, are asking when the hen will lay and what sort of egg it will be. There seem to be indications that I may possibly get one or two small concessions in the way of export trades and some claims settled. But the old ones I think will have to be left until a future occasion. It will scarcely be possible, at the rate at wch. things go at Fez, for me to leave again for Tangier for another fortnight.

As far as my observation goes, the Sultan's position is being gradually consolidated, and the G.V. has this part of the country well in hand. The F.M. Gharnit is quite powerless for good, but as his hostility might be serious, I have tried to conciliate him. There is one very anti-foreign member of the Govt. Abselam Tazi, who is responsible for the advice to ask crowned heads to withdraw their vice-consuls; he sent a message that he did not wish to receive a present from me. The others are mere figureheads, B.H. is the one man.

I went over the Italian arms factory yesterday.[39] It never can be of any use to the Sultan, and the arms turned out (Martini) are entirely untrustworthy. To close it, as the Moors are desirous of doing, wld. be a triumph for Linarès, and a snub for the Italians, and the latter will strain every effort to keep it going.

Linarès is said to have told the Mh. Govt. that France was ready to remove the Vi[ce]-

---

[39] Sultan Mulay al-Hassan I set up the arms factory in 1886 near his palace in Fez Jdid and hired Italian officers to manage it. Only five rifles per day were produced (Hamid Irbouh, *Art in the Service of Colonialism*, I.B. Tauris, 2005. pp. 93-94) See also Satow's diary for November 7, 1894.

PRO 30/33 14/7 Semi-official Letters from Morocco (July 10, 1894 to November 22, 1894)

Co[nsul]. & the Military mission as well, in return for some bits of land at Tuat and Figuig. Fr. the way on wch. B.H. spoke to me of Tuat, incidentally, I am disposed to think that no such gilded bait as Linarès offers is likely to be swallowed.

   y.v.t

61. Satow to Monbel

Monbel

12 Nov. 94

My d[ea]r. Coll[eague]:

In the Diario de T[anger]. over the signature of K.[Kerdec?] I observe an absurd statement that at the end of my audience with the Sultan I handed him a sealed letter, the signature of wch. was inspected, etc. etc. I am sure I need not tell you that nothing of the kind occurred. I handed my credentials to the Sultan in the usual way after a short complimentary discourse of the ordinary kind, & that was all. But as I perceive that the same rubbish has been repeated by the Mogreb al Akra & is given currency by the Epoca also, I feel bound to tell you there is nothing in it.

Up to this day I have had no business discussion with the Court. They have not mentioned the subject of the V-Cs, but I am told they will speak of it later on. I have once or twice lent our Spanish friends a helping hand, but my own affairs have remained untouched. De Vismes, the legation interpreter, has been in bed for a week & is not yet able to get up, so that I am obliged to delay my departure. And indeed it is only when one gets to Fez that one realizes the difficulty of getting away again.

The Débats[40] it appears has attached serious importance to my being here with our friend Gentile. Govts. one knows are not misled by newspapers, but MPs & deputies & other people who are "not in the swim", I fear often take their misstatements for gospel.

I shall see what can be done abt. the money due to the Conseil Sanitaire, but will not undertake to be successful.

Fez is very uninteresting [interesting?] & there are many pleasant rides in the environs,

---

[40] The *Journal des Débats* was a French newspaper published between 1789 and 1944.

PRO 30/33 14/7 Semi-official Letters from Morocco (July 10, 1894 to November 22, 1894)

but M[ooris]h. houses are not built for cold weather, & I shall be glad to be back in my comfortable Q[uarte]rs. at Tangier.

Kind regards, especially to Ojeda.

62. Satow to Sanderson

Fez.

Nov. 12. 1894.

My dear Sanderson,

B.H. sent Maclean to me yesterday to say that one of the cobs, the larger, kicks, & as he was being driven yesterday morning got his leg over the pole. They are afraid the young Sultan will not be able to drive them, so wld. I take the animal back & send them another.

I told him I cld. not do that, it wld. look so bad, but that when I go to Engl[and]. I will get him a quiet pair not too big for the carriage. The fact is, the Sultan has the horses led, & for that he needs a very quiet kind of animal. The harness was too small when we came to put it on, & here there is no one who cld. make the needful alterations.

I hope you will approve of my giving this promise, wch. indeed under the circs. I cld. not help giving. When I come home I will consult c. the coachmaker abt. the matter, & I dare say he cld. help me to find the proper pair.

[End of letter]

63. Satow to Sanderson

Fez.

12/11/94.

My dr. Sanderson,

There is very little to add to what I wrote on the 12th to Ld. K[imberley]. De Vismes is still in bed with a bilious fever, & B.H. puts off any official talk until after the great feats he is giving us tonight. He returned my call on the 8th late in the afternoon, & was very friendly. He is very greedy of flattery, & has absorbed all the functions of govt. No one else has any authority whatever. I hope however that I may get a few things settled, in spite of his aversion to doing business.

PRO 30/33 14/7   Semi-official Letters from Morocco (July 10, 1894 to November 22, 1894)

Things are evidently going much better for the Sultan at Morocco City. The Govt. gives out publicly that he will go there in the spring, & I partly believe it. It is necessary for him to make an attempt to subdue the Zemmour tribe, & afterwds. he will I expect, go S.

I propose telling B.H. that I will come back in the spring to settle all the old claims with him, if he has no time to go into them now. I very carefully examined them all before I left Tangier, & think the whole cld. be done for $13,598 excluding one or two bogus ones. But I shall not press them.

De V. has bilious fever but is getting better.

y.v.t.

64. Satow to Lord Kimberley

15 Nov. 1894

Dr. Ld. K.,

I had my first business talk with the G[rand]. V[izier]. yesterday evening,[41] Kaid Maclean acting as interpreter, De Vismes being ill in bed with fever. After exchanging compliments and thanking him for an entertainment he had given me on the 12th, I spoke to him abt. my not having been told to put my hat on by Sultan at public audience, as is usual. He immediately assured me that the Sultan had asked me to cover, and had expressed surprise at my not doing so. The only possible ans[wer]. was that my interpreter had not heard the words, & I said of course that it did not matter, for one got so into the habit of putting a cocked hat under the arm that I had not noticed the omission. In fact, I rather excused my own inadvertence, & I am quite sure that the Sultan really forgot, just as I did myself. So the position is saved for the coll[eague]s: who may come after. I have written a short desp[atch]. on the subject.

After all, I do not feel that the ceremony is humiliating; the Sultan alone is on horseback, all the viziers being on foot and uncovered. That is to say, they remove the hoods wch. on all other occasions they wear on their turbans. In my own opinion, the manner of the Sultan is what decides whether the F.R. [Foreign Representative] is properly treated or not. Some

---

[41] Satow mentions this meeting in his diary for November 14, 1894.

PRO 30/33 14/7   Semi-official Letters from Morocco (July 10, 1894 to November 22, 1894)

people complain that it is humiliating to have to stand bare headed in the sun, but in South America I have had to do the same thing, with even more discomfort, & it never occurred to any of my colleagues that there was a loss of dignity.

The information the G.V. gave me abt. the policy of the govt. regarding the tribes abt. D.a.B. & in the South as recorded in my No. [   ] may be relied on. I feel certain that it is true, because it is so exactly in accordance with Moorish practice. The Sultan will be lenient with the first named, and having thus got them over to his side, will be able to be more severe with those further along the line of march. The Fr[ench]. legation & consul at D.a.B., with Dr. Linares, predict all sorts of evils, and I daresay they might not be sorry to see general anarchy. But I do not observe the signs of that. All the reports fr. the coast are tinged with a feeling that merchants will for some time be unable to recover their advances on produce, & they judge the situation to be bad accordingly.

I spoke to him abt. the best way of obtaining the arrest of the assailants of Mr. Madden & his companions, and suggested the employment of the usual plan in such cases, wch. is when the culprit is not forthcoming, to imprison his relatives, on the principle of collective responsibility. He said that the Govr. of Zuata had been told to make every effort to capture the fugitives, & if necessary to seize their families as hostages. He added that the app[ointmen]t. of a strong man like Kaid el Arbi to be govr. of DaB had already produced a good effect, wch. was shown by the stolen property being given up.

I then said to him that my mission to the Court was one of courtesy, to present my credentials & congratulate the Sultan on his accession. It was a fortunate omen for the harmony of our relations that he, whose father, Cid Morsa, had been a great friend of Sir John Hay's, shld. have been made gr. V. just at the time that I had been apptd. to Morocco. If on the occasion of my visit to the Court I cld. do anything to render our intercourse smoother, I was to take the opportunity & listen to anything the M[ooris]h. Govt. might wish to say, and that at the same time there were one or two matters of business on wch. I desired to converse with him.

He replied that he also had some subjects in his mind abt. wch. he wished to speak, but had deferred doing so lest I might imagine that he was anxious to see my visit soon over, & so he had said nothing until after he had been able to show me some hospitality.

PRO 30/33 14/7   Semi-official Letters from Morocco (July 10, 1894 to November 22, 1894)

I then said that there were a number of claims of BSs. [British Subjects] wch. it was very desirable to settle, so as to remove all friction betw. the two govts. A claimant of course had to show by some kind of proof that his demands were legitimate, & on examining the claims, wch. was a very long process, I had found that some of them were not supported by the necessary proofs, & these I had first put aside. Others were of a complicated nature, necessitating detailed consid[eratio]n. of documents, and I thought they might be conveniently deferred to a future occasion. A third class were of recent origin, such as those agst. Fez merchants and Mr. Forde's Habassi claim (on wch. a report was made to the F.O. by Sir W. Ridgeway). These I thought a word fr. him wld. be sufficient to settle.

The Vizier replied that if I wld. give him a note of each separate affair, he wld. let me know what he cld. do. It was lastly arranged that in case of disagreement we shld. discuss the merits together.

I have not written officially abt. this part of the conversation, but in the meantime I thought Y.L. [Your Lordship] might like to know exactly what I have been doing, especially as newspaper people & telegraph agents have already begun the game of misrepresentation. I have been very careful to confine myself to our own affairs, and to avoid all mention or disparagement of other nationalities or legations. There is one thing I regret, that in telling my colleagues at Tangier that I did not expect to remain more than ten days at Fez, I reckoned without the Moors. They are not to be hurried, and wld. have felt much surprised and annoyed if I had cut short my stay. Now the illness of De Vismes has come to justify my remaining. The Dr. says he cannot be fit to travel for another ten days or more. The V-C. has yet to come on the tapis [under consideration], and I have as yet no indications of the line the M[ooris]h. Govt. will take. One way or another I may be able next week to form an idea of when it will be possible to leave. But as long as the G.V. is friendly, & willing to talk, the longer I stay, the better for our future business relations.

 Believe me
 Dr. Ld. K.
 y.v.f.

65. Satow to Sanderson

PRO 30/33 14/7 Semi-official Letters from Morocco (July 10, 1894 to November 22, 1894)

Fez. 17.11.94

My dear Sanderson,

I have today drawn on the Secy. of State for £300, of wch. I have given £200 to Maclean for himself in accordance with the arrange[men]t. I made with Currie, & £100 for presents here to people for whom I had no specific gifts. An exact account will reach you as soon as the whole business is over.

   y.v.t.

66. Satow to Lord Kimberley

Fez

19.11.94

Dr. Ld. K,

As soon as I heard of the murder of Neumann at DaB, I asked for an interview with the G.V., of wch. I have given an acct. in my desp[atch]. No. 126 of yesterday. I said to him that I cld. not say what wld. be the nature of the reparation to be demanded, wch. it was for the German Min. [Tattenbach] to inform them, but I advised him to send some one to meet him on his way, & to express in the Sultan's name regret at what had occurred, & that he shld. let the Moorish people know how much he detested these outrages agst. foreigners. Today I saw him again, when he told me that the V[ice Minister]. for F.A. [Foreign Affairs] wld. be deputed to meet the Germ. Minister, & that the letters suggested had already been written. He thanked me very much for the advice I had given, wch. he said was a proof of true friendship. Orders have been sent for the arrest of the murderer or murderers, who are to be brought in chains to Fez. The effect of the Germ. Min's demand for the execution of the murderers has already been discounted by Dr. L., who at once told the court. I trust the advice I have given will be approved by Y.L.

I also handed to the G.V. a list of claims that have been presented since I took charge at Tangier, & a memo. on the old claims, embodying the gist of my desp[atch]. on the subject. I trust that this desp[atch]. will reach England in time for telegraphic instructions to find me still at Fez, shld. it be thought that I have taken too lenient a view of the obligations of the M[ooris]h. Govt. With Mr. De Vismes still confined to his bed with fever, I cannot well

PRO 30/33 14/7   Semi-official Letters from Morocco (July 10, 1894 to November 22, 1894)

leave Fez before the 3rd or 4th Dec. The G.V. after reading the memo. said he cld. promise me that I shld. be satisfied in the matter, & tho' one must not trust too much to Mh. promises, I think he must be relieved to find how moderate the demand is. Linares is reported to have told the Mh. Govt. that Engl. had not forgiven the refusal of my predecessor's [Euan-Smith's] proposals, & that I had been sent to lull them to sleep with soft words, preparing all the time to play off some disagreeable trick on them. He has played the part of spoilsport so long, that it is quite natural for him to try the game again.

I am to see the Sultan again privately the day after tomorrow, but it will not be necessary to talk business with him.[42]

The thorny question of the V-C. lies still ahead of me, & I do not yet see how it can be satisfactorily settled. As it was the Fr[ench]. who by sending an official consul here to make a fuss abt. protégés & so forth, really were the origin of the present difficulty, I shld. not be sorry to leave the discussion to begin with them.

The proposed embassy to Spain has not yet started, but the ambassador is on his way here to receive his instructions, & Dr. Cortes tells me he hopes to get all the money due [Melilla indemnity?] up to the present paid thro' the Amb[assado]r.

Gentile is still here, trying to settle the accts. of the arms factory & the cruiser that is being built in Italy. He is also trying to persuade the G.V. to place their other vessel the "Hassani" in Italian hands. At present it is captained & manned by Spaniards. But I doubt the negotiations being successful.

      y.v.f.

67. Satow to Ojeda

Fez.

22 11 94

My dear Colleague,

Y[ou]r. letter of the 14th was handed to me by Dr Cortes the evening before last, & we agreed that I shld. communicate its contents to B.H. yesterday morning. I had to pay a visit

---

[42] See Satow's diary for November 21, 1894.

PRO 30/33 14/7   Semi-official Letters from Morocco (July 10, 1894 to November 22, 1894)

to the Sultan, & afterwds. I drew the Vizier aside & asked him on what date Torres had informed you of the desp[atch]. of the Embassy; he replied that he had sent instructions the day he had informed me thro' Gh[arnit]. & that he had already heard that you had been much pleased. I then told him that on the 14th you had not yet recd. any communication. Also that you considered it desirable for the Embassy to reach Madrid when the Cortes [Generales] opened, taking the money [Melilla indemnity] c. it. He ans[were]d. that the money wld. leave here <u>in 3 days</u> time. Dr. Cortes has since told me that you have heard of the embassy going, & he is trying to obtain some written assurance abt. the money.

Our German coll. arr[ived]. today, but I have not yet seen him. De V. is still in bed, & it will be at least a week yet before he gets up. I hope however to get away fr. here in 10 or 12 days more, for I miss the society of my Tangier friends, & the comforts of civilization.

    y.v.t.

List of letters

PRO 30/33 14/8   Semi-Official Letters from Morocco (30 November 1894 to 3 June 1895)

PRO 30/33 14/8   Satow's Semi-Official Correspondence

Letters from Morocco beginning 30 November 1894.

Letters from Japan beginning 15 August 1895 (stamped p.69 to end of file) are in a separately transcribed volume with the following title:

Ian Ruxton (ed.) *The Semi-Official Letters of British Envoy Sir Ernest Satow from Japan and China (1895-1906)*, Lulu.com, 2007.

1. Satow to French Minister Monbel

30. 11. 94

My dear Colleague,

Many thanks for your note of the 21st, wch. was delivered to me by M. de Marcilly, and for having caused the "Diario" to contradict the statement abt. the supposed sealed packet.

Yesterday B.H. talked to me about our V-C [Vice-Consul] but without making any allusion to the Queen's letter or to the Sultan. He said that a consular officer was like a ball round wch. gathered others of his nation, but (that being manifestly not borne out by facts hitherto), explained that 'protections' were the great objection. I replied that my V-C. cld. not grant protections. He was under the Consul at Tangier, who in his turn was under the Minister, so that he holds a very unimportant position, his functions being chiefly to help visitors find lodgings, wch. as he knew they often had difficulty in obtaining for themselves, & to recover debts contracted by Fez merchants with houses of business in Engl. as he was also aware. He said finally that he wld. give me a written memo. on the subject, & I promised that I wld. send it to my Govt. I suppose that it may be necessary for me to remain here until I can hear fr. home whether Ld. K[imberley]. desires to pursue the subject any further at present. I have had a desp[atch]. approving that part of the memo. of our conversation with Ojeda, stating the course I proposed to pursue here – one of non-committal of my colls.

De V[ismes] is better but unable to leave his bed, & the Dr. says it will be weeks before he is able to do any work. Under these circs. I propose to send him to Tangier under the Dr's care, as soon as the roads are safe. Our postal courier fr. here to Tangier who started on the 26th was robbed abt 45 miles away, at the ford over the Warra, & all the correspce. carried off.

I am getting very tired of Fez, & wish it were already time for me to turn my back on

PRO 30/33 14/8   Semi-Official Letters from Morocco (30 November 1894 to 3 June 1895)

the place. Tattenbach also talked of a week, but I do not think he will be able to carry out his plans. I wish you were here, for without actual experience of the Viziers, it is difficult to realize how hardly they can be moved to transact even the simplest routine business.

    y.v.t.

      E.S.

2. Satow to Lord Kimberley (stamped p.3)

Dec. 2[?] 1894.

Dr. Lord K.

I am very much obliged for your note of the 14th Nov. All the news that reaches me here points to the gradual settling down of the people round Morocco, but as there is no regular service of couriers between DaB & Fez, my information mostly comes round by Tangier, and is older than what is sent forward by White.

Our Bubker tries to claim the credit of the pacification for himself & our other protégé Mulai el Hadj, but I find other people are also making out that the merit belongs to them, and the Govt. maintains that it was by force of arms that the Rehanma were subdued. But I have a private letter from Allan Maclean of the 27th reporting things much quieter everywhere, only one Taher Ben Shinan continues to levy blackmail where he can in the neighbourhood of Morocco. The real truth I believe to be that they brought over some of the other tribes, & the R. being outnumbered chose the better part of valour & gave in. Altho' I had written to our 2 protégés to exert their influence, I don't think they cld. do much.[1]

I had not expected to have any discussion abt. Cape Juby [on the coast opposite the Canary Islands] with the Vizier, & left all the papers behind me at Tangier, except some protocols of conversations betw. Euan Smith and the late Sultan. Fr[om]. them it wld. appear that the question is still regarded as unsettled, whether Juby belongs to the Sultan or not, & whether the Co. are to be left in undisturbed possession, and allowed to trade without interference. The Sultan seems to have said that he had forbidden all the tribes who acknowledge him to trade there. On the 2nd & 3rd occasions when he recurred to the subject Euan-Smith replied that he wld. not discuss it till the Commercial

---

[1] This paragraph may have been deleted. It has a vertical line through it.

PRO 30/33 14/8   Semi-Official Letters from Morocco (30 November 1894 to 3 June 1895)

Treaty was agreed to. So, altho' I think the Vizier has been advised to try to get the NWA Co[2] out of Juby, I shld. not be surprised at his talking abt. it spontaneously.

[The Co. I am told is in a bad way financially, & the £10,000 wch. for the last 4 yrs. they have been receiving has just enabled them to keep their heads above water. They will get another £10,000 next year & then be left to their own resources. D. Mack. [Donald Mackenzie] has told me that he was going to get a lot of money fr. financial people, but I have not yet heard of his success.][3] Perh. the Co. might be willing to go away for a cons[ideratio]n.

Then as far as the Fr[ench]. feeling in the matter is concerned, they probably regard Juby as about on a par with Tuat. At least the Sultan's claims to have them recognized as within his 'sphere of influence' wld. appear to them to possess abt. the same degree of validity. Could the one be set off agst. the other.

Suppose the Sultan were willing to (1) indemnify the Co. for the buildings, (2) to enter into an agreement to assume jurisdiction as far as Cape Bojador & to exercise authority at Juby by app[oin]ting a gov[erno]r. & customs adm[inistrat]ors (3) to keep the place open to Foreign Trade of all nations equally, applying the general Morocco tariff (4) to give us the refusal before ceding the territory to any other power. Wld. that be a basis of agreement wch. we might get the Fr[ench]. to enter into, namely to respect on our side the Sultan's sovereignty as far as Cape Bojador, on theirs, his title to Tuat and Figuig? I am inclined to think that as far as the Sultan at least is concerned we might be able to arrange on the above terms.

Our postal courier fr. here of the 26th returned a few days later, stating that he had been robbed of the mail. Macleod is trying to recover it, but is not sanguine of success. There is some risk therefore in writing.

The doctor has decided that De Vismes must be moved, presumably to the Hospital at Gib. and I hope to get him started in a few days. He has been in bed now four weeks and is very weak. I am making shift to do my work as best I can, but it goes on very slowly, and I fear it will hardly be possible to get away fr. here for some time to come. I

---

[2] The North West Africa Company was a British company which established a trading post near Cape Juby called Port Victoria. On March 26, 1888 Moroccan soldiers attacked the post. The company sold the post to the Sultan of Morocco on March 13, 1895 (see Satow's diary).

[3] Satow's parentheses.

have written privately to Monbel [on November 12th – see 14/7] all that has passed betw. the Vizier & myself on the subject to the V-Cs. He knew before I left that if a favourable opportunity presented itself, I shld. try to arrange the claims of BSs. [British Subjects] It is a pity he shld. have been misled by the maresnest [illusion, hoax] of my handing to the Sultan a sealed packet containing proposals for a treaty of commerce and I am almost afraid he may also have in turn misled the Fr. Govt.

y.v.f.

3. Satow to Lord Kimberley
9/12/94

Dear Ld. Kimberley,

I began to think it was time the G.V. [Grand Vizier] shld. show whether he intended to carry out his promises of attending to certain of my requests, one of them being for an exequatur[4] for [Allan] Maclean's new commission wch. includes Rabat. I called on him by apptmt. on the 6th and after speaking to him on the subject of smuggling arms & ammunition, and one or two other matters, inquired whether he had thought any more abt. the two questions on wch. he had spoken to me a week earlier, (Cape Juby & the Vice consulates at Fez). He replied that he was not yet ready. I then said that I had now been 6 weeks in Fez, that I was much obliged for the hospitality & good treatment I had recd. but thought the time had now come for me to take my leave. A visit of ceremony ought not to be extended too long. So as soon as the weather improved & the roads were dry enough, I shld. leave Fez. He replied that the weather was still rainy, and we cld. talk of that when it cleared up. I rejoined that the necessity of moving De Vismes was great; he had now been ill for nearly 5 weeks, & I must take the first opportunity of conveying him to Tangier.

The Vizier replied that he wld. inform the Sultan.

A couple of days later Kaid Maclean took an opportunity of letting him know that I was much hurt at the way in wch. the promises made to me had remained without fulfilment, & recd. assurances that everything shld. be done as I wished, & that I shld. leave Fez entirely satisfied.

---

[4] Exequatur: an official recognition by a government of a consul or other representative of a foreign state, authorizing them to exercise office.

PRO 30/33 14/8 Semi-Official Letters from Morocco (30 November 1894 to 3 June 1895)

Gharnit has also promised that he will tomorrow bring me various letters containing the orders I had asked for. One of these I am told is for the new Ghetto at Mogador. The old claims and debts of Fez merchants to houses of business in England I have treated separately, and promises have been made that they shall be settled, but I am not pressing them.

When the troubles round Morocco City began, I wrote to Bubeker and the Sherif of Tamshloht, another of our protégés, who seems to be a man of consideration among the Berber tribes in that part of the country, to use their influence on behalf of peace & good order. I have now heard fr. Bubeker that their efforts had been effectual, & that the Sherif is coming here with a deputation from the Rehanma tribe to implore the Sultan's pardon. If possible I shld. like to be here when they arrive, as I have not seen the Sherif. If all that Bubeker writes abt. his action is true, the knowledge of English influence having been exerted on behalf of the Sultan ought to produce a good effect.

The German Min[ister]. tells me he intends to remain here until he gets reports fr. Daralbaida showing that efforts are really being made to capture the assassins of Neumann. One man now in prison has confessed to being accomplice before the fact, & has accused two others, one of these is also under arrest. Sig[no]r. Gentile is still here. He has arranged I believe for the Arms factory to be continued for two years more under Italian superintendence, at the end of wch. time, if it goes [does] not give satisfactory results, the M[ooris]h. Govt. will take it over.

As an example of M[ooris]h. procrastination, I have only today received the promised copy of the Sultan's reply at my public audience on the 29 Oct.

My present calculation is that I cannot well leave Fez for another fortnight. That will give me time to know whether Y.L. [Your Lordship] wishes me to discuss Cape Juby.

    I remain

        D. Ld. K.

          y.v.f.

4. Satow to Sir Thomas Sanderson

Fez,

9.12.94

My dr. Sanderson,

I send the copy of your private letter of the 22nd Sept. wch. you asked for.

PRO 30/33 14/8   Semi-Official Letters from Morocco (30 November 1894 to 3 June 1895)

Our courier who left here on the 26th returned a few days later saying that he had been robbed. There was some fighting going on in the district he had to pass thro', & it is quite probable that being afraid to go on, he may have thrown his bag of letters into the river, & then returned with a plausible story of having been robbed. Such things have happened before. I made a fuss abt. it, & the 3 following couriers were escorted thro' the disturbed districts by mounted soldiers of the Sultan. I hope ∴ [therefore] that my despp. will have got safe to Tangier. This cover I am sending by Morant, who starts tomorrow with the Dr. in charge of De Vismes, whom they are taking to Laraiche. He has been now 5 wks. in bed c. fever, & the Dr. has decided that the only thing is to move him fr. here. If the fever leaves him en route, well & good; if not, the Dr. wants to take him to Gib. & after consultation, prob. will order him to England. I am telegraphing to ask that a man-of-war may be sent to Laraiche to meet them, as that will save 3 days.

Beyond making a couple of translations of letters fr. Bubeker, De Vismes has been unable to do any work. Consequently I have had to use Kaid Maclean as my interpreter, wch. perh. may have been advantageous, as he is persona grata c. B.H. Most of my written communications have been done for me by Macleod with the aid of a native scribe; for 2 of the important ones I used a Moor belonging to the govt. who understands Engl.

Up to the present I have accomplished no results. But Maclean assures me that the various requests I have made are being favourably considered, & that I shall get nearly all the small things asked for. That the principal Fez debtors of Engl. firms at home will be brought to book, & that B.H. will give me his word to pay the old claims after my return to Tangier. My long desp[atch]. on this subject will have shown that yr. instructions to make specific demands on acct. of specific claims have been adhered to. I gave B.H. a detailed list of what I considered to be really due to B.Ss., but the offer to pay (made thro' Maclean) came fr. him. I have not been in a great hurry to accept, because I hoped my report might be forwarded fr. here, & an ans[wer]. reach me fr. L.K. [Lord Kimberley] But I was disapptd. in this because White had not had time to go thro' my rough dft. wch. I left c. him & have it copied. His clerk & constable have both been ill. Then when I had got back the notes fr. him, & had the report copied here, it was lost in the alleged 'courier robbery'. Whether the promises of B.H. on these matters will be fulfilled or not is a matter that seems to me highly problematical. The Moors are given

PRO 30/33 14/8   Semi-Official Letters from Morocco (30 November 1894 to 3 June 1895)

to procrastinating, & put off everything till the last moment. So until I finally leave Fez it cannot be known whether my mission is an entire failure or not.

By way of stimulating B.H.'s sluggishness I told him 3 days ago that having been here 6 [3?] wks,[5] it seemed time for me to go, & that as soon as the weather was sufficiently settled I must start Tangier-wards. He did not seem at all desirous however that I shld. leave Fez. Our personal relations have been very friendly, & I shall endeavour to keep them so. For wishing to remain a little longer I have several reasons. I want to give time for some indication to reach me fr. home as to the desirability of my discussing Cape Juby. Then I have heard fr. Bubker that the chiefs of the Rahanma are on their way here with our new protégé the Sherif of Tamsloht, & I shld. like to be here if possible when they arrive. And also, I have some stores coming up fr. Tangier for the return journey, wch. may be here in another 10 days. I calculate my prob. stay here at another fortnight, subject to my receiving instructions to discuss Cape Juby. That wld. prob. be a longish business.

   y.v.t.

5. Satow to Lord Kimberley (stamped p.9)

Fez, Dec. 20. 1894

Dr. Ld. K,

I am still apparently as far as ever from getting away from Fez, altho' most of the small requests alluded to in my previous letter of the 9th have been accorded. A promise has been given to me that ground shall be set apart for a new Mella at Mogador, but the question who is to build has not been settled. The Vizier is not willing to provide the money fr. the Sultan's Treasury, & I do not know whether the rich & influential Jews at home, who have interested themselves in this matter, wld. advance what is necessary. I have suggested the apptmt. of a Commission of 5 respectable persons at Mogador, including our Vice Consul Johnston, & Mr. Reuben Elmaleh, to distribute the land among those who will build, and to establish regulations for preventing rackrenting by the richer Jews. It is this practice wch. leads to the overcrowding that has been complained of. I have obtained the exequatur of Maclean as superintending Consul at

---

[5] The handwriting is unclear. Satow reached Fez on October 25th (diary). Hence 6 seems more likely here.

459

PRO 30/33 14/8   Semi-Official Letters from Morocco (30 November 1894 to 3 June 1895)

Rabat, besides confirmation of our tenure of the consular houses on the coast mentioned in a report I wrote some time ago. But the addition of a piece of garden-ground to the Signal Station at Cap Spartel & one or two other small improvements suggested by Col. Hozier to Mr. White have been refused, as were requests that the export duty on millet might be assimilated to that on bird-seed, & that tourists might be allowed to pass M[ooris]h guns thro' the C.H. [Custom House] These two trifling things show the attitude of the govt. towards anything like commercial concessions. Of the import duties there is nothing to complain, but the exports tariff is undoubtedly too high to allow of the trade taking a natural development. I have carefully refrained however fr. mentioning the subject of treaties of commerce, as there is nothing the Moors hold so much in horror. If they made concessions to Powers whose aims are chiefly commercial they fear that those who have mainly political interests wld. demand in their turn concessions of another sort.

At the last interview I had with the Vizier, on the 16th, I reminded him of the short memos. I placed in his hands on the 19 Nov. abt. claims, & asked whether he had considered them. He replied that the subjects they dealt with were complicated, & that he must look into them himself, but he assured me his answer wld. be satisfactory to me. These claims are of two classes (1) the old ones that are a legacy of the past, dealt with in my recent despatch & (2) for money due by merchants of Fez to bankers & merchants in London & Manchester. With a little good will on the part of the M[ooris]h. Govt. these latter might speedily be settled, & I think I ought to insist upon their being put in a way of settlement now as I have been corresponding abt. them for the past 9 mos. Otherwise I shld. have to make another visit to Fez very shortly for the purpose.

Unluckily too, in the recent punitive expedition agst. the Gharb, of wch. mention I see has been made in the press, two semsars of Br[itish]. S[ubject]s. & an "agent" were looted. On receiving official information fr. the V-C. at Laraiche I spoke to the Vizier, & remonstrated very plainly. A circular note had been addressed to the FRR [Foreign Representatives] at Tangier by Torres, giving warning of the expedition, & asking that foreigners shld. withdraw their property. But 3 days before the date of Torres' note, these people of ours had already been attacked & plundered. Further reports having reached me, I again wrote to the Vizier, & proposed that a joint commission shld. proceed to the spot to ascertain the amount of property taken. My intention was to send V-C. Macleod who is very competent in matters of this kind. No formal ans[wer]. has

PRO 30/33 14/8 Semi-Official Letters from Morocco (30 November 1894 to 3 June 1895)

come from the Vz. but I was told by Maclean that the Govt. proposed on their side to send some one fr. Tangier. I have intimated that I will not consent to anything but a joint commission fr. Fez. In the meantime I have obtained fr. the plundered men, who have come here to see me, pretty accurate statements of what has been taken fr. them; fr. one man property worth abt. £250, fr. the 2nd about £100 worth, fr. the 3rd abt. £2000. But this last prob. includes property of his relatives. I think I ought to stay here until a proper settle[men]t. is at least in prospect.

One of these men was raided abt. 4 yrs. ago V.C. Forde presented a claim for some £300, wch. was afterwds. inquired into by Allan Maclean & Gleichen, & their report was sent home by Sir W. Ridgeway. There seems however reason to think that the property was not really Forde's, but that of his "agent", who by treaty is not entitled to protection. I am asking Forde for an explanation, & shall prob. have to report on the case. These unfortunate Moors, whenever they get into the black b[oo]ks. of their Kaid, go to a foreigner & execute a declaration that all they have is the foreigner's, & get an "agent's" certificate. This is issued on the faith of the foreigner's word, and the Moor fancies that it confers on him protection. Later on he is cruelly undeceived, as seems to be the case with this man of Forde's.

The Germ. Min. is still here. He has asked for the execution of one only of the 3 men engaged in the murder of Neumann at DaB, the other 2 to be imprisoned for life. Acc. to the M[ooris]h. view all three are equally guilty, & I think Tattenbach has made a mistake in allowing himself to be influenced by sentiment in this matter. I believe he is now engaged in trying to get some accts. settled in connection with the fort erected at Rabat by a German engineer & the wages paid of the crew of a steam tug at Rabat the order for wch. was given to him by the late Sultan.

Gentile has settled the accts. of the cruiser built at Leghorn [Livorno], and is trying to get the M[ooris]h. Govt. to carry on the Arms factory under the superintendance [superintendence] of Col. Ferrara. But the Moors, who are dissatisfied with the poor results hitherto obtained, want to get rid of the military man, and put the factory under the charge of the foreneman [foreman?] Notari. The latter was formerly at Mandalay doing similar work for King Thubaw. Gentile is also trying to obtain the transfer of the Sultan's st[eame]r. "Hassani" at present officered by Spaniards, and of the str. that brought out the 2 Krupp guns for Rabat and the tug just mentioned, wch. are in German hands. Then with the cruiser, also commanded by an Italian officer, there wld. be a small squadron all in the hands of Italy. But I am convinced that the Sp. will not consent to giving up the Hsssani, and the Fr. I believe have warned the Vizier not to put an Italian officer in command of the cruiser.

The rumour abt. Peregil [Perejil Island near Ceuta] was prob. sent to the "Tribuna" by an Italian at Tangier named Petri. This man is a sort of protégé of Cantagalli, and was sent by him to Morocco as a secret agent last March when Martinez Campos was negotiating his Melilla convention.

The embassy to Spain has not yet started. Cortes is trying to insist on the remaining $400,000 of the 1st instalment being sent fr. here, the $200,000 due in Nov. having been already despatched to Tangier. Ojeda not having asked my assistance in this matter, I have left Cortes to his own resources.

I believe the difficulties with the Rahanma tribe are in process of settlement, but no govt. officials can travel, nor govt. despatches be openly conveyed betw. the coast towns & Morocco City. The Govt. send their despp. by private hands, often entrusting them to the Jews. It is said that this is the cause of the frequent robberies of the French couriers betw. this & Tangier, some friends of the Rehanma people having found out that the Govt. despp. went that way. I have not yet recovered the bag that was robbed fr. our courier during the Gharb disturbances 4 wks. ago. Some of the Rehanma people arr. here yesterday, but the Sherif of Tamsloht has not yet made his appearance. The long illness of De Vismes & the necessity of sending him to Tangier have been a great inconvenience, as I have no European who can read confidential Arabic correspce. much less write the answers. Several letters fr. Bubker have consequently had to remain untranslated.

The Vizier has not said a word more abt. either Cape Juby or the Vice-consuls, and I have no idea what he proposes to do. His evil genius in all matters relating to F.A. [Foreign Affairs] is the Treasurer (Amin) Abdsulain Tazi. Gharnit seems disposed to take a more reasonable view of things. The Vizier reserves to himself the decision of every question, as the late Sultan did before him, and that is no doubt the chief explanation of the delays in business. Gharnit has but one clerk. Even under favourable circs. I do not think it wld. be easy or even practicable to settle the arrears of several years in a few weeks, as the extraordinary missions of the Powers always try to do.

Believe me &c.

PRO 30/33 14/8   Semi-Official Letters from Morocco (30 November 1894 to 3 June 1895)

6. Satow to Lord Kimberley

21 Dec. 94.

Dr. Ld. K,

After despatching yesterday's courier I personally examined the <u>semsar</u>[6] who is the greatest loser by the recent raids, & came to the conclusion that it is necessary to speak strongly to the Vizier on the subject. The omission to give me information abt. what was on foot agst. our protégés may perh. have been the result of heedlessness or stupidity, but it seems to me that the M[ooris]h. Govt. ought to be reminded that when the Br. Min. is at Fez he is the proper person to address with respect to such a matter as complaints agst. protégés & "agents". If the Vizier had spoken to me, instead of sending a communication thro' the Sultan's Tangier agent, I cld. at once have prevented what has happened. Habassi's impunity on a previous occasion has encouraged him to repeat his violence on an extended scale. No Fr. protégés have as far as I can learn been touched, & only one Italian protégé or agent. I hope that I may be strongly supported, not because I am in favour of "protection", but because the evil will grow if not checked, & our "prestige" will certainly suffer. As the Vizier is practically Sultan, I am endeavouring to throw the blame on Torres & the Kaid Habassi formisinterpreting instructions, tho' it seems as if the V. were very much to blame also. But it wld. be impolitic to hurt his feelings, as he is at present outwardly friendly.

It is easy to see fr. two out of the 3 cases that extortion on the part of the Kaid has been the motive for seeking protection. One of the men plundered has possessed a sort of paper of protection fr. the Sultan for the past 7 yrs. but finding that it was of no use to him, he 3 yrs. later obtained a semsar's certificate. He said to me that the only effective protection is that of "Xtians". As soon as a well-to-do native like this man gets protection, he is exempt fr. taxation, & as he expressed himself, fr. that moment he was at loggerheads with the Kaid. At the Madrid Convention it was agreed that protégés shld. pay agricultural & other regular taxes, but the provision remained a dead letter. It is a terrible imboglio out of wch. I see no escape, for the Fr. are quite impracticable on the matter of protection.

   E.S.

---

[6] semsar: native commercial agent, or broker enjoying consular protection.

PRO 30/33 14/8 Semi-Official Letters from Morocco (30 November 1894 to 3 June 1895)

7. Satow to Lord Kimberley (stamped p.15)

Fez

27.12.94

Dr. Ld. K

With reference to my desp[atch]. of the 21st, I saw the Vizier on the 23rd, and after talking to him very plainly abt. the violation of treaty committed by Kaid Habassi, handed him a Note protesting agst. what had been done and proposing to him the dismissal of the Kaid after making him responsible for all the plundered property. He agreed to everything, including the apptmt. of a representative of the Legation to assist in the inquiry, but objected to my demand for the dismissal of the Kaid, on the ground that it wld. pave the way to similar demands fr. other legations, for trivial causes. I said that I wld. not press this, but suggested that he shld. do it spontaneously, as then no precedent wld. be created, and he gave a solemn promise that the Kaid shld. be removed later on. On the 25th I recd. fr. him a very satisfactory letter expressing the concern of the M[ooris]h. Govt. agreeing to my sending some one to represent the Legation on the local inquiry, and promising that if the charge agst. the Kaid be proved of wantonly attacking a Br. protégé he shall be severely punished. I have not time today to forward the correspce. as I am very shorthanded, but the Vizier sent me a message expressing the hope that I wld. without loss of time inform H.M.G. of his readiness to afford redress. I am sending Mr. Macleod, as there is no one else at hand, and propose to remain at Fez until he returns with his report.

I notice a remarkable improvement in the tone of the two Tangier papers that are known to be more or less inspired by the Fr. legation. My circular note to my colleagues abt. the suppression of the trade in arms has been favourably commented on, and the notion that my lengthened stay here was for the purpose of obtaining concessions contrary to the political interests of others seems to have been completely dispelled. Personally speaking, I should be very glad to get away fr. Fez before the rains begin, especially as the discomfort of a Mh. house in cold weather is very great, but I am convinced that it is better to wait until I see the end of this affair of our protégés and get some sort of promise with regard to the old claims that they shall at least be attended later on. The notion has sedulously been instilled into the Vizier's mind that he must not settle Br. claims dating from the late reign, lest all the legations shld. at once follow suit; and it is advice wch. he will be only too glad to act upon. [End of letter]

PRO 30/33 14/8 Semi-Official Letters from Morocco (30 November 1894 to 3 June 1895)

8. Satow to Lord Kimberley

31.12.94

Dear Ld. Kimberley,

I am sending a report of further proceedings in regard to the plundered protégés, and regret that it shld. have to be so voluminous. But it seemed necessary to place the whole on record. The language of the translations of my Notes to the Vizier will perh. appear excessively complimentary, but the Arabic style is extremely ornate, and I have had to have recourse to the aid of the Moor already mentioned to put my drafts into Arabic, and these have been retranslated literally by Mr. Macleod.

I had thought it was all arranged satisfactorily abt. Mr. Macleod going alone for the inquiry. On the 24th I had informed the Min. for F.A. that he wld. be sent, and I understood that he was accepted. On the morning of the 29th however just as he was ready to start, I recd. a message fr. the Vizier thro' Kaid Maclean begging me to choose some one else. On inquiry I found that if I insisted, the impression wld. get abroad that I had by this means tried to force his recognition as Vice-consul on the M[ooris]h. Govt. by a side wind as it were, and that the Vizier wld. be accused of having allowed himself to be made victim of a clever trick. In fact very disagreeable things were being said. Partly, I think, these ideas had been put into the heads of the court people by a foreigner. I thought it wld. be better therefore to compromise the matter, in order to show that may action was without arrière pensée, and I arranged therefore to substitute Mr. Madden's name in the Note I had already addressed to the Vizier, and to send Mr. Macleod nominally as an interpreter, Mr. Madden's very slight knowledge of Arabic not enabling him to conduct the inquiry personally. My giving way on this point has caused great satisfaction to the Vizier, and I think that the intrigue wch. was intended either to bring about an open quarrel between us, or to weaken his position with his own people, has thus been frustrated for the moment.

Mr. Macleod is naturally much disappointed, but he has taken it very well, and I am confident that he will work in complete harmony with his coadjutor. It is somewhat inconvenient to be deprived of Mr. Madden's assistance just now, as I am thus left quite alone, but I saw no other way of arranging the matter. Mr. Macleod's position as an unpaid V-C. wld. I suppose have entitled him to consider himself free from rendering such services as he has given me almost from the first moment when Mr. De Vismes

PRO 30/33 14/8   Semi-Official Letters from Morocco (30 November 1894 to 3 June 1895)

was taken ill, and I shld. be glad to think that some way might be found of acknowledging them by a gratuity.

My last news from Morocco City, of the 18th inst. fr. a native source was in the highest degree satisfactory. The city gates were open, and the streets crowded with caravans. [End of letter]

Start of 1895

9. Satow to Lord Kimberley (stamped p.18)

Fez,

17.1.95

Dr. Ld. K,

Very many thanks for yr. telegram of the 8th approving my proceedings with regard to the plundered protégés. It has greatly strengthened my hands, & I am inclined to hope that tho' it may take a little time the affair will be satisfactorily settled.

I sent in a Note yesterday abt. the "Mayer" piracy,[7] & this afternoon recd. a verbal assurance fr. the Vizier that he accepted the responsibility, & wld. pay the indemnity without delay. He had sounded me thro' Gh[arnit]. as to postponing the pay[men]t. for 6 mo[nth]s. but I said that they cld. have no difficulty in finding this trifling sum, & that I had no instructions on the point. I wld. telegraph if he really desired it. On getting this reply he saw how absurd the proposal was.

The arch-obstructionist Tazzi has lost, it seems, some of the influence he had over the Vizier, with respect to F.A. [Foreign Affairs] & Gh's position is much stronger.

This afternoon I had a talk c. the Vizier abt. the necessity of having a small but well-disciplined force of abt. 5000 men to keep the peace among the tribes, & enforce the Sultan's authority over the provincial governors. He asked me to put my ideas on paper. I also suggested a plan for regulating the receipt of taxes, so as to ensure the collection of the revenue & prevent the governors fr. robbing the people. As he said to me the other day, it is the robbery & oppression of the governors that drives the people to take foreign protection. Certainly much more is to be hoped fr. good govt. than from a

---

[7] This was first mentioned in Satow's diary on August 5, 1894. He spoke to Torres and demanded reparation from the Moorish Government on August 23rd.

PRO 30/33 14/8   Semi-Official Letters from Morocco (30 November 1894 to 3 June 1895)

conference of the Powers for the abolition of protection.

He spoke to me also of his desire to send some Moorish youths abroad, in fact to England, to study & be variously trained. This suggestion was entirely spontaneous on his part, & it is a good sign. I applauded the idea, & said I shld. be very glad to assist him.

Altho' there have been rumours of renewed trouble at or near Morocco City, I believe that things are going on well. The people are coming in fr. Rahanma, also fr. Figuig all up to Morocco City, & the principal rebel will probably be captured before long.

A ridiculous story has been in circulation among the townspeople during the past week that I had bribed some one to hoist the Engl. flag on a mosque tower, & this canard [false rumour] will no doubt find its way into the Tangier papers. The U.S. consular agent at Laraiche, by birth a M[ooris]h. Jew, who is here abt. some claims, appears to have used a threat of hoisting the stars & stripes, if his affairs were not better attended to, and the Vizier actually gave an order for a guard of 20 additional men to be placed on his house. As he is lodged close by me, the idea got abroad that a 2nd row abt. the flag was impending.

Mr. Morant rejoined me from Tangier a few days ago, & perh. in a week or ten days I may see Mr. Madden & Mr. Macleod back fr. the inquiry into the plundering of our protégés. I calculate that it will require another month to finish this affair & to settle a commercial claim that has been pending for a year past.

   E.S.

10. Satow to Lord Cromer[8]

Fez.

19 1 95

Dr. Ld. Cromer,

The Vizier has recently been speaking to me abt. organizing a small but compact army, so as to provide the Sultan with force sufficient to keep order & to enable him to carry out various reforms in the administration.

Kaid Maclean, who has been with the late Sultan 18 years & possesses the confidence

---

[8] Evelyn Baring, 1st Earl of Cromer (1841-1917). 1st Consul-General of Egypt, 1883-1907.

467

PRO 30/33 14/8   Semi-Official Letters from Morocco (30 November 1894 to 3 June 1895)

of the Vizier will continue to command the infantry, the artillery remaining under Fr. instructors. There is no idea at present of bringing any more European officers, but what is greatly needed is drill-books in Arabic. If you could help me to procure a set of these as are in use in the Egyptian army for presentation to the Min[ister]. of War, who is the Vizier's brother, I shld. be very greatly obliged, & the bks. wld. be highly appreciated. The arm adopted here is the Martini-Henry.[9]

The reforms at present contemplated relate chiefly to taxation & the collection of revenue. I hope something may also be done to improve the administration of justice & the condition of the prisons. Taxation is more or less arbitrarily imposed by the district gov[erno]rs. who give no receipts, & defraud the Sultan on the one hand, robbing the people on the other, & driving them to seek foreign protection. In some parts of the country all the well-to-do people are under the protection of one or other Legation. The Vizier sees that the only way to amend this state of things & to establish the Sultan's authority is to make reforms in the collection of revenue. Negotiation with the Powers for restricting the abuses of protection was tried in 1880, and found to have the contrary result of increasing their number and variety.

Perh. you may have seen Sir W. Ridgeway's report on this country in the confidential print of July 1893. It gives a very good idea of the condition of Morocco.

I am very anxious to forward the present good intentions of the Vizier, & no doubt his attention has been aroused by reports that have reached him of what has been done in Egypt. Would it be possible to procure for him a set of the forms that are used in the collection of internal and Customs revenue in Egypt, as well as reports & other papers in Arabic relating to the organization of native courts & the prison administration. Mixed Courts like those of Alexandria are out of the question here, & the fanaticism of the people is so great that I wld. not even mention the subject to them. But anything that is native Musulman Arabic they wld. study with interest.

I send this letter thro' the F.O. the only safe channel for anything of a confidential nature. In the same way I would beg that anything you send me may be transmitted. It wld. be unfortunate if any one were to suspect that I was offering advice to the Vizier of this kind, & our French friends wld. probably be excessively annoyed if they thought there was any danger of the introduction into Morocco of ideas that have been

---

[9] The Martini-Henry rifle first entered service in the British Army in 1871.

successful in Egypt.

    B[est]. w[ishes] &c.

11. Satow to Boleslawski[10]

Boleslawski

Fez

23/1/95

My dr. Friend & Colleague,

Y[ou]r. letter of the 11th reached me only yesterday. For nearly a week we had been without news fr. Tangier, & were in a state of despair, for the arrival of the post is the only event of interest in this dull place.

It was not correct that Mr. McL. went to Marakesh to inquire into the drowning of a missionary lady. In Novr. some <u>semsars</u> of ours were raided in the district of Beni Malek, & after agreeing with the Vizier, I despatched Mr. Madden (my clerk) and Mr. McL. to hold an inquiry in conjunction c. a Moorish official. You know how long it takes to get anything put thro' in this country, & moreover the bad weather has impeded travelling, so the commission of inquiry has not yet returned.

With regard to the other matter you ask abt. I have not been able to settle anything, & indeed do not see how I can, for the consent of all the P.P. [Powers] wld. be necessary. It is only a day or two ago that I have been put in poss[essio]n. of the views of the Vizier,[11] & I must take some days to reflect what is the best step to take next. In the meantime tho' it takes time to arrange the smallest matters, I have made a little progress with my current business. Neither politically nor commercially am I attempting anything. I am trying to obtain the repayment of that money spent at Mogador by the Conseil Sanitaire, but cannot yet say whether I am likely to be successful.

    y.v.s.

12. Satow to Italian Minister Cantagalli

Cantagalli

27.1.95

---

[10] Karl von Boleslawski, Austro-Hungarian head of mission in Morocco, 1890-96.
[11] Satow met the Vizier on January 17, 1895.

PRO 30/33 14/8   Semi-Official Letters from Morocco (30 November 1894 to 3 June 1895)

My dr. Fr[iend]. & Coll[eague].

Y[ou]r. letter of the 11th for wch. very many thanks, reached me only yesterday, our courier having taken 11 days on the road. It was with the greatest satisfaction that I heard of your return to Tangier thoroughly restored in health & spirits, & I hope we may now keep you with us. Better pleased shld. I be if we could be here together, tho' just now is hardly the time for being on the road. Even if my affairs were settled, I shld. hesitate about embarking on a sea of mud. But as they are not, I am not called on to take a decision. Mr. Madden and Mr. Macleod who went just four w[ee]ks. ago down to the Gharb to inquire into the plundering of 2 <u>semsars</u> are still out. Owing to the soldier who carried the Sultan's orders to Alcazar having turned aside to spend a week with his relations, they did not get to work for about a fortnight, & then it turned out that the orders were not sufficient for the case. When I learnt this, it took me another week to get them amended. I felt that the mere statements of the injured semsars was [were] insufficient to demonstrate the extent of the wrong that had been done them, & that a careful investigation on the spot was necessary. I am glad to say I find the Court willing to do what is right, but as in many other countries of wch. I have experience, time is necessary to get the wheels to move. Certainly things go no slower here than in a South American Repub[lic]. The anomaly is our position vis à vis the central govt. wch. makes it necessary for us to try to dispose of the accumulated business of several years in a few weeks.

The political situation seems to be improving. I hear that Taher ben Shiman, the principal head of the disturbances round Marakesh, is dead, & the leaders of the Rehanma are here. That being the case, I doubt whether we are to fear a recrudescence of the late troubles. Owing however to the want of organized postal communication in this country, news fr. that part of the country reaches Fez mostly by Tangier. The Tangier papers I see talk a good deal abt. the impaired authority of the Vizier, but I distrust the impartiality of the source whence many of the rumours proceed. There are one or two intriguing persons among the natives who make it a business to talk to foreigners in this fashion, officious fellows too who want something for themselves, wch. they cannot hope for under the existing régime, & they fancy foreigners will be induced to help their schemes in return for a pretended exercise of influence.

As for the rumour abt. Tuat, I heard of it at the time it was started, but not attaching much credit to it, made no report to my govt. It reached me from various sources. On further inquiry, it appeared to be of the same character as much we have heard during the past few years, wch. turned out in the end to be false alarms. The Vizier has not mentioned the subject to me.

I am very pleased to hear that some steps have been taken for further considering what is to be done with the concessions obtained by d'Aubigny, & hope that in the end something of practical value may be achieved. When leaving for Fez, I was requested by the Com[mission] d'Hygiène to ask the Sultan for a subvention towards paving the streets, but having perceived no readiness on the part of the Treasurer to part with money for any purpose, have not said anything abt. the matter. The repay[men]t. of the Mogador expenses to the Conseil Sanitaire comes a long way first, & I have made representations on this point wch. I hope may be listened to.

But you will be tired of so long a letter, so I will bring it to an end. Aurevoir à bientôt. y.v.s.

13. Satow to Lord Kimberley (stamped p.24)

Fez

29.1.95

Dear Ld. K,

I hope it will not seem that I have gone beyond my instructions in the remarks I made to Gh[arnit]. on the M[ooris]h. memo. abt. V.Cs. He told me the Fr[ench]. Govt. had expressed their willingness to withdraw Marcilly if MacL[eo]d. were removed. This was done verbally, I know, thro' Dr. Linares, who has also tried to persuade the Vizier that I had powers to arrange the whole question. I therefore emphatically assured Gh. that the Fr. Govt. had stated they had no intention of withdrawing Marcilly, & I also satisfied him that all I cld. do was to transmit home the Sultan's wishes.

Gh[arnit]. said that only Engl[and]. & Fr[ance]. had as yet answered. The Ital[ian]. ans[wer]. is still in the hands of Gentile, who tells him he wishes to deliver it to the Sultan in person. I suspect that it is favourable, & that he is keeping it back to use as a quidproquo in his negotiations about the Arms Factory and the cruiser. He has I fancy settled nothing yet. He says the cruiser will cost £10,000 to £12,000 a year, and the Moors don't want to spend so much money on a useless toy.

The German Min. on his recent visit here seems to have said that his govt. wld. not reply. At least that is what Gh. tells me. But I think he is only waiting to see wch. way

PRO 30/33 14/8 Semi-Official Letters from Morocco (30 November 1894 to 3 June 1895)

things go. He dangled before Macleod's eyes the prospect of appt[ointin]g. him Germ. V-C, while abusing MacL. to me as dealing longly [for a long time; largely?] in protections in an underhand manner. I repudiated this accusation with some warmth.

Gh[arnit]. complained of the rémuant disposition displayed by Marcilly when he first came. Among other things he had made great fuss about some melon peel accidentally thrown fr. the roof of a house as he was passing; on that occasion Gh. had said to him that he shld. take an example by MacL. who all the time he had been in Fez had never made any trouble. Since that time Marcilly had been quieter. But he asked me whether the Fr. Govt. did not want M. to provoke a row, perh. get himself killed by some rough mountaineer, in order to afford them a pretext for coming to Oujda. I told him such an idea was absurd.

His testimony to MacL.[MacLeod's] tact & discretion is valuable.

Marcilly coming straight fr. Tunis was doubtless a little overbearing at first.

Gh. said that a Moor named Omar Barada who was formerly Sp. consular agent here used to keep a brothel. It is very likely, for the man is a bad character. Both he & the Fr. Algerian agent used to manufacture protections.

The Portuguese min. and all his Portuguese & Brazilian V.C. are without doubt most corrupt. Of the U.S. Consul-genl. Barclay my colls. have a low opinion: they have nicknamed him le faux bonhomme. All his consular agents deal largely in protections. Gh. said that the Laraiche man, whom I mentioned in my last private letter, has 200 employés. But this is possibly an exaggeration.

Gh. is both untruthful & indiscreet in the highest degree.

Our position with regard to this question wld. be much better if MacL. were a paid V-C. instead of being a merchant & thus having a direct interest in the existence of protection. I shld. think £300 a year besides his office allowance, & permission to receive 5% (acc. to the fee-table) for all sums he recovered for Br. creditors, wld. content him. I have however carefully abstained fr. giving him any encouragement to expect a change in his position.

If it were possible to get France & one or two other PP. [Powers] to agree that all protégés including <u>semsars</u> shld. pay the same taxes as town Moors, I think the difficulty wld. be solved. The V-Cs. wld. see that they did not pay more. Regarding Country semsars & employés I think the same arrangement desirable, but doubt its being feasible.

PRO 30/33 14/8   Semi-Official Letters from Morocco (30 November 1894 to 3 June 1895)

The complaint that the Madrid convention is not observed is quite just, even as regards ourselves. We have given <u>semsars</u> to small traders and English houses of business not established in Morocco, who are not entitled to them. And men like Forde the V.C. at Laraiche undoubtedly make a business of apptg. so-called employés. The numerous cases of so-called partnerships betw. Moors & BSs. [British Subjects] are of a very suspicious character.

The rumour abt. my wanting to hoist the flag on a mosque-tower is still the talk of the town, and takes the most grotesque forms. But I do not think it of any importance.

Madden & MacL. have not yet returned fr. their mission of inquiry, but fr. the reports they have sent me, I conclude that they are doing their work well & with a considerable measure of success. I hope to have them here soon. The rains have lately much impeded communication with them as well as with Tangier. [End of letter]

14. Satow to Sanderson (stamped p.27)

30 Jan. 1895

My dear Sanderson,

Many thanks for your letter of the 2nd. I have not been able to have any further talk with the Vizier abt. Juby, but he told Maclean that he intended to speak again on that subject.

I have written to Ld. K. some further details of Gh[arnit]'s talk abt. the V.C. question. The fear of the Portuguese & Americans & their shameless traffic in protections seems to be the principal difficulty. If we could get France, Spain & one or two other PP to agree that protégés including semsars & employés here shld. pay the same taxes as town Moors, I think that wld. afford a solution. E.g. at present our protégés who deal in slippers escape the market tax, & hence have a great advantage over other traders, who are driven to give them commissions to buy. This diminishes the revenue locally collected. Something in the way of a written agree[men]t., including also a clearer statement of the XI art[icle]. of the Madrid convention relating to the exclusive competence of the Mh. Courts in suits relating to real property wld. seem to meet the case. And as I have said to Ld. K. our position as to the V-C. question wld. be much better if McL. were a paid man, instead of being a merchant interested in the protection system as at present practised. The more I see of this place & the people, the more injudicious Euan-Smith's proceedings seem to have been. It was he who wrote to the

PRO 30/33 14/8   Semi-Official Letters from Morocco (30 November 1894 to 3 June 1895)

M[ooris]h. Govt. that MacL. wld. be entitled to hoist his flag & have a place of worship allotted to him, & Fez is the last place in the world where one wld. have wished to have a merchant V.C., even as discreet a man as MacL. on the whole is.   Whether a man bears the title of Consul or Vice Consul is to the Moors a matter of indifference.

I am sorry to say that the last accounts of poor De Vismes are not satisfactory. He was operated on successfully for abscess on the liver, but a week later the discharges still continued copiously, & the doctor feared the formation of a second one. I am afraid that under the most favourable circs. it will be a month before he can resume work.

Nahon writes again fr. Tetuan that he is too unwell to discharge his duties as Consular agent, & begs me to give him leave of absence. I cannot expect Morant to go back there, and Nahon besides being an incapable is in a ruined condition of health. Morant tells me there is absolutely no B.S. there wld. [who] cld. be apptd. The missionary Mensink whom I have formerly mentioned as a possible locum tenens will not return to Tetuan. But there is a Spaniard, at present clerk to the Sp. Consul, who is dissatisfied with his position, & M. thinks he could be got to take the post for £100 besides the fee allowance. I don't quite like a Sp. in such a post, but he wld. be cheaper than an Englishman.

I am beginning to think that the end of Feb. may see me start for Tangier. They have promised to pay the "Mayer" indemnity, and I have some hopes of being able to get a settle[men]t. of the old claims, on the lines laid down in my instructions. There remains the affair of the raided <u>semsars</u> wch. as far as can be judged fr. the reports that come in fr. M. & M. is going on as fairly as cld. be expected.

Tattenb[ach]. After having accepted $5000 for the widow of the Germ. subject murdered at DaB was met on his way back to Tangier by instructions to ask for another $15,000. I imagine that there will be some hesitation on the part of the M[ooris]h. Govt. abt. conceding this.

y.v.t.

P.S. There is a small detach[men]t. of 600 men on the way to Oujda, where there has been some fighting betw. the townspeople & the Angat tribe close by. Eventually they are to go to Melilla. Another body is being got ready in, it is supposed, abt. 3 wks. time, partly to make a show of force, but prob. in the main to fetch the Vizier's women.

E.S.

PRO 30/33 14/8   Semi-Official Letters from Morocco (30 November 1894 to 3 June 1895)

15. Satow to Boleslawski (stamped p.29)

8/2/95

[See pencil marks in letter of 23 Jany.

My dr. fr. & coll.]¹²

I wrote to you on 23 Jan. in reply to yrs. of 11, but my letter was unluckily in the bag that was taken fr. our courier on 30. It is very vexatious that these things shld. happen, & yet I do not see how it is to be prevented in a country like this.

It was not ... necessary.¹³ I have been put in possn. of the views of the Vizier, wch. I have laid before my Govt. In my own mind the most valid objection that he has put forward to the apptmt. of other cons. officers here is that certain PP. are in the habit of dealing out protection broadcasts[?], & the protégés are exempt fr. taxation. That is a wrong of daily increasing magnitude. For my own p[ar]t. I do not see how it is to be combatted except by the M[ooris]h. Govt. establishing fixed rates of taxation for its own people, & then the 12th & 13th Art. of the Madrid convention cld. be carried out by the PP.

Whilst waiting here all these weary weeks I have been able to make a little progress with my current business, but have not attempted anything else. I have tried however to obtain the repay[men]t. of that money spent at Mogador by the Cons[eil]. Sanit[aire]. but cannot yet say whether I am likely to be successful.

I was very much amused by the attempt to persuade the public that I had been threatening to hoist a flag, & had been invited to leave Fez etc. etc. The extravagant variations on this theme are quite worthy of Münchhausen. At the same time it all

---

¹² Satow's parentheses

¹³ This part is repeated from Satow's letter to Boleslawski of January 23ʳᵈ.

"It was not correct that Mr. McL. went to Marakesh to inquire into the drowning of a missionary lady. In Novr. some <u>semsars</u> of ours were raided in the district of Beni Malek, & after agreeing with the Vizier, I despatched Mr. Madden (my clerk) and Mr. McL. to hold an inquiry in conjunction c. a Moorish official. You know how long it takes to get anything put thro' in this country, & moreover the bad weather has impeded travelling, so the commission of inquiry has not yet returned.

With regard to the other matter you ask abt. I have not been able to settle anything, & indeed do not see how I can, for the consent of all the P.P. [Powers] wld. be necessary."

PRO 30/33 14/8   Semi-Official Letters from Morocco (30 November 1894 to 3 June 1895)

shows great poverty of imagination on the part of the inventors. Their 1st canard abt. the sealed packet containing proposals for a commercial treaty having fallen flat, they next started the 2nd[?] of Perejil[?]: & now this very obvious plagiarism of the incidents of 1892.

We have had a great deal of rain &c.

E.S.

16. Satow to Sir Percy Anderson (stamped p.30)

Fez

11.2.95

My dr. Anderson,

Mr. Nahon of Tetuan has returned to the charge, & asked to be allowed what he calls sick leave. He had 5 mos. last yr, but was not able to get himself put right, & in fact he never will. He has a y[ounge]r. br[other]. who has some times acted, but is afflicted c. even a worse form of constitutional syphilis. I am sending an official on the subject, wch. I hope may receive y[ou]r. support. The Br. Ss. who frequent Tetuan are nearly all Gibraltarians engaged in smuggling, & can only be kept in order by a man of some energy. Morant has spoken to me of a Span[iar]d. who is clerk at present to the Sp. Cons[ul]. He might do as a 'pis-aller', but there wld. prob. be a great outcry, & he wld. be sure to make things look as black as possible for Gib[raltar]. in acc[ordance]. c. the natural temper of all Spaniards. I have 2 Englishmen in my eye, either of whom wld. do. a Mr. W.S. Bewicke,[14] who acts as Secy. here to Kaid Maclean, & Reader, formerly legn. clerk, whose venture in cattle exporting seems to have been unsuccessful. I daresay the latter might be glad to come back to us, & he is a good honest boy. B[ewicke]. is an older man, of 35 or 40. a member of the St. Stephen's Club, & of good family. He lived in Madrid the earlier part of his life with an invalid father. Eventually he came into about £300 a year, wch. is now rather diminished by unlucky investments. He is discreet & trsutworthy. He wld. live at Rio Martin, the port of Tetuan, & be at hand for overhauling any vessel suspected of smuggling. With the native Basha an

---

[14] Satow records his death in his diary for August 16, 1912: "William Standert Bewicke, whom I got apptd. vice-consul at Tetuan in 1895, died of heart disease in the Gibraltar Hospital on the 10th…"

PRO 30/33 14/8   Semi-Official Letters from Morocco (30 November 1894 to 3 June 1895)

Englishman wld. of course have much more weight than a Jew of Barbary like Nahon, who is not even a B[ritish]. S[ubject].

    y.v.t.

17. Satow to Lord Kimberley (stamped p.31)

11.2.95

Dr. Ld. K,

 The 3 Fr. newspapers of Tangier have vied with each other in giving currency to the most absurd stories of my having offered bribes to Muezzins [prayer leaders at mosques] to hoist the Br. flag on the top of a mosque-tower, & one of them went so far as to hint that the M[ooris]h. Govt. had started the rumour with the object of frightening me out of the place. The Vizier having heard of this sent me today a very friendly message to say how vexed he was, & that he was certain I shld. not suppose he or any other responsible person wld. be guilty of such an intrigue agst. the repres[entati]ve of a great P[owe]r. like England. He said that if he cld. discover the author of these rumours, he wld. have him severely punished. He also proposed to have a letter written to some Tangier paper by a Moor in authority denying the whole thing.

 I replied that I did not for a moment suspect him or any other member of the Govt. of setting such stories abt. & that the Tangier newspapers were not worth taking notice of.

 I hear that a teleg. containing the most ridiculous details was sent fr. Tangier to the "Imparcial" at Madrid. The correspt. mayoral who sent it is Kerdec's collaborateur on the "Diario de Tanger".

 As I said before these things do not harm but rather the contrary, & the tone of the Court people could not be better. More than all, they are gradually settling all my business.

  [End of letter]

18. Satow to Lord Kimberley (stamped p.32)

Feb. 17. 1895

Dr. Ld. K,

 I have not had an opportunity till today of speaking to the Vizier abt. Cape Juby, tho' I had sounded him thro' Kaid Maclean 1ce. or 2ce. after receiving your telegram of the 9th Jany. Maclean thought the Vizier did not really care abt. the question. However,

PRO 30/33 14/8   Semi-Official Letters from Morocco (30 November 1894 to 3 June 1895)

when I went to him today he showed very great interest in it. I abstained fr. mentioning the amt. required, as I think it is the really difficult p[oin]t. as usual in these cases. I began by showing him the F.M.'s letter to White of 22/4/91 recording the settle[men]t. made c. Sir Wm. Green abt the indemnity of £50,000 of wch £10,000 is yet unpaid. I then said that the Co. had recd. a good offer, & wished to know as soon as possible whether the M[ooris]h. Govt. were disposed to treat. I said that on a former occasion the Co, after first proposing to pay duties a[t] 8%, with a monopoly of the trade, had offered to pay 10, but c. the same condition. The proposal now was that the trade shld. be open to everybody on the same terms as at the other ports. In ans[wer]. to a question whether the Co. offered to sell the land only, I said that the M[ooris]h. Govt. wld. acquire the town on shore, the fort, & the heavy guns, the company retaining their private property, such as merchandise & small arms. I thought I might safely say this, as being included in the words of yr. teleg. "buy them out". I also informed him that the Sultan's sovereignty would be recognized as far as the Sp. possns. beginning at Cape Bogador, c. the final condition that he shld. not part with it to any other power without the consent of Gt. Britain. He eagerly replied that they wld. never give to others what they had acquired fr. us, so I explained that the undertaking wld. not be so much in our favour, as a guarantee agst. any other Power, G.B. thus standing behind them as it were. He seemed very pleased, & promised to let me hear fr. him in a few days, as there was much he wished to talk to me about, including the recent incident at Madrid.

The news reached Fez on the 11th. On the following day I saw the Vizier, who seemed much pre-occupied. Linares had been at him already, & had given a contorted version, saying that the Envoy had refused to have his audience, & had been hissed by the Sp. troops. I was able to give him the true story, fr. Sir H.D. W[olff]'s teleg. to me, & next day I sent him a paraphrase thro' Kaid Maclean. The day before yesterday the Min. for F.A. brought me [Moorish Ambassador Sidi] Brisha's letter, in wch. he makes light of the incident, attributing it to a madman, & wisely says nothing abt. the blow having struck him on the face.[15] Gh. added that the Fr[ench]. had been urging them to treat it as a very serious matter. Whether L. & Sch. are acting on their own initiative or upon instructions fr. Monbel I do not know, but the latter (Schlum[berge]r) has talked at

---

[15] "News arrived of insult to Brisha at Madrid by an insane Genl. Fuentes, who slapped him on the face." (Satow's diary, 11 February 1895)

his own table in very strong terms. I think the Vizier is sensible enough to see that more is to be gained by accepting the excuses that have been offered to Brisha, than by making a grievance of the affair.

The Report I am sending abt. the raiding of British "semsars" contains the exact facts, & I have addressed a Note to the Vizier accordingly, claiming full restitution & inquiring what the punish[men]t. of the Kaid will be. But there is not time to have this copied for the special courier. In consequence of the recent robbery of our post under rather suspicious circs. I have given up using it, & employ other means of sending my correspce.

It seems prob. that the Sultan will go to Mequinez abt. 5 wks. hence & after staying there a while, go on to Rabat. The expedition for Oujda & the Riff has finally left today. [End of letter]

19. Satow to Sanderson (stamped p.34)
20.2.95

My dear Sanderson,

Sir H[enr]y. Burford-Hancock who has just been transferred fr. Gib. to Jamaica, writed to me abt. a personal matter. He says he has fr. many years past acted as a sort of legal adviser to my predecessors on many points connected c. their duties, & besides the part he took in the preparation of the Morocco O. in C. [Order in Council] & the rules under it, he has actively assisted in the organization of the Courts & in every way in his power helped those who had to carry on the work. Altho' he has worked long at these labours, & his position in respect of them has been recognized by the F.O., wch. on more than one occasion has called on him for assistance, he has never either wished for or accepted any pecuniary recompense, or even his expenses. Now that he is severing his connexion c. the Tangier legation, it wld. be a lasting gratification to him to receive some mark of HM's recognition of the services he has been able to render, & he asks me to make a recommendation to that effect.

I feel some diffidence in mentioning this to you, but I am sure that Sir H. has worked indefatigably for the improvement of the Consular Courts in Morocco, & I am inclined to hope that some way may be found of recognizing his services.

    y.v.t.

PRO 30/33 14/8   Semi-Official Letters from Morocco (30 November 1894 to 3 June 1895)

20. Satow to Col. Hozier[16]

20.2.95

Dr. Col. Hozier,

Yr. letter of the 2nd reached me here yesterday. I regret very greatly that my absence fr. Tangier during your visit has prevented our meeting.

With regard to the Agency wch. it is proposed to establish at Tangier, I beg to say that if the Committee at Lloyd's shld. decide upon its establish[men]t. I shld. view with satisfaction the transference of the duties fr. the Consular clerk to a business house of standing. The recent case of the "Benalder" [17]seems to show how necessary it is that Lloyd's agent shld. be a man of energy.

I do not know of anyone at Tangier who wld. be better able to discharge the functions of the office than the pres[en]t. agent for Forwood Bros & Co.[18]

y.f.

21. Satow to Sanderson (stamped p.35)

21.2.95

My dr. S,

The Juby negotiation is going on well, as you will have learnt fr. my teleg. It was Tazy,[19] the antiforeign member of the Govt, who objected to keeping the place open,[20] but when the Vizier heard what he had said to me on the subject, he was not at all pleased at his having taken such a line, as he had only instructed him to hear what I had to say, & not to argue. I hope this objection is overcome.

T. is also making difficulties abt. the settle[men]t. of the affair of the raided semsars. If we were to admit that the M[ooris]h. Govt. cld. at any moment deal c. protected

---

[16] Satow had met Colonel Hozier of Lloyds at the Foreign Office on December 3, 1891 (diary entry).

[17] SS Benalder ran aground and was wrecked when five nautical miles South of Cape Arat, Morocco on the 9th August 1894, when en route from Safi to Gibraltar with a cargo of beans. At the time of sinking she was owned by Whittles, Pallister & Co. of South Shields. (https://www.wrecksite.eu/wreck.aspx?201524   accessed 5 February 2019).

[18] Apparently Eugene Chappory. See diary for January 9, 1894.

[19] Presumably Abdselam Tazi.

[20] Tazi's objections were on grounds of distance and expense. (See Satow's diary for February 18, 1895.)

PRO 30/33 14/8 Semi-Official Letters from Morocco (30 November 1894 to 3 June 1895)

Moors as if they were under M[ooris]h. jurisdiction we might as well have no treaty at all. If a semsar has been made without proper reason or justification on the part of the foreign employer, an objection shld. be lodged at once. It is too late however when a man has had protection for 4 yrs. c. the knowledge of the M[ooris]h. Auth. to pretend that he shld. not have had it.[21] I hope that T's opposition may be overcome on this point also.

Prob. the Juby business will keep me here another 2 or 3 wks. In any case I suppose I ought not to leave until the semsar's affair is satisfactorily settled. The "Benalder" claim being of less urgent importance, I shld. incline to content myself c. presenting a Note, dwelling on the proofs we have of the plundering & demanding the $6000. I am a little disposed to think that Forde, who was extremely lethargic in the 1st instance & neglected to ask for guards to be placed near the wreck, has made a liberal estimate of the value of what was plundered.

y.v.t.

22. Satow to Lord Kimberley (stamped p.36)

Fez.

5.3.95.

Dr. Ld. Kimberley,

Since the date of my last private letter of the 17th Feb. I have seen Gh[arnit]. & Tazi 2ce. abt. the Cape Juby business. The latter tried hard to induce me to give way on the point of the place remaining open to trade, but I told him it was useless, & that I was certain H.M.G. wld. not consent to its being closed to trade. Moreover it was contrary to the Sultan's interest, as then Cape Juby wld. become a sort of Noman's Land as it was before the N W Africa Co. went there. I was to have had another interview c. them, but afterwds. on reflection I declined to have any more talk with Tazi, who is a most impracticable man, & sent a message to the Vizier thro' Maclean that if they insisted on closing the port I wld. drop the negotiation. This brought him round, as he is anxious for it to be arranged, not only on acct. of the prestige the Sultan will gain thereby, but also because of the present he expects to receive, in accordance with Moorish custom. He then asked that I wld. put the terms on paper, wch. I did, & on the 2nd Gh. came to me,

---

[21] See diary for February 18, 1895.

& took down a translation fr. Maclean's dictation. Today he brought me an Arabic version, the effect of wch. wld. be that the port wld. not remain open, & that no one wld. be allowed to trade there without the Sultan's express permission. I told him that this was altogether inadmissible, & that if they wld. not restore my wording the negotiation had better be dropped. He thereupon amended his draft, & took it up to the Vizier. Maclean has just returned to tell me that this point is settled satisfactorily.

An attempt was also made to induce me to accept pay[men]t. in five annual instalments, but I told Maclean that I cld. not agree to it, & this idea has been given up.

I have compromised the largest of the claims of our raided protégés for $10,000, his claim being abt. $14,500, but the evidence for his losses was incomplete, & I did not press for the whole sum. The other two men are to be paid in full. As soon as I get the Vizier's written undertaking, I shall be able to regard this affair as settled.

It is only Cape Juby wch. now keeps me at Fez. I hear that my Fr[ench]. colleague is coming here abt. the end of March, & it will be better for me to leave before his arrival, as the Moors are not accustomed to deal with more than one Minr. at a time. [End of letter]

23. Satow to Lord Kimberley

13.3.95

Dr. Ld. K,

I shld. have very much preferred to wait for a reply to my teleg. of the 10th transmitting my draft of the Cape Juby agreet. before signing, but the Vizier was ready, & moreover I had private intimation of renewed opposition to the whole business on the part of the Treasurer Tazy, & I thought it better to take the responsibility of signing without delay. I hope this step will not meet c. Y.L. disapproval, & I shall be on tenterhooks till I get a teleg. The Co. gets abt. £54,000 including presents, & £25,000 down insteading [instead] of only £10,000 at once. I do not think it wld. be possible to get better terms for them.

Gh[arnit]. asked me today abt. the V.C. ? [question] I replied that the PP [Powers] were being consulted.

I have recd. a very satisfactory note recording the arranget. for compensating the raided "semsars", & I have little left to keep me at Fez, beyond obtaining the actual payts. promised.

PRO 30/33 14/8   Semi-Official Letters from Morocco (30 November 1894 to 3 June 1895)

I hear that my Fr. coll: is to arr[ive]. here abt the 4th April.

24. Satow to Mackenzie of the North West Africa Co. (stamped p.38)
15.3.95

Dr. Mr. Mackenzie (Donald M.)

Part of the arrange[men]t. abt. Cape Juby is that the M[ooris]h. Govt. shall be allowed to send some officials there, to see that they get the buildings & guns delivered to them intact. I think it wld. be desirable if you cld. give a hint to yr. officials there to abstain fr. saying anything to make them think that Cape Juby is a disagreeable place to live in, or that the M[ooris]h. Govt. are not get[ting] a very valuable piece of property. Fr. the political point of view it wld. of course be difficult to exaggerate the value of the concession they are obtaining, as it must greatly add to the prestige of the young Sultan.

The idea as regards the property the M[ooris]h. Govt. are to receive is something like that wch. has formed the basis of the proposed arrange[men]t. between the E.A. Co.[22] & HMG, of drawing a distinction betw. public & private assets.

y.v.f.

25. Satow to Lord Kimberley
Fez

20/3/95

Dr. Ld/ K,

I had a very satisfactory talk c. the Vizier yesterday. He has agreed to settle everything, including the old claims on the basis of my Report, but with the exception of the claims of the underwriters for the plunder of the wrecked "Benalder". I hope however to get that also. If so, I shall come away c. no arrears but the commercial claims at Fez, wch. will take some time yet, as the def[endan]ts. are at Tangier.

Gentile has managed to get round Tazzi respecting the cruiser. Gh[arnit]. says Tazzi is to get $20,000 out of the $100,000 wch. are to be allowed for the annual cost, but one has to take all he says with a large grain of salt. Some time ago Gh. brought me a letter fr. Torres to the Vizier, wch. I suspect was inspired by the Fr. Legn. urging the

---

[22] Presumably the Imperial British East Africa Company, founded in 1888 and defunct in 1896.

uselessness & great expense of the cruiser, & he asked my opinion knowing the ambitious projects of Gentile for obtaining the transfer of the Hassani fr. Sp. to Ital. control, & of the two small st[eame]rs. at Rabat under Germ. manage[men]t. to Ital. hands also. I said I did not see what use the cruiser cld. be. He told me the Vizier had decided to write to the Ital. Govt. asking them to take the cruiser off their hands. He then asked me what they shld. do abt. the Arms Factory. I said they shld. carefully avoid wounding Ital[ian]. susceptibilities, & that it wld. be better to carry on the factory with an increased staff of Ital. foremen. I have since heard that an arrange[men]t. has been come to by wch. Col. Ferrara is to remain in charge, c. two Italian foremen, the present man[a]ger Notari being dismissed, & that Gh. told Gentile I had advised the Sultan to keep the factory going.

G. told me he was now going to discuss Italian commercial claims, and a case of piracy similar to that of the "Mayer". If he carries out this programme he will remain here some time longer, & that will enable him to watch the proceedings of Monbel when the latter comes up.

Linares, besides doing all he cld. to frustrate Gentile's plans, has also been trying to persuade the Moors that they have made an exceedingly bad bargain abt. Juby. Fortunately he knew nothing of the negotiations until they were concluded, otherwise his suggestions wld. prob. have found an echo in the mind of Tazzi, who also tried to oppose the agree[men]t. on the same ground. This & his failure to upset G. seems to show that Fr. influence is not very great at present.

The willingness of the Vizier to settle our affairs, even to the old claims, wch. I have not pressed, and the friendliness of all his proceedings, seem to indicate a real desire on his part to stand well with England, wch. will be greatly strengthened if his request to be allowed to send an Embassy were granted. Spain entertained Brisha during the whole of his stay, & 80,000 ps. [pesetas] were voted for the purpose. I hope ∴ [therefore] that if an Embassy goes to England the same treatment wld. be accorded to them. Spain sent a man-of-war to Tangier to convey the ambassador & his suite to Cadiz. Could we do something similar?

The only question wch. he wld. be instructed to treat wld. I think be that of the V-C. at Fez. This is naturally a very delicate matter. Mr. Macleod wld. undoubtedly be a great loser, even in his position as a trader, if the V-C were taken away fr. him. This seems to make it much more difficult to do what the Vizier desires, for the Fr[ench]. whose idea,

PRO 30/33 14/8   Semi-Official Letters from Morocco (30 November 1894 to 3 June 1895)

in the case of the withdrawal being agreed to, is to give Marcilly leave of absence, putting in an Algerian as locum-tenens, & then appt. Marcilly somewhere else. It is however possible that Monbel may come to change his views after some experience of Fez & of the M[ooris]h. Govt. At present he sees everything thro' Linares' eyes, who wishes to be the sole European agent here.

I hear that several persons connected with Morocco are aspiring to be apptd. in Mr. De Vismes' place. If it shld. be decided to app[oin]t. a local man I hope I may be consulted as to the choice to be made. What is needed at Tangier is a competent scholar in written Arabic, a man of some education and also that he shld. be thoroughly honest.

Speaking of De Vismes, I trust that means may be found of granting a compassionate allowance to his widow & children, besides the pay[men]t. of medical expenses. They will otherwise have only abt. £50 a year to live on. There can be little doubt that his illness originated on the way to Fez, when he separated fr. me & went by way of Laraiche to hurry up the presents for the Sultan. He took to his bed a fortnight after his arrival. Luckily none of the other members of the mission have suffered seriously, tho' all have been more or less troubled by the climate & bad sanitary conditions.

I am making efforts to wind up everything so as to get away before the great feast on the 28th of this month. Otherwise I shld. be kept here till the 4 or 5 of May[?].

The talk abt. the Sultan's starting on an expedition to Mequinez Rabat & Morocco has died away for the present. [End of letter]

26. Satow to Sanderson

Fez

25/3/95

My dear Sanderson,

In my reply to Ld. K's desp[atch]. No. 30 abt. V-Cs at Fez I have tried to be as discreet as possible, but I could not avoid saying something about the abuses of protection committed by other Legations. And I have also said nothing abt. another difficulty, wch. is that the M[ooris]h. Govt. & especially Tazzi, do not want to have VCs here on any terms if they can avoid it. This will appear fr. the Note addressed to Euan-Smith in 1892, of wch. no copy was sent home at the time.

This question at one time threatened to be my chief stumbling block, & I have endeavoured all along to temporize. At pres[en]t. the feeling of the Court seems to be

PRO 30/33 14/8   Semi-Official Letters from Morocco (30 November 1894 to 3 June 1895)

that the question depends on Monbel's attitude, & it will do no harm to let him try his hand when he comes up. For that reason I have not taken advantage of the authorization conveyed in Ld. K's No 30 of Mar 2 to repeat as fr. H.M.G. the observations I made to Gharnit. In my private letter to you of 30 Jany. & one of the 29th to Ld. K. I said that if the PP [Powers] wld. consent to semsars & agents at Fez & Mequinez paying the same taxes as Moors I thought the difficulty wld. be solved. Less than that I think wld. be insufficient.

y.v.t.

27. Satow to Sanderson (stamped p.42)
Secret
2.4.95
My dr. Sanderson,

I have given Kaid Maclean a cheque for £200, and have today drawn a bill on the Secretary of State for that amount.

y.v.t.   E.S.

28. Satow to Sir Robert Biddulph[23]
Fez.
5 April 95.
Dr. Sir Rbt. [Biddulph],

I am sending you officially a desp[atch]. abt. the inferiority of our courier services betw. Fez & Tangier to that kept up by the Fr[ench]. The latter treat it as a branch of their G.P.O. & it is consequently kept at a high standard of efficiency. From a pol[itica]l. p[oin]t. of view it is of importance to GB to maintain an efficient postal service here, because the natives, even officials make use of it, & our weight with the Moors depends on our showing that we are not behindhand as compared with others. I daresay Miss Cresswell[24] may not care to incur any increase of expenditure. In that case I wld. as [ask?] the F.O. to sanction my giving a subsidy for the purpose of increasing the speed of our post to Fez.   y.v.t.

---

[23] General Sir Robert Biddulph (1835-1918). Governor of Gibraltar, 1893-1900.
[24] Margaret Susan Creswell, Postmistress of Gibraltar.

PRO 30/33 14/8   Semi-Official Letters from Morocco (30 November 1894 to 3 June 1895)

29. Satow to Sanderson (stamped p.43)

Fez

10.5.95 [10.4.95 is correct.]

My dr. Sanderson,

I see in a local paper the reproduction of a teleg. fr. Tangier to the "Debats" that the M[ooris]h. Govt. had agreed to buy Juby for 1¼ million francs. The price is therefore public property, and I do not think anything further can be done to meet the wishes expressed by the chairman & secretary.

The agree[men]t. or rather the M[ooris]h. version of it, was sent by the M[ooris]h. Govt. to Torres who communicated it to Tattenb[ach]. & Monbel, I suppose also to other colls: The former criticised it severely to Torres, but his interpreter, whom he left behind here last Xmas, informed Gh. that he had instructions to say that it was an excellent arrangement. Gh. in telling this added that they now knew what sort of a man Tatt: was, not to be relied upon. M's attitude you will have learnt fr. my teleg. His agent here seems to have used rather theatrical language, & to have said that now they had placed themselves under English protection, France would through [throw?] them over. He accused the G.V. & Gh. in particular of having taken Engl. protection. Prob. much of the annoyance displayed is due to the colls: in question having been kept in the dark.

I hope my recommendation on behalf of Macleod for an allowance as translator will be favourably entertained. He has been most useful to me, and he gave up his own affairs to go away on that mission of inquiry, of wch. he was the real head, tho' to soothe the Govt, I made him interpreter to it; a mission too wch. was successful in every way. Without him it cld. not have been done, and the claims wld. not have been proved nor settled.

        y.v.t.

        E.S.

30. Satow to Sir Percy Anderson (stamped p.44)

10.4.95

My dr. Anderson,

I am exceedingly pleased that my recommendations with regard to Tetuan have been adopted, & I have proposed Mr. Bewicke for the apptmt. He is well known to Mr.

PRO 30/33 14/8   Semi-Official Letters from Morocco (30 November 1894 to 3 June 1895)

Justice Henn Collins, Mr. Macartney MP & to Mr. Richard Martin. He is a y[ounge]r. br[other]. of Mr. C.T. Bewicke of Hallaton Hall Leicestershire & another brother is Major in the Manchester Regiment. If it cld. be managed, I shld. be glad if you cld. excuse him the usual exam. for I do not think his French is very good, but he is better than most men in arithmetic, & his handwriting & spelling are what they should be.

  y.v.t.
   E.S.

PS. I shld. have said that he has been acting as private Sec. to Kaid Maclean for a year past, & during the last six months I have had plenty of opportunity of judging of his character.

31. Satow to Wodehouse[25]

Fez

15.4.95

Dr. Mr. Wodehouse,

 I hear that amongst the applicants for the vacant post of interpreter to the Legation at Tangier will be a Mr. Cecil Snow, in the employ of the Egyptian Govt. at Port Said, and I have been told that he is a capital man for the post. I shld. like to say one thing with regard to the choice that may be made, namely that a knowledge of epistolary Arabic, enough to enable a man to read & write without the aid of a scribe, is all-important, for it often happens that we receive confidential letters & have to send answers to them, for wch. it wld. not be safe to employ native assistance. Poor De V. possessed this knowledge in perfection, & I have much felt the inconvenience of being deprived of such assistance during my stay here.

 If I might make another suggestion it wld. be that the new man shld. not have the rank of V-C, but be simply styled dragoman,[26] because the functions he usually

---

[25] This is the Hon. Armine Wodehouse (1860-1901), son and principal private secretary of John Wodehouse (Lord Kimberley) when the latter was Foreign Secretary, 1894-5. Satow had previously written to him using the incorrect name 'Woodhouse' (PR0 30/33 14/7 No. 47, October 3, 1894).

[26] A dragoman was an interpreter, translator and official guide between Turkish, Arabic and Persian-speaking countries and European embassies, consulates, vice-consulates and trading posts. A dragoman had to have knowledge of Arabic, Persian, Turkish and European languages.

performs are not consular, & the possn. of the title of V-C. under such circs. is rather apt to lead to misunderstandings.

    y.v.t.

32. Satow to Wodehouse (stamped p.45)
Tangier 30 April 1895.
Dr. Mr. Wodehouse,

 Yr. letter of the 3rd reached me only a day or two ago, having been sent to Fez & back again here. So mine of the 15th was not a reply to it.

 If Mr. Snow possesses the necessary knowledge of epistolary Arabic, I shld. be quite satisfied, & I have telegd. to Gould at Pt. Said [Egypt] to inquire. Shld. he not come up to the standard, then the person I shld. be disposed to suggest for the vacabcy wld. be Mr. Alfred Irwin of DaB [Dar al Baida] at present in the employ of Messrs. Lamb Bros., the most respectable Br[itish]. firm in Morocco. He writes Arabic perfectly, & is also thoroughly acquainted c. Spanish. I know him personally, & can vouch for his character. But I have said nothing to him on the subject of the apptmt. & he has not put himself forward as a candidate.

 Ceteris paribus [all other things being equal], a man who knows the M[ooris]h. Arabic wld. be more useful than one acquainted only c. the Arabic of Egypt or Syria.

 Many thanks for what you say abt. the results of my work at Fez, in so kind a manner. It had to be carried on under unusual difficulties, & but for Kaid Maclean, I shld. have been helpless.

   Believe me
    y.v.t.

33. Satow to Sanderson (stamped p.46)
30 April to Sanderson. A short note saying that I had recd. orders for $15,000 on the old claims, the mistake of K.M. also "Mayer" indemnity, and promise abt. "Benalder" & odd $377.57.

34. Satow to Sanderson
Secret
Tangier May 1/95

PRO 30/33 14/8   Semi-Official Letters from Morocco (30 November 1894 to 3 June 1895)

My dear Sanderson,

I send you my account of various sums disbursed on acct. of secret service since the date of my letter of Aug. 7 last, enclosing Kaid Maclean's acct. up to that date. It includes $1300 given to Gharnit, of wch. $300 were for his services in connexion with the settlement of the Beni Malek raids. He is now very friendly.

Maclean found me an excellent source of information in a man named Gabbas[27], fr. whom I was able to learn all abt. the doings of Linares & Gentile. I gave him a present of $100 and $30 a month as long as he continues to be of service. I also gave a present now & then to Gharnit's y[ounge]r. br[other]. Si Mehédi, who was very useful also. The barley was for the Sultan's agent here.

I am drawing a bill on the Secy. of State for £8242.7.6 accordingly.

    y.v.t.

    1894-5

Kaid Maclean for couriers &c.

No. 1 account	$85.60
No. 2 "	353.10
Present to Gharnit	1300. –
" to Ci M. Gabbas	100. –
2 summer sheets for Sultan's horses	9. –
Barley for Hadj Mohd. Torres	11.12
Gharnit's br. Dec 31/94	10. –
Do Jan 6/95	10. –
Presents to people who brought supplies to H.M.S. Amphion	30. –
	$1908.82

In sterling at $575.5 = £100		
(May 1. 1895)	=	£333.7.5
Tennis set presented to Sultan		8.19.7
		£342.7.0

---

[27] Si Mahd. Gabbas is first mentioned in Satow's diary for November 18, 1894, being used as a translator.

PRO 30/33 14/8   Semi-Official Letters from Morocco (30 November 1894 to 3 June 1895)

Less £100 drawn for Aug. 7/94   100.
                                  £242.7.0

35. Satow to Kaid Maclean (stamped p.47)

May 1, 1895

My dear Maclean,

Many thanks for your No.2 of April 23. I am sending to Coutts' for you a bill at 3 days sight on the Ch[ief]. Clerk F.O. for £139.15.7 and a cheque on my bankers for £26.4.0, the equivalent of $950 balce. Due to you @ 572.50 = £100, the rate of the day. I trust this will prove correct.

   y.v.t.

36. Satow to Sanderson

Tangier

May 2. 95

My dr. Sanderson,

In reply to your private letter of 10/4/, I think the M[ooris]h. Govt. wld. feel it very much if they were not allowed to send a Mission. With the exception of the "Benalder" case, as to wch. I got a promise fr. the Vizier that, judging fr. his past acts, he is not likely to repudiate, they have settled everything I put before them, & in every possible way manifested their desire to renew the ancient friendship c. Engl. & to bury the recent past. Over the old claims I had no difficulty or discussion whatever, the V[izier]. simply accepted them & said they shld. be paid.

My instructions when I came out here implied that the question depended on the reestablishment of good relations, & when the subject was mentioned to me first by Maclean I told him that the Mh. Govt. had first to prove their friendly disposition. I think he will have said something of the sort to the Vizier, of course as fr. himself, & it prob. influenced his line of action. To refuse therefore under present circs. wld. I think lessen his goodwill towards us, while to accord permission wld. strengthen his position with his own people, & encourage him to go on as he has been doing in regard to our affairs.

   y.v.t.

PRO 30/33 14/8   Semi-Official Letters from Morocco (30 November 1894 to 3 June 1895)

37. Satow to Kaid Maclean

No. 1

Tangier

3/5/95

My dear Maclean,

I was asked privately fr. Engl. abt. the proposed 6139[28] and recommended it strongly. It wld. produce a good effect if I cld. teleg. that I had recd. a Note fr. Vizier agreeing to settle the "Benalder" affair. I am quite sure the people swam on board & got the stuff carried away on donkeys in sacks & swarries [?]. Prob. they used ropes fr. the ship to sling it along to where the animals stood waiting. The "Benalder" was a big ship carrying at least 20,000 fanegas.[29] Only 692½ fanegas were saved by our people.

We have had bad news fr. Morocco City of wch. I enclose a copy.

Frost reports on the 26 Apr. the arrival of Mulai el Amin[Amûr?] with 1500 men. Officially they are said to be 200 horse & 1800 infantry, but Frost thinks lesser number nearer the mark.

The above please tell the Vizier fr. me.

I have read all the correspce. abt. the Abdul Wahed case. It appears that his countrymen made grave charges agst. him, wch. were believed by the Egyptian Govt.

He was only <u>ookeel</u> *ookeel* [attorney? agent?][30] of the Moors in Egypt, & had no exequatur as consul fr. the Sultan of Turkey. So he was treated as any ordinary person, as coming under the jurisdiction of the Egyptian Courts. Twice he was fined 500 fr. for assault and misappropriation of property. There is no trace of its having been a question of whether he shld. pay taxes or not. It was in 1887 that the row abt. him began, so that it clearly was not in consequence of the Br. occupation, wch. began in 1882, that he was refused recognition as a consul.

Under the circs. I do not think there is any chance of his being recd. there again as Mh. Consul. & I cld. not conscientiously advise the Mh. Govt. to notify us or the Eg[yptian]. Govt. that the present Sultan has reappointed him. It wld. be merely to

---

[28] 'mission' is written above the numbers. Are they code for 'mission'?
[29] A Spanish measure of grain, beans etc. Roughly 55.5 litres.
[30] This word may be an alternative form of the Arabic 'wakil' meaning 'agent'.

expose him to a rebuff. Will you kindly tell him this fr. me. The summary of his case given above you need not mention, except to the Vizier in case he asks you abt. the matter.

I shld. be glad if you would ask the Vizier for the promised letters, in order that if possible they may reach me before I go on leave. The date of that event is not yet fixed, but I hope it will not be long *frist*.[31]

Kind regards to Mrs. & Miss Maclean, I asked you the date of Kaid Jilali's[?] birthday but you have not told me, O faithless one.

The Co's secretary will be here on the 9th, so please ask the Vizier to hurry up his people.

in cypher   I think it will be best to send the £6000 to your banker to your credit. They can get 5000 new sovereigns, and the box & its freight to Tangier out of the bal[an]ce. of say $725 after deducting the $5000 for Gh[arnit]. Please write them a letter of instructions to that effect, & send it to me by a safe hand. The box shld. be addressed to White, as I shall prob. be away when it comes.

   y.v.t.

P.S. Please say all sorts of nice things to the Vizier, and say we had a very pleasant journey down.

38. Satow to Sanderson (stamped p.50)

Tangier

4.5.95

My dear Sanderson,

I know the F.O. takes no cognisance of the Bushta Fund, but I do not like to deal with it, without telling you. Last year I spent, besides the two sums of $500 given to the English Jewish school & Hope House Hospital, $110 in repairing the Consular House at Tetuan. The balce. now left in the hands of the Legation Banker is $1085.35. If you see no objection, I shld. like to give £100, say $575, towards the erection of the new church, wch. when finished will be a credit to England, and deserves help.

   y.v.t.

---

[31] Apparently 'frist', an obsolete word for period of time, or delay.

PRO 30/33 14/8   Semi-Official Letters from Morocco (30 November 1894 to 3 June 1895)

39. Satow to Kimberley

5/5/95

Dr. Ld. Kimberley,

I showed the draft of my desp[atch]. abt. the Ital[ian]. cruiser to Monbel, who was quite satisfied with it. He is anxious he says to avoid giving the Fr[ench]. press any pretext for making trouble abt. the matter. If the pres[en]t. plan is adhered to of the vessel having an état-major of Italian officers, the Fr. Govt. will insist on the Sultan having a ship built in Fr[ance]. to be commanded by Fr. officers. He admits frankly that this wld. be to impose on the Sultan another useless piece of property.

All he desires here he says is equality of influence, & a preponderant position given to any Power wld. of course be resisted by France.

Ojeda, who came to see me yesterday afternoon, spoke of the cruiser in much the same way as Monbel. He tells me that abt. the end of Feb. he wrote to Madrid a desp[atch]. urging the necessity of a common understanding betw. Engl. Fr. & Spain with regard to Morocco, believing that such a combination wld. have immense weight with the Sultan. In this view I agree, but am not sure whether the Fr. wld. act straightly with us. Monbel is evidently very much afraid of the press.

He told me that Martinière[32] was the composer of the letters published in the Débats wch. purport to come fr. Tangier. I am quite certain that L[inares]. furnished Martinière with news fr. Fez, for in those letters I have seen falsehoods that Gh[arnit]. boasted of having told L. in order to put him off the scent. Notably with regard to C[ape]. Juby he told L. I was asking the Sultan for letters to the tribes to carry on trade with the Co. When he learnt that the sale had been effected he was of course furious.

Maclean learnt fr. Gabbas that L. has again told the Mh. Govt. that neither Fr. nor any other Power will consent to the clause binding the Sultan not to cede the Juby territory without consulting Engl. & has recommended them, when they get possession, to inform the PP of the arrange[men]t. omitting this clause. One does not quite see what good that wld. do.

It seems that I was in error in supposing that the text of the arrangement was

---

[32] Probably Henri de la Martinière (1859-1922). French explorer, archaeologist and diplomat.

PRO 30/33 14/8   Semi-Official Letters from Morocco (30 November 1894 to 3 June 1895)

communicated to Monbel & Tatt: thro' Torres. Judging fr. what Boleslaw[ski]. has told me, I think none of them have seen the text. I have not shown it to anyone. Monbel's only allusion to the matter was to say that he wld. be at a disadvantage at Fez, because [he] had nothing similar to give the Sultan. He seems to think the V-C. question will give him trouble. The day after Marcilly started fr. Fez, a Note arrd. fr. Gh[arnit]. in such pressing terms that if it had come a day earlier, d'Aub[igny]. cld. not possibly have sent M[arcilly]. He fears that the Mh. Govt. may believe that M[arcilly]. was sent in spite of that Note. His intention is to follow the line I took, & say that the question must be referred to a genl. agreet. of the PP. [Powers] He is vexed at the Spaniards having pro[mise]d. not to appt. a V-C. as long as those already apptd. are not recognized, thus encouraging the Mh. Govt. in their present attitude.

Ojeda thinks the recent agreement with regard to the indemnity & other clauses of the Martinez Campos agree[men]t. was a great blunder, & that Brisha successfully hoodwinked Groizard.[33]

The result of a calculation sent in by Mr. MacL. after I left Fez is that the gain to the Moors is only $70,000, but they have got rid of the clause abt. the intervention in the C.H. [Custom House] to wch. they had a very lively objection.

The last thing I hear abt. the cruiser is that the G.V. [Grand Vizier] has put before Gentile an agree[men]t. that that ['that' repeated] the Ital. officers of the cruiser shall take their orders fr. the Mh. Govt. & fr. no one else.

Tatt: came back the day before yesterday, without having succeeded in obtaining the arrest of Rockstroh's murderers.[34] His landing armed men fr. the "Alexandrine" was not necessary for his safety, & is condemned by all my colls: The Sp. Min. spoke to me very strongly abt. it.

I thank Y.L. [Your Lordship] very sincerely for the high compliment of offering me the legation at Tokio, the responsibilities of wch. are so great at the present moment. It is an apptmt. for wch. I had not ventured to hope.[35]

---

[33] Don Alejandro Groizard (1830-1919). Spanish noble and Minister of State, 1894-95.
[34] See diary for April 11, 1895. Rockstroh, a German subject, was murdered by one of his camel drivers between Mazagan and Saffi.
[35] A telegram from Lord Kimberley offering Satow the Tokyo post reached him on May 2, 1895. (Diary)

PRO 30/33 14/8 Semi-Official Letters from Morocco (30 November 1894 to 3 June 1895)

40. Satow to Maclean (stamped p.53)

Tangier

5.5.95

My dear Maclean,

Many thanks for your 2 letters of 28 & 30 April, both of them numbered 3.

Yr. conversation with Gabbas abt. C.J. [Cape Juby] is interesting, but I do not intend to show the agree[men]t. to any of my colls, & they have not asked me abt. it. The Br. Govt. will doubtless do that in good time.

Tatt: came back the day before yesterday. It appears he landed a dozen armed sailors at Saffi for his personal protection agst. the wish of the governor, who convened the consuls & asked them to protest.

Another Riff piracy occurred on the 25 Apr. 7 miles fr. Alhucemas, agst. a Dutch sailing vessel laden with oil fr. Oran. The Capt. a Dutchman was shot, & died of his wounds, & the mate who is Engl. is now in hospital at Gib. with a bullet in his belly. The pirates are prob. the same people who sacked the "Mayer". I don't suppose the Vizier can do anything, but if this sort of thing goes on, we shall not be able to prevent Europe taking the matter into her own hands.

I think you might tell B.H. [Ba Hamed] if you have a good opportunity that I consider it unwise to have Italian officers on the cruiser.[36] You know why.

y.v.t.

P.S. Our camels have not turned up, & Hadj el Arbi says many people have come in, & can give no news of them. I shld. be much obliged if you wld. kindly make a stir abt. them, as Morant & I cannot go away on leave till they arrive.   E.S.

P.S. I think you shld. order for yourself the Diario de Tanger, Eco Mauritano, Reveil du Maroc, Moghreb al Aksa & Crónica, & charge the cost in your acct. c. us.

41. Satow to Sanderson (stamped p.54)

Secret

Tangier

7.5.1895.

---

[36] "Italian officers on the cruiser" is given in numerical code, written above the words: "7579 1448 2529 2413". Presumably this cypher was used in the letter sent to Maclean.

496

PRO 30/33 14/8   Semi-Official Letters from Morocco (30 November 1894 to 3 June 1895)

My dr. Sanderson,

I have paid all the medical expenses connected with poor De Vismes' last illness, as authorised, and have drawn a bill at 1 mos. sight on the Secy. of State for £94.3.3 (the total amount) in favour of Parr's Banking Co. & the Alliance Bank, Ld [London].

Mrs. De Vismes is very grateful to Ld. K. for relieving her of what wld. otherwise have been a heavy drain upon her extremely limited resources.

  y.v.t.

42. Satow to Maclean

Tangier

7.5.95

My dear Maclean,

I do not believe there is a word of truth in the story told you by P abt. Germ. Min. wanting to pocket the money, but I have been told here that the extra sum was paid. I shld. not like by asking a question to give even the slightest ground to anyone to think that I regarded it as possible.

Thanks for the three letters abt. [Nicholas] Dassoy's land. But I am rather vexed that the letter for the balance of the old claims has not come. I think Ci Said would do very well, because he can be nice when he likes.

I expect to be off to Engl. very soon, but will let you know as soon as the date is fixed.

  y.v.t.

P.S.   Your no.5 recd. this morning. I hope we have at last got the truth about the desp[atch]. of the C.J. [Cape Juby] money. We have heard so many diff[erent]. stories, that I begin to fancy something is going on that we are not cognizant of.

I send you a Note for delivery to the Vizier abt. the plunder of the goods washed ashore fr. the "Mequinez" lighter at Laraiche, together with an Arabic copy for our other friend, and Engl. copies of that & a preceding Note for your information. These you shld. keep by you. The goods were insured by an Engl. Co. & the loss in consequence of the robbery falls ∴ [therefore] on our people, & we are obliged to claim it fr. the robber vill. [village?]

The horses & mules all stood the journey very well. Our camels are announced as being today at Akbat al Hamra.   E.S.

PRO 30/33 14/8 Semi-Official Letters from Morocco (30 November 1894 to 3 June 1895)

43. Satow to Maclean (stamped p.55)

4.   7 May

My dr. Maclean,

Torres says they find the loss on Hassani coin in amount like the $15,000 & the $17,076 [   ] for the "Mayer" indemnity & the Conseil Sanitaire is 6 or 7%, not ½% as the Makhzen seem to have supposed, & he has sent off a courier to inform the Court and ask for instructions. Of course I cannot accept anything less than the full amount in good Sp. dolls; for I have officially reported that orders to that effect have been given me by the Court. Please do what you think best about quickening the desp[atch]. of fresh instructions, as I want to square up matters before leaving.

   y.v.t.
    E.S.

44. Satow to Maclean

5.   May 9.

My dr. Maclean,

The Secy. of Cape Juby [Mr. Raynor?] has arr[ive]d. [Margin: in cypher] Please tell B.H. & say that no time shld. be lost in paying over the £35,000 here, & sending down the officials & soldiers that they may start thither at once. It is all the more necessary to hasten, as I am obliged to go to Engl. at once, but wish to see this put thru', as he requested me, before I go.

   y.v.t.

45. Satow to Sanderson (stamped p.56)

9.5.95

My dr. Sanderson,

I think there can be no doubt that the piece of land spoken of in yr. teleg. of yesterday is Khankosh, as I suggested in my reply. Jack Green does not possess an acre, tho' abt. 18 mos. ago he got his mother to advance $400 towards paying off a mortgage on a piece he talked of buying.

Neither Morant nor I knew of the existence of cypher E, & it was White who cleared up the difficulty today.

PRO 30/33 14/8   Semi-Official Letters from Morocco (30 November 1894 to 3 June 1895)

Tattenbach's escapade at Saffi is condemned by most of the colls: It appears that when he first got there, he used to have a Mrs. Russi & a Miss Jennings to lunch & dine c. him almost daily at his encampment, & it was only after the arrival of the "Alexandrine" that he found the spot unsafe without a doz. sailors to guard him.

Mr. Raynor turned up today,[37] so I sent off a courier to Fez to hurry the Vizier with the pay[men]t. of the money, & the despatch of the people who are to take the place over. I am not quite comfortable in my mind abt. Monbel. He has scarcely mentioned Cape Juby to me & I am inclined to think that when he reaches Fez he will try to upset the agreement. He is, acc. to present arrangements, to start on the 15th. I hear nothing of Ojeda's going to Fez at the moment, & think he does not wish to be there at the same time as Monbel, to whom he wld. in a measure have to play 2nd fiddle.

I am very pleased at the prospect of going to Japan, & hope it will soon be settled. I wanted to come on leave on my return fr. Fez, but cannot move as long as things are uncertain, so propose to wait until I hear fr. you. I shld. have a great deal of packing to do, besides disposing of my furniture & horses.

y.v.t.

46. Satow to Maclean (stamped p.57)

[No.6]

12.5.95

My dr. Maclean,

I was very glad to receive your No. 6 yesterday with the letter fr. Gh[arnit]. enclosing orders for the $377.57. I think I have already acknowledged the 3 letters abt. [Nicholas] Dassoy's land.

Torres told White yesterday that the bal[an]ce. of the C.J. money has arr[ive]d. & that they wld. begin paying it over today. So that what is now needed is that the officials who are to take possn. shld. speedily arrive here.

---

[37] "Raynor came. Discussed with him the ? [question] of taking over Juby. He is disposed to urge that the N.W. Afr. Co. shld. hold the house on the reef until the bal[an]ce. is paid. I said I thought the Moors had always been pretty punctual in the pay[men]ts. of the indemnity, and that therefore there was no ground for supposing they wld. fail to carry out their engagement. Then I sent off an express to Fez with letter to Maclean to hurry up the money and the despatch of the officials who are to take over Juby." (Diary,) May 1895).

I think that by my last special I sent a Note for B.H. abt. the robbery of the lighter at Laraiche. Please tell him that I had orders fr. home to put in this claim.

Today I am sending to him a note on closing a correspce. c. Torres abt. <u>semsars</u> & "agents" taking part in local rows. I suppose this means really what has taken place at DaB [Dar al Baida]. There an Ital. protégé shared in the robbery of Fernan's cattle, & owing to the supineness of the Ital. cons. agent was allowed to escape. What I want the V[izier]. to do, please tell him, is to <u>name</u> the individuals, & we will do our best to second his efforts to check this lawlessness.

It is indeed necessary for the V: to take energetic steps to quell the disaffection in the S.

Thanks for the skins. Can you tell us what we owe you for them.

   y.v.t.

47. Satow to Maclean

[No.7]

Tangier

12.5.95

My dr. Maclean,

I enclose a copy of an extract fr. a letter of Nairn's to y[ou]r. br[other]. dated the 4th. It is evident that things are very serious at Morocco City, & if the hands of El-Marani are not strengthened there will be a disaster.

Mulai el Amin's men do not number more than 800, as you told me at Fez.

Will you kindly tell the Vizier of this fr. me. Add that I was much relieved to hear that he intended to take energetic steps to put down the present anarchy, & I trust he will lose no time in taking the necessary measures. What those shld. be he can best judge, but for my own part I have no doubt that liberality & regularity of pay wld. bring plenty of men to the Sultan's standard.

The Germ[an]. Min[ister]. returned here today in the "Alexandrine". Your brother [Allan Maclean] writes to me fr. DaB abt. the business wch. took him there. As I shld. like you to know all about it, I send you a full extract of his letter. My object is not to volunteer any information to the Vizier, but that if he shld. ask you, you will be in a position to tell him the facts, & that your br[other]. only intervened in order to prevent serious trouble to the Mh. Govt. Bet[ween]. you & me, I do not like this bustling activity of the Germ. coll: wch. when it becomes known, will I fancy be severely commented on by the others.

y.v.t.

48. Satow to Lord Kimberley

Private

13.5.95

Dr. Ld. K,

My Germ[an]. coll[eague]: has been displaying great activity lately. A few days after his return fr. Saffi, he started again for the coast in his corvette, and proceeding to Rabat, presented certain demands for pay[men]t. of debts due to Germ[an]. S[ubject]s., wch. under pressure of threats that force wld. be used, he got settled. Flushed c. success, he next proceeded to DaB [Dar al Baida], where he repeated the same process, but found the Govr. by no means so ready to yield. So he sent for Mr. [Allan] Maclean, & induced him to see the Govr. & bring him round. Thus what will be represented in Germany as a triumph of Germ[an]. diplomatic energy is really due to the influence of a Br[itish]. consul.

C[oun]t. Tatt[enbach] said nothing to his colls: abt. the steps he was going to take. If he had said to me beforehand that a man-of-war was to be used for the purpose of enforcing a trifling claim on behalf of a protégé, I shld. have given him to understand that we have no sympathy with that method. It seemed to me that he was not acting in acc[ordance]. with etiquette, to make use of Maclean to pull the chestnuts out of the fire for him, & I gave him that to understand pretty clearly. It is not the 1st time he has held communication c. Maclean on diplomatic matters without informing me of his wish.

The explan[ation]. of all this activity at Rabat & DaB prob[ably] is to be found in the attacks made on him in the Germ. press wch. originated in letters written fr. the latter place wch. were publ[ished]. in the "Tägliche Rundschau", accusing him of having mismanaged the Neumann murder case. 3 men were concerned in that murder, but one only was executed & that too in a hole-&-corner fashion, so that it had no deterrent effect. I think that another motive is to alarm the Sultan's Court, & to make them feel that Germany can be disagreeable if necessary. Lastly my coll: hopes that the Vizier will be stirred up to take energetic actions to restore the authority of the Sultan.

Monbel thinks, & I agree with him, that naval demonstrations & landing marines are

PRO 30/33 14/8   Semi-Official Letters from Morocco (30 November 1894 to 3 June 1895)

proceedings calculated rather to diminish than to support the prestige of the Sultan. At the same time it is not necessary to take Tatt: "au grand sérieux" & I have said as little as poss. in my desp[atch]. on the subject.

I hear fr. Fez that Linares has told the Court that he has written a letter to the "Débats" severely criticizing Tatt's proceedings, so the press will come to know of it before long. Of course L. did not, when he wrote, know of this second escapade.

When I protested to Tatt: agst. his making use of M[aclean]. without consulting me beforehand, he refused to admit that he had done anything irregular, & said rather rudely that he was not going to take instructions fr. me. I told him that if that was his opinion, I was sure it wld. not be that of H.M.G. I added that I wld. take care H.M.G. shld. know how useful M. had been to him.

The C.J. money or rather the moiety due at once has arrd. here & is being paid over. By the end of the week the Sec. of the Co. will have recd. the whole of what is due on the pres[en]t. occasion. I have written urgently to Fez to ask that the officials who are to take over the buildings etc. shld. be sent here at once, in order to proceed to C.J. c. Mr. Raynor.

y.v.t.

49. Satow to Maclean
No. 8
15/5/95
My dear Maclean,

Your No. 7 by Allal reached me the day before yesterday. Many thanks for the 3 alternative letters enclosed. The greater part of the C.J. money has been paid in to Pariente, & that part of the transaction will, I hope, be completed by the end of the week.

[In cypher]   I enclose a cutting fr. the Cronica. As the Mh. Govt. have given away abt. the indemnity in the former case, I do not see how they can refuse it for this new one. It is regrettable. As to the execution of the 12 men, I shld. think those who actually inflicted the wounds shld. be put to death, the others imprisoned.

Monbel leaves [for Fez] tomorrow. he will have with him Gauderax & Couget (secretaries) Malpertuy (dragoman) Capt. Moncoq fr. Rabat & Dr. Spirakoff. I do not know what he will have to talk about beyond claims & some incursions said to have

PRO 30/33 14/8   Semi-Official Letters from Morocco (30 November 1894 to 3 June 1895)

been made by frontier Moors into Algerian territory.

I enclose 2 letters for the Vizier, one abt. a scoundrel at Rabat who pretends to be bankrupt. I fear Suezy[?] *Swezy* is not straight. The other is to ask for a letter for Manuel Bonich & his secy. to go to Maraksh as soon as the roads are safe, to get rid of Bonich's property and a house he bought in his servant's name. As Bo. wants to leave Maraksh & go elsewhere, I presume to the coast, it wld. be good policy to further his plans. If you can get a copy besides the Sherifian letter I ask for, I shld. be much obliged.

[End of letter]

50. Satow to Maclean (stamped p.61)

No. 9   (by post)

17.5.95

My dear Maclean,

Bewicke's apptmt. reached me yesterday, & we are sending him an official notification of it. I hope it will be convenient to you to let him go pretty soon, as I am anxious to have him installed.

All the C.J. money has now been paid with the exception of £1000, wch. we shall get in a few days, I suppose.

I am sending the Vizier a Note, of wch. the usual copies for yourself & Gh. are also sent, abt. a cattle robbery at Salé. I have put "responsible auth[ority]." in the Note because I do not know who ought to pay, the Govr. of Rabat or him of Salé. Will you kindly tell the Vizier that I shld. be glad if he wld. decide who is to make good the loss suffered by Abensur, who is a very respectable man, and not one of those who ever ask for more than their due.

You will have heard fr. y[ou]r. brother of the murder of Tubudi. I shall be curious to learn what line will be taken by Monbel.

y.v.t.

P.S. The Fr. mission started at 7 yesterday morning. Ojeda, [Belgian envoy Edward] Ansp[ach]. & I did not go to see him off, as he had told us he was starting early on purpose to avoid the usual ceremonial, & it does not indicate any coldness betw. Monbel and us three. E.S.

PRO 30/33 14/8   Semi-Official Letters from Morocco (30 November 1894 to 3 June 1895)

P.P.S.   I have just heard fr. yr. br[other]. that the missing Fr. man has turned up.

3P.S.   I send also a Note about a claim of the Tangier Cattle Co. wch. is, White tells me, completely substantiated.

51. Satow to Sir Percy Anderson (stamped p.62)

Tang.

May 18, 1895.

My dear Anderson,

I am sending a desp[atch]. enclosing dft. of the instructions for Allan Maclean wch. I was told in Nr. 4 Cons. of Mar. 20/94 to frame. The delay is due to my long absence at Fez & the dilatoriness of the Mh. Govt. with regard to the exequaturs for the new commissions.

I consulted Maclean abt. them. He thinks that in the case of a special occurrence requiring a visit fr. him to any particular port or to any place in the interior, He shld. not be obliged to obtain the Min's sanction beforehand. He says it goes without saying that he wld. not undertake any journey involving risk without consulting the head of the Mission.

With regard to correspce. he wishes that the V[ice]-C[onsul]s shld. not corresp[ond]. with the Head of the Mission except in cases of urgency. If they do it will lessen the Consul's influence and prestige with his subordinates. He regards the whole system as consisting of the Legn. & two units. One unit is the Tangier consulate, the other is DaB. Each shld. be responsible for its own organization, but, he adds "a greater centralization than that I do not think wld. be of advantage to the efficiency of the public service".

However, it will be for you to judge. Fr. what I have seen of Maclean's proceedings, I incline to think that he likes playing off his own bat, & honestly thinks he ought to govern his own province without interference fr. the legation, & that if he were left too free a hand he might commit indiscretions, wch. are natural enough in a man who has had no official training.

    y.v.t.

52. Satow to Coutts & Co. (bank) (stamped p.63)

Coutts & Co.

May 1895

PRO 30/33 14/8   Semi-Official Letters from Morocco (30 November 1894 to 3 June 1895)

Dear Sirs,

I enclose a letter fr. Kaid Harry Maclean with reference to a sum of £6000 wch. I am remitting to you to his credit.

Please be so good as to obtain £5000 new sovereigns fr. the Mint, of this y[ea]r's coinage if possible. Please purchase a very handsome suitable iron box with good lock & pack the above coins in it. The box & freight & insurance of the contents shld. not exceed £100. Put the iron box into a strong wooden case & ship it insured, addressed

   H.E. White Esq.

   H.B.M. Consul

    Tangier.

c/o H.E. The Govr. of Gib[raltar].

Please inform Mr. White of its shipment and send the key in a registered letter to Mr. White.

The £5000 and all other expenses to be debited to the acct. of Kaid Harry Maclean.

   y.f.

53. Satow to Maclean (summary)

Maclean.   18.5

Telling him of my departure.

54. Satow to Lord Kimberley (stamped p.64)

19/5/95[?]

Dr. Ld. K.

I think there is a good deal in what the C.J. [Cape Juby] co's people on the spot say abt. the possibility of trouble when the transfer takes place, & so I have written an official desp[atch]. on the subj. The presence of the [torpedo gunboat H.M.S.] "Hebe" wld. I think be suff[icien]t. to keep the tribesmen quiet.

Maclean writes fr. Fez at request of Vizier that the Mh. officials for C.J. wld. leave for Tangier on the 15th, but I think there may still be some delay.

Monbel started for Fez on morn[in]g. of 16th very early, and as he had given me to understand he wished to leave unobserved, neither Ojeda the Belgian nor I got up to see him off. He seemed not very happy abt. his mission, & the question of the V-C will give him some trouble, as L. has been telling the Vizier that Fr[ance]. was quite willing to

PRO 30/33 14/8   Semi-Official Letters from Morocco (30 November 1894 to 3 June 1895)

withdraw their man if we took away MacLeod, & I do not think he quite takes the same view. L. has also been stirring up the Vizier's mind agst Tatt: while Monbel has been disposed to minimize what Tatt has been doing at Saffi & elsewhere. Altogether it must be unpleasant for him to have an Agent at Court who writes direct to Hanotaux,[38] & as a rule acts independently of the Legn.

A curious story comes fr. DaB. It seems Tatt told his 'confidant' Fernan, who tho' a B.S. is Swedish V-C, that before leaving Tangier he had obtained a free hand fr. the colls: to take any steps he liked at Saffi. An occupation had been determined on, but the anchorage being a bad one, & the landing sometimes impossible, an ultimatum had been forwarded to the Sultan, stating that if Rockstroh's murderers were not delivered up within a fortnight Germ. troops wld. occupy some port. Fernan was under the impression that the port selected wld. be DaB.

As far as we, the Span[iard]s. & A-H[Austro-Hungarians] are concerned there was no such understanding, & I think Tatt was merely trying thro' F. to frighten the Gov. of DaB. Still it seems to me poss[ible]. that Monbel may have encouraged Tatt, in the hope of a row ensuing, as wld. certainly happen if troops were landed. Monbel, who is not on very cordial terms with Ojeda, was daily at the Germ. Legn. paying great court to Mme Tatt who is not an attractive woman. Ojeda says he has found Monbel false to him on more than one occasion, & I conclude that the attempt to form an alliance with the Sp. to the exclusion of Engl. has failed at least as far as Tangier diplomacy is concerned. Ojeda says that Moret warned him not to put his confidence in Monbel.

Fr. Fez I learn that the Germ. demands are 1° publ[ic]. execut[io]n. of 12 men concerned in murder   2° imprison[men]t of 2 Kaids whose men they are   3 $20,000 indemnity   4 salute of 21 guns to Germ. flag at Tangier. Vizier has offered [to] execute men proved guilty or to pay $20,000, but refuses to do both. He also undertakes [to] punish 2 Kaids, but refuses [to] salute flag. Think he is acting on L's advice.

Vizier thro' M[aclean]. asked my advice abt 1° & 3°. Wrote on 15th to say that thought cld. not get out of paying indemnity besides punishing murderers c. death, as they had already admitted principle in Neumann case. thought those who actually

---

[38] Gabriel Hanotaux (1853-1944). French Foreign Minister, May 1894 - October 1895, 1896-8.

PRO 30/33 14/8   Semi-Official Letters from Morocco (30 November 1894 to 3 June 1895)

inflicted wounds on R[ockstroh]. shld. be executed & rest of robbers imprisoned. But this advice will not reach Fez till today.

Vizier greatly hoping mission to Engl[and]. will be allowed. In that case his br[other]. the Min. for War will prob. be sent, & he wld. prob. be with him. This I think wld. be good combination.

   y.v.f.

55. Satow to Maclean (stamped p.66)

[No.] 10

20 May

My dear Maclean,

Your no. 9 just recd. Please pay Ci Fdul the $5000. It is only today that I have recd. the £6000, the £29000 having been paid on the 18th. A cheque for the former sum goes forward tomorrow to your banker with instructions about £5000 and box, wch. will be addressed to White c/o Govr. of Gib. [See No. 52 above.] whom I shall ask to send it over here in a gunboat. Of the claims, Mayer indemnity and Sanitary Board money I have not yet recd. anything, owing to the question of the exchanges not beong settled. As soon as the claims are paid, White will write to you to pay Si Fdul,[39] & will remit the equivalent to your banker.

The rest of your news is very interesting – I am writing again to urge the Abdurrahman Bengelum claim being paid by Rishdi the late Basha of Fez.[40]

Perh[aps]. what you have been told abt. the shares given to O & another is inspired by envy?

Y[ou]r. advice on the subject of Rockstroh's murder is just what I shld. have given myself.

I am going to give the Sultan's mule to Torres & the horse to the Basha, as I do not like selling gifts. I tell you this in case you shld. be asked.

When I arrive in England I will try to get the bags you want & have them sent out.

Most of the colls: seem to think the demand for a salute to the flag unreasonable. That is only done when one <u>nation</u> or <u>govt.</u> does something to another wch. has hurt its

---

[39] Note the inconsistent spelling of Ci/Si Fdul in the same paragraph.
[40] This paragraph has a wavy line through it.

PRO 30/33 14/8   Semi-Official Letters from Morocco (30 November 1894 to 3 June 1895)

honour.

I sincerely hope the plan abt. the Mog[ador]. Mellah[41] will be carried thro'.

We have not yet heard who is to be my successor. But whoever it is, he will be told to pursue the same line of conduct as myself, that was laid down for me by Ld. Rosebery & Ld. K. & has been fully approved. My app[ointmen]t. to Japan, wch. is a post of higher rank & 2ce. the pay is the evidence of this. I hope the V[izier]. will understand how much I esteem him & the great value I put on his friendship. It is with the greatest regret that I leave this country, & I wish to say to him how grateful I am to the Sultan & himself for the friendly & courteous reception that was accorded to me at Fez. I shall never forget this, & constantly desire their happiness & prosperity.

Oya Maheb, I cannot sufficiently express to you the obligations I am under to yourself for the altogether invaluable help you gave me in a task that but for you wld. have entirely failed of success, & if I have an opportunity of seeing my successor will tell him he may always rely on you to the utmost.

y.v.s.

56. Satow to Kaid Harry Maclean

3 June [18]95.

My dear Maclean,

Many thanks for yr. letters nos. 10 to 13, & one without a no. of May 23. The advice you gave to the Vizier abt. strengthening the army was excellent. Unless they do something of the kind the country south will certainly go to pieces. The complaint ag[ain]st. Bubeker is very vexatious; I hope it is not true, but those protégés are a very uncertain lot.

I have almost decided abt. the bag for the Vizier, & it will be made by Rodrigues of Piccadilly, a very good man, & sent to you thro' White. They are however to give me an estimate. I took fr. Tangier the words "F.A." & "H A" in Arabic, & hope they will come out all right.

No decision has yet been come to abt. my successor, at least had not last Friday. I am afraid however that the Vizier's suggestion is not likely to be adopted, as the F.O. want to send a member of the Diplomatic Service if possible. That you w[ou]ld. be a most

---

[41] A 'mellah' is a walled Jewish quarter in a city of Morocco.

efficient Bashador [ambassador] I have no doubt, but just think how jealous the other PP [Powers] wld. be.

I said on the 29th if nothing occurs in the meantime, & am coming back to town on the 18th to make my final preparations I will go & see y[ou]r. people if I can possibly manage it, but cannot be certain so far ahead.

P.S. I think the consent to an embassy being sent to London will be conveyed to the M[ooris]h. Gov[ernmen]t. by my successor. But perh[aps]. you had better keep this to yourself for the present, or at any rate mention it only as your own idea.

[End of letters from Morocco. The remaining letters in the file are from Japan.]